# WEBSTER'S
## UNIVERSAL
# ENGLISH
# DICTIONARY

Published 2004 by Geddes & Grosset, David Dale House,
New Lanark, ML11 9DJ, Scotland

Copyright © 2004 Geddes & Grosset

ISBN 1 84205 441 4

Printed and bound in Canada

# WEBSTER'S
## UNIVERSAL
# ENGLISH
# DICTIONARY

**GEDDES&
GROSSET**

# Abbreviations Used In This Book

| | | | |
|---|---|---|---|
| *abbr* | abbreviation | *n* | noun |
| *adj* | adjective | *naut* | nautical |
| *adv* | adverb | *neut* | neuter |
| *anat* | anatomy | *news* | news media |
| *approx* | approximately | *nf* | noun feminine |
| *arch* | archaic | *npl* | noun plural |
| *archit* | architecture | *n sing* | noun singular |
| *astrol* | astrology | *orig* | original, |
| *astron* | astronomy | | originally, origin |
| *Austral* | Australia, Australasia | *p* | participle |
| *aux* | auxiliary | *pers* | person, personal |
| *biol* | biology | *philos* | philosophy |
| *bot* | botany | *photog* | photography |
| *Brit* | Britain, British | *pl* | plural |
| *c* | *circa*, about | *poet* | poetical |
| *cap* | capital | *poss* | possessive |
| *cent* | century | *pp* | past participle |
| *chem* | chemical, chemistry | *prep* | preposition |
| *compar* | comparative | *pres t* | present tense |
| *comput* | computing | *print* | printing |
| *conj* | conjunction | *pron* | pronoun |
| *demons* | demonstrative | *pr p* | present participle |
| *derog* | derogatory, | *psychol* | psychology |
| | derogatorily | *pt* | past tense |
| *econ* | economics | *RC* | Roman Catholic |
| *eg* | *exempli gratia*, | *reflex* | reflexive |
| | for example | *Scot* | Scotland |
| *elect* | electricity | *sing* | singular |
| *esp* | especially | *sl* | slang |
| *fig* | figuratively | *superl* | superlative |
| *geog* | geography | *theat* | theatre |
| *geol* | geology | *TV* | television |
| *geom* | geometry | *UK* | United Kingdom |
| *gram* | grammar | *US* | United States |
| *her* | heraldry | *USA* | United States |
| *hist* | history | | of America |
| *ie* | *id est*, that is | *usu* | usually |
| *imper* | imperative | *vb* | verb |
| *incl* | including | *vb aux* | auxiliary verb |
| *inf* | informal | *vi* | intransitive verb |
| *interj* | interjection | *vt* | transitive verb |
| *math* | mathematics | *vti* | transitive |
| *mech* | mechanics | | or instransitive verb |
| *med* | medicine | *vulg* | vulgar, vulgarly |
| *mil* | military | *zool* | zoology |
| *myth* | mythology | | |

# A

**A** *abbr* = ampere(s).

**a** *adj* the indefinite article; one; any; per.

**AA** *abbr* = Alcoholics Anonymous; anti-aircraft; Automobile Association.

**aback** *adv* **taken aback** startled.

**abandon** *vt* to leave behind; to desert; to yield completely to an emotion or urge. • *n* freedom from inhibitions.—**abandonment** *n*.

**abate** *vti* to make or become less; (*law*) to end.—**abatement** *n*.

**abattoir** *n* a slaughterhouse.

**abbey** *n* a building occupied by monks or nuns; a church attached to an abbey; the community of monks or nuns.

**abbot** *n* the head of an abbey of monks.

**abbreviate** *vt* to make shorter, esp to shorten (words) by omitting letters.

**abbreviation** *n* the process of abbreviating; a shortened form of a word.

**abdicate** *vti* to renounce an official position or responsibility, etc.—**abdication** *n*.

**abdomen** *n* the region of the body below the chest containing the digestive organs; the belly; (*insects, etc*) the section of the body behind the thorax.—**abdominal** *adj*.

**abduct** *vt* to carry off (a person) by force.—**abduction** *n*.—**abductor** *n*.

**abet** *vt* (*pt* **abetted**) to encourage or assist.—**abetter**.

**abhor** *vt* (*pt* **abhorred**) to detest, despise.

**abide** *vt* (*pt* **abode** *or* **abided**) to endure; to put up with.

**ability** *n* being able; power to do; talent; skill.

**ablaze** *adj* burning, on fire.

**able** *adj* having the competence or means (to do); talented; skilled.—**ably** *adv*.

**abnormal** *adj* unusual, not average or typical; irregular.—**abnormality** *n*.

**aboard** *adv* on or in an aircraft, ship, train, etc.—*also prep*.

**abolish** *vt* to bring to an end, do away with.

**abolition** *n* the act of abolishing; (*with cap*) in UK, the ending of the slave trade (1807) or slavery (1833), in US, the emancipation of the slaves (1863).—**abolitionist** *n*.

**abominable** *adj* despicable, detestable; (*inf*) very unpleasant.—**abominably** *adv*.

**aborigine** *n* any of the first known inhabitants of a region; (*with cap*) one of the original inhabitants of Australia.

**abort** *vti* to undergo or cause an abortion; to terminate or cause to terminate prematurely. • *n* the premature termination of a rocket flight, etc.

**abortion** *n* the premature expulsion of a foetus, esp if induced.

**abortive** *adj* failing in intended purpose; fruitless; causing abortion.

**abound** *vi* to be in abundance; to have in great quantities.

**about** *prep* on all sides of; near to; with; on the point of; concerning. • *adv* all around; near; to face the opposite direction.

**above** *prep* over, on top of; better or more than; beyond the reach of; too complex to understand. • *adv* in or to a higher place; in addition; (*text*) mentioned earlier.

**abrasive** *adj* causing abrasion; harsh, irritating. • *n* a substance or tool used for grinding or polishing, etc.

**abreast** *adv* side by side and facing the same way; informed (of); aware.

**abridge** *vt* to shorten by using fewer words but keeping the substance.—**abridgement, abridgment** *n*.

**abroad** *adv* in or to a foreign country; over a wide area; out in the open; in circulation, current.

**abrupt** *adj* sudden; unexpected; curt.—**abruptly** *adv*.

**abscess** *n* an inflamed area of the body containing pus.

**abscond** *vi* to hide, run away, esp to avoid punishment.

**absence** *n* the state of not being present; the time of this; a lack; inattention.

**absent**[1] *adj* not present; not existing; inattentive.

**absent**[2] *vt* to keep (oneself) away.

**absentee** *n* a person who is absent, as from work or school.

**absenteeism** *n* persistent absence from work, school, etc.

**absent-minded** *adj* inattentive; forgetful.

**absolute** *adj* unrestricted, unconditional; complete; positive; perfect, pure; not relative; (*inf*) utter, out-and-out.

**absolutely** *adv* completely; unconditionally; (*inf*) I completely agree, certainly.

**absolve** *vt* to clear from guilt or blame; to give religious absolution to; to free from a duty, obligation, etc.

**absorb** *vt* to take in; to soak up; to incorporate; to pay for (costs, etc); to take in (a shock) without recoil; to occupy one's interest completely.—**absorber** *n*.—**absorption** *n*.

**absorbent** *adj* capable of absorbing moisture, etc.—**absorbency** *n*.

**abstain** *vi* to keep oneself from some indulgence, esp alcohol; to refrain from using one's vote.—**abstainer** *n*.—**abstention** *n*.

**abstemious** *adj* sparing in consuming food or alcohol.

**abstinence** *n* an abstaining or refraining, esp from food or alcohol.—**abstinent** *adj*.

**abstract** *adj* having no material existence; theoretical; (*art*) non-representational. • *n* (*writing, speech*) a summary or condensed version. • *vt* to remove or extract; to separate; to summarize.

**absurd** *adj* against reason or common sense; ridiculous.—**absurdity** *n*.

**abundance** *n* a plentiful supply; a considerable amount.

**abundant** *adj* plentiful; rich (in).—**abundantly** *adv*.

**abuse** *vt* to make wrong use of; to mistreat; to insult, attack verbally. • *n* misuse; mistreatment; insulting language.

**abusive** *adj* insulting.

**abysmal** *adj* extremely bad, deplorable.

**abyss** *n* a bottomless depth; anything too deep to measure.

**academic** *adj* pertaining to a school, college or university; scholarly; purely theoretical in nature. • *n* a member of a college or university; a scholarly person.

**academy** *n* a school for specialized training; (*Scot*) a secondary school; (*with cap*) a society of scholars, etc.

**accede** *vi* to take office; to agree or assent to (a suggestion).

**accelerate** *vti* to move faster; to happen or cause to happen more quickly; to increase the speed of (a vehicle).

**acceleration** *n* the act of accelerating or condition of being accelerated; the rate of increase in speed or change in velocity; the power of accelerating.

**accelerator** *n* a device for increasing speed; a throttle; (*physics*) an apparatus that imparts high velocities to elementary particles.

**accent** *n* emphasis on a syllable or word; a mark used to indicate this; any way of speaking characteristic of a region, class, or an individual; the emphasis placed on something; rhythmic stress in music or verse.

**accept** vt to receive, esp willingly; to approve; to agree to; to believe in; to agree to pay.—**acceptance** n.

**acceptable** adj satisfactory; welcome; tolerable.

**access** n approach, or means of approach; the right to enter, use, etc. • vt (comput) to retrieve (information) from a storage device; to gain access to.

**accessory** adj additional; extra. • n a supplementary part or item, esp of clothing; a person who aids another in a crime.

**accident** n an unexpected event; a mishap or misfortune, esp one resulting in death or injury; chance.

**accidental** adj occurring or done by accident; non-essential; (mus) a sign prefixed to a note indicating a departure from the key signature.—**accidentally** adv.

**acclaim** vt to praise publicly; to welcome enthusiastically. • vi to shout approval. • n a shout of welcome or approval.—**acclamation** n.

**acclimatize** vt to adapt to a new climate or environment • vi to become acclimatized.—**acclimatization** n.

**accommodate** vt to provide lodging for; to oblige, supply; to adapt, harmonize.

**accommodating** adj obliging, willing to help.

**accommodation** n lodgings; the process of adapting; willingness to help.

**accompaniment** n an instrumental part supporting a solo instrument, a voice, or a choir; something that accompanies.—**accompanist** n.

**accompany** vt (person) to go with; (something) to supplement.

**accomplice** n a partner, esp in committing a crime.

**accomplish** vt to succeed in carrying out; to fulfil.

**accomplished** adj done; completed; skilled, expert; polished.

**accomplishment** n a skill or talent; the act of accomplishing; something accomplished.

**accord** vi to agree; to harmonize (with). • vt to grant. • n consent; harmony.

**accordance** n agreement; conformity.

**accordingly** adv consequently; therefore.

**accordion** n a portable keyboard instrument with manually operated folding bellows that force air through metal reeds.—**accordionist** n.

**accost** vt to approach and speak to.

**account** n a description; explanatory statement; business record or statement; a credit arrangement with a bank, department store, etc; importance, consequence. • vt to think of as; to consider. • vi to give a financial reckoning (to); (with for) to give reasons (for); (with for) to kill, dispose of.

**accountable** adj liable; responsible.—**accountability** n.

**accountancy** n the profession or practice of an accountant.

**accountant** n one whose profession is auditing business accounts.

**accumulate** vti to collect together in increasing quantities, to amass.—**accumulation** n.—**accumulative** adj.

**accurate** adj conforming with the truth or an accepted standard; done with care, exact.— **accuracy** n.—**accurately** adv.

**accusation** n the act of accusing or being accused; an allegation.

**accuse** vt to charge with a crime, fault, etc; to blame.—**accuser** n.—**accusingly** adv.

**accustom** vt to make used (to) by habit, use, or custom.

**accustomed** *adj* usual, customary.

**ace** *n* the one spot in dice, cards, etc; a point won by a single stroke; an expert. • *adj* (*inf*) excellent.

**ache** *n* a dull, continuous pain. • *vi* to suffer a dull, continuous mental or physical pain; (*inf*) to yearn.

**achieve** *vt* to perform successfully, accomplish; to gain, win. —**achievable** *adj*.—**achiever** *n*.

**acid** *adj* sharp, tart, sour; bitter. • *n* a sour substance; (*chem*) a corrosive substance that turns litmus red; (*sl*) LSD.

**acknowledge** *vt* to admit that something is true and valid; to show that one has noticed or recognized.—**acknowledgement** *n*.

**acne** *n* inflammation of the skin glands producing pimples.

**acorn** *n* the nut of the oak tree.

**acoustic** *adj* of the sense of hearing or sound; of acoustics.

**acoustics** *npl* (*room, concert hall, etc*) properties governing how clearly sounds can be heard in it; (*in sing*) the physics of sound.—**acoustical** *adj*.—**acoustically** *adv*.

**acquaint** *vt* to make (oneself) familiar (with); to inform.

**acquaintance** *n* a person whom one knows only slightly.

**acquire** *vt* to gain by one's own efforts; to obtain.

**acquisition** *n* gaining, acquiring; something that is acquired.

**acquisitive** *adj* eager or greedy for possessions.—**acquisitively** *adv*.—**acquisitiveness** *n*.

**acquit** *vt* (*pt* **acquitted**) to free from an obligation; to behave or conduct (oneself); to declare innocent.—**acquittal** *n*.

**acre** *n* land measuring 4840 sq yards.

**acrimony** *n* bitterness of manner or language.—**acrimonious** *adj*.—**acrimoniously** *adv*.

**acrobat** *n* a skilful performer of spectacular gymnastic feats.—**acrobatic** *adj*.—**acrobatically** *adv*.

**acrobatics** *npl* acrobatic feats.

**across** *prep* from one side to the other of; on or at an angle; on the other side of. • *adv* crosswise; from one side to the other.

**act** *vi* to perform or behave in a certain manner; to perform a specific function; to have an effect; to perform on the stage. • *vt* to portray by actions, esp on the stage; to pretend, simulate; to take the part of, as a character in a play. • *n* something done, a deed; an exploit; a law; a main division of a play or opera; the short repertoire of a comic, etc; something done merely for effect or show.

**acting** *n* the art of an actor. • *adj* holding an office or position temporarily.

**action** *n* process of doing something; an operation; a movement of the body, gesture; a land or sea battle; a lawsuit; the unfolding of events in a play, etc.

**activate** *vt* to make active; to set in motion.—**activation** *n*.—**activator** *n*.

**active** *adj* lively, physically mobile; engaged in practical activities; energetic, busy; (*volcano*) liable to erupt; capable of producing an effect; radioactive; (*armed forces*) in full-time service. • *n* (*gram*) the verb form having as its subject the doer of the action.—**actively** *adv*.

**activity** *n* being active; energetic, lively action; specific occupations (*indoor activities*).

**actor** *n* a person who acts in a play, film, etc.—**actress** *nf*.

**actual** *adj* real; existing in fact or reality.—**actually** *adv*.

**acumen** *n* sharpness of mind, perception.

**acupuncture** *n* the insertion of the tips

of fine needles into the skin at certain points to treat various common ailments.—**acupuncturist** *n*.

**acute** *adj* (*hearing*) sensitive; (*pain*) severe; very serious; (*angles*) less than 90 degrees; (*disease*) severe but not long lasting.—**acutely** *adv*.—**acuteness** *n*.

**ad** *abbr* = *anno Domini* (in the year of Our Lord) in dates of the Christian era, indicating the number of years since the birth of Christ.

**Adam's apple** *n* the hard projection of cartilage in the front of the neck.

**adapt** *vti* to make or become fit; to adjust to new circumstances.—**adaptability** *n* —**adaptable** *adj*.

**adaptation** *n* the process or condition of being adapted; something produced by modification; a version of a literary composition rewritten for a different medium.

**adapter, adaptor** *n* a device that allows an item of equipment to be put to new use; a device for connecting parts of differing size and shape.

**add** *vt* to combine (two or more things together); to combine numbers or amounts in a total; to remark or write further. • *vi* to perform or come together by addition.

**adder** *n* the venomous viper.

**addict** *n* a person who is dependent upon a drug.—**addiction** *n*.

**addition** *n* the act or result of adding; something to be added; an extra part.—**additional** *adj*.

**additive** *adj* produced by addition. • *n* a substance added (to food, etc) to improve texture, flavour, etc.

this on a letter for delivery; a speech, esp a formal one; (*comput*) a specific memory location where information is stored.

**adenoids** *npl* enlarged masses of tissue in the throat behind the nose.

**adept** *adj* highly proficient. • *n* a highly skilled person.

**adequate** *adj* sufficient for requirements; barely acceptable. —**adequacy** *n* —**adequately** *adv*.

**adhere** *vi* to stick, as by gluing or suction; to give allegiance or support (to); to follow.—**adherence** *n*.—**adherent** *n*.

**adhesion** *n* the action or condition of adhering; the attachment of normally separate tissues in the body.

**adhesive** *adj* sticky; causing adherence. • *n* a substance used to stick, such as glue, paste, etc.—**adhesiveness** *n*.

**adjacent** *adj* nearby; adjoining.

**adjective** *n* a word used to add a characteristic to a noun or pronoun.—**adjectival** *adj*.

**adjoining** *adj* beside, in contact with.

**adjourn** *vt* to suspend (a meeting) temporarily. • *vi* (*inf*) to retire (to another room, etc).—**adjournment** *n*.

**adjust** *vt* to arrange in a more proper or satisfactory manner; to regulate or modify by minor changes; to decide the amount to be paid in settling (an insurance claim). • *vi* to adapt oneself. —**adjustable** *adj*.—**adjuster** *n*.—**adjustment** *n*.

**adjutant** *n* a military staff officer who assists the commanding officer.—**adjutancy** *n*.

**ad-lib** *vti* (*pt* **ad-libbed**) (*speech, etc*) to improvise. • *n* an ad-libbed remark. • *adv* spontaneously, freely.

**address** *vt* to write directions for delivery on (a letter, etc); to speak or write directly to; to direct one's skills or attention (to); (*golf*) to adjust one's stance and aim before hitting the ball; • *n* a place where a person or business resides, the details of

**administer** *vt* to manage, direct; to give out as a punishment; to dispense (medicine, punishment, etc); to tender (an oath, etc).

**administration** n management; the people who administer an organization; the government; (with cap) the executive officials of a government, their policies, and term of office.—**administrative** adj.

**administrator** n a person who manages or supervises; (law) one appointed to settle an estate.

**admiral** n the commanding officer of a fleet; a naval officer of the highest rank.

**admiration** n a feeling of pleasurable and often surprised respect; an admired person or thing.

**admire** vt to regard with honour and approval; to express admiration for.—**admirer** n.—**admiring** adj. —**admiringly** adv.

**admission** n an entrance fee; a conceding, confessing, etc; a thing conceded, confessed, etc.

**admit** vb (pt **admitted**)vt to allow to enter or join; to concede or acknowledge as true. • vi to give access; (with of) to allow or permit.

**admittance** n the act of admitting; the right to enter.

**admittedly** adv acknowledged as fact, willingly conceded.

**admonish** vt to remind or advise earnestly; to reprove gently.—**admonition** n.—**admonitory** adj.

**ado** n fuss, excitement, esp over trivia.

**adolescent** adj between childhood and maturity; (inf) immature. • n an adolescent person.—**adolescence** n.

**adopt** vt to take legally into one's family and raise as one's child; to take as one's own.—**adoption** n.

**adore** vt to worship; to love deeply.—**adoringly** adv.

**adorn** vt to decorate; to make more pleasant or attractive.—**adornment** n.

**adrenaline** n a hormone that stimulates the heart rate, blood pressure, etc in response to stress and that is secreted by the adrenal glands or manufactured synthetically.

**adrift** adj, adv afloat without mooring, drifting; loose.

**adroit** adj skilful and clever.—**adroitly** adv.—**adroitness** n.

**adult** adj fully grown; mature; suitable only for adults, as in pornography, etc. • n a mature person, etc.

**adulterate** vt to make impure or inferior, etc by adding an improper substance.—**adulteration** n.

**adultery** n sexual intercourse between a married person and someone other than their legal partner.—**adulterous** adj.

**advance** vt to bring or move forward; to promote; to raise the rate of; (money) to lend. • vi to go forward; to make progress; to rise in rank, price, etc. • n progress; improvement; a rise in value; payment beforehand; (pl) friendly approaches. • adj in front; beforehand.

**advanced** adj in front; old; superior in development.

**advancement** n promotion to higher rank; progress in development.

**advantage** n superiority of position or condition; a gain or benefit; (tennis) the first point won after deuce. • vt to produce a benefit or favour to.

**advantageous** adj producing advantage, beneficial.—**advantageously** adv.

**advent** n an arrival or coming.

**adventure** n a strange or exciting undertaking; an unusual, stirring, often romantic, experience.—**adventurous** adj.—**adventurously** adv.

**adventurer** n a person who seeks adventure; someone who seeks money or power by unscrupulous means.—**adventuress** nf.

**adverb** n a word that modifies a verb, adjective, another adverb, phrase, clause or sentence and indicates how, why, where, etc.—**adverbial** adj.

**adversary** *n* an enemy or opponent.

**adverse** *adj* hostile; contrary or opposite; unfavourable.—**adversely** *adv*.

**adversity** *n* trouble, misery, misfortune.

**advert** *n* (*inf*) an advertisement.

**advertise** *vt* to call public attention to by buying space or time in the media, etc. • *vi* to call public attention to things for sale; to ask (for) by public notice.—**advertiser** *n*.

**advertisement** *n* advertising; a public notice, usu paid for by the provider of a good or service.

**advertising** *n* the promotion of goods or services by public notices; advertisements; the business of producing adverts.

**advice** *n* recommendation with regard to a course of action; formal notice or communication.

**advisable** *adj* prudent, expedient.—**advisability** *n*.

**advise** *vt* to give advice to; to caution; to recommend; to inform. • *vi* to give advice.—**adviser, advisor** *n*.

**advisory** *adj* having or exercising the power to advise; containing or giving advice.

**advocate** *n* a person who argues or defends the cause of another, esp in a court of law; a supporter. • *vt* to plead in favour of.

**aegis** *n* protection, sponsorship.

**aerial** *adj* belonging to or existing in the air; of aircraft or flying. • *n* a metal device for transmitting and receiving radio waves, an antenna.

**aerie, aery** *n* variant spellings of **eyrie**.

**aeroplane, airplane** (*US*) *n* a power-driven aircraft.

**aerosol** *n* a suspension of fine solid or liquid particles in gas, esp as held in a container under pressure, with a device for releasing it in a fine spray.

**aesthetics, esthetics** (*US*) *n* the philosophy of art and beauty.—**aesthetic** *adj*.—**aesthetically** *adv*.

**affable** *adj* friendly; approachable.—**affability** *n* —**affably** *adv*.

**affair** *n* a thing done or to be done; (*pl*) public or private business; (*inf*) an event; a temporary romantic or sexual relationship.

**affect**[1] *vt* to have an effect on; to produce a change in; to act in a way that alters or affects the feelings of.

**affect**[2] *vt* to pretend or feign (an emotion); to incline to or show a preference for.

**affect**[3] *n* an emotion, feeling or desire associated with a certain stimulus.

**affectation** *n* a striving after or an attempt to assume what is not natural or real; pretence.

**affected** *adj* (*manner, etc*) assumed artificially.

**affection** *n* tender feeling; liking.

**affectionate** *adj* showing affection, loving.—**affectionately** *adv*.

**affiliate** *vt* to connect as a subordinate member or branch; to associate (oneself with). • *vi* to join. • *n* an affiliated person, club, etc.—**affiliation** *n*.

**affinity** *n* attraction, liking; a close relationship, esp by marriage; similarity, likeness; (*chem*) a tendency in certain substances to combine.

**affirmation** *n* affirming; an assertion; a solemn declaration made by those declining to swear an oath, eg on religious grounds.

**affix** *vt* to fasten; to add, esp in writing; to attach.

**afflict** *vt* to cause persistent pain or suffering to; to trouble greatly.

**affliction** *n* persistent pain, suffering; a cause of this.

**affluent** *adj* rich, well provided for.—**affluence** *n* —**affluently** *adv*.

**afford** *vt* to be in a position to do or bear without much inconvenience; to have enough time, money, or resources for; to supply, produce.

**affront** vi to insult or offend openly or deliberately. • n a deliberate insult.

**afield** adv far away from home; to or at a distance; astray.

**afloat** adj floating; at sea, on board a ship; debt-free; flooded.—also adv.

**afraid** adj full of fear or apprehension; regretful.

**afresh** adv anew, starting again.

**aft** adv at, near, or toward the stern of a ship or rear of an aircraft.

**after** prep behind in place or order; following in time, later than; in pursuit of; in imitation of; in view of, in spite of; according to; about, concerning; subsequently. • adv later; behind. • conj at a time later than. • adj later, subsequent; nearer the stern of a ship or aircraft.

**aftereffect** n an effect that occurs some time after its cause.

**afterlife** n life after death.

**aftermath** n the result, esp an unpleasant one.

**afternoon** n the time between noon and sunset or evening.—also adj.

**aftershave** n lotion for use after shaving.

**afterthought** n a thought or reflection occurring later.

**afterwards** adv at a later time.

**again** adv once more; besides; on the other hand.

**against** prep in opposition to; unfavourable to; in contrast to; in preparation for; in contact with; as a charge on.

**age** n the period of time during which someone or something has lived or existed; a stage of life; later years of life; a historical period; a division of geological time; (inf: often pl) a long time. • vti (pr p ageing or aging, pt aged) to grow or make old, ripe, mature, etc.

**aged** adj very old; of a specified age.

**agency** n action; power; means; a firm,

etc, empowered to act for another; an administrative government division.

**agenda** n a list of items or matters of business that need attention.

**agent** n a person or thing that acts or has an influence; a substance or organism that is active; one empowered to act for another; a government representative; a spy.

**aggravate** vt to make worse; (inf) to annoy, irritate.—aggravation n.

**aggregate** adj formed of parts combined into a mass or whole; taking all units as a whole. • n a collection or sum of parts; sand, stones, etc, mixed with cement to form concrete. • vt to collect or form into a mass or whole; to amount to (a total).

**aggression** n an unprovoked attack; a hostile action or behaviour.

**aggressive** adj boldly hostile; quarrelsome; self-assertive, enterprising.—aggressively adv.—aggressiveness n.

**aghast** adj utterly horrified.

**agile** adj quick and nimble in movement; mentally acute.—agility n.

**agitate** vt to shake, move; to disturb or excite the emotions of. • vi to stir up public interest for a cause, etc.—agitation n.—agitator n.

**ago** adv in the past. • adj gone by; past.

**agony** n extreme mental or physical suffering.

**agree** vb (pt agreed)vi to be of similar opinion; to consent or assent (to); to come to an understanding about; to be consistent; to suit a person's digestion; (gram) to be consistent in gender, number, case, or person. • vt to concede, grant; to bring into harmony; to reach terms on.

**agreeable** adj likeable, pleasing; willing to agree.—agreeably adv.

**agreement** n harmony in thought or

opinion, correspondence; an agreed settlement between two people, etc.

**agriculture** n the science or practice of producing crops and raising livestock; farming.—**agricultural** adj.—**agriculturally** adv.

**aground** adj on or onto the shore.—also adv.

**ahead** adj in or to the front; forward; onward; in advance; winning or profiting.—also adv.

**aid** vti to help, give assistance to. • n anything that helps; a specific means of assistance, eg money; a helper.

**aide** n an aide-de-camp; assistant.

**AIDS, Aids** n (acronym for acquired immune deficiency syndrome) a condition caused by a virus, in which the body loses immunity to infection.

**ailment** n a slight illness.

**aim** vti to point or direct towards a target so as to hit; to direct (one's efforts); to intend. • n the act of aiming; purpose, intention.

**air** n the mixture of invisible gases surrounding the earth; the earth's atmosphere; empty, open space; a light breeze; aircraft, aviation; outward appearance, demeanour; a pervading influence; (mus) a melody; (pl) an affected manner. • vt to expose to the air for drying; to expose to public notice; (clothes) to place in a warm place to finish drying.

**airborne** adj carried by or through the air; aloft or flying.

**air conditioning** n regulation of air humidity and temperature in buildings, etc.

**air-cooled** adj cooled by having air passed over, into, or through.

**aircraft** n (pl aircraft) any machine for travelling through air.

**aircraft carrier** n a warship with a large flat deck, for carrying aircraft.

**airgun** n a gun that fires pellets by compressed air.

**air hostess** n a stewardess on a passenger aircraft.

**air letter** n a sheet of light writing paper that is folded and sealed for sending by airmail.

**airline** n a system or company for transportation by aircraft.

**airlock** n a blockage in a pipe caused by an air bubble; an airtight compartment giving access to a pressurized chamber.

**airmail** n mail transported by aircraft.

**airplane** n the US spelling of **aeroplane**.

**airport** n a place where aircraft can land and take off, with facilities for repair, etc.

**air raid** n an attack by military aircraft on a surface target.

**airship** n a self-propelled steerable aircraft that is lighter than air.

**airstrip** n an area of land cleared for aircraft to land on; a runway.

**airtight** adj too tight for air or gas to enter or escape; (alibi, etc) invulnerable.

**airy** adj (**airier, airiest**) open to the air; breezy; light as air; graceful; lighthearted; flippant.—**airily** adv.

**aisle** n a passageway, as between rows of seats; a side part of a church.

**ajar** adv partly open, as a door.

**alarm** n a signal warning of danger; an automatic device to arouse from sleep or to attract attention; fear arising from apprehension of danger. • vt to give warning of danger; to fill with apprehension or fear.

**album** n a book with blank pages for the insertion of photographs, autographs, etc; a long-playing record, cassette, or CD.

**alchemy** n chemistry as practised during medieval times, with the aim of transmuting base metals into gold.—**alchemist** n.

**alcohol** n a liquid, generated by distillation

and fermentation, that forms the intoxicating agent in wine, beer and spirits; a liquid containing alcohol; a chemical compound of this nature.

**alcoholic** *adj* of or containing alcohol; caused by alcohol. • *n* a person suffering from alcoholism.

**alcoholism** *n* a disease caused by excessive consumption of alcohol.

**alcove** *n* a recess off a larger room.

**ale** *n* beer.

**alert** *adj* watchful; active, brisk. • *n* a danger signal. • *vt* to warn of impending danger, put in a state of readiness.—**alertly** *adv*.—**alertness** *n*.

**algebra** *n* the branch of mathematics dealing with the properties and relations of numbers; the generalization and extension of arithmetic.—**algebraic** *adj*.

**alias** *adv* otherwise called. • *n* (*pl* **aliases**) an assumed name.

**alibi** *n* (*pl* **alibis**) (*law*) the plea that a person charged with a crime was elsewhere when it was committed; (*inf*) any excuse.

**alien** *adj* foreign; strange. • *n* a person from another country, place, etc; a person of foreign birth who has not been naturalized; a being from outer space.

**alienate** *vt* to render hostile or unfriendly; to make less affectionate or interested.—**alienation** *n*.

**alight**[1] *vi* to come down, as from a bus; to descend after a flight.

**alight**[2] *adj* on fire; lively.

**align** *vt* to place in a straight line, to bring into agreement, etc. • *vi* to line up.—**alignment** *n*.

**alike** *adj* like one another. • *adv* equally; similarly.

**alimony** *n* an allowance for support made by one spouse to the other; maintenance.

**alive** *adj* having life; active, alert; in existence, operation, etc.

**alkali** *n* (*pl* **alkalis**) (*chem*) any salt or mixture that neutralizes acids.—**alkaline** *adj*.

**all** *adj* the whole amount or number of; every one of. • *adv* wholly; supremely, completely; entirely. • *n* the whole number, quantity; everyone; everything.

**allay** *vt* to lighten, alleviate; to pacify or make calm.

**allege** *vt* to assert or declare, esp without proof; to offer as an excuse.—**allegation** *n*.

**allegedly** *adv* asserted without proof.

**allegiance** *n* the obligation of being loyal to one's country, etc; devotion, as to a cause.

**allegory** *n* a fable, story, poem, etc, in which events depicted are used to convey a deeper, usu moral or spiritual, meaning.—**allegorical** *adj*.

**allergy** *n* an abnormal reaction of the body to substances (certain foods, pollen, etc) normally harmless; antipathy.—**allergic** *adj*.

**alleviate** *vt* to lessen or relieve (pain, worry, etc).—**alleviation** *n*.

**alley** *n* a narrow street between or behind buildings; a bowling lane.

**alliance** *n* a union by marriage or treaty for a common purpose; an agreement for this; the countries, groups, etc in such an association.

**alligator** *n* a large reptile similar to the crocodile but having a short, blunt snout.

**all-in** *adj* (*inf*) exhausted.

**allocate** *vt* to distribute or apportion in shares; to set apart for a specific purpose.—**allocation** *n*.

**allot** *vt* (*pt* **allotted**) to distribute, allocate.

**allotment** *n* allotting; a share allotted; a small area of land rented for cultivation.

**all-out** *adj* using maximum effort.

**allow** *vt* to permit; to acknowledge,

admit as true; (*money*) to give, grant as an allowance at regular intervals; to estimate as an addition or deduction. • *vi* to admit the possibility (of).

**allowance** *n* an amount or sum allowed; a discount; a portion of income not subject to income tax; permission; admission, concession.

**alloy** *n* a solid substance comprising a mixture of two or more metals; something that degrades the substance to which it is added. • *vt* to make into an alloy; to degrade or spoil by mixing with an inferior substance.

**all-round** *adj* efficient in all respects, esp sport.

**all-time** *adj* unsurpassed until now.

**allude** *vi* to refer indirectly to.

**allure** *vt* to entice, charm. • *n* fascination; charm.

**alluring** *adj* attractive.

**allusion** *n* alluding; an implied or indirect reference.—**allusive** *adj*.

**ally** *vti* to join or unite for a specific purpose; to relate by similarity of structure, etc. • *n* a country or person joined with another for a common purpose.

**almighty** *adj* all-powerful. • *n* (*with cap*) God, the all-powerful.

**almond** *n* the edible kernel of the fruit of a tree of the rose family; the tree bearing this fruit. • *adj* (*eyes, etc*) oval and pointed.

**almost** *adv* all but, very nearly but not quite all.

**alms** *npl* money, food, etc, given to the poor.

**alone** *adj* isolated; without anyone or anything else; unassisted; unique. • *adv* exclusively.

**along** *adv* onward, forward; over the length of; in company and together with; in addition. • *prep* in the direction of the length of; in accordance with.

**alongside** *prep* close beside. • *adv* at the side.

**aloof** *adv* at a distance; apart. • *adj* cool and reserved.—**aloofness** *n*.

**aloud** *adv* with a normal voice; loudly.

**alphabet** *n* the characters used in a language arranged in conventional order.—**alphabetical** *adj*.—**alphabetically** *adv*.

**alpine** *adj* of the Alps; of high mountains. • *n* a mountain plant, esp a small herb.

**already** *adv* by or before the time specified; before the time expected.

**also** *adv* in addition, besides.

**altar** *n* a table, etc for sacred purposes in a place of worship.

**alter** *vti* to make or become different in a small way; to change.—**alteration** *n*.

**alternate**[1] *vt* to do or use by turns. • *vi* to act, happen, etc, by turns; to take turns regularly.

**alternate**[2] *adj* occurring or following in turns.—**alternately** *adv*.

**alternating current** *n* an electric current that reverses its direction at regular intervals.

**alternative** *adj* presenting a choice between two things. • *n* either of two possibilities.—**alternatively** *adv*.

**alternator** *n* an electric generator that produces alternating current.

**although** *conj* though; in spite of that.

**altitude** *n* height, esp above sea level.

**alto** *n* (*pl* **altos**) the range of the highest male voice; a singer with this range.

**altogether** *adv* in all; on the whole; completely.

**aluminium, aluminum** (*US*) *n* a silvery-white malleable metallic element notable for its lightness.

**always** *adv* at all times; in all cases; repeatedly; forever.

**am** *see* **be**.

**a.m.** *abbr* = *ante meridiem,* before noon.

**amalgamate** *vt* to combine, unite.—
**amalgamation** *n*.

**amass** *vt* to bring together in a large quantity; to accumulate.

**amateur** *n* one who engages in a particular activity as a hobby, and not as a profession. • *adj* of or done by amateurs.

**amateurish** *adj* lacking expertise.—
**amateurishly** *adv*.

**amaze** *vt* to fill with wonder, astonish.—**amazement** *n*.—**amazing** *adj*.

**ambassador** *n* the highest-ranking diplomatic representative from one country to another; an authorized messenger.—**ambassadorial** *adj*.

**amber** *n* a hard yellowish fossil resin, used for jewellery and ornaments, etc; the colour of amber; a yellow traffic light used to signal "caution."

**ambiguous** *adj* capable of two or more interpretations; indistinct, vague.—
**ambiguity** *n*.—**ambiguously** *adv*.

**ambition** *n* desire for power, wealth and success; an object of ambition.

**ambitious** *adj* having or governed by ambition; resulting from or showing ambition; requiring considerable effort or ability.—**ambitiously** *adv*.

**amble** *vi* to walk in a leisurely way.

**ambulance** *n* a special vehicle for transporting the sick or injured.

**ambush** *n* the concealment of soldiers, etc to make a surprise attack; the bushes or other cover in which they are hidden. • *vti* to lie in wait; to attack from an ambush.

**amenable** *adj* easily influenced or led, tractable; answerable to legal authority.—**amenably** *adv*.

**amend** *vt* to remove errors, esp in a text; to modify, improve; to alter in minor details.—**amendment**.

**amends** *npl* (*used as sing*) compensation or recompense for some loss, harm, etc.

**amenity** *n* pleasantness, as regards situation or convenience.

**amethyst** *n* a gemstone consisting of bluish-violet quartz.

**amiable** *adj* friendly in manner, congenial.—**amiably** *adv*.

**amicable** *adj* friendly; peaceable.—
**amicably** *adv*.

**amid, amidst** *prep* in or to the middle of; during.

**amiss** *adj* wrong, improper. • *adv* in an incorrect manner.

**ammunition** *n* bullets, shells, rockets, etc; any means of attack or defence; facts and reasoning used to prove a point in an argument.

**amnesia** *n* a partial or total loss of memory.—**amnesiac** *n*.

**amnesty** *n* a general pardon, esp of political prisoners.

**among, amongst** *prep* in the number of, surrounded by; in the group or class of; within a group, between; by the joint efforts of.

**amoral** *adj* neither moral nor immoral; without moral sense.

**amorous** *adj* displaying or feeling love or desire.—**amorously** *adv*.—**amorousness** *n*.

**amorphous** *adj* lacking a specific shape, shapeless; unrecognizable, indefinable.

**amount** *vi* to be equivalent (to) in total, quantity or significance. • *n* the total sum; the whole value or effect; a quantity.

**ampere** *n* the standard SI unit by which electric current is measured.

**amphibious** *adj* living on both land and water; (*mil*) involving both sea and land forces.

**amphitheatre** *n* an oval or circular building with rising rows of seats around an open arena.

**ample** *adj* large in size, scope, etc; plentiful.—**amply** *adv*.

**amplifier** *n* a device that increases electric voltage, current, or power, or the loudness of sound.

**amplify** *vt* to expand more fully, add details to; (*electrical signals, etc*) to strengthen.—**amplification** *n*.

**amputate** *vt* to cut off, esp by surgery.—**amputation** *n*.

**amuse** *vt* to entertain or divert in a pleasant manner; to cause to laugh or smile.—**amusement** *n*.

**an** *adj* the indefinite article ("a"), used before words beginning with the sound of a vowel except "u" as pronounced "y."

**anaemia, anemia** (*US*) *n* a condition in which the blood is low in red cells or in haemoglobin, resulting in paleness, weakness, etc.

**anaemic, anemic** (*US*) *adj* suffering from anaemia; weak; pale; listless.

**anaesthetic, anesthetic** (*US*) *n* a drug, gas, etc used to produce anaesthesia, as before surgery. • *adj* of or producing anaesthesia.

**anaesthetist, anesthetist** (*US*) *n* a person trained to give anaesthetics.

**analogy** *n* a similarity or correspondence in certain respects between two things.

**analyse, analyze** (*US*) *vt* to separate (something) into its constituent parts to investigate its structure and function, etc; to examine in detail; to psychoanalyse.

**analysis** *n* (*pl* **analyses**) the process of analysing; a statement of the results of this; psychoanalysis.

**analyst** *n* a person who analyses; a psychoanalyst.

**analytic, analytical** *adj* pertaining to analysis.—**analytically** *adv*.

**anarchist** *n* a person who believes that all government is unnecessary and should be abolished.—**anarchism** *n*.

**anarchy** *n* the absence of government; political confusion; disorder, lawlessness.—**anarchic** *adj*.

**anathema** *n* anything greatly detested; an ecclesiastical denunciation with excommunication.

**anatomy** *n* the science of the physical structure of plants and animals; the structure of an organism.—**anatomical** *adj*.—**anatomically** *adv*.

**ancestor** *n* one from whom a person is descended, a forefather; an early animal or plant from which existing types are descended; something regarded as a forerunner.—**ancestral** *adj*.—**ancestress** *nf*.

**ancestry** *n* ancestors collectively; lineage.

**anchor** *n* a heavy metal implement that lodges at the bottom of the sea or a river to hold a ship in position; something that gives support or stability. • *vt* to fix by an anchor; to secure firmly.

**anchorage** *n* a safe anchoring place for ships; the charge for anchoring.

**anchovy** *n* a small Mediterranean fish resembling a herring with a very salty taste.

**ancient** *adj* very old; dating from the distant past; of the period and civilizations predating the fall of the Roman Empire; old-fashioned. • *n* a person who lived in the ancient period; (*pl*) the members of the classical civilizations of antiquity.

**and** *conj* in addition to; together with; plus; increasingly; as a consequence, afterwards; expressing contrast.

**anecdote** *n* a short entertaining account about an amusing or interesting event or person.

**anew** *adv* afresh; again, once more; in a new way or form.

**angel** *n* a messenger of God; an image of a human figure with wings and a halo; a very beautiful or kind person.—**angelic** *adj*.

**anger** *n* strong displeasure, often because of opposition, a hurt, etc. • *vti* to make or become angry.

**angina** *n* sharp stabbing pains in the chest, usu caused by angina pectoris.

**angle**[1] *n* a corner; the point from which two lines or planes extend or diverge; a specific viewpoint; an individual method or approach (eg to a problem). • *vt* to bend at an angle; to move or place at an angle; to present, news, etc from a particular point of view.

**angle**[2] *vi* to fish with a hook and line; to use hints or artifice to get something.—**angler** *n*.

**Anglican** *adj* belonging to or of the Church of England or churches in communion with it. • *n* a member of the Anglican Church.—**Anglicanism** *n*.

**angry** *adj* (**angrier, angriest**) full of anger; inflamed.—**angrily** *adv*.

**anguish** *n* agonizing physical or mental distress.

**angular** *adj* having one or more angles; forming an angle; measured by an angle; stiff and clumsy in manner, thin and bony.—**angularity** *n*.

**animal** *n* any living organism except a plant or bacterium, typically able to move about; a lower animal as distinguished from man, esp mammals; a brutish person. • *adj* of or like an animal; bestial; sensual.

**animate** *vt* to give life to; to liven up; to inspire, encourage. • *adj* alive; lively.

**animosity** *n* strong dislike; hostility.

**aniseed** *n* the seed of the anise plant, used as a flavouring.

**ankle** *n* the joint between the foot and leg, the part of the leg between the foot and calf.

**annex** *vt* to attach, esp to something larger; to incorporate into a state the territory of (another state).—**annexation** *n*.

**annihilate** *vt* to destroy completely; (*inf*) to defeat convincingly, as in an argument.—**annihilation** *n*.

**anniversary** *n* the yearly return of the date of some event; a celebration of this.—*also adj*.

**annotate** *vti* to provide with explanatory notes.—**annotation** *n*.

**announce** *vt* to bring to public attention; to give news of the arrival of; to be an announcer for. • *vi* to serve as an announcer.—**announcement** *n*.

**annoy** *vt* to vex, tease, irritate, as by a repeated action.—**annoyance** *n*.

**annual** *adj* of or measured by a year; yearly; coming every year; living only one year or season. • *n* a plant that lives only one year; a periodical published once a year.—**annually** *adv*.

**annuity** *n* an investment yielding fixed payments, esp yearly; such a payment.

**annul** *vt* (*pt* **annulled**) to do away with; to deprive of legal force, nullify.—**annulment** *n*.

**anoint** *vt* to rub with oil; to apply oil in a sacred ritual as a sign of consecration.—**anointment** *n*.

**anomaly** *n* abnormality; anything inconsistent or odd.—**anomalous** *adj*.

**anonymous** *adj* having or providing no name; written or provided by an unnamed person; lacking individuality.—**anonymity** *n*.—**anonymously** *adv*.

**anorak** *n* a waterproof jacket with a hood.

**another** *adj* a different or distinct (thing or person); an additional one of the same kind; some other.—*also pron*.

**answer** *n* a spoken or written reply or response; the solution to a problem; a reaction, response. • *vt* to speak or write in reply; to satisfy or correspond to (eg a specific need); to justify, offer a refutation of. • *vi* to reply; to act in response (to); to be responsible (for); to conform (to).

**answerable** *adj* capable of being refuted; (*with* **for** *or* **to**) responsible, accountable.

**ant** *n* any of a family of small, generally wingless insects of many species, all of which form and live in highly organized groups.

**antagonism** *n* antipathy, hostility; an opposing force, principle, etc.

**antagonist** *n* an adversary; an opponent.—**antagonistic** *adj.*—**antagonistically** *adv.*

**antagonize** *vt* to arouse opposition.

**Antarctic** *adj* of the South Pole or its surroundings. • *n* the Antarctic regions; the Antarctic Ocean.

**antelope** *n* any of the family of fast-running and graceful deer-like animals of Africa and Asia.

**antenatal** *adj* occurring or present before birth.

**antenna** *n* (*pl* **antennae**) either of a pair of feelers on the head of an insect, etc; (*pl* **antennas**) an aerial.

**anthem** *n* a religious choral song; a song of praise or devotion, as to a nation.

**anthill** *n* a mound thrown up by ants or termites in digging their nests.

**anthology** *n* a collection of poetry or prose.—**anthologist** *n*.

**anthropology** *n* the scientific study of human beings, their origins, distribution, physical attributes and culture.—**anthropological** *adj.*—**anthropologist** *n*.

**anti-** *prefix* opposed to; against.

**antibiotic** *n* any of various chemical, fungal or synthetic substances used against bacterial or fungal infections.

**anticipate** *vt* to give prior thought and attention to; to use, spend, act on in advance; to foresee and take action to thwart another; to expect. • *vi* to speak, act, before the appropriate time.—**anticipation** *n*.

**anticlimax** *n* a sudden drop from the important to the trivial; an ending to a story or series of events that disappoints one's expectations.

**anticlockwise** *adj* moving in a direction contrary to the hands of a clock as viewed from the front.—*also adv.*

**anticyclone** *n* a body of air rotating about an area of high atmospheric pressure.

**antidote** *n* a remedy that counteracts a poison; something that counteracts harmful effects.

**antifreeze** *n* a substance used, as in car radiator, to prevent freezing up.

**antipathy** *n* a fixed dislike; aversion; an object of this.

**antiquated** *adj* old-fashioned; obsolete.

**antique** *adj* from the distant past; old-fashioned. • *n* a relic of the distant past; a piece of furniture, pottery, etc dating from an earlier historical period and sought after by collectors.

**antiquity** *n* the far distant past, esp before the Middle Ages; (*pl*) relics dating from the far distant past.

**antiseptic** *n* a substance that destroys or prevents the growth of disease-producing microorganisms. • *adj* destroying harmful organisms; very clean.

**antisocial** *adj* avoiding the company of other people, unsocial; contrary to the interests of society in general.

**antler** *n* the branched horn of a deer or related animal.—**antlered** *adj*.

**anus** *n* the excretory orifice of the alimentary canal.

**anvil** *n* the heavy iron block on which metal objects are shaped with a hammer.

**anxiety** *n* the condition of being anxious; eagerness, concern; a cause of worry.

**anxious** *adj* worried; uneasy; eagerly wishing; causing anxiety.—**anxiously** *adv.*

**any** *adj* one out of many, some; every.

**anybody** *pron* any person; an important person.

**anyhow** *adv* in any way whatever; in any case.

**anymore** *adv* now; nowadays.

**anyone** *pron* any person; anybody.

**anything** *pron* any object, event, fact, etc. • *n* a thing, no matter what kind.

**anyway** *adv* in any manner; at any rate; haphazardly.

**anywhere** *adv* in, at, or to any place.

**apart** *adv* at a distance, separately, aside; into two or more pieces.

**apartheid** *n* a policy of racial segregation implemented in South Africa.

**apartment** *n* a room or rooms in a building; a flat.

**apathy** *n* lack of feeling; lack of concern, indifference.—**apathetic** *adj*.—**apathetically** *adv*.

**ape** *n* a chimpanzee, gorilla, orangutan, or gibbon; any monkey; a mimic. • *vt* to imitate.

**apéritif** *n* an alcoholic drink taken before a meal.

**aperture** *n* an opening; a hole.

**apex** *n* the highest point, the tip; the culminating point; the vertex of a triangle.

**aphrodisiac** *adj* arousing sexually. • *n* a food, drug, etc that excites sexual desire.

**apiece** *adv* to, by, or for each one.

**aplomb** *n* poise; self-possession.

**apologetic** *adj* expressing an apology; contrite; presented in defence.—**apologetically** *adv*.

**apologize** *vi* to make an apology.

**apology** *n* an expression of regret for wrongdoing; a defence or justification of one's beliefs, etc; (*with* **for**) a poor substitute.

**apoplexy** *n* a sudden loss of consciousness and subsequent partial paralysis, usu caused by a broken or blocked artery in the brain.

**apostle** *n* the first or principal supporter of a new belief or cause.

**apostrophe** *n* a mark (') showing the omission of letters or figures, also a sign of the possessive case or the plural of letters and figures.

**appal, appall** (*US*) *vt* (*pt* **appalled**) to fill with terror or dismay.

**appalling** *adj* shocking, horrifying.—**appallingly** *adv*.

**apparatus** *n* the equipment used for a specific task; any complex machine, device, or system.

**apparent** *adj* easily seen, evident; seeming, but not real.—**apparently** *adv*.

**apparition** *n* an appearance or manifestation, esp something unexpected or unusual; a ghost.

**appeal** *vi* to take a case to a higher court; to make an earnest request; to refer to a witness or superior authority for vindication, confirmation, etc; to arouse pleasure or sympathy. • *n* the referral of a lawsuit to a higher court for rehearing; an earnest call for help; attraction, the power of arousing sympathy; a request for public donations to a charitable cause.

**appear** *vi* to become or be visible; to arrive, come in person; to be published; to present oneself formally (before a court, etc); to seem, give an impression of being.

**appearance** *n* the act or occasion of appearing; that which appears; external aspect of a thing or person; outward show, semblance.

**appease** *vt* to pacify; to allay; to conciliate by making concessions.—**appeasement** *n*.

**appendage** *n* something appended; an external organ or part, as a tail.

**appendicitis** *n* inflammation of the appendix of the intestine.

**appendix** *n* (*pl* **appendixes, appendices**) a section of supplementary information at the back of a book, etc; a small tube of tissue that forms an outgrowth of the intestine.

**appetite** n sensation of bodily desire, esp for food; (with **for**) a strong desire or liking, a craving.

**appetizing** adj stimulating the appetite.—**appetizingly** adv.

**applaud** vt to show approval, esp by clapping the hands.

**applause** n approval expressed by clapping; acclamation.

**apple** n a round, firm, fleshy, edible fruit.

**appliance** n a device or machine, esp for household use.

**applicable** adj that may be applied; appropriate, relevant (to).—**applicability** n.

**applicant** n a person who applies, esp for a job.

**application** n the act of applying; the use to which something is put; a petition, request; concentration, diligent effort; relevance or practical value.

**apply** vt to bring to bear; to put to practical use; to spread, lay on; to devote (oneself) with close attention. • vi to make a formal, esp written, request; to be relevant.

**appoint** vt to fix or decide officially; to select for a job; to prescribe.

**appraise** vt to estimate the value or quality of.—**appraisal** n.

**appreciable** adj capable of being perceived or measured; fairly large.—**appreciably** adv.

**appreciate** vt to value highly; to recognize gratefully; to understand, be aware of; to increase the value of. • vi to rise in value.

**appreciation** n gratitude, approval; sensitivity to aesthetic values; an assessment or critical evaluation; a favourable review; an increase in value.—**appreciative** adj.

**apprehend** vt to arrest, capture; to understand, to perceive.

**apprehension** n anxiety; the act of arresting; understanding; an idea.

**apprehensive** adj uneasy; anxious.—**apprehensively** adv.

**apprentice** n one being taught a trade or craft; a novice.—**apprenticeship** n.

**approach** vi to draw nearer. • vt to make a proposal to; to set about dealing with; to come near to. • n the act of approaching; a means of entering or leaving; a move to establish relations; the final descent of an aircraft.—**approachable** adj.

**appropriate** adj fitting, suitable. • vt to take for one's own use, esp illegally; (money, etc) to set aside for a specific purpose.—**appropriately** adv.—**appropriateness** n.

**approval** n approving; favourable opinion; official permission.

**approve** vt to express a good opinion of; to authorize. • vi (with **of**) to consider to be favourable or satisfactory.

**approximate** adj almost exact or correct. • vt to come near to; to be almost the same as. • vi to come close.—**approximately** adv.

**approximation** n a close estimate; a near likeness.

**apricot** n a small, oval orange-pink fruit resembling the plum and peach.

**apron** n a garment worn to protect clothing; anything resembling the shape of an apron used for protection; the paved surface on an airfield where aircraft are parked, etc.

**apt** adj ready or likely (to); suitable, relevant; able to learn easily.—**aptness** n.

**aptitude** n suitability; natural talent, esp for learning.

**aqualung** n portable diving gear comprising air cylinders connected to a face mask.

**aquarium** n (pl **aquariums**) a tank, pond, etc for keeping aquatic animals or plants; a building where collections of aquatic animals are exhibited.

**Aquarius** n (astrol) the eleventh sign of the zodiac, the Water-carrier, operative 20 January–18 February.

**aquatic** adj of or taking place in water; living or growing in water.

**aqueduct** n a large pipe or conduit for carrying water; an elevated structure supporting this.

**arbiter** n an arbitrator.

**arable** adj (land) suitable for ploughing or planting crops.—also n.

**arbitrary** adj not bound by rules; despotic, absolute; capricious, unreasonable.—**arbitrarily** adv.—**arbitrariness** n.

**arbitrate** vi to act as an arbitrator. • vt to submit to or act as an arbitrator.

**arbitration** n the settlement of disputes by arbitrating.

**arbitrator** n a person chosen to settle a dispute between contending parties.

**arc** n a portion of the circumference of a circle or other curve; a luminous discharge of electricity across a gap between two electrodes or terminals. • vi (pt **arced** or **arcked**) to form an electric arc.

**arcade** n an arched passageway; a covered walk or area lined with shops.

**arch**[1] n a curved structure spanning an opening; the curved underside of the foot. • vti to span or cover with an arch; to curve, bend into an arch.

**arch**[2] adj (criminal, etc) principal, expert; clever, sly; mischievous.

**archaeology, archeology** n the study of past human societies through their extant remains.—**archaeological, archeological** adj.—**archaeologist, archeologist** n.

**archaic** adj belonging to ancient times; (language) no longer in use.

**archbishop** n a bishop of the highest rank.

**archer** n a person who shoots with a bow and arrow.

**archery** n the art or sport of shooting arrows from a bow.

**archetype** n the original pattern or model; a prototype.—**archetypal** adj.

**archipelago** n (pl **archipelagos**) a sea filled with small islands; a group of small islands.

**architect** n a person who designs buildings and supervises their erection; someone who plans something.

**architecture** n the art, profession, or science of designing and constructing buildings; the style of a building or buildings.—**architectural** adj.—**architecturally** adv.

**archives** npl the location in which public records are kept; the public records themselves.

**archway** n an arched or vaulted passage, esp leading into a castle.

**arctic** adj (often with cap) of, near, or relating to the North Pole or its surroundings; (inf) very cold, icy.

**ardent** adj passionate; zealous.—**ardently** adv.

**arduous** adj difficult, laborious; steep, difficult to climb.—**arduously** adv.

**are** see **be**.

**area** n an expanse of land; a total outside surface, measured in square units; a part of a house, district, etc; scope or extent.

**arena** n an area within a sports stadium, etc where events take place; a place or sphere of contest or activity.

**aren't** = are not.

**arguable** adj able to be asserted; plausible.—**arguably** adv.

**argue** vt to try to prove by reasoning; to debate, dispute; to persuade (into, out of). • vi to offer reasons for or against something; to disagree, exchange angry words.

**argument** n a disagreement; a debate, discussion; a reason offered in debate; an abstract, summary.

**arid** adj very dry, parched; uninteresting; dull.—**aridity** n.—**aridly** adv.—**aridness** n.

**Aries** n (astrol) the first sign of the zodiac, the Ram, operative 21 March–21 April.

**aright** adv correctly.

**arise** vi (pt **arose**, pp **arisen**) to get up, as from bed; to rise, ascend; to come into being, to result (from).

**aristocracy** n (a country with) a government dominated by a privileged minority class; the privileged class in a society, the nobility; those people considered the best in their sphere.

**aristocrat** n a member of the aristocracy; a supporter of aristocratic government; a person with the manners or taste of a privileged class.

**aristocratic** adj relating to or characteristic of the aristocracy; elegant, stylish in dress and manners.—**aristocratically** adv.

**arithmetic** n (math) computation (addition, subtraction, etc) using real numbers; calculation.—**arithmetic, arithmetical** adj.—**arithmetically** adv.

**ark** n (Bible) the boat in which Noah and his family and two of every kind of creature survived the flood; an enclosure in a synagogue for the scrolls of the Torah.

**arm**[1] n the upper limb from the shoulder to the wrist; something shaped like an arm, as a support on a chair; a sleeve; power, authority; an administrative division of a large organization.

**arm**[2] n (usu pl) a weapon; a branch of the military service; (pl) heraldic bearings. • vt to provide with weapons, etc; to provide with something that protects or strengthens, etc; to set a fuse ready to explode. • vi to prepare for war or any struggle.

**armchair** n a chair with side rests for the arms. • adj lacking practical experience.

**armful** n as much as the arms can hold.

**armistice** n a truce, preliminary to a peace treaty.

**armour, armor** (US) n any defensive or protective covering.

**armpit** n the hollow underneath the arm at the shoulder

**arms** see **arm**[2].

**army** n a large body of soldiers for waging war, esp on land; any large number of persons, animals, etc.

**aroma** n a pleasant smell; a fragrance.—**aromatic** adj.

**arose** see **arise**.

**around** prep on all sides of; on the border of; in various places in or on; approximately, about. • adv in a circle; in every direction; in circumference; to the opposite direction.

**arouse** vt to wake from sleep; to stir, as to action; to evoke.

**arrange** vt to put in a sequence or row; to settle, make preparations for; (mus) to prepare a composition for different instruments other than those intended. • vi to come to an agreement; to make plans.—**arrangement** n.—**arranger** n.

**array** n an orderly grouping, esp of troops; an impressive display; fine clothes; (comput) an ordered data structure that allows information to be easily indexed. • vt to set in order, to arrange; to dress, decorate.

**arrears** npl overdue debts; work, etc still to be completed.

**arrest** vt to stop; to capture, apprehend esp by legal authority; to catch and hold the attention of. • n a stoppage; seizure by legal authority.

**arrival** n arriving; a person or thing that has arrived.

**arrive** vi to reach any destination; to come; to achieve success, celebrity.

**arrogance** n an exaggerated assumption of importance.

**arrogant** adj overbearing; aggressively self-important.—**arrogantly** adv.

**arrow** *n* a straight, pointed weapon, made to be shot from a bow; a sign used to indicate direction.

**arsenal** *n* a workshop or store for weapons and ammunition.

**arsenic** *n* a soft grey metallic element, highly poisonous.

**arson** *n* the crime of using fire to destroy property deliberately.—**arsonist** *n*.

**art** *n* human creativity; skill acquired by study and experience; any craft and its principles; the making of things that have form and beauty; any branch of this, as painting, sculpture, etc; drawings, paintings, statues, etc; (*pl*) the creative and nonscientific branches of knowledge, esp as studied academically.

**artefact, artifact** *n* a product of human craftsmanship, esp a simple tool or ornament.

**artery** *n* a tubular vessel that conveys blood from the heart; any main channel of transport or communication.—**arterial** *adj*.

**artful** *adj* skilful at attaining one's ends; clever, crafty.—**artfully** *adv*.—**artfulness** *n*.

**arthritis** *n* painful inflammation of a joint.—**arthritic** *adj*.

**artichoke** *n* a thistle-like plant with a scaly flower head, parts of which are eaten as a vegetable.

**article** *n* a separate item or clause in a written document; an individual item on a particular subject in a newspaper, magazine, etc; a particular or separate item; (*gram*) a word placed before a noun to identify it as definite or indefinite.

**articulate** *adj* capable of distinct, intelligible speech, or expressing one's thoughts clearly; jointed. • *vti* to speak or express clearly; to unite or become united (as) by a joint.

**artificial** *adj* lacking natural qualities; man-made.—**artificiality** *n*.—**artificially** *adv*.

**artillery** *n* large, heavy guns; the branch of the army that uses these.

**artisan** *n* a skilled workman.

**artist** *n* one who practises fine art, esp painting; one who does anything very well.—**artistic** *adj*.

**artistry** *n* artistic quality, ability, work, etc.

**artless** *adj* simple, natural; without art or skill.—**artlessly** *adv*.—**artlessness** *n*.

**as** *adv* equally; for instance; when related in a certain way. • *conj* in the same way that; while; because. • *prep* in the role or function of.

**asbestos** *n* a fine fibrous mineral used for making incombustible and chemical-resistant materials.

**ascend** *vti* to go up; to succeed to (a throne).

**ascendancy, ascendency** *n* dominating influence.

**ascent** *n* ascending; an upward slope, means of ascending.

**ascertain** *vt* to acquire definite knowledge of.—**ascertainable** *adj*.

**ascetic** *adj* self-denying, austere. • *n* a person who practises rigorous self-denial as a religious discipline; any severely abstemious person.—**ascetically** *adv*.—**asceticism** *n*.

**ascribe** *vt* to attribute.—**ascribable** *adj*.

**ash**[1] *n* a tree with silver-grey bark; the wood of this tree.

**ash**[2] *n* powdery residue of anything burnt; fine, volcanic lava.

**ashamed** *adj* feeling shame or guilt.

**ashen** *adj* like ashes, esp in colour; pale.

**ashore** *adv* to or on the shore; to or on land.—*also adj*.

**ashtray** *n* a small receptacle for tobacco ash and cigarette stubs.

**aside** *adv* on or to the side; in reserve;

notwithstanding. • *n* words uttered and intended as inaudible, esp as spoken by an actor to the audience and supposedly unheard by the others on the stage.

**ask** *vt* to put a question to, inquire of; to make a request of or for; to invite; to demand, expect. • *vi* to inquire about.

**askance, askant** *adv* with a sideways glance; with distrust.

**askew** *adv, adj* to one side; awry.

**asleep** *adj* sleeping; inactive; numb. • *adv* into a sleeping condition.

**asparagus** *n* a plant cultivated for its edible young shoots.

**aspect** *n* the look of a person or thing to the eye; a particular feature of a problem, situation, etc; the direction something faces; (*astrol*) the position of the planets with respect to one another, regarded as having an influence on human affairs.

**aspersions** *npl* slander; an attack on a person's reputation.

**asphalt** *n* a hard, black bituminous substance, used for paving roads, etc. • *vt* to surface with asphalt.

**asphyxiate** *vt* to suffocate.—**asphyxiation** *n*.

**aspiration** *n* strong desire; ambition; aspirating; the act of breathing; the withdrawal of air or fluid from a body cavity.

**aspire** *vi* to desire eagerly; to aim at high things.

**aspirin** *n* a pain-relieving drug.

**ass** *n* a donkey; a silly, stupid person; (*sl*) the arse, the buttocks.

**assail** *vt* to attack violently either physically or verbally.

**assailant** *n* an attacker.

**assassin** *n* a murderer, esp one hired to kill a leading political figure, etc.

**assassinate** *vt* to kill a political figure, etc; to harm (a person's reputation, etc).—**assassination** *n*.

**assault** *n* a violent attack; (*law*) an unlawful threat or attempt to harm another physically. • *vti* to make an assault (on).

**assemble** *vti* to bring together; to collect; to fit together the parts of; (*comput*) to translate.

**assembly** *n* assembling or being assembled; a gathering of persons, esp for a purpose; the fitting together of parts to make a whole machine, etc.

**assembly line** *n* a series of machines, equipment and workers through which a product passes in successive stages to be assembled.

**assent** *vi* to express agreement to something. • *n* consent or agreement.

**assert** *vt* to declare, affirm as true; to maintain or enforce (eg rights).

**assertion** *n* asserting; a statement that something is a fact, usu without evidence.

**assertive** *adj* self-assured, positive, confident.—**assertively** *adv*.—**assertiveness** *n*.

**assess** *vt* to establish the amount of, as a tax; to impose a tax or fine; to value, for the purpose of taxation; to estimate the worth, importance, etc of.—**assessment** *n*.

**asset** *n* anything owned that has value; a desirable thing; (*pl*) all the property, accounts receivable, etc of a person or business; (*pl: law*) property usable to pay debts.

**assign** *vt* to allot; to appoint to a post or duty; to ascribe; (*law*) to transfer (a right, property, etc).—**assignable** *adj*.

**assignment** *n* the act of assigning; something assigned to a person, such as a share, task, etc.

**assimilate** *vt* to absorb; to digest; to be ascribed; to be like.—**assimilation** *n*.

**assist** *vti* to support or aid.—**assistance** *n*.—**assistant** *n*.

**associate** *vt* to join as a friend, business partner or supporter; to bring together; to unite; to connect in the mind. • *vi* to combine or unite with others; to come together as friends, business partners or supporters. • *adj* allied or connected; having secondary status or privileges. • *n* a companion, business partner, supporter, etc; something closely connected with another; a person admitted to an association as a subordinate member.

**association** *n* an organization of people with a common aim; the act of associating or being associated; a connection in the mind, etc.

**assorted** *adj* distributed according to sorts; miscellaneous.

**assortment** *n* a collection of people or things of different sorts.

**assume** *vt* to take on, to undertake; to usurp; to take as certain or true; to pretend to possess.

**assumption** *n* something taken for granted.

**assurance** *n* a promise, guarantee; a form of life insurance; a feeling of certainty, self-confidence.

**assure** *vt* to make safe or certain; to give confidence to; to state positively; to guarantee, ensure.

**asterisk** *n* a sign (•) used in writing or printing to mark omission of words, etc. • *vt* to mark with an asterisk.

**astern** *adv* behind a ship or aircraft; at or toward the rear of a ship, etc; backward.

**asthma** *n* a chronic respiratory condition causing difficulty with breathing.—**asthmatic** *adj*.—**asthmatically** *adv*.

**astir** *adv* moving or bustling about; out of bed.

**astonish** *vt* to fill with sudden or great surprise.—**astonishing** *adj*.—**astonishment** *n*.

**astound** *vt* to astonish greatly.—**astounding** *adj*.

**astray** *adv* off the right path; into error.

**astride** *adv* with a leg on either side. • *prep* extending across.

**astrology** *n* the study of planetary positions and motions to determine their supposed influence on human affairs.—**astrologer** *n*.—**astrological** *adj*.—**astrologically** *adv*.

**astronaut** *n* one trained to make flights in outer space.

**astronomy** *n* the scientific investigation of the stars and other planets.—**astronomer** *n*.

**astute** *adj* crafty, shrewd.—**astutely** *adv*.—**astuteness** *n*.

**asylum** *n* a place of safety, a refuge; (*formerly*) an institution for the blind, the mentally ill, etc.

**at** *prep* on; in; near; by; used to indicate location or position.

**ate** *see* **eat**.

**atheism** *n* belief in the nonexistence of God.—**atheist** *n*.

**athlete** *n* a person trained in games or exercises requiring skill, speed, strength, stamina, etc.

**athletic** *adj* of athletes or athletics; active, vigorous.—**athletically** *adv*. —**athleticism** *n*.

**athletics** *n* (*used as sing or pl*) running, jumping, throwing sports, games, etc.

**atlas** *n* a book containing maps, charts and tables.

**atmosphere** *n* the gaseous mixture that surrounds the earth or the other stars and planets; a unit of pressure equal to the pressure of the atmosphere at sea level; any dominant or surrounding influence.—**atmospheric** *adj*.

**atom** *n* the smallest particle of a chemical element; a tiny particle, bit.

**atomic bomb** *n* a bomb whose

explosive power derives from the atomic energy released during nuclear fission or fusion.

**atomizer** *n* a device for atomizing liquids, usu perfumes or cleaning agents.

**atone** *vi* to give satisfaction or make amends (for).

**atrocious** *adj* extremely brutal or wicked; (*inf*) very bad, of poor quality.—**atrociously** *adv*.

**atrocity** *n* a cruel act; something wicked or repellent.

**attach** *vt* to fix or fasten to something; to appoint to a specific group; to ascribe, attribute. • *vi* to become attached; to adhere.—**attachable** *adj*.

**attack** *vt* to set upon violently; to assault in speech or writing; to invade, as of a disease. • *vi* to make an assault. • *n* an assault; a fit of illness; severe criticism; a beginning of a performance, undertaking, etc.

**attain** *vt* to succeed in getting or arriving at; to achieve. • *vi* to come to or arrive at by growth or effort.—**attainable** *adj*.

**attainment** *n* something attained; an accomplishment.

**attempt** *vt* to try to accomplish, get, etc. • *n* an endeavour or effort to accomplish; an attack, assault.

**attend** *vt* to take care of; to go with, accompany; to be present at. • *vi* to apply oneself (to); to deal with, give attention to.

**attendance** *n* attending; the number of people present; the number of times a person attends.

**attendant** *n* a person who serves or accompanies another; someone employed to assist or guide. • *adj* accompanying, following as a result; being in attendance.

**attention** *n* the application of the mind to a particular purpose, aim, etc; awareness, notice; care, consideration;

(*usu pl*) an act of civility or courtesy; (*mil*) a soldier's formal erect posture.

**attentive** *adj* observant, diligent; courteous.—**attentively** *adv*.—**attentiveness** *n*.

**attest** *vt* to state as true; to certify, as by oath; to give proof of. • *vi* to testify, bear witness (to).—**attestation** *n*.

**attic** *n* the room or space just under the roof; a garret.

**attire** *vt* to clothe; to dress up. • *n* dress, clothing.

**attitude** *n* posture, position of the body; a manner of thought or feeling; the position of an aircraft or spacecraft in relation to certain reference points.

**attorney** *n* (*pl* **attorneys**) one legally authorized to act for another; a lawyer.

**attract** *vt* to pull towards oneself; to get the admiration, attention, etc of. • *vi* to be attractive.

**attraction** *n* the act of attraction; the power of attracting, esp charm; (*physics*) the mutual action by which bodies tend to be drawn together.

**attractive** *adj* pleasing in appearance, etc; arousing interest; able to draw or pull.—**attractively** *adv*.—**attractiveness** *n*.

**attribute** *vt* to regard as belonging to; to ascribe, impute (to) • *n* a quality, a characteristic of.—**attributable** *adj*.—**attribution** *n*.

**attrition** *n* a grinding down by or as by friction; a relentless wearing down and weakening.

**aubergine, eggplant** (*US*) *n* the dark purple fruit of the egg plant used as a vegetable; its colour.

**auburn** *adj* reddish brown.

**auction** *n* a public sale of items to the highest bidder. • *vt* to sell by or at an auction.

**auctioneer** *n* one who conducts an auction.

**audacious** *adj* daring, adventurous; bold; rash; insolent.—**audaciously** *adv*.—**audacity** *n*.

**audible** *adj* heard or able to be heard. —**audibly** *adv*.—**audibility** *n*.

**audience** *n* a gathering of listeners or spectators; the people addressed by a book, play, film, etc; a formal interview or meeting.

**audiovisual** *adj* using both sound and vision, as in teaching aids.

**audit** *n* the inspection and verification of business accounts by a qualified accountant. • *vt* to make such an inspection.

**audition** *n* a trial to test a performer. • *vti* to test or be tested by audition.

**auditor** *n* a person qualified to audit business accounts.

**auditorium** *n* the part of a building allotted to the audience; a building or hall for speeches, concerts, etc.

**augment** *vti* to increase.—**augmentation** *n*.

**augur** *vti* to prophesy; to be an omen (of).

**August** *n* the eighth month of the year, having 31 days.

**august** *adj* imposing; majestic.

**aunt** *n* a father's or mother's sister; an uncle's wife.

**au pair** *n* a person, esp a young woman, from abroad who performs domestic chores, child-minding, etc, in return for board and lodging.

**aura** *n* a particular quality or atmosphere surrounding a person or thing.

**auspice** *n* an omen; (*pl*) sponsorship; patronage.

**auspicious** *adj* showing promise, favourable.—**auspiciously** *adv*.

**austere** *adj* stern, forbidding in attitude or appearance; abstemious; severely simple, plain.—**austerely** *adv*.—**austerity** *n*.

**authentic** *adj* genuine, conforming to truth or reality; trustworthy, reliable.—**authentically** *adv*.—**authenticity** *n*.

**author** *n* a person who brings something into existence; the writer of a book, article, etc. • *vt* to be the author of. —**authoress** *nf*.

**authoritarian** *adj* favouring strict obedience; dictatorial. • *n* a person advocating or practising authoritarian principles.

**authoritative** *adj* commanding or possessing authority; accepted as true; official.—**authoritatively** *adv*.

**authority** *n* the power or right to command; (*pl*) officials with this power; influence resulting from knowledge, prestige, etc; a person, writing, etc cited to support an opinion; an expert.

**authorize** *vt* to give authority to, to empower; to give official approval to, sanction.—**authorization** *n*.

**auto** *n* (*pl* **autos**) (*US inf*) a motor car.

**autobiography** *n* the biography of a person written by himself or herself.—**autobiographer** *n*.—**autobiographical** *adj*.

**autocrat** *n* an absolute ruler; any domineering person.—**autocratic** *adj*.—**autocratically** *adv*.

**autograph** *n* a person's signature. • *vt* to write one's signature in or on.

**automate** *vt* to control by automation; to convert to automatic operation.

**automatic** *adj* involuntary or reflexive; self-regulating; acting by itself. • *n* an automatic pistol or rifle.—**automatically** *adv*.

**automation** *n* the use of automatic methods, machinery, etc, in industry.

**automaton** *n* (*pl* **automatons**, **automata**) any automatic device, esp a robot; a human being who acts like a robot.

**automobile** *n* a motor car.

**autonomy** *n* freedom of self-determination; independence, self-government.—**autonomous** *adj*.

**autopsy** *n* a post-mortem examination to determine the cause of death.

**autumn** *n* the season between summer and winter; in US, fall.—**autumnal** *adj*.

**auxiliary** *adj* providing help, subsidiary; supplementary. • *n* a helper; (*gram*) a verb that helps form tenses, moods, voices, etc of other verbs, as *have*, *be*, *may*, *shall*, etc.

**avail** *vti* to be of use or advantage to. • *n* benefit, use or help.

**available** *adj* ready for use; obtainable, accessible.—**availability** *n*.

**avalanche** *n* a mass of snow, ice, and rock tumbling down a mountainside; a sudden overwhelming accumulation or influx.

**avant-garde** *n* (*arts*) those ideas and practices regarded as in advance of those generally accepted. • *adj* pertaining to these and their creators.

**avarice** *n* greed for wealth.—**avaricious** *adj*.—**avariciously** *adv*.

**Ave, ave** *abbr* = avenue.

**avenge** *vt* to get revenge for.—**avenger** *n*.

**avenue** *n* a street, drive, etc, esp when broad; means of access.

**average** *n* the result of dividing the sum of two or more quantities by the number of quantities; the usual kind, amount, etc. • *vt* to calculate the average of; to achieve an average number of.

**averse** *adj* unwilling; opposed (to).

**aversion** *n* antipathy; hatred; something arousing hatred or repugnance.

**avert** *vt* to turn away or aside from; to prevent, avoid.

**aviation** *n* the art or science of flying aircraft.

**avid** *adj* eager, greedy.—**avidly** *adv*.

**avocado (pear)** *n* a thick-skinned, pear-shaped fruit with yellow buttery flesh.

**avoid** *vt* to keep clear of, shun; to refrain from.

**avoidable** *adj* able to be avoided.

**await** *vti* to wait for; to be in store for.

**awake** *vb* (*pt* **awoke** *or* **awaked**, *pp* **awoken** *or* **awaked**) *vi* to wake; to become aware. • *vt* to rouse from sleep; to rouse from inaction. • *adj* roused from sleep, not asleep; active; aware.

**award** *vt* to give, as by a legal decision; to give (a prize, etc); to grant. • *n* a decision, as by a judge; a prize.

**aware** *adj* realizing, having knowledge; conscious.—**awareness** *n*.

**awash** *adj* filled or overflowing with water.

**away** *adv* from a place; in another place or direction; off, aside; far. • *adj* absent; at a distance.

**awe** *n* a mixed feeling of fear, wonder and dread. • *vt* to fill with awe.

**awesome** *adj* inspiring awe.

**awful** *adj* very bad; unpleasant. • *adv* (*inf*) very.—**awfulness** *n*.

**awhile** *adv* for a short time.

**awkward** *adj* lacking dexterity, clumsy; graceless; embarrassing; embarrassed; inconvenient; deliberately obstructive or difficult to deal with.—**awkwardly** *adv*.—**awkwardness** *n*.

**awning** *n* a structure, as of canvas, extended above or in front of a window, door, etc to provide shelter against the sun or rain.

**awoke, awoken** *see* **awake**.

**awry** *adv* twisted to one side. • *adj* contrary to expectations, wrong.

**axe, ax** (*US*) *n* a tool with a long handle and bladed head for chopping wood, etc. • *vt* to trim, split, etc with an axe.

**axiom** *n* a widely held or accepted truth or principle.—**axiomatic** *adj*.

**axis** *n* (*pl* **axes**) a real or imaginary straight line about which a body rotates; the centre line of a symmetrical figure; a reference line of a coordinate system; a partnership, alliance.—**axial** adj.

**axle** n a rod on or with which a wheel turns; a bar connecting two opposite wheels, as of a car.

# B

**babble** vi to make sounds like a baby; to talk incoherently; to murmur, as a brook. • n incoherent talk; chatter; a murmuring sound.—**babbler** n.

**baby** n a newborn child or infant; a very young animal; (sl) a girl or young woman; a personal project. • vt to pamper.—also adj.—**babyish** adj.

**baby-sit** vti to look after a baby or child while the parents are out.—**baby-sitter** n.

**bachelor** n an unmarried man; a person who holds a degree from a college or university.—**bachelorhood** n.

**back** n the rear surface of the human body from neck to hip; the corresponding part in animals; a part that supports or fits the back; the part farthest from the front; (sport) a player or position behind the front line. • adj at the rear; (streets, etc) remote or inferior; (pay, etc) of or for the past; backward. • adv at or toward the rear; to or toward a former condition, time, etc; in return or requital; in reserve or concealment. • vti to move or go backward; to support; to bet on; to provide or be back for; (with **down**) to withdraw from a position or claim; (with **off**) to move back (or away, etc); (with **out**) to withdraw from an enterprise; to evade keeping a promise, etc; (with **up**) to support; to move

backward; to accumulate because of restricted movement; (comput) to make a copy (of a data file, etc) for safekeeping.

**backache** n an ache or pain in the back.

**backbencher** n a Member of Parliament who does not hold an important office.

**backbiting** n spiteful talk behind a person's back.—**backbite** vt.

**backbone** n the spinal column; main support; strength, courage.

**backdate** vt to declare valid from some previous date.

**backfire** vi (automobiles) to ignite prematurely causing a loud bang from the exhaust; to have the opposite effect from that intended, usu with unfortunate consequences.—also n.

**backgammon** n a board game played by two people with pieces moved according to throws of the dice.

**background** n the distant part of a scene or picture; an inconspicuous position; social class, education, experience; circumstances leading up to an event.

**backhand** n (tennis, etc) a stroke played with the hand turned outwards.

**backhanded** adj backhand; (compliment) indirect, ambiguous.—also adv.

**backhander** n a backhanded stroke; (inf) a backhanded remark; (sl) a bribe.

**backing** n support; supporters; a lining to support or strengthen the back of something; musical accompaniment to a (esp pop) singer.

**backlash** n a violent and adverse reaction; a recoil in machinery.

**backlog** n an accumulation of work, etc still to be done.

**backside** n (inf) buttocks.

**backstroke** n (swimming) a stroke using backward circular sweeps of the arms whilst lying face upward.

**backward** adj turned toward the rear or opposite way; shy; slow or retarded. • *adv* backwards.—**backwardness** *n*.

**backwards** *adv* towards the back; with the back foremost; in a way opposite the usual; into a less good or favourable state or condition; into the past.

**backwater** *n* a pool of still water fed by a river; a remote, backward place.

**backyard** *n* a yard at the back of a house.

**bacon** *n* salted and smoked meat from the back or sides of a pig

**bacteria** *npl* (*sing* **bacterium**) microscopic unicellular organisms.—**bacterial** *adj*.

**bad** *adj* (**worse, worst**) not good; not as it should be; inadequate or unfit; rotten or spoiled; incorrect or faulty; wicked; immoral; mischievous; harmful; ill; sorry, distressed.—**badness** *n*.

**bade** *see* **bid**.

**badge** *n* an emblem, symbol or distinguishing mark.

**badger** *n* a hibernating, burrowing black and white mammal related to the weasel. • *vt* to pester or annoy persistently.

**badly** *adv* poorly; inadequately; unsuccessfully; severely; (*inf*) very much.

**badminton** *n* a court game for two or four players played with light rackets and a shuttlecock volleyed over a net.

**baffle** *vt* to bewilder or perplex; to frustrate; to make ineffectual. • *n* a plate or device used to restrict the flow of sound, light or fluid.—**bafflement** *n*.—**baffling** *adj*.

**bag** *n* a usu flexible container of paper, plastic, etc that can be closed at the top; a satchel, suitcase, etc; a handbag; game taken in hunting; a bag-like shape or part; (*derog*) an old woman; (*inf: in pl*) plenty (of). • *vti* (*pt* **bagged**) to place in a bag; to kill in hunting; (*inf*) to get; to make a claim on; to hang loosely.

**baggage** *n* suitcases; luggage.

**baggy** *adj* (**baggier, baggiest**) hanging loosely in folds.—**baggily** *adv*.—**bagginess** *n*.

**bagpipe** *n* (*often pl*) a musical instrument consisting of an air-filled bag fitted with pipes.

**bail**[1] *n* money lodged as security that a prisoner, if released, will return to a court to stand trial; such a release; the person pledging such money. • *vt* to free a person by providing bail; (*with* **out**) to help out of financial or other difficulty.

**bail**[2] *vti* (*usu with* **out**) to scoop out (water) from (a boat).

**bail**[3] *n* (*cricket*) either of two wooden cross-pieces that rest on the three stumps; a bar separating horses in an open stable; a metal bar that holds the paper against the roller of a typewriter.

**bailiff** *n* in UK, the agent of a landlord or landowner; a sheriff's officer who serves writs and summonses; a minor official in some US courts.

**bait** *n* food attached to a hook to entice fish or make them bite; any lure or enticement. • *vt* to put food on a hook to lure; to set dogs upon (a badger, etc); to persecute, worry or tease, esp by verbal attacks; to lure, to tempt; to entice.

**bake** *vt* (*pottery*) to dry and harden by heating in the sun or by fire; (*food*) to cook by dry heat in an oven. • *vi* to do a baker's work; to dry and harden in heat; (*inf*) to be very hot.

**baker** *n* a person who bakes and sells bread, cakes, etc.

**bakery** *n* a room or building for baking; a shop that sells bread, cakes, etc; baked goods.

**baking powder** *n* a leavening agent containing sodium bicarbonate and an acid-forming substance.

**balance** *n* a device for weighing, consisting of two dishes or pans hanging from a pivoted horizontal beam; equilibrium; mental stability; the power to influence or control; a remainder. • *vt* to weigh; to compare; to equalize the debit and credit sides of an account. • *vi* to be equal in power or weight, etc; to have the debits and credits equal.

**balance sheet** *n* a statement of assets and liabilities.

**balcony** *n* a projecting platform from an upper storey enclosed by a railing; an upper floor of seats in a theatre, etc.—**balconied** *adj*.

**bald** *adj* lacking a natural or usual covering, as of hair, vegetation, nap; (*tyre*) having little or no tread; (*truth*) plain or blunt; bare, unadorned.—**baldly** *adv*.—**baldness** *n*.

**bale**[1] *n* a large bundle of goods, as raw cotton, compressed and bound. • *vt* (*hay etc*) to make into bales. • *vi* (*with* out) to parachute from an aircraft.

**bale**[2] *n* great evil; woe.—**baleful** *adj*.

**balk** *vt* to obstruct or foil. • *vi* to stop and refuse to move and act.—*also* **baulk**.

**ball**[1] *n* a spherical or nearly spherical body or mass; a round object for use in tennis, football, etc; a throw or pitch of a ball; a missile for a cannon, rifle, etc; (*pl*) testicles; any rounded part or protuberance of the body. • *vti* to form into a ball.

**ball**[2] *n* a formal social dance; (*inf*) a good time.—**ballroom** *n*.

**ballad** *n* a narrative song or poem; a slow, sentimental, esp pop, song.

**ballast** *n* heavy material carried in a ship or vehicle to stabilize it when it is not carrying cargo; crushed rock or gravel, etc used in railway tracks.

**ballerina** *n* a female ballet dancer.

**ballet** *n* a theatrical representation of a story, set to music and performed by dancers; the troupe of dancers.

**ballistics** *n* (*used as sing*) the scientific study of projectiles and firearms.

**balloon** *n* a large airtight envelope that rises up when filled with hot air or light gases, usu with a basket for passengers; a small inflatable rubber pouch used as a toy; a balloon-shaped line enclosing speech or thoughts in a strip cartoon. • *vti* to inflate; to swell, expand; to travel in a balloon.—**balloonist** *n*.

**ballot** *n* a paper used in voting; the process of voting; the number of votes cast. • *vi* (*pt* **balloted**) to vote.

**ballot box** *n* a secure container for ballot papers.

**ballpoint pen** *n* a pen with a tiny ball, which rotates against an inking cartridge, as its writing tip.

**balsam** *n* a fragrant, resinous substance or the tree yielding it.

**bamboo** *n* any of various, often tropical, woody grasses, used for furniture.

**bamboozle** *vt* (*inf*) to deceive; to mystify.

**ban** *n* a condemnation, an official prohibition. • *vt* (*pt* **banned**) to prohibit, esp officially; to forbid.

**banal** *adj* trite, commonplace.—**banality** *n*.

**banana** *n* a herbaceous plant bearing its fruit in compact, hanging bunches.

**band**[1] *n* a strip of material used for binding; a stripe; (*radio*) a range of wavelengths.

**band**[2] *n* a group of people with a common purpose; a group of musicians. • *vti* to associate together for a particular purpose.

**bandage** *n* a strip of cloth for binding wounds and fractures. • *vt* to bind a wound.

**bandit** *n* a robber.

**bandwagon** *n* a wagon for carrying a

band in a parade; a movement, idea, etc that is (thought to be) heading for success.

**bandy**[1] *vt* to pass to and fro; (*often with* **about**) (*rumours, etc*) to spread freely; to exchange words, esp angrily.

**bandy**[2] *adj* (**bandier, bandiest**) having legs curved outward at the knee.— *also* **bandy-legged**.

**bang** *n* a hard blow; a sudden loud sound. • *vt* to hit or knock with a loud noise; (*door*) to slam. • *vi* to make a loud noise; to hit noisily or sharply. • *adv* with a bang, abruptly; (*inf*) precisely.

**bangle** *n* a bracelet worn on the arm or ankle.

**banish** *vt* to exile from a place; to drive away; to get rid of.—**banishment** *n*.

**banister** *n* the railing or supporting posts in a staircase.—*also* **bannister**.

**banjo** *n* (*pl* **banjos**) a stringed musical instrument with a drum-like body and a long fretted neck.

**bank**[1] *n* a mound or pile; the sloping side of a river; elevated ground in a lake or the sea; a row or series of objects, as of dials, switches. • *vti* to form into a mound; to cover (a fire) with fuel so that it burns more slowly; (*aircraft*) to curve or tilt sideways.

**bank**[2] *n* an institution that offers various financial services, such as the safekeeping, lending and exchanging of money; the money held by the banker or dealer in a card game; any supply or store. • *vti* (*cheques, cash, etc*) to deposit in a bank.

**banker** *n* a person who runs a bank; the keeper of the bank at a gaming table.

**banking** *n* the activity or occupation of running a bank. • *adj* of or concerning a bank.

**banknote** *n* a note issued by a bank, which serves as money.

**bankrupt** *n* a person, etc legally declared unable to pay his debts; one who becomes insolvent. • *adj* judged to be insolvent; financially ruined. • *vt* to make bankrupt.— **bankruptcy** *n*.

**banner** *n* a flag or ensign; a headline running across a newspaper page; a strip of cloth bearing a slogan or emblem carried between poles in a parade.

**bannister** *see* **banister**.

**banns** *npl* public declaration of intention, esp in church, to marry.

**banquet** *n* a feast; an elaborate and sometimes formal dinner in honour of a person or occasion. • *vt* to hold a banquet.

**banter** *vt* to tease good-humouredly.

**baptise, baptize** *vt* to immerse in or sprinkle with water, esp as a religious rite; to christen, name.

**baptism** *n* the sprinkling of water on the forehead, or complete immersion in water, as a rite of admitting a person to a Christian church; an initiating experience.—**baptismal** *adj*.—**baptismally** *adv*.

**bar**[1] *n* a straight length of wood or metal; a counter where drinks etc are served; a place with such a counter; an oblong piece, as of soap; anything that obstructs or hinders; a band or strip; barristers or lawyers collectively; the legal profession; (*mus*) a vertical line dividing a staff into measures; (*mus*) a measure. • *vt* (*pt* **barred**) to secure or fasten as with a bar; to exclude or prevent; to oppose. • *prep* except for.

**bar**[2] *n* a unit of atmospheric pressure.

**barbecue** *n* a metal frame for grilling food over an open fire; an open-air party where barbecued food is served. • *vt* to cook on a barbecue.

**barber** *n* a person who cuts hair and shaves beards.

**barbiturate** *n* a sedative drug.

**bare** *adj* without covering; unclothed, naked; simple, unadorned; mere; without furnishings. • *vt* to uncover; to reveal.—**bareness** *n*.

**bareback** *adj* on a horse with no saddle.—*also adv*.

**barefaced** *adj* with the face shaven or uncovered; shameless.

**barefoot, barefooted** *adj* with the feet bare.—*also adv*.

**barely** *adv* openly; merely, scarcely.

**bargain** *n* an agreement laying down the conditions of a transaction; something sold at a price favourable to the buyer. • *vt* to make a bargain, haggle.

**barge** *n* a flat-bottomed vessel, used to transport freight along rivers and canals; a large boat for excursions or pleasure trips. • *vi* to lurch clumsily; (*with* in) to interrupt (a conversation) rudely; (*with* into) to enter abruptly.

**baritone** *n* the adult male voice ranging between bass and tenor; a singer with such a voice.

**bark**¹ *n* the harsh or abrupt cry of a dog, wolf, etc; a similar sound, such as one made by a person. • *vi* to make a loud cry like a dog; to speak sharply.

**bark**² *n* the outside covering of a tree trunk. • *vt* to remove the bark from; (*inf*) to scrape; to skin (the knees, etc).

**barley** *n* a grain used in making beer and whisky, and for food.

**barmaid** *n* a woman serving alcohol in a bar.

**barman** *n* a man serving alcohol in a bar.

**barmy** *adj* (**barmier, barmiest**) (*sl*) crazy.

**barn** *n* a farm building used for storing grain, hay, etc.

**barnacle** *n* a hard-shelled marine animal that attaches itself to rocks and ship-bottoms.

**barometer** *n* an instrument for measuring atmospheric pressure and imminent changes in the weather; anything that marks change.—**barometric** *adj*.

**baron** *n* a member of a rank of nobility, the lowest in the British peerage; a powerful businessman.—**baroness** *nf*.

**barracks** *n* (*used as sing*) a building for housing soldiers.

**barrage** *n* a man-made dam across a river; heavy artillery fire; (*of protests*) continuous and heavy delivery.

**barrel** *n* a cylindrical container, usu wooden, with bulging sides held together with hoops; the amount held by a barrel; a tubular structure, as in a gun. • *vt* (*pt* **barrelled**) to put into barrels.

**barrel organ** *n* a mechanical piano or organ played by a revolving cylinder with pins that operate the keys or valves to produce sound.

**barren** *adj* infertile; incapable of producing offspring; unable to bear crops; unprofitable.

**barricade** *n* a barrier or blockade used in defence to block a street; an obstruction. • *vt* to block with a barricade.

**barrier** *n* anything that bars passage, prevents access, controls crowds, etc.

**barrister** *n* a qualified lawyer who has been called to the bar in England.

**barrow** *n* a wheelbarrow or hand-cart used for carrying loads.

**barter** *vt* to trade commodities or services without exchanging money. • *vi* to haggle or bargain. • *n* trade by the exchanging of commodities.

**base**¹ *n* the bottom part of anything; the support or foundation; the fundamental principle; the centre of operations (eg military); (*baseball*) one of the four corners of the diamond. • *vt* to use as a basis; to found (on).—**basal** *adj*.

**base**[2] *adj* low in morality or honour; worthless; menial.—**basely** *adv*.—**baseness** *n*.

**baseball** *n* the US national game, involving two teams that score runs by hitting a ball and running round four bases arranged in a diamond shape on the playing area.

**basement** *n* the part of a building that is partly or wholly below ground level.

**bash** *vt* (*inf*) to hit hard.

**bashful** *adj* easily embarrassed, shy.—**bashfully** *adv*.

**basic** *adj* fundamental. • *n* (*often pl*) a basic principle, factor, etc.—**basically** *adv*.

**basil** *n* a plant with aromatic leaves used for seasoning food.

**basin** *n* a wide shallow container for liquid; its contents; any large hollow, often with water in it; a tract of land drained by a river.

**basis** *n* (*pl* **bases**) a base or foundation; a principal constituent; a fundamental principle or theory.

**bask** *vi* to lie in sunshine or warmth; to enjoy someone's approval.

**basket** *n* a container made of interwoven cane, wood strips, etc; the hoop through which basketball players throw the ball to score.

**basketball** *n* a game in which two teams compete to score by throwing the ball through an elevated net basket or hoop; this ball.

**bass**[1] *n* (*mus*) the range of the lowest male voice; a singer or instrument with this range. • *adj* of, for or in the range of a bass.

**bass**[2] *n* any of numerous freshwater food and game fishes.

**bassoon** *n* an orchestral, deep-toned woodwind instrument.—**bassoonist** *n*.

**bastard** *n* a person born of unmarried parents; (*offensive*) an unpleasant person; (*inf*) a person (*lucky bastard*). • *adj* illegitimate (by birth); false; not genuine.—**bastardy** *n*.

**baste**[1] *vt* to drip fat over (roasting meat, etc).

**baste**[2] *vt* to sew with long loose stitches as a temporary seam.

**bat**[1] *n* a wooden club used in cricket, baseball, etc; one who bats; a paddle used in table tennis. • *vb* (*pt* **batted**) *vt* to hit as with a bat. • *vi* to take one's turn at bat.

**bat**[2] *n* a mouse-like flying mammal with forelimbs modified to form wings.

**bat**[3] *vt* (*pt* **batted**) (*one's eyelids*) to wink or flutter.

**batch** *n* the quantity of bread, etc produced at one time; one set, group, etc; an amount of work for processing by a computer in a single run.

**bath** *n* water for washing the body; a bathing; a tub for bathing; (*pl*) a building with baths for public use; a municipal swimming pool. • *vti* to give a bath to; to bathe.

**bathe** *vt* to dampen with any liquid. • *vi* to have a bath; to go swimming; to become immersed.—**bather** *n*.

**bathroom** *n* a room with a bath or shower and usually a toilet and washbasin.

**baton** *n* a staff serving as a symbol of office; a thin stick used by the conductor of an orchestra to beat time; a hollow cylinder carried by each member of a relay team in succession; a policeman's truncheon.

**battalion** *n* an army unit consisting of three or more companies; a large group.

**batter** *vt* to beat with repeated blows; to wear out with heavy use. • *vi* to strike heavily and repeatedly. • *n* a mixture of flour, egg, and milk or water used in cooking.

**battery** *n* a set of heavy guns; a small unit of artillery; an electric cell that supplies current; unlawful beating.

**battle** *n* a combat or fight between two opposing individuals or armies; a contest. • *vti* to fight; to struggle.

**battlefield** *n* the land on which a battle is fought.

**battlement** *n* a parapet or wall with indentations, from which to shoot.

**battleship** *n* a large, heavily armoured warship.

**baulk** *see* **balk**.

**bawdy** *adj* (**bawdier, bawdiest**) humorously indecent; obscene, lewd.— **bawdily** *adv*.—**bawdiness** *n*.

**bawl** *vti* to shout; to weep loudly. • *n* a loud shout; a noisy weeping.— **bawler** *n*.—**bawling** *n*.

**bay**[1] *n* a type of laurel tree.

**bay**[2] *n* a wide inlet of a sea or lake; an inward bend of a shore.

**bay**[3] an alcove or recess in a wall; a compartment used for a special purpose.

**bay**[4] *vti* to bark (at). • *n* the cry of a hound or a pursuing pack; the position of one forced to turn and fight.

**bay**[5] *adj* reddish brown. • *n* a horse of this colour.

**bayonet** *n* a blade for stabbing attached to the muzzle of a rifle. • *vt* (*pt* **bayoneted** *or* **bayonetted**) to kill or stab with a bayonet.

**bay window** *n* a window projecting from the outside wall of a house.

**bazaar** *n* a market-place; a street full of small shops; a benefit sale for a church, etc.

**BBC** *abbr* = British Broadcasting Corporation.

**BC** *abbr* = Before Christ.

**be** *vi* (*pres* **t am, are, is**, *pt* **was, were**, *pp* **been**) to exist; to live; to take place.

**beach** *n* a flat, sandy shore of the sea. • *vi* to bring (a boat) up on the beach from the sea.

**beacon** *n* a light for warning or guiding.

**bead** *n* a small ball pierced for stringing; (*pl*) a string of beads; (*pl*) a rosary; a bubble or droplet of liquid; the sight of a rifle.—**beaded** *adj*.

**beading** *n* moulding or edging in the form of a series of beads; a wooden strip, rounded on one side, used for trimming.—*also* **beadwork**.

**beak** *n* a bird's bill; any projecting part; the nose.—**beaked** *adj*.

**beaker** *n* a large drinking cup, or the amount it holds; a cylindrical vessel with a pouring lip used by chemists and pharmacists.

**beam** *n* a long straight piece of timber or metal; the crossbar of a balance; a ship's breadth at its widest point; a slender shaft of light, etc; a radiant look, smile, etc; a steady radio or radar signal for guiding aircraft or ships. • *vt* (*light, etc*) to send out; to smile with pleasure.

**bean** *n* a plant bearing kidney-shaped seeds; a seed or pod of such a plant; any bean-like seed.

**bear**[1] *vb* (*pt* **bore**, *pp* **borne**) *vt* to carry; to endure; to support, to sustain; to conduct (oneself); to produce or bring forth; (*with* **out**) to confirm. • *vi* to be productive; (*with* **down**) to press or weigh down; to overwhelm; (*with* **on** *or* **upon**) to have reference to; (*with* **up**) to endure with courage.

**bear**[2] *n* a large mammal with coarse fur, short legs, strong claws and feeding mainly on fruit and insects; a gruff or ill-mannered person; a teddy bear; a speculator who sells stock in anticipation of a fall in price.

**bearable** *adj* endurable.—**bearably** *adv*.

**beard** *n* hair covering a man's chin; similar bristles on an animal or plant. • *vt* to defy, oppose openly.— **bearded** *adj*.

**bearer** *n* a person who bears or presents; a person who carries something (a coffin, etc).

**bearing** *n* demeanour; conduct; a compass direction; (*followed by* **to** *or* **upon**) relevance; a machine part on which another part slides, revolves, etc.

**beast** *n* a large, wild, four-footed animal; a brutal, vicious person; (*inf*) something difficult, an annoyance.

**beastly** *adj* (**beastlier, beastliest**) (*inf*) disagreeable. • *adv* (*inf*) very (*beastly cold*).

**beat** *vb* (*pt* **beat**, *pp* **beaten**) *vt* to strike, dash or pound repeatedly; to flog; to overcome or counteract; to find too difficult for; (*mus*) to mark (time) with a baton, etc; (*eggs, etc*) to mix by stirring vigorously; (*esp wings*) to move up and down; (*a path, way, etc*) to form by repeated trampling; (*sl*) to baffle. • *vi* to hit, pound, etc repeatedly; to throb; (*naut*) to sail against the wind. • *n* a recurrent stroke, pulsation, as in a heartbeat or clock ticking; rhythm in music or poetry; the area patrolled by a police officer.

**beater** *n* an implement for beating, such as an attachment for an electric food mixer.

**beating** *n* the act of striking or thrashing; throbbing, pulsation; a defeat.

**beautician** *n* one who offers cosmetic treatments.

**beautiful** *adj* having beauty; very enjoyable.—**beautifully** *adv*.

**beauty** *n* the combination of qualities in a person or object that cause delight or pleasure; an attractive woman or girl; good looks.

**beaver** *n* a large semi-aquatic dam-building rodent; its fur; a hat made from beaver fur. • *vi* (*often with* **away**) to work hard (at).

**became** *see* **become**.

**because** *conj* since; for the reason that.

**beckon** *vti* to summon by a gesture.

**become** *vb* (*pt* **became**, *pp* **become**) *vi* to come or grow to be. • *vt* to be suitable for.

**becoming** *adj* appropriate; seemly; suitable to the wearer.—**becomingly** *adv*.

**bed** *n* a piece of furniture for sleeping on; a plot of soil where plants are raised; the bottom of a river, lake, etc; any flat surface used as a foundation; a stratum. • *vt* (*pt* **bedded**) to put to bed; to embed; to plant in a bed of earth; to arrange in layers.

**bedraggle** *vt* to make untidy or dirty by dragging in the wet or dirt.—**bedraggled** *adj*.

**bedridden** *adj* confined to bed through illness.

**bedroom** *n* a room for sleeping in. • *adj* suggestive of sexual relations; inhabited by commuters.

**bedside** *n* the space beside a bed. • *adj* situated or conducted at the bedside; suitable for someone bedridden.

**bedsit, bedsitter, bedsitting room** *n* a single room with sleeping and cooking facilities.

**bee** *n* a social, stinging four-winged insect that is often kept in hives to make honey; any of numerous insects that also feed on pollen and nectar and are related to wasps.

**beech** *n* a tree with smooth silvery-grey bark; its wood.

**beef** *n* the meat of a full-grown cow, steer, etc; (*inf*) muscular strength; (*inf*) a complaint, grudge; (*pl* **beeves**) cows, ox, steers, etc bred for their meat. • *vt* (*with* **up**) to add weight, strength or power to.

**beeline** *n* a direct line or course.

**been** *see* **be**.

**beer** *n* an alcoholic drink made from malt, sugar, hops and water fermented with yeast.

**beetle** *n* any of an order of insects having hard wing covers.

**beetroot** *n* the fleshy root of beet used as a vegetable, in salads, etc.

**befall** *vti* (*pt* befell, *pp* befallen) to happen or occur to.

**before** *prep* ahead of; in front of; in the presence of; preceding in space or time; in preference to; rather than. • *adv* beforehand; previously; until now. • *conj* earlier than the time that; rather than.

**befriend** *vt* to be a friend to, to favour.

**beg** *vti* (*pt* begged) to ask for money or food; to ask earnestly; to implore.

**began** *see* begin.

**beggar** *n* a person who begs or who lives by begging; a pauper; (*inf*) a person. • *vt* to reduce to poverty; (*description*) to render inadequate.

**begin** *vti* (*pr p* beginning, *pt* began, *pp* begun) to start doing, acting, etc; to originate.

**beginner** *n* one who has just started to learn or do something; a novice.

**beginning** *n* source or origin; commencement.

**begrudge** *vt* to grudge; to envy.

**begun** *see* begin.

**behalf** *n*: in *or* on behalf of in the interest of; for.

**behave** *vti* to act in a specified way; to conduct (oneself) properly.

**behaviour, behavior** (*US*) *n* way of behaving; conduct or action.—**behavioural** *adj*.

**beheld** *see* behold.

**behind** *prep* at the rear of; concealed by; later than; supporting. • *adv* in the rear; slow; late.

**behold** *vb* (*pt* beheld) *vt* to look at; to observe. • *vi* to see.—**beholder** *n*.

**beige** *n* a very light brown.

**being** *n* life; existence; a person or thing that exists; nature, substance.

**belated** *adj* coming late.—**belatedly** *adv*.

**belch** *vti* to expel gas from the stomach by the mouth; to eject violently from inside.—*also n*.

**belfry** *n* the upper part of a tower in which bells are hung.

**belie** *vt* to show to be a lie; to misrepresent; to fail to live up to (a hope, promise).

**belief** *n* a principle or idea considered to be true; religious faith.

**believe** *vt* to accept as true; to think; to be convinced of. • *vi* to have religious faith.—**believer** *n*.

**belittle** *vt* (*a person*) to make feel small; to disparage.

**bell** *n* a hollow metal object which rings when struck; anything bellshaped; the sound made by a bell.

**belligerent** *adj* at war; of war; warlike; ready to fight or quarrel.—**belligerence** *n*.

**bellow** *vi* to roar; to make an outcry. • *vt* to utter loudly. • *n* the roar of a bull; any deep roar.

**bellows** *n* (*used as pl or sing*) a device for creating and directing a stream of air by compression of its collapsible sides.

**belly** *n* the lower part of the body between the chest and the thighs; the abdomen; the stomach; the underside of an animal's body; the deep interior, as of a ship. • *vti* to swell out; to bulge.

**belong** *vi* to have a proper place; to be related (to); (*with* to) to be a member; to be owned.

**belongings** *npl* personal effects, possessions.

**beloved** *adj* dearly loved. • *n* one who is dearly loved.

**below** *prep* lower than; unworthy of. • *adv* in or to a lower place; beneath; later (in a book, etc).

**belt** *n* a band of leather, etc worn around the waist; any similar encircling thing; a continuous moving strap passing over pulleys and so driving machinery; a distinctive region or strip; (*sl*) a hard blow. • *vt* to surround, attach with a belt; to thrash with a belt; (*sl*) to deliver a hard blow; (*sl*) to hurry; (*with* out) (*sl*) to sing or play loudly; (*with* up) to fasten with a belt. • *vi* (*with* up) (*inf*) to wear a seat-belt; (*sl: often imper*) to be quiet.

**bench** *n* a long hard seat for two or more persons; a long table for working at; the place where judges sit in a court of law; the status of a judge; judges collectively; (*sport*) the place where reserves, etc, sit during play.

**bend** *vb* (*pt, pp* bent) *vt* to form a curve; to make crooked; to turn, esp from a straight line; to adapt to one's purpose, distort. • *vi* to turn, esp from a straight line; to yield from pressure to form a curve; (*with* over or down) to curve the body; to give in. • *n* a curve, turn; a bent part; (*pl*) decompression sickness.

**beneath** *prep* underneath; below; unworthy. • *adv* in a lower place; underneath.—*also adj*.

**benefactor** *n* a patron.

**beneficial** *adj* advantageous.—**beneficially** *adv*.

**benefit** *n* advantage; anything contributing to improvement; (*often pl*) allowances paid by a government, employer, etc; a public performance etc, whose proceeds are to help some person or cause. • *vb* (*pt* **benefited**) *vt* to help. • *vi* to receive advantage.

**benevolence** *n* inclination to do good; kindness; generosity.—**benevolent** *adj*.—**benevolently** *adv*.

**bent**[1] *see* bend.

**bent**[2] *n* aptitude; inclination of the mind. • *adj* curved or crooked; (*with* on) strongly determined; (*sl*) dishonest.

**bequeath** *vt* (*property, etc*) to leave by will; to pass on to posterity.

**bequest** *n* act of bequeathing; something that is bequeathed, a legacy.

**bereave** *vt* to deprive (of) a loved one through death.—**bereaved** *adj*.—**bereavement** *n*.

**beret** *n* a flat, round, soft cap.

**berry** *n* any small, juicy, stoneless fruit (eg blackberry, holly berry).

**berserk** *adj* frenzied; destructively violent.—*also adv*.

**berth** *n* a place in a dock for a ship at mooring; a built-in bed. • *vt* to put into or furnish with a berth; to moor a ship. • *vi* to occupy a berth.

**beseech** *vt* (*pt* besought) to implore, to entreat; to beg earnestly for.

**beset** *vt* (*pr p* besetting, *pt* beset) to surround or hem in; to attack from all sides; to harass.

**beside** *prep* at, by the side of, next to; in comparison with; in addition to; aside from.

**besides** *prep* other than; in addition; over and above. • *adv* in addition; except for that mentioned; moreover.

**besiege** *vt* to hem in with armed forces; to close in on; to overwhelm, harass.

**besought** *see* beseech.

**best** *adj* (*superl of* good) most excellent; most suitable, desirable, etc; largest; above all others. • *n* one's utmost effort; the highest state of excellence. • *adv* (*superl of* well) in or to the highest degree. • *vt* to defeat, outdo.

**best man** *n* the principal attendant of the bridegroom at a wedding.

**bestow** *vt* to present as a gift.—**bestowal** *n*.

**best seller** *n* a book or other commodity that sells in vast numbers; the author of such a book.—**best-selling** *adj*.

**bet** *n* a wager or stake; the thing or sum staked; a person or thing likely to bring about a desired result. • *vti* (*pt* bet *or* betted) to declare as in a bet; to stake (money, etc) in a bet (with someone).

**betray** vt to aid an enemy; to expose treacherously; to be a traitor to; to reveal unknowingly.—**betrayal** n.— **betrayer** n.

**better**[1] adj (compar of **good**) more excellent; more suitable; improved in health; larger. • adv (compar of **well**) in a more excellent manner; in a higher degree; more. • n a person superior in position, etc; a more excellent thing, condition, etc. • vt to outdo; to surpass.

**better**[2] n someone who bets.

**between** prep the space, time, etc separating (two things); (bond, etc) connecting from one or the other.

**beverage** n a drink, esp one other than water.

**beware** vti to be wary or careful (of).

**bewilder** vt to perplex; to confuse hopelessly.—**bewilderment** n.

**bewitching** adj fascinating, enchanting.

**beyond** prep further on than; past; later than; outside the reach of (beyond help). • adv further away.

**bias** n a slanting or diagonal line, cut or sewn across the grain in cloth; partiality; prejudice. • vt (pt **biased** or **biassed**) to prejudice.

**bib** n a cloth or plastic cover tied around a baby or child to prevent food spillage on clothes; the upper part of dungarees or an apron.

**Bible** n the sacred book of the Christian Church; the Old and New Testaments.

**bicker** vi to squabble, quarrel.—also n.

**bicycle** n a vehicle consisting of a metal frame on two wheels, driven by pedals and having handlebars and a seat. • vti to ride or travel on a bicycle.— **bicyclist** n.

**bid**[1] n an offer of an amount one will pay or accept; (cards) a statement of the number of tricks that a player intends to win. • vi (pr p **bidding**, pt **bid**) to make a bid.—**bidder** n.

**bid**[2] vt (pr p **bidding**, pt **bade** or **bid**, pp **bidden** or **bid**) to command or ask; (farewell, etc) to express.

**bide** vi to wait; to dwell.

**bier** n a portable framework on which a coffin is put.

**big** adj (**bigger**, **biggest**) large; of great size; important; grown-up; boastful.—**bigness** n.

**bigamy** n the act of marrying a second time when one is already legally married.—**bigamous** adj.—**bigamously** adv.

**bigot** n an intolerant person who blindly supports a particular political view or religion.—**bigoted** adj.— **bigotry** n.

**bike** n (inf) a bicycle; a motorcycle.

**bikini** n (pl **bikinis**) a scanty two-piece swimsuit for women.

**bile** n a thick bitter fluid secreted by the liver; bad temper.—**bilious** adj.—**biliousness** n.

**bilingual** adj written in two languages; able to speak two languages.

**bill**[1] n a bird's beak.

**bill**[2] n a statement for goods supplied or services rendered; a list, as a menu or theatre programme; a poster or handbill; a draft of a proposed law, to be discussed by a legislature; a bill of exchange; a piece of paper money; (law) a written declaration of charges and complaints filed. • vt to make out a bill of (items); to present a statement of charges to; to advertise by bills; (performer) to book.

**billet** n a written order to provide lodging for military personnel; the lodging; a position or job. • vt (pt **billeted**) to assign to lodging by billet.

**billiards** n a game in which hard balls are driven by a cue on a felt-covered table with raised, cushioned edges.

**billion** *n* a thousand millions, the numeral 1 followed by 9 zeros; (UK) a million million.—**billionaire** *n*.

**bin** *n* a box or enclosed space for storing grain, coal, etc; a dustbin.

**bind** *vb* (*pt* **bound**) *vt* to tie together, as with rope; to hold or restrain; to encircle with a belt, etc; (*often with* **up**) to bandage; to fasten together the pages of (a book) and protect with a cover; to obligate by duty, love, etc; to compel, as by oath or legal restraint. • *vi* to become tight or stiff; to stick together; to be obligatory. • *n* anything that binds; (*inf*) a difficult situation.

**binding** *n* the covering of a book holding the pages together.

**bingo** *n* a game of chance in which players cover numbers on their cards according to the number called aloud.

**binoculars** *npl* a viewing device for use with both eyes, consisting of two small telescope lenses joined together.

**biochemistry** *n* the chemistry of living organisms.—**biochemical** *adj*.—**biochemist** *n*.

**biography** *n* an account of a person's life written by another; biographical writings in general.—**biographer** *n*.—**biographical** *adj*.

**biology** *n* the study of living organisms.—**biological** *adj*.—**biologically** *adv*.—**biologist** *n*.

**birch** *n* a tree with a smooth white bark and hard wood; a bundle of birch twigs used for thrashing. • *vt* to flog.

**bird** *n* any class of warm-blooded, egg-laying vertebrates with a feathered body, scaly legs, and forelimbs modified to form wings; (*sl*) a woman.

**birth** *n* the act of being born; childbirth; the origin of something; ancestry.

**birth control** *n* the use of contraceptive drugs or devices to limit reproduction.

**birthday** *n* the day of birth; the anniversary of the day of birth.

**birth rate** *n* the number of births per thousand of population per year.

**biscuit** *n* a small, flat, dry, sweet or plain cake baked from dough. • *adj* pale brown in colour.

**bishop** *n* a high-ranking clergyman governing a diocese or church district; a chessman that can move in a diagonal direction.

**bit**[1] *n* a small amount or piece; a small part in a play, film, etc.

**bit**[2] *n* a metal mouthpiece in a bridle used for controlling a horse; a cutting or boring attachment for use in a brace, drill, etc.

**bit**[3] *n* (*comput*) a unit of information equivalent to either of two digits, 0 or 1.

**bitch** *n* a female dog or wolf; (*sl*) a spiteful woman; (*inf*) an unpleasant or difficult situation. • *vi* (*inf*) to grumble.

**bite** *vti* (*pt* **bit**, *pp* **bitten**) to grip or tear with the teeth; to sting or puncture, as an insect; to cause to smart; to take the bait. • *vi* to press or snap the teeth (into, at, etc). • *n* the act of biting with the teeth; a sting or puncture by an insect.

**biting** *adj* severe; critical, sarcastic.

**bitter** *adj* having an acrid or sharp taste; sorrowful; harsh; resentful; cynical.—**bitterly** *adj*.—**bitterness** *n*.

**bivouac** *n* a temporary camp, esp one without tents. • *vi* (*pt* **bivouacked**) to spend the night in a bivouac.

**bizarre** *adj* odd, unusual.

**blab** *vti* (*pt* **blabbed**) to reveal (a secret); to gossip. • *n* a gossip.—**blabber** *n*.

**black** *adj* of the darkest colour, like coal or soot; having dark-coloured skin and hair, esp Negro; without light; dirty; evil, wicked; sad, dismal; sullen. • *n* black colour; (*often with* *cap*) a Negro, Australian Aborigine;

black clothes, esp as mourning; (*chess, draughts*) black pieces. • *vt* to make black; to blacken; (*shoes*) to polish; to boycott; (*with* **out**) (*lights*) to extinguish, obliterate; (*broadcast*) to prevent transmission. • *vi* (*with* **out**) to lose consciousness or vision.—**blackness** *n*.

**blackberry** *n* a woody bush with thorny stems and berry-like fruit; its black or purple edible fruit. • *vt* to gather blackberries.

**blackboard** *n* a black or dark green board written on with chalk.

**blacken** *vt* to make black; to defame.

**black eye** *n* (*inf*) bruising around the eye caused by a blow.

**blackjack** *see* **pontoon**[2].

**blacklist** *n* a list of those censored, refused employment, etc.—*also vt*.

**blackmail** *vt* to extort money by threatening to disclose discreditable facts. • *n* the crime of blackmailing.— **blackmailer** *n*.

**black market** *n* the illegal buying and selling of goods.—**black marketeer** *n*.

**blackout** *n* the darkness when all lights are switched off; temporary loss of consciousness or electricity.

**black sheep** *n* a person regarded as disreputable or a disgrace by their family.

**blacksmith** *n* a metal worker, esp one who shoes horses.

**bladder** *n* a sac that fills with fluid, esp one that holds urine flowing from the kidneys; any inflatable bag.

**blade** *n* the cutting edge of a tool or knife; the broad, flat surface of a leaf; a straight, narrow leaf of grass; the flat part of an oar or paddle; the runner of an ice skate.—**bladed** *adj*.

**blame** *vt* to hold responsible for; to accuse. • *n* responsibility for an error; reproof.—**blamable, blameable** *adj*.

**blameless** *adj* innocent; free from

blame.—**blamelessly** *adv*.—**blamelessness** *n*.

**bland** *adj* mild; gentle; insipid.— **blandly** *adv*.—**blandness** *n*.

**blank** *adj* (*paper*) bearing no writing or marks; vacant; (*mind*) empty of thought; (*denial, refusal*) utter, complete; (*cheque*) signed but with no amount written in. • *n* an empty space, esp one to be filled out on a printed form; an empty place or time; a powder-filled cartridge without a bullet.—**blankly** *adv*.—**blankness** *n*.

**blanket** *n* a large, soft piece of cloth used for warmth, esp as a bed cover; (*of snow, smoke*) a cover or layer. • *adj* applying to a wide variety of cases. • *vt* (*pt* **blanketed**) to cover.

**blare** *vti* to sound harshly or loudly. • *n* a loud, harsh sound.

**blasphemy** *n* speaking irreverently of God, a divine being or sacred things.

**blast** *n* a sharp gust of air; the sound of a horn; an explosion; an outburst of criticism. • *vt* to wither; to blow up, explode; to criticize sharply. • *vi* to make a loud, harsh sound; to set off explosives; (*with* **off**) to be launched.

**blastoff** *n* the launch of a space vehicle or rocket.

**blatant** *adj* noisy; glaringly conspicuous.—**blatantly** *adv*.

**blaze** *n* an intensive fire; a bright light; splendour; an outburst (*of emotion*). • *vi* to burn brightly; to shine with a brilliant light; to be excited, as with anger.

**blazer** *n* a lightweight jacket, often in a bright colour representing membership of a sports club, school, etc.

**bleach** *vti* to make or become white or colourless. • *n* a substance for bleaching.

**bleak** *adj* cold; exposed; bare; harsh; gloomy; not hopeful.—**bleakly** *adv*.—**bleakness** *n*.

**bleat** *vi* to cry as a sheep, goat or calf.
• *n* a bleating cry or sound.

**bleed** *vb* (*pt* **bled**) *vi* to lose blood; to ooze sap, colour or dye. • *vt* to remove blood or sap from; (*inf*) to extort money or goods from.

**bleep** *vi* to emit a high-pitched sound or signal (eg a car alarm). • *n* a small portable electronic radio receiver that emits a bleep to convey a message (— *also* **bleeper**).

**blemish** *n* a flaw or defect, as a spot.
• *vt* to mar; to spoil.

**blend** *vt* (*varieties of tea, etc*) to mix or mingle; to mix so that the components cannot be distinguished.
• *vi* to mix, merge; to shade gradually into each other, as colours; to harmonize. • *n* a mixture.

**bless** *vt* (*pt* **blessed** *or* **blest**) to consecrate; to praise; to call upon God's protection; to grant happiness; to make the sign of the cross over.

**blessed** *adj* holy, sacred; fortunate; blissful.—**blessedly** *adv.*—**blessedness** *n*.

**blessing** *n* a prayer or wish for success or happiness; a cause of happiness; good wishes or approval; a grace said before or after eating.

**blew** *see* **blow**[2].

**blight** *n* any insect, disease, etc that destroys plants; anything that prevents growth or destroys. • *vt* to destroy; to frustrate.

**blind** *adj* sightless; unable to discern or understand; not directed by reason; (*exit*) hidden, concealed; closed at one end. • *n* something that deceives; a shade for a window. • *vti* to make sightless, to deprive of insight; to dazzle (with facts, a bright light, etc); to deceive.—**blindly** *adv.*—**blindness** *n*.

**blindfold** *adj* having the eyes covered, so as not to see. • *n* a cloth or bandage used to cover the eyes.—*also vt*.

**blind spot** *n* a point on the retina of the eye that is insensitive to light; a place where vision is obscured; a subject on which one is ignorant.

**blink** *vi* to open and close the eyes rapidly; (*light*) to flash on and off; (*with* **at**) to ignore. • *vt* (*with* **at**) to be amazed or surprised. • *n* a glance, a glimpse; a momentary flash.

**bliss** *n* supreme happiness; spiritual joy.—**blissful** *adj.*—**blissfully** *adv*.

**blister** *n* a raised patch on the skin, containing water, as caused by burning or rubbing; a raised bubble on any other surface. • *vti* to cause or form blisters; to lash with words.

**blithe** *adj* happy, cheerful, gay.—**blithely** *adv*.

**blitz** *n* any sudden destructive attack.
• *vt* to subject to a blitz.

**blizzard** *n* a severe storm of wind and snow.

**bloat** *vti* to swell as with water or air; to puff up, as with pride.—**bloated** *adj*.

**blob** *n* a drop of liquid; a round spot (of colour, etc).

**block** *n* a solid piece of stone or wood, etc; a piece of wood used as a base (for chopping, etc); a group or row of buildings; a number of things as a unit; the main body of a petrol engine; a building divided into offices; an obstruction. • *vt* to impede or obstruct; to shape; (*often with* **out**) to sketch roughly. • *vi* to obstruct an opponent in sports.

**blockade** *n* (*mil*) the obstruction of an enemy seaport by warships; any strategic barrier.— *also vt*.

**blockage** *n* an obstruction.

**block letter** *n* a handwritten capital letter similar to a printed letter.

**bloke** *n* (*inf*) a man.

**blond, blonde** *adj* having light-coloured hair and skin; light-coloured.
• *n* a blonde person.

**blood** *n* the red fluid that circulates in

the arteries and veins of animals; the sap of a plant; the essence of life; kinship; descent; hatred; bloodshed.

**blood donor** n a person who donates blood for transfusion.

**blood group** n any of the classes of human blood.

**bloodshed** n killing.

**bloodshot** adj (eye) suffused with blood, red and inflamed.

**bloodstream** n the flow of blood through the blood vessels in the human body.

**bloodthirsty** adj eager for blood, warlike.— **bloodthirstiness** n.

**bloody** adj (**bloodier**, **bloodiest**) stained with or covered in blood; bloodthirsty; cruel, murderous; (sl) as an intensifier (a bloody good hiding). • vt to cover with blood.

**bloody-minded** adj (inf) deliberately obstructive.—**bloody-mindedness** n.

**bloom** n a flower or blossom; the period of being in flower; a period of most health, vigour, etc; a youthful, healthy glow; the powdery coating on some fruit and leaves. • vi to blossom; to be in one's prime; to glow with health etc.

**blossom** n a flower, esp one that produces edible fruit; a state or time of flowering. • vi to flower; to begin to develop.

**blot** n a spot or stain, esp of ink; a blemish in reputation. • vt (pt **blotted**) to spot or stain; to obscure; to disgrace; to absorb with blotting paper.

**blotch** n a spot or discoloration on the skin; any large blot or stain. • vt to cover with blotches.—**blotched** adj.—**blotchy** adj.

**blotting paper** n absorbent paper used to dry freshly written ink.

**blouse** n a shirt-like garment worn by women.

**blow**[1] n a hard hit, as with the fist; a sudden attack; a sudden misfortune; a setback.

**blow**[2] vb (pt **blew**, pp **blown**) vi to cause a current of air; to be moved or carried (by air, the wind, etc); (mus) to make a sound by forcing in air with the mouth; (often with **out**) to burst suddenly; to breathe hard; (with **out**) to become extinguished by a gust of air; (gas or oil well) to erupt out of control. • vt to move along with a current of air; to make a sound by blowing; to inflate with air; (a fuse, etc) to melt; (inf) to spend (money) freely; (sl) to bungle; (with **out**) to extinguish by a gust; (storm) to dissipate (itself) by blowing; (with **over**) to pass over or pass by; (with **up**) to burst by an explosion; to enlarge a photograph; (inf) to lose one's temper.

**blowlamp**, **blowtorch** n a gas-powered torch that produces a hot flame for welding, etc.

**blowout** n (inf) a festive social event; a bursting of (a tyre) by pressure on a weak spot; an uncontrolled eruption of a gas or oil well.

**blubber**[1] n whale fat; excessive fat on the body.

**blubber**[2] vi to weep loudly.

**bludgeon** n a short, heavy stick used for striking. • vti to strike with a bludgeon; to bully or coerce.

**blue** adj (**bluer**, **bluest**) of the colour of the clear sky; depressed; (film) indecent, obscene. • n the colour of the spectrum lying between green and violet; (with **the**) the sky, the sea; (pl: with **the**) (inf) a depressed feeling; a style of vocal and instrumental jazz.

**bluebottle** n a large fly.

**blueprint** n a blue photographic print of plans; a detailed scheme, template of work to be done.

**bluff**[1] adj rough in manner; abrupt, outspoken; ascending steeply with a flat front. • n a broad, steep bank or cliff.—**bluffness** n.

**bluff**[2] *vti* to mislead or frighten by a false, bold front. • *n* deliberate deception.—**bluffer** *n*.

**blunder** *vi* to make a foolish mistake; to move about clumsily. • *n* a foolish mistake.—**blunderer** *n*.

**blunt** *adj* not having a sharp edge or point; rude, outspoken. • *vti* to make or become dull.—**bluntly** *adv*.—**bluntness** *n*.

**blur** *n* a stain, smear; an ill-defined impression. • *vti* (*pt* **blurred**) to smear; to make or become indistinct in shape, etc; to dim.

**blurt** *vt* (*with* **out**) to utter impulsively.

**blush** *n* a red flush of the face caused by embarrassment; any rosy colour. • *vi* (*with* **for, at**) to show embarrassment, modesty, joy, etc, involuntarily by blushing; to become rosy.

**bluster** *vi* to make a noise like the wind; to bully. • *n* a blast, as of the wind; bullying or boastful talk.—**blusterer** *n*.—**blustery** *adj*.—**blusteringly, blusterously** *adv*.

**boar** *n* a male pig, a wild hog.

**board** *n* meals, esp when provided regularly for pay; a long, flat piece of sawed wood, etc; a flat piece of wood, etc for some special purpose; a council; a group of people who supervise a company; the side of a ship. • *vt* to provide with meals and lodging at fixed terms; to come onto the deck of (a ship); to get on (a train, bus, etc). • *vi* to provide room and/or meals, regularly for pay; (*with* **up**) to cover with boards.

**boarding house** *n* a house where board is provided.

**boardroom** *n* a room where meetings of a company's board are held.

**boast** *vi* to brag. • *vt* to speak proudly of; to possess with pride. • *n* boastful talk.—**boaster** *n*.—**boastful** *adj*.—**boastfully** *adv*.

**boat** *n* a small, open, waterborne craft; a ship. • *vi* to travel in a boat, esp for pleasure.

**boater** *n* a stiff flat straw hat.

**boating** *n* rowing, sailing, etc.

**bob** *vb* (*pt* **bobbed**) *vi* to move abruptly up and down; to curtsey. • *vt* (*hair*) to cut short. • *n* a jerking motion up and down; the weight on a pendulum, plumb line, etc; a woman's or girl's short haircut.

**bobbin** *n* a reel or spool on which yarn or thread is wound.

**bobby clip** *n* a grip for holding hair in position.

**bobsleigh, bobsled** (*US*) *n* a long racing sledge. • *vi* to ride or race on a bobsleigh.

**bodice** *n* the upper part of a dress.

**bodily** *adj* physical; relating to the body. • *adv* in the flesh; as a whole; altogether.

**body** *n* the whole physical substance of a person, animal, or plant; the trunk of a person or animal; a corpse; the principal part of anything; a distinct mass; substance or consistency, as of liquid; a richness of flavour; a person; a distinct group. • *vt* to give shape to.

**bodyguard** *n* a person or persons assigned to guard someone.

**bog** *n* wet, spongy ground; quagmire.—**boggy** *adj*.

**boggle** *vi* to be surprised; to hesitate (at). • *vt* to confuse (the imagination, mind, etc).

**bogus** *adj* counterfeit, spurious.

**boil**[1] *vi* to change rapidly from a liquid to a vapour by heating; to bubble when boiling; to cook in boiling liquid; to be aroused with anger; (*with* **down**) to reduce by boiling; to condense; (*with* **over**) to overflow when boiling; to burst out in anger. • *vt* to heat to boiling point; to cook in boiling water.

**boil**[2] *n* an inflamed, pus-filled, painful swelling on the skin.

**boiler** *n* a container in which to boil things; a tank in which water is heated and steam generated; a device for providing central heating and hot water.

**boisterous** *adj* wild, noisy; stormy; loud and exuberant.—**boisterously** *adv*.

**bold** *adj* daring or courageous; fearless; impudent; striking to the eye.—**boldly** *adv*.—**boldness** *n*.

**bollard** *n* a strong post on a wharf around which mooring lines are secured; one of a line of posts closing off a street to traffic; an illuminated marker on a traffic island.

**bolster** *n* a long narrow pillow; any bolster-like object or support. • *vt* (*often with* up) to support or strengthen.

**bolt** *n* a bar used to lock a door, etc; a type of arrow; a flash of lightning; a threaded metal rod used with a nut to hold parts together; a roll (of cloth, paper, etc); a sudden dash. • *vt* to lock with a bolt; to eat hastily; to say suddenly; to blurt (out); to abandon (a party, group, etc). • *vi* (*horse*) to rush away suddenly • *adv* erectly upright.

**bomb** *n* a projectile containing explosives, incendiary material, or chemicals used for destruction; (*sl*) a lot of money. • *vt* to attack with bombs.

**bombard** *vt* to attack with bombs or artillery; to attack verbally.—**bombardment** *n*.

**bombast** *n* pretentious or boastful language.—**bombastic** *adj*.

**bomber** *n* a person who bombs; an aeroplane that carries bombs.

**bombshell** *n* a shocking surprise.

**bona fide** *adj* in good faith; genuine or real.

**bond** *n* anything that binds, fastens, or unites; (*pl*) shackles; an obligation imposed by a contract, promise, etc; the status of goods in a warehouse until taxes are paid; an interest-bearing certificate issued by the government or business, redeemable on a specified date; surety against theft, absconding, etc. • *vt* to join, bind, or otherwise unite; to provide a bond for; to place or hold (goods) in bond. • *vi* to hold together by means of a bond.

**bone** *n* the hard material making up the skeleton; any constituent part of the skeleton. • *vti* to remove the bones from, as meat; (*with* up) (*inf*) to study hard.—**boneless** *adj*.

**bonnet** *n* a hat with a chin ribbon, a cap.

**bonus** *n* an amount paid over the sum due as interest, dividend, or wages.

**bony** *adj* (**bonier, boniest**) of or resembling bones; having large or prominent bones; full of bones.

**booby trap** *n* a trap for playing a practical joke on someone; a camouflaged explosive device triggered by an unsuspecting victim.

**book** *n* a bound set of printed or blank pages; a literary composition of fact or fiction; (*pl*) written records of accounts. • *vt* to make a reservation in advance; to note a person's name and address for an alleged offence. • *vi* to make a reservation.

**bookcase** *n* a piece of furniture with shelves for books.

**book-keeping** *n* the systematic recording of business accounts.—**book-keeper** *n*.

**booklet** *n* a small book, usu with a paper cover; a pamphlet.

**bookmaker** *n* a person who takes bets on horse races, etc, and pays out winnings.

**boom**[1] *n* a spar on which a sail is stretched; a barrier across a harbour; a long pole carrying a microphone.

**boom**[2] *vi* to make a deep, hollow sound. • *n* a resonant sound, as of the sea.

**boom**[3] *vi* to flourish or prosper suddenly. • *n* a period of vigorous growth (eg in business, sales, prices).

**boomerang** *n* a curved stick that, when thrown, returns to the thrower; an action that unexpectedly rebounds and harms the agent.—*also vi*.

**boon** *n* something useful or helpful.

**boost** *vt* (*sales etc*) to increase; to encourage, to improve; to push. • *n* a push.

**boot** *n* a strong covering for the foot and lower part of the leg; (*sl*; *with* **the**) dismissal from employment; the rear compartment of a car used for holding luggage, etc. • *vt* to kick; (*comput*) to bring a program from a disc into the memory.

**booth** *n* a stall for selling goods; a small enclosure for voting; a public telephone enclosure.

**booty** *n* spoils obtained as plunder.

**booze** *vi* (*inf*) to drink alcohol excessively. • *n* alcohol.—**boozy** *adj*.

**border** *n* the edge, rim, or margin; a dividing line between two countries; a narrow strip along an edge. • *vi* (*with* **on**, **upon**) to be adjacent. • *vt* to form a border.

**borderline** *n* a boundary. • *adj* on a boundary; doubtful, indefinite.

**bore**[1] to drill so as to form a hole; to weary, by being dull or uninteresting. • *n* a hole made by drilling; the diameter of a gun barrel; a dull or uninteresting person.

**bore**[2] *see* **bear**[1].

**boring** *adj* dull, tedious; making holes.

**born** *adj* by birth, natural.

**borne** *see* **bear**[1].

**borough** *n* a self-governing, incorporated town; an administrative area of a city, as in London or New York.

**borrow** *vt* to obtain (an item) with the intention of returning it; (*an idea*) to adopt as one's own; (*loan, money*) to obtain from a financial institution at definite rates of interest.—**borrower** *n*.

**bosom** *n* the breast of a human being, esp a woman; the part of a dress that covers it; the seat of the emotions. • *adj* (*friend*) very dear, intimate.

**boss** *n* (*inf*) the manager or foreman; a powerful local politician. • *vt* to domineer.

**botany** *n* the scientific study of plants.—**botanical** *adj*.—**botanist** *n*.

**botch** *n* a poorly done piece of work. • *vt* to mend or patch clumsily; to put together without sufficient care.

**both** *adj*, *pron* the two together; the one and the other. • *conj* together equally.—*also adv*.

**bother** *vt* to perplex or annoy; to take time or trouble. • *n* worry; trouble; someone who causes problems, etc.

**bottle** *n* a glass or plastic container for holding liquids; its contents; (*sl*) courage, nerve. • *vt* to put in bottles; to confine as if in a bottle.

**bottleneck** *n* a narrow stretch of a road where traffic is held up; a congestion in any stage of a process.

**bottom** *n* the lowest or deepest part of anything; the base or foundation; the lowest position (eg in a class); the buttocks; (*naut*) the part of a ship's hull below water; the seabed. • *vt* to be based or founded on; to bring to the bottom, to get to the bottom of. • *vi* to become based; to reach the bottom; (*with* **out**) to flatten off after dropping sharply.

**bottomless** *adj* very deep.

**bough** *n* a branch of a tree.

**bought** *see* **buy**.

**boulder** *n* a large stone or mass of rock rounded by the action of erosion.

**bounce** *vi* to rebound; to jump up suddenly; (*sl*: *cheque*) to be returned. • *vt* to cause a ball to bounce; (*sl*) to put (a person) out by force; (*sl*) to fire from a job. • *n* a leap or springiness; capacity for bouncing.

**bouncer** *n* (*sl*) a man hired to remove people from nightclubs, etc.

**bound**[1] *see* **bind**.

**bound**[2] *n* (*usu pl*) the limit or boundary. • *vt* to limit, confine or surround; to name the boundaries of.

**bound**[3] *n* a jump or leap. • *vi* to jump or leap.

**bound**[4] *adj* intending to go to, on the way to.

**boundary** *n* the border of an area; the limit.

**boundless** *adj* unlimited, vast.

**bout** *n* a spell, a turn, a period spent in some activity; a contest or struggle.

**bovine** *adj* relating to cattle; dull, sluggish. • *n* an ox, cow, etc.

**bow**[1] *vi* to lean the head (and chest) forward as a form of greeting or respect; to submit. • *vt* to bend downwards; to weigh down; to usher in or out with a bow. • *n* a lowering of the head (and chest) in greeting.

**bow**[2] *n* a weapon for shooting arrows; an implement for playing the strings of a violin; a decorative knot of ribbon, etc. • *vti* to bend, curve.

**bow**[3] *n* the forward part of a ship.

**bowel** *n* the intestine; (*pl*) the deep and remote part of anything.

**bowl**[1] *n* a wooden ball having a bias used in bowling; (*pl*) a game played on a smooth lawn with bowls. • *vti* to play the game of bowls; to send a ball to a batsman; (*cricket*) to dismiss by hitting the wicket with a bowled ball; (*with* **over**) to knock over; (*inf*) to astonish.

**bowl**[2] *n* a deep, rounded dish; the rounded end of a pipe; a sports stadium.

**bowler**[1] *n* a person who plays bowls or cricket.

**bowler**[2] *n* a stiff felt hat.

**bowling** *n* a game in which a heavy wooden ball is bowled along a bowling alley at ten wooden skittles; the game of bowls.

**bowling alley** *n* a long narrow wooden lane, usu one of several in a building designed for them.

**bowling green** *n* a smooth lawn for bowls.

**bow tie** *n* a tie tied in the shape of a bow.

**box**[1] *n* a container or receptacle for holding anything; (*theatre*) a compartment with seats; (*inf*) a television set. • *vt* to put into a box; to enclose.

**box**[2] *vt* to hit using the hands or fists. • *vi* to fight with the fists. • *n* a blow on the head or ear with the fist.

**boxer** *n* a person who engages in boxing; a breed of dog with smooth hair and a stumpy tail.

**boxing** *n* the skill or sport of fighting with the fists.

**box office** *n* a theatre ticket office; the popularity of a play, film, etc.—*also adj*.

**boy** *n* a male child; a son; a lad; a youth. • *interj* an exclamation of surprise or joy.—**boyish** *adj*.

**boycott** *vt* to refuse to deal with or trade with in order to punish or coerce.—*also n*.

**boyfriend** *n* a male friend with whom a person is romantically or sexually involved.

**bra** *n* a woman's undergarment for protecting and supporting the breasts, a brassiere.

**brace** *n* a prop; a support to stiffen a framework; a hand tool for drilling; (*pl* **brace**) a pair, esp of game; (*pl*) straps for holding up trousers; a dental appliance for straightening the teeth. • *vt* to steady.

**bracelet** *n* an ornamental chain or band for the wrist.

**bracing** *adj* refreshing, invigorating.

**bracken** *n* a large, coarse fern.

**bracket** *n* a projecting metal support for a shelf; a group or category of people classified according to income; (*pl*) a pair of characters ( ), [ ], { }, used in printing or writing as parentheses. • *vt* (*pt* **bracketed**) to support with brackets; to enclose by brackets; (*people*) to group together.

**brag** *vti* (*pt* **bragged**) to boast. • *n* a boast or boastful talk.

**braid** *vt* to weave three or more strands (of hair, straw, etc) together; to make in this way. • *n* a narrow band made for decorating clothing; a plait.

**brain** *n* nervous tissue contained in the skull of vertebrates that controls the nervous system; intellectual ability; (*inf*) a person of great intelligence; (often *pl*) the chief planner of an organization or enterprise. • *vt* to shatter the skull of; (*sl*) to hit on the head.

**brainwash** *vt* to change a person's ideas or beliefs by physical or mental conditioning, usu over a long period.—**brainwashing** *n*.

**brain wave** *n* an electrical impulse in the brain; (*inf*) a bright idea.

**braise** *vt* (*meat, vegetables, etc*) to fry lightly and cook slowly in liquid in a covered pan.

**brake** *n* a device for slowing or stopping the motion of a wheel by friction. • *vt* to retard or stop by a brake. • *vi* to apply the brake on a vehicle; to become checked by a brake.

**bramble** *n* a prickly shrub or vine, esp of raspberries and blackberries.

**bran** *n* the husks of cereal grain separated from the flour by sieving.

**branch** *n* an offshoot extending from the trunk or bough of a tree or from the parent stem of a shrub; a separately located subsidiary or office of an enterprise or business; a part of something larger. • *vi* to possess branches; to divide into branches; to come out (from a main part) as a branch; (*with* **out**) to extend one's interests, activities, etc.

**brand** *n* an identifying mark on cattle, imprinted with hot iron; a burning piece of wood; a mark of disgrace; a trademark; a particular make (of goods). • *vt* to burn a mark with a hot iron; to denounce.

**brandish** (*a weapon, etc*) *vt* to wave or flourish in a threatening manner.

**brand-new** *adj* entirely new and unused.

**brandy** *n* an alcoholic liquor made from distilled wine or fermented fruit juice.

**brash** *adj* bold; reckless.—**brashly** *adv*.—**brashness** *n*.

**brass** *n* an alloy of copper and zinc; (*inf*) showy; impudent; nerve; cheek; (often *pl*) the brass instruments of an orchestra or band; (*sl*) officers or officials of high rank.

**brass band** *n* a band that uses brass and percussion instruments.

**brasserie** *n* a bar and restaurant.

**brassiere** *n* a bra.

**brat** *n* an ill-mannered, annoying child.

**bravado** *n* pretended confidence; swaggering.

**brave** *adj* showing courage; not timid or cowardly; fearless. • *vt* to confront boldly; to defy. • *n* a North American Indian warrior.—**bravely** *adv*.—**bravery** *n*.

**brawl** *vi* to quarrel loudly.—*also n*.

**brawn** *n* strong, well-developed muscles; physical strength.

**brawny** *adj* (**brawnier, brawniest**) muscular.

**bray** *n* the sound of a donkey; any harsh sound. • *vi* to make similar sounds.

**brazen** *adj* made of brass; shameless. • *vt* to face a situation boldly and shamelessly.

**brazier** *n* a metal container for hot coals.

**breach** *n* a break or rupture; violation of a contract, promise etc; a break in friendship. • *vt* to make an opening in.

**bread** *n* a dough, made from flour,

yeast and milk, that is baked; nourishment; (*sl*) money.

**breadth** *n* measurement from side to side, width; liberality (eg of interests).

**breadwinner** *n* the principal wage-earner of a family.

**break** *vb* (*pt* **broke**, *pp* **broken**) *vt* to smash or shatter; to tame; (*rules*) to violate; to discontinue; to cause to give up a habit; to ruin financially; (*news*) to impart; to decipher or solve; (*with* **down**) to crush or destroy; to analyse; (*with* **in**) to intervene; to train. • *vi* to fall apart; (*voice*) to assume a lower tone at puberty; to cut off relations with; to suffer a collapse, as of spirit; (*news*) to become public in a sudden and sensational way; (*with* **down**) to fail completely; to succumb emotionally; (*with* **even**) to suffer neither profit nor loss (after taking certain action); (*with* **in**) to force a way in; (*with* **out**) to appear, begin; to erupt; to throw off restraint, escape; (*with* **up**) to disperse; to separate; to collapse. • *n* a breaking; an interruption; a gap; a sudden change, as in weather; an escape; (*snooker, billiards*) a continuous run of points; (*sl*) a fortunate opportunity.

**breakable** *adj* able to be broken. • *n* a fragile object.

**breakage** *n* the action of breaking; something broken.

**breakdown** *n* a mechanical failure; failure of health; nervous collapse; an analysis.

**breakfast** *n* the first meal of the morning; the food consumed. • *vi* to have breakfast.

**break-out** *n* an escape, esp from prison.

**breakthrough** *n* the action of breaking through an obstruction; an important advance or discovery.

**breakwater** *n* a barrier that protects a harbour or area of coast against the force of the waves.

**breast** *n* the chest; one of the two mammary glands; the seat of the emotions. • *vt* to oppose, confront.

**breaststroke** *n* a swimming stroke in which both arms are brought out sideways from the chest.

**breath** *n* the inhalation and exhalation of air in breathing; the air taken into the lungs; life; a slight breeze.

**Breathalyser, Breathalyzer** *n* (*trademark*) a device for measuring the amount of alcohol in a person's breath.—**breathalyze, breathalyse** *vt*.

**breathe** *vi* to inhale and exhale, to respire air; to take a rest or pause; to exist or live; to speak or sing softly; to whisper. • *vt* to emit or exhale; to whisper or speak softly.

**breather** *n* a pause during exercise to recover one's breath.

**breathless** *adj* out of breath; panting; gasping; unable to breathe easily because of emotion.—**breathlessness** *n*.

**breathtaking** *adj* very exciting.

**breed** *vb* (*pt* **bred**) *vt* to engender; to bring forth; (*dogs*) to raise; to give rise to. • *vi* to produce young; to be generated. • *n* offspring; origin or race; species (of animal).—**breeder** *n*.

**breeze** *n* a light gentle wind. • *vi* (*inf*) to move quickly or casually.

**breezy** *adj* (**breezier, breeziest**) windy; nonchalant; light-hearted.

**brevity** *n* briefness; conciseness.

**brew** *vt* to make (beer, ale, etc) from malt and hops by boiling and fermenting; to infuse (tea, etc); to plot, scheme. • *vi* to be in the process of being brewed. • *n* a brewed drink.

**brewer** *n* a person who brews, usu beer.

**brewery** *n* a place where beer, etc is brewed.

**bribe** *n* money or gifts offered illegally

to gain favour or influence; the gift to do this. • *vt* to offer or give a bribe to.

**bribery** *n* the process of giving or taking bribes.

**brick** *n* a baked clay block for building; a similar shaped block of other material. • *vt* to lay or wall up with brick.

**bricklayer** *n* a person who lays bricks.

**bridal** *adj* relating to a bride or a wedding.

**bride** *n* a woman about to be married or recently married.

**bridegroom** *n* a man about to be married or recently married.

**bridesmaid** *n* a young girl or woman attending the bride during a wedding.

**bridge**[1] *n* a structure built to convey people or traffic over a river, road, railway line, etc; the platform on a ship where the captain gives directions; the hard ridge of bone in the nose; an arch to raise the strings of a guitar, etc; a mounting for false teeth.—*also vt.*

**bridge**[2] *n* a card game based on whist.

**bridle** *n* the headgear of a horse; a restraint or check. • *vt* to put a bridle on (a horse); to restrain or check. • *vi* to draw one's head back as an expression of anger, scorn, etc.

**bridle path** *n* a trail suitable for horse riding.

**brief** *n* a summary of a client's case for the instruction of a barrister in a trial at law; an outline of an argument, esp that setting out the main contentions; (*pl*) snug, legless underpants. • *vt* to provide with a precise summary of the facts. • *adj* short, concise.—**briefly** *adv.*—**briefness** *n.*

**briefcase** *n* a flat case for carrying documents, etc.

**brigade** *n* an army unit, smaller than a division; a group of people organized to perform a particular function.

**bright** *adj* clear, shining; brilliant in colour or sound; favourable or hopeful; intelligent, illustrious. • *adv* brightly.—**brightly** *adv.*—**brightness** *n.*

**brighten** *vti* to make or become brighter.

**brilliant** *adj* sparkling, bright; splendid; very intelligent.—**brilliantly** *adv.*—**brilliance** *n.*

**brim** *n* the rim of a hollow vessel; the outer edge of a hat. • *vti* (*pt* **brimmed**) to fill or be filled to the brim; (*with* **over**) to overflow.

**brine** *n* salt water.

**bring** *vt* (*pt* **brought**) to fetch, carry or convey "here" or to the place where the speaker will be; (*rain, relief, etc*) to cause to happen, to result in; to lead to an action or belief; to sell for; (*with* **about**) to induce, to effect; (*with* **down**) to cause to fall by or as if by shooting; (*with* **round, around**) to restore to consciousness; (*with* **up**) to educate, rear; to raise (a matter) for discussion; to vomit.— **bringer** *n.*

**brink** *n* the verge of a steep place; the point of onset; the threshold of danger.

**brisk** *adj* alert; vigorous; sharp in tone.—**briskly** *adv.*—**briskness** *n.*

**bristle** *n* a short, coarse hair. • *vi* to stand up, as bristles; to have the bristles standing up; to show anger or indignation; to be thickly covered (with).

**brittle** *adj* easily cracked or broken; fragile.—**brittleness** *n.*

**broach** *vt* (*a topic*) to introduce for discussion; to pierce (a container) and draw out liquid.

**broad** *adj* of large extent from side to side; wide; spacious; strongly marked in dialect or pronunciation. • *n* (*sl*) a woman.—**broadly** *adv.*

**broadcast** *n* a programme on radio or

television. • *vti* (*pt* **broadcast**) to transmit on radio or television; to make known widely.—**broadcaster** *n*.

**broaden** *vti* to grow or make broad.

**brochure** *n* a booklet.

**broil** *vti* to cook by exposure to direct heat; to grill.

**broke** *pt* of **break**. • *adj* (*inf*) hard up, having no money.

**broken** *pp* of **break**. • *adj* splintered, fractured; violated; ruined; tamed; disconnected, interrupted; (*speech*) imperfect.—**brokenly** *adv*.

**broken-down** *adj* extremely infirm; worn out.

**broker** *n* an agent who negotiates contracts of purchase and sale; a power broker.

**bronchitis** *n* inflammation of the lining of the windpipe.—**bronchitic** *adj*.

**bronze** *n* a copper and tin alloy, sometimes other elements; any object cast in bronze; a reddish-brown colour. • *adj* made of, or like, bronze.

**brooch** *n* an ornament held by a pin or a clasp and usu worn near the neck.

**brood** *vi* to incubate or hatch (eggs); to ponder over or worry about. • *n* a group having a common nature or origin, esp the children in a family; the number produced in one hatch.

**brook**[1] *n* a freshwater stream.

**brook**[2] *vt* to tolerate.

**broom** *n* a bundle of fibres or twigs attached to a long handle for sweeping.

**broomstick** *n* the handle of a broom.

**broth** *n* a thin soup made by boiling meat, etc in water.

**brothel** *n* a house where prostitutes work.

**brother** *n* a male sibling; a friend who is like a brother; a fellow member of a group, profession or association; a lay member of a men's religious order; (*pl* **brethren**) used chiefly in formal address or in referring to the members of a society or sect.

**brother-in-law** *n* the brother of a husband or wife; the husband of a sister.

**brotherly** *adj* like a brother; kind; affectionate.—**brotherliness** *n*.

**brought** *see* **bring**.

**brow** *n* the forehead; the eyebrows; the top of a cliff; the jutting top of a hill.

**browbeat** *vt* (*pt* **browbeat**, *pp* **browbeaten**) to intimidate with threats, to bully.

**brown** *adj* having the colour of chocolate, a mixture of red, black and yellow; tanned. • *n* a brown colour. • *vti* to make or become brown.—**brownish** *adj*.

**brownie** *n* a square of flat, rich chocolate cake; a friendly helpful elf; (*with cap*) a junior Guide.

**browse** *vti* to nibble, graze; to examine casually.

**bruise** *vt* to injure and discolour (body tissue) without breaking the skin; to break down (as leaves and berries) by pounding; to inflict psychological pain on. • *vi* to inflict a bruise; to undergo bruising. • *n* contusion of the skin; a similar injury to plant tissue; an injury, esp to the feelings.

**brunette** *n* a girl or woman with black or dark-brown hair, often with dark eyes and complexion.—*also adj*.

**brunt** *n* the main force or shock of a blow; the hardest part.

**brush** *n* a device made of bristles set in a handle, used for grooming the hair, painting or sweeping; a fox's, etc bushy tail; a light stroke or graze, made in passing. • *vt* to groom or sweep with a brush; to remove with a brush. • *vi* to touch lightly or graze.

**brush-off** *n* a curt dismissal.

**Brussels sprout** *n* a plant with a small edible green head.

**brutal** *adj* inhuman; savage, violent; severe.—**brutality** *n*.—**brutally** *adv*.

**brute** *n* any animal except man; a brutal

person; (*inf*) an unpleasant or difficult person or thing. • *adj* (*force*) sheer.

**bubble** *n* a film of liquid forming a ball around air or gas; a tiny ball of gas or air in a liquid or solid; a transparent dome; a scheme that collapses. • *vi* to boil; to rise in bubbles; to make a gurgling sound.

**buck** *n* the male of animals such as the deer, hare, rabbit, antelope; (*inf*) a dashing young man; (*sl*) a dollar. • *vti* (*horse*) to rear upward quickly; (*inf*) to resist; (*with* **up**) (*inf*) to make or become cheerful; to hurry up.

**bucket** *n* a container with a handle for carrying liquids, etc.

**buckle** *n* a fastening or clasp for a strap or band; a bend or bulge. • *vti* to fasten with a buckle; to bend under pressure, etc; (*with* **down**) (*inf*) to apply oneself.

**bud** *n* an embryo shoot, flower, or flower cluster of a plant; an early stage of development. • *vi* (*pt* **budded**) to produce buds; to begin to develop.

**Buddha** *n* the state of perfect enlightenment; an image of Siddharta Gautama, founder of Buddhism.— **Buddhist** *adj, n.*

**budding** *n* being in an early stage of development; promising.

**buddy** *n* (*inf*) a friend; a term of informal address.

**budge** *vti* to shift or move.

**budgerigar** *n* a small Australian parrot.—*also* (*coll*) **budgie**.

**budget** *n* an estimate of income and expenditure within specified limits; the total amount of money for a given purpose; a stock or supply. • *vb* (*pt* **budgeted**) *vi* to make a budget. • *vt* to put on a budget; to plan.

**buff** *n* a heavy, soft, brownish-yellow leather; a dull brownish yellow; (*inf*) a devotee, fan; (*inf*) a person's bare skin. • *adj* made of buff; of a buff colour. • *vt* to clean or shine, orig with leather or a leather-covered wheel.

**buffer** *n* anything that lessens shock, as of collision; something that serves as a protective barrier; a temporary storage area in a computer.

**buffet**[1] *n* a blow with the hand or fist. • *vb* (*pt* **buffeted**) *vt* to hit with the hand or fist; to batter (as of the wind). • *vi* to make one's way esp under difficult conditions.

**buffet**[2] *n* a counter where refreshments are served; a meal at which guests serve themselves food.

**buffoon** *n* a clown, a jester.

**bug**[1] *n* a continuing source of irritation.

**bug**[2] *n* an insect with sucking mouth parts; any insect; (*inf*) a germ or virus; (*sl*) a defect, as in a machine; (*sl*) a hidden microphone. • *vt* (*sl*) to plant a hidden microphone; (*sl*) to annoy, anger, etc.

**bugbear** *n* an object that causes great fear and anxiety.

**bugle** *n* a valveless brass instrument like a small trumpet, used esp for military calls. • *vti* to signal by blowing a bugle.—**bugler** *n.*

**build** *vb* (*pt* **built**) *vt* to make or construct, to establish, base; (*with* **up**) to create or develop gradually. • *vi* to put up buildings; (*with* **up**) to grow or intensify; (*health, reputation*) to develop. • *n* the way a thing is built or shaped; the shape of a person.—**builder** *n.*

**building** *adj* the skill or occupation of constructing houses, boats, etc; something built with walls and a roof.

**building society** *n* a company that pays interest on deposits and issues loans to enable people to buy their own houses.

**built-in** *adj* incorporated as an integral part of a main structure; inherent.

**built-up** *adj* made higher, stronger, etc with added parts; having many buildings on it.

**bulb** *n* the underground bud of plants such as the onion and daffodil; a glass bulb in an electric light.—**bulbous** *adj*.

**bulge** *n* a swelling; a rounded projected part. • *vti* to swell or bend outward.—**bulgy** *adj*.

**bulk** *n* magnitude; great mass; volume; the main part. • *adj* total, aggregate; not packaged.

**bulkhead** *n* a wall-like partition in the interior of a ship, aircraft or vehicle.

**bulky** *adj* (**bulkier, bulkiest**) large and unwieldy.—**bulkiness** *adj*.

**bull**[1] *n* an adult male bovine animal; a male whale or elephant; a speculator who buys in anticipation of reselling at a profit; the bull's-eye; (*sl*) nonsense. • *adj* male; rising in price.

**bull**[2] *n* an official edict issued by the pope, with the papal seal on it.

**bulldozer** *n* an excavator with caterpillar tracks for moving earth.

**bullet** *n* a small metal missile fired from a gun or rifle.

**bulletin** *n* an announcement; a short statement of news or of a patient's progress.

**bullfighting** *n* the sport of goading and then killing bulls, popular in Spain, etc.—**bullfighter** *n*.

**bullion** *n* gold or silver in mass before coinage.

**bullock** *n* a gelded bull; steer.

**bull's-eye** *n* (*darts, archery*) the centre of a target; something resembling this; a direct hit.

**bully** *n* a person, esp a child, who hurts or intimidates others weaker than himself. • *vt* to intimidate, oppress or hurt.

**bum** *n* (*inf*) a tramp; (*inf*) a devotee, as of skiing, etc; (*sl*) buttocks or anus.

**bumblebee** *n* a large, furry bee.

**bump** *vi* to knock with a jolt. • *vt* to hurt by striking or knocking; (*with off*) (*sl*) to murder. • *n* a jolt; a knock; a swelling or lump.

**bumper** *n* a shock-absorbing bar fixed to the front and rear of a motor vehicle. • *adj* exceptionally large.

**bumptious** *adj* offensively conceited or self-assertive.—**bumptiously** *adv.*—**bumptiousness** *n*.

**bun** *n* a roll made of bread dough and currants, spices and sugar; a bun-shaped coil of hair at the neck.

**bunch** *n* a cluster; a number of things growing or fastened together; (*inf*) a group of people. • *vi* to group together. • *vt* to make into a bunch.

**bundle** *n* a number of things fastened together; a fastened package; (*sl*) a large sum of money. • *vt* to put together in bundles; to push hurriedly into.

**bung** *n* a cork or rubber stopper. • *vt* to close up with a bung; (*sl*) to throw, toss.

**bungalow** *n* a one-storey house.

**bungle** *n* a mistake or blunder; something carried out clumsily. • *vt* to spoil something through incompetence or clumsiness.—**bungler** *n*.

**bunion** *n* a lump on the side of the first joint of the big toe.

**bunk**[1] *n* a narrow, shelf-like bed.

**bunk**[2] *n* (*sl*) a hurried departure.

**bunker** *n* a large storage container, esp for coal; a sand pit forming an obstacle on a golf course; an underground shelter.

**bunting** *n* a cotton fabric used for making flags; a line of pennants and decorative flags.

**buoy** *n* a bright, anchored, marine float used for mooring. • *vt* to keep afloat; (*usu with* **up**) to hearten or raise the spirits of; to mark with buoys.

**buoyancy** *n* ability to float or rise; cheerfulness; resilience.—**buoyant** *adj*.

**burden** *n* a load; something worrisome that is difficult to bear; responsibility. • *vt* to weigh down, to oppress.—**burdensome** *adj*.

**bureau** *n* (*pl* **bureaus, bureaux**) a writing desk; a chest of drawers; a branch of a newspaper, magazine or wire service in an important news centre; a government department.

**bureaucracy** *n* a system of government where the administration is organized in a hierarchy; the government collectively; excessive paperwork and red tape.

**bureaucrat** *n* an official in a bureaucracy.—**bureaucratic** *adj*.

**burglar** *n* a person who trespasses in a building with the intention of thieving.—**burglary** *n*.

**burgle, burglarize** *vt* to commit burglary.

**burial** *n* the act of burying.

**burly** *adj* (**burlier, burliest**) heavily built; sturdy.—**burliness** *n*.

**burn** *vb* (*pt* **burned** *or* **burnt**) *vt* to destroy by fire; to injure by heat. • *vi* to be on fire, to feel hot; to feel passion; (*inf*) to suffer from sunburn. • *n* a mark or injury caused by burning.

**burnish** *vt* to make shiny by rubbing; to polish. • *n* lustre; polish.

**burnt** *see* **burn**.

**burp** *vi* to belch. • *vt* to pat a baby on the back to cause it to belch.—*also n*.

**burrow** *n* an underground hide or tunnel dug by a rabbit, badger or fox, etc for shelter. • *vi* to dig a burrow; to live in a burrow; to hide (oneself).

**bursar** *n* a treasurer; a student holding a bursary.

**bursary** *n* a scholarship awarded to a student.

**burst** *vb* (*pt* **burst**) *vt* to break open; to cause to explode. • *vi* to emerge suddenly; to explode; to break into pieces; to give vent to. • *n* an explosion; a burst; a volley of shots.

**bury** *vt* (*bone, corpse*) to place in the ground; to conceal, to cover; to blot out of the mind.

**bus** *n* a motor coach for public transport. • *vti* (*pt* **bused** *or* **bussed**) to transport or travel by bus.

**bush** *n* a low shrub with many branches; a cluster of shrubs forming a hedge; woodland; uncultivated land.

**bushy** *adj* (**bushier, bushiest**) covered with bushes; (*hair*) thick.—**bushiness** *n*.

**business** *n* trade or commerce; occupation or profession; a firm; one's concern or responsibility; a matter.

**businesslike** *adj* efficient, methodical, practical.

**businessman** *n* a person who works for an industrial or commercial company.—**businesswoman** *nf*.

**busker** *n* a street entertainer.

**bust**[1] *n* the chest or breast of a human being, esp a woman; a sculpture of the head and chest.

**bust**[2] *vti* (*pt* **busted** *or* **bust**) (*inf*) to burst or break; to make or become bankrupt or demoted; to hit; to arrest. • *n* (*inf*) a failure; financial collapse; a punch; a spree; an arrest.

**bustle**[1] *vi* to move or act noisily or fussily. • *n* noisy activity, stir.

**bustle**[2] *n* a pad placed beneath a skirt to cause it to puff up at the back.

**busy** *adj* (**busier, busiest**) occupied; active; industrious; (*painting*) having too much detail; (*room, telephone*) in use. • *vt* to occupy; to make or keep busy (esp oneself).—**busily** *adv*.

**busybody** *n* a meddlesome person.

**but** *prep* save; except. • *conj* in

contrast; on the contrary, other than.
• *adv* only; merely; just.

**butane** *n* a flammable gas used as fuel.

**butcher** *n* a person who slaughters meat; a retailer of meat; a ruthless murderer. • *vt* to slaughter; to murder ruthlessly; to make a mess of or spoil.

**butler** *n* a male servant, esp the head servant of a household with several servants.

**butt**[1] *vti* to strike or toss with the head or horns, as a bull, etc.—*also n.*

**butt**[2] *n* a large cask for wine or beer.

**butt**[3] *n* a mound of earth behind targets; a person who is the target of ridicule or jokes; (*pl*) the target range.

**butt**[4] *n* the thick or blunt end; the stump; (*sl*) a cigarette; (*sl*) the buttocks. • *vti* to join end to end.

**butter** *n* a solidified fat made from cream by churning. • *vt* to spread butter on; (*with* up) (*inf*) to flatter.

**butterfly** *n* an insect with a slender body and four usu brightly coloured wings; a swimming stroke.

**buttock** *n* one half of the human rump.

**button** *n* a disc or knob of metal, plastic, etc used as a fastening; a badge. • *vti* to fasten with a button or buttons.

**buttonhole** *n* the slit through which a button is passed; a flower in the buttonhole. • *vt* to keep in conversation.

**buttress** *n* a projecting structure for strengthening a wall. • *vt* to support.

**buxom** *adj* plump and healthy; (*woman*) big-bosomed.

**buy** *vt* (*pt* **bought**) to purchase (for money); to bribe, corrupt; to acquire in exchange; (*inf*) to believe.—**buyer** *n*.

**buzz** *vi* to hum like an insect; to gossip; to hover (about). • *vt* to spread gossip secretly; (*inf*) to telephone. • *n* the humming of bees or flies; a

rumour; (*sl*) a telephone call; (*sl*) a thrill.

**buzzard** *n* a large bird of prey.

**buzzer** *n* a device producing a buzzing sound.

**by** *prep* beside; next to; via; through the means of; not later than. • *adv* near to; past; in reserve.

**bye-bye** *interj* (*inf*) goodbye.

**by-election, bye-election** *n* an election other than a general election.

**bylaw, bye-law** *n* a rule or law made by a local authority or a company.

**bypass** *n* a main road avoiding a town; a channel redirecting the flow of something; (*med*) an operation to redirect the flow of blood into the heart. • *vt* to go around; to avoid.

**by-product** *n* a secondary product in the process of making something else.

**bystander** *n* a chance onlooker.

**byte** *n* (*comput*) a set of eight bits treated as a unit.

**byword** *n* a familiar saying; a perfect example; an object of derision.

# C

**C** *abbr* = Celsius, centigrade; (*chem symbol*) = carbon.

© (*symbol*) = copyright.

**cab** *n* a taxicab; the place where the driver sits in a truck, crane, etc.

**cabaret** *n* entertainment given in a restaurant or nightclub.

**cabbage** *n* a garden plant with thick leaves formed usu into a compact head, used as a vegetable.

**cabin** *n* a small house, a hut; a room in a ship; the area where passengers sit in an aircraft.

**cabin cruiser** *n* a powerful motorboat with living accommodation.

**cabinet** *n* a case with drawers or shelves; a case containing a TV, radio, etc; a body of official advisers to a government.

**cabinetmaker** *n* a person who makes fine furniture.

**cable** *n* a strong thick rope often of wire strands; an anchor chain; an insulated cord that carries electric current; a cablegram; a bundle of insulated wires for carrying cablegrams, TV signals, etc. • *vti* to send a message by cablegram.

**cable car** *n* a car drawn by a moving cable, as up a steep incline.

**cablegram** *n* a message transmitted by telephone line, submarine cable, etc, a cable.

**cache** *n* a secret hiding place; a store of food left for use by travellers, etc. • *vt* to place in a cache.

**cackle** *n* the clucking sound of a hen; shrill or silly talk or laughter. • *vti* to utter with a cackle.

**cactus** *n* (*pl* **cacti, cactuses**) a plant with a fleshy stem that stores water and is often studded with prickles.

**caddie, caddy**[1] *n* a person who carries a golfer's clubs. • *vi* to perform as a caddie.

**caddy**[2] *n* a small box or tin for storing tea.

**cadet** *n* a student at an armed forces academy.

**cadge** *vti* to beg or get by begging.— **cadger** *n*.

**Caesarean section** *n* the removal of a child from the womb by a surgical operation.

**café** *n* a small restaurant, a coffee bar, a nightclub, etc.

**cafeteria** *n* a self-service restaurant.

**caffeine** *n* a stimulant present in coffee and tea.

**cage** *n* a box or enclosure with bars for confining an animal, bird, prisoner, etc; a car for raising or lowering miners. • *vt* to shut in a cage, to confine.

**cagey, cagy** *adj* (**cagier, cagiest**) (*inf*) wary, secretive, not frank.—**cagily** *adv*.—**caginess** *n*.

**cajole** *vti* to persuade or soothe by flattery or deceit.

**cake** *n* a mixture of flour, eggs, sugar, etc baked in small, flat shapes or a loaf; a small block of compacted or congealed matter. • *vti* to encrust; to form into a cake or hard mass.

**calamity** *n* a disastrous event, a great misfortune; adversity.—**calamitous** *adj*.

**calcium** *n* the chemical element prevalent in bones and teeth.

**calculate** *vti* to reckon or compute by mathematics; to suppose or believe; to plan.—**calculable** *adj*.

**calculating** *adj* shrewd, scheming.

**calculation** *n* the act of calculating; the result obtained; an estimate.

**calculator** *n* a device, esp a small, electronic, hand-held one, for doing mathematical calculations rapidly; one who calculates.

**calculus** *n* (*pl* **calculi, calculuses**) an abnormal, stony mass in the body; (*math*) a mode of calculation using symbols.

**calendar** *n* a system of determining the length and divisions of a year; a chart or table of months, days and seasons; a list of scheduled events.

**calf**[1] *n* (*pl* **calves**) the young of a cow, seal, elephant, whale, etc; the leather skin of a calf.

**calf**[2] *n* (*pl* **calves**) the fleshy back part of the leg below the knee.

**calibre, caliber** (*US*) *n* the internal diameter of a gun barrel or tube; capacity, standing, moral weight.

**call** *vi* to shout or cry out; to pay a short visit; to telephone; (*with* **in**) to pay a brief or informal visit; (*with* **on**) to pay a visit; to ask, to appeal to. • *vt* to summon; to name; to describe as specified; to awaken; to give orders for; (*with* **down**) to invoke; (*with* **in**) to summon for advice or help; to bring out of circulation; to demand payment of (a loan); (*with* **off**) to cancel; (*an animal*) to call away in order to stop; (*with* **out**) to cry aloud; (*workers*) to order to strike; (*troops*) to summon to action; (*with* **up**) to telephone; to summon to military action, as in time of war; to recall. • *n* a summons; the note of a bird; a vocation, esp religious; occasion; a need; a demand; a short visit; the use of a telephone; a cry, shout.

**call box** *n* a telephone box.

**caller** *n* one who calls, esp by telephone.

**call girl** *n* a prostitute who is called by telephone to assignations.

**callous** *adj* (*skin*) hardened; (*person*) unfeeling.—**calloused** *adj*.—**callously** *adv*.—**callousness** *n*.

**calm** *adj* windless; still, unruffled; quiet, peaceful. • *n* the state of being calm; stillness; tranquillity. • *vti* to become or make calm.—**calmly** *adv*.—**calmness** *n*.

**calorie, calory** *n* a unit of heat; a measure of food energy.

**calve** *vti* to give birth to a calf.

**camber** *n* a slight upward curve in the surface of a road, etc. • *vti* to curve upwards slightly.—**cambered** *adj*.

**came** *see* **come**.

**camel** *n* a large four-footed, long-necked animal with a humped back; a fawny-beige colour.—*also adj*.

**cameo** *n* an onyx or other gem carved in relief; an outstanding bit role, esp in a motion picture; a short piece of fine writing.

**camera** *n* the apparatus used for taking still photographs or television or motion pictures; a judge's private chamber.

**cameraman** *n* a film or television camera operator.

**camouflage** *n* a method (esp using colouring) of disguise or concealment used to deceive an enemy; a means of putting people off the scent. • *vt* to conceal by camouflage.

**camp**[1] *n* the ground on which tents or temporary accommodation is erected; the occupants of this, such as holiday-makers or troops; the supporters of a particular cause. • *vi* to lodge in a camp; to pitch tents.—**camper** *n*.

**camp**[2] *adj* (*sl*) theatrical, exaggerated; effeminate.

**campaign** *n* a series of military operations; a series of operations with a particular objective, such as election of a candidate or promotion of a product; organized course of action. • *vi* to take part in or conduct a campaign.—**campaigner** *n*.

**camp site** *n* a camping ground, often with facilities for holiday-makers.

**campus** *n* (*pl* **campuses**) the grounds, and sometimes buildings, of a college or university.

**can**[1] *vt* (**could**) to be able to; to have the right to; to be allowed to.

**can**[2] *n* a container, usu metal, with a separate cover in which petrol, film, etc is stored; a tin in which meat, fruit, drinks, etc, are hermetically sealed; the contents of a can; (*sl*) jail; (*sl*) a toilet. • *vti* (*pt* **canned**) to preserve (foods) in a can.—**canner** *n*.

**canal** *n* an artificial waterway cut across land; a duct in the body.

**canary** *n* a small finch, usu greenish to yellow in colour, kept as a songbird.

**cancel** *vt* (*pt* **cancelled**) to cross out; to obliterate; to annul, suppress; (*reservation, etc*) to call off; to countermand.

**cancellation** *n* the act of cancelling; annulment; something cancelled; the mark made by cancelling.

**Cancer** *n* (*astron*) the Crab, a northern

constellation; (*astrol*) the 4th sign of the zodiac, operative 21 June–21 July.

**cancer** *n* the abnormal and uncontrollable growth of the cells of living organisms, esp a malignant tumour; an undesirable or dangerous expansion of something.—**cancerous** *adj*.

**candela** *n* a unit of luminous intensity.

**candid** *adj* frank, outspoken; unprejudiced; (*photograph*) informal.—**candidly** *adv*—**candidness** *n*.

**candidate** *n* a person who has nomination for an office or qualification for membership or award; a student taking an examination.—**candidacy** *n*.—**candidature** *n*.

**candle** *n* a stick of wax with a wick that burns to give light.

**candlelight** *n* the light produced by a candle or candles.

**candour, candor** (*US*) *n* sincerity, openness, frankness.

**candy** *n* a solid confection of sugar or syrup with flavouring, fruit, nuts, etc, a sweet.

**candyfloss** *n* a confection of spun sugar.

**cane** *n* the slender, jointed stem of certain plants, as bamboo; a plant with such a stem, as sugar cane; a stick of this used for corporeal punishment (*usu with* **the**) or supporting plants; strips of this used in furniture making etc; a walking stick. • *vt* to thrash with a cane; to weave cane into.

**canine** *adj* of or like a dog; of the family of animals that includes wolves, dogs and foxes; pertaining to a canine tooth. • *n* a dog or other member of the same family of animals; in humans, a pointed tooth next to the incisors.

**canister** *n* a small box or container for storing tea, flour, etc; a tube containing tear gas which explodes and releases its contents on impact.

**cannabis** *n* a narcotic drug obtained from the hemp plant; the hemp plant.—also **hashish, marijuana**.

**canned** *adj* stored in sealed tins; recorded for reproduction; (*sl*) drunk.

**cannibal** *n* a person who eats human flesh; an animal that feeds on its own species. • *adj* relating to or indulging in this practice.—**cannibalism** *n*.—**cannibalistic** *adj*.

**cannon** *n* (*pl* **cannon**) a large mounted piece of artillery; (*pl* **cannons**) an automatic gun on an aircraft; (*billiards*) a shot in which the cue ball hits two others successively. • *vi* to collide with great force (*with* **into**); to rebound; (*billiards*) to make a cannon.

**cannonball** *n* the heavy, round shot fired from a cannon. • *vi* to move along at great speed.

**cannot** = can not.

**canoe** *n* a narrow, light boat propelled by paddles.—*also vi*.—**canoeist** *n*.

**canon** *n* a decree of the Church; a general rule or standard, criterion; a list of the books of the Bible accepted as genuine; the works of any author recognized as genuine; a member of a cathedral chapter; a part of the mass containing words of consecration; (*mus*) a round.—**canonical** *adj*.—**canonically** *adv*.

**canonize** *vt* (*RC Church*) to officially declare (a person) a saint. —**canonization** *n*.

**canopy** *n* a tent-like covering over a bed, throne, etc; any roof-like projection.

**cant**[1] *n* insincere or hypocritical speech; language specific to a group (eg thieves, lawyers); cliched talk, jargon. • *vi* to talk in or use cant.

**cant**[2] *n* an inclination or tilt; a slanting surface, bevel. • *vti* to slant, to tilt.

**can't** = can not.

**cantaloupe, cantaloup** *n* a variety of melon with orange flesh.

**cantankerous** *adj* ill-natured, bad-tempered, quarrelsome.—**cantankerously** *adv*.—**cantankerousness** *n*.

**canteen** *n* a restaurant attached to factory, school, etc, catering for large numbers of people; a flask for carrying water; (a box containing) a set of cutlery.

**canter** *n* a horse's 3-beat gait resembling a slow, smooth gallop.—*also vti*.

**cantilever** *n* a projecting beam that supports a balcony, etc.

**canvas** *n* a strong coarse cloth of hemp or flax, used for tents, sails, etc, and for painting on; sails; a tent or tents; an oil painting on canvas.

**canvass** *vti* to go through (places) or among (people) asking for votes, opinions, orders, etc.—*also n*.—**canvasser** *n*.

**canyon** *n* a long, narrow valley between high cliffs.

**cap** *n* any close-fitting head gear, visored or brimless; a cap-like thing, as an artificial covering for a tooth; a top, a cover; a percussion cap in a toy gun; a type of contraceptive device; (*sport*) the head gear presented to a player chosen for a team. • *vt* (*pt* **capped**) to put a cap on; to cover (the end of); to seal (an oil or gas well); to equal, outdo or top; (*sport*) to choose a player for a team.

**capability** *n* the quality of being capable; an undeveloped faculty.

**capable** *adj* able or skilled to do; competent, efficient; susceptible (of); adapted to.—**capably** *adv*.

**capacity** *n* the power of holding or grasping; cubic content; mental ability or power; character; legal competence; the greatest possible output or content.

**cape**[1] *n* a headland or promontory running into the sea.

**cape**[2] *n* a sleeveless garment fastened at the neck and hanging over the shoulders and back.

**capital**[1] *adj* of or pertaining to the head; (*offence*) punishable by death; serious; chief, principal; leading, first-class; of, or being the seat of government; of capital or wealth; relating to a large letter, upper case; (*inf*) excellent. • *n* a city that is the seat of government of a country; a large letter; accumulated wealth used to produce more; stock or money for carrying on a business; a city, town, etc pre-eminent in some special activity.

**capital**[2] *n* the head or top part of a column or pillar.

**capital gain** *n* the profit made on the sale of an asset.

**capitalism** *n* the system of individual ownership of wealth; the dominance of such a system.

**capitalist** *n* a person who has money invested in business for profit; a supporter of capitalism. • *adj* of or favouring capitalism.—**capitalistic** *adj*.

**capital punishment** *n* the death penalty for a crime.

**capitulate** *vi* to surrender on terms; to give in.—**capitulation** *n*.

**capricious** *adj* unstable, inconstant; unreliable.—**capriciously** *adv*.—**capriciousness** *n*.

**Capricorn** *n* (*astron*) the Goat, a southern constellation; (*astrol*) the tenth sign of the zodiac, operative 21 December–19 January.

**capsize** *vti* to upset or overturn.

**capstan** *n* an upright drum around which cables are wound to haul them in; the spindle in a tape recorder that winds the tape past the head.

**capsule** *n* a small gelatin case enclosing a drug to be swallowed; a metal or plastic container; (*bot*) a seed case; the orbiting and recoverable part of a spacecraft.

**captain** *n* a chief, leader; the master of a ship; the pilot of an aircraft; a rank of army, naval and marine officer; the leader of a team, as in sports. • *vt* to be captain of.—**captaincy** *n*.

**caption** *n* a heading in a newspaper, to a chapter, etc ; a legend or title describing an illustration; a subtitle. • *vti* to provide with a caption.

**captivate** *vt* to fascinate; to charm.—**captivating** *adj*.—**captivation** *n*.

**captivity** *n* the state of being a captive; a period of imprisonment.

**capture** *vt* to take prisoner; *(fortress, etc)* to seize; to catch; to gain or obtain by skill, attraction, etc, to win. • *n* the act of taking a prisoner or seizing by force; anything or anyone so taken.

**car** *n* a self-propelled motor vehicle, an automobile, a motorcar; the passenger compartment of a train, airship, lift, cable railway, etc; a railway carriage.

**carafe** *n* an open-topped bottle for serving water or wine at table.

**caramel** *n* burnt sugar, used in cooking to colour or flavour; a type of sweet tasting of this.

**carat** *n* a measure of weight for precious stones; a measure of the purity of gold.—*also* **karat**.

**caravan** *n* a large enclosed vehicle equipped to be lived in (—*also* **trailer**); a band of merchants travelling together for safety. • *vi* (*pt* **caravanned**) to travel with a caravan, esp on holiday.

**caraway** *n* a biennial plant with pungent aromatic seeds used as a flavouring.

**carbohydrate** *n* a compound of carbon, hydrogen and oxygen, esp in sugars and starches as components of food. • *npl* starchy foods.

**carbon** *n* a nonmetallic element, a constituent of all organic matter; a duplicate made with carbon paper.

**carbon copy** *n* a copy of typed or written material made by using carbon paper; an exact copy.

**carburettor** *n* a device in an internal-combustion engine for making an explosive mixture of air and fuel vapour.

**carcass, carcase** *n* the dead body of an animal; a framework, skeleton or shell.

**card**[1] *n* a small piece of cardboard; a piece of this with a figure or picture for playing games or fortune-telling; a piece of this with a person or firm's name, address or with an invitation, greeting, message, etc; (*inf*) an entertaining or eccentric person; a small piece of plastic identifying a person for banking purposes (eg a cheque card, credit card); (*pl*) card games; (*pl*) card playing; (*pl*) employees' documents held by the employer.

**card**[2] *n* a toothed instrument for combing cotton, wool or flax fibres off. • *vt* (*wool, etc*) to comb.

**cardboard** *n* thick stiff paper, often with a clay coating. • *adj* made of this; lacking substance.

**cardiac** *adj* relating to the heart.

**cardigan** *n* a knitted sweater fastening up the front.

**cardinal** *adj* of chief importance, fundamental; of a bright red. • *n* an official appointed by the Pope to his councils; bright red.

**cardinal numbers** *npl* numbers that express how many (1, 2, 3, etc).

**care** *n* anxiety; concern; serious attention, heed; consideration; charge, protection; the cause or object of concern or anxiety. • *vt* to feel concern; to agree or be willing (to do something). • *vi* (*usu with* **for**, **about**) to feel affection or regard; to have a desire (for); to provide for, have in one's charge.

**career** *n* progress through life; a profession, occupation, esp with prospects for promotion. • *vi* to rush rapidly or wildly.

**carefree** *adj* without cares, lively, light-hearted.

**careful** *adj* painstaking; cautious; thoughtful.—**carefully** *adv*.—**carefulness** *n*.

**careless** *adj* not careful; unconcerned, insensitive; carefree.—**carelessly** *adv*.—**carelessness** *n*.

**caress** *vt* to touch or stroke lovingly.—*also n*.

**caretaker** *n* a person put in charge of a place or thing; (*government*) one temporarily in control.

**cargo** *n* (*pl* **cargoes**) the load carried by a ship, truck, aircraft, etc; freight.

**Caribbean** *adj* of or pertaining to the Caribbean Sea and its islands. • *n* the Caribbean Sea.

**caricature** *n* a likeness made ludicrous by exaggeration or distortion of characteristic features. • *vt* to make a caricature of, to parody.—**caricaturist** *n*.

**carnal** *adj* of the flesh; sexual; sensual; worldly.—**carnally** *adv*.

**carnation** *n* a garden flower.

**carnival** *n* public festivities and revelry; a travelling fair with sideshows, etc.

**carnivore** *n* a flesh-eating mammal.

**carnivorous** *adj* (*animals*) feeding on flesh; (*plants*) able to trap and digest insects.

**carol** *n* a joyful song of joy; a Christmas hymn. • *vi* (*pt* **carolled**) to sing carols.

**carp**[1] *vi* to find fault, esp continually.

**carp**[2] *n* a brown and yellow freshwater fish.

**car park, parking lot** (*US*) *n* land or premises intended for parking cars.

**carpenter** *n* a person skilled in woodwork, esp house building.—**carpentry** *n*.

**carpet** *n* a woven fabric for covering floors; any thick covering. • *vt* (*pt* **carpeted**) to cover with carpet.

**carriage** *n* the act of carrying, transport; the cost of this; deportment, bearing; behaviour; a railway coach or compartment; the moving part of a typewriter.

**carriageway** *n* a road bearing single-line traffic.

**carrier** *n* one who carries or transports goods, esp for hire; a device for carrying; a person or animal transmitting an infectious disease without being affected by it; an aircraft carrier; a carrier bag.

**carrier bag** *n* a plastic bag with handles for holding shopping, etc.

**carrot** *n* a plant grown for its edible, fleshy orange root; an induccment, often illusory.

**carry** *vt* to convey or transport; to support or bear; to involve, have as a result; to hold (oneself); to extend or prolong; to gain by force; to win over; to stock; (*with* **off**) to cause to die; to remove by force; (*situation*) to handle successfully; (*with* **out**) to perform (a task, etc); to accomplish. • *vi* (*with* **on**) to persevere; to conduct a business, etc; (*inf*) to have an affair; (*inf*) to cause a fuss.

**carrycot** *n* a baby's portable cot.

**carry-on** *n* (*inf*) a fuss.

**carry-out** *n* food or drink sold by a restaurant but consumed elsewhere.—*also adj*.

**cart** *n* a two-wheeled vehicle drawn by horses; any small vehicle for carrying loads. • *vt* to carry in a cart; (*inf*) to transport with effort.

**cartilage** *n* tough, elastic tissue attached to the bones of animals; gristle.

**carton** *n* a cardboard box or container.

**cartoon** *n* a humorous picture dealing with current events; a comic-strip; an animated cartoon; a full-size preparatory sketch for reproduction on a fresco, etc.—**cartoonist** *n*.

**cartridge** *n* the case that contains the explosive charge and bullet in a gun or rifle; a sealed case of film for a camera; the device containing the stylus on the end of the pick-up arm of a record player.

**carve** *vt* to shape by cutting; to adorn with designs; to cut up (meat, etc).

**carving** *n* a figure or design carved from wood, stone, etc; the act of carving.

**cascade** *n* a small, steep waterfall; a shower, as of sparks, etc. • *vti* to fall in a cascade.

**case**[1] *n* a covering; a suitcase; its contents.

**case**[2] *n* an instance; a state of affairs; a condition, circumstance; a lawsuit; an argument for one side; (*sl*) character; (*med*) a patient under treatment; (*gram*) the relationship between nouns, pronouns and adjectives in a sentence.

**cash** *n* money in coins or notes; immediate payment, as opposed to that by cheque or on credit. • *vt* to give or get cash for.

**cashew** *n* the small, edible nut of a tropical tree.

**cashier** *n* a person in charge of the paying and receiving of money in a bank, shop, etc.

**cashmere** *n* a fine wool from Kashmir goats; a material made from this.

**cash register** *n* an automatic or electronic till that shows and records the amount placed in it.

**casing** *n* a protective or outer covering; the material for this.

**casino** *n* (*pl* **casinos**) a room or building where gambling takes place.

**cask** *n* a barrel of any size, esp one for liquids; its contents.

**casket** *n* a small box or chest for jewels, etc; a coffin.

**casserole** *n* a covered dish for cooking and serving; the food so cooked and served. • *vt* to cook in a casserole.

**cassette** *n* a usu plastic box that holds an audio or video tape.

**cast** *vb* (*pt* **cast**) *vt* to throw or fling; to throw off or shed; to record; to direct; to shape in a mould; to calculate; to select actors, etc for a play. • *vi* to throw, hurl; (*with* **off**) to untie a ship from its moorings; (*knitting*) to loop off stitches from a needle without letting them unravel; (*with* **on**) to loop the first row of stitches onto a needle. • *n* act of casting; a throw; a plaster form for immobilizing an injured limb; a mould for casting; type or quantity; a tinge of colour; the actors assigned roles in a play; the set of actors; a slight squint in the eye.

**castanets** *npl* hollow shell-shaped pieces of wood held between the fingers and rattled together, esp to accompany Spanish dancing.

**castaway** *n* a shipwrecked person.

**caste** *n* any of the Hindu hereditary social classes; an exclusive social group.

**casting vote** *n* the deciding vote used by the chairman of a meeting when the the votes on each side are equal.

**cast iron** *n* iron melted and run into moulds.—*also adj.*

**castle** *n* a fortified building; a chess piece (—*also* **rook**).

**castor** *n* a small container with a perforated top for sprinkling salt, sugar, etc; a small swivelled wheel on a table leg, etc.

**castor oil** *n* a vegetable oil used as a purgative and lubricant.

**castor sugar** *n* finely ground sugar.

**castrate** *vt* to remove the testicles of, to geld.—**castration** *n.*

**casual** *adj* accidental, chance; unplanned; occasional; careless, unmethodical; informal.—**casually** *adv.*

**casualty** *n* a person injured or killed in a war or in an accident; something damaged or destroyed.

**cat** *n* a small, domesticated feline mammal kept as a pet; a wild animal related to this; lions, tigers, etc (*inf*) a spiteful person.

**catalogue, catalog** (*US*) *n* a list of books, names, etc in systematic order. • *vti* to list, to make a catalogue of.—**cataloguer** *n*.

**catalyst** *n* a substance which accelerates or retards a chemical reaction without itself undergoing any permanent chemical change; a person or thing which produces change.

**catapult** *n* a contraption with elastic for shooting small stones (—*also* **slingshot**); a device for launching aircraft from the deck of an aircraft carrier. • *vt* to shoot forward as from a catapult.

**cataract** *n* a waterfall, esp a large sheet one; a disease of the eye causing dimming of the lens and loss of vision.

**catarrh** *n* inflammation of a mucous membrane, esp in the nose.—**catarrhal** *adj*.

**catastrophe** *n* a great disaster.—**catastrophic** *adj*.—**catastrophically** *adv*.

**catch** *vb* (*pt* **caught**) *vt* to take hold of, to grasp; to capture; to ensnare or trap; to be on time for; to detect; to apprehend; to become infected with (a disease); (*inf*) to see, hear, etc; to grasp (a meaning); (*with* **out**) (*inf*) to detect (a person) in a mistake; (*cricket*) to catch a ball hit by a batsman before it touches the ground, making him "out." • *vi* to become entangled; to begin to burn; (*with* **on**) (*inf*) to become popular; to understand; (*with* **up**) to reach or come level with (eg a person ahead); to make up for lost time, deal with a backlog. • *n* the act of catching; a device for fastening; someone worth catching; a hidden difficulty.

**catching** *adj* infectious; attractive.

**catchment area** *n* a geographic area served by an institution.

**catch phrase** *n* a well-known phrase or slogan, esp one associated with a particular group or person.

**catchup** *see* **ketchup**.

**catchy** *adj* (**catchier, catchiest**) easily remembered, as a tune.

**catechism** *n* a simple summary of the principles of religion in question and answer form, used for instruction.

**categorical** *adj* unconditional, absolute; positive, explicit.—**categorically** *adv*.

**categorize** *vt* to place in a category.

**category** *n* a class or division of things.

**cater** *vi* (*with* **for, to**) to provide with what is needed or desired, esp food and service, as for parties.—**caterer** *n*.

**caterpillar** *n* the worm-like larvae of a butterfly or moth; the ribbed band in place of wheels on a heavy vehicle; a vehicle (eg tank, tractor) equipped with such tracks.

**cathedral** *n* the chief church of a diocese. • *adj* of a cathedral.

**Catholic** *n* a member of the Roman Catholic Church. • *adj* relating to the Roman Catholic Church; embracing the whole body of Christians.—**Catholicism** *n*.

**catholic** *adj* universal, all-embracing; broad-minded, liberal; general, not exclusive.

**catsup** *see* **ketchup**.

**cattle** *npl* domesticated bovine mammals such as bulls and cows.

**caught** *see* **catch**.

**cauliflower** *n* a kind of cabbage with an edible white flower-head used as a vegetable.

**cause** *n* that which produces an effect; reason, motive, justification; a principle for which people strive; a lawsuit. • *vt* to bring about, to effect; to make (to do something).

**causeway** *n* a raised road across wet ground or water.

**caustic** *adj* burning tissue, etc by chemical action; corrosive; sarcastic, cutting. • *n* a caustic substance.—**caustically** *adv*.—**causticity** *n*.

**caution** *n* care for safety, prudence; warning. • *vt* to warn (against); to admonish.

**cautious** *adj* careful, circumspect.—**cautiously** *adv*.—**cautiousness** *n*

**cavalry** *n* combat troops originally mounted on horseback.

**cave** *n* a hollow place inside the earth open to the surface. • *vti* (*with* in) to collapse or make collapse.

**caveman** *n* a prehistoric cave dweller; (*inf*) a person who acts in a primitive or crude manner.

**cavern** *n* a cave, esp a large cave.—**cavernous** *adj*.

**caviar, caviare** *n* pickled roe of the sturgeon.

**cavity** *n* a hole; a hollow place, esp in a tooth.

**cavort** *vi* to frolic, prance.

**CBI** *abbr* = Confederation of British Industry; Central Bureau of Investigation

**cc** *abbr* = carbon copy; cubic centimetre(s).

**cease** *vti* to stop, to come to an end; to discontinue.

**ceasefire** *n* a period of truce in a war, uprising, etc.

**ceaseless** *adj* without ceasing; incessant.—**ceaselessly** *adv*.

**cedar** *n* a large coniferous evergreen tree; its wood.—**cedarwood** *n*.

**cede** *vt* to yield to another, give up, esp by treaty; to assign or transfer the title of.

**ceiling** *n* the inner roof of a room; the lining of this; an upper limit; the highest altitude a particular aircraft can fly.

**celebrate** *vt* to make famous; to praise, extol; to perform with proper rites; to mark with ceremony; to keep (festival).—**celebrant** *n*.

**celebrated** *adj* famous.

**celebration** *n* the act of celebrating; an observance or ceremony to celebrate anything.

**celebrity** *n* fame; a famous or well-known person.

**celery** *n* a vegetable with long juicy edible stalks.

**celestial** *adj* in or of the sky; heavenly; divine.

**celibacy** *n* the unmarried state; complete sexual abstinence.

**cell** *n* a small room for one in a prison or monastery; a small cavity as in a honeycomb; a device that converts chemical energy into electricity; a microscopic unit of living matter; a small group of people bound by common aims within an organization or political party.—**cellular** *adj*.

**cellar** *n* a basement; a stock of wines.

**cello** *n* (*pl* **cellos**) a large bass instrument of the violin family.—**cellist** *n*.

**cellophane** *n* a thin transparent paper made from cellulose.

**cellulose** *n* a starch-like carbohydrate forming the cell walls of plants, used in making paper, textiles, film, etc.

**Celtic** *adj* of or relating to the Celts; the language of the Celts, including Scots or Irish Gaelic, Manx, Welsh, Cornish and Breton.

**cement** *n* a powdered substance of lime and clay, mixed with water, etc to make mortar or concrete, which hardens upon drying; any hard drying substance. • *vt* to bind or glue together with or as if with cement; to cover with cement.

**cemetery** *n* a place for the burial of the dead.

**cenotaph** *n* a monument to a person who is buried elsewhere.

**censor** *n* an official with the power to

examine literature, mail, etc and remove or prohibit anything considered obscene, objectionable, etc. • *vt* to act as a censor.—**censorship** *n*.

**censure** *n* an expression of disapproval or blame. • *vt* to condemn as wrong; to reprimand.—**censurable** *adj*.

**cent** *n* a hundredth of a dollar; (*inf*) a negligible amount of money.

**centenary** *n* a hundredth anniversary or its celebration. • *adj* of a hundred years.

**centi-** *prefix* one hundredth.

**centigrade** *adj* of a scale of a hundred degrees, of the Celsius scale. • *n* a hundredth part of a grade.

**centimetre, centimeter** (*US*) *n* one hundredth of a metre.

**centipede** *n* a a crawling creature with a long body divided into numerous segments each with a pair of legs.

**central** *adj* in, at, from or forming the centre; main, principal; important.—**centrally** *adv*.—**centrality** *n*.

**central heating** *n* a system of heating by pipes carrying hot water from a central boiler.

**centralize** *vt* to draw to the centre; to place under the control of a central authority, esp government.—**centralization** *n*.

**centre, center** (*US*) *n* the approximate middle point or part of anything, a pivot; interior; point of concentration, source; political moderation; (*sport*) a player at the centre of the field, etc, a centre-forward. • *adj* of or at the centre. • *vt* (*pr p* **centring**, *pt* **centred**) to place in the centre; to concentrate; to be fixed; (*football, hockey*) to kick or hit the ball into the centre of the pitch.

**centre forward** *n* (*football, hockey*) the central player in the forward attack.

**centrifugal** *adj* moving away from the centre of rotation.

**century** *n* a period of a hundred years;

a set of a hundred; (*cricket*) 100 runs made by a batsman in a single innings; a company of a Roman legion.

**ceramic** *adj* of earthenware, porcelain, or brick. • *n* something made of ceramic; (*pl*) the art of pottery.

**cereal** *n* a grass grown for its edible grain, e.g. wheat, rice; the grain of such grasses; a breakfast food made from such grains. • *adj* of corn or edible grain.

**ceremony** *n* a sacred rite; formal observance or procedure; behaviour that follows rigid etiquette.

**certain** *adj* sure, positive; unerring, reliable; sure to happen, inevitable; definite, fixed; some; one.

**certainly** *adv* without doubt; yes.

**certainty** *n* something undoubted, inevitable; the condition of being certain.

**certificate** *n* a document formally attesting a fact; a testimonial of qualifications or character.—**certificated** *adj*.

**certify** *vt* to declare in writing or attest formally; to endorse with authority.

**cervix** *n* the neck of the womb.

**cessation** *n* a stoppage; a pause.

**cesspit, cesspool** *n* a covered cistern for collecting liquid waste or sewage.

**cf.** *abbr* = compare (Latin *confer*).

**chafe** *vti* to restore warmth by rubbing; to make or become sore by rubbing; to irritate; to feel irritation, to fret.

**chaffinch** *n* a European songbird.

**chain** *n* a series of connected links or rings; a continuous series; a series of related events; a bond; a group of shops, hotels, etc owned by the same company; a unit of length equal to 66 feet. • *vt* to fasten with a chain or chains.

**chain reaction** *n* a process in which a chemical, atomic or other reaction stimulates further reactions, eg combustion or nuclear fission; a series of events, each of which stimulates the next.

**chain-smoke** *vti* to smoke (cigarettes) one after the other.—**chain-smoker** *n*.

**chain store** *n* one of a series of shops owned by one company.

**chair** *n* a separate seat for one; a seat of authority; a chairman; a professorship; the electric chair. • *vt* to preside as chairman of.

**chair lift** *n* a series of seats suspended from a cable for carrying sightseers or skiers uphill.

**chairman** *n* a person who presides at a meeting; the president of a board or committee.—**chairwoman** *nf*.—*also* **chairperson**.

**chalet** *n* a Swiss hut; any similar building used in a holiday camp, as a ski lodge, etc.

**chalice** *n* a large cup with a base; a communion cup.

**chalk** *n* calcium carbonate, a soft white limestone; such a stone or a substitute used for drawing or writing. • *vt* to write, mark or draw with chalk; (*with* up) (*inf*) to score, get, achieve; to charge or credit.—**chalky** *adj*.

**challenge** *vt* to summon to a fight or contest; to call in question; to object to; to hail and interrogate. • *n* the act of challenging; a summons to a contest; a calling in question; a problem that stimulates effort.—**challenger** *n*.—**challenging** *adj*.

**chamber** *n* a room, esp a bedroom; a deliberative body or a division of a legislature; a room where such a body meets; a compartment; a cavity in the body of an organism; (*pl*) a judge's office.

**chambermaid** *n* a woman employed to clean bedrooms in a hotel, etc.

**chamber music** *n* music for performance by a small group, as a string quartet.

**chamois** *n* a small antelope found in Europe and Asia; a piece of chamois leather.

**chamois leather** *n* soft, pliable leather formerly made from chamois skin, and now obtained from sheep, goats and deer.

**champagne** *n* a sparkling white wine; a pale straw colour.

**champion** *n* a person who fights for another; one who upholds a cause; a competitor successful against all others. • *adj* first-class; (*inf*) excellent. • *vt* to defend; to uphold the cause of.

**championship** *n* the act of championing; the process of determining a champion; a contest held to find a champion.

**chance** *n* a course of events; fortune; an accident, an unexpected event; opportunity; possibility; probability; risk. • *vti* to risk; to happen. • *adj* accidental, not planned.

**chancel** *n* the part of a church around the altar, for the clergy and the choir.

**chancellor** *n* a high government official, as, in certain countries, a prime minister; in some universities, the president or other executive officer.—**chancellorship** *n*.

**chandelier** *n* an ornamental hanging frame with branches for holding lights.

**change** *vt* to make different, to alter; to transform; to exchange; to put fresh clothes on. • *vi* to become different, to undergo alteration; to put on fresh clothes; to continue one's journey by leaving one station, etc, or mode of transport and going to and using another. • *n* alteration, modification; substitution; variety; a fresh set, esp clothes; money in small units; the balance of money returned when given in a larger denomination as payment.

**changeable** *adj* able to be changed;

altering rapidly between different conditions; inconstant.

**channel** n the bed or the deeper part of a river, harbour, etc; a body of water joining two larger ones; a navigable passage; a means of passing or conveying; a band of radio frequencies reserved for a particular purpose, eg television station; a path for an electrical signal; a groove or line along which liquids, etc may flow. • vt (pt **channelled**) to form a channel in; to groove; to direct.

**chant** vti to sing; to recite in a singing manner; to sing or shout (a slogan) rhythmically. • n sacred music to which prose is sung; sing-song intonation; a monotonous song; a rhythmic slogan, esp as sung or shouted by sports fans, etc.

**chaos** n utter confusion, muddle.

**chaotic** adj completely without order or arrangement.—**chaotically** adv.

**chap**[1] vti (pt **chapped**) (skin) to make or become split or rough in cold weather. • n a chapped place in the skin.

**chap**[2] n (inf) a man.

**chapel** n a building for Christian worship, not as large as a church; an association of printers in a printing office.

**chaperon, chaperone** n a woman who accompanies a girl at social occasions for propriety. • vt to attend as a chaperon.

**chaplain** n a clergyman serving in a religious capacity with the armed forces, or in a prison, hospital, etc.—**chaplaincy** n.

**chapter** n a main division of a book; the body or meeting of canons of a cathedral or members of a monastic order; a sequence of events; an organized branch of a society or association.

**char**[1] n a charwoman. • vt (pt **charred**) to work as a charwoman.

**char**[2] vb (pt **charred**) vt to burn to charcoal or carbon. • vti to scorch.

**char**[3] n (sl) tea.

**character** n the combination of qualities that distinguishes an individual person, group or thing; moral strength; reputation; disposition; a person of marked individuality; a person in a play or novel; a guise, role; a letter or mark in writing, printing, etc.

**characteristic** adj marking or constituting the particular nature (of a person or thing). • n a characteristic feature.

**characterize** vt to describe in terms of particular qualities; to designate; to be characteristic of, mark.—**characterization** n.

**charade** n a game of guessing a word from the acted representation of its syllables and the whole; a travesty; an absurd pretence.

**charcoal** n the black carbon matter obtained by partially burning wood and used as fuel, as a filter or for drawing.

**charge** vt to ask as the price; to record as a debt; to load, to fill, saturate; to lay a task or trust on; to burden; to accuse; to attack at a run; to build up an electric charge (in). • n a price charged for a good or service; a build-up of electricity; the amount which a receptacle can hold at one time; the explosive required to fire a weapon; trust, custody; a thing or person entrusted; a task, duty; accusation; an attack.

**chariot** n a two-wheeled vehicle driven by two or more horses in ancient warfare, races, etc.—**charioteer** n.

**charitable** adj of or for charity; generous to the needy, benevolent; lenient in judging others, kindly.—**charitably** adv.

**charity** n leniency or tolerance towards

others; generosity in giving to the needy; a benevolent fund or institution.

**charm** n an alluring quality, fascination; a magic verse or formula; something thought to possess occult power; an object bringing luck; a trinket on a bracelet. • vt to delight, captivate; to influence as by magic.—**charmer** n.

**chart** n a map, esp for use in navigation; an information sheet with tables, graphs, etc; a table, graph, etc; (pl with **the**) a list of the most popular music recordings. • vt to make a chart of; to plan (a course of action).

**charter** n a document granting rights, privileges, ownership of land, etc; the hire of transportation. • vt to grant by charter; to hire.

**chartered accountant** n an accountant who has qualified by passing the examinations of the Institute of Chartered Accountants.

**charwoman** n a woman employed to clean a house.

**chase** vt to pursue; to run after; to drive (away); to hunt; (inf: usu with **up**) to pursue in a determined manner. • n pursuit; a hunt; a quarry hunted; a steeplechase.

**chasm** n a deep cleft, an abyss, a gaping hole; a wide difference in opinions, etc.

**chassis** n (pl **chassis**) the frame of a car, aeroplane or other vehicle.

**chastity** n sexual abstinence; virginity.

**chat** vi (pt **chatted**) to talk in an easy or familiar way. • n informal conversation.

**chatter** vi to talk aimlessly and rapidly; (animal, etc) to utter rapid cries; (teeth) to rattle together. • n idle rapid talk; the sound of chattering.—**chatterer** n.

**chatterbox** n an incessant talker.

**chatty** adj (**chattier, chattiest**) talkative, full of gossip.—**chattily** adv.—**chattiness** n.

**chauffeur** n a person who drives a car for someone else. • vt to drive as a chauffeur.—**chauffeuse** nf.

**cheap** adj low-priced, inexpensive; good value; of little worth, inferior.—**cheaply** adv.—**cheapness** n.

**cheapen** vti to make or become cheap.

**cheat** vti to defraud, to swindle; to deceive; to play unfairly. • n a fraud, deception, a person who cheats.—**cheater** n.

**check** vti to bring or come to a stand; to restrain or impede; to admonish, reprove; to test the accuracy of, verify; (with **out**) to settle the bill and leave a hotel; to investigate. • n repulse; stoppage; a pattern of squares; a control to test accuracy; a tick against listed items; a bill in a restaurant; a cheque; (chess) a threatening of the king.

**checker**[1] n a cashier in a supermarket (esp in US); a cloakroom attendant.

**checker**[2] see **draughtsman**[2].

**checkers** n the game of draughts.

**checkmate** n (chess) the winning position when the king is threatened and unable to move; defeat. • vt (chess) to place in checkmate; to defeat, foil.

**checkroom** n a left luggage office.

**cheek** n the side of the face below the eye; (sl) buttock; impudence.

**cheeky** adj (**cheekier, cheekiest**) disrespectful, impudent.—**cheekily** adv.—**cheekiness** n.

**cheer** n a shout of applause or welcome; a frame of mind, spirits; happiness. • vt to gladden; to encourage; to applaud.

**cheerful** n in good spirits; happy.—**cheerfully** adv.—**cheerfulness** n.

**cheese** n the curds of milk pressed into a firm or hard mass.

**chef** n a professional cook.

**chemical** n a substance used in, or arising from, a chemical process. • adj of, used in, or produced by chemistry.—**chemically** adv.

**chemist** n a pharmacy; a manufacturer of medicinal drugs; a person skilled in chemistry.

**chemistry** n the science of the properties of substances and their combinations and reactions; chemical structure.

**cheque, check** (US) n a money order to a bank.

**chequebook, checkbook** (US) n a book containing blank cheques to be drawn on a bank.

**chequered, checkered** (US) adj marked with a variegated pattern; having a career of fluctuating fortunes.

**cherish** vt to tend lovingly, foster; to keep in mind.

**cherry** n a small red, pitted fruit; the tree bearing it; a bright red colour.

**chess** n a game played by two people with 32 pieces on a chessboard.

**chessboard** n a board chequered with 64 squares used for playing chess or draughts.

**chessman** n any of the 16 pieces used by each player in chess.

**chest** n a large strong box; the part of the body enclosed by the ribs, the thorax.

**chestnut** n a tree or shrub of the beech family; the edible nut of a chestnut; the wood of the chestnut; a horse with chestnut colouring. • adj of the colour of a chestnut, a deep reddish brown.

**chest of drawers** n a piece of furniture containing several drawers.

**chew** vt to grind between the teeth, to masticate; to ponder, think over. • n the act of chewing; something to chew, as a sweet.

**chewing gum** n a flavoured gum made from chicle, for chewing.

**chic** n elegance, style. • adj stylish.

**chick** n a young bird; (sl) a youthful person.

**chicken** n a young, domestic fowl; its flesh. • adj cowardly, timorous.

**chicken feed** n poultry food; (inf) a trifling amount.

**chickenpox** n a contagious viral disease that causes a rash of red spots on the skin.

**chicory** n a salad plant; its dried, ground, roasted root used to flavour coffee.

**chief** adj principal, most important. • n a leader; the head of a tribe or clan.

**chiefly** adv especially; mainly; for the most part.

**chiffon** n a thin gauzy material.

**chilblain** n an inflamed swelling on the hands, etc, due to cold.

**child** n (pl **children**) a young human being; a son or daughter; offspring.

**childbirth** n the process of giving birth to children.

**childhood** n the period between birth and puberty in humans.

**childish** adj of, like or suited to a child; foolish.—**childishly**.—**childishness** n.

**childlike** adj like a child; innocent, simple, candid.

**child minder** n a person employed to look after children.

**chill** n a sensation of coldness; an illness caused by exposure to cold and marked by shivering; anything that dampens or depresses. • adj shivering with cold; feeling cold; unemotional, formal. • vti to make or become cold; to harden by cooling; to depress.

**chilly** adj (**chillier, chilliest**) cold; unfriendly.—**chilliness** n.

**chime** n the harmonious sound of a bell; accord; harmony; (pl) a set of bells or metal tubes, etc tuned in a scale; their ringing. • vi to ring (a bell); (*with* **with**) to agree. • *vt* to indicate the hour by chiming, as a clock.

**chimney** *n* (*pl* **chimneys**) a passage for smoke, hot air or fumes, a funnel.

**chimpanzee** *n* an African anthropoid ape.

**chin** *n* the part of the face below the mouth.

**china** *n* fine porcelain; articles made from this.

**chink**[1] *n* a narrow opening; a crack or slit.

**chink**[2] *n* the sound of coins clinking together.

**chip** *vt* (*pt* **chipped**) to knock small pieces off; to shape or make by chipping. • *n* a small piece cut or broken off; a thin strip of fried potato; a potato crisp; a counter used in games; a tiny piece of semi-conducting material, such as silicon, printed with a microcircuit and used as part of an integrated circuit.

**chirp** *n* the sharp, shrill note of some birds or a grasshopper. • *vi* to make this sound.

**chisel** *n* a tool with a square cutting end. • *vt* (*pt* **chiselled**) to cut or carve with a chisel; (*sl*) to defraud.

**chit**[1] *n* a voucher or a sum owed for drink, food, etc; a note; a requisition.

**chit**[2] *n* a child; (*derog*) an impudent girl.

**chivalry** *n* the medieval system of knighthood; knightly qualities, bravery, courtesy, respect for women.—**chivalrous** *adj*.—**chivalrously**.

**chive, chives** *n* a plant whose onion-flavoured leaves are used in cooking and salads.

**chloride** *n* any compound containing chlorine.

**chlorine** *n* a non-metallic element, a yellowish-green poisonous gas used in bleaches, disinfectants, and in industry.

**chock** *n* a block of wood or other material used as a wedge. • *vt* to secure with a chock.

**chock-a-block, chock-full** *adj* completely full.

**chocolate** *n* a powder or edible solid made of the roasted, pounded cacao bean; a drink made by dissolving this powder in boiling water or milk; a sweet with a centre and chocolate coating. • *adj* flavoured or coated with chocolate; dark reddish brown.

**choice** *n* act of choosing; the power to choose; selection; alternative; a thing chosen; preference; the best part. • *adj* of picked quality, specially good; fastidious.

**choir** *n* an organized group of singers, esp of a church; the part of a church used by them.

**choke** *vti* to stop the breath of, stifle; to throttle; to suffocate; to block (up). • *n* a fit of choking; a choking sound; a valve that controls the flow of air in a carburettor.

**cholera** *n* a severe, infectious intestinal disease.

**choose** *vt* (*pt* **chose**, *pp* **chosen**) to select (one thing) rather than another. • *vi* to decide, to think fit.—**chooser** *n*.

**chop** *vt* (*pt* **chopped**) to cut by striking; to cut into pieces. • *n* a cut of meat and bone from the rib, loin, or shoulder; a downward blow or motion.

**choppy** *adj* (**choppier, choppiest**) (*sea*) running in rough, irregular waves; jerky.—**choppiness** *n*.

**chopsticks** *n* a pair of wooden or plastic sticks used in Asian countries to eat with.

**choral** *adj* relating to, sung by, or written for, a choir or chorus.

**chord**[1] *n* (*mus*) three or more notes played simultaneously.

**chord**[2] *n* a straight line joining the ends of an arc.

**chore** n a piece of housework; a regular or tedious task.

**choreography** n the art of devising ballets or dances.—**choreographer** n. — **choreographic** adj.

**chorister** n a member of a choir.

**chortle** vi to chuckle exultantly.—also n.

**chorus** n a group of singers and dancers in the background to a play, musical, etc; a group of singers, a choir; music sung by a chorus; a refrain; an utterance by many at once. • vt to sing, speak or shout in chorus.

**chose, chosen** see **choose**.

**Christ** n Jesus of Nazareth, regarded by Christians as the Messiah. • interj (taboo) an oath expressing annoyance.

**christen** vt to enter the Christian Church by baptism; to give a name to; (inf) to use for the first time.— **christening** n.

**Christian** n a person who believes in Christianity. • adj relating to, believing in, or based on the doctrines of Christianity; kind, gentle, humane.

**Christianity** n the religion based on the teachings of Christ.

**Christian name** n a name given when one is christened; (loosely) any forename.

**Christmas** n an annual festival (25 December) in memory of the birth of Christ.

**Christmas tree** n an evergreen tree decorated at Christmas; an imitation tree.

**chrome** n chromium; a chromium pigment; something plated with an alloy of chromium.

**chromium** n a hard metallic element used in making steel alloys and electroplating to give a tough surface.

**chromosome** n any of the microscopic rod-shaped bodies bearing genes.

**chronic** adj (disease) long-lasting; (sl) bad, extremely unpleasant.—**chronically** adv.

**chronicle** n a record of events in chronological order; an account; a history. • vt to record in a chronicle.—**chronicler** n.

**chronological** adj arranged in order of occurrence.—**chronologically** adv.

**chrysanthemum** n a plant with a brightly coloured flower head.

**chubby** adj (chubbier, chubbiest) plump.—**chubbiness** n.

**chuck**[1] vt to throw, to toss; (inf) to stop, to give up.

**chuck**[2] n a device on a lathe, etc, that holds the work or drill; a cut of beef from the neck to the ribs.

**chuckle** vt to laugh softly; to gloat. • n a quiet laugh.

**chum** n (inf) a close friend, esp of the same sex.

**chunk** n a short, thick piece or lump, as wood, bread, etc.—**chunky** adj.

**church** n a building for public worship, esp Christian worship; the clerical profession; a religious service; (with cap) all Christians; (with the) a particular Christian denomination.

**churchyard** n the yard around a church often used as a burial ground.

**churn** n a large metal container for milk; a device that can be vigorously turned to make milk or cream into butter. • vt to agitate in a churn; to make (butter) this way; to stir violently.

**chute** n an inclined trough or a passage for sending down water, logs, rubbish, etc; a fall of water, a rapid.

**CID** abbr = Criminal Investigation Department.

**cider** n fermented apple juice as a drink.

**cigar** n a compact roll of tobacco leaf for smoking.

**cigarette** n shredded tobacco rolled in fine paper for smoking.

**cinch** n (sl) a firm hold, an easy job.

**cinder** n a tiny piece of partly burned

wood, etc; (*pl*) ashes from wood or coal.

**cine-** *prefix* motion picture or cinema, as *cinecamera*, *cinefilm*.

**cinema** *n* a place where motion pictures are shown; film as an industry or art form.

**cinnamon** *n* a tree of the laurel family; its aromatic edible bark; a spice made from this; a yellowish brown colour.—*also adj*.

**cipher** *n* the numeral 0, zero; any single Arabic numeral; a thing or person of no importance, a nonentity; a method of secret writing. • *vt* to convert (a message) into cipher.—*also* **cypher**.

**circle** *n* a perfectly round plane figure; the line enclosing it; the curved seating area above the stalls in a theatre; a group, set or class (of people); extent, scope, as of influence. • *vti* to encompass; to move in a circle; to revolve (round).

**circuit** *n* a distance round; a route or course; an area so enclosed; the path of an electric current; a visit to an area by a judge to hold courts; the area itself; a chain or association.

**circuitous** *adj* roundabout, indirect.

**circular** *adj* shaped like a circle, round; (*argument*) using as evidence the conclusion which it is seeking to prove; moving round a circle. • *n* an advertisement, etc addressed to a number of people.

**circulate** *vti* to pass from hand to hand or place to place; to spread or be spread about; to move round, finishing at the starting point.—**circulatory** *adj*.

**circulation** *n* the act of circulating; a movement to and fro; the number of copies sold of a newspaper, etc; currency.

**circumcise** *vt* to cut off the foreskin of (a male) or the clitoris of (a female),

esp as a religious rite.—**circumcision** *n*.

**circumference** *n* the line bounding a circle, a ball, etc; the length of this line.

**circumstance** *n* an occurrence, an incident; a detail; ceremony; (*pl*) a state of affairs; condition in life.

**circus** *n* a large arena for the exhibition of games, feats of horsemanship etc; a travelling show of acrobats, clowns, etc; a company of people travelling round giving displays.

**cistern** *n* a tank or reservoir for storing water, esp in a toilet.

**cite** *vt* to summon officially to appear in court; to quote; to give as an example or authority.

**citizen** *n* a member of a city, state or nation.—**citizenship** *n*.

**citrus** *n* a genus of trees including the lemon, orange, etc; the fruit of these.

**city** *n* an important or cathedral town; a town created a city by charter; the people of a city; business circles, esp financial services.

**civic** *adj* of a city, citizen or citizenship. • *npl* the principles of good citizenship; the study of citizenship.

**civil** *adj* of citizens or the state; not military or ecclesiastical; polite, obliging; (*law*) relating to crimes other than criminal ones or to private rights.

**civil engineer** *n* an engineer who designs and constructs roads, bridges, etc.

**civilian** *n* a person who is not a member of the armed forces.

**civilization, civilisation** *n* the state of being civilized; the process of civilizing; an advanced stage of social culture; moral and cultural refinement.

**civil service** (*Brit*) *n* those employed in the service of a state apart from the military.

**civil war** *n* a war between citizens of the same state or country.

**claim** *vt* to demand as a right; to call for; to require; to profess (to have); to assert. • *n* the act of claiming; a title, right to something; a thing claimed, esp a piece of land for mining.

**claimant** *n* one who makes a claim.

**clam** *n* an edible marine bivalve mollusc.

**clamber** *vi* to climb with difficulty, using the hands as well as the feet. • *n* a climb performed in this way.—**clamberer** *n*.

**clammy** *adj* (**clammier**, **clammiest**) damp and sticky.—**clamminess** *n*.

**clamp** *n* a device for gripping objects tightly together. • *vt* to grip with a clamp; to attach firmly.

**clan** *n* a group of people with a common ancestor, under a single chief; people with the same surname; a party or clique.

**clang** *n* a loud metallic sound. • *vti* to make or cause to make a clang.

**clap**[1] *vti* (*pt* **clapped**) to strike (the hands) together sharply; to applaud in this way; to slap; to put or place suddenly or vigorously. • *n* the sound of hands clapping; a sudden sharp noise; a sudden sharp slap.

**clap**[2] *n* (*vulg*) venereal disease, gonorrhoea.

**claret** *n* a dry red wine of Bordeaux in France.

**clarify** *vti* to make or become clear or intelligible; to free or become free from impurities.—**clarification** *n*.

**clarinet** *n* an orchestral woodwind instrument.—**clarinettist** *n*.

**clarity** *n* clearness.

**clash** *n* a loud noise of striking weapons, cymbals, etc; a contradiction, disagreement; a collision. • *vti* to make or cause to make a clash by striking together; to conflict; to collide; to be at variance (with).

**clasp** *n* a hold, an embrace; a catch or buckle. • *vt* to grasp firmly, to embrace; to fasten with a clasp.

**class** *n* a division, a group; a kind; a set of students who are taught together; a grade of merit or quality; standing in society, rank. • *vt* to put into a class.

**classic** *adj* of the highest class or rank, esp in literature; of the best Greek and Roman writers; of music conforming to certain standards of form, complexity, etc; traditional; authoritative. • *n* a work of literature, art, cinema, etc, of the highest excellence; a definitive work of art.

**classical** *adj* influenced by, of or relating to ancient Roman and Greek art, literature and culture; traditional; serious; refined.—**classically** *adv*.

**classification** *n* the organization of knowledge into categories; a category or a division of a category into which knowledge or information has been put.

**classify** *vt* to arrange in classes, to categorize; to restrict for security reasons.

**classmate** *n* a member of the same class in a school, college, etc.

**classroom** *n* a room where pupils or students are taught.

**clatter** *n* a rattling noise; noisy talk. • *vti* to make or cause a clatter.

**clause** *n* a single article or stipulation in a treaty, law, contract, etc; (*gram*) a short sentence; a part of a sentence.

**claustrophobia** *n* a morbid fear of confined spaces.—**claustrophobic** *adj*.

**claw** *n* the sharp hooked nail of an animal or bird; the pointed end or pincer of a crab, etc; a claw-like thing. • *vti* to seize or tear with claws or nails; to clutch (at).

**clay** *n* a sticky ductile earthy material.

**clean** adj free from dirt or impurities; unsoiled; morally or ceremonially pure; complete, decisive. • adv entirely; outright; neatly. • vti to remove dirt from.—**cleanness** n.

**cleaner** n a substance or device used for cleaning; a person employed to clean; (pl) a dry cleaner.

**cleanse** vt to make clean or pure.

**cleanser** n something that cleanses, esp a detergent, face cream, etc.

**clear** adj bright, not dim; transparent; without blemish; easily seen or heard; unimpeded, open; free from clouds; quit (of); plain, distinct, obvious; keen, discerning; positive, sure. • adv plainly; apart from. • vti to make or become clear; to rid (of), remove; to to free from suspicion, vindicate; to disentangle; to pass by or over without touching; to make as a profit.—**clearness** n.

**clearance** n the act of clearing; permission, authority to proceed; the space between two objects in motion.

**clearing** n a tract of land cleared of trees, etc for cultivation.

**clearly** adv in a clear manner; evidently.

**clearway** n a main road where it is illegal for vehicles to stop.

**clef** n a sign on a music stave that indicates the pitch of the notes.

**clench** vt (teeth, fist) to close tightly; to grasp. • n a firm grip.

**clergy** n ministers of the Christian church collectively.

**clergyman** n a member of the clergy.

**clerical** adj of or relating to the clergy or a clergyman; of or relating to a clerk or a clerk's work.

**clerk** n an office worker who types, keeps files, etc; a layman with minor duties in a church; a public official who keeps the records of a court, town, etc.

**clever** adj able; intelligent; ingenious; skilful, adroit.—**cleverly** adv.—**cleverness** n.

**cliché** n a hackneyed phrase; something that has become commonplace.—**cliché'd, clichéd** adj.

**click** n a slight, sharp sound. • vi to make such a sound.

**client** n a person who employs another professionally; a customer.

**clientele** n clients, customers.

**cliff** n a high steep rock face.

**climate** n the weather characteristics of an area; the prevailing attitude, feeling, atmosphere.—**climatic** adj.

**climax** n the highest point; a culmination; sexual orgasm. • vti to reach, or bring to a climax.—**climactic** adj.

**climb** vti to mount with an effort; to ascend; (plants) to grow upwards by clinging onto walls, fences or other plants. • n an ascent.

**climber** n a mountaineer or rock climber; a climbing plant.

**clinch** vt (argument, etc) to confirm or drive home. • vi (boxing) to grip the opponent with the arms to hinder his punching. • n the act of clinching; (inf) an embrace.

**cling** vi (pt clung) to adhere, to be attached (to); to keep hold by embracing or entwining.

**clinic** n a place where outpatients are given medical care or advice; a place where medical specialists practice as a group; a private or specialized hospital; the teaching of medicine by treating patients in the presence of students.

**clinical** adj of or relating to a clinic; based on medical observation; plain, simple; detached, cool, objective.—**clinically** adv.

**clink**[1] n a slight metallic ringing sound. • vti to make or cause to make such a sound.

**clink**[2] n (sl) prison.

**clip**[1] *vt* (*pt* **clipped**) to cut or trim with scissors or shears; to punch a small hole in, esp a ticket; (*words*) to shorten or slur; (*inf*) to hit sharply. • *n* the piece clipped off; a yield of wool from sheep; an extract from a film; (*inf*) a smart blow; speed.

**clip**[2] *vt* (*pt* **clipped**) to hold firmly; to secure with a clip. • *n* any device that grips, clasps or hooks; a magazine for a gun; a piece of jewellery held in place by a clip.

**clique** *n* a small exclusive group, a set.—**cliquey** *adj*.—**cliquish** *adj*.

**cloak** *n* a loose sleeveless outer garment; a covering; something that conceals, a pretext. • *vt* to cover as with a cloak; to conceal.

**cloakroom** *n* a room where overcoats, etc, may be left.

**clock** *n* a device for measuring time; any timing device with a dial and displayed figures. • *vt* to time (a race, etc) using a stopwatch or other device; (*inf*) to register a certain speed; (*sl*) to hit.

**clockwise** *adv* moving in the direction of a clock's hands.—*also adj*.

**clockwork** *n* the mechanism of a clock or any similar mechanism with springs and gears. • *adj* mechanically regular.

**clog** *n* a wooden-soled shoe. • *vt* (*pt* **clogged**) to cause a blockage in; to impede, obstruct.

**cloister** *n* a roofed pillared walk, usu with one side open, in a convent, college, etc; a religious retreat. • *vt* to confine or keep apart as if in a convent.

**close**[1] *adj* near; reticent, secret; nearly alike; nearly even or equal; dense, compact; sultry, airless; narrow; restricted. • *adv* closely; near by. • *n* a courtyard; the entrance to a courtyard; the precincts of a cathedral.—**closely** *adv*.—**closeness** *n*.

**close**[2] *vt* to make closed; to stop up (an opening); to draw together; to conclude; to shut. • *vi* to come together; to complete; to finish. • *n* a completion, end.

**closed** *adj* shut up; with no opening; restricted; not open to question or debate; not open to the public, exclusive.

**closet** *n* a small room or a cupboard for clothes, supplies, etc; a small private room. • *vt* (*pt* **closeted**) to enclose in a private room for a confidential talk.

**close-up** *n* a film or television shot taken from very close range; a close examination.

**closure** *n* closing; the condition of being closed; something that closes; (*parliament, etc*) a decision to end further debate and move to an immediate vote.

**clot** *n* a thickened mass, esp of blood; (*sl*) an idiot. • *vti* (*pt* **clotted**) to form into clots, to curdle, coagulate.

**cloth** *n* woven, knitted or pressed fabric from which garments, etc are made; a piece of this; a tablecloth; clerical dress.

**clothe** *vt* (*pt* **clothed** or **clad**) to cover with a garments; to dress; to surround, endow (with).

**clothes** *npl* garments, apparel.

**clothesline** *n* a rope on which washing is hung to dry.

**clothespeg, clothespin** *n* a plastic, wooden or metal clip for attaching washing to a line.

**clothing** *n* clothes.

**cloud** *n* a visible mass of water vapour floating in the sky; a mass of smoke, etc; a threatening thing, a gloomy look; a multitude. • *vt* to darken or obscure as with clouds.—**cloudless** *adj*.

**cloudburst** *n* a sudden rainstorm.

**cloudy** *adj* (**cloudier, cloudiest**) of or

full of clouds; not clear; gloomy.— **cloudiness** n.

**clout** n a blow; (sl) power, influence.

**clove**[1] n a segment of a bulb, as garlic.

**clove**[2] n the dried flower bud of a tropical tree, used as a spice.

**clover** n a low-growing plant with three leaves used as fodder; a trefoil; (inf) luxury.

**clown** n a person who entertains with jokes, antics, etc, esp in a circus; a clumsy or boorish person. • vi to act the clown, behave comically or clumsily.—**clownish** adj.

**club** n a heavy stick used as a weapon; a stick with a head for playing golf, etc; an association of people for athletic, social, or common purposes; its premises; a suit of playing cards with black clover-like markings. • vt to beat with or use as a club. • vi to form into a club for a common purpose.

**clubhouse** n premises used by a club.

**cluck** n the call of a hen. • vi to make such a noise.

**clue** n a guide to the solution of a mystery or problem. • vt (pt **clued**) to provide with helpful information.

**clump** n a cluster of trees; a lump; (of hair) a handful; the sound of heavy footsteps.

**clumsy** adj (**clumsier, clumsiest**) unwieldy; awkward; lacking tact, skill or grace.—**clumsily** adv.—**clumsiness** n.

**clung** see **cling**.

**cluster** n a bunch; a swarm; a group. • vti to form or arrange in a cluster.

**clutch**[1] vt to seize, to grasp tightly; to snatch at. • n a tight grip; a device for throwing parts of a machine into or out of action; the pedal operating this device.

**clutch**[2] n a nest of eggs; a brood of chicks.

**clutter** n a disordered mess; confusion. • vti to litter; to put into disorder.

**Co.** abbr = Company; County.

**c/o** abbr = care of.

**coach** n a long-distance bus; a railway carriage; a large, covered four-wheeled horse-drawn carriage; a sports instructor; a tutor in a specialized subject. • vti to teach or train.

**coagulate** vti to change from a liquid to partially sold state, to clot, curdle.—**coagulation** n.

**coal** n a black mineral used for fuel; a piece of this; an ember.

**coalfield** n a region yielding coal.

**coalition** n a temporary union of parties or states.

**coarse** adj rough; large in texture; rude, crude; inferior.—**coarsely** adv.—**coarseness** n.

**coast** n an area of land bordering the sea; the seashore. • vi to sail along a coast; to travel down a slope without power; to proceed with ease.—**coastal** adj.

**coastguard** n an organization which monitors the coastline and provides help for ships in difficulties, prevents smuggling, etc.

**coat** n a sleeved outer garment; the natural covering of an animal; a layer. • vt to cover with a layer or coating.

**coating** n a surface coat; material for coats.

**coat of arms** n the heraldic bearings of a family, city, institution, etc.

**coax** vt to persuade gently; to obtain by coaxing.—**coaxingly** adv.

**cobble**[1] n a cobblestone, a rounded stone used for paving. • vt to pave with cobblestones.

**cobble**[2] vt to repair, to make (shoes); to put together roughly or hastily.

**cobra** n a venomous hooded snake of Africa and India.

**cobweb** n a spider's web; a flimsy thing; an entanglement.

**cocaine** n an intoxicating addictive

drug obtained from coca leaves, used in anaesthesia.

**cock** *n* the adult male of the domestic fowl; the male of other birds; a tap or valve; the hammer of a gun; a cocked position; (*vulg*) the penis. • *vt* to set erect, to stick up; to set at an angle; to bring the hammer (of gun) to firing position.

**cockerel** *n* a young cock.

**cockeyed** *adj* (*inf*) having a squint; slanting; daft, absurd.

**cockle** *n* an edible shellfish with a rounded shell.

**cockney** *n* a person born in the East End of London; the dialect of this area.

**cockpit** *n* the compartment of a small aircraft for the pilot and crew, the flight deck; an arena for cock fighting; the driver's seat in a racing car.

**cockroach** *n* a nocturnal beetle-like insect.

**cocktail** *n* an alcoholic drink containing a mixture of spirits or other liqueurs; an appetizer, usu containing shellfish, served as the first course of a meal.

**cocoa** *n* a powder of ground cacao seeds; a drink made from this.

**coconut** *n* the fruit of the coconut palm.

**cocoon** *n* a silky case spun by some insect larvae for protection in the chrysalis stage; a cosy covering. • *vt* to wrap in a cocoon.

**cod** *n* a large edible fish of the North Atlantic.

**code** *n* a system of letters, numbers or symbols used to transmit secret messages, or to simplify communication; a systematic body of laws; a set of rules or conventions; (*comput*) a set of program instructions. • *vt* to put into code.

**codify** *vt* to collect or arrange (laws, rules, regulations, etc) into a system.—**codifier** *n*.—**codification** *n*.

**coeducation** *n* the teaching of students of both sexes in the same institution.—**coeducational** *adj*.

**coerce** *vt* to compel; to force by threats.—**coercion** *n*.

**coexist** *vi* to exist together at the same time; to live in peace together.—**coexistence** *n*.—**coexistent** *adj*.

**coffee** *n* a drink made from the seeds of the coffee tree; the seeds, or the shrub; a light-brown colour.

**coffee table** *n* a low table for holding drinks, books, etc. • *adj* (*book*) large and for looking at, not reading.

**coffin** *n* a chest for a dead body to be buried in.

**cog** *n* a tooth-like projection on the rim of a wheel.

**cogent** *adj* persuasive, convincing.—**cogently** *adv*.—**cogency** *n*.

**cogwheel** *n* a wheel with a toothed rim for gearing.

**coherent** *adj* cohering; capable of intelligible speech; consistent.—**coherently** *adv*.—**coherence** *n*.

**coil** *vti* to wind in rings or folds; to twist into a circular or spiral shape. • *n* a coiled length of rope; a single ring of this; (*elect*) a spiral wire for the passage of current; an intra-uterine contraceptive device.

**coin** *n* a piece of legally stamped metal used as money. • *vt* to invent (a word, phrase); to make into money, to mint.

**coinage** *n* the act of coining; the issue of coins, currency; a coined word.

**coincide** *vi* to occupy the same portion of space; to happen at the same time; to agree exactly, to correspond.

**coincidence** *n* the act of coinciding; the occurrence of an event at the same time as another without apparent connection.

**coke**[1] *n* coal from which gas has been expelled. • *vt* to convert (coal) into coke.

**coke**$^2$ *n* (*sl*) cocaine.

**colander** *n* a bowl with holes in the bottom for straining cooked vegetables, pasta, etc.

**cold** *adj* lacking heat or warmth; lacking emotion, passion or courage; unfriendly; (*scent*) faint; (*sl*) unconscious. • *n* absence of heat; the sensation caused by this; cold weather; a virus infection of the respiratory tract.—**coldly** *adv*.—**coldness** *n*.

**cold feet** *n* (*inf*) fear.

**coleslaw** *n* raw shredded cabbage in a dressing, used in salads.

**collaborate** *vi* to work jointly or together, esp in literature; to side with the invaders of one's country.—**collaboration** *n*.—**collaborator** *n*.

**collage** *n* art made up from scraps of paper, material and other odds and ends pasted onto a hard surface.

**collapse** *vi* to fall down; to come to ruin, to fail; to break down physically or mentally. • *n* the act of collapsing; a breakdown, prostration.

**collapsible** *adj* designed to fold compactly.

**collar** *n* the band of a garment round the neck; a decoration round the neck, a choker; a band of leather or chain put round an animal's neck. • *vt* to put a collar on; (*inf*) to seize.

**collarbone** *n* one of the two bones that connect the shoulder blades with the breast bone, the clavicle.

**colleague** *n* an associate in the same profession or office; a fellow worker.

**collect** *vti* to bring together, gather or assemble; to regain command of (oneself); to concentrate (thoughts, etc). • *n* a short prayer for a particular occasion.

**collected** *adj* self-possessed, cool.—**collectedly** *adv*.

**collection** *n* act of collecting; an accumulation; money collected at a meeting, etc; a group of things collected for beauty, interest, rarity or value; the periodic showing of a designer's fashions.

**collector** *n* a person who collects things, eg stamps, butterflies, as a hobby or so as to inspect them, as tickets.

**college** *n* an institution of higher learning; a school offering specialized knowledge; the buildings housing a college; an organized body of professionals.

**collide** *vi* to come into violent contact (with); to dash together; to conflict.

**colliery** *n* a coal mine and its associated buildings.

**collision** *n* state of colliding together; a violent impact of moving bodies, a crash; a clash of interests, etc.

**colloquial** *adj* used in familiar but not formal talk, not literary.—**colloquially** *adv*.

**colon**$^1$ *n* the part of the large intestine from the caecum to the rectum.—**colonic** *adj*.

**colon**$^2$ *n* a punctuation mark (:) between the semicolon and the full stop.

**colonel** *n* a commissioned officer junior to a brigadier but senior to a lieutenant colonel.

**colonial** *adj* of or pertaining to a colony or colonies; (*with cap*) pertaining to the thirteen British colonies that became the US. • *n* a person who takes part in founding a colony, a settler.

**colonize** *vt* to establish a colony in; to settle in a colony.

**colony** *n* an area of land acquired and settled by a distant state and subject to its control; a community of settlers; a group of people of the same nationality or interests living in a particular area; a collection of organisms in close association.

**colossal** *adj* gigantic, immense; (*inf*) amazing, wonderful.

**colour, color** (*US*) *n* the eye's perception of wavelengths of light with different colours corresponding to different wavelengths; the attribute of objects to appear different according to their differing ability to absorb, emit, or reflect light of different wavelengths; colour of the face or skin; pigment; dye; paint; (*literature*) use of imagery, vividness; (*mus*) depth of sound; (*pl*) a flag. • *vt* to give colour to, paint; to misrepresent; to influence. • *vi* to emit colour; to blush.—**coloration** *n*.

**colour bar** *n* discrimination based on race, esp by white races against other races.

**colour-blind** *adj* unable to distinguish colours, esp red and green.

**coloured, colored** (*US*) *adj* possessing colour; biased, not objective; of a darker skinned race. • *n* a person of a darker skinned race.

**colourful, colorful** (*US*) *adj* full of colour; vivid.—**colourfully** *adv*.

**colt** *n* a young male horse.

**column** *n* a round pillar for supporting or decorating a building; something of this shape; a vertical division of a page; a narrow-fronted deep formation of troops; a feature article appearing regularly in a newspaper, etc.

**columnist** *n* a journalist who contributes a regular column.

**coma** *n* deep prolonged unconsciousness.

**comb** *n* a toothed instrument for separating hair, wool, etc; a part of a machine like this; the crest of a cock; a honeycomb. • *vt* to arrange (hair) or dress (wool) with a comb; to seek for thoroughly.

**combat** *vti* (*pt* **combated**) to strive against, oppose; to do battle. • *n* a contest; a fight; struggle.

**combination** *n* the act of combining; a union of separate parts; persons allied for a purpose; a sequence of numbers which opens a combination lock.

**combine** *vti* to join together; to unite intimately; to possess together; to cooperate; (*chem*) to form a compound with. • *n* an association formed for commercial or political purposes; a machine for harvesting and threshing grain.

**combustible** *adj* capable of burning; easily set alight; excitable. • *n* a combustible thing.—**combustibility** *n*.

**combustion** *n* the process of burning; the process in which substances react with oxygen in air to produce heat.

**come** *vi* (*pt* **came**, *pp* **come**) to approach; to arrive; to reach; to happen (to); to originate; to turn out (to be); to occur in a certain order; to be derived or descended; to be caused; to result; to be available; (*sl*) to experience a sexual orgasm.

**comeback** *n* (*inf*) a return to a career or to popularity; (*inf*) a witty answer.

**comedian** *n* an actor of comic parts; an entertainer who tells jokes; a person who behaves in a humorous manner.

**comedy** *n* an amusing play or film; drama consisting of amusing plays; an amusing occurrence; humour.

**comet** *n* a celestial body that travels round the sun, with a visible nucleus and a luminous tail.

**comfort** *vti* to bring consolation to; to soothe; to cheer. • *n* consolation; relief; bodily ease; (*pl*) things between necessities and luxuries.

**comfortable** *adj* promoting comfort; at ease; adequate; (*inf*) financially well off.—**comfortably** *adv*.

**comic** *adj* of comedy; causing amusement. • *n* a comedian; an entertaining person; a paper or book with strip cartoons.

**comical** *adj* funny, laughable; droll, ludicrous.—**comically** *adv*.

**comic strip** *n* a series of drawings that depict a story in stages.

**coming** *adj* approaching next; of future importance.

**comma** *n* a punctuation mark (,) indicating a pause or break in a sentence, or separating items in a list.

**command** *vti* to order; to bid; to control; to have at disposal; to evoke, compel; to look down over; to be in authority (over), to govern. • *n* an order; control; disposal; position of authority; something or someone commanded; an instruction to a computer.

**commandeer** *vt* to seize for military purposes; to appropriate for one's own use.

**commander** *n* a person who commands, a leader; a naval officer ranking next below a captain.

**commando** *n* (*pl* **commandos**) a member of an elite military force trained to raid enemy territory.

**commemorate** *vt* to keep in the memory by ceremony or writing; to be a memorial of.—**commemoration** *n*.—**commemorative** *adj*.

**commence** *vti* to begin.

**commend** *vt* to speak favourably of, to praise; to recommend; to entrust.—**commendable** *adj*.

**commendation** *n* the act of com-mending, praise; an award.

**commensurate** *adj* having the same extent or measure; proportionate.

**comment** *n* a remark, observation, criticism; an explanatory note; talk, gossip. • *vi* to make a comment (upon); to annotate.

**commentary** *n* a series of explanatory notes or remarks.

**commentator** *n* one who reports and analyses events, trends, etc, as on TV.

**commerce** *n* trade in goods and services on a large scale between nations or individuals.

**commercial** *adj* of or engaged in commerce; sponsored by an advertiser; intended to make a profit. • *n* a broadcast advertisement.

**commercialize** *vt* to put on a business basis; to exploit for profit.—**commercialization** *n*.

**commiserate** *vti* to sympathize (with); to feel pity for.—**commiseration** *n*.

**commission** *n* authority to act; a document bestowing this; appointment as a military officer of the rank of lieutenant or above; a body of people appointed for specified duties; business committed to someone; a percentage on sales paid to a salesman or agent; brokerage. • *vt* to empower or appoint by commission; to employ the service of; to authorize.

**commissionaire** *n* a uniformed attendant at the entrance to an office building, shop, etc.

**commissioner** *n* a person empowered by a commission; various types of civil servant; a member of a commission.

**commit** *vti* (*pt* **committed**) to entrust; to consign (to prison); to do, to perpetrate; to pledge, to involve.

**commitment** *n* the act of committing; an engagement that restricts freedom; an obligation; an order for imprisonment or confinement in a mental institution.—**committal** *n*.

**committee** *n* a body of people appointed from a larger body to consider or manage some matter.

**commodity** *n* an article of trade; a useful thing; (*pl*) goods.

**common** *adj* belonging equally to more than one; public; usual, ordinary; widespread; familiar; frequent; easily obtained, not rare; low, vulgar; (*noun*) applying to any of a class. • *n* a tract of open public land; (*pl*) the common people; the House of

Commons.—**commonly** *adv.*—**commonness** *n.*

**commoner** *n* an ordinary person, not a member of the nobility.

**common law** *n* the body of law based on custom and judicial precedent, as distinct from statute law. • *adj* denoting a marriage recognized in law not by an official ceremony, but after a couple have cohabited for a number of years.

**Common Market** *n* (*with* **the**) an unofficial name for the European Community, a grouping of nations formed to facilitate trade by removing tariff barriers.

**commonplace** *adj* ordinary, unremarkable. • *n* a platitude; an ordinary thing.

**common sense** *n* ordinary, practical good sense.—**common-sense** *adj.*

**commonwealth** *n* a political community; a sovereign state, republic; a federation of states; (*with cap*) an association of sovereign states and dependencies ruled or formerly ruled by Britain.

**commotion** *n* a violent disturbance; agitation; upheaval.

**communal** *adj* of a commune or community; shared in common.—**communally** *adv.*

**commune**[1] *n* a group of people living together and sharing possessions; the smallest administrative division in several European countries.

**commune**[2] *vi* to converse intimately; to communicate spiritually.

**communicate** *vti* to impart, to share; to succeed in conveying information; to be connected.

**communication** *n* the act of communicating; information; a connecting passage or channel; (*pl*) connections of transport; (*pl*) means of imparting information, as in newspapers, TV.

**communication cord** *n* a cord, by pulling which a passenger can stop a train in an emergency.

**communion** *n* common possession, sharing; fellowship; union in a religious body; (*with cap*) Holy Communion, the Christian sacrament of the Eucharist when bread and wine are consecrated and consumed.

**communiqué** *n* an official communication, esp to the press or public.

**communism** *n* a social system under which private property is abolished and the means of production are owned by the people; (*with cap*) a political movement seeking the overthrow of capitalism based on the writings of Karl Marx; the system as instituted in the former USSR and elsewhere.—**communist** *n, adj.*

**community** *n* an organized political or social body; a body of people in the same locality; the general public, society; any group having work, interests, etc in common; joint ownership; common character.

**community centre** *n* a place providing social and recreational facilities for a local community.

**commute** *vti* to travel daily from a suburban home to a city office; to exchange (for); to change (to); to reduce (a punishment) to one less severe.—**commutation** *n*.

**commuter** *n* a person who commutes to and from work.

**compact**[1] *n* an agreement; a contract, a treaty.

**compact**[2] *adj* closely packed; condensed; terse. • *vt* to press or pack closely; to compose (of). • *n* a small cosmetic case, usu containing powder and a mirror.—**compactly** *adv.*—**compactness** *n.*

**companion** *n* an associate in an activity; a partner; a friend; one of a pair of matched things.—**companionship** *n.*

**company** *n* any assembly of people; an association of people for carrying on a business, etc; a society; a military unit; the crew of a ship; companionship, fellowship.

**comparable** *adj* able or suitable to be compared (*with* **with**); similar.— **comparably** *adv*.—**comparability** *n*.

**comparative** *adj* estimated by comparison; relative, not absolute; (*gram*) expressing more.—**comparatively** *adv*.

**compare** *vt* to make one thing the measure of another; to observe similarity between, to liken; to bear comparison; (*gram*) to give comparative and superlative forms of (an adjective). • *vi* to make comparisons; to be equal or alike.

**comparison** *n* the act of comparing; an illustration; (*gram*) the use of *more* or *er* with an adjective.

**compartment** *n* a space partitioned off; a division of a railway carriage; a separate section or category.— **compartmental** *adj*.

**compass** *n* a circuit, circumference; an extent, area; the range of a voice; an instrument with a magnetic needle indicating north, south, east, west; (*often pl*) a two-legged instrument for drawing circles, etc.

**compassion** *n* sorrow for another's sufferings; pity.

**compassionate** *adj* showing compassion; merciful.— **compassionately** *adv*.

**compatible** *adj* agreeing or fitting in (with); consistent.—**compatibly** *adv*.—**compatibility** *n*.

**compel** *vt* (*pt* **compelled**) to force, constrain; to oblige; to obtain by force.

**compendium** *n* (*pl* **compendiums, compendia**) an abridgement; a summary; a collection.

**compensate** *vti* to counterbalance; to make up for; to recompense.—**compensatory** *adj*.

**compensation** *n* the act of compensating; a sum given to compensate.

**compere, compère** *n* a person who introduces cabaret performers, television acts, etc. • *vt* to act as a compere (for).

**compete** *vi* to strive; to contend; to take part in a competition.

**competence** *n* the quality of being capable; sufficiency; capacity; an adequate income to live on.

**competent** *adj* fit, capable; adequate; legally qualified.—**competently** *adv*.

**competition** *n* act of competing; rivalry; a contest in skill or knowledge; a match.

**competitive** *adj* of, or involving, competition; of sufficient value in terms of price or quality to ensure success against rivals.—**competitively** *adv*.— **competitiveness** *n*.

**competitor** *n* a person who competes; an opponent; a rival.

**compile** *vt* to collect or make up from various sources; to amass; (*comput*) to translate high-level programme instructions into machine code using a compiler.—**compilation** *n*.

**complacent** *adj* self-satisfied.—**complacently** *adv*.—**complacency** *n*.

**complain** *vi* to find fault, to grumble; to be ill; (*poet*) to express grief, to make a mourning sound.

**complaint** *n* a statement of some grievance; a cause of distress or dissatisfaction; an illness.

**complement** *n* something making up a whole; a full allowance (of equipment or number). • *vt* to make complete.

**complementary** *adj* completing; together forming a balanced whole.

**complete** *adj* entire; free from deficiency; finished; thorough. • *vt* to make complete; to finish.—**completeness** *n*.

**completely** *adv* entirely, utterly.

**completion** n the act of completing; accomplishment; fulfilment.

**complex** adj having more than one part; intricate, not simple; difficult. • n a complex whole; a collection of interconnected parts, buildings or units; a group of mostly unconscious impulses, etc strongly influencing behaviour.—**complexity** n.

**complexion** n a colour, texture and look of the skin; aspect, character.

**compliance** n the act of complying with another's wishes; acquiescence.

**compliant** adj yielding, submissive.—**compliantly** adv.

**complicate** vt to make intricate or involved; to mix up.

**complicated** adj intricately involved; difficult to understand.

**complication** n a complex or intricate situation; a circumstance that makes (a situation) more complex; (med) a condition or disease following an original illness.

**compliment** n a polite expression of praise, a flattering tribute; (pl) a formal greeting or expression of regard. • vt to pay a compliment to, to flatter; to congratulate (on).

**complimentary** adj conveying or expressing a compliment; given free of charge.

**comply** vi to act in accordance (with); to yield, to agree.

**component** adj going to the making of a whole, constituent. • n a component part.

**compose** vt to make up, to form; to construct in one's mind, to write; to arrange, to put in order; to settle, to adjust; to tranquillize; (print) to set up. • vi to create musical works, etc.

**composed** adj calm, self-controlled.—**composedly** adv.

**composer** n a person who composes, esp music.

**composition** n the act or process of composing; a work of literature or music, a painting; a short written essay; the general make-up of something; a chemical compound.

**compost** n a mixture of decomposed organic matter for fertilizing soil.

**composure** n the state of being composed, calmness.

**compound**[1] n a substance or thing made up of a number of parts or ingredients, a mixture; a compound word. • vt to combine (parts, ingredients) into a whole, to mix; to intensify by adding new elements; to settle (debt) by partial payment. • vi to become joined in a compound; to come to terms of agreement. • adj compounded or made up of several parts; not simple.

**compound**[2] n an enclosure in which a building stands.

**compound fracture** n a fracture in which the bone pierces the skin.

**compound interest** n interest paid on the principal sum of capital and the interest that it has accrued.

**comprehend** vt to grasp with the mind, to understand; to include, to embrace.—**comprehension** n.

**comprehensive** adj wide in scope or content, including a great deal. • n a comprehensive school.—**comprehensively** adv.—**comprehensiveness** n.

**comprehensive school** n in Britain, a secondary school for local pupils of all abilities.

**compress** vt to press or squeeze together; to bring into a smaller bulk; to condense. • n a soft pad for compressing an artery, etc; a wet bandage to for relieving inflammation.

**compression** n the act of compressing; the increase in pressure in an engine to compress the gases so that they explode.

**comprise** vt to consist of, to include.

**compromise** n a settlement of a dispute

by mutual concession; a middle course or view between two opposed ones. • *vti* to adjust by compromise; to lay open to suspicion, disrepute, etc.

**compulsion** *n* the act of compelling; something that compels; an irresistible urge.

**compulsive** *adj* compelling; acting as if compelled.—**compulsively** *adv*.

**compulsory** *adj* enforced, obligatory, required by law, etc; involving compulsion; essential.—**compulsorily** *adv*.

**computer** *n* an electronic device that processes data in accordance with programmed instructions.

**computerize** *vt* to equip with computers; to control or perform (a process) using computers; to store or process data using a computer.—**computerization** *n*.

**comrade** *n* a companion; a fellow member of a Communist party.—**comradely** *adv*.—**comradeship** *n*.

**con**[1] *vt* (*pt* **conned**) (*inf*) to swindle, trick. • *n* (*inf*) a confidence trick.

**con**[2] *n* against, as in **pro and con**.

**con**[3] *prep* with.

**concave** *adj* curving inwards, hollow. • *n* a concave line or surface.—**concavity** *n*.

**conceal** *vt* to hide, to keep from sight; to keep secret.—**concealment** *n*.

**concede** *vt* to grant; to admit to be true, to allow.

**conceit** *n* an over-high opinion of oneself; vanity; a far-fetched comparison, a quaint fancy.

**conceited** *adj* full of conceit, vain.—**conceitedly** *adv*.

**conceivable** *adj* capable of being imagined or believed.—**conceivably** *adv*.

**conceive** *vti* to become pregnant (with); to form in the mind; to think out, to imagine; to understand; to express.

**concentrate** *vt* to bring or converge together to one point; to direct to a single object or purpose; to collect one's thoughts or efforts; (*chem*) to increase the strength of by diminishing bulk, to condense. • *n* a concentrated product, esp a food reduced in bulk by eliminating fluid; a foodstuff relatively high in nutrients.

**concentration** *n* the act or process of concentrating; the direction of attention to a single object.

**concern** *vt* to relate or apply to, to fill with anxiety; to interest (oneself) in; to take part, to be mixed up (in). • *n* a thing that concerns one; anxiety, misgiving; interest in or regard for a person or thing; a business or firm.

**concerned** *adj* troubled, worried; interested.—**concernedly** *adv*.

**concerning** *prep* about; regarding.

**concert** *n* a musical entertainment; harmony; agreement or union.

**concerted** *adj* planned or arranged by mutual agreement; combined; (*mus*) arranged in separate parts for musicians or singers.

**concertina** *n* a hexagonal musical instrument, which produces sound by squeezing bellows that pass air over metal reeds. • *vi* to collapse or fold like the bellows of a concertina.

**concerto** *n* (*pl* **concertos**) a musical composition for a solo instrument and orchestra.

**concession** *n* the act of conceding; something conceded; a grant of rights, land, etc by a government, corporation, or individual; a reduction in price (of admission, travel, etc) for certain people.—**concessionary** *adj*.

**conciliate** *vt* to win over from hostility; to make friendly; to appease; to reconcile.—**conciliation** *n*.—**conciliator** *n*.—**conciliatory** *adj*.

**concise** *adj* brief, condensed, terse.—**concisely** *adv*.—**conciseness** *n*.

**conclave** *n* a private or secret meeting; a meeting of cardinals in seclusion to choose a pope; the meeting place.

**conclude** *vti* to bring or come to an end, to finish; to effect, to settle; to infer; to resolve.

**conclusion** *n* concluding; the end or close; an inference; a final opinion; (*logic*) a proposition deduced from premises.

**conclusive** *adj* decisive; convincing.—**conclusively** *adv*.

**concoct** *vt* to make by combining ingredients; to devise, to plan; to invent (a story).

**concourse** *n* an open space or hall where crowds gather, eg a railway or airport terminal.

**concrete** *adj* having a material existence; (*gram*) denoting a thing, not a quality, not abstract; made of concrete. • *n* anything concrete; a mixture of sand, cement, etc, used in building. • *vti* to form into a mass, to solidify; to cover with concrete.

**concur** *vi* (*pt* **concurred**) to happen together, to coincide; to cooperate; to be of the same opinion, to agree.—**concurrence** *n*.

**concurrent** *adj* existing, acting or occurring at the same time; coinciding.—**concurrently** *adv*.

**concussion** *n* the violent shock of an impact or explosion; loss of consciousness caused by a violent blow to the head.

**condemn** *vt* to express strong disapproval of; to find guilty; to blame or censure; to declare unfit for use.—**condemnation** *n*.—**condemnatory** *adj*.

**condense** *vt* to reduce to a smaller compass, to compress; to change from a gas into a liquid; to concentrate; to express in fewer words. • *vi* to become condensed.—**condenser** *n*.—**condensation** *n*.

**condensed milk** *n* milk that has been reduced by evaporation and sweetened.

**condescend** *vi* to waive one's superiority; to deign, to stoop; to act patronizingly.—**condescension** *n*.

**condiment** *n* a seasoning or relish.

**condition** *n* anything required for the performance, completion or existence of something else; physical state of health; an abnormality, illness; a prerequisite; (*pl*) attendant circumstances. • *vt* to be essential to the happening or existence of; to stipulate; to agree upon; to make fit; to make accustomed (to).—**conditioner** *n* a person or thing that conditions; a creamy substance for bringing the hair into a glossy condition.

**conditional** *adj* depending on conditions; not absolute; (*gram*) expressing condition. • *n* a conditional clause or conjunction.—**conditionally** *adv*.

**condolence** *n* sympathy.

**condone** *vt* to overlook, to treat as nonexistent.

**conducive** *adj* leading or helping to cause or produce.

**conduct** *vti* to lead; to convey; to direct (an orchestra); to carry on or manage (a business); to transmit (electricity, heat); to behave (oneself). • *n* management, direction; behaviour.

**conductor** *n* a person who conducts an orchestra; one in charge of passengers on a train, or who collects fares on a bus; a substance that conducts heat or electricity.—**conductress** *nf*.

**conduit** *n* a channel or pipe that carries water, etc.

**cone** *n* a solid pointed figure with a circular or elliptical base; any cone-shaped object; the scaly fruit of the pine, fir, etc.

**confectionery** *n* sweets.

**confederation** n the act or state of confederating; an alliance of individuals, organizations or states.

**confer** vt (pt **conferred**) to grant or bestow; to compare views or take counsel; to consult.

**conference** n a meeting for discussion or consultation.

**confess** vt to acknowledge or admit; to disclose (sins) to a confessor; (priest) to hear confession of. • vi to make or hear a confession.

**confession** n admission or acknowledgement of a fault or sin, esp to a confessor; a thing confessed; a statement of one's religious beliefs, creed.

**confessional** n an enclosure in a church where a priest hears confessions.

**confessor** n a priest who hears confessions and grants absolution; one who confesses.

**confetti** npl bits of coloured paper thrown at weddings.

**confide** vti to put confidence (in); to entrust; to impart.

**confidence** n firm trust, faith; belief in one's own abilities; boldness; something revealed confidentially.

**confidence trick** n the persuading of a victim to hand over valuables as proof of confidence.

**confident** adj full of confidence; positive, assured.—**confidently** adv.

**confidential** adj spoken or written in confidence, secret; entrusted with secrets.- **confidentially** adv.—**confidentiality** n.

**confine** vt to restrict, to keep within limits; to keep shut up, as in prison, a sickbed, etc; to imprison. • n (pl) borderland, edge, limit.

**confined** adj narrow, enclosed.

**confinement** n a being confined; the period of childbirth.

**confirm** vt to make stronger; to establish firmly; to make valid, to ratify; to corroborate; to administer rite of confirmation to.

**confirmation** n the act of confirming; convincing proof; the rite by which people are admitted to full communion in Christian churches.

**confirmed** adj habitual; have undergone the rite of confirmation.

**confiscate** vt to appropriate to the state as a penalty; to seize by authority.—**confiscation** n.

**conflict** n a fight; a contest; strife, quar-rel; emotional disturbance. • vi to be at variance; to clash (with); to struggle.

**conform** vi to comply, to be obedient (to); to act in accordance with. • vt to adapt; to make like.

**conformist** n one who conforms to established rules, standards, etc; compliance with the rites and doctrines of an established church.—**conformism** n.

**confound** vt to mix up, to obscure; to perplex, to astound; to overthrow; to mistake one thing for another.

**confounded** adj astonished; confused; annoying; (inf) damned.—**confoundedly** adv.

**confront** vt to stand in front of, face; to bring face to face (with); to encounter; to oppose.—**confrontation** n.

**confuse** vt to throw into disorder; to mix up; to mistake one thing for another; to perplex, to disconcert; to embarrass; to make unclear.—**confusedly** adv.

**confusion** n the act or state of being confused; disorder; embarrassment, discomfiture; lack of clarity.

**congeal** vti to change from a liquid to a solid by cooling, to jell.—**congealment** n.

**congenial** adj of a similar disposition or with similar tastes, kindred; suited, agreeable (to).—**congenially** adv.—**congeniality** n.

**congenital** *adj* existing or dating since birth, as in certain defects.—**congenitally** *adv*.

**conger eel** *n* a large marine eel.

**congestion** *n* an overcrowding; (*med*) an excessive accumulation of blood in any organ; an accumulation of traffic causing obstruction.

**congratulate** *vt* to express sympathetic pleasure at success or good fortune of, to compliment.—**congratulation** *n*.—**congratulatory** *adj*.

**congratulations** *npl* an expression of joy or pleasure.

**congregate** *vti* to flock together, to assemble; to gather into a crowd or mass.

**congregation** *n* a gathering, an assembly; a body of people assembled for worship.

**congress** *n* an association or society; an assembly or conference, esp for discussion and action on some question; (*with cap*) the legislature of the US, comprising the Senate and the House of Representatives.

**Congressman** *n* a member of Congress.—**Congresswoman** *nf*.

**conic, conical** *adj* of a cone; cone-shaped.

**conifer** *n* any evergreen trees and shrubs with true cones (as pines) and other (as yews).—**coniferous** *adj*.

**conjecture** *n* a guess, guesswork. • *vt* to make a conjecture, to guess, surmise.—**conjectural** *adj*.

**conjugal** *adj* of or relating to marriage.—**conjugally** *adv*.

**conjunction** *n* (*gram*) a word connecting words, clauses or sentences; a union; a simultaneous occurrence of events; the apparent proximity of two or more planets.

**conjunctivitis** *n* inflammation of the membrane (conjunctiva) that covers the eyeball and inner eyelid.

**conjure** *vti* to practise magical tricks; to call up (spirits) by invocation.—**conjurer, conjuror** *n*.

**conk** *n* (*sl*) the nose or head. • *n* a blow to the nose or head.

**con man** *n* (*inf*) a swindler, one who defrauds by means of a confidence trick.

**connect** *vti* to fasten together, to join; to relate together, to link up; (*trains, buses, etc*) timed to arrive as another leaves so that passengers can continue their journey; to establish a link by telephone.—**connector, connecter** *n*.

**connection, connexion** *n* the act of connecting; the state of being connected; a thing that connects; a relationship, bond; a train, bus, etc timed to connect with another; an opportunity to transfer between trains, buses, etc; context; a link between components in an electric circuit; a relative; (*pl*) clients, customers.

**connive** *vi* to permit tacitly; to wink (at); to plot.—**connivance** *n*.

**connoisseur** *n* a trained discriminating judge, esp of the fine arts.

**connotation** *n* a consequential meaning, an implication—**connotative** *adj*.

**conquer** *vt* to gain victory (over), to defeat; to acquire by conquest; to overcome, to master. • *vi* to be victor.—**conqueror** *n*.

**conquest** *n* conquering; the winning of a person's affection; a person or thing conquered.

**conscience** *n* the knowledge of right and wrong that affects action and behaviour; the sense of guilt or virtue induced by actions, behaviour, etc; an inmost thought; conscientiousness.

**conscientious** *adj* following the dictates of the conscience; scrupulous; careful, thorough.—**conscientiously** *adv*.—**conscientiousness** *n*.

**conscientious objector** *n* a person who refuses to serve in the military forces on moral or religious grounds.

**conscious** *adj* aware (of); awake to one's surroundings; (*action*) realized by the person who does it.—**consciously** *adv*.

**consciousness** *n* the state of being conscious; perception; the whole body of a person's thoughts and feelings.

**conscript** *adj* enrolled into service by compulsion; drafted. • *n* a conscripted person (as a military recruit). • *vt* to enlist compulsorily.—**conscription** *n*.

**consecrate** *vt* to set apart as sacred, to sanctify; to devote (to).—**consecration** *n*.

**consecutive** *adj* following in regular order without a break; successive; (*gram*) expressing consequence.—**consecutively** *adv*.

**consensus** *n* an opinion held by all or most; general agreement, esp in opinion.

**consent** *vi* to agree (to); to comply; to acquiesce • *n* agreement, permission; concurrence.

**consequence** *n* a result, an outcome; importance; (*pl*) a game in which each player writes part of a story without knowing what has gone before.

**consequent** *adj* occurring as a result.—**consequently** *adv*.

**conservation** *n* conserving; preservation of the environment and natural resources.—**conservationist** *n*.

**conservative** *adj* traditional; cautious; moderate. • *n* a conservative person; (*with cap*) a member of the Conservative Party in Britain and other countries.—**conservatively** *adv*.

**conservatory** *n* a greenhouse attached to a house; a conservatoire.

**conserve** *vt* to keep from loss or injury; to preserve (food) with sugar.

• *n* a type of jam using whole fruit.

**consider** *vti* to reflect (upon), to contemplate; to examine, to weigh the merits of; to take into account; to regard as; to be of the opinion.

**considerable** *adj* a fairly large amount; worthy of respect.—**considerably** *adv*.

**considerate** *adj* careful of the feelings of others.—**considerately** *adv*.

**consideration** *n* the act of considering; deliberation; a point of importance; an inducement; thoughtfulness; deference.

**considering** *prep* in view of. • *adv* all in all. • *conj* seeing that.

**consign** *vt* to hand over, to commit; to send goods addressed (to).

**consignment** *n* consigning; goods, etc consigned.

**consist** *vi* to be made up (of); to be comprised (in).

**consistency** *n* degree of density, esp of thick liquids; the state of being consistent.

**consistent** *adj* compatible, not contradictory; uniform in thought or action.—**consistently** *adv*.

**consolation** *n* someone or something that offers comfort in distress.

**console**[1] *vt* to bring consolation to, to cheer in distress.—**consolable** *adj*.

**console**[2] *n* a desk containing the controls of an electronic system; the part of an organ containing the pedals, stops, etc; an ornamental bracket supporting a shelf or table.

**consolidate** *vti* to solidify; to establish firmly, to strengthen; to combine into a single whole.—**consolidation** *n*.

**consonant** *n* a letter of the alphabet that is not a vowel; the sound representing such a letter. • *adj* consistent, in keeping (with).

**consortium** *n* (*pl* **consortia**) an international banking or financial combination.

**conspicuous** *adj* easily seen, prominent; outstanding, eminent.—**conspicuousness** *n*.—**conspicuously** *adv*.

**conspiracy** *n* a secret plan for an illegal act; the act of conspiring.

**conspire** *vti* to combine secretly for an evil purpose; to plot, to devise.

**constable** *n* a policeman or policewoman of the lowest rank.

**constant** *adj* fixed; unchangeable; faithful; continual.—**constancy** *n*.

**constellation** *n* a group of fixed stars.

**consternation** *n* surprise and alarm; shock; dismay.

**constipation** *n* infrequent and difficult movement of the bowels.

**constituency** *n* a body of electors; the voters in a particular district.

**constituent** *adj* forming part of a whole, component; having the power to revise the constitution. • *n* a component part; a member of an elective body; a voter in a district.

**constitute** *vt* to set up by authority, to establish; to frame, to form; to appoint; to compose, to make up.

**constitution** *n* fundamental physical condition; disposition; temperament; structure, composition; the system of basic laws and principles of a government, society, etc; a document stating these specifically.

**constitutional** *adj* of or pertaining to a constitution; authorized or limited by a constitution, legal; inherent, natural. • *n* a walk for the sake of one's health.—**constitutionally** *adv*.—**constitutionality** *n*.

**constrain** *vt* to compel, to force; to hinder by force; to confine, to imprison.

**constrained** *adj* enforced; embarrassed, inhibited; showing constraint.

**constraint** *n* compulsion; forcible confinement; repression of feeling; embarrassment.

**constrict** *vt* to draw together, to squeeze, to compress.

**construct** *vt* to make, to build, to fit together; to compose. • *n* a structure; an interpretation; an arrangement, esp of words in a sentence.—**constructible** *adj*.—**constructor, constructer** *n*.

**construction** *n* constructing; anything constructed; a structure, building; interpretation, meaning; (*gram*) two or more words grouped together to form a phrase, clause or sentence.—**constructional** *adj*.

**constructive** *adj* helping to improve, promoting development.—**constructively** *adv*.

**construe** *vti* to translate word for word; to analyse grammatically; to take in a particular sense, to interpret.

**consul** *n* a person appointed to live in a foreign city to attend to the interests of his country's citizens and business there.—**consular** *adj*.

**consulate** *n* the official residence of a consul; the office of a Roman consul.

**consult** *vti* to seek advice from, esp a doctor or lawyer; to deliberate, to confer.

**consultant** *n* a specialist who gives professional or technical advice; a senior physician or surgeon in a hospital; a person who consults another.—**consultancy** *n*.

**consultation** *n* the act of consulting; a conference, esp with a doctor or lawyer.—**consultative** *adj*.

**consume** *vti* to destroy; to use up; to eat or drink up; to waste away; to utilize economic goods.—**consumable** *adj*.

**consumer** *n* a person who uses goods and services, the end user.

**consummate**[1] *vt* to bring to perfection, to be the crown of; (*marriage*) to complete by sexual intercourse.— **consummation** n.

**consummate**[2] adj complete, perfect.

**consumption** n the act of consuming; the state of being consumed or used up; (econ) expenditure on goods and services by consumers; tuberculosis.

**contact** n touch, touching; connection; an acquaintance, esp in business; a connection allowing the passage of electricity; (med) a person who has been in contact with a contagious disease.• vti to establish contact with.

**contact lens** n a thin correctional lens placed over the cornea of the eye.

**contagious** adj (disease) spread by contact; capable of spreading disease by contact; (influence) catching, infectious.

**contain** vt to hold, to enclose; to comprise, to include; to hold back or restrain within fixed limits.

**container** n a receptacle, etc designed to contain goods or substances; a standardized receptacle used to transport commodities.

**contaminate** vt to render impure, to pollute.—**contaminant** n.—**contamination** n.—**contaminator** n.

**contemplate** vti to look at steadily; to reflect upon, to meditate; to have in view, to intend.—**contemplation** n.

**contemporary** adj living or happening at the same time; of about the same age; present day. • n a person living at the same time; a person of the same age.

**contempt** n the feeling one has toward someone or something considered low, worthless etc; the condition of being despised.

**contemptible** adj deserving contempt.—**contemptibly** adv.—**contemptibility** n.

**contemptuous** adj showing or feeling contempt; disdainful.—**contemptuously** adv.—**contemptuousness** n.

**contend** vti to take part in a contest, to strive (for); to quarrel; to maintain (that), to assert.—**contender** n.

**content**[1] n (usu pl) what is in a container; (usu pl) what is in a book; substance or meaning.

**content**[2] adj satisfied (with), not desiring more; willing (to); happy; pleased. • n satisfaction. • vt to make content; to satisfy.—**contentment** n.

**contention** n contending, struggling, arguing; a point in dispute; an assertion in an argument.

**contest** vti to call in question, to dispute; to fight to gain, to compete for; to strive. • n a struggle, an encounter; a competition; a debate; a dispute.

**contestant** n a competitor in a contest; a person who contests.

**context** n the parts of a written work or speech that precede and follow a word or passage, contributing to its full meaning; associated surroundings, setting.—**contextual** adj.

**continent**[1] n one of the six or seven main divisions of the earth's land; (with cap) the mainland of Europe, excluding the British Isles; a large extent of land.

**continent**[2] adj able to control urination and defecation; practising self-restraint; chaste.—**continence** n.

**continental** adj of a continent; (with cap) of or relating to Europe, excluding the British Isles; of or relating to the former 13 British colonies later forming the USA. • n an inhabitant of the Continent.

**contingency** n a possibility of a future event or condition; something dependent on a future event.

**contingent** adj possible, that may happen; chance; dependent (on); incidental (to). • n a possibility; a quota of troops.—**contingently** adv.

**continual** *adj* frequently repeated, going on all the time.—**continually** *adv*.

**continuation** *n* a continuing; prolongation; resumption; a thing that continues something else, a sequel, a further instalment.

**continue** *vt* to go on (with); to prolong; to extend; to resume, to carry further. • *vi* to remain, to stay; to last; to preserve.

**continuity** *n* continuousness; uninterrupted succession; a script or scenario in a film or broadcast.

**continuous** *adj* continuing; occurring without interruption.—**continuously** *adv*.—**continuousness** *n*.

**contort** *vti* to twist out of a normal shape, to pull awry.—**contortion** *n*.

**contortionist** *n* a person who can twist his or her body into unusual postures.

**contour** *n* the outline of a figure, land, etc; the line representing this outline; a contour line.

**contour line** *n* a line on a map that passes through all points at the same altitude.

**contra-** *prefix* against.

**contraband** *n* smuggled goods; smuggling. • *adj* illegal to import or export.

**contraception** *n* the deliberate prevention of conception, birth control.

**contraceptive** *n* a contraceptive drug or device.—*also adj*.

**contract** *vt* to draw closer together; to confine; to undertake by contract; (*debt*) to incur; (*disease*) to become infected by; (*word*) to shorten by omitting letters. • *vi* to shrink; to become smaller or narrower; to make a contract. • *n* a bargain; an agreement to supply goods or perform work at a stated price; a written agreement enforceable by law.

**contraction** *n* the act of contracting; the state of being contracted; a contracted word; a labour pain in childbirth.

**contractor** *n* a person who makes a business contract, esp a builder.

**contractual** *adj* of a contract.—**contractually** *adv*.

**contradict** *vti* to assert the contrary or opposite of; to deny; to be at variance (with).

**contradiction** *n* the act of contradicting; a denial.—**contradictory** *adj*.

**contralto** *n* (*pl* **contraltos**) a singing voice having a range between tenor and mezzo-soprano; a person having this voice.

**contraption** *n* (*inf*) a device, a gadget.

**contrary** *adj* opposed; opposite in nature; wayward, perverse. • *n* the opposite. • *adv* in opposition to; in conflict with.—**contrarily** *adv*.—**contrariness** *n*.

**contrast** *vi* to show marked differences. • *vt* to compare so as to point out the differences. • *n* the exhibition of differences; difference of qualities shown by comparison; the degree of difference between colours or tones.

**contravene** *vt* to infringe (a law), to transgress; to conflict with, to contradict.—**contravention** *n*.

**contribute** *vti* to give to a common stock or fund; to write (an article) for a magazine, etc; to furnish ideas, etc.—**contributory** *adj*.

**contribution** *n* the act of contributing; something contributed; a literary article; a payment into a collection.

**contributor** *n* a person who contributes, esp the writer of a newspaper article, etc; a contributing factor.

**contrite** *adj* deeply repentant, feeling guilt.—**contritely** *adv*.—**contrition** *n*.

**contrivance** *n* something contrived, esp a mechanical device, invention; inventive ability; an artificial construct; a stratagem.

**contrive** *vt* to plan ingeniously; to devise, to design, to manage; to achieve, esp by some ploy; to scheme.—**con-triver** n.

**control** n restraint; command, authority; a check; a means of controlling; a standard of comparison for checking an experiment. • vt (pt **controlled**) to check; to restrain; to regulate; to govern; (experiment) to verify by comparison.

**controversial** adj causing controversy, open to argument.

**controversy** n a discussion of contrary opinions; dispute, argument.

**convalesce** vi to recover health and strength after an illness; to get better. —**convalescence** n.

**convalescent** adj recovering health; aiding the recovery of full health. • n a patient recovering after an illness.

**convector** n a heater that circulates warm air.

**convene** vti to call together for a meeting.—**convener** n.

**convenience** n what suits one; a useful appliance; a public lavatory.

**convenient** adj handy; suitable; causing little or no trouble.—**conveniently** adv.

**convent** n a house of a religious order, esp an establishment of nuns.

**convention** n a political or ecclesiastical meeting; an agreement between nations, a treaty; established usage, social custom.

**conventional** adj of or based on convention or social custom; not spontaneous; following accepted rules; (weapons) non-nuclear.—**conventionality** n —**conventionally** adj.

**converge** vti to come or bring together.—**convergence** n.—**convergent** adj.

**conversant** adj well acquainted; proficient; familiar (with).

**conversation** n informal talk or exchange of ideas, opinions, etc

between people.—**conversational** adj.—**conversationally** adv.

**converse**[1] vi to engage in conversation (with). • n familiar talk, conversation.

**converse**[2] adj opposite, contrary. • n something that is opposite or contrary.—**conversely** adv.

**conversion** n change from one state, or from on religion, to another; something converted from one use to another; an alteration to a building undergoing a change in function; (rugby) a score after a try by kicking the ball over the crossbar.

**convert** vt to change from one thing, condition or religion to another; to alter; to apply to a different use; (rugby) to make a conversion after a try. • n a converted person, esp one who has changed religion.—**convertibility** n.

**convertible** adj able to be converted. • n a car with a folding or detachable roof.

**convex** adj curving outward like the surface of a sphere.—**convexly** adv.—**convexity** n.

**convey** vt to transport; to conduct, to transmit; to make known, to communicate; (law) to make over (property). —**conveyable** adj.—**conveyor** n.

**conveyor belt** n a continuous moving belt or linked plates for moving objects in a factory.

**convict** vt to prove or pronounce guilty. • n a convicted person serving a prison sentence.

**conviction** n act of convicting; a settled opinion; a firm belief.

**convince** vt to persuade by argument or evidence; to satisfy by proof.

**convincing** adj compelling belief.—**convincingly** adv.

**convivial** adj sociable, jovial.—**conviviality** n.—**convivially** adv.

**convulse** vt to agitate violently; to

shake with irregular spasms. • *vi* (*inf*) to cause to shake with uncontrollable laughter.—**convulsive** *adj*.—**convulsively** *adv*.

**convulsion** *n* a violent involuntary contraction of a muscle or muscles; an agitation, tumult; (*pl*) a violent fit of laughter.

**cook** *vt* to prepare (food) by heat; (*inf*) to fake (accounts, etc); to subject to great heat. • *vi* to be a cook; to under go cooking. • *n* a person who cooks; one whose job is to cook.

**cookbook, cookery book** *n* a book of recipes and other information for preparing food.

**cooker** *n* an electric or gas appliance for cooking.

**cookery** *n* the art or practice of cooking.

**cookie** *n* a biscuit.

**cool** *adj* moderately cold; calm; indifferent. • *vti* to make or become cool. • *n* coolness; composure.—**cooler** *n*.—**coolly** *adv*.—**coolness** *n*.

**coop**[1] *n* a small pen for poultry. • *vt* to confine as in a coop.

**coop**[2]**, co-op** *n* a cooperative society or shop run by a cooperative society.

**cooperate, co-operate** *vi* to work together, to act jointly.—**cooperation, co-operation** *n*.—**cooperator, co-operator** *n*.

**cooperative, co-operative** *adj* willing to cooperate; helpful. • *n* an organization or enterprise owned by, and operated for the benefit of, those using its services.—**cooperatively, co-operatively** *adv*.

**coordinate, co-ordinate** *vt* to integrate (different elements, etc) into an efficient relationship; to adjust to; to function harmoniously. • *n* an equal person or thing; any of a series of numbers that, in a given frame of reference, locate a point in space; (*pl*) separate items of clothing

intended to be worn together. • *adj* equal in degree or status.—**coordinately, co-ordinately** *adv*.

**coordination, co-ordination** *n* the act of coordinating; the state of being coordinated; balanced and harmonious movement of the body.

**coot** *n* a European water-bird with dark plumage, similar to a duck.

**cop** *vb* (*pt* **copped**) *vt* (*sl*) to arrest, catch. • *vi* (*with* **out**) (*sl*) to fail to perform, to renege. • *n* (*sl*) capture; a policeman.

**cope** *vi* to deal successfully with; to contend on even terms (with).

**copilot** *n* a second pilot in an aircraft.

**copious** *adj* plentiful, abundant.—**copiously** *adv*.

**copper**[1] *n* a reddish ductile metallic element; a bronze coin. • *adj* made of, or of the colour of, copper.

**copper**[2] *n* (*sl*) a police officer.

**copulate** *vi* to have sexual intercourse.—**copulation** *n*.—**copulative** *adj*.

**copy** *n* a reproduction; a transcript; a single specimen of a book; a model to be copied; a manuscript for printing; text for an advertisement; subject matter for a writer. • *vt* to make a copy of, to reproduce; to take as a model, to imitate.

**copyright** *n* the exclusive legal right to the publication and sale of a literary, dramatic, musical, or artistic work in any form. • *adj* protected by copyright.

**copywriter** *n* a writer of advertising or publicity copy.—**copywriting** *n*.

**coral** *n* the hard skeleton secreted by certain marine polyps. • *adj* made of or like coral.

**cord** *n* a thick string or thin rope; something that binds; a slender electric cable; a ribbed fabric, esp corduroy; (*pl*) corduroy trousers.

**cordial** *adj* hearty, warm; friendly;

affectionate. • *n* a fruit-flavoured drink.—**cordiality** *n*.—**cordially** *adv*.

**cordon** *n* a chain of police or soldiers preventing access to an area; a piece of ornamental cord or ribbon given as an award. • *vt* (*with* **off**) (*area*) to prevent access to.

**corduroy** *n* a strong cotton fabric with a velvety ribbed surface; (*pl*) trousers of this.

**core** *n* the innermost part, the heart; the inner part of an apple, etc containing seeds; the region of a nuclear reactor containing the fissile material; (*comput*) a form of magnetic memory used to store one bit of information. • *vt* to remove the core from.

**cork** *n* the outer bark of the cork oak used esp for stoppers and insulation; a stopper for a bottle, esp made of cork. • *adj* made of cork. • *vt* to stop up with a cork; to give a taste of cork to (wine).

**corkage** *n* a charge made by a restaurant for serving wine, esp when brought in by the customer from outside.

**corkscrew** *n* a tool for drawing corks from wine bottles. • *adj* resembling a corkscrew.

**cormorant** *n* a large voracious sea bird with dark plumage and webbed feet.

**corn**[1] *n* a grain or seed of a cereal plant; plants that yield grain; maize; (*sl*) something corny.

**corn**[2] *n* a small hard painful growth on the foot.

**corn cob** *n* the central part of an ear of maize to which the corn kernels are attached.

**cornea** *n* the transparent membrane in front of the eyeball.—**corneal** *adj*.

**corner** *n* the point where sides or streets meet; an angle; a secret or confined place; a difficult or dangerous situation; (*football, hockey*) a free kick from the corner of the

pitch; a monopoly over the supply of a good or service giving control over the market price; one of the opposite angles in a boxing ring. • *vt* to force into a corner; to monopolize supplies of (a commodity). • *vi* to turn round a corner; to meet at a corner or angle.

**cornerstone** *n* the principal stone, esp one at the corner of a foundation; an indispensable part.

**cornet** *n* a tapering valved brass musical instrument; a cone-shaped wafer for ice cream.

**cornflour** *n* a type of maize flour used for thickening sauces.

**cornice** *n* a plaster moulding round a ceiling or on the outside of a building.

**corny** *adj* (**cornier, corniest**) (*inf*) hackneyed; banal; trite; overly sentimental.—**cornily** *adv*.—**corniness** *n*.

**corollary** *n* an additional inference from a proposition already proved; a result.

**coronary** *adj* pertaining to the arteries supplying blood to the heart. • *n* a coronary artery.

**coronation** *n* the act or ceremony of crowning a sovereign.

**coroner** *n* a public official who inquires into the causes of sudden or accidental deaths.

**coronet** *n* a small crown; an ornamental headdress.

**corporal**[1] *n* a non-commissioned officer below the rank of sergeant.

**corporal**[2] *adj* of or relating to the body; physical, not spiritual.—**corporally** *adv*.

**corporal punishment** *n* physical punishment, such as beating.

**corporate** *adj* legally united into a body; of or having a corporation; united.—**corporately** *adv*.

**corporation** *n* a group of people authorized by law to act as one individual; a city council.

**corps** *n* (*pl* **corps**) an organized subdivision of the military establishment; a group or organization with a special function (*medical corps*).

**corpse** *n* a dead body.

**corpuscle** *n* a red or white blood cell.—*also* **corpuscule**.—**corpuscular** *adj*.

**corral** *n* a pen for livestock; an enclosure with wagons; a strong stockade. • *vt* (*pt* **corralled**) to form a corral; to put or keep in a corral.

**correct** *vt* to set right, to remove errors from; to reprove, to punish; to counteract, to neutralize. • *adj* free from error; right, true, accurate; conforming to a fixed standard; proper.—**correctly** *adv*.—**correctness** *n*.

**correction** *n* the act of correcting; punishment.—**correctional** *adj*.

**correlate** *vti* to have or to bring into mutual relation; to correspond to one another.—**correlation** *n*.—**correlative** *adj*.

**correspond** *vi* to answer, to agree; to be similar (to); to communicate by letter.

**correspondence** *n* communication by writing letters; the letters themselves; agreement.

**correspondent** *n* a person who writes letters; a journalist who gathers news for newspapers, radio or television from a foreign country. • *adj* similar, analogous.

**corridor** *n* a long passage into which compartments or rooms open.

**corroborate** *vt* to confirm; to make more certain; to verify.—**corroboration** *n*.—**corroborative** *adj*.—**corroborator** *n*.

**corrode** *vti* to eat into or wear away gradually, to rust; to disintegrate.—**corrosion** *n*.

**corrugated iron** *n* sheet iron pressed in alternate parallel ridges and grooves and galvanized.

**corrupt** *adj* dishonest; taking bribes; depraved; rotten, putrid. • *vti* to make or become corrupt; to infect; to taint.—**corruptly** *adv*.—**corruptness** *n*.

**corset** *n* a close-fitting undergarment, worn to support the torso.

**cortege, cortège** *n* a train of attendants; a retinue; a funeral procession.

**cosmetic** *n* a preparation for improving the beauty, esp of the face. • *adj* beautifying or correcting faults in the appearance.—**cosmetically** *adv*.

**cosmonaut** *n* a Russian astronaut.

**cosmopolitan** *adj* of all parts of the world; free from national prejudice; at home in any part of the world.—**cosmopolitanism** *n*.

**cosmos** *n* the universe as an ordered whole; any orderly system.

**cosset** *vt* (*pt* **cosseted**) to make a pet of; to pamper.

**cost** *vt* (*pt* **cost**) to involve the payment, loss, or sacrifice of; to have as a price; (*pt* **costed**) to fix the price of. • *n* a price; expenditure of time, labour, etc; (*pl*) the expenses of a lawsuit.

**costly** *adj* (**costlier, costliest**) expensive; involving great sacrifice.—**costliness** *n*.

**costume** *n* a style of dress, esp belonging to a particular period, fashion, etc; clothes of an unusual or historical nature, as worn by actors in a play, etc.

**costume jewellery** *n* imitation gems or cheap jewellery worn for decorative effect.

**cosy, cozy** (*US*) *adj* (**cosier, cosiest**) warm and comfortable; snug.

**cot** *n* a child's box-like bed; a narrow collapsible bed.

**cottage** *n* a small house, esp in the country.

**cottage cheese** *n* a soft cheese made from loose milk curds.

**cotton** n soft white fibre of the cotton plant; fabric or thread made of this; thread. • adj made of cotton.

**cotton wool** n raw cotton that has been bleached and sterilized for use as a dressing, etc; a state of being protected.

**couch** n a piece of furniture, with a back and armrests, for seating several persons; a bed, esp as used by psychiatrists for patients. • vt to express in words in a particular way.

**cough** vi to expel air from the lungs with a sudden effort and noise. • n the act of coughing; a disease causing a cough.

**could** see can[1].

**council** n an elected or appointed legislative or advisory body; a central body uniting a group of organizations; an executive body whose members are equal in power and authority.

**councillor, councilor** (US) n a member of a council.

**counsel** n advice; consultation, deliberate purpose or design; a person who gives counsel, a lawyer or a group of lawyers; a consultant. • vb (pt **counselled**) vt to advise; to recommend. • vi to give or take advice.

**counsellor, counselor** (US) n an adviser; a lawyer.

**count**[1] n a European noble.

**count**[2] vt to number, add up; to reckon; to consider to be; to call aloud (beats or time units); to include or exclude by counting. • vi to name numbers or add up items in order; to mark time; to be of importance; to rely (upon). • n act of numbering or reckoning; the total counted; a separate and distinct charge in an indictment; rhythm.

**countdown** n the descending count backwards to zero, eg to the moment a rocket lifts off.

**countenance** n the whole form of the face; appearance; support. • vt to favour, give approval to.

**counter**[1] n one who or that which counts; a disc used for scoring, a token; a table in a bank or shop across which money or goods are passed.

**counter**[2] adv contrary; adverse; in an opposite direction; in the wrong way. • adj opposed; opposite. • n a return blow or parry; an answering move. • vti to oppose; to retort; to give a return blow; to retaliate.

**counteract** vt to act in opposition to so as to defeat or hinder; to neutralize.—**counteraction** n.—**counteractive** adj.

**counterattack** n an attack in response to an attack. • vt to make a counterattack.

**counterbalance** n a weight balancing another. • vt to act as a counterbalance; to act against with equal power.

**counterespionage** n spying on or exposing enemy spies.

**counterfeit** vt to imitate; to forge; to feign, simulate. • adj made in imitation, forged; feigned, sham. • n an imitation, a forgery.

**counterfoil** n a detachable section of a cheque or ticket, kept as a receipt or record.

**counterpart** n a thing exactly like another, a duplicate; a corresponding or complementary part or thing.

**countess** n a woman with the rank of count or earl; the wife or widow of an earl or count.

**countless** adj innumerable.

**country** n a region or district; the territory of a nation; a state; the land of one's birth or residence; rural parts; country-and-western. • adj rural.

**countryman** n a person who lives in the country; a person from the same country as another.—**countrywoman** nf.

**countryside** n a rural district.

**county** n an administrative subdivision for local government.—*also adj.*

**coup** n a sudden telling blow; a masterstroke; a coup d'état.

**coup d'état** n a sudden and unexpected bold stroke of policy; the sudden overthrow of a government.

**coupé** n a closed, four-seater, two-door car with a sloping back.

**couple** n two of the same kind connected together; a pair; a husband and wife; a pair of equal and parallel forces. • *vt* to link or join together. • *vi* to copulate.

**couplet** n two consecutive lines of verse that rhyme with each other.

**coupling** n a device for joining parts of a machine or two railway carriages.

**coupon** n a detachable certificate on a bond, presented for payment of interest; a certificate entitling one to a discount, gift, etc; an entry form, as for a competition.

**courage** n bravery; fortitude; spirit.— **courageous** *adj.*—**courageously** *adv.*—**courageousness** n.

**courier** n a messenger; a tourist guide; a carrier of illegal goods between countries.

**course** n a race; a path or track; a career; a direction or line of motion; a regular sequence; the portion of a meal served at one time; conduct; behaviour; the direction a ship is steered; a continuous level range of brick or masonry of the same height; the chase of a hare by greyhounds; a series of studies; any of the studies. • *vt* to hunt. • *vi* to move swiftly along an indicated path; to chase with greyhounds.

**court** n an uncovered space surrounded by buildings or walls; a short street; a playing space, as for tennis, etc; a royal palace; the retinue of a sovereign; (*law*) a hall of justice; the judges, etc engaged there; address; civility; flattery. • *vt* to seek the friendship of; to woo; to flatter; to solicit. • *vi* to carry on a courtship.

**courteous** *adj* polite; obliging.—**courteously** *adv.*—**courteousness** n.

**courtesan, courtezan** n (*formerly*) a prostitute, or mistress of a courtier.

**courtesy** n politeness and kindness; civility; a courteous manner or action.

**courthouse** n a public building that houses law courts or local authority offices.

**courtier** n one in attendance at a royal court.

**court martial** n (*pl* **courts martial**) a court of justice composed of naval or military officers for the trial of disciplinary offences.

**court-martial** *vt* (*pt* **court-martialled**) to try by court martial.

**cousin** n the son or daughter of an uncle or aunt.

**cove** n a small sheltered bay or inlet in a body of water; a curved moulding at the juncture of a wall and ceiling (—*also* **coving**).

**covenant** n a written agreement; a solemn agreement of fellowship and faith between members of a church. • *vt* to promise by a covenant. • *vi* to enter into a formal agreement.— **covenanted** *adj.*

**cover** *vt* to overspread the top of anything with something else; to hide; to save from punishment; to shelter; to clothe; to understudy; to insure against damage, loss, etc; to report for a newspaper; (*male animal*) to copulate. • *vi* to spread over, as a liquid does; to provide an excuse (for). • n that which is laid on something else; a shelter; a covert; an understudy; something used to hide one's real actions, etc; insurance against loss or damage; a place laid at a table for a meal.

**coverage** *n* the amount, extent, etc covered by something; the amount of reporting of an event for newspaper, television, etc.

**cover charge** *n* a charge made by a restaurant over and above the cost of the food and service.

**covet** *vt* (*pt* **coveted**) to desire earnestly; to lust after; to long to possess (what belongs to another).—**covetous** *adj*.—**covetousness** *n*.

**coving** *see* **cove**.

**cow**[1] *n* the mature female of domestic cattle; the mature female of various other animals, as the whale, elephant, etc; (*sl*) a disagreeable woman.

**cow**[2] *vt* to take the spirit out of, to intimidate.

**coward** *n* a person lacking courage; one who is afraid.

**cowardice** *n* lack of courage.

**cowardly** *adj* of, or like, a coward.—**cowardliness** *n*.

**cowboy** *n* a person who tends cattle or horses.—*also* **cowhand**.

**cower** *vi* to crouch or sink down through fear, etc; to tremble.

**coxswain** *n* a person who steers a boat, esp in a race.

**coy** *adj* playfully demure; bashful.—**coyly** *adv*.—**coyness** *n*.

**cozy** *see* **cosy**.

**crab** *n* any of numerous chiefly marine broadly built crustaceans. • *vi* (*pt* **crabbed**) to fish for crabs; to complain.

**crack** *vt* to burst, break or sever; to utter a sharp, abrupt cry; to injure; to damage mentally; to open a bottle; (*sl*) to make (a joke); (*inf*) to break open (a safe); to decipher (a code). • *vi* to make a sharp explosive sound; (*inf*) to lose control under pressure; to shift erratically in vocal tone. • *n* a chink or fissure; a narrow fracture; a sharp sound; a sharp resonant blow; an altered tone of voice; a chat, gossip; a wisecrack.

**cracker** *n* a firework that explodes with a crack; a paper tube that when pulled explodes harmlessly and releases a paper hat, etc; a thin, crisp biscuit.

**crackle** *vi* to make a slight, sharp explosive noise. • *vt* to cover with a delicate network of minute cracks. • *n* a noise of frequent and slight cracks and reports; a surface glaze on glass or porcelain.—**crackly** *adj*.

**crackling** *n* the browned crisp rind of roast pork.

**cradle** *n* a baby's crib or a small bed, often on rockers; infancy; birthplace or origin; a case for a broken limb; a framework of timbers, esp for supporting a boat. • *vt* to rock or place in a cradle; to nurse or train in infancy.

**craft** *n* manual skill; a skilled trade; the members of a skilled trade; cunning; (*pl* **craft**) a boat, ship, or aircraft.

**craftsman** *n* a person skilled in a particular craft.—**craftsmanship** *n*.

**crag** *n* a rough steep rock or cliff.—**craggy** *adj* (**craggier**, **craggiest**).—**cragginess** *n*.

**cram** *vt* (*pt* **crammed**) to pack tightly; to stuff; to fill to overflowing; (*inf*) to prepare quickly for an examination. • *vi* to eat greedily.

**cramp** *n* a spasmodic muscular contraction of the limbs; (*pl*) abdominal spasms and pain; a clamp. • *vt* to affect with muscular spasms; to confine narrowly; to hamper; to secure with a cramp. • *vi* to suffer from cramps.

**cramped** *adj* restricted, narrow; (*handwriting*) small and irregular.

**crampon, crampoon** *n* a metal frame with spikes attached to boots for walking or climbing on ice.

**cranberry** n a small red sour berry; the shrub it grows on.

**crane** n a large wading bird with very long legs and neck, and a long straight bill; a machine for raising, shifting, and lowering heavy weights. • vti to stretch out (the neck).

**cranium** n (pl **craniums, crania**) the skull, esp the part enclosing the brain.—**cranial** adj.

**crank** n a right-angled arm attached to a shaft for turning it; (inf) an eccentric person. • vt to provide with a crank; to turn or wind.

**cranny** n a fissure, crack, crevice.

**crash** n a loud, sudden confused noise; a violent fall or impact; a sudden failure, as of a business or a computer; a collapse, as of the financial market. • adj done with great speed, suddenness or effort. • vti to clash together with violence; to make a loud clattering noise; (aircraft) to land with a crash; to collapse, to ruin; (inf) to intrude into (a party).

**crash helmet** n a cushioned helmet worn by airmen, motorcyclists, etc for protection.

**crash-land** vti (aircraft) to make an emergency landing without lowering the undercarriage, or to be landed in this way.—**crash-landing** n.

**crate** n an open box of wooden slats, for shipping; (sl) an old car or aircraft. • vt to pack in a crate.

**crater** n the mouth of a volcano; a cavity caused by the explosion of a bomb, shell, etc; an ancient Greek goblet.

**cravat** n a neckcloth.

**crave** vt to have a strong desire (for); to ask humbly, to beg.—**craving** n.

**crawl** vi to move along the ground on hands and knees; to move slowly and with difficulty; to creep; (inf) to seek favour by servile behaviour; to swarm (with). • n the act of crawling; a

slow motion; a racing stroke in swimming.—**crawler** n.

**crayfish** n any of numerous freshwater crustaceans; the spiny lobster.

**crayon** n a stick or pencil of coloured chalk; a drawing done with crayons. • vt to draw with a crayon.

**craze** n a passing infatuation; excessive enthusiasm; a crack in pottery glaze. • vt to produce cracks; to render insane.

**crazy** adj (**crazier, craziest**) (inf) mad, insane; foolish; ridiculous; unsound; (paving) composed of irregular pieces.—**crazily** adv.—**craziness** n.

**creak** vi to make a shrill grating sound. • n such a sound.—**creaky** adj.

**cream** n the rich, fatty part of milk; the choicest part of anything; a yellowish white colour; a type of face or skin preparation. • vt to add or apply cream to; to beat into a soft, smooth consistency; to skim cream from; to remove the best part of. • vi to form cream or scum; to break into a creamy froth. —**creamy** adj.—**creaminess** n.

**cream cheese** n soft cheese made from soured milk or cream.

**crease** n a line made by folding; (cricket) a line made by a batsman or bowler marking the limits of their position. • vti to make or form creases; to become creased.

**create** vt to cause to come into existence; to form out of nothing. • vi to make something new, to originate; (sl) to make a fuss.

**creation** n the act of creating; the thing created; the whole world or universe; a production of the human mind.

**creative** adj of creation; having the power to create; imaginative, original, constructive.—**creatively** adv.—**creativeness** n.—**creativity** n.

**creator** n one who creates, esp God.

**creature** n a living being; a created

thing; one dependent on the influence of another.

**crèche** *n* a day nursery for very young children.

**credence** *n* belief or trust, esp in the reports or testimony of another.

**credentials** *npl* documents proving the identity, honesty or authority of a person.

**credible** *adj* believable; trustworthy.—**credibility** *n*.—**credibly** *adv*.

**credit** *n* belief; trust; honour; good reputation; trust in a person's ability to pay; time allowed for payment; a sum at a person's disposal in a bank; the entry in an account of a sum received; the side of the account on which this is entered; (*educ*) a distinction awarded for good marks in an examination; (*pl*) a list of those responsible for a film, television programme, etc. • *vt* to believe; to trust; to have confidence in; to attribute to; to enter on the credit side of an account.

**creditable** *adj* worthy of praise.—**creditably** *adv*.

**credit card** *n* a card issued by a bank, department store, etc authorizing the purchase of goods and services on credit.

**creditor** *n* a person to whom money is owed.

**creed** *n* a system of religious belief or faith; a summary of Christian doctrine; any set of principles or beliefs.

**creek** *n* a natural stream of water smaller than a river.

**creep** *vi* (*pt* **crept**) to move slowly along the ground, as a worm or reptile; (*plant*) to grow along the ground or up a wall; to move stealthily or slowly; to fawn; to cringe; (*flesh*) to feel as if things were creeping over it. • *n* (*inf*) a dislikable or servile person; (*pl: inf*) shrinking horror.

**creeper** *n* a creeping or climbing plant.

**creepy** *adj* (**creepier**, **creepiest**) making one's flesh crawl; causing fear or disgust.—**creepily** *adv*.—**creepiness** *n*.

**cremate** *vt* to burn (a corpse) to ashes.—**cremation** *n*.

**crematorium** *n* (*pl* **crematoriums, crematoria**) a place where bodies are cremated.

**creosote** *n* an oily substance derived from tar used as a wood preservative. • *vt* to treat with creosote.

**crepe, crêpe** *n* a thin, crinkled cloth of silk, rayon, wool, etc; thin paper like crepe; a thin pancake.

**crept** *see* **creep**.

**crescendo** *adv* (*mus*) gradually increasing in loudness or intensity; moving to a climax. • *n* (*pl* **crescendos**) a crescendo passage or effect.

**crescent** *n* the figure of the moon in its first or last quarter; a narrow, tapering curve; a curving street. • *adj* crescent-shaped, increasing.

**cress** *n* any of various plants with pungent leaves, used in salads.

**crest** *n* a plume of feathers on the head of a bird; the ridge of a wave; the summit of a hill; a distinctive device above the shield on a coat of arms. • *vti* to mount to the top of; to take the form of a crest; to provide or adorn with a crest, to crown.

**crestfallen** *adj* dejected.

**crevasse** *n* a deep cleft in a glacier; a deep crack.

**crevice** *n* a crack, a fissure.

**crew** *n* the people operating a ship or aircraft; a group of people working together. • *vi* to act as a member of the crew of a ship, etc.

**crib** *n* a rack for fodder, a manger; a child's cot with high sides; a model of the manger scene representing the birth of Jesus; (*inf*) something copied from someone else; (*inf*) a literal translation of foreign texts used (usu illicitly) by students in examinations, etc. • *vti* (*pt* **cribbed**) (*inf*) to copy illegally, plagiarize.

**crick** *n* a painful stiffness of the muscles of the neck. • *vt* to produce a crick in.

**cricket**[1] *n* a leaping grasshopper-like insect.

**cricket**[2] *n* a game played with wickets, bats, and a ball, by eleven players on each side.—**cricketer** *n*.

**crime** *n* a violation of the law; an offence against morality or the public welfare; wrong-doing; (*inf*) a shame, disappointment.

**criminal** *adj* of the nature of, or guilty of, a crime. • *n* a person who has committed a crime.

**crimson** *n* a deep-red colour inclining to purple. • *adj* crimson-coloured. • *vti* to dye with crimson; to blush.

**cringe** *vi* to shrink in fear or embarrassment; to cower; to behave with servility; to fawn.

**crinkle** *vt* to wrinkle; to corrugate; to crimp. • *vi* to curl; to be corrugated or crimped. • *n* a wrinkle.—**crinkly** *adj*.

**cripple** *vt* to deprive of the use of a limb; to disable. • *n* a lame or otherwise disabled person. • *adj* lame.

**crisis** *n* (*pl* **crises**) a turning point; a critical point in a disease; an emergency; a time of serious difficulties or danger.

**crisp** *adj* dry and brittle; bracing; brisk; sharp and incisive; decided. • *n* a potato snack; in US, a potato chip. • *vt* to make crisp.

**criterion** *n* (*pl* **criteria**) a standard, law or rule by which a correct judgment can be made.

**critic** *n* a person skilled in judging the merits of literary or artistic works; one who passes judgment; a faultfinder.

**critical** *adj* skilled in criticism; censorious;

relating to the turning point of a disease; crucial.—**critically** *adv*.

**criticism** *n* a being critical; a critical comment; a review or analysis of a book, play, work of art, etc, by a critic.

**criticize** *vt* to pass judgment on; to find fault with; to examine critically.

**croak** *n* a deep hoarse discordant cry. • *vti* to utter a croak; (*inf*) to die, to kill.

**crochet** *n* a kind of knitting done with a hooked needle. • *vti* to do this; to make crochet articles.

**crockery** *n* china dishes, earthenware vessels, etc.

**crocodile** *n* large amphibious reptile, similar to an alligator; its skin, used to make handbags, shoes, etc; a line of schoolchildren walking in pairs.

**crocus** *n* a bulbous plant with yellow, purple, or white flowers.

**croft** *n* a small plot of land with a rented farmhouse, esp in Scotland.—**crofter** *n*.

**crook** *n* a shepherd's hooked staff; a bend, a curve; a swindler, a dishonest person. • *vti* to bend or to be bent into the shape of a hook.

**crooked** *adj* bent, twisted; dishonest. —**crookedly** *adv*.—**crookedness** *n*.

**crop** *n* a year's or a season's produce of any cultivated plant; harvest; a pouch in a bird's gullet; a hunting whip; hair cut close or short. • *vti* (*pt* **cropped**) to clip short; to bite off or eat down (grass); (*land*) to yield; to sow, to plant; (*geol*) to come to the surface; to appear unexpectedly; to sprout.

**croquet** *n* a game played with mallets, balls and hopes.

**croquette** *n* a ball of minced meat, fish or potato seasoned and fried brown.

**cross** *n* a figure formed by two intersecting lines; a wooden structure, consisting of two beams placed across each other, used in ancient times for crucifixion; the emblem of the Christian faith; a burden, or affliction; a device resembling a cross; a cross-shaped medal; a hybrid. • *vti* to pass across; to intersect; to meet and pass; to place crosswise; to make the sign of the cross over; to thwart, to oppose; to modify (a breed) by intermixture (with). • *adj* transverse; reaching from side to side; intersecting; out of temper, peevish.—**crossly** *adv.*—**crossness** *n*.

**crossbar** *n* a horizontal bar, as that across goal posts or as bicycle frame.

**crossbreed** *vt* (*pt* **crossbred**) to breed animals by mating different varieties. • *n* an animal produced in this way.

**cross-country** *adj* across fields; denoting cross-country racing or skiing.

**cross-examine** *vt* to question closely; (*law*) to question (a witness) who has already been questioned by counsel on the other side.—**cross-examination** *n*.

**cross-eyed** *adj* squinting.

**crossing** *n* an intersection of roads or railway lines; a place for crossing a street.

**crossroad** *n* a road crossing another; (*pl*) where two roads cross; (*fig*) the time when a decisive action has to be made.

**cross section** *n* a cutting at right angles to length; the surface then shown; a random selection of the public.

**crossword** *n* a puzzle in which interlocking words to be inserted vertically and horizontally in a squared diagram are indicated by clues.

**crotch** *n* the region of the body where the legs fork, the genital area; any forked region.

**crotchet** *n* (*mus*) a note equal to a half-minim.

**crotchety** *adj* peevish, whimsical.

**crouch** *vi* to squat or lie close to the ground; to cringe.

**crouton** *n* a small piece of fried or toasted bread, sprinkled onto soups.

**crow** *n* any of various usu large, glossy, black birds; a cawing cry, the shrill sound of a cock. • *vi* (*pt* **crowed** *or* **crew**) to make a sound like a cock; to boast in triumph; to utter a cry of pleasure.

**crowbar** *n* an iron bar used to lever.

**crowd** *n* a number of people or things collected closely together; a dense multitude, a throng; (*inf*) a set; a clique. • *vti* to crowd closely together; to fill to excess; to push, to thrust; to importune.—**crowded** *adj*.

**crown** *n* a wreath worn on the head; the head covering of a monarch; regal power; the sovereign; the top of the head; a summit; a reward; the part of a tooth above the gum. • *vt* to invest with a crown; to adorn or dignify; to complete; to reward.

**crucial** *adj* decisive; severe; critical. — **crucially** *adv*.

**crucifix** *n* a cross with the sculptured figure of Christ.

**crucifixion** *n* a form of execution by being nailed or bound to a cross by the hands and feet; (*with cap*) the death of Christ in this manner.

**crucify** *vt* to put to death on a cross; to cause extreme pain to; to utterly defeat in an argument.

**crude** *adj* in a natural state; unripe; raw; immature; harsh in colour; unfinished, rough; lacking polish; blunt; vulgar. • *n* crude oil.— **crudely** *adv.*—**crudity** *n*.

**cruel** *adj* (**crueller**, **cruellest**) disposed to give pain to others; merciless; hard-hearted; fierce; painful; unrelenting. —**cruelly** *adv.*—**cruelty** *n*.

**cruet** *n* a small glass bottle for vinegar and oil, used at the table.

**cruise** *vi* to sail to and fro; to wander about; to move at the most efficient speed for sustained travel. • *vt* to

**cruise** over or about. • *n* a voyage from place to place for military purposes or for pleasure.

**crumb** *n* a fragment of bread; the soft part of bread; a little piece of anything.

**crumble** *vt* to break into crumbs; to cause to fall into pieces. • *vi* to disappear gradually, to disintegrate.— **crumbly** *adj*.

**crumpet** *n* a soft cake, usu eaten toasted; (*sl*) a sexually attractive woman.

**crumple** *vti* to twist or crush into wrinkles; to crease; to collapse. • *n* a wrinkle or crease made by crumpling.

**crunch** *vti* to crush with the teeth; to tread underfoot with force and noise; to make a sound like this; to chew audibly. • *n* the sound or act of crunching.

**crusade** *n* a medieval Christian military expedition to recover the Holy Land; a vigorous concerted action defending a cause or advancing an idea. • *vi* to engage in a crusade.— **crusader** *n*.

**crush** *vt* to press between two opposite bodies; to squeeze; to break by pressure; to bruise; to ruin; to quell. • *vi* to be pressed out of shape or into a smaller compass. • *n* a violent compression or collision; a dense crowd; (*inf*) a large party; a drink made from crushed fruit; (*sl*) an infatuation.

**crust** *n* a hard external coating or rind; the exterior solid part of the earth's surface; a shell or hard covering. • *vti* to cover or become covered with a crust.—**crusty** *adj*.—**crustily** *adv*.—**crustiness** *n*.

**crutch** *n* a staff with a crosswise head to support the weight of a lame person; a prop; the crotch.

**crux** *n* (*pl* **cruxes, cruces**) a difficult problem; the essential or deciding point.

**cry** *vi* to call aloud; to proclaim; to exclaim vehemently; to implore; to shed tears. • *vt* to utter loudly and publicly. • *n* an inarticulate sound; an exclamation of wonder or triumph; an outcry; clamour; an urgent appeal; a spell of weeping; a battle cry; a catchword.

**crypt** *n* an underground chamber or vault, esp under a church, used as a chapel or for burial.

**cryptic** *adj* hidden, secret; mysterious.

**crystal** *n* very clear, brilliant glass; articles of such glass, as goblets. • *adj* made of crystal.—**crystalline** *adj*.

**crystallize** *vti* to form crystals; to give definite form.—**crystallization** *n*.

**cu.** *abbr* = cubic.

**cub** *n* a young carnivorous mammal; a young, inexperienced person; (*with cap*) a Cub Scout.

**cube** *n* a solid body with six equal square sides or faces; a cube-shaped block; the product of a number multiplied by itself twice. • *vt* to raise (number) to the third power, or cube; to cut into cube-shaped pieces.

**cubic** *adj* having the form or properties of a cube; three-dimensional.

**cubicle** *n* a small separate sleeping compartment in a dormitory, etc.

**cuckoo** *n* a bird with a dark plumage, a curved bill and a characteristic call that lays its eggs in the nests of other birds.

**cuckoo clock** *n* a clock that strikes the hours with a cuckoo call.

**cucumber** *n* a long juicy fruit used in salads and as a pickle; the creeping plant that bears it.

**cud** *n* the food that a ruminating animal brings back into the mouth to chew again.

**cuddle** *vt* to embrace or hug closely.

• *vt* to nestle together. • *n* a close embrace.

**cudgel** *n* a short thick stick for beating.

**cue**[1] *n* the last word of a speech in a play, serving as a signal for the next actor to enter or begin to speak; any signal to do something; a hint. • *vt* (*pr p* **cuing** *or* **cueing**) to give a cue to.

**cue**[2] *n* a tapering rod used in snooker, billiards, and pool to strike the cue ball.

**cuff**[1] *n* a blow with the fist or the open hand. • *vt* to strike such a blow.

**cuff**[2] *n* the end of a sleeve; a covering round the wrist; the turn-up on a trouser leg.

**cufflink** *n* a decorative clip for fastening the edges of a shirt cuff.

**cuisine** *n* a style of cooking or preparing food; the food prepared.

**cul-de-sac** *n* a street blocked off at one end; a blind alley.

**culinary** *adj* of or relating to cooking.

**culminate** *vti* to reach the highest point of altitude, rank, power, etc; (*astron*) to reach the meridian; to bring to a head or the highest point.—**culmination** *n*.

**culpable** *adj* deserving censure; criminal; blameworthy.—**culpably** *adv*.— **culpability** *n*.

**culprit** *n* a person accused, or found guilty, of an offence.

**cult** *n* a system of worship; devoted attachment to a person, principle, etc; a religion regarded as unorthodox or spurious; its body of adherents.

**cultivate** *vt* to till; to improve by care, labour, or study; to seek the society of; to civilize or refine.

**cultivation** *n* the act of cultivating; the state of being cultivated; tillage; culture.

**cultural** *adj* pertaining to culture.— **culturally** *adv*.

**culture** *n* appreciation and understanding of the arts; the skills, arts, etc of a given people in a given period; the customary beliefs, social forms, and material traits of a religious, social, or racial group; improvement of the mind, manner, etc; a growth of bacteria, etc in a prepared substance. • *vt* to cultivate bacteria for study or use.

**cultured** *adj* educated to appreciate the arts; having good taste; artificially grown, as cultured pearls.

**cumbersome** *adj* inconveniently heavy or large, unwieldy.

**cunning** *adj* ingenious; sly; designing; subtle. • *n* slyness, craftiness.

**cup** *n* a small, bowl-shaped container for liquids, usu with a handle; the amount held in a cup; an ornamental cup used as a trophy. • *vt* (*pt* **cupped**) to take or put as in a cup; to curve (the hands) into the shape of a cup.

**cupboard** *n* a closet or cabinet with shelves for cups, plates, utensils, food etc.

**cupola** *n* a dome.

**curate** *n* an assistant of a vicar or rector.

**curator** *n* a superintendent of a a museum, art gallery, etc.

**curb** *vt* to restrain; to check; to keep in subjection. • *n* that which checks, restrains, or subdues; a kerb.

**curd** *n* the coagulated part of soured milk, used to make cheese.

**curdle** *vti* to turn into curds; to coagulate.

**cure** *n* the act or art of healing; a remedy; restoration to health. • *vt* to heal; to rid of; to preserve, as by drying, salting, etc.—**curable** *adj*.

**curfew** *n* a signal, as a bell, at a fixed evening hour as a sign that everyone must be indoors; the signal or hour.

**curio** *n* (*pl* **curios**) an item valued as rare or unusual.

**curiosity** *n* the quality of being curious; inquisitiveness; a rare, strange or interesting object.

curious                    106                    cut

**curious** *adj* anxious to know; prying, inquisitive; strange, remarkable, odd.—**curiously** *adv.*—**curiousness** *n.*

**curl** *vti* to form into a curved shape, to coil; to twist into ringlets; to proceed in a curve, to bend; to play at curling. • *n* a ringlet of hair; a spiral form, a twist; a bend or undulation.

**curler** *n* a small pin or roller used for curling the hair; a person who plays curling.

**curling** *n* a game in which two teams slide large smooth stones on ice into a target circle.

**curly** *adj* (**curlier, curliest**) full of curls.—**curliness** *n.*

**currant** *n* a small variety of dried grape; a shrub that yields a red or black fruit.

**currency** *n* the time during which a thing is current; the state of being in use; the money current in a country.

**current** *adj* generally accepted; happening now; presently in circulation. • *n* a body of water or air in motion, a flow; the transmission of electricity through a conductor; a general tendency.

**currently** *adv* at the present time.

**curriculum** *n* (*pl* **curricula, curriculums**) a prescribed course of study.

**curriculum vitae** *n* a brief survey of one's career.

**curry** *n* a spicy dish with a hot sauce; curry seasoning. • *vt* to flavour with curry.

**curse** *n* a calling down of destruction or evil; a profane oath; a swear word; a violent exclamation of anger; a scourge. • *vti* to invoke a curse on; to swear, to blaspheme; to afflict, to torment.

**cursor** *n* a flashing indicator on a computer screen indicating position; the transparent slide on a slide-rule.

**cursory** *adj* hasty, passing; superficial, careless.—**cursorily** *adv.*

**curt** *adj* short; abrupt; concise; rudely brief.—**curtly** *adv.*—**curtness** *n.*

**curtail** *vt* to cut short; to reduce; to deprive of part (of).—**curtailment** *n.*

**curtain** *n* a cloth hung as a screen at a window, etc; the movable screen separating the stage from the auditorium; (*pl*) (*sl*) the end. • *vt* to enclose in, or as with, curtains.

**curtsy, curtsey** *n* a formal gesture of greeting, involving bending the knees, made by women and children. • *vi* to make a curtsy.

**curve** *n* a bending without angles; a bent form or thing; (*geom*) a line of which no part is straight. • *vti* to form into a curve, to bend.—**curvy** *adj.*

**cushion** *n* a case stuffed with soft material for resting on; the elastic border around a snooker table; the air mass supporting a hovercraft. • *vt* to furnish with cushions; to protect by padding.

**custard** *n* a sauce mixture of milk, eggs and sugar.

**custody** *n* guardianship; imprisonment; security.—**custodial** *adj.*—**custodian** *n.*

**custom** *n* a regular practice; usage; frequent repetition of the same act; business patronage; (*pl*) duties on imports.

**customary** *adj* habitual; conventional; common.—**customarily** *adv.*

**customer** *n* a person who buys from a shop or business, esp regularly.

**cut** *vb* (*pr p* **cutting**, *pt* **cut**) *vb* to cleave or separate with a sharp instrument; to make an incision in; to divide; to trim; to intersect; to abridge; to diminish; to pass deliberately without recognition; to wound deeply; to reduce or curtail; to grow a new tooth through the gum; to divide (a pack of cards) at random; (*inf*) to stay away from class, school, etc. • *vi* to make an incision; to perform the work of an edged instrument; to grow through the gums; (*cinema*) to change to another scene, to stop photographing. • *n* an incision or wound made by a sharp instrument; a gash; a sharp stroke; a sarcastic remark; a passage or channel cut out; a slice; a block on which an engraving is cut; the fashion or shape of a garment; the deliberate ignoring of an acquaintance; the division of a pack of cards; a diminution in price below another merchant; (*sl*) a share, as of profits • *adj* divided or separated; gashed; having the surface ornamented or fashioned; not wrought or hand-made.

**cutback** *n* a reduction, esp in expenditure.

**cute** *adj* (*inf*) acute, shrewd; pretty or attractive, esp in a dainty way.— **cutely** *adv*.—**cuteness** *n*.

**cuticle** *n* the skin at the base of the fingernail or toe nail; epidermis.

**cutlery** *n* knives, forks, etc for eating and serving food.

**cutlet** *n* a neck chop of lamb, etc; a small slice cut off from the ribs or leg; minced meat in the form of a cutlet.

**cutthroat** *n* a murderer. • *adj* merciless; (*razor*) having a long blade in a handle.

**cutting** *n* a piece cut off or from; an incision; a newspaper clipping; a slip from a plant for propagation; a passage or channel cut out; the process of editing a film or recording; a recording. • *adj* (*remarks*) hurtful.

**cuttlefish** *n* a marine creature with a flattened body that squirts ink when threatened.

**CV** *abbr* = curriculum vitae.

**cwt.** *abbr* = hundredweight.

**cyanide** *n* a poison.

**cyclamen** *n* a plant of the primrose family, with pink, purple or white flowers.

**cycle** *n* a recurring series of events or phenomena; the period of this; a body of epics or romances with a common theme; a bicycle, motorcycle, or tricycle. • *vi* to go in cycles; to ride a bicycle or tricycle.

**cyclic, cyclical** *adj* moving or recurring in cycles.—**cyclically** *adj*.

**cyclist** *n* a person who rides a bicycle.

**cyclone** *n* a violent circular storm; an atmospheric movement in which the wind blows spirally round towards a centre of low barometric pressure.— **cyclonic** *adj*.

**cygnet** *n* a young swan.

**cylinder** *n* a hollow figure or object with parallel sides and circular ends; an object shaped like a cylinder; any machine part of this shape; the piston chamber in an engine.—**cylindrical** *adj*.

**cymbal** *n* (*mus*) one of a pair of two brass plates struck together to produce a ringing or clashing sound.— **cymbalist** *n*.

**cynic** *n* a morose, surly, or sarcastic person; one of a sect of ancient Greek philosophers.—**cynicism** *n*.

**cynical** *adj* sceptical of or sneering at goodness; shameless in admitting unworthy motives.—**cynically** *adv*.

**cypher** *see* **cipher**.

**cypress** *n* an evergreen tree with hard wood.

**cyst** *n* a closed sac developing abnormally in the structure of plants or animals.—**cystic** *adj*.

**czar** *see* **tsar**.

# D

**dab**[1] *vt* (*pt* **dabbed**) to touch lightly with something moist or soft. • *n* a quick light tap; a small lump of anything moist or soft.

**dab**[2] *n* a species of European flounder.

**dabble** *vi* to move hands, feet etc gently in water or another liquid; (*usu* *with* **at, in, with**) to do anything in a superficial or dilettante way. • *vt* to splash.—**dabbler** *n*.

**dad, daddy** *n* (*inf*) father.

**daddy-longlegs** *n* (*inf*) a crane fly; (*inf*) in US, any of various spiders or insects with long, slender legs.

**daffodil** *n* a yellow spring flower, a narcissus; its pale yellow colour.

**daft** *adj* (*inf*) silly, weak-minded; giddy; mad.—**daftness** *n*.

**dagger** *n* a short weapon for stabbing; a reference mark used in printing (†).—*also* **obelisk.**

**daily** *adj*, *adv* (happening) every day; constantly, progressively. • *n* a newspaper published every weekday; (*inf*) a charwoman.

**dainty** *adj* (**daintier, daintiest**) delicate; choice; nice, fastidious. • *n* a titbit, a delicacy.—**daintily** *adv*.—**daintiness** *n*.

**dairy** *n* a building or room where milk is stored and dairy products made; a shop selling these; a company supplying them.

**daisy** *n* any of various plants with a yellow centre and white petals, esp the English daisy.

**dale** *n* a valley.

**dally** *vi* to lose time by idleness or trifling; to play or trifle (with); to flirt.

**dam**[1] *n* an artificial embankment to retain water; water so contained. • *vt* (*pt* **dammed**) to retain (water) with such a barrier; to stem, obstruct, restrict.

**dam**[2] *n* the mother of a four-footed animal.

**damage** *n* injury, harm; loss; (*inf*) price, cost; (*pl*) (*law*) payment in compensation for loss or injury. • *vt* to do harm to, to injure.—**damaging** *adj*.

**damn** *vt* to condemn, censure; to ruin; to curse; to consign to eternal punishment. • *vti* to prove guilty. •

*interj* (*sl*) expressing irritation or annoyance. • *n* (*sl*) something having no value. • *adj*, *adv* damned.—**damnatory** *adj*.

**damp** *n* humidity, moisture; in mines, poisonous or foul gas. • *adj* slightly wet, moist. • *vt* to moisten; (*with* **down**) to stifle, reduce.—**dampness** *n*.

**dampen** *vti* to make or become damp. • *vt* to stifle.—**dampener** *n*.

**damson** *n* a small, dark-purple variety of plum; the colour of this; the tree on which this fruit grows.

**dance** *vti* to move rhythmically, esp to music; to skip or leap lightly; to execute (steps); to cause to dance or to move up and down. • *n* a piece of dancing; a dance performance of an artistic nature; a party with music for dancing; music for accompanying dancing.—**dancer** *n*.

**dandelion** *n* a common wild plant with ragged leaves, a yellow flower and a fluffy seed head.

**dandruff** *n* scales of skin on the scalp, under the hair, scurf.

**danger** *n* exposure to injury or risk; a source of harm or risk.

**dangerous** *adj* involving danger; unsafe; perilous.—**dangerously** *adv*.

**dangle** *vi* to hang and swing loosely. • *vt* to carry something so that it hangs loosely; to display temptingly.

**dapper** *adj* nimble; neat in appearance, spruce.

**dare** *vti* to be bold enough; to venture, to risk; to defy, to challenge. • *n* a challenge.

**daredevil** *n* a rash, reckless person. • *adj* daring, bold; courageous.

**daring** *adj* fearless; courageous; unconventional. • *n* adventurous courage.

**dark** *adj* having little or no light; of a shade of colour closer to black than white; (*person*) having brown or black skin or hair; gloomy; (*inf*) secret, unknown; mysterious. • *n* a dark state or colour; ignorance; secrecy.—**darkly** *adv*.—**darkness** *n*.

**darken** *vti* to make or become dark or darker.

**darkroom** *n* a room for processing photographs in darkness or safe light.

**darling** *n* a dearly loved person; a favourite. • *adj* lovable; much admired.

**darn**[1] *vt* to mend a hole in fabric or a garment with stitches. • *n* an area that has been darned.

**darn**[2] *interj* a form of **damn** as a mild oath.—*also adj*.

**dart** *n* a small pointed missile; a sudden movement; a fold sewn into a garment for shaping it; (*pl*) an indoor game in which darts are thrown at a target. • *vti* to move rapidly; to send out rapidly.

**dartboard** *n* a circular cork or wooden target used in the game of darts.

**dash** *vti* to fling violently; to rush quickly; (*hopes*) to shatter; (*one's spirits, etc*) to depress, confound; to write quickly. • *n* a short race; a rush; a small amount of something added to food; a tinge; a punctuation mark (—); a dashboard; vigour, verve; display.

**dashboard** *n* an instrument panel in a car.

**dashing** *adj* spirited, stylish, dapper.

**data** *npl* (*sing* **datum**) (*often used as sing*) facts, statistics, or information either historical or derived by calculation or experimentation.

**data processing** *n* the analysis of information stored in a computer for various uses, eg stock control, statistical research, mathematical modelling, etc.

**date**[1] *n* a day or time of occurrence; a statement of this in a letter, etc; a period to which something belongs;

a duration; an appointment, esp with a member of the opposite sex. • *vt* to affix a date to; to note the date of; to reckon the time of; (*inf*) to make a date with; (*inf*) to see frequently a member of the opposite sex. • *vi* to reckon from a point in time; to show signs of belonging to a particular period.

**date**[2] *n* the sweet fruit of the date palm, a palm tree of tropical regions.

**date line** *n* the line running north to south along the 180-degree meridian, east of which is one day earlier than west of it; a line on a newspaper story giving the date and place of writing.

**daub** *vt* to smear or overlay (with clay, etc); to paint incompetently. • *n* a smear; a poor painting.

**daughter** *n* a female child or descendant.

**daughter-in-law** *n* the wife of one's son.

**dauntless** *adj* intrepid.—**dauntlessly** *adv*.

**dawdle** *vi* to move slowly and waste time, to loiter.—**dawdler** *n*.

**dawn** *vi* (*day*) to begin to grow light; to begin to appear. • *n* daybreak; a first sign.

**day** *n* the time when the sun is above the horizon; the twenty-four hours from midnight to midnight; daylight; a particular period of success or influence; (*usu pl*) a period, an epoch.

**daybreak** *n* the first appearance of daylight, dawn.

**daydream** *n* a reverie. • *vi* to have one's mind on other things; to fantasize.—**daydreamer** *n*.

**daylight** *n* the light of the sun; dawn; publicity; a visible gap; the dawning of sudden realization or understanding.

**daytime** *n* the time of daylight.

**daze** *vt* to stun, to bewilder. • *n* confusion, bewilderment.

**dazzle** vt to confuse the sight of or be partially blinded by strong light; to overwhelm with brilliance. • n an overpoweringly strong light; bewilderment. —**dazzler** n.—**dazzling** adj.—**dazzlingly** adv.

**dead** adj without life; inanimate, inert; no longer used; lacking vegetation; emotionally or spiritually insensitive; without motion; (fire, etc) extinguished; (limb, etc) numb; (colour, sound etc) dull; (a ball) out of play; complete, exact; unerring. • adv in a dead manner; completely; utterly. • n a dead person; the quietest time.

**deaden** vt to render numb or insensible; to deprive of vitality; to muffle.

**dead-end** n a cul-de-sac; a hopeless situation.

**dead heat** n a race in which two or more finish equal, a tie.

**deadline** n the time by which something must be done.

**deadlock** n a clash of interests making progress impossible; a standstill.—also vt.

**deadly** adj (**deadlier, deadliest**) fatal; implacable; (inf) tedious. • adv death-like; intensely.

**deadpan** adj (inf) deliberately expressionless or emotionless.—also adv.

**deaf** adj unable to hear; hearing badly; not wishing to hear.—**deafness** n.

**deafen** vt to deprive of hearing.—**deafeningly** adv.

**deal**[1] vb (pt **dealt**) vt (a blow) to deliver, inflict; (cards, etc) to distribute; (with **with**) to do business with; (problem, task) to solve. • vi to do business (with); to trade (in). • n a portion, quantity; (inf) a large amount; a dealing of cards; a business transaction.

**deal**[2] n fir or pine wood.—also adj.

**dealer** n a trader; a person who deals cards; (sl) a seller of illegal drugs.

**dealings** npl personal or business transactions.

**dean** n the head of a cathedral chapter; a college fellow in charge of discipline; the head of a university or college faculty.

**dear** adj loved, precious; charming; expensive; a form of address in letters. • n a person who is loved. • adv at a high price.—**dearly** adv.—**dearness** n.

**dearth** n scarcity, lack.

**death** n the end of life, dying; the state of being dead; the destruction of something.

**deathbed** n the bed in which a person dies or is about to die.

**death certificate** n an official document with details of the date, place and cause of a person's death.

**death duties** npl taxes paid on an inheritance after a death.

**deathly** adj like death, pale still; deadly.—also adv.

**debar** vt (pt **debarred**) to exclude, bar.—**debarment** n.

**debase** vt to lower in character or value; (coinage) to degrade.—**debasement** n.

**debatable, debateable** adj open to question, disputed.

**debate** n a formal argument; a discussion, esp in parliament. • vt to consider, contest. • vi to discuss thoroughly; to join in debate.—**debater** n.

**debauchery** n depraved over-indulgence; corruption; profligacy.

**debit** n the entry of a sum owed, opposite to the credit; the left side of a ledger used for this. • vt to charge to the debit side of a ledger.

**debris, débris** n broken and scattered remains, wreckage.

**debt** n a sum owed; a state of owing; an obligation.

**debtor** n a person, company, etc who owes money to another.

**debut** *n* a first appearance as a public performer or in society.

**decade** *n* a period of ten years; a group of ten.

**decadence, decadency** *n* a state of deterioration in standards, esp of morality.

**decadent** *adj* deteriorating; self-indulgent.

**decay** *vti* to rot, decompose; to deteriorate, wither. • *n* the act or state of decaying; a decline, collapse.

**decease** *n* death. • *vi* to die.

**deceased** *adj* dead. • *n* the dead person.

**deceit** *n* the act of deceiving; cunning; treachery; fraud.

**deceitful** *adj* treacherous; insincere; misleading.—**deceitfully** *adv.*—**deceitfulness** *n*.

**deceive** *vt* to cheat; to mislead; to delude; to impose upon.—**deceiver** *n*.

**December** *n* the twelfth and last month of the year with 31 days.

**decency** *n* being decent; conforming to accepted standards of behaviour.

**decent** *adj* respectable, proper; moderate; not obscene; (*inf*) quite good; (*inf*) kind, generous.—**decently** *adv*.

**decentralize** *vt* (*government, organization*) to divide among local centres.—**decentralization** *n*.

**deception** *n* the act of deceiving or the state of being deceived; illusion; fraud.

**deceptive** *adj* apt to mislead; ambiguous; unreliable.—**deceptively** *adv.*—**deceptiveness** *n*.

**decibel** *n* a unit for measuring sound level.

**decide** *vti* to determine, to settle; to give a judgment on; to resolve.

**decided** *adj* unhesitating; clearly marked.

**decidedly** *adv* definitely, certainly.

**deciduous** *adj* (*trees, shrubs*) shedding all leaves annually, at the end of the growing season.

**decimal** *adj* of tenths, of numbers written to the base 10.

**decimal point** *n* a dot written before the numerator in a decimal fraction (eg $0.5 = {}^1\!/2$).

**decimate** *vt* to kill every tenth person; to reduce by one tenth; to kill a great number.—**decimation** *n*.

**decipher** *vt* to decode; to make out (indistinct writing, meaning, etc).—**decipherable** *adj.*—**decipherment** *n*.

**decision** *n* a settlement; a ruling; a judgment; determination, firmness.

**decisive** *adj* determining the issue, positive; conclusive, final.—**decisively** *adv*.

**deck** *n* the floor on a ship, aircraft, bus or bridge; a pack of playing cards; the turntable of a record-player; the playing mechanism of a tape recorder; (*sl*) the ground, the floor. • *vt* to cover; to adorn.

**deck chair** *n* a folding chair made of canvas suspended in a frame.

**declare** *vt* to affirm, proclaim; to admit possession of (dutiable goods). • *vi* (*law*) to make a statement; (*with* **against, for**) to announce one's support; (*cricket*) to choose to close an innings before ten wickets have fallen.—**declaration** *n.*—**declarative** *adj.*—**declaratory** *adj*.

**decline** *vi* to refuse; to move down; to deteriorate, fall away; to fail; to diminish; to draw to an end; to deviate. • *vt* to reject, to refuse; (*gram*) to give the cases of a declension. • *n* a diminution; a downward slope; a gradual loss of physical and mental faculties.

**decode** *vt* to translate a code into plain language.—**decoder** *n*.

**decompose** *vti* to separate or break up into constituent parts, esp as part of a chemical process; to resolve into its elements. • *vi* to decay.—**decomposition** *n*.

**decontaminate** *vt* to free from (radioactive, etc) contamination.—**decontamination** *n*.

**décor, decor** *n* general decorative effect, eg of a room; scenery and stage design.

**decorate** *vt* to ornament; to paint or wallpaper; to honour with a badge or medal.

**decoration** *n* decorating; an ornament; a badge or an honour.

**decorative** *adj* ornamental, pretty to look at.—**decoratively** *adv*.

**decorator** *n* a person who decorates, esp houses.

**decoy** *vt* to lure into a trap. • *n* anything intended to lure into a snare.

**decrease** *vti* to make or become less. • *n* a decreasing; the amount of diminution.

**decree** *n* an order, edict or law; a judicial decision. • *vt* (*pt* **decreed**) to decide by sentence in law; to appoint.

**decrepit** *adj* worn out by the infirmities of old age; in the last stage of decay.—**decrepitude** *n*.

**dedicate** *vt* to consecrate (to some sacred purpose); to devote wholly or chiefly; to inscribe (to someone) — **dedication** *n*.—**dedicator** *n*.—**dedicatory** *adj*.

**deduce** *vt* to derive (knowledge, a conclusion) from reasoning; infer.—**deducible** *adj*.

**deduct** *vt* to take (from); to subtract.

**deduction** *n* deducting; the amount deducted; deducing; a conclusion that something is true because it necessarily follows from a set of general premises known to be valid.—**deductive** *adj*.

**deed** *n* an act; an exploit; a legal document recording a transaction.

**deep** *adj* extending or placed far down or far from the outside; fully involved; engrossed; profound, intense; heartfelt; penetrating; diffi-cult to understand; secret; cunning; sunk low; low in pitch; (*colour*) of high saturation and low brilliance. • *adv* in a deep manner; far in, into. • *n* that which is deep; the sea.—**deeply** *adv*.—**deepness** *n*.

**deepen** *vt* to make deeper in any sense; to increase. • *vi* to become deeper.

**deepfreeze** *n* a refrigerator in which food is frozen and stored.

**deep-freeze** *vt* to freeze (food) so that it keeps for a long period of time. • *n* a freezer.

**deer** *n* (*pl* **deer, deers**) a four-footed animal with antlers, esp on the males, including stag, reindeer, etc.

**deface** *vt* to disfigure; to obliterate. — **defacement** *n*.

**default** *n* neglect to do what duty or law requires; failure to fulfil a financial obligation; (*comput*) a basic setting or instruction to which a program reverts. • *vi* to fail in one's duty (as honouring a financial obligation, appearing in court).—**defaulter** *n*.

**defeat** *vt* to frustrate; to win a victory over; to baffle. • *n* a frustration of plans; overthrow, as of an army in battle; loss of a game, race, etc.

**defeatism** *n* disposition to accept defeat.—**defeatist** *n*.

**defect** *n* a deficiency; a blemish, fault. • *vi* to desert one's country or a cause.

**defective** *adj* having a defect; faulty; incomplete. • *n* a person defective in physical or mental powers.—**defectively** *adv*.—**defectiveness** *n*.

**defence, defense** (*US*) *n* resistance or protection against attack; a means of resisting an attack; protection; vindication; (*law*) a defendant's plea; the defending party in legal proceedings; (*sport*) defending (the goal, etc) against the attacks of the opposing side; the defending players in a team.—**defenceless** *adj*.

**defend** *vt* to guard or protect; to maintain against attack; (*law*) to resist, as a claim; to contest (a suit).

**defendant** *n* a person accused or sued in a lawsuit.

**defensive** *adj* serving to defend; in a state or posture of defence.—**defensively** *adv*.

**defer**[1] *vt* (*pt* **deferred**) to put off to another time; to delay.—**deferment**, **deferral** *n*.—**deferrable, deferable** *adj*.

**defer**[2] *vi* (*pt* **deferred**) to yield to another person's wishes, judgment or authority.

**deference** *n* a deferring or yielding in judgment or opinion; polite respect.

**defiance** *n* the act of defying; wilful disobedience; a challenge.—**defiant** *adj*.

**deficiency** *n* being deficient; lack, shortage; deficit.

**deficient** *adj* insufficient, lacking.

**deficit** *n* the amount by which an amount falls short of what is required; excess of expenditure over income, or liabilities over assets.

**defile**[1] *vt* to pollute or corrupt.

**defile**[2] *n* a long, narrow pass or way, through which troops can pass only in single file. • *vt* to march in single file.

**define** *vt* to fix the bounds or limits of; to mark the limits or outline of clearly; to describe accurately; to fix the meaning of.—**definable** *adj*.

**definite** *adj* defined; having distinct limits; fixed; exact; clear.—**definitely** *adv*.

**definition** *n* a description of a thing by its properties; an explanation of the exact meaning of a word, term, or phrase; sharpness of outline.

**definitive** *adj* defining or limiting; decisive, final.—**definitively** *adv*.

**deflate** *vt* to release gas or air from; to reduce in size or importance; to reduce the money supply, restrict credit, etc to reduce inflation in the economy. —**deflation** *n*.—**deflationary** *adj*.

**deflect** *vti* to turn or cause to turn aside from a line or proper course.—**deflection** *n*.—**deflector** *n*.

**deform** *vt* to spoil the natural form of; to put out of shape.—**deformation** *n*.

**deformity** *n* the condition of being deformed; a deformed part of the body; a defect.

**defraud** *vt* to remove (money, rights, etc) from a person by cheating or deceiving.—**defrauder** *n*.

**defray** *vt* to provide money (to pay expenses, etc).—**defrayal, defrayment** *n*.

**defrost** *vt* to unfreeze; to free from frost or ice.—*also vi*.

**deft** *adj* skilful, adept; nimble.—**deftly** *adv*.—**deftness** *n*.

**defunct** *adj* no longer being in existence or function or in use.

**defuse** *vt* to disarm an explosive (bomb or mine) by removing its fuse; to decrease tension in a (crisis) situation.

**defy** *vt* to resist openly and without fear; to challenge (a person) to attempt something considered dangerous or impossible; to resist attempts at, to elude.

**degenerate** *adj* having declined in physical or moral qualities; sexually deviant. • *vi* become or grow worse. • *n* a degenerate person.—**degeneracy** *n*.—**degeneration** *n*.

**degrading** *adj* humiliating.

**degree** *n* a step in a series; a stage in intensity; the relative quantity in intensity; a unit of measurement in a scale; an academic title awarded as of right or as an honour.

**dehydrate** *vt* to remove water from. • *vi* to lose water, esp from the bodily tissues.—**dehydration** *n*.

**de-ice** *vt* to prevent the formation of

or to remove ice from a surface.—**de-icer** n.

**deign** vi to condescend; to think it worthy to do (something).

**deity** n a god or goddess; the rank or essence of a god; (with cap and the) God.

**dejected** adj morose, depressed.—**dejectedly** adv.

**dejection** n depression; lowness of spirits.

**delay** vt to postpone; to detain, obstruct. • vi to linger. • n a delaying or being delayed; the time period during which something is delayed.

**delectable** adj delightful, delicious.—**delectably** adv.

**delegate** vt to appoint as a representative; to give powers or responsibilities to (an agent or assembly). • n a deputy or an elected representative.

**delegation** n the act of delegating; a group of people empowered to represent others.

**delete** vt to strike out (something written or printed); to erase.—**deletion** n.

**deliberate** vt to consider carefully. • vi to discuss or debate thoroughly; to consider. • adj well thought out; intentional; cautious.—**deliberately** adv.

**delicacy** n delicateness; sensibility; a luxurious food.

**delicate** adj fine in texture; fragile, not robust; requiring tactful handling; of exquisite workmanship; requiring skill in techniques.—**delicately** adv.—**delicateness** n.

**delicatessen** n a store selling prepared foods, esp imported delicacies.

**delicious** adj having a pleasurable effect on the senses, esp taste; delightful.—**deliciously** adv.—**deliciousness** n.

**delight** vt to please greatly. • vi to have or take great pleasure (in). • n great pleasure; something that causes this.

**delightful** adj giving great pleasure.—**delightfully** adv.

**delinquent** adj negligent; guilty of an offence. • n a person guilty of a misdeed, esp a young person who breaks the law.—**delinquency** n.

**delirium** n a state of mental disorder, esp caused by a feverish illness; wild enthusiasm.—**delirious** adj.

**deliver** vt (goods, letters, etc) to transport to a destination; to distribute regularly; to liberate; to rescue; to give birth; to assist at a birth; (blow) to launch; (baseball) to pitch; (speech) to utter.—**deliverer** n.

**delivery** n act of delivering; anything delivered or communicated; the manner of delivering (a speech, etc); the manner of bowling in cricket, etc; the act of giving birth.

**delta** n the fourth letter of the Greek alphabet; an alluvial deposit at the mouth of a river.

**delude** vt to mislead, to deceive.

**deluge** n a flood; anything happening in a heavy rush. • vt to inundate.

**delusion** n a false belief; a persistent false belief that is a symptom of mental illness.—**delusive** adj.—**delusory** adj.

**delve** vti to search deeply; to dig.

**demagogue, demagog** n a political orator who derives power from appealing to popular prejudices.—**demagogic** adj.—**demagogy** n.

**demand** vt to ask for in an authoritative manner. • n a request or claim made with authority for what is due; an urgent claim; desire for goods and services shown by consumers.

**demanding** adj constantly making demands; requiring great skill, concentration or effort.

**demarcation, demarkation** n the act of marking off a boundary or setting a limit to; a limit; the strict separation of the type of work done by members of different trade unions.

**demean** *vt* to lower in dignity.—**demeaning** *adj*.

**demeanour, demeanor** (*US*) *n* behaviour; bearing.

**demented** *adj* crazy, insane.—**dementedly** *adv*.

**demise** *n* (*formal*) death; termination, end.

**demobilize** *vt* to discharge from the armed forces.—**demobilization** *n*.

**democracy** *n* a form of government by the people through elected representatives; a country governed by its people; political, social or legal equality.

**democrat** *n* a person who believes in or promotes democracy; (*with cap*) a member of the Democratic Party in the US.

**democratic** *adj* of, relating to, or supporting the principles of democracy; favouring or upholding equal rights.—**democratically** *adv*.

**demolish** *vt* (*a building*) to pull down or knock down; (*an argument*) to defeat; (*inf*) to eat up.—**demolition** *n*.

**demonstrate** *vt* to indicate or represent clearly; to provide certain evidence of, to prove; to show how something (a machine, etc) works. • *vi* to show one's support for a cause, etc by public parades and protests; to act as a demonstrator of machinery, etc.—**demonstrator** *n*.

**demonstration** *n* proof by evidence; a display or exhibition; a display of feeling; a public manifestation of opinion, as by a mass meeting, march, etc; a display of armed force.

**demonstrative** *adj* displaying one's feelings openly and unreservedly; indicative; conclusive; (*gram*) describing an adjective or pronoun indicating the person or thing referred to.—**demonstratively** *adv*.—**demonstrativeness** *n*.

**demoralize** *vt* to lower the morale of, discourage.—**demoralization** *n*.

**demote** *vt* to reduce in rank or position.—**demotion** *n*.

**demur** *vi* (*pt* **demurred**) to raise objections.

**den** *n* a cave or lair of a wild beast; a place where people gather for illegal activities; a room in a house for relaxation or study.

**denial** *n* the act of denying; a refusal of a request, etc; a refusal or reluctance to admit the truth of something.

**denigrate** *vt* to disparage the character of; to belittle.—**denigration** *n*.

**denim** *n* a hard-wearing cotton cloth, esp used for jeans; (*pl*) denim trousers or jeans.

**denomination** *n* a name or title; a religious group comprising many local churches, larger than a sect; one of a series of related units, esp monetary.—**denominational** *adj*.

**denominator** *n* the part of a fractional expression written below the fraction line.

**denote** *vt* to indicate, be the sign of; to mean.—**denotation** *n*.

**denounce** *vt* to condemn or censure publicly; to inform against; to declare formally the ending of (treaties, etc). —**denouncement** *n*.

**dense** *adj* difficult to see through; massed closely together; dull-witted, stupid.—**densely** *adv*.—**denseness** *n*.

**density** *n* the degree of denseness or concentration; stupidity; the ratio of mass to volume.

**dent** *n* a depression made by pressure or a blow. • *vti* to make a dent or become dented.

**dental** *adj* of or for the teeth.

**dentifrice** *n* toothpowder or toothpaste.

**dentist** *n* a person qualified to treat tooth decay, gum disease, etc.—**dentistry** *n*.

**denture** *n* (*usu pl*) a set of artificial teeth.

**deny** *vt* to declare to be untrue; to repudiate; to refuse to acknowledge; to refuse to assent to a request, etc.

**deodorant** *n* a substance that removes or masks unpleasant odours.

**depart** *vi* to go away, leave; to deviate (from).

**department** *n* a unit of specialized functions into which an organization or business is divided; a province; a realm of activity.—**departmental** *adj*.

**department store** *n* a large shop divided into various departments selling different types of goods.

**departure** *n* departing; deviating from normal practice; a new venture, course of action, etc.

**depend** *vi* to be determined by or connected with anything; to rely (on), put trust (in); to be reliant on for support, esp financially.

**dependable** *adj* able to be relied on.—**dependably** *adv*.—**dependability** *n*.

**dependant** *n* a person who is dependent on another, esp financially.

**dependence, dependance** *n* the state of being dependent; reliance, trust; a physical or mental reliance on a drug, person, etc.

**dependent** *adj* relying on another person, thing etc for support, money, etc; contingent; subordinate.

**depict** *vt* to represent pictorially; to describe.—**depiction** *n*.

**deplete** *vt* to use up a large quantity of. —**depletion** *n*.

**deplorable** *adj* shocking; extremely bad.—**deplorably** *adv*.

**deplore** *vt* to regret deeply; to complain of; to deprecate.

**deploy** *vt* (*military forces*) to distribute and position strategically. • *vi* to adopt strategic positions within an area.—**deployment** *n*.

**depopulate** *vt* to reduce the population of.—**depopulation** *n*.

**deport** *vt* to expel (an undesirable person) from a country; to behave (in a certain manner).—**deportation** *n*.

**deportment** *n* manners; behaviour.

**depose** *vt* to remove from power; to testify, esp in court.

**deposit** *vt* to place or lay down; to pay money into a bank or other institution for safekeeping, to earn interest, etc; to pay as a first instalment; to let fall, leave. • *n* something deposited for safekeeping; money put in a bank; money given in part payment or security; material left in a layer, eg sediment.

**depositor** *n* a person who deposits money in a bank, etc.

**depot** *n* a warehouse, storehouse; a place for storing military supplies; a military training centre; a bus or railway station.

**deprave** *vt* to pervert; to corrupt morally.—**depravation** *n*.—**depraved** *adj*.

**depravity** *n* moral corruption; extreme wickedness.

**depreciate** *vti* to make or become lower in value.

**depreciation** *n* a fall in value, esp of an asset through wear and tear; an allowance for this deducted from gross profit; disparagement.

**depress** *vt* to push down; to sadden, dispirit; to lessen the activity of.—**depressing** *adj*.—**depressingly** *adv*.

**depression** *n* excessive gloom and despondency; an abnormal state of physiological inactivity; a phase of the business cycle characterized by stagnation, widespread unemployment, etc; a falling in or sinking; a lowering of atmospheric pressure, often signalling rain.

**deprive** *vt* to take a thing away from;

to prevent from using or enjoying.— **deprivation** n.

**deprived** adj lacking the essentials of life, such as adequate food, shelter, education, etc.

**depth** n deepness; the distance downwards or inwards; the intensity of emotion or feeling; the profundity of thought; intensity of colour; the mid point of the night or winter; the lowness of sound or pitch; the quality of being deep.

**depth-charge** n a bomb designed to explode under water, used against submarines.

**deputation** n a person or group appointed to represent others.

**deputize** vi to act as deputy.

**deputy** n a delegate, representative, or substitute.

**derail** vti (train) to cause to leave the rails.—**derailment** n.

**derange** vt to throw into confusion; to disturb; to make insane.—**derangement** n.

**derelict** adj abandoned, deserted and left to decay; negligent. • n a person abandoned by society; a wrecked ship or vehicle.

**deride** vt to scorn, mock.

**derision** n ridicule.

**derisive** adj full of derision; mocking, scornful.

**derisory** adj showing or deserving of derision.

**derivation** n the tracing of a word to its root; origin; descent.

**derivative** adj derived from something else; not original. • n something that is derived; a word formed by derivation; (math) the rate of change of one quantity with respect to another.

**derive** vt to take or receive from a source; to infer, deduce (from). • vi to issue as a derivative (from).

**derogatory** adj disparaging; deliberately offensive.

**derrick** n any crane-like apparatus; a tower over an oil well, etc, holding the drilling machinery.

**descend** vi to come or climb down; to pass from a higher to a lower place or condition; (with **on**, **upon**) to make a sudden attack upon, or visit unexpectedly; to sink in morals or dignity; to be derived. • vt to go, pass, or extend down.

**descendant** n a person who is descended from an ancestor; something derived from an earlier form.

**descent** n a descending; a downward motion or step; a way down; a slope; a raid or invasion; lineage, ancestry.

**describe** vt to give a verbal account of; to trace out.

**description** n a verbal or pictorial account; sort, kind.

**descriptive** adj tending to or serving to describe.

**desecrate** vt to violate a sacred place by destructive or blasphemous behaviour.—**desecration** n.

**desert**[1] n (often pl) a deserved reward or punishment.

**desert**[2] vt to leave, abandon, with no intention of returning; to abscond from the armed forces without permission.—**deserter** n.—**desertion** n.

**desert**[3] n a dry, barren region, able to support little or no life; a place lacking in some essential quality.

**deserve** vt to merit or be suitable for (some reward, punishment, etc).—**deservedly** adv.

**deserving** adj worthy of support, esp financially.

**design** vt to plan; to create; to devise; to make working drawings for; to intend. • n a working drawing; a mental plan or scheme; the particular form or disposition of something; a decorative pattern; purpose; (pl) dishonest intent.

**designate** vt to indicate, specify; to

name; to appoint to or nominate for a position, office. • adj (*after noun*) appointed to office but not yet installed.

**designation** n the act of designating; nomination; a distinguishing name or title.

**designer** n a person who designs things; a person who is renowned for creating high-class fashion clothes. • adj (*inf*) trendy, of the latest, esp expensive, fashion.

**desirable** adj arousing (sexual) desire; advisable or beneficial; worth doing.—**desirably** adv.—**desirability** n.

**desire** vt to long or wish for; to request, to ask for. • n a longing for something regarded as pleasurable or satisfying; a request; something desired; sexual craving.—**desirous** adj.

**desk** n a piece of furniture with a writing surface and usu drawers; a counter behind which a cashier, etc sits; the section of a newspaper responsible for a particular topic.

**desolate** adj solitary, lonely; devoid of inhabitants; laid waste.

**desolation** n destruction, ruin; a barren state; loneliness; wretchedness.

**despair** vi to have no hope. • n utter loss of hope; something that causes despair.

**despatch** see **dispatch**.

**desperate** adj (almost) hopeless; reckless through lack of hope; urgently requiring (money, etc); (*remedy*) extreme, dangerous.—**desperately** adv.

**desperation** n loss of hope; recklessness from despair.

**despicable** adj contemptible, worthless.—**despicably** adv.

**despise** vt to regard with contempt or scorn; to consider as worthless, inferior.

**despite** prep in spite of.

**despondent** adj dejected; lacking hope.—**despondence, despondency** n.—**despondently** adv.

**dessert** n the sweet course at the end of a meal.

**dessertspoon** n a spoon in between a teaspoon and a tablespoon in size, used for eating desserts.

**destination** n the place to which a person or thing is going.

**destine** vt to set aside for some specific purpose; to predetermine; intend.

**destiny** n the power supposedly determining the course of events; the future to which any person or thing is destined; a predetermined course of events.

**destitute** adj (*with* of) lacking some quality; lacking the basic necessities of life, very poor.

**destroy** vt to demolish, ruin, to put an end to; to kill.

**destroyer** n a fast small warship.

**destructible** adj able to be destroyed.

**destruction** n the act or process of destroying or being destroyed; ruin.

**destructive** adj causing destruction; (*with* of or to) ruinous; (*criticism*) intended to discredit, negative.—**destructively** adv.—**destructiveness** n.

**detach** vt to release; to separate from a larger group; (*mil*) to send off on special assignment.

**detachable** adj able to be detached.

**detached** adj separate; (*house*) not joined to another; aloof; free from bias or emotion.

**detachment** n indifference; freedom from emotional involvement or bias; the act of detaching; a thing detached; a body of troops detached from the main body and sent on special service.

**detail** vt to describe fully; (*mil*) to set apart for a particular duty. • n an item; a particular or minute account; (*art*) treatment of smaller parts; a reproduction of a smaller part of a picture, statue, etc; a small detachment for special service.

**detailed** *adj* giving full details; thorough.

**detain** *vt* to place in custody or confinement; to delay.

**detect** *vt* to discover the existence or presence of; to notice.

**detection** *n* a discovery or being discovered; the job or process of detecting.

**detective** *n* a person or a police officer employed to find evidence of crimes.

**detector** *n* a device for detecting the presence of something.

**detention** *n* the act of detaining or withholding; a being detained; confinement; being kept in (school after hours) as a punishment.

**deter** *vt* (*pt* **deterred**) to discourage or prevent (from acting).—**determent** *n*.

**detergent** *n* a cleaning agent—*also adj*.

**deteriorate** *vt* to make or become worse.—**deterioration** *n*.

**determination** *n* the act or process of making a decision; a decision resolving a dispute; firm intention; resoluteness.

**determine** *vt* to fix or settle officially; to find out; to regulate; to impel. • *vi* to come to a decision.

**determined** *adj* full of determination, resolute.—**determinedly** *adv*.

**deterrent** *n* something that deters; a nuclear weapon that deters attack through fear of retaliation. • *adj* deterring.—**deterrence** *n*.

**detest** *vt* to dislike intensely.—**detestation** *n*.

**detestable** *adj* intensely disliked, abhorrent.—**detestably** *adv*.

**detonate** *vti* to explode or cause to explode rapidly and violently.—**detonation** *n*.

**detonator** *n* a device that sets off an explosion.

**detour** *n* a deviation from an intended course, esp one serving as an alternative to a more direct route. • *vti* to make or send by a detour.

**detract** *vt* to take away. • *vi* to take away (from).—**detraction** *n*.—**detractor** *n*.

**detriment** *n* (a cause of) damage or injury.—**detrimental** *adj*.

**devalue, devaluate** *vt* to reduce the exchange value of (a currency).—**devaluation** *n*.

**devastate** *vt* to lay waste; to destroy; to overwhelm.—**devastation** *n*.

**develop** *vt* to evolve; to bring to maturity; to show the symptoms of (eg a habit, a disease); to treat a photographic film or plate to reveal an image; to improve the value of. • *vi* to grow (into); to become apparent.

**developer** *n* a person who develops; a person or organization that develops property; a reagent for developing photographs.

**developing country** *n* a poor country that is attempting to improve its social conditions and encourage industrial growth.

**development** *n* the process of growing or developing; a new situation that emerges; a piece of land or property that has been developed.

**deviate** *vi* to diverge from a course, topic, principle, etc. **deviation** *n*.

**device** *n* a machine, implement, etc for a particular purpose; an invention; a scheme, a plot.

**devil** *n* (*with cap*) in Christian and Jewish theology, the supreme spirit of evil, Satan; any evil spirit; an extremely wicked person; (*inf*) a reckless, high-spirited person; (*inf*) someone or something difficult to deal with; (*inf*) a person. • *vb* (*pt* **devilled**) *vt* to cook food with a hot seasoning. • *vi* to act as a drudge to someone; to do research for an author or barrister.

**devilish** *adj* fiendish; mischievous.
• *adv* (*inf*) very.

**devious** *adj* indirect; not straightforward; underhand, deceitful.—**deviously** *adv*.—**deviousness** *n*.

**devise** *vt* to invent, contrive; to plan.—**deviser, devisor** *n*.

**devoid** *adj* lacking (*with* **of**); free from.

**devote** *vt* to give or use for a particular activity or purpose.

**devoted** *adj* zealous; loyal; loving. —**devotedly** *adv*.

**devotion** *n* given to religious worship; piety; strong affection or attachment (to); ardour; (*pl*) prayers. —**devotional** *adj*.

**devour** *vt* to eat up greedily; to consume; to absorb eagerly by the senses or mind.

**devout** *adj* very religious, pious; sincere, dedicated.—**devoutly** *adv*.—**devoutness** *n*.

**dew** *n* air moisture, deposited on a cool surface, esp at night.

**dexterity** *n* manual skill, adroitness.

**diabetes** *n* a medical disorder marked by the persistent and excessive discharge of urine.

**diabetic** *adj* suffering from diabetes.—*also n*.

**diagnose** *vt* to ascertain by diagnosis.

**diagnosis** *n* (*pl* **diagnoses**) the identification of a disease from its symptoms; the analysis of the nature or cause of a problem.—**diagnostic** *adj*.—**diagnostician** *n*.

**diagonal** *adj* slanting from one corner to an opposite corner of a polygon. • *n* a straight line connecting opposite corners.—**diagonally** *adv*.

**diagram** *n* a figure or plan drawn in outline to illustrate the form or workings of something.—**diagrammatic** *adj*.

**dial** *n* the face of a watch or clock; a graduated disc with a pointer used in various instruments; the control on a radio or television set indicating wavelength or station; the numbered disc on a telephone used to enter digits to connect calls; an instrument for telling the time by the sun's shadow. • *vt* (*pt* **dialled**) to measure or indicate by a dial; to make a telephone connection by using a dial or numbered keypad.

**dialect** *n* the form of language spoken in a particular region or social class.

**dialogue, dialog** (*US*) *n* a conversation, esp in a play or novel; an exchange of opinions, negotiation.

**diameter** *n* a straight line bisecting a circle; the length of this line.

**diamond** *n* a valuable gem, a crystallized form of pure carbon; (*baseball*) the playing field, esp the infield; a suit of playing cards denoted by a red lozenge. • *adj* composed of, or set with diamonds; shaped like a diamond.

**diaper** *n* a nappy.

**diaphragm** *n* the midriff, a muscular structure separating the chest from the abdomen; any thin dividing membrane; a device for regulating aperture of a camera lens; a contraceptive cap covering the cervix; a thin vibrating disc used in a telephone receiver, microphone, etc.

**diarrhoea, diarrhea** (*US*) *n* excessive looseness of the bowels.

**diary** *n* a daily record of personal thoughts, events, or business appointments; a book for keeping a daily record.

**dice** *n* (*the pl of* **die**[2] *but used as sing*) a small cube with numbered sides used in games of chance. • *vt* to gamble using dice; to cut (food) into small cubes.

**dictate** *vt* to say or read for another person to write or for a machine to record; to pronounce, order with authority. • *vi* to give dictation; to give orders (to). • *n* an order, rule, or command; (*usu pl*) an impulse, ruling principle.—**dictation** *n*.

**dictator** *n* a ruler with absolute authority, usu acquired by force.

**dictatorship** *n* the office or government of a dictator; a country governed by a dictator; absolute power.

**diction** *n* a way of speaking, enunciation; a person's choice of words.

**dictionary** *n* a reference book containing the words of a language or branch of knowledge alphabetically arranged, with their meanings, pronunciation, origin, etc.

**did** *see* **do**.

**die**[1] *vi* (*pr p* **dying**, *pt* **died**) to cease existence; to become extinct; to stop functioning; to feel a deep longing.

**die**[2] *n* a dice.

**die**[3] *n* an engraved stamp for pressing coins; a casting mould.

**diesel** *n* a vehicle driven by diesel engine.

**diesel engine** *n* an internal combustion engine in which ignition is produced by the heat of highly compressed air alone.

**diet**[1] *n* food selected to adjust weight, to control illness, etc; the food and drink usually consumed by a person or animal. • *vt* to put on a diet. • *vi* to eat according to a special diet.—**dieter** *n*.

**diet**[2] *n* a legislative assembly in some countries.

**differ** *vi* to be unlike, distinct (from); to disagree.

**difference** *n* the act or state of being unlike; disparity; a distinguishing feature; the amount or manner of being different; the result of the subtraction of one quantity from another; a disagreement or argument.

**different** *adj* distinct, separate; unlike, not the same; unusual.—**differently** *adv*.

**differential** *adj* of or showing a difference; (*math*) relating to increments in given functions. • *n* something that marks the difference between comparable things; the difference in wage rates for different types of labour, esp within an industry.

**differentiate** *vt* to make different; to become specialized; to note differences; (*math*) to calculate the derivative of.—**differentiation** *n*.

**difficult** *adj* hard to understand; hard to make, do, or carry out; not easy to please.

**difficulty** *n* being difficult; a problem, etc that is hard to deal with; an obstacle; a troublesome situation; a disagreement.

**diffident** *adj* shy, lacking self-confidence, not assertive.—**diffidence** *n*.—**diffidently** *adv*.

**diffuse**[1] *vt* to spread widely in all directions. • *vti* (*gases, fluids, particles*) to intermingle.—**diffuser, diffusor** *n*.

**diffuse**[2] *adj* spread widely, not concentrated; wordy, not concise.—**diffusely** *adv*.

**dig** *vt* (*pr p* **digging**, *pt* **dug**) to use a tool or hands, claws, etc in making a hole in the ground; to unearth by digging; to excavate; to investigate; to thrust (into); to nudge; (*sl*) to understand, approve. • *n* (*sl*) a thrust; an archaeological excavation; a cutting remark.

**digest**[1] *vt* to convert (food) into assimilable form; to reduce (facts, laws, etc) to convenient form by classifying or summarizing; to form a clear view of (a situation) by reflection. • *vi* to become digested.

**digest**[2] *n* an abridgment of any written matter; a periodical synopsis of published or broadcast material.

**digestible** *adj* capable of being digested.—**digestibility** *n*.

**digestion** *n* the act or process of digesting.

**digit** *n* any of the basic counting units of a number system, including zero; a human finger or toe.

**digital** *adj* of or using digits.—**digitally** *adv*.

**dignified** *adj* possessing dignity; noble; serious.

**dignitary** *n* a person in a high position or rank.

**dignity** *n* noble, serious, formal in manner and appearance; sense of self-respect, worthiness; a high rank, eg in the government.

**digress** *vi* to stray from the main subject in speaking or writing.—**digression** *n*.

**digs** *npl* (*inf*) lodgings.

**dilapidated** *adj* in a state of disrepair; shabby.

**dilate** *vti* to enlarge or become enlarged.—**dilation** *n*.—**dilator, dilater** *n*.

**dilatory** *adj* tardy; causing or meant to cause delay.—**dilatorily** *adv*.—**dilatoriness** *n*.

**dilemma** *n* a situation where each of two alternative courses is undesirable; any difficult problem or choice.

**diligent** *adj* industrious; done with proper care and effort.—**diligently** *adv*.—**diligence** *n*.

**dilute** *vt* to thin down, esp by mixing with water; to weaken the strength of. • *adj* diluted.—**dilution** *n*.

**dim** *adj* (**dimmer, dimmest**) faintly lit; not seen, heard, understood, etc clearly; gloomy; unfavourable; (*inf*) stupid. • *vti* to make or cause to become dark.—**dimly** *adv*.—**dimness** *n*.

**dime** *n* a US or Canadian coin worth ten cents.

**dimension** *n* any linear measurement of width, length, or thickness; extent; size.—**dimensional** *adj*.

**diminish** *vti* to make or become smaller in size, amount, or importance.

**diminutive** *adj* very small. • *n* a word formed by a suffix to mean small (eg *duckling*) or to convey affection (eg *Freddie*).

**dimple** *n* a small hollow, usu on the cheek or chin. • *vti* to make or become dimpled; to reveal dimples.

**din** *n* a loud persistent noise. • *vt* (*pt* **dinned**) to make a din; (*with* **into**) to instil by continual repetition.

**dine** *vi* to eat dinner. • *vt* to entertain to dinner.

**dinghy** *n* a small open boat propelled by oars or sails; a small inflatable boat.

**dingy** *adj* (**dingier, dingiest**) dirty-looking, shabby.—**dinginess** *n*.

**dinner** *n* the principal meal of the day; a formal meal in honour of a person or occasion.

**dinner jacket** *n* a man's usu black jacket for semiformal evening wear.

**diocese** *n* the district over which a bishop has authority.—**diocesan** *adj*.

**dip** *vt* (*pt* **dipped**) to put (something) under the surface (of a liquid) and lift quickly out again; to immerse (sheep) in an antiseptic solution. • *vi* to go into water and come out quickly; to drop down or sink out of sight; to read superficially; to slope downward. • *n* a dipping of any kind; a sudden drop; a mixture in which to dip something.

**diphtheria** *n* an acute infectious disease causing inflammation of the throat and breathing difficulties.

**diphthong** *n* the union of two vowel sounds pronounced in one syllable; a ligature.

**diploma** *n* a certificate given by a college or university to its graduating students.

**diplomacy** *n* the management of relations between nations; skill in handling affairs without arousing hostility.

**diplomat** *n* a person employed or skilled in diplomacy.

**diplomatic, diplomatical** *adj* of diplomacy; employing tact and conciliation; tactful.—**diplomatically** *adv*.

**dipstick** *n* a rod with graduated markings to measure fluid level.

**dire** *adj* dreadful; ominous; desperately urgent.

**direct** *adj* straight; in an unbroken line, with nothing in between; frank; truthful. • *vt* to manage, to control; to tell or show the way; to point to, to aim at; (*a letter or parcel*) to address; to carry out the organizing and supervision of; to train and lead performances; to command. • *vi* to determine a course; to act as a director.—**directness** *n*.

**direct current** *n* an electric current that flows in one direction only.

**direction** *n* management, control; order, command; a knowing or telling what to do, where to go, etc; any way in which one may face or point; (*pl*) instructions.

**directly** *adv* in a direct manner; immediately; in a short while.

**director** *n* person who directs, esp the production of a show for stage or screen; one of the persons directing the affairs of a company or an institution.—**directorial** *adj*.— **directorship** *n*.

**directory** *n* an alphabetical or classified list, as of telephone numbers, members of an organization, charities, etc.

**dirt** *n* filth; loose earth; obscenity; scandal.

**dirt-cheap** *adj* (*inf*) very cheap.

**dirty** *adj* (**dirtier, dirtiest**) filthy; unclean; dishonest; mean; (*weather*) stormy; obscene. • *vti* to make or become dirty.—**dirtily** *adv*.—**dirtiness** *n*.

**disability** *n* a lack of physical, mental or social fitness; something that disables, a handicap.

**disabled** *adj* having a physical handicap.

**disadvantage** *n* an unfavourable condition or situation; loss, damage. • *vt* to put at a disadvantage.

**disadvantageous** *adj* causing disadvantage.

**disagree** *vi* to differ in opinion; to quarrel; (*with* **with**) to have a bad effect on.—**disagreement** *n*.

**disagreeable** *adj* nasty, bad tempered. —**disagreeably** *adv*.

**disallow** *vt* to refuse to allow or to accept the truth or value of.

**disappear** *vi* to pass from sight completely; to fade into nothing.—**disappearance** *n*.

**disappoint** *vt* to fail to fulfil the hopes of (a person).—**disappointed** *adj*.—**disappointing** *adj*.—**disappointingly** *adv*.

**disappointment** *n* the frustration of one's hopes; annoyance due to failure; a person or thing that disappoints.

**disapprove** *vti* to express or have an unfavourable opinion (of).—**disapproval** *n*.

**disarm** *vt* to deprive of weapons or means of defence; to defuse (a bomb); to conciliate. • *vi* to abolish or reduce national armaments.

**disarmament** *n* the reduction or abolition of a country's armed forces and weaponry.

**disaster** *n* a devastating and sudden misfortune; utter failure.—**disastrous** *adj*.—**disastrously** *adv*.

**disband** *vt* to disperse; to break up and separate.—**disbandment** *n*.

**disc** *n* any flat, thin circular body; something resembling this, as the sun; a cylindrical pad of cartilage between the vertebrae; a gramophone record; (*comput*) a variant spelling of **disk**.

**discard** vti to cast off, get rid of; (cards) to throw away a card from one's hand. • n something discarded; (cards) a discarded card.

**disc brake** n one in which two flat discs press against a central plate on the wheel hub.

**discern** vt to perceive; to see clearly. —**discernible** adj.—**discernibly** adv.

**discerning** adj discriminating; perceptive.—**discernment** n.

**discharge** vt to unload; to send out, emit; to release, acquit; to dismiss from employment; to shoot a gun; to fulfil, as duties. • vi to unload; (gun) to be fired; (fluid) to pour out. • n the act or process of discharging; something that is discharged; an authorization for release, acquittal, dismissal, etc.

**disciple** n a person who believes in and helps to spread another's teachings, a follower; one of the twelve apostles of Christ.

**disciplinary** adj of or for discipline.

**discipline** n a field of learning; training and conditioning to produce obedience and self-control; punishment; the maintenance of order and obedience as a result of punishment; a system of rules of behaviour. • vt to punish to enforce discipline; to train by instruction; to bring under control.

**disc jockey** n (inf) a person who announces records on a programme of broadcast music, or in discotheques.

**disclaim** vi to deny connection with; to renounce all legal claim to.

**disclose** vt to bring into the open, to reveal.—**disclosure** n.

**disco** n (inf) a discotheque.

**discolour, discolor** (US) vti to ruin the colour of; to fade, stain.—**discoloration** n.

**discomfort** n uneasiness; something causing this. • vt to make uncomfortable; to make uneasy.

**disconcert** vt to confuse; to upset.

**disconnect** vt to separate or break the connection of.

**disconnected** adj disjointed; incoherent.

**disconsolate** adj miserable; dejected. —**disconsolately** adv.

**discontent** n lack of contentment, dissatisfaction.—**discontentment** n.

**discontented** adj feeling discontent; unhappy, unsatisfied.

**discontinue** vti to stop or come to a stop; to give up.—**discontinuance** n.

**discord** n lack of agreement, strife; (mus) a lack of harmony; harsh clashing sounds.—**discordance** n.— **discordant** adj.—**discordantly** adv.

**discotheque** n an occasion when people gather to dance to recorded pop music; a club or party, etc where this takes place; equipment for playing such music.

**discount** n a reduction in the amount or cost; the percentage charged for doing this. • vt to deduct from the amount, cost; to allow for exaggeration; to disregard; to make less effective by anticipation. • vi to make and give discounts.

**discourage** vt to deprive of the will or courage (to do something); to try to prevent; to hinder.—**discouraging** adj.—**discouraged** adj.—**discouragement** n.

**discourteous** adj lacking in courtesy, rude.—**discourteously** adv.—**discourtesy** n.

**discover** vt to see, find or learn of for the first time.—**discoverable** adj.— **discoverer** n.

**discovery** n the act of discovering or being discovered; something discovered.

**discredit** n damage to a reputation; doubt; disgrace; lack of credibility. • vt to damage the reputation of; to cast doubt on the authority or credibility of.

**discreet** *adj* wisely cautious, prudent; unobtrusive.—**discreetly** *adv*.—**discreetness** *n*.

**discrepancy** *n* difference; a disagreement, as between figures in a total.

**discretion** *n* the freedom to judge or choose; prudence; wise judgment; skill.

**discriminate** *vi* to be discerning in matters of taste; to make a distinction; to treat differently, esp unfavourably due to prejudice.—**discrimination** *n*.—**discriminatory** *adj*.

**discriminating** *adj* judicious; discerning; discriminatory.

**discus** *n* a heavy disc with a thickened middle, thrown by athletes.

**discuss** *vt* to talk over; to investigate by reasoning or argument.—**discussion** *n*.

**disdain** *vt* to scorn, treat with contempt. • *n* scorn; a feeling of contemptuous superiority.—**disdainful** *adj*.—**disdainfully** *adv*.

**disease** *n* an unhealthy condition in an organism caused by infection, poisoning, etc; sickness; a harmful condition or situation.—**diseased** *adj*.

**disembark** *vti* to land from a ship, debark.—**disembarkation** *n*.

**disembodied** *adj* (*soul, spirit, etc*) free of the body.

**disembowel** *vt* (*pt* **disembowelled**) to remove the entrails of; to remove the substance of.

**disenchant** *vt* to disillusion.—**disenchantment** *n*.

**disengage** *vt* to separate or free from engagement or obligation; to detach, to release.—**disengaged** *adj*.—**disengagement** *n*.

**disentangle** *vt* to untangle; to free from complications.—**disentanglement** *n*.

**disfavour, disfavor** (*US*) *n* dislike; disapproval. • *vt* to treat with disfavour.

**disfigure** *vt* to spoil the beauty or appearance of.—**disfigurement** *n*.

**disgrace** *n* a loss of trust, favour, or honour; something that disgraces. • *vt* to bring disgrace or shame upon.

**disgraceful** *adj* causing disgrace, shameful.—**disgracefully** *adv*.

**disgruntled** *adj* dissatisfied, resentful.

**disguise** *vt* to hide what one is by appearing as something else; to hide what (a thing) really is. • *n* the use of a changed appearance to conceal identity; a false appearance.

**disgust** *n* sickening dislike. • *vt* to cause disgust in. —**disgustedly** *adv*.

**dish** *n* any of various shallow concave vessels to serve food in; the amount of food served in a dish; the food served; a shallow concave object, as a dish aerial; (*inf*) an attractive person.

**dishcloth** *n* a cloth for washing dishes.

**dishearten** *vt* to discourage.

**dishevelled, disheveled** (*US*) *adj* rumpled, untidy.—**dishevelment** *n*.

**dishonest** *adj* not honest.—**dishonestly** *adv*.—**dishonesty** *n*.

**dishonour, dishonor** (*US*) *n* loss of honour; disgrace, shame. • *vt* to bring shame on, to disgrace; to refuse to pay, as a cheque.

**dishonourable, dishonorable** (*US*) *adj* lacking honour, disgraceful.—**dishonourably** *adv*.

**dishwasher** *n* an appliance for washing dishes; a person employed to wash dishes.

**disillusion** *vt* to free from (mistaken) ideals or illusions. • *n* the state of being disillusioned.—**disillusionment** *n*.

**disinfect** *vt* to destroy germs.—**disinfection** *n*.

**disinfectant** *n* any chemical agent that inhibits the growth of or destroys germs.

**disintegrate** *vti* to break or cause to break into separate pieces.—**disintegration** *n*.

**disinterested** *adj* impartial; objective.—**disinterestedly** *adv*.

**disjointed** *adj* incoherent, muddled, esp of speech or writing.

**disk** *n* an alternative spelling of **disc**; (*comput*) a storage device in a computer, either floppy or hard.

**dislike** *vt* to consider unpleasant. • *n* aversion, distaste.—**dislikable, dislikeable** *adj*.

**dislocate** *vt* to put (a joint) out of place, to displace; to upset the working of.—**dislocation** *n*.

**dislodge** *vt* to force or move out of a hiding place, established position, etc.—**dislodgement, dislodgment** *n*.

**dismal** *adj* gloomy, miserable, sad; (*inf*) feeble, worthless. —**dismally** *adv*.

**dismantle** *vt* to pull down; to take apart.

**dismay** *n* apprehension, discouragement. • *vt* to fill with dismay.

**disobedient** *adj* failing or refusing to obey.—**disobediently** *adv*.—**disobedience** *n*.

**disobey** *vt* to refuse to follow orders.

**disorder** *n* lack of order; untidiness; a riot; an illness or interruption of the normal functioning of the body or mind. • *vt* to throw into confusion; to upset.—**disorderly** *adj*.

**disorganize** *vt* to confuse or disrupt an orderly arrangement.—**disorganization** *n*.

**disown** *vt* to refuse to acknowledge as one's own.

**disparage** *vt* to belittle.—**disparagingly** *adv*.—**disparagement** *n*.

**disparity** *n* essential difference; inequality.

**dispassionate** *adj* unemotional; impartial.—**dispassionately** *adv*.

**dispatch** *vt* to send off somewhere; to perform speedily; to kill. • *n* a sending off (of a letter, a messenger etc); promptness; haste; a written message, esp of news.—*also* **despatch**.

**dispel** *vt* (*pt* **dispelled**) to drive away and scatter.

**dispensary** *n* a place in a hospital, a chemist shop, etc where medicines are made up and dispensed.

**dispense** *vt* to deal out, distribute; to prepare and distribute medicines; to administer.

**disperse** *vt* to scatter in different directions. • *vi* to separate, become dispersed.—**dispersal** *n*.

**dispirited** *adj* depressed, discouraged.

**displace** *vt* to take the place of, to oust; to remove from a position of authority.—**displacement** *n*.

**display** *vt* to show, expose to view; to exhibit ostentatiously. • *n* a displaying; an eye-catching arrangement, exhibition; a computer monitor for presenting visual information.

**displease** *vt* to cause offence or annoyance to.

**displeasure** *n* a feeling of being displeased; dissatisfaction.

**disposable** *adj* designed to be discarded after use; available for use. • *n* something disposable, eg a baby's nappy.

**disposal** *n* a disposing of something; order, arrangement.

**dispose** *vt* to place in order, arrange; to influence. • *vi* to deal with or settle; to give, sell or transfer to another; to throw away.

**disposed** *adj* inclined (towards something).

**disposition** *n* a natural way of behaving towards others; tendency; arrangement.

**disproportionate** *adj* out of proportion.—**disproportionately** *adv*.

**disprove** *vt* to prove (a claim, etc) to be incorrect.

**dispute** *vt* to make the subject of an argument or debate; to query the validity of. • *vi* to argue. • *n* an argument; a quarrel.

**disqualify** *vt* to make ineligible because of a violation of rules; to make unfit or unsuitable, to disable.—**disqualification** n.

**disquiet** n anxiety, worry.—also vt.—**disquieting** adj.—**disquietude** n.

**disregard** vt to pay no attention to; to consider as of little or no importance. • n lack of attention, neglect.

**disrepair** n a worn-out condition through neglect of repair.

**disreputable** adj of bad reputation.

**disrespect** n lack of respect, rudeness.—**disrespectful** adj.—**disrespectfully** adv.

**disrupt** vti to break up; to create disorder or confusion; to interrupt.—**disruption** n.

**dissect** vt to cut apart (a plant, animal, etc) for scientific examination; to analyse and interpret in fine detail.—**dissection** n.—**dissector** n.

**disseminate** vt to spread or scatter (ideas, information, etc) widely.—**dissemination** n.

**dissent** vi to hold a different opinion; to withhold assent. • n a difference of opinion.—**dissenter** n.

**dissident** adj disagreeing. • n a person who disagrees strongly with government policies, esp one who suffers harassment or imprisonment as a result.—**dissidence** n.

**dissipate** vt to scatter, dispel; to waste, squander (money, etc). • vi to separate and vanish.

**dissipated** adj dissolute, indulging in excessive pleasure; scattered, wasted.

**dissociate** vti to separate or cause to separate the association of (people, things, etc) in consciousness; to repudiate a connection with.—**dissociation** n.

**dissolute** adj lacking moral discipline.

**dissolve** vt to cause to pass into solution; to disperse (a legislative assembly); to melt; (partnership, marriage) to break up legally, annul. • vi to

become liquid; to fade away; to be overcome by emotion.

**dissuade** vt to prevent or discourage by persuasion.—**dissuasion** n.—**dissuasive** adj.

**distance** n the amount of space between two points or things; a distant place or point; remoteness, coldness of manner. • vt to place at a distance, physically or emotionally; to outdistance in a race, etc.

**distant** adj separated by a specific distance; far-off in space, time, place, relation, etc; not friendly, aloof.—**distantly** adv.

**distaste** n aversion; dislike.

**distasteful** adj unpleasant, offensive.—**distastefully** adv.

**distemper** n an infectious and often fatal disease of dogs and other animals; a type of paint made by mixing colour with egg or glue instead of oil; a painting made with this.

**distend** vti to swell or cause to swell, esp from internal pressure.

**distil, distill** (US) vti (pt **distilled**) to treat by, or cause to undergo, distillation; to purify; to extract the essence of; to let or cause to fall in drops.

**distillery** n a place where distilling, esp of alcoholic spirits, is carried on.

**distinct** adj different, separate (from); easy to perceive by the mind or senses.—**distinctly** adv.—**distinctness** n.

**distinction** n discrimination, separation; a difference seen or made; a distinguishing mark or characteristic; excellence, superiority; a mark of honour.

**distinctive** adj clearly marking a person or thing as different from another; characteristic.

**distinguish** vt to see or recognize as different; to mark as different, characterize; to see or hear clearly; to

confer distinction on; to make eminent or known. • *vi* to perceive a
difference. —**distinguishable** *adj*.

**distinguished** *adj* eminent, famous;
dignified in appearance or manners.

**distort** *vt* to pull or twist out of shape;
to alter the true meaning of, misrepresent.—**distortion** *n*.

**distract** *vt* to draw (eg the mind or attention) to something else; to confuse.

**distracted** *adj* bewildered, confused.

**distraction** *n* something that distracts
the attention; an amusement; perplexity; extreme agitation.

**distraught** *adj* extremely distressed.

**distress** *n* physical or emotional suffering, as from pain, illness, lack of
money, etc; a state of danger, desperation. • *vt* to cause distress to.

**distribute** *vt* to divide and share out;
to spread, disperse throughout an
area.—**distribution** *n*.

**distributor** *n* an agent who sells goods,
esp wholesale; a device for distrib-
uting current to the spark plugs in
an engine.

**district** *n* a territorial division defined
for administrative purposes; a region
or area with a distinguishing character.

**distrust** *n* suspicion, lack of trust.—
also *vt*.—**distrustful** *adj*.

**disturb** *vt* to interrupt; to cause to
move from the normal position or
arrangement; to destroy the quiet or
composure of.

**disturbance** *n* a disturbing or being
disturbed; an interruption; an outbreak of disorder and confusion.

**ditch** *n* any long narrow trench dug in
the ground. • *vt* to make a ditch in;
(*sl*) to drive (a car) into a ditch; (*sl*)
to make a forced landing of (an aircraft); (*sl*) to get rid of.

**dither** *vi* to hesitate, vacillate.—**dith-
erer** *n*.

**ditto** *n* the same again, as above—used
in written lists and tables to avoid
repetition. • *vt* to repeat.

**divan** *n* a long couch without back or
sides; a bed of similar design.

**dive** *vi* (*pt* **dived** *or* **dove**) to plunge
headfirst into water; (*aircraft*) to
descend or fall steeply; (*diver, submarine*) to submerge; to plunge (eg
the hand) suddenly into anything; to
dash headlong, lunge. • *n* a headlong plunge; a submerging of a submarine, etc; a sharp descent; a steep
decline; (*sl*) a disreputable public
place.

**diver** *n* a person who dives; a person
who works or explores underwater
from a diving bell or in a diving suit;
any of various aquatic birds.

**diverge** *vi* to branch off in different
directions from a common point; to
differ in character, form, etc; to deviate from a path or course.—**diver-
gent** *adj*.—**divergence** *n*.

**diverse** *adj* different; assorted, various.

**diversify** *vt* to vary; to invest in a broad
range of securities to lessen risk of
loss. • *vi* to engage in a variety of
commercial operations to reduce
risk.—**diversification** *n*.

**diversion** *n* turning aside from a
course; a recreation, amusement; a
drawing of attention away from the
principal activity; a detour when a
road is temporarily closed to traffic.—**diversionary** *adj*.

**diversity** *n* variety.

**divert** *vt* to turn aside from one course
onto another; to entertain, amuse.

**divide** *vt* to break up into parts; to distribute, share out; to sort into categories; to cause to separate from
something else; to separate into opposing sides; (*Parliament*) to vote or
cause to vote by division; (*math*) to
ascertain how many times one quantity contains another. • *vi* to become

separated; to diverge; to vote by separating into two sides. • *n* a watershed; a split.

**dividend** *n* a number which is to be divided; the money earned by a company and divided among the shareholders; a bonus derived from some action.

**divine** *adj* of, from, or like God or a god; (*inf*) excellent. • *n* a clergyman; a theologian. • *vt* to foretell the future by supernatural means; to discover intuitively; to dowse. • *vi* to practise divination.—**divinely** *adv.*—**diviner** *n.*

**diving board** *n* a platform or springboard for diving from.

**divinity** *n* any god; theology; the quality of being God or a god.

**division** *n* a dividing or being divided; a partition, a barrier; a portion or section; a military unit; separation; (*Parliament*) a separation into two opposing sides to vote; a disagreement; (*math*) the process of dividing one number by another.—**divisional** *adj.*

**divorce** *n* the legal dissolution of marriage; separation. • *vt* to terminate a marriage by divorce; to separate.

**divorcé, divorcee** *n* a divorced person.—**divorcée** *nf.*

**divulge** *vt* to tell or reveal.—**divulgence** *n.*

**DIY** *abbr* = do-it-yourself.

**dizzy** *adj* (**dizzier, dizziest**) confused; causing giddiness or confusion; (*sl*) silly; foolish. • *vt* to make dizzy; to confuse.—**dizzily** *adv.*

**DJ** *abbr* = disc jockey; dinner jacket.

**do** *vt* (*pres t* **does**, *pt* **did**, *pp* **done**) to perform; to work; to end, to complete; to make; to provide; to arrange, to tidy; to perform; to cover a distance; to visit; (*sl*) to serve time in prison; (*sl*) to cheat, to rob; (*sl*) to assault. • *vi* to act or behave; to be

satisfactory; to manage. • *n* (*pl* **dos, do's**) (*inf*) a party; (*inf*) a hoax. *Do* has special uses where it has no definite meaning, as in asking questions (*Do you like milk?*), emphasizing a verb (*I do want to go*), and standing for a verb already used (*My dog goes where I do*).

**docile** *adj* easily led; submissive.— **docilely** *adv.*—**docility** *n.*

**dock**[1] *vt* (*an animal's tail*) to cut short; (*wages, etc*) to deduct a portion of.

**dock**[2] *n* a wharf; an artificial enclosed area of water for ships to be loaded, repaired, etc; (*pl*) a dockyard. • *vt* to come or bring into dock; to join (spacecraft) together in space.

**dock**[3] *n* an enclosed area in a court of law reserved for the accused.

**docker** *n* a labourer who works at the docks.

**dockyard** *n* an area with docks and facilities for repairing and refitting ships.

**doctor** *n* a person qualified to treat diseases or physical disorders; the highest academic degree; the holder of such a degree. • *vt* to treat medically; (*machinery, etc*) to patch up; to tamper with, falsify; (*inf*) to castrate or spay. —**doctoral** *adj.*

**doctrine** *n* a principle of belief.—**doctrinal** *adj.*

**document** *n* a paper containing information or proof of anything. • *vt* to provide or prove with documents. — **documentation** *n.*

**documentary** *adj* consisting of documents; presenting a factual account of an event or activity. • *n* a non-fiction film.

**dodge** *vi* to move quickly in an irregular course. • *vt* to evade (a duty) by cunning; to avoid by a sudden movement or shift of position; to trick. • *n* a sudden movement; (*inf*) a clever trick.—**dodger** *n.*

**dog** *n* a canine mammal of numerous breeds, commonly kept as a domestic pet; the male of the wolf or fox; a despicable person; a device for gripping things. • *vt* (*pt* **dogged**) to pursue relentlessly.—**dog-like** *adj*.

**dog-collar** *n* (*inf*) a clerical collar.

**dog-eared** *adj* (*book*) having the corners of the pages turned down; worn, shabby.

**dogma** *n* a belief taught or held as true, esp by a church; a doctrine.

**dogmatic, dogmatical** *adj* pertaining to a dogma; forcibly asserted as if true; overbearing.—**dogmatically** *adv*.

**doings** *npl* things done; actions.

**doldrums** *npl* inactivity; depression; boredom; the regions of the ocean about the equator where there is little wind.

**dole** *n* (*inf*) money received from the state while unemployed; a small portion. • *vt* to give (out) in small portions.

**doleful** *adj* sad, gloomy.—**dolefully** *adv*.

**doll** *n* a toy in the form of a human figure; a ventriloquist's dummy; (*sl*) a woman

**dollar** *n* the unit of money in the US, Canada, Australia and many other countries.

**dolphin** *n* a marine mammal with a beak-like snout, larger than a porpoise but smaller than a whale.

**domain** *n* an area under the control of a ruler or government; a field of thought, activity, etc.

**dome** *n* a large, rounded roof; something high and rounded.—*also vt*.

**domesday** *see* **doomsday**.

**domestic** *adj* belonging to the home or family; not foreign; (*animals*) tame. • *n* a servant in the home.—**domestically** *adv*.

**domesticate** *vt* to tame; to make home-loving and fond of household duties.—**domestication** *n*.

**domicile** *n* a house; a person's place of residence.—**domiciliary** *adj*.

**dominant** *adj* commanding, prevailing over others; overlooking from a superior height. • *n* (*mus*) the fifth note of a diatonic scale.—**dominance** *n*.

**dominate** *vt* to control or rule by strength; to hold a commanding position over; to overlook from a superior height.—**domination** *n*.

**dominion** *n* a territory with one ruler or government; the power to rule, authority.

**domino** *n* (*pl* **dominoes, dominos**) a flat oblong tile marked with up to six dots; (*pl*) a popular game usu using a set of 28 dominoes; a loose cloak, usu worn with an eye mask, at masquerades.

**don**[1] *vt* (*pt* **donned**) to put on.

**don**[2] *n* a head, fellow or tutor at Oxford or Cambridge universities; (*loosely*) any university teacher.

**donate** *vt* to give as a gift or donation, esp to a charity.—**donator** *n*.

**donation** *n* donating; a contribution.

**done** *see* **do**.

**donkey** *n* a small animal resembling a horse.

**donor** *n* a person who donates something, a donator; a person who gives blood, organs, etc, for medical use.

**don't** = do not.

**donut** *n* (*inf*) a doughnut.

**doom** *n* a grim destiny; ruin. • *vt* to condemn to failure, destruction, etc.

**doomsday** *n* the day of God's Last Judgment of mankind.—*also* **domesday**.

**door** *n* a movable barrier to close an opening in a wall; a doorway; a means of entry or approach.

**doorman** *n* a uniformed attendant stationed at the entrance to large hotels, offices, etc.

**doormat** *n* a mat placed at the entrance to a doorway for wiping one's feet;

(*inf*) a submissive or easily bullied person.

**dope** *n* a thick pasty substance used for lubrication; (*inf*) any illegal drug, such as cannabis or narcotics; (*sl*) a stupid person; (*sl*) information. • *vt* to treat with dope. • *vi* to take addictive drugs.

**dopey, dopy** *adj* (**dopier, dopiest**) (*sl*) stupid; (*inf*) half asleep.—**dopiness** *n*.

**dormant** *adj* sleeping; quiet, as if asleep; inactive.—**dormancy** *n*.

**dormitory** *n* a large room with many beds, as in a boarding school.

**dormouse** *n* (*pl* **dormice**) a small mouse-like creature that hibernates in winter.

**dose** *n* the amount of medicine, radiation, etc administered at one time; a part of an experience; (*sl*) a venereal disease. • *vt* to administer a dose (of medicine) to.—**dosage** *n*.

**dosshouse** *n* (*sl*) a cheap lodging house.

**dot** *n* a small round speck, a point; the short signal in Morse code. • *vt* (*pt* **dotted**) to mark with a dot; to scatter (about).

**dote** *vi* (*with* **on** *or* **upon**) to show excessive affection.

**double** *adj* twice as large, as strong, etc; designed or intended for two; made of two similar parts; having two meanings, characters, etc; (*flowers*) having more than one circle of petals. • *adv* twice; in twos. • *n* a number or amount that is twice as much; a person or thing identical to another; (*film*) a person closely resembling an actor and who takes their place to perform stunts, etc; (*pl*) a game between two pairs of players. • *vti* to make or become twice as much or as many; to fold, to bend; to bend sharply backwards; to sail around; to have an additional purpose.—**doubly** *adv*.

**double bass** *n* the largest instrument of the violin family.

**double-breasted** *adj* (*suit*) having one half of the front overlap the other.

**double-cross** *vt* to betray an associate, to cheat.—*also n*.

**double-park** *vt* to park alongside a car which is already parked beside the kerb.

**doubt** *vi* to be uncertain or undecided. • *vt* to hold in doubt; to distrust; to be suspicious of. • *n* uncertainty; (*often pl*) lack of confidence in something, distrust.—**doubter** *n*.

**doubtful** *adj* feeling doubt; uncertain; suspicious.—**doubtfully** *adv*.

**doubtless** *adv* no doubt.

**dough** *n* a mixture of flour and water, milk, etc used to make bread, pastry, or cake; (*inf*) money.—**doughy** *adj*.

**doughnut** *n* small, fried, usu ring-shaped, cake.

**dove**[1] *see* **dive**.

**dove**[2] *n* a small bird of the pigeon family; (*politics, diplomacy*) an advocate of peace or a peaceful policy.

**dovetail** *n* a wedge-shaped joint used in woodwork. • *vt* to fit or combine together.

**dowdy** *adj* (**dowdier, dowdiest**) poorly dressed, not stylish.—**dowdily** *adv*.—**dowdiness** *n*.

**down**[1] *n* soft fluffy feathers or fine hairs.

**down**[2] *adv* toward or in a lower physical position; to a lying or sitting position; toward or to the ground, floor, or bottom; to a source or hiding place; to or in a lower status or in a worse condition; from an earlier time; in cash; to or in a state of less activity. • *adj* occupying a low position, esp lying on the ground; depressed, dejected. • *prep* in a descending direction in, on, along, or through. • *n* a low period (as in activity, emotional life, or fortunes); (*inf*) a dislike, prejudice. • *vti* to go or cause to go or come down; to defeat; to swallow.

**downcast** *adj* dejected; (*eyes*) directed downwards.

**downfall** *n* a sudden fall (from power, etc); a sudden or heavy fall of rain, etc.

**down payment** *n* a deposit.

**downpour** *n* a heavy fall of rain.

**downright** *adj* frank; absolute. • *adv* thoroughly.

**downtown** *n* the main business district of a town or city.—*also adj*.

**downward**[1] *adj* moving from a higher to a lower level, position or condition. • *adv* downwards.

**downwards, downward**[2] *adv* towards a lower place, position, etc; from an earlier time to a later.

**dowry** *n* the money or possessions that a woman brings to her husband at marriage.

**doze** *vi* to sleep lightly. • *n* a light sleep, a nap.—**dozer** *n*.

**dozen** *n* a group of twelve.—**dozenth** *adj*.

**Dr** *abbr* = Doctor; debtor.

**drab** *adj* (**drabber, drabbest**) dull, uninteresting.—**drably** *adv*.—**drabness** *n*.

**draft** *n* a rough plan, preliminary sketch; an order for the payment of money by a bank; a smaller group selected from a larger for a specific task; in US, conscription; a draught. • *vt* to draw a rough sketch or outline of; to select for a special purpose; in US, to conscript.

**drain** *vt* to draw off liquid gradually; to make dry by removing liquid gradually; to exhaust physically or mentally; to drink the entire contents of a glass • *vi* to flow away gradually; to become dry as liquid trickles away. • *n* a sewer, pipe etc

by which water is drained away; something that causes exhaustion or depletion.

**drainage** *n* a draining; a system of drains; something drained off.

**draining-board** *n* a sloping, usu grooved, surface beside a sink for draining washed dishes.

**drainpipe** *n* a pipe that carries waste liquid, sewage, etc out of a building.

**drama** *n* a play for the stage, radio or television; dramatic literature as a genre; a dramatic situation or a set of events.

**dramatic** *adj* of or resembling drama; exciting, vivid.—**dramatically** *adv*.

**dramatist** *n* a person who writes plays.

**drank** *see* **drink**.

**drape** *vt* to cover or hang with cloth; to arrange in loose folds; to place loosely or untidily. • *n* a hanging cloth or curtain; (*pl*) curtains.

**draper** *n* a seller of cloth.

**drastic** *adj* acting with force and violence.—**drastically** *adv*.

**draught, draft** (*US*) *n* a current of air, esp in an enclosed space; the pulling of a load using an animal, etc; something drawn; a dose of medicine or liquid; an act of swallowing; the depth of water required to float a ship; beer, wine, etc stored in bulk in casks; a flat counter used in the game of draughts.

**draughts** *n* a board game for two players using 24 round pieces.—*also* **checkers**.

**draughtsman**[1], **draftsman** (*US*) *n* a person who makes detailed drawings or plans.—**draughtsmanship** *n*.

**draughtsman**[2] *n* a flat counter used in the game of draughts.—*also* **checker**.

**draw** *vti* (*pt* **drew**, *pp* **drawn**) to haul, to drag; to cause to go in a certain direction; to pull out; to attract; to delineate, to sketch; to receive (as a salary); to bend (a bow) by pulling back the string; to leave (a contest) undecided; to write up, to draft (a will); to produce or allow a current of air; to draw lots; to get information from; (*ship*) to require a certain depth to float. • *n* the act of drawing; (*inf*) an event that attracts customers, people; the drawing of lots; a drawn game.

**drawback** *n* a hindrance, handicap.

**drawbridge** *n* a bridge (eg over a moat) designed to be drawn up.

**drawer** *n* a person who draws; a person who draws a cheque; a sliding box-like compartment (in a table, chest, or desk); (*pl*) knickers, underpants.

**drawing** *n* a figure, plan, or sketch drawn by using lines.

**drawing pin** *n* a flat-headed pin used for fastening paper, drawings, etc, to a board.

**drawing room** *n* a room where visitors are entertained, a living room.

**drawl** *vt* to speak slowly and with elongated vowel sounds.—*also n*.

**drawn** *pp of* **draw**. • *adj* looking strained because of tiredness or worry.

**dread** *n* great fear or apprehension. • *vt* to fear greatly. —**dreadful** *adj.*— **dreadfully** *adv.*

**dream** *n* a stream of thoughts and images in sleep; a day-dreaming state, a reverie; an ambition; an ideal. • *vb* (*pt* **dreamt** *or* **dreamed**) *vi* to have a dream in sleep; to fantasize. • *vt* to dream of; to imagine as a reality.— **dreamer** *n.*

**dreamy** *adj* (**dreamier, dreamiest**) given to dreaming, unpractical; (*inf*) attractive, wonderful.

**dreary** *adj* (**drearier, dreariest**) dull; cheerless.—**drearily** *adv.*—**dreariness** *n.*

**dredge**[1] *n* a device for scooping up material from the bottom of a river, harbour, etc.—*also vt*.

**dredge**[2] *vt* to coat (food) by sprinkling.

**dredger**[1] *n* a vessel fitted with dredging equipment.

**dredger**[2] *n* a container with a perforated lid for sprinkling.

**dregs** *npl* solid impurities that settle on the bottom of a liquid; residue; (*inf*) a worthless person or thing.

**drench** *vt* to soak, saturate.

**dress** *n* clothing; a one-piece garment worn by women and girls comprising a top and skirt; a style or manner of clothing. • *vt* to put on or provide with clothing; to decorate; (*wound*) to wash and bandage; (*animal*) to groom; to arrange the hair; to prepare food (eg poultry, fish) for eating by cleaning, gutting, etc. • *vi* to put on clothes; to put on formal wear for an occasion.

**dress circle** *n* the first tier of seats in a theatre above the stalls.

**dresser** *n* a person who assists an actor to dress; a type of kitchen sideboard.

**dressing** *n* a sauce or stuffing for food; manure spread over the soil; dress or clothes; the bandage, ointment, etc applied to a wound.

**dressing-down** *n* a severe scolding.

**dressing-gown** *n* a loose garment worn when one is partially clothed.

**dress rehearsal** *n* rehearsal in full costume.

**drew** *see* **draw**.

**dribble** *vi* to flow in a thin stream or small drips; to let saliva to trickle from the mouth. • *vt* (*soccer, basketball, hockey*) to move (the ball) along little by little with the foot, hand, stick, etc. • *n* the act of dribbling; a thin stream of liquid.—**dribbler** *n.*

**drier** *see* **dryer**.

**drift** *n* a heap of snow, sand, etc deposited by the wind; natural course, tendency; the general meaning or intention (of what is said); the extent of deviation (of an aircraft, etc) from a course; an aimless course; the action or motion of drifting. • *vt* to cause to drift. • *vi* to be driven or carried along by water or air currents; to move along aimlessly; to be piled into heaps by the wind.

**drill**[1] *n* an implement with a pointed end that bores holes; the training of soldiers, etc; repetitious exercises or training as a teaching method; (*inf*) correct procedure or routine. • *vt* to make a hole with a drill; to instruct or be instructed by drilling.

**drill**[2] *n* a machine for planting seeds in rows; a furrow in which seeds are planted; a row of seeds planted in this way.—*also vt.*

**drink** *vb* (*pt* **drank**, *pp* **drunk**) *vt* to swallow (a liquid); to take in, absorb; to join in a toast. • *vi* to consume alcoholic liquor, esp to excess. • *n* liquid to be drunk; alcoholic liquor; (*sl*) the sea.—**drinker** *n*.

**drip** *vti* (*pt* **dripped**) to fall or let fall in drops. • *n* a liquid that falls in drops; the sound of falling drops; (*med*) a device for injecting a fluid slowly and continuously into a vein; (*inf*) a weak or ineffectual person.

**drip-dry** *adj* (*clothing*) drying easily and needing little ironing.—*also vti.*

**dripping** *n* fat that drips from meat during roasting.

**drive** *vb* (*pt* **drove**, *pp* **driven**) *vt* to urge, push or force onward; to direct the movement or course of; to convey in a vehicle; to carry through strongly; to impress forcefully; to propel (a ball) with a hard blow. • *vi* to be forced along; to be conveyed in a vehicle; to work, to strive (at). • *n* a trip in a vehicle; a stroke to drive a ball (in golf, etc); a driveway; a mili-

tary attack; an intensive campaign; dynamic ability; the transmission of power to machinery.

**driver** *n* one who or that which drives; a chauffeur; (*golf*) a wooden club used from the tee.

**driveway** *n* a road for vehicles, often on private property.

**drizzle** *n* fine light rain.—*also vi.*—**drizzly** *adj*.

**droll** *adj* oddly amusing; whimsical. —**drolly** *adv*.

**dromedary** *n* a one-humped camel.

**drone** *n* a male honey-bee; a lazy person; a deep humming sound; a monotonous speaker or speech; an aircraft piloted by remote control. • *vi* to make a monotonous humming sound; to speak in a monotonous manner.

**drool** *vi* to slaver, dribble; to show excessive enthusiasm for.

**droop** *vi* to bend or hang down; to become weak or faint. • *n* the act or an instance of drooping.—**droopy** *adj*.

**drop** *n* a small amount of liquid in a roundish shape; something shaped like this; a tiny quantity; a sudden fall; the distance down. • *vb* (*pt* **dropped**) *vi* to fall in drops; to fall suddenly; to go lower, to sink; to come (in); (*with* **in**) to visit (with) informally; (*with* **out**) to abandon or reject (a course, society, etc). • *vt* to let fall, to cause to fall; to lower or cause to descend; to set down from a vehicle; to mention casually; to cause (the voice) to be less loud; to give up (as an idea).—**dropper** *n*.

**dropout** *n* a student who abandons a course of study; a person who rejects normal society.—*also vi.*

**droppings** *npl* animal dung.

**dross** *n* a surface scum on molten metal; rubbish, waste matter.

**drought** *n* a long period of dry weather.

**drove**[1] *see* **drive**.

**drove**[2] *n* a group of animals driven in a herd or flock, etc; a large moving crowd of people.

**drown** *vti* to die or kill by suffocation in water, etc. • *vt* to flood; to drench; to become immersed in some activity; to blot out (a sound) with a louder noise; to remove (sorrow, etc) with drink.

**drowse** *vi* to be nearly asleep.

**drowsy** *adj* (**drowsier, drowsiest**) sleepy.—**drowsily** *adv*.—**drowsiness** *n*.

**drudge** *vi* to do boring or very menial work.—*also n*.—**drudgery** *n*.

**drug** *n* any substance used in medicine; a narcotic. • *vt* (*pt* **drugged**) to administer drugs to; to stupefy

**druggist** *n* a pharmacist.

**drugstore** *n* a retail store in the US selling medicines and other miscellaneous articles such as cosmetics, film, etc.

**drum** *n* a round percussion instrument, played by striking a membrane stretched across a hollow cylindrical frame; the sound of a drum; anything shaped like a drum, as a container for liquids. • *vb* (*pt* **drummed**) *vi* to play a drum; to beat or tap rhythmically. • *vt* (*with* **in**) to instil (knowledge) into a person by constant repetition; (*with* **up**) to summon as by drum.

**drummer** *n* a person who plays a drum.

**drunk**[1] *see* **drink**.

**drunk**[2] *adj* intoxicated with alcohol. • *n* a drunk person.

**drunkard** *n* an habitual drunk.

**drunken** *adj* intoxicated; caused by excessive drinking.—**drunkenly** *adv*.—**drunkenness** *n*.

**dry** *adj* (**drier, driest**) free from water or liquid; thirsty; marked by a matter-of-fact, ironic or terse manner of expression; uninteresting, wearisome; (*bread*) without butter, etc; (*wine*) not sweet; not selling alcohol. • *vti* to make or become dry.—**drily, dryly** *adv*.—**dryness** *n*.

**dry-clean** *vt* to clean with solvents as opposed to water.—**dry-cleaner** *n*.—**dry-cleaning** *n*.

**dryer** *n* a device for drying, as a tumble-drier; a clothes horse.—*also* **drier**.

**dry rot** *n* decay of timber caused by a fungus; any form of moral decay or corruption.

**dual** *adj* double; consisting of two.—**duality** *n*.

**dubious** *adj* doubtful (about, of); uncertain as to the result; untrustworthy. —**dubiously** *adv*.

**duchess** *n* the wife or widow of a duke; a woman having the same rank as a duke in her own right.

**duck**[1] *vt* to dip briefly in water; to lower the head suddenly, esp to avoid some object; to avoid, dodge. • *vi* to dip or dive; to move the head or body suddenly; to evade a duty, etc. • *n* a ducking movement.

**duck**[2] *n* a water bird related to geese and swans; the female of this bird; its flesh used as food.

**duct** *n* a channel or pipe for fluids, electric cable, etc; a tube in the body for fluids to pass through.

**dud** *n* (*sl*) anything worthless.—*also adj*.

**due** *adj* owed as a debt; immediately payable; fitting, appropriate; appointed or expected to do or arrive. • *adv* directly, exactly. • *n* something due or owed; (*pl*) fees.

**duel** *n* combat with weapons between two persons over a matter of honour, etc; conflict of any kind between two people, sides, ideas, etc. • *vi* (*pt* **duelled**) to fight in a duel.—**duellist** *n*.

**duet** *n* a musical composition for two performers.

**dug** *see* **dig**.

**duke** *n* the highest order of British nobility; the title of a ruler of a European duchy.—**dukedom** *n*.

**dull** *adj* not sharp or pointed; not bright or clear; stupid; boring; not active. • *vti* to make or become dull.—**dully** *adv*.—**dullness** *n*.

**duly** *adv* properly; suitably.

**dumb** *adj* not able to speak; silent; (*inf*) stupid.—**dumbly** *adv*.—**dumbness** *n*.

**dumbfound, dumfound** *vti* to astonish, surprise.

**dummy** *n* a figure of a person used to display clothes; (*sl*) a soother or pacifier for a baby; a stupid person; an imitation; (*bridge*) the exposed cards of the dealer's partner.

**dump** *vt* to drop or put down carelessly in a heap; to deposit as rubbish; to abandon or get rid of; to sell goods abroad at a price lower than the market price abroad. • *n* a place for refuse; a temporary store; (*inf*) a dirty, dilapidated place.

**dumpling** *n* a rounded piece of dough cooked by boiling or steaming; a short, fat person.

**dunce** *n* a person who is stupid or slow to learn.

**dune** *n* a hill of sand piled up by the wind.

**dung** *n* excrement; manure.

**dungarees** *npl* overalls or trousers made from a coarse cotton cloth.

**dungeon** *n* an underground cell for prisoners.

**dupe** *n* a person who is cheated. • *vt* to deceive; to trick.

**duplicate** *adj* in pairs, double; identical; copied exactly from an original. • *n* one of a pair of identical things; a copy. • *vt* to make double; to make an exact copy of; to repeat.—**duplication** *n*.

**durable** *adj* enduring, resisting wear, etc.—**durability** *n*.—**durably** *adv*.

**duration** *n* the time in which an event continues.

**duress** *n* compulsion by use of force or threat; unlawful constraint; imprisonment.

**during** *prep* throughout the duration of; at a point in the course of.

**dusk** *n* (the darker part of) twilight.

**dusky** *adj* (**duskier, duskiest**) having a dark colour.—**duskiness** *n*.

**dust** *n* fine particles of solid matter. • *vt* to free from dust; to sprinkle with flour, sugar, etc.

**dustbin** *n* a container for household refuse.

**dust jacket** *n* a paper cover for a book.

**dustman** *n* a person employed to empty dustbins.

**Dutch** *adj* pertaining to Holland, its people, or language. • *n* the Dutch language.

**duty** *n* an obligation that must be performed for moral or legal reasons; respect for one's elders or superiors; actions and responsibilities arising from one's business, occupation, etc; a tax on goods or imports, etc.

**duty-free** *adj* free from tax or duty.

**dwarf** *n* (*pl* **dwarfs**) a person, animal, plant of abnormally small size. • *vt* to stunt; to cause to appear small.

**dwell** *vi* (*pt* **dwelt** *or* **dwelled**) to live (in a place); (*with* **on**) to focus the attention on; to think, talk, or write at length about.—**dweller** *n*.

**dwelling** *n* the house, etc where one lives, habitation.

**dwindle** *vi* to shrink, diminish; to become feeble.

**dye** *vt* (*pr p* **dyeing**, *pt* **dyed**) to give a new colour to. • *n* a colouring substance, esp in solution; a colour or tint produced by dyeing.

**dynamic** *adj* relating to force that produces motion; (*person*) forceful, energetic.—**dynamically** *adv*.

**dynamics** *n* (*used as sing*) the branch

of science that deals with forces and their effect on the motion of bodies.

**dynamite** *n* a powerful explosive; a potentially dangerous situation; (*inf*) an energetic person or thing. • *vt* to blow up with dynamite.

**dynamo** *n* (*pl* **dynamos**) a device that generates electric current.

**dynasty** *n* a line of hereditary rulers or leaders of any powerful family or similar group —**dynastic** *adj*.

**dysentery** *n* painful inflammation of the large intestine with associated diarrhoea.

# E

**E.** *abbr* = east; eastern.

**each** *adj* every one of two or more.

**eager** *adj* enthusiastically desirous (of); keen (for); marked by impatient desire or interest.—**eagerly** *adv*.—**eagerness** *n*.

**eagle** *n* a bird of prey with keen eyes and powerful wings; (*golf*) a score of two strokes under par.

**ear**[1] *n* (the external part of) the organ of hearing; the sense or act of hearing; attention; something shaped like an ear.

**ear**[2] *n* the part of a cereal plant (eg corn, maize) that contains the seeds.

**earache** *n* a pain in the ear.

**eardrum** *n* the membrane within the ear that vibrates in response to sound waves.

**earl** *n* a member of the British nobility ranking between a marquis and a viscount.—**countess** *nf*.

**early** *adj* (**earlier**, **earliest**) before the expected or normal time; of or occurring in the first part of a period or series; of or occurring in the distant past or near future.—*also adv*.—**earliness** *n*.

**earmark** *vt* to set aside for a specific use; to put an identification mark on. • *n* a distinguishing mark.

**earn** *vt* to gain (money, etc) by work or service; to acquire; to deserve; to earn interest (on money invested, etc).

**earnest** *adj* sincere in attitude or intention.—**earnestly** *adv*.—**earnestness** *n*.

**earnings** *npl* wages or profits; something earned.

**earring** *n* an ornament worn on the ear lobe.

**earth** *n* the world that we inhabit; solid ground, as opposed to sea; soil; the burrow of a badger, fox, etc; a connection between an electric device or circuit with the earth; (*inf*) a large amount of money. • *vt* to cover with or bury in the earth; to connect an electrical circuit or device to earth.

**earthenware** *n* pottery, etc made from baked clay.

**earthquake** *n* a violent tremor of the earth's crust.

**earthy** *adj* (**earthier**, **earthiest**) of or resembling earth; crude.—**earthiness** *n*.

**earwig** *n* a small insect with a pincer-like appendage at the end of its body.

**ease** *n* freedom from pain, discomfort or disturbance; rest from effort or work; effortlessness; lack of inhibition or restraint, naturalness. • *vt* to relieve from pain, trouble, or anxiety; to relax, make less tight, release; to move carefully and gradually. • *vi* (*often with* **off**) to become less active, intense, or severe.

**easel** *n* a supporting frame, esp one used by artists to support their canvases while painting.

**easily** *adv* with ease; by far; probably.

**east** *n* the direction of the sunrise; the compass point opposite west; (*with cap and* **the**) the area of the world east of Europe. • *adj, adv* in, towards, or from the east.

**Easter** *n* the Christian festival observed on a Sunday in March or April in commemoration of the resurrection of Christ.

**easterly** *adj* situated towards or belonging to the east, coming from the east. • *n* a wind from the east.

**eastern** *adj* of or in the east.

**eastward** *adj* towards the east.—**eastwards** *adv*.

**easy** *adj* (**easier, easiest**) free from pain, trouble, anxiety; not difficult or requiring much effort; (*manner*) relaxed; lenient; compliant; unhurried; (*inf*) open to all alternatives. • *adv* with ease.—**easiness** *n*.

**easy chair** *n* a comfortable chair.

**easygoing** *adj* placid, tolerant, relaxed.

**eat** *vt* (*pt* **ate**, *pp* **eaten**) to take into the mouth, chew and swallow as food; to have a meal; to consume, to destroy bit by bit; (*also with* **into**) to corrode; (*inf*) to bother, cause anxiety to; (*pl: inf*) food.—**eater** *n*.

**eatable** *adj* suitable for eating; fit to be eaten. • *n* (*pl*) food.

**eaves** *npl* the overhanging edge of a roof.

**eavesdrop** *vi* (*pt* **eavesdropped**) to listen secretly to a private conversation.—**eavesdropper** *n*.

**ebb** *n* the flow of the tide out to sea; a decline. • *vi* (*tide water*) to flow back; to become lower, to decline.

**ebony** *n* a hard heavy wood. • *adj* black as ebony.

**ebullient** *adj* exuberant, enthusiastic; boiling.—**ebullience, ebulliency** *n*.—**ebulliently** *adv*.

**EC** *abbr* = European Community; East Central.

**eccentric** *adj* deviating from a usual pattern; unconventional in manner or appearance, odd; (*circles*) not concentric; off centre. • *n* an eccentric person.—**eccentrically** *adv*.—**eccentricity** *n*.

**ecclesiastic**[1] *n* a member of the clergy.

**ecclesiastic**[2], **ecclesiastical** *adj* of or relating to the Christian Church or clergy.

**echo** *n* (*pl* **echoes**) a repetition of sound caused by the reflection of sound waves; imitation; the reflection of a radar signal by an object. • *vb* (*pr p* **echoing**, *pt* **echoed**) *vi* to resound; to produce an echo. • *vt* to repeat; to imitate; to send back (a sound) by an echo.

**eclipse** *n* the obscuring of the light of the sun or moon by the intervention of the other; a decline into obscurity, as from overshadowing by others. • *vt* to cause an eclipse of; to overshadow, darken; to surpass.

**ecology** *n* (the study of) the relationships between living things and their environments.—**ecological** *adj*.—**ecologist** *n*.

**economic** *adj* pertaining to economics or the economy; (*business, etc*) capable of producing a profit.

**economical** *adj* thrifty.—**economically** *adv*.

**economics** *n* (*used as sing*) the social science concerned with the production, consumption and distribution of goods and services; (*as pl*) financial aspects.—**economist** *n*.

**economize** *vti* to spend money carefully; to save; to use prudently.—**economization** *n*.

**economy** *n* careful use of money and resources to minimize waste; an instance of this; the management of the finances and resources, etc of a business, industry or organization; the economic system of a country.

**ecstasy** *n* intense joy; (*sl*) a synthetic amphetamine-based drug that reduces social and sexual inhibitions. —**ecstatic** *adj*.—**ecstatically** *adv*.

**ecumenical** *adj* of the whole Christian Church; seeking Christian unity worldwide.—**ecumenicalism** *n*.

**eczema** *n* inflammation of the skin causing itching and the formation of scaly red patches.—**eczematous** *adj*.

**eddy** *n* a swiftly revolving current of air, water, fog, etc. • *vi* to move round and round.

**edge** *n* the border, brink, verge, margin; the sharp cutting side of a blade; sharpness, keenness; force, effectiveness. • *vt* to supply an edge or border to; to move gradually.

**edgeways, edgewise** *adv* with the edge forwards; sideways.

**edgy** *adj* (**edgier, edgiest**) irritable.—**edginess** *n*.

**edible** *adj* fit or safe to eat.

**edict** *n* a decree.

**edifice** *n* a substantial building; any large or complex organization or institution.

**edit** *vt* to prepare (text) for publication; to be in charge of a publication; (*cinema*) to prepare a final version of a film by selection and arrangement of sequences.

**edition** *n* a whole number of copies of a book, etc printed at a time; the form of a particular publication.

**editor** *n* a person in charge of a newspaper or other publication; a person who edits written material for publication; one who prepares the final version of a film; a person in overall charge of the form and content of a radio or television programme.

**editorial** *adj* of or produced by an editor. • *n* an article expressing the opinions of the editor or publishers of a newspaper or magazine.—**editorially** *adv*.

**educate** *vt* to train the mind, to teach; to provide schooling for.—**educator** *n*.

**education** *n* the process of learning and training; instruction as imparted in schools, colleges and universities; a course or type of instruction; the theory and practice of teaching,—**educational** *adj*.—**educationally** *adv*.

**EEC** *abbr* = (*formerly*) European Economic Community.

**eel** *n* a snake-like fish.

**eerie** *adj* (**eerier, eeriest**) causing fear; weird.—**eerily** *adv*.—**eeriness** *n*.

**effect** *n* the result of a cause or action by some agent; the power to produce some result; the fundamental meaning; an impression on the senses; an operative condition; (*pl*) personal belongings; (*pl: theatre, cinema*) sounds, lighting, etc to accompany a production. • *vt* to bring about, to accomplish.—**effectible** *adj*.

**effective** *adj* producing a specified effect; forceful, striking in impression; actual, real; operative.—**effectively** *adv*.—**effectiveness** *n*.

**effeminate** *adj* (*man*) displaying what are regarded as feminine qualities.—**effeminately** *adv*.—**effeminacy** *n*.

**efficacious** *adj* achieving the desired result.—**efficacy** *n*.

**efficient** *adj* achieving results without waste of time or effort; competent.—**efficiently** *adv*.—**efficiency** *n*.

**effigy** *n* a sculpture or portrait; a crude figure of a person, esp for exposure to public contempt and ridicule.

**effort** *n* exertion; an attempt, try; a product of great exertion.

**effortless** *adj* done with little effort, or seemingly so.—**effortlessly** *adv*.—**effortlessness** *n*.

**effrontery** *n* impudent boldness, insolence.

**e.g., eg, eg.** *abbr* = for example (Latin *exempli gratia*).

**egalitarian** *adj* upholding the principle of equal rights for all.—*also n*.—**egalitarianism** *n*.

**egg**[1] *n* the oval hard-shelled reproductive cell laid by birds, reptiles and fish; the egg of the domestic poultry used as food; ovum.—**eggy** adj.

**egg**[2] vt (with **on**) to incite (someone to do something).

**eggplant** n a plant producing a smooth, dark-purple fruit; this fruit used as a vegetable, aubergine.

**eggshell** n the hard outer covering of an egg. • adj fragile; (paint) having a slight sheen.

**ego** n the self; self-image, conceit.

**eiderdown** n the down of the eider duck used for stuffing quilts, etc; a thick quilt with a soft filling.

**eight** n, adj one more than seven; the symbol for this (8, VIII, viii); (the crew of) an eight-oared rowing boat.

**eighteen** n, adj one more than seventeen; the symbol for this (18, XVIII, xviii).—**eighteenth** adj.

**eighth** adj, n one after seventh; one of eight equal parts.

**eighty** n eight times ten; the symbol for this (80, LXXX, lxxx); (pl) the numbers from 80 to 89.—**eightieth** adj, n.

**either** adj, n the one or the other of two; each of two. • conj correlative to or.

**eject** vt to turn out, to expel by force. • vi to escape from an aircraft or spacecraft using an ejector seat.—**ejection** n.—**ejector** n.

**ejector seat** n an escape seat, esp in combat aircraft, that can be ejected with its occupant in an emergency by means of explosive bolts.

**eke** vt (with **out**) to supplement; to use (a supply) frugally; to make (a living) with difficulty.

**elaborate** adj highly detailed; planned with care and exactness. • vt to work out, explain in detail.—**elaborately** adv.—**elaboration** n.

**elapse** vi (time) to pass by.

**elastic** adj returning to the original size and shape if stretched or squeezed; springy; adaptable. • n fabric, tape, etc incorporating elastic thread.—**elastically** adv.—**elasticity** n.

**elbow** n the joint between the forearm and upper arm; the part of a piece of clothing covering this; any sharp turn or bend, as in a pipe. • vt to shove away rudely with the elbow; to jostle.

**elder**[1] n a tree or shrub with flat clusters of white or pink flowers.

**elder**[2] n an older person; an office bearer in some churches.

**elderly** adj quite old.

**eldest** n oldest, first born.

**elect** vti to choose by voting; to make a selection (of); to make a decision on. • adj chosen for an office but not installed.

**election** n the public choice of a person for office, esp a politician.

**elector** n a person who has a vote at an election.

**electoral** adj of elections or electors.

**electorate** n the whole body of qualified electors.

**electric** adj of, producing or worked by electricity; exciting, thrilling. • npl electric fittings.

**electrical** adj of or relating to electricity.—**electrically** adv.

**electric blanket** n a blanket heated by an internal electric element.

**electrician** n a person who installs and repairs electrical devices.

**electricity** n a form of energy comprising certain charged particles; an electric current.

**electrify** vt to charge with electricity; to modify or equip for the use of electric power; to astonish or excite.—**electrification** n.

**electrode** n a conductor through which an electric current enters or leaves a gas discharge tube, etc.

**electromagnetic** adj having electric

and magnetic properties.—**electro-magnetism** n.

**electron** n a negatively charged elementary particle that forms the part of the atom outside the nucleus.

**electronic** adj of or worked by streams of electrons flowing through devices, vacuum or gas; of or concerned with electrons or electronics. —**electronically** adv.

**electronics** n (used as sing) the study, development and application of electronic devices; (as pl) electronic circuits.

**elegant** adj graceful; refined; dignified, tasteful in manner and appearance.—**elegantly** adv.—**elegance** n.

**element** n a constituent part; any of the 105 known substances composed of atoms with the same number of protons in their nuclei; a favourable environment for a plant or animal; a wire that produces heat in an electric cooker, kettle, etc; any of the four substances (earth, air, fire, water) that in ancient and medieval thought were believed to constitute the universe; (pl) atmospheric conditions (wind, rain, etc); (pl) the basic principles, rudiments.

**elementary** adj concerned with the basic principles of a subject.

**elephant** n a large heavy mammal with a long trunk, thick skin, and ivory tusks.

**elevate** vt to lift up; to raise in rank; to improve in intellectual or moral stature.

**elevation** n a raised place; the height above the earth's surface or above sea level; the angle to which a gun is aimed above the horizon; a drawing that shows the front, rear, or side view of something.

**elevator** n a cage or platform for moving something from one level to another; a moveable surface on the tail-plane of an aircraft to produce motion up and down; a lift; a building for storing grain.

**eleven** adj, n one more than ten; the symbol for this (11, XI, xi); (cricket, football, etc) a team of eleven players. —**eleventh** adj, n.

**elevenses** npl (inf) a light snack taken around mid-morning.

**elf** n (pl **elves**) a mischievous fairy. — **elfin** adj.—**elfish** adj.

**elicit** vt to draw out (information, etc).

**eligible** adj suitable to be chosen, legally qualified; desirable, esp as a marriage partner.—**eligibility** n.

**eliminate** vt to expel, get rid of; to eradicate completely; (sl) to kill; to exclude (eg a competitor) from a competition, usu by defeat.—**elimination** n.—**eliminator** n.

**elite, élite** n a superior group; (typewriting) a letter size having twelve characters to the inch.

**ellipse** n (geom) a closed plane figure formed by the plane section of a right-angled cone; a flattened circle.

**elm** n a tall deciduous shade tree with spreading branches and broad top; its hard heavy wood.

**elocution** n skill in public speaking.—**elocutionary** adj.—**elocutionist** n.

**elongate** vti to make or become longer.—**elongation** n.

**elope** vi to run away secretly with a lover, esp to get married.

**eloquence** n skill in the use of words; speaking with fluency, power or persuasiveness.

**eloquent** adj (speaking, writing, etc) fluent and powerful.

**else** adv besides; otherwise.

**elucidate** vt to make clear, to explain. —**elucidation** n.—**elucidatory** adv.

**elude** vt to avoid stealthily; to escape the understanding or memory of a person.

**elusive** adj escaping; baffling; solitary, difficult to contact.

**emanate** *vi* to issue from a source.—
**emanation** *n*.

**emancipate** *vt* to liberate, esp from
bondage or slavery.—**emancipation**
*n*.—**emancipator** *n*.

**embalm** *vt* to preserve (a dead body)
with drugs, chemicals, etc.—**em-
balment** *n*.

**embankment** *n* an earth or stone
mound made to hold back water or
to carry a roadway.

**embargo** *n* (*pl* **embargoes**) an order of
a government forbidding ships to
enter or leave its ports; any ban or
restriction on commerce by law; a
prohibition, ban. • *vt* to lay an embargo on; to requisition.

**embark** *vti* to put or go on board a ship
or aircraft to begin a journey; to
make a start in any activity or enterprise.—**embarkation** *n*.

**embarrass** *vt* to make (a person) feel
confused, uncomfortable or discon-
certed.—**embarrassment** *n*.

**embassy** *n* a person or group sent
abroad as ambassadors; the official
residence of an ambassador.

**embed** *vt* (*pt* **embedded**) to fix firmly
in surrounding matter.

**embellish** *vt* to decorate, to adorn.—
**embellishment** *n*.

**ember** *n* a piece of glowing coal or
wood in fire; (*pl*) the smouldering
remains of a fire.

**embezzle** *vt* to steal (money, securities, etc entrusted to one's care).—
**embezzlement** *n*.—**embezzler** *n*.

**embitter** *vt* to cause to feel bitter.—
**embitterment** *n*.

**emblem** *n* a symbol; a figure adopted
and used as an identifying mark.

**embody** *vt* to express in definite form;
to incorporate in a single book, law,
system, etc.—**embodiment** *n*.

**emboss** *vt* to ornament with a raised
design.—**embossment** *n*.

**embrace** *vt* to take and hold tightly in
the arms as a sign of affection; to
accept eagerly (eg an opportunity);
to adopt (eg a religious faith); to include.—*also n*.

**embroider** *vt* to ornament with decorative stitches; to embellish (eg a
story).

**embroidery** *n* decorative needlework;
elaboration or exaggeration.

**embryo** *n* (*pl* **embryos**) an animal during the period of its growth from a
fertilized egg up to the third month;
a human product of conception up
to about the second month of
growth; a thing in a rudimentary
state.

**emerald** *n* a rich green gemstone; its
colour.

**emerge** *vi* to appear up out of, to come
into view; to be revealed as the result of investigation.—**emergence**
*n*.—**emergent** *adj*.

**emergency** *n* an unforeseen situation
demanding immediate action; a serious medical condition requiring
instant treatment.

**emery** *n* a hard granular mineral used
for grinding and polishing; a hard
abrasive powder.

**emery board** *n* a nailfile made from
cardboard covered with crushed
emery.

**emery paper** *n* a stiff paper covered
with powdered emery.

**emetic** *n* a medicine that induces vomiting.—*also adj*.

**emigrant** *n* a person who emigrates.

**emigrate** *vi* to leave one's country for
residence in another.—**emigration** *n*.

**eminence, eminency** *n* high rank or
position; a person of high rank or
attainments; (*with cap: RC Church*)
the title for a cardinal; a raised piece
of ground, a high place.

**eminent** *adj* famous; conspicuous; distinguished.—**eminently** *adv*.

**emit** *vt* (*pt* **emitted**) to send out (light,

heat, etc); to put into circulation; to express, to utter.—**emission** n.—**emissive** adj.—**emitter** n.

**emotion** n a strong feeling of any kind.

**emotional** adj of emotion; inclined to express excessive emotion.—**emotionally** adv.—**emotionalism** n.

**emotive** adj characterized by or arousing emotion.

**emperor** n the sovereign ruler over an empire.—**empress** nf.

**emphasis** n (pl **emphases**) particular stress or prominence given to something; force or vigour of expression; clarity of form or outline.

**emphasize** vt to place stress on.

**emphatic** adj spoken, done or marked with emphasis; forceful, decisive.—**emphatically** adv.

**empire** n a large state or group of states under a single sovereign, usu an emperor; nations governed by a single sovereign state; a large and complex business organization.

**empirical** adj based on observation, experiment or experience only, not theoretical.—**empirically** adv.

**employ** vt to give work and pay to; to make use of.

**employee** n a person who is hired by another person for wages.

**employer** n a person, business, etc that employs people.

**employment** n an employing; a being employed; occupation or profession.

**empower** vt to give official authority to.

**empress** n the female ruler of an empire; the wife or widow of an emperor.

**empty** adj (**emptier, emptiest**) containing nothing; not occupied; lacking reality, substance, or value; hungry. • vt to make empty; to transfer or discharge (the contents of something) by emptying. • vi to become empty; to discharge contents. • n

empty containers or bottles.—**emptily** adv.—**emptiness** n.

**emulate** vt to try to equal or do better than; to imitate; to rival or compete.—**emulation** n.—**emulative** adj.—**emulator** n.

**emulsion** n a mixture of mutually insoluble liquids in which one is dispersed in droplets throughout the other; a light-sensitive substance on photographic paper or film.

**enable** vt to give the authority or means to do something; to make easy or possible.

**enamel** n a glasslike substance used to coat the surface of metal or pottery; the hard outer layer of a tooth; a usu glossy paint that forms a hard coat. • vt (pt **enamelled**) to cover or decorate with enamel.

**enamour, enamor** (US) vt to inspire with love.—**enamoured** adj.

**enchant** vt to bewitch, to delight.—**enchanter** n.—**enchantment** n.—**enchantress** nf.

**encircle** vt to surround; to move or pass completely round.—**encirclement** n.

**enclose** vt to shut up or in; to put in a wrapper or parcel, usu together with a letter.

**enclosure** n an enclosing; an enclosed area; something enclosed with a letter in a parcel, etc.

**encore** interj once more! • n a call for the repetition of a performance.—also vt.

**encounter** vt to meet, esp unexpectedly; to fight, engage in battle with; to be faced with (problems, etc). • n a meeting; a conflict, battle.

**encourage** vt to inspire with confidence or hope; to urge, incite; to promote the development of.—**encouragement** n.

**encroach** vi to infringe another's territory, rights, etc; to advance beyond an established limit.—**encroachment** n.

**encyclopaedia, encyclopedia** n a book or books containing information on all branches of knowledge, or treating comprehensively a particular branch.

**end** n the last part; the place where a thing stops; purpose; result, outcome. • vt to bring to an end; to destroy. • vi to come to an end; to result (in). • adj final; ultimate.

**endanger** vt to put in danger.

**endear** vt to make loved or more loved.—**endearing** adj.

**endeavour, endeavor** (US) vi to try or attempt (to). • n an attempt.

**ending** n reaching or coming to an end; the final part.

**endless** adj unending; uninterrupted; extremely numerous.

**endorse** vt to write one's name, comment, etc, on the back of to approve; to record an offence on a driving licence; to support.—**endorsement** n.

**endow** vt to give money or property to provide an income for; to provide with a special power or attribute.

**endurance** n the ability to withstand pain, hardship, strain, etc.

**endure** vt to undergo, tolerate (hardship, etc) esp with patience. • vi to continue in existence, to last out.—**endurable** adj.—**endurably** adv.

**enemy** n a person who hates or dislikes and wishes to harm another; a military opponent; something harmful or deadly.

**energetic** adj lively, active; done with energy.—**energetically** adv.

**energy** n capacity of acting or being active; vigour, power; (physics) capacity to do work.

**enforce** vt to compel obedience by threat; to execute with vigour.—**enforceable** adj.—**enforcement** n.

**engage** vt to pledge as security; to promise to marry; to keep busy; to hire; to attract and hold, esp attention or sympathy; to cause to participate; to bring or enter into conflict; to begin or take part in a venture; to connect or interlock, to mesh.

**engaged** adj entered into a promise to marry; reserved, occupied or busy.

**engagement** n the act or state of being engaged; a pledge; an appointment agreed with another person; employment; a battle.

**engaging** adj pleasing, attractive.

**engender** vt to bring into existence.

**engine** n a machine by which physical power is applied to produce a physical effect; a locomotive; (formerly) a mechanical device, such as a large catapult, used in war.

**engineer** n a person trained in engineering; a person who operates an engine, etc; a member of a military group devoted to engineering work; a designer or builder of engines. • vt to contrive, plan, esp deviously.

**engineering** n the art or practice of constructing and using machinery; the art and science by which natural forces and materials are utilized in structures or machines.

**English** adj of, relating to, or characteristic of, England, the English people, or the English language. • n the language of the British people, the US and other areas; English language and literature as a subject of study.

**engrained** see **ingrained**.

**engrave** vt to produce by cutting or carving a surface; to cut to produce a representation that may be printed from; to lodge deeply (in the mind, etc).—**engraver** n.

**engraving** n a print made from an engraved surface.

**engulf** vt to flow over and enclose; to overwhelm.

**enhance** *vt* to increase in value, importance, attractiveness, etc; to heighten.—**enhancement** *n*.

**enigma** *n* someone or something that is puzzling or mysterious.—**enigmatic** *adj*.—**enigmatically** *adv*.

**enjoy** *vt* to get pleasure from, take joy in; to use or have the advantage of; to experience.—**enjoyment** *n*.

**enjoyable** *adj* giving enjoyment.—**enjoyably** *adv*.

**enlarge** *vti* to make or grow larger; to reproduce (a photograph) in a larger form; to speak or write at length (on).

**enlargement** *n* an act, instance, or state of enlarging; a photograph, etc that has been enlarged.

**enlighten** *vt* to instruct; to inform.—**enlightenment** *n*.

**enlightened** *adj* well-informed, tolerant, unprejudiced.

**enlist** *vt* to engage for service in the armed forces; to secure the aid or support of. • *vi* to register oneself for the armed services.—**enlistment** *n*.

**enmity** *n* hostility, esp mutual hatred.

**enormity** *n* great wickedness; a serious crime; huge size, magnitude.

**enormous** *adj* extremely large.—**enormously** *adv*.

**enough** *adj* adequate, sufficient. • *adv* so as to be sufficient; very; quite. • *n* a sufficiency. • *interj* stop!

**enquire** *see* **inquire**.

**enrich** *vt* to make rich or richer; to ornament; to improve in quality by adding to.—**enrichment** *n*.

**enrol, enroll** (*US*) *vti* (*pt* **enrolled**) to enter or register on a roll or list; to become a member of a society, club, etc; to admit as a member.—**enrolment** *n*.

**ensign** *n* a flag; the lowest commissioned officer in the US Navy.

**enslave** *vt* to make into a slave; to subjugate.—**enslavement** *n*.

**ensue** *vi* to occur as a consequence or in time.

**ensure** *vt* to make certain, sure or safe.

**entail** *vt* to involve as a result; to restrict the inheritance of property. • *n* the act of entailing or the estate entailed.

**enter** *vi* to go or come in or into; to come on stage; to begin, start; (*with* **for**) to register as an entrant. • *vt* to come or go into; to pierce, penetrate; (*organization*) to join; to insert; (*proposal, etc*) to submit; to record (an item) in a diary, etc.

**enterprise** *n* a difficult or challenging undertaking; a business project; readiness to engage in new ventures.

**entertain** *vt* to show hospitality to; to amuse, please (a person or audience); to have in mind; to consider.

**entertainer** *n* a person who entertains in public, esp professionally.

**entertainment** *n* entertaining; amusement; an act or show intended to amuse and interest.

**enthusiasm** *n* intense interest or liking; something that arouses keen interest.

**enthusiast** *n* a person filled with enthusiasm for something.

**enthusiastic** *adj* filled with enthusiasm.—**enthusiastically** *adv*.

**entice** *vt* to attract by offering some pleasure or reward.—**enticement** *n*.

**entire** *adj* whole; complete.—**entirely** *adv*.

**entirety** *n* completeness; the total.

**entitle** *vt* to give a title to; to give a right (to).—**entitlement** *n*.

**entrance**[1] *n* the act of entering; the power or authority to enter; a means of entering; an admission fee.

**entrance**[2] *vt* to put into a trance; to fill with great delight.—**entrancement** *n*.—**entrancing** *adj*.

**entrant** *n* a person who enters (eg a competition, profession).

**entreat** *vt* to request earnestly; to implore, beg.—**entreaty** *n*.

**entrench** *vt* to dig a trench as a defensive perimeter; to establish (oneself) in a strong defensive position.—**entrenchment** *n*.

**entrust** *vt* (*with* **with**) to confer as a responsibility, duty, etc; (*with* **to**) to place something in another's care.

**entry** *n* the act of entering; a place of entrance; an item recorded in a diary, journal, etc; a person or thing taking part in a contest.

**entwine** *vt* to twine together or around.

**enumerate** *vt* to count; to list.—**enumeration** *n*.—**enumerator** *n*.

**enunciate** *vt* to state definitely; to pronounce clearly.—**enunciation** *n*.

**envelop** *vt* (*pt* **enveloped**) to enclose completely (as if) with a covering.—**envelopment** *n*.

**envelope** *n* something used to wrap or cover, esp a gummed paper container for a letter.

**envious** *adj* filled with envy.—**enviously** *adv*.

**environment** *n* external conditions and surroundings, esp those that affect the quality of life of plants, animals and human beings.—**environmental** *adj*.

**envisage** *vt* to have a mental picture of.

**envoy** *n* a diplomatic agent; a representative.

**envy** *n* resentment or discontent at another's achievements, possessions, etc; an object of envy. • *vt* to feel envy of.

**enzyme** *n* a complex protein, produced by living cells, that induces or speeds chemical reactions in plants and animals.

**ephemeral** *adj* existing only for a very short time.

**epic** *n* a long poem narrating the deeds of a hero; any literary work, film, etc in the same style. • *adj* relating to or resembling an epic.

**epidemic** *adj, n* (a disease) attacking many people at the same time in a community or region.

**epilepsy** *n* a disorder of the nervous system marked typically by convulsive attacks and loss of consciousness.—**epileptic** *adj, n*.

**epilogue** *n* the concluding section of a book or other literary work; a short speech addressed by an actor to the audience at the end of a play.

**epiphany** *n* a moment of sudden revelation or insight; (*with cap*) a festival of the Christian Church in commemoration of the coming of the Magi to Christ.

**episode** *n* a piece of action in a dramatic or literary work; an incident in a sequence of events.

**epistle** *n* (*formal*) a letter; (*with cap*) a letter written by one of Christ's Apostles.

**epitaph** *n* an inscription in memory of a dead person, usu on a tombstone.

**epitome** *n* a typical example; a paradigm; personification; a condensed account of a written work.

**epitomize** *vt* to be or make an epitome of.

**epoch** *n* a date in time used as a point of reference; an age in history associated with certain characteristics; a unit of geological time.—**epochal** *adj*.

**equable** *adj* level, uniform; (*climate*) free from extremes of hot and cold; even-tempered.—**equably** *adv*.

**equal** *adj* the same in amount, size, number, or value; impartial; regarding or affecting all objects in the same way; capable of meeting a task or situation. • *n* a person that is equal. • *vt* (*pt* **equalled**) to be equal to, esp to be identical in value; to make or do something equal to.—**equality** n.—**equally** adv.

**equalize** vti to make or become equal; (*games*) to even the score.—**equalization** n.

**equanimity** n evenness of temper; composure.

**equate** vt to make, treat, or regard as comparable. • vi to correspond as equal.

**equation** n an act of equalling; the state of being equal; (*logic, math*) a usu formal statement of equivalence with the relations denoted by the sign =; (*chem*) an expression representing a reaction in symbols.

**equator** n an imaginary circle passing round the globe, equidistant from the poles.—**equatorial** n.

**equilibrium** n (*pl* **equilibriums, equilibria**) a state of balance of weight, power, force, etc.

**equinox** n the two times of the year when night and day are equal in length (around 21 March and 23 September).—**equinoctial** adj.

**equip** vt (*pt* **equipped**) to provide with all the necessary tools or supplies.

**equipment** n the tools, supplies and other items needed for a particular task, expedition, etc.

**equitable** adj just and fair; (*law*) pertaining to equity as opposed to common or statute law.—**equitably** adv.

**equity** n fairness; (*law*) a legal system based on natural justice developed into a body of rules supplementing the common law; (*pl*) ordinary shares in a company.

**equivalent** adj equal in amount, force, meaning, etc; virtually identical, esp in effect or function. • n an equivalent thing.

**equivocal** adj ambiguous; uncertain; questionable; arousing suspicion.—**equivocally** adv.

**era** n an historical period typified by some special feature; a chronological order or system of notation reckoned from a given date as a basis.

**eradicate** vt to obliterate.—**eradication** n.—**eradicator** n.

**erase** vt to rub out, obliterate; to remove a recording from magnetic tape; to remove data from a computer memory or storage medium.

**erect** adj upright; not leaning or lying down; (*sexual organs*) rigid and swollen with blood from sexual stimulation. • vt to construct, set up.—**erecter, erector** n.—**erectness** n.

**erection** n construction; something erected, as a building; swelling, esp of the penis, due to sexual excitement.

**ermine** n (*pl* **ermines, ermine**) the weasel in its winter coat; the white fur of the winter coat; a rank or office whose official robe is edged with ermine.

**erode** vt to eat or wear away gradually.—**erosion** n.—**erosive** adj.

**erotic** adj of sexual love; sexually stimulating.—**erotically** adv.

**eroticism** n erotic nature; sexually arousing themes in literature and art; sexual desire.

**err** vi to be or do wrong.

**errand** n a short journey to perform some task, usu on behalf of another; the purpose of this journey.

**erratic** adj capricious; irregular; eccentric, odd.—**erratically** adv.

**erroneous** adj incorrect; mistaken.—**erroneously** adv.

**error** n a mistake, an inaccuracy; a mistaken belief or action.

**erudite** adj scholarly, having great knowledge.—**erudition** n.

**erupt** vi to burst forth; to break out into a rash; (*volcano*) to explode, ejecting ash and lava into the air.—**eruption** n.—**eruptive** adj.

**escalate** *vi* to increase rapidly in magnitude or intensity.—**escalation** *n*.

**escalator** *n* a motorized set of stairs arranged to ascend or descend continuously.

**escapade** *n* a wild or mischievous adventure.

**escape** *vt* to free oneself from confinement, etc; to avoid, remain unnoticed; to be forgotten. • *vi* to achieve freedom; (*gas, liquid*) to leak. • *n* an act or instance of escaping; a means of escape; a leakage of liquid or gas; a temporary respite from reality.—**escaper** *n*.

**escort** *n* a person, group, ship, aircraft, etc accompanying a person or thing to give protection, etc. • *vt* to attend as escort.

**espionage** *n* spying or the use of spies to obtain information.

**esquire** *n* a general courtesy title used instead of Mr in addressing letters.

**essay** *n* a short prose work usu dealing with a subject from a limited or personal point of view; an attempt. • *vt* to try, to attempt.

**essence** *n* that which makes a thing what it is; a substance extracted from another substance and having the special qualities of the original; a perfume.

**essential** *adj* of or containing the essence of something; indispensable, of the greatest importance. • *n* (*often pl*) indispensable elements or qualities.—**essentially** *adv*.

**establish** *vt* to set up (eg a business) permanently; to settle (a person) in a place or position; to get generally accepted; to place beyond dispute, prove as a fact.

**establishment** *n* the act of establishing; a commercial organization or other large institution; the staff and resources of an organization; a household; (*with cap*) those in

power who work to preserve the status quo.

**estate** *n* landed property; a large area of residential or industrial development; a person's total possessions, esp at their death; a social or political class.

**estate agent** *n* a person whose business is selling and leasing property.

**estate car** *n* a car with extra carrying space reached through a rear door.

**esteem** *vt* to value or regard highly; to consider or think. • *n* high regard, a favourable opinion.

**estimate** *vt* to judge the value, amount, significance of; to calculate approximately. • *n* an approximate calculation; a judgment or opinion; a preliminary calculation of the cost of a particular job.

**estimation** *n* estimating; an opinion, judgment; esteem.

**estuary** *n* an arm of the sea at the mouth of a river.

**etching** *n* the art or process of producing designs on and printing from etched plates; an impression made from an etched plate.

**eternal** *adj* continuing forever without beginning or end, everlasting; unchangeable; (*inf*) seemingly endless. —**eternally** *adv*.

**eternity** *n* infinite time; the timelessness thought to constitute life after death; (*inf*) a very long time.

**ether** *n* (*chem*) a light flammable liquid used as an anaesthetic or solvent; the upper regions of space.

**ethic** *n* a moral principle or set of principles. • *adj* ethical.

**ethical** *adj* of or pertaining to ethics; conforming to the principles of proper conduct, as established by society, a profession, etc; (*med*) legally available only on prescription.—**ethically** *adv*.

**ethics** *n* (*used as sing*) the philosophical analysis of human morality and conduct; system of conduct or behaviour, moral principles.

**ethnic** *adj* of races or large groups of people classed according to common traits and customs.—**ethnically** *adv*.

**etiquette** *n* the form of conduct or behaviour prescribed by custom or authority to be observed in social, official or professional life.

**eulogy** *n* a speech or piece of writing in praise or celebration of someone or something.

**euphemism** *n* a mild or inoffensive word substituted for a more unpleasant or offensive term; the use of such words.—**euphemistic** *adj*.—**euphemistically** *adv*.

**euthanasia** *n* the act or practice of killing painlessly, esp to relieve incurable suffering.

**evacuate** *vti* to move (people, etc) from an area of danger to one of safety; to leave or make empty; to discharge wastes from the body.—**evacuation** *n*.

**evade** *vt* to manage to avoid, esp by dexterity or slyness.—**evadable, evadible** *adj*.—**evader** *n*.

**evaluate** *vt* to determine the value of; to assess.—**evaluation** *n*.—**evaluator** *n*.

**evangelist** *n* a person who preaches the gospel; one of the writers of the four Gospels.—**evangelistic** *adj*.

**evaporate** *vti* to change into a vapour; to remove water from; to give off moisture; to vanish; to disappear.—**evaporation** *n*.

**evasion** *n* the act of evading; a means of evading, esp an equivocal reply or excuse.—**evasive** *adj*.—**evasively** *adv*.—**evasiveness** *n*.

**eve** *n* the evening or the whole day, before a festival; the period immediately before an event; (*formerly*) evening.

**even** *adj* level, flat; smooth; regular, equal; balanced; exact; divisible by two. • *vti* to make or become even; (*with*

up) to balance (debts, etc). • *adv* exactly; precisely; fully; quite; at the very time; used as an intensive to emphasize the identity of something (*he looked content, even happy*), to indicate something unexpected (*she refused even to look at him*), or to stress the comparative degree (*she did even better*).—**evenly** *adv*.—**evenness** *n*.

**even-handed** *adj* impartial, fair.

**evening** *n* the latter part of the day and early part of the night.

**event** *n* something that happens; a social occasion; contingency; a contest in a sports programme.

**eventful** *adj* full of incidents; momentous

**eventual** *adj* happening at some future unspecified time; ultimate.—**eventually** *adv*.

**eventuality** *n* a possible occurrence.

**ever** *adv* always, at all times; at any time; in any case.

**evergreen** *adj* (*plants, trees*) having foliage that remains green all year.—*also n*.

**everlasting** *adj* enduring forever; (*plants*) having flowers that may be dried without loss of form or colour.—**everlastingly** *adv*.

**every** *adj* being one of the total.

**everybody, everyone** *pron* every person.

**everyday** *adj* happening daily; commonplace; worn or used on ordinary days.

**everything** *pron* all things, all; of the utmost importance.

**everywhere** *adv* in every place.

**evict** *vt* to expel from land or from a building by legal process; to expel.—**eviction** *n*.

**evidence** *n* an outward sign; proof, testimony, esp matter submitted in court to determine the truth of alleged facts. • *vt* to demonstrate clearly; to give proof or evidence for.

**evident** *adj* easy to see or understand.—**evidently** *adv*.

**evil** *adj* wicked; causing or threatening distress or harm. • *n* a sin; a source of harm or distress.—**evilly** *adv*.

**evoke** *vt* to call forth or up.—**evocation** *n*.—**evocative** *adj*.

**evolution** *n* a process of change in a particular direction; the process by which something attains its distinctive characteristics; a theory that existing types of plants and animals have developed from earlier forms.—**evolutionary** *adj*.

**evolve** *vi* to develop by or as if by evolution.—**evolvement** *n*.

**ewe** *n* a female sheep.

**ex**[1] *n* (*inf*) a former husband, wife, etc.

**ex**[2] *prep* out of, from.

**ex-** *prefix* out, forth; quite, entirely; formerly.

**exact** *adj* without error, absolutely accurate; detailed. • *vt* to compel by force, to extort; to require.—**exactness** *n*.

**exacting** *adj* greatly demanding; requiring close attention and precision.

**exactitude** *n* (the state of) being exact.

**exactly** *adv* in an exact manner; precisely. • *interj* quite so!

**exaggerate** *vt* to enlarge (a statement, etc) beyond what is really so or believable.—**exaggeration** *n*.

**exalt** *vt* to raise up, esp in rank, power, or dignity.—**exaltation** *n*.

**exam** *n* (*inf*) an examination.

**examination** *n* an examining, close scrutiny; a set of written or oral questions designed as a test of knowledge; the formal questioning of a witness on oath.

**examine** *vt* to look at closely and carefully, to investigate; to test, esp by questioning.—**examiner** *n*.

**example** *n* a representative sample; a model to be followed or avoided; a problem to be solved in order to show the application of some rule; a warning to others.

**exasperate** *vt* to annoy intensely.—**exasperation** *n*.

**excavate** *vt* to form a hole or tunnel by digging; to unearth; to expose to view (remains, etc) by digging away a covering.—**excavation** *n*.—**excavator** *n*.

**exceed** *vt* to be greater than or superior to; to go beyond the limit of.

**exceedingly** *adv* very, extremely.

**excellence** *n* that in which one excels; superior merit or quality; (*with cap*) a title of honour given to certain high officials (—*also* **Excellency**).

**excellent** *adj* very good, outstanding.—**excellently** *adv*.

**except** *vt* to exclude, to take or leave out. • *prep* not including; other than.

**exception** *n* the act of excepting; something excepted; an objection.

**exceptional** *adj* unusual, forming an exception; superior.

**excerpt** *n* an extract from a book, film, etc.

**excess** *n* the exceeding of proper established limits; the amount by which one thing or quantity exceeds another; (*pl*) overindulgence in eating or drinking; unacceptable conduct.

**excessive** *adj* greater than what is acceptable, too much.—**excessively** *adv*.

**exchange** *vt* to give and take (one thing in return for another); to give to and receive from another person. • *n* the exchanging of one thing for another; the thing exchanged; the conversion of money from one currency to another; the system of settling commercial debts between foreign governments; a place where things and services are exchanged, esp a marketplace for securities; a centre or device in which telephone lines are interconnected.—**exchangeable** *adj*.

**exchequer** *n* (*with cap*) the British governmental department in charge of finances; (*inf*) personal finances.

**excise**[1] *n* a tax on the manufacture, sale, or use of certain articles within a country.

**excise**[2] *vt* to remove by cutting out.— **excision** *n*.

**excitable** *adj* easily excited.—**excitability** *n*.

**excite** *vt* to arouse the feelings of, esp to generate feelings of pleasurable anticipation; to cause to experience strong emotion; to stir up, agitate; to rouse to activity; to stimulate a response, eg in a bodily organ.

**excited** *adj* experiencing or expressing excitement.—**excitedly** *adv*.

**excitement** *n* a feeling of strong, esp pleasurable, emotion; something that excites.

**exciting** *adj* causing excitement; stimulating.

**exclaim** *vti* to shout out or utter suddenly and with strong emotion.

**exclamation** *n* a sudden crying out; a word or utterance exclaimed.

**exclamation mark, exclamation point** *n* the punctuation mark (!) placed after an exclamation.

**exclude** *vt* to shut out, to keep out; to reject or omit; to eject.—**exclusion** *n*.

**exclusive** *adj* excluding all else; reserved for particular persons; snobbishly aloof; fashionable, high-class, expensive; unobtainable or unpublished elsewhere; sole, undivided. — **exclusively** *adv*.—**exclusiveness** *n*.—**exclusivity** *n*.

**excommunicate** *vt* to bar from association with a church; to exclude from fellowship.—**excommunication** *n*.

**excrement** *n* waste matter discharged from the bowels.—**excremental** *adj*.

**excruciating** *adj* intensely painful or distressful; (*inf*) very bad.

**excursion** *n* a pleasure trip; a short journey.

**excuse** *vt* to pardon; to forgive; to give a reason or apology for; to be a reason or explanation of; to let off.—*also n*.

**execute** *vt* to carry out, put into effect; to perform; to produce (eg a work of art); to make legally valid; to put to death by law.

**execution** *n* the act or process of executing; the carrying out or suffering of a death sentence; the style or technique of performing, eg music.

**executioner** *n* a person who executes a death sentence upon a condemned prisoner.

**executive** *n* a person or group concerned with administration or management of a business or organization; the branch of government with the power to put laws, etc into effect. • *adj* having the power to execute decisions, laws, decrees, etc.

**exemplary** *adj* deserving imitation; serving as a warning.

**exemplify** *vt* to illustrate by example; to be an instance or example of.— **exemplification** *n*.

**exempt** *adj* not liable, free from the obligations required of others.—*also vt*.—**exemption** *n*.

**exercise** *n* the use or application of a power or right; regular physical or mental exertion; something performed to develop or test a specific ability or skill; (*often pl*) manoeuvres for military training. • *vt* to use, exert, employ; to engage in regular physical activity; to train (troops) by drills and manoeuvres; to engage the attention of; to perplex.

**exert** *vt* to bring (eg strength, influence) into use.

**exhaust** *vt* to use up completely; to make empty; to use up, tire out; (*subject*) to deal with or develop completely. • *n* the escape of waste gas or steam from an engine; the device through which these escape. —**exhausted** *adj*.—**exhaustible** *adj*. —**exhausting** *adj*.

**exhaustion** *n* the act of exhausting or being exhausted; extreme weariness.

**exhaustive** *adj* comprehensive, thorough.—**exhaustively** *adv*.

**exhibit** *vt* to display, esp in public; to present to a court in legal form. • *n* an act or instance of exhibiting, something exhibited; something produced and identified in court for use as evidence.—**exhibitor** *n*.

**exhibition** *n* a showing, a display; a public show.

**exhilarate** *vt* to make very happy; to invigorate.—**exhilaration** *n*.

**exhort** *vt* to urge or advise strongly. — **exhortation** *n*.—**exhortative** *adj*. — **exhortatory** *adj*.

**exile** *n* prolonged absence from one's own country, either through choice or as a punishment; an exiled person.—*also vt*.

**exist** *vi* to have being; to just manage a living; to occur in a specific place under specific conditions.

**existence** *n* the state or fact of existing; continuance of life; everything that exists.

**exit** *n* a way out of an enclosed space; death; a departure from a stage. • *vi* to leave, withdraw; to go offstage.

**exonerate** *vt* to absolve from blame; to relieve from a responsibility, obligation.—**exoneration** *n*.

**exorcise** *vt* to expel an evil spirit (from a person or place) by ritual and prayer.—**exorcism** *n*.—**exorcist** *n*.

**exotic** *adj* foreign; strange; excitingly different or unusual.—**exotically** *adv*.

**expand** *vt* to increase in size, bulk, extent, importance; to describe in fuller detail. • *vi* to become larger; to become more genial and responsive.

**expanse** *n* a wide area of land, etc; the extent of a spread-out area.

**expansion** *n* the act of expanding or being expanded; something expanded; the amount by which something expands; the fuller development of a theme, etc.

**expatriate** *adj* living in another country; self-exiled or banished. • *n* an expatriate person. • *vti* to exile (oneself) or banish (another person).—**expatriation** *n*.

**expect** *vt* to anticipate; to regard as likely to arrive or happen; to consider necessary, reasonable or due; to think, suppose.

**expectant** *adj* expecting, hopeful; filled with anticipation; pregnant.—**expectantly** *adv*.—**expectancy** *n*.

**expectation** *n* the act or state of expecting; something that is expected to happen; (*pl*) prospects for the future, esp of inheritance.

**expediency, expedience** *n* fitness, suitability; an inclination towards expedient methods.

**expedient** *adj* suitable or desirable under the circumstances. • *n* a means to an end; a means devised or used for want of something better.—**expediently** *adv*.

**expedite** *vt* to carry out promptly; to facilitate.—**expediter, expeditor** *n*.

**expedition** *n* a journey to achieve some purpose, as exploration, etc; the party making this journey; speedy efficiency, promptness.

**expel** *vt* (*pt* **expelled**) to drive out, to eject; to banish.

**expend** *vt* to spend (money, time, energy, etc); to use up, consume.

**expenditure** *n* the act or process of

expending money, etc; the amount expended.

**expense** *n* a payment of money for something, expenditure; a cause of expenditure; (*pl*) money spent on some business activity; reimbursement for this.

**expense account** *n* an account of expenses to be repaid to an employee.

**expensive** *adj* causing or involving great expense; costly.—**expensively** *adv.*—**expensiveness** *n.*

**experience** *n* observation or practice resulting in or tending towards knowledge; knowledge gained by seeing and doing; a state of being affected from without (as by events); an affecting event. • *vt* to have experience of.

**experienced** *adj* wise or skilled through experience.

**experiment** *n* any test or trial to find out something; a controlled procedure carried out to discover, test, or demonstrate something. • *vi* to carry out experiments.—**experimentation** *n.*

**experimental** *adj* of, derived from, or proceeding by experiment; empirical; provisional.—**experimentalism** *n.*

**expert** *adj* thoroughly skilled; knowledgeable through training and experience. • *n* a person with special skills or training in any art or science.—**expertly** *adv.*

**expertise** *n* expert knowledge or skill.

**expire** *vti* to come to an end; to lapse or become void; to breathe out; to die.—**expiration** *n.*

**explain** *vt* to make plain or clear; to give a reason for, account for.

**explanation** *n* an act or process of explaining; something that explains, esp a statement.

**explanatory** *adj* serving as an explanation.

**explicit** *adj* clearly stated, not merely implied; outspoken, frank; graphically detailed.—**explicitly** *adv.*—**explicitness** *n.*

**explode** *vti* to burst or cause to blow up with a loud noise, as in the detonation of a bomb; (*emotions*) to burst out; (*population*) to increase rapidly; to expose (a theory, etc) as false.

**exploit** *n* a bold achievement. • *vt* to utilize, develop (raw materials, etc); to take unfair advantage of, esp for financial gain.—**exploitation** *n.*

**exploratory, explorative** *adj* for the purpose of exploring or investigating.

**explore** *vti* to examine or inquire into; to travel through (a country) for the purpose of discovery; to examine minutely.—**exploration** *n.*—**explorer** *n.*

**explosion** *n* an act or instance of exploding; a sudden loud noise caused by this; an outburst of emotion; a rapid increase or expansion.

**explosive** *adj* liable to or able to explode; liable or threatening to burst out with violence and noise. • *n* an explosive substance.—**explosively** *adv.*

**exponent** *n* a person who explains or interprets something; a person who champions, advocates, or exemplifies; (*math*) an index of the power to which an expression is raised.

**export** *vt* to send out (goods) of one country for sale in another. • *n* the act of exporting; the article exported.—**exportable** *adj.*—**exportation** *n.*—**exporter** *n.*

**expose** *vt* to deprive of protection or shelter; to subject to an influence (as light, weather); to display, reveal; to uncover or disclose.

**exposure** *n* an exposing or state of being exposed; time during which light reaches and acts on a photographic film, paper or plate; publicity.

**expound** *vt* to explain or set forth in detail.

**express** *vt* to represent in words; to make known one's thoughts, feelings, etc; to represent by signs, symbols, etc; to squeeze out. • *adj* firmly stated, explicit; (*train, bus, etc*) travelling at high speed with few or no stops. • *adv* at high speed, by express service. • *n* an express train, coach, etc; a system or company for sending freight, etc at rates higher than standard.

**expression** *n* an act of expressing, esp by words; a word or phrase; a look; intonation; a manner of showing feeling in communicating or performing (eg music); (*math*) a collection of symbols serving to express something. —**expressionless** *adj*.

**expressive** *adj* serving to express; full of expression.

**expressly** *adv* explicitly; for a specific purpose.

**expulsion** *n* the act of expelling or being expelled.—**expulsive** *adj*.

**exquisite** *adj* very beautiful, refined; sensitive, showing discrimination; acutely felt, as pain or pleasure.—**exquisitely** *adv*.

**extend** *vt* to stretch or spread out; to stretch fully; to prolong in time; to cause to reach in distance, etc; to enlarge, increase the scope of; to hold out (eg the hand); to accord, grant; to give, offer, (eg sympathy). • *vi* to prolong in distance or time; to reach in scope.

**extension** *n* act of extending or state of being extended; extent, scope; an added part, eg to a building; an extra period; a programme of extramural teaching provided by a college, etc; an additional telephone connected to the principal line.

**extensive** *adj* large; having a wide scope or extent.— **extensively** *adv*. — **extensiveness** *n*.

**extent** *n* the distance over which a thing is extended; the range or scope of something; the limit to which something extends.

**exterior** *adj* of, on, or coming from the outside; external; (*paint, etc*) suitable for use on the outside. • *n* the external part or surface; outward manner or appearance.

**exterminate** *vt* to destroy completely.— **extermination** *n*.—**exterminator** *n*.

**external** *adj* outwardly perceivable; of, relating to, or located on the outside or outer part. • *n* an external feature. —**externally** *adv*.

**extinct** *adj* (*animals*) not alive, no longer existing; (*fire*) not burning, out; (*volcano*) no longer active.— **extinction** *n*.

**extinguish** *vt* to put out (a fire, light, etc); to bring to an end.

**extinguisher** *n* a device for putting out a fire.

**extort** *vt* to obtain (money, promises, etc) by force or improper pressure.—**extortion** *n*.—**extortioner** *n*.

**extortionate** *adj* excessively high in price.

**extra** *adj* additional. • *adv* unusually; in addition. • *n* something extra or additional, esp a charge; a special edition of a newspaper; a person who plays a non-speaking role in a film.

**extra-** *prefix* outside, beyond.

**extract** *vt* to take or pull out by force; to withdraw by chemical or physical means; to abstract. • *n* the essence of a substance obtained by extraction; a passage taken from a book, play, film, etc.

**extraction** *n* the act of extracting; lineage; something extracted.

**extradite** *vt* to surrender (an alleged criminal) to the country where the offence was committed.—**extradition** *n*.

**extramarital** *adj* occurring outside marriage, esp sexual relationships.

**extraneous** *adj* coming from outside; not essential.—**extraneously** *adv*.

**extraordinary** *adj* not usual or regular; remarkable, exceptional.—**extraordinarily** *adv*.

**extravagant** *adj* lavish in spending; (*prices*) excessively high; wasteful; (*behaviour, praise, etc*) lacking in restraint, flamboyant, profuse.—**extravagantly** *adv*.—**extravagance** *n*.

**extravert** *see* **extrovert**.

**extreme** *adj* of the highest degree or intensity; excessive, immoderate, unwarranted; very severe, stringent; outermost. • *n* the highest or furthest limit or degree; (*often pl*) either of the two points marking the ends of a scale or range.—**extremely** *adv*.

**extremist** *n* a person of extreme views, esp political.—**extremism** *n*.

**extremity** *n* the utmost point or degree; the most remote part; the utmost violence, vigour, or necessity; the end; (*pl*) the hands or feet.

**extricate** *vt* to release from difficulties; to disentangle.—**extrication** *n*.

**extrovert** *n* a person more interested in the external world than his own feelings. —*also* **extravert**.

**exuberant** *adj* lively, high-spirited; profuse.—**exuberantly** *adv*.—**exuberance** *n*.

**exude** *vt* to cause or allow to ooze through pores or incisions, as sweat, pus; to display (confidence, emotion) freely.—**exudation** *n*.

**exult** *vi* to rejoice greatly.—**exultation** *n*.

**eye** *n* the organ of sight; the iris; the faculty of seeing; the external part of the eye; something resembling an eye. • *vt* (*pr p* **eyeing** *or* **eying**, *pt* **eyed**) to look at; to observe closely.

**eyeball** *n* the ball of the eye. • *vt* (*sl*) to stare at.

**eyebrow** *n* the hairy ridge above the eye.

**eye-catching** *adj* attractive or striking in appearance.

**eyelash** *n* the fringe of fine hairs along the edge of each eyelid.

**eyelid** *n* the lid of skin and muscle that moves to cover the eye.

**eye-opener** *n* something that comes as a shock or surprise.

**eye-shadow** *n* a coloured powder applied to accentuate or decorate the eyelids.

**eyesight** *n* the faculty of seeing.

**eyesore** *n* anything offensive to the sight.

**eye-witness** *n* a person who sees an event.

**eyrie** *n* the nest of an eagle or other bird of prey; any high inaccessible place or position.

# F

**F** *abbr* = Fahrenheit; (*chem symbol*) fluorine.

**fable** *n* a story, often with animal characters, conveying a moral; a lie, fabrication; a story involving mythical, legendary or supernatural characters or events.

**fabric** *n* cloth made by knitting, weaving, etc; framework, structure.

**fabulous** *adj* told in fables; incredible, astonishing; (*inf*) very good.—**fabulously** *adv*.

**façade, facade** *n* the main front or face of a building; an outward appearance, esp concealing something.

**face** *n* the front part of the head containing the eyes, nose, etc; facial expression; the front or outer surface of anything; external show or appearance; dignity, self-respect; impudence, effrontery; a coal face. • *vt* to be confronted by (a problem, etc); to deal with (an opponent, etc) resolutely; to be opposite to; to turn (a card) face upwards; to cover with a new surface. • *vi* to turn the face in a certain direction; to be situated in or have a specific direction.

**face-lift** *n* plastic surgery to smooth and firm the face; an improvement or renovation, esp to the outside of a building.

**facet** *n* a small plane surface (as on a cut gem); an aspect of character, a problem, issue, etc.

**facetious** *adj* joking, esp in an inappropriate manner.—**facetiously** *adv.*—**facetiousness** *n.*

**facia** *see* **fascia**.

**facial** *adj* of or pertaining to the face. • *n* a beauty treatment for the face.—**facially** *adv.*

**facile** *adj* easy to do; superficial.

**facilitate** *vt* to make easier.

**facility** *n* the quality of being easily done; aptitude, dexterity; something, eg a service or equipment, that makes it easy to do something.

**facsimile** *n* an exact copy of a book, document, etc; a method of transmitting printed matter through the telephone system.—*also* **fax**.

**fact** *n* a thing known to have happened or to exist; reality; a piece of verifiable information; (*law*) an event, occurrence, etc as distinguished from its legal consequences.

**faction**[1] *n* a small group of people in an organization working together in a common cause against the main body; dissension within a group or organization.—**factional** *adj.*—**factionally** *adv.*—**factious** *adj.*

**faction**[2] *n* a book, film, etc based on facts but presented as a blend of fact and fiction.

**factor** *n* any circumstance that contributes towards a result; (*math*) any of two or more numbers that, when multiplied together, form a product; a person who acts for another.

**factory** *n* a building or buildings where things are manufactured.

**factual** *adj* based on, or containing, facts; actual.—**factually** *adv.*

**faculty** *n* any natural power of a living organism; special aptitude; a teaching department of a college or university, or the staff of such a department.

**fad** *n* a personal habit or idiosyncrasy; a craze.—**faddish, faddy** *adj.*

**fade** *vi* to lose vigour or brightness of colour gradually; to vanish gradually. • *vt* to cause (an image or a sound) to increase or decrease in brightness or intensity gradually.—*also n.*

**fag** *vti* (*pt* **fagged**) to become or cause to be tired by hard work. • *n* (*formerly*) a British public schoolboy who performs chores for senior pupils; (*inf*) drudgery; (*sl*) a homosexual; (*sl*) a cigarette.

**fag-end** *n* the useless remains of anything; (*sl*) a cigarette-end.

**fail** *vi* to weaken, to fade or die away; to stop operating; to fall short; to be insufficient; to be negligent in duty, expectation, etc; (*exam, etc*) to be unsuccessful; to become bankrupt. • *vt* to disappoint the expectations or hopes of; to be unsuccessful in an exam, etc; to leave, to abandon; to grade (a candidate) as not passing a test, etc. • *n* failure in an examination.

**failing** *n* a fault, weakness. • *prep* in default or absence of.

**failure** *n* failing, non-performance, lack of success; the ceasing of normal operation of something; a deficiency; bankruptcy; an unsuccessful person or thing.

**faint** *adj* dim, indistinct; weak, feeble; timid; on the verge of losing consciousness. • *vi* to lose consciousness temporarily from a decrease in the supply of blood to the brain, as from shock. • *n* an act or condition of fainting.—**faintly** *adv.*—**faintness** *n.*

**faint-hearted** *adj* lacking courage and resolution.

**fair**[1] *adj* pleasing to the eye; clean, unblemished; (*hair*) light-coloured; (*weather*) clear and sunny; (*handwriting*) easy to read; just and honest; according to the rules; moderately large; average. • *adv* in a fair manner; squarely.—**fairness** *n*.

**fair**[2] *n* a gathering for the sale of goods, esp for charity; a competitive exhibition of farm, household, or manufactured goods; a fun-fair.

**fairly** *adv* in a fair manner; justly; moderately.

**fairy** *n* an imaginary supernatural being, usu in human form; (*sl*) a male homosexual.

**fairy story, fairy tale** *n* a story about fairies; an incredible story; a fabrication.

**faith** *n* trust or confidence in a person or thing; a strong conviction, esp a belief in a religion; any system of religious belief; fidelity to one's promises, sincerity.

**faithful** *adj* loyal; true; true to the original, accurate.—**faithfully** *adv*.

**fake** *vt* to make (an object) appear more real or valuable in order to deceive; to pretend, simulate. • *n* a faked article, a forgery; an impostor. • *adj* counterfeit, not genuine.— **faker** *n*.

**falcon** *n* a type of hawk trained for use in falconry.

**fall** *vi* (*pt* **fell**, *pp* **fallen**) to descend by force of gravity; to come as if by falling; to collapse; to drop to the ground; to become lower, weaker, less; to lose power, status, etc; to lose office; to slope downwards; to be wounded or killed in battle; to pass into a certain state; to become pregnant; to take place, happen; to be directed by chance; to come by inheritance; (*with* **back**) to retreat; (*with*

**out**) to quarrel; to leave one's place in a military formation. • *n* act or instance of falling; something which falls; the amount by which something falls; a decline in status, position; overthrow; a downward slope; a decrease in size, quantity, value; in US, autumn; (*wrestling*) a scoring move by pinning both shoulders of an opponent to the floor at once.

**fallacy** *n* a false idea; a mistake in reasoning.

**fallible** *adj* liable to make mistakes.— **fallibly** *adv*.— **fallibility** *n*.

**fall-out** *n* a deposit of radioactive dust from a nuclear explosion; a by-product.

**fallow**[1] *adj* (*lan d*) ploughed and left unplanted for a season or more.

**fallow**[2] *adj* yellowish-brown.

**false** *adj* wrong, incorrect; deceitful; artificial; disloyal, treacherous; misleading, fallacious.—**falsely** *adv*.— **falseness** *n*.

**falsehood** *n* a being untrue; the act of deceiving; a lie.

**falter** *vi* to move or walk unsteadily, to stumble; to hesitate or stammer in speech; to be weak or unsure, to waver.

**fame** *n* the state of being well known; good reputation.—**famed** *adj*.

**familiar** *adj* well-acquainted; friendly; common; well-known; too informal, presumptuous. • *n* a spirit or demon supposed to aid a witch, etc; an intimate.—**familiarly** *adv*.—**familiarity** *n*.

**familiarize** *vt* to make well known or acquainted; to make (something) well known.—**familiarization** *n*.

**family** *n* parents and their children; a person's children; a set of relatives; the descendants of a common ancestor; any group of persons or things related in some way; a group of related plants or animals; a unit of a crime syndicate (as the Mafia).

**famine** *n* an acute scarcity of food in a particular area; an extreme scarcity of anything.

**famous** *adj* renowned; (*inf*) excellent.—**famously** *adv*.

**fan**[1] *n* a handheld or mechanical device used to set up a current of air. • *vt* (*pt* **fanned**) to cool, as with a fan; to ventilate; to stir up, to excite; to spread out like a fan.

**fan**[2] *n* an enthusiastic follower of some sport, hobby, person, etc.

**fanatic** *n* a person who is excessively enthusiastic about something.— **fanatical** *adj*.—**fanatically** *adv*.

**fan belt** *n* the belt that drives the cooling fan in a car engine.

**fanciful** *adj* not factual, imaginary; indulging in fancy; elaborate or intricate in design.—**fancifully** *adv*.

**fancy** *n* imagination; a mental image; a whim; fondness. • *adj* (**fancier**, **fanciest**) not based on fact, imaginary; elegant or ornamental. • *vt* to imagine; to have a fancy or liking for; (*inf*) to be sexually attracted to.

**fancy dress** *n* a costume worn at masquerades or parties, usu representing an animal, historical character, etc.

**fang** *n* a long sharp tooth, as in a canine; the long hollow tooth through which venomous snakes inject poison.

**fanlight** *n* a semicircular window with radiating bars like the ribs of a fan.

**fantastic** *adj* unrealistic, fanciful; unbelievable; imaginative; (*inf*) wonderful.—**fantastically** *adv*.

**fantasy** *n* imagination; a product of the imagination, esp an extravagant or bizarre notion or creation; an imaginative poem, play or novel.

**far** *adj* (**farther**, **farthest** *or* **further**, **furthest**) remote in space or time; long; (*political views, etc*) extreme • *adv* very distant in space, time, or degree; to or from a distance in time or position, very much.

**faraway** *adj* distant, remote; dreamy.

**farce** *n* a style of light comedy; a drama using such comedy; a ludicrous situation.—**farcical** *adj*.

**fare** *n* money paid for transportation; a passenger in public transport; food. • *vi* to be in a specified condition.

**farewell** *interj* goodbye.—*also n*.

**far-fetched** *adj* unlikely.

**farm** *n* an area of land (with buildings) on which crops and animals are raised. • *vt* to grow crops or breed livestock; to cultivate, as land; to breed fish commercially; (*with* **out**) to put out (work, etc) to be done by others, to subcontract.

**farmer** *n* a person who manages or operates a farm.

**farmhouse** *n* a house on a farm.

**farmyard** *n* a yard close to or surrounded by farm buildings.

**far-reaching** *adj* having serious or widespread consequences.

**far-seeing** *adj* having foresight.

**fart** *vi* (*vulg*) to expel wind from the anus.—*also n*.

**farther** *adj* at or to a greater distance. • *adv* to a greater degree.

**farthest** *adj* at or to the greatest distance. • *adv* to the greatest degree.

**fascia** *n* (*pl* **fasciae**) the instrument panel of a motor vehicle, the dashboard; the flat surface above a shop front, with the name, etc.—*also* **facia**.

**fascinate** *vt* to hold the attention of, to attract irresistibly.—**fascination** *n*.

**fashion** *n* the current style of dress, conduct, speech, etc; the manner or form of appearance or action. • *vt* to make in a particular form; to suit or adapt.

**fashionable** *adj* conforming to the current fashion; attracting or frequented by people of fashion.— **fashionably** *adv*.

**fast**[1] *adj* swift, quick; (*clock*) ahead of time; firmly attached, fixed; (*colour, dye*) non-fading; wild, promiscuous. • *adv* firmly, thoroughly, rapidly, quickly.

**fast**[2] *vi* to go without all or certain foods. • *n* a period of fasting.

**fasten** *vti* to secure firmly; to attach; to fix (the eyes, attention) steadily.

**fastener, fastening** *n* a clip, catch, etc for fastening.

**fastidious** *adj* hard to please; daintily refined; over-sensitive.—**fastidiously** *adv.*—**fastidiousness** *n.*

**fat** *adj* (**fatter, fattest**) plump; thick; fertile; profitable. • *n* an oily or greasy material found in animal tissue and plant seeds; the richest or best part of anything; a superfluous part.—**fatness** *n.*

**fatal** *adj* causing death; disastrous (to); fateful.—**fatally** *adv.*

**fatalism** *n* belief that all events are predetermined by fate and therefore inevitable; acceptance of this doctrine. —**fatalist** *n.*—**fatalistic** *adj.*

**fatality** *n* a death caused by a disaster or accident; a person killed in such a way; a fatal power or influence.

**fate** *n* the ultimate power that predetermines events, destiny; the ultimate end, outcome; misfortune, doom, death.

**fateful** *adj* having important, usu unpleasant, consequences.—**fatefully** *adv.*

**father** *n* a male parent; an ancestor; a founder or originator; (*with cap*) God; a title of respect applied to monks, priests, etc. • *vt* to be the father of; to found, originate.—**fatherhood** *n.*

**father-in-law** *n* the father of one's husband or wife.

**fathom** *n* a nautical measure of 6 feet (1.83 m). • *vt* to measure the depth of; to understand.

**fatigue** *n* tiredness from physical or mental effort; the tendency of a material to break under repeated stress; any of the menial or manual tasks performed by military personnel; (*pl*) the clothing worn on fatigue or in the field. • *vti* to make or become tired.

**fatten** *vt* to make fat or fleshy; to make abundant.—**fattening** *adj.*

**fatty** *adj* (**fattier, fattiest**) resembling or containing fat. • *n* (*inf*) a fat person.

**fatuous** *adj* foolish, idiotic.—**fatuously** *adv.*—**fatuousness** *n.*—**fatuity** *n.*

**faucet** *n* a fixture for draining off liquid (as from a pipe or cask); a tap.

**fault** *n* a failing, defect; a minor offence; (*tennis, etc*) an incorrect serve or other error; a fracture in the earth's crust causing displacement of strata. • *vt* to find fault with, blame. • *vi* to commit a fault.

**faultless** *adj* without fault.—**faultlessly** *adv.*—**faultlessness** *n.*

**faulty** *adj* (**faultier, faultiest**) imperfect.—**faultily** *adv.*—**faultiness** *n.*

**fauna** *n* (*pl* **faunas, faunae**) the animals of a region, period, or specific environment.

**favour, favor** (*US*) *n* goodwill; approval; a kind or helpful act; partiality; a gift given out at a party; (*usu pl*) a privilege conceded, esp sexual. • *vt* to regard or treat with favour; to show support for; to oblige (with); to afford advantage to, facilitate.

**favourable, favorable** (*US*) *adj* expressing approval; pleasing; propitious; conducive (to).—**favourably** *adv.*

**favourite, favorite** (*US*) *n* a favoured person or thing; a competitor expected to win. • *adj* most preferred.

**favouritism, favoritism** (*US*) *n* the showing of unfair favour.

**fawn**[1] *n* a young deer; a yellowish-brown colour. • *adj* fawn-coloured.

**fawn**[2] *vi* (*dogs, etc*) to crouch to show affection; to flatter obsequiously.— **fawner** *n*.—**fawning** *n*.

**fax** *see* **facsimile.**

**fear** *n* an unpleasant emotion excited by danger, pain, etc; a cause of fear; anxiety; deep reverence. • *vt* to feel fear, be afraid of; to be apprehensive, anxious; to be sorry. • *vi* to be afraid or apprehensive.—**fearless** *adj*.— **fearlessly** *adv*.—**fearlessness** *n*.

**fearful** *adj* causing intense fear; timorous; apprehensive (of); (*inf*) very great, very bad.—**fearfully** *adv*.

**feasible** *adj* able to be done or implemented, possible.—**feasibly** *adv*.— **feasibility** *n*.

**feast** *n* an elaborate meal prepared for a special occasion; something that gives abundant pleasure; a periodic religious celebration. • *vi* to have or take part in a feast. • *vt* to entertain with a feast.

**feat** *n* an action of remarkable strength, skill, or courage.

**feather** *n* any of the light outgrowths forming the covering of a bird, a hollow central shaft with a vane of fine barbs on each side; a plume; something resembling a feather; the water thrown up by the turn of the blade of an oar. • *vt* to ornament with feathers; to turn (a blade) so that the edge is foremost.—**feathering** *n*.—**feathery** *adj*.

**feature** *n* any of the parts of the face; a characteristic trait of something; a special attraction or distinctive quality of something; a prominent newspaper article, etc; the main film in a cinema programme. • *vti* to make or be a feature of (something).

**featureless** *adj* lacking prominent or distinctive features.

**February** *n* the second month of the year, having 28 days (or 29 days in leap years).

**federal** *adj* designating, or of a union of states, etc, in which each member surrenders some of its power to a central authority; of a central government of this type.—**federalism** *n*.—**federalist** *n*.—**federally** *adv*.

**federation** *n* a union of states, groups, etc, in which each subordinates its power to a central authority; a federated organization.

**fee** *n* the price paid for the advice or service of a professional; a charge for some privilege, as membership of a club; (*law*) an inheritance in land.

**feeble** *adj* weak, ineffective.—**feebly** *adv*.—**feebleness** *n*.

**feeble-minded** *adj* mentally defective; of low intelligence.

**feed** *vb* (*pt* **fed**) *vt* to give food to; to give as food to; to supply with necessary material; to gratify. • *vi* to consume food. • *n* food for animals; material fed into a machine; the part of a machine supplying this material.

**feedback** *n* a return to the input of part of the output of a system; information about a product, service, etc returned to the supplier for evaluation.

**feel** *vb* (*pt* **felt**) *vt* to perceive or explore by the touch; to find one's way by cautious trial; to be conscious of, experience; to have a vague or instinctual impression of; to believe, consider. • *vi* to be able to experience the sensation of touch; to be affected by; to convey a certain sensation when touched. • *n* the sense of touch; feeling; a quality as revealed by touch.

**feeler** *n* a tactile organ (as a tentacle or antenna) of an animal; a tentative approach or suggestion to test another person's reactions.

**feeling** *n* the sense of touch; mental or physical awareness; a physical or mental impression; a state of mind;

sympathy; emotional sensitivity; a belief or opinion arising from emotion; (*pl*) emotions, sensibilities.

**feet** *see* **foot**.

**feign** *vt* to invent; to pretend.

**fell**[1] *see* **fall**.

**fell**[2] *vt* to cut, beat, or knock down; to kill, to sew (a seam) by folding one raw edge under the other.

**fell**[3] *n* a skin, hide, pelt.

**fell**[4] *adj* (*poet*) cruel, fierce, bloody, deadly.

**fellow** *n* an associate; a comrade; an equal in power, rank, or position; the other of a pair, a mate; a member of the governing body in some colleges and universities; a member of a learned society; (*inf*) a man or boy. • *adj* belonging to the same group or class.

**fellowship** *n* companionship; a mutual sharing; a group of people with the same interests; the position held by a college fellow.

**felony** *n* (*formerly*) a grave crime.

**felt**[1] *see* **feel**.

**felt**[2] *n* a fabric made from woollen fibres, often mixed with fur or hair, pressed together. • *vti* to make into or become like felt.

**female** *adj* of the sex that produces young; of a woman or women; (*pipe, plug, etc*) designed with a hollow part for receiving an inserted piece. • *n* a female animal or plant.

**feminine** *adj* of, resembling, or appropriate to women; (*gram*) of that gender to which words denoting females belong.—**femininity** *n*.

**feminism** *n* the movement to win political, economic and social equality for women.—**feminist** *adj*, *n*.

**fence** *n* a barrier put round land to mark a boundary, or prevent animals, etc from escaping; a receiver of stolen goods. • *vt* to surround with a fence; to keep (out) as by a fence.

• *vi* to practise fencing; to make evasive answers; to act as a fence for stolen goods.—**fencer** *n*.

**fencing** *n* fences; material for making fences; the art of fighting with foils or other types of sword.

**fend** *vi* (*with* **for**) to provide a livelihood for.

**fender** *n* anything that protects or fends off something else, as old tyres along the side of a vessel, or the part of a car body over the wheel.

**ferment** *n* an agent causing fermentation, as yeast; excitement, agitation. • *vti* to (cause to) undergo fermentation; to (cause to) be excited, agitated.

**fermentation** *n* the breakdown of complex molecules in organic components caused by the influence of yeast or other substances.

**fern** *n* any of a large class of non-flowering plants having roots, stems, and fronds, and reproducing by spores.—**ferny** *adj*.

**ferocious** *adj* savage, fierce.—**ferociously** *adv*.—**ferocity** *n*.

**ferry** *vt* to convey (passengers, etc) over a stretch of water; to transport from one place to another, esp along a regular route. • *n* a boat used for ferrying; a ferrying service; the location of a ferry.—**ferryman** *n*.

**fertile** *adj* able to bear offspring; (*land*) easily supporting plants and vegetation; (*animals*) capable of breeding; (*eggs*) able to grow and develop; prolific; (*mind, brain*) inventive.—**fertility** *n*.

**fertilize** *vt* to make (soil) fertile by adding nutrients; to impregnate; to pollinate.—**fertilization** *n*.

**fertilizer** *n* natural organic or artificial substances used to enrich the soil.

**fervent, fervid** *adj* passionate; zealous.—**fervently, fervidly** *adv*.—**fervency** *n*.

**fester** *vti* to become or cause to become infected; to suppurate; to rankle.

**festival** *n* a time of celebration; performances of music, plays, etc given periodically.

**festive** *adj* merry, joyous.

**fetch** *vt* to go for and bring back; to cause to come; (*goods*) to sell for (a certain price); (*inf*) to deal (a blow, slap, etc).

**fetching** *adj* attractive.

**fête, fete** *n* a festival; a usu outdoor sale, bazaar or entertainment in aid of charity. • *vt* to honour or entertain (as if) with a fête.

**fetish** *n* an object believed by primitive peoples to have magical properties; any object or activity regarded with excessive devotion.

**fetus,** *n* (*pl* **fetuses**) the unborn young of an animal, esp in its later stages; in humans, the offspring in the womb from the fourth month until birth.—*also* **foetus** (*pl* **foetuses**).—**fetal, foetal** *adj*.

**feud** *n* a state of hostilities, esp between individuals, families, or clans; a dispute.—*also vi*.

**feudal** *adj* pertaining to feudalism; (*inf*) old-fashioned, redundant.

**feudalism** *n* the economic and social system in medieval Europe, in which land, worked by serfs, was held by vassals in exchange for military and other services to overlords.

**fever** *n* an abnormally increased body temperature; any disease marked by a high fever; a state of restless excitement.—**fevered** *adj*.

**feverish** *adj* having a fever; indicating a fever; restlessly excited.—**feverishly** *adv*.—**feverishness** *n*.

**few** *adj, n* a small number, not many.—**fewness** *n*.

**fiancé** *n* a person engaged to be married.—**fiancée** *nf*.

**fiasco** *n* (*pl* **fiascos, fiascoes**) a complete and humiliating failure.

**fib** *n* a lie about something unimportant.—*also vi*.—**fibber** *n*.

**fibre, fiber** (*US*) *n* a natural or synthetic thread, eg from cotton, nylon, which is spun into yarn; a material composed of such yarn; texture; strength of character; a fibrous substance, roughage.—**fibrous** *adj*.

**fibreglass, fiberglass** (*US*) *n* glass in fibrous form, often bonded with plastic, used in making various products.

**fickle** *adj* inconstant; capricious.—**fickleness** *n*.

**fiction** *n* an invented story; any literary work with imaginary characters and events, as a novel, play, etc; such works collectively.—**fictional** *adj*.—**fictionally** *adv*.

**fictitious** *adj* imaginary, not real; feigned.—**fictitiously** *adv*.

**fiddle** *n* (*inf*) a violin; (*sl*) a swindle. • *vt* (*inf*) to play on a violin; (*sl*) to swindle; to falsify. • *vi* to handle restlessly, to fidget.—**fiddler** *n*.

**fidelity** *n* faithfulness, loyalty; truthfulness; accuracy in reproducing sound.

**fidget** *vi* to (cause to) move restlessly.—*also n*.—**fidgety** *adj*.

**field** *n* an area of land cleared of trees and buildings, used for pasture or crops; an area rich in a natural product (eg gold, coal); a battlefield; a sports ground; an area affected by electrical, magnetic or gravitational influence, etc; the area visible through an optical lens; a division of activity, knowledge, etc; all competitors in a contest; (*comput*) a section of a record in a database. • *vt* (*cricket, baseball, etc*) to catch or stop and return the ball as a fielder; to put (eg. a team) into the field to play; (*inf*) to handle (eg questions) successfully.

**field glasses** *npl* small, portable binoculars for use outdoors.

**fieldwork** *n* research done outside the laboratory or place of work by scientists, archaeologists, social workers, etc. —**fieldworker** *n*.

**fiend** *n* an evil spirit; an inhumanly wicked person; (*inf*) an avid fan.— **fiendish** *adj*.—**fiendishly** *adv*.

**fierce** *adj* ferociously hostile; angry, violent; intense; strong, extreme.— **fiercely** *adv*.—**fierceness** *n*.

**fiery** *adj* (**fierier, fieriest**) like or consisting of fire; the colour of fire; intensely hot; spicy; passionate, ardent; impetuous; irascible.—**fierily** *adv*.—**fieriness** *n*.

**fifteen** *adj, n* one more than fourteen; the symbol for this (15, XV, xv); the first point scored by a side in a game of tennis.—**fifteenth** *adj, n*.

**fifth** *adj, n* last of five; being one of five equal parts.

**fifty** *adj, n* five times ten; the symbol for this (50, L, l).—**fiftieth** *adj*.

**fig** *n* a tree yielding a soft, pear-shaped fruit; a thing of little or no importance.

**fight** *vb* (*pt* **fought**) *vi* to engage in battle in war or in single combat; to strive, struggle (for). • *vt* to engage in or carry on a conflict with; to achieve (one's way) by fighting; to strive to overcome. • *n* fighting; a struggle or conflict of any kind; a boxing match.

**fighter** *n* a person who fights; a person who does not yield easily; an aircraft designed to destroy enemy aircraft.

**figment** *n* something imagined or invented.

**figurative** *adj* metaphorical; using figures of speech.—**figuratively** *adv*.

**figure** *n* a character representing a number; a number; value or price; bodily shape or form; a graphic representation of a thing, person or animal; a design; a geometrical form; a statue; appearance; a personage; (*dancing, skating*) a set of steps or movements; (*pl*) arithmetic. • *vt* to represent in a diagram or outline; to imagine; (*inf*) to consider; (*inf*) to believe. • *vi* to take a part (in), be conspicuous (in); to calculate.

**figurehead** *n* a carved figure on the bow of a ship; a nominal head or leader.

**filament** *n* a slender thread or strand; a fibre; the fine wire in a light bulb.

**file**[1] a container for keeping papers, etc, in order; an orderly arrangement of papers; a line of persons or things; (*comput*) a collection of related data under a specific name. • *vt* to dispatch or register; to put on public record. • *vi* to move in a line; to apply.

**file**[2] *n* a tool, usu steel, with a rough surface for smoothing or grinding. • *vt* to cut or smooth with, or as with, a file; to polish, improve.

**filing** *n* a particle rubbed off with a file.

**fill** *vt* to put as much as possible into; to occupy wholly; to put a person into (a position or job, etc); to supply the things called for (in an order, etc); to close or plug (holes, etc). • *vi* to become full. • *n* enough to make full or to satisfy; anything that fills.

**fillet** *n* a thin boneless strip of meat or fish; a ribbon, etc worn as a headband; (*archit*) a narrow band used between mouldings. • *vt* to bone and slice (fish or meat).

**filling** *n* a substance used to fill a tooth cavity; the contents of a sandwich, pie, etc. • *adj* (*meal, etc*) substantial.

**filling station** *n* a place where petrol is sold to motorists, a service station.

**fillip** *n* a blow with the nail of the finger; a stimulus.

**film** *n* a fine, thin skin, coating, etc; a flexible cellulose material covered with a light-sensitive substance used in photography; a haze or blur; a motion picture. • *vti* to cover or be covered as with a film; to photograph or make a film (of).

**filter** *n* a device or substance straining out solid particles, impurities, etc, from a liquid or gas; a device for removing or minimizing electrical oscillations, or sound or light waves, of certain frequencies; a traffic signal that allows cars to turn left or right while the main lights are red. • *vti* to pass through or as through a filter; to remove with a filter.

**filth** *n* dirt; obscenity.

**filthy** *adj* (**filthier, filthiest**) dirty, disgusting; obscene; (*inf*) extremely unpleasant.—**filthily** *adv*.—**filthiness** *n*.

**fin** *n* an organ by which a fish, etc steers itself and swims; a rubber flipper used for underwater swimming; any fin-shaped object used as a stabilizer, as on an aircraft or rocket.

**final** *adj* of or coming at the end; conclusive. • *n* (*often pl*) the last of a series of contests; a final examination. —**finally** *adv*.

**finale** *n* the concluding part of any public performance; the last section in a musical composition.

**finalist** *n* a contestant in a final.

**finalize** *vt* to make complete, to bring to an end.—**finalization** *n*.

**finance** *n* the management of money; (*pl*) money resources. • *vt* to supply or raise money for.—**financial** *adj*.—**financially** *adv*.

**financier** *n* a person skilled in finance.

**find** *vb* (*pt* **found**) *vt* to discover by chance; to come upon by searching; to perceive; to recover (something lost); to reach, attain; to decide and declare to be. • *vi* to reach a decision (as by a jury). • *n* a discovery, something found.

**finding** *n* a discovery; the conclusion reached by a judicial enquiry.

**fine**[1] *adj* very good; with no impurities, refined; (*weather*) clear and bright; not heavy or coarse; very thin or small; sharp; subtle; elegant. • *adv* in a fine manner; (*inf*) very well.—**finely** *adv*.—**fineness** *n*.

**fine**[2] *n* a sum of money imposed as a punishment. • *vt* to punish by a fine.

**fine arts** *npl* painting, sculpture, music, etc valued for their aesthetic qualities.

**finery** *n* elaborate clothes, jewellery, etc.

**finesse** *n* delicacy or subtlety of performance; skilfulness, diplomacy in handling a situation; (*bridge*) an attempt to take a trick with a card lower than a higher card held by an opponent. • *vt* to achieve by finesse; to play (a card) as a finesse.

**finger** *n* one of the digits of the hand, usu excluding the thumb; anything shaped like a finger; (*inf*) the breadth of a finger. • *vt* to touch with fingers; (*mus*) to use the fingers in a certain way when playing.

**fingernail** *n* the nail on a finger.

**fingerprint** *n* the impression of the ridges on a fingertip, esp as used for purposes of identification.—*also vt*.

**finicky, finicking** *adj* too particular, fussy.

**finish** *vt* to bring to an end, to come to the end of; to consume entirely; to perfect; to give a desired surface effect to. • *vi* to come to an end. • *n* the last part, the end; anything used to finish a surface; the finished effect; means or manner of completing or perfecting; polished manners, speech, etc.—**finisher** *n*.

**finite** *adj* having definable limits; (*verb form*) having a distinct grammatical person and number.

**fiord** *see* **fjord**.

**fir** *n* a kind of evergreen, cone-bearing tree; its timber.

**fire** n the flame, heat and light of combustion; something burning; burning fuel in a grate to heat a room; an electric or gas fire; a destructive burning; a strong feeling; a discharge of firearms. • vti to ignite; to supply with fuel; to bake (bricks, etc) in a kiln; to excite or become excited; to shoot (a gun, etc); to hurl or direct with force; to dismiss from a position.

**fire alarm** n a device that uses a bell, hooter, etc to warn of a fire.

**firearm** n a handgun.

**fire brigade** n an organization of men trained and equipped to fight fires.

**fire escape** n a means of exit from a building, esp a stairway, for use in case of fire.

**fireman** n a member of a fire brigade; a person employed to tend furnaces.

**fireplace** n a place for a fire, esp a recess in a wall; the surrounding area.

**fireside** n the area in a room nearest the fireplace; home.

**firework** n a device packed with explosive and combustible material used to produce noisy and colourful displays; (pl) such a display; (pl) a fit of temper, an outburst of emotions.

**firing squad** n a detachment with the task of firing a salute at a military funeral or carrying out an execution.

**firm**[1] adj securely fixed; solid, compact; steady; resolute; definite. • vti to make or become firm.—**firmly** adv.—**firmness** n.

**firm**[2] n a business partnership; a commercial company.

**first** adj before all others in a series; 1st; earliest; foremost, as in rank, quality, etc. • adv before anyone or anything else; for the first time; sooner. • n any person or thing that is first; the beginning; the winning place, as in a race; low gear; the highest award in a university degree.

**first aid** n emergency treatment for an injury, etc, before regular medical aid is available.

**first-class** adj of the highest quality, as in accommodation, travel.—also n.

**firsthand** adj obtained directly.

**First Lady** n the wife of the US president.

**firstly** adv in the first place.

**first-rate** adj, adv of the best quality; (inf) excellent.

**fiscal** adj of or relating to public revenue; financial. • n a prosecuting official in some countries.

**fish** n (pl **fish**, **fishes**) any of a large group of cold-blooded animals living in water, having backbones, gills and fins; the flesh of fish used as food. • vi to catch or try to catch fish; (with for) to try to obtain by roundabout methods. • vt (often with out) to grope for, find, and bring to view.

**fisherman** n a person who fishes for sport or for a living; a ship used in fishing.

**fishery** n the fishing industry; an area where fish are caught.

**fish finger** n a small oblong piece of fish covered in breadcrumbs.

**fishmonger** n a shop that sells fish.

**fishy** adj (**fishier**, **fishiest**) like a fish in odour, taste, etc; (inf) creating doubt or suspicion.—**fishily** adv.—**fishiness** n.

**fission** n a split or cleavage; the reproductive division of biological cells; the splitting of the atomic nucleus resulting in the release of energy, nuclear fission.—**fissionable** adj.

**fissure** n a narrow opening or cleft.—also vti.

**fist** n the hand when tightly closed or clenched.

**fit**[1] adj (**fitter**, **fittest**) suited to some purpose, function, etc; proper, right; healthy; (sl) inclined, ready. • n the manner of fitting. • *vb* (*pt* **fitted**) *vt* to be suitable to; to be the proper size or shape for; to adjust so as to fit; to equip, to outfit. • *vi* to be suitable or proper; to have the proper size or shape.—**fitly** *adv.*—**fitness** *n*.

**fit**² *n* any sudden, uncontrollable attack, as of coughing; an outburst, as of anger; a short period of impulsive activity; a seizure involving convulsions or loss of consciousness.

**fitful** *adj* marked by intermittent activity; spasmodic.—**fitfully** *adv.*—**fitfulness** *n*.

**fitment** *n* a piece of equipment, esp fixed furniture.

**fitter** *n* a person who specializes in fitting clothes; a person skilled in the assembly and operation of a particular piece of machinery.

**fitting** *adj* appropriate. • *n* an act of one that fits, esp a trying on of altered clothes; a small often standardized electrical part.—**fittingly** *adv*.

**five** *adj, n* one more than four; the symbol for this (5, V, v).

**fiver** *n* (*inf*) a £5 note.

**fix** *vt* to fasten firmly; to set firmly in the mind; to direct (one's eyes) steadily at something; to make rigid; to make permanent; to establish (a date, etc) definitely; to set in order; to repair; to prepare (food or meals); (*inf*) to influence the result or action of (a race, jury, etc) by bribery; (*inf*) to punish. • *vi* to become fixed; (*inf*) to prepare or intend. • *n* the position of a ship, etc, determined from the bearings of two known positions; (*inf*) a predicament; (*inf*) a situation that has been fixed; (*inf*) something whose supply becomes continually necessary or greatly desired, as a drug, activity, etc.

**fixture** *n* what is fixed to anything, as to land or to a house; a fixed article of furniture; a firmly established

person or thing; a fixed or appointed time or event.

**fizz** *vi* to make a hissing or sputtering sound. • *n* this sound; any effervescent drink.—**fizzy** *adj.*—**fizziness** *n*.

**fizzle** *vi* to make a weak fizzing sound; (*with* **out**) (*inf*) to end feebly, die out, esp after a promising start.

**fjord** *n* a long, narrow inlet of the sea between high cliffs, esp in Norway. —*also* **fiord**.

**flabbergast** *vt* (*inf*) to astonish, startle.

**flabby** *adj* (**flabbier, flabbiest**) fat and soft; weak and ineffective.—**flabbiness** *n*.

**flag**¹ *vi* (*pt* **flagged**) to grow limp; to become weak, listless.

**flag**² *n* a piece of cloth, usu with a design, used to show nationality, party, a particular branch of the armed forces, etc, or as a signal. • *vt* (*pt* **flagged**) to decorate with flags; to signal to (as if) with a flag; (*usu with* **down**) to signal to stop.

**flag**³ *n* a hard, flat stone used for paving, a flagstone. • *vt* (*pt* **flagged**) to pave.

**flagon** *n* a pottery or metal container for liquids with a handle and spout and often a lid.

**flagrant** *adj* conspicuous, notorious.—**flagrantly** *adv.*—**flagrancy** *n*.

**flair** *n* natural ability, aptitude; discernment; (*inf*) stylishness, sophistication.

**flake** *n* a small piece of snow; a small thin layer chipped from a larger mass of something. • *vt* to form into flakes.—**flaky** *adj*.

**flamboyant** *adj* brilliantly coloured; ornate; strikingly elaborate; dashing, exuberant.—**flamboyantly** *adv.*—**flamboyance** *n*.

**flame** *n* the burning gas of a fire, appearing as a tongue of light; the state of burning with a blaze; a thing like a flame; an intense emotion; (*inf*) a sweetheart. • *vi* to burst into flame; to become bright red with emotion.

**flamingo** *n* any of several wading birds with rosy-white plumage and long legs and neck.

**flammable** *adj* easily set on fire.—**flammability** *n*.

**flan** *n* an open case of pastry or sponge cake with a sweet or savoury filling.

**flange** *n* a projecting or raised edge.

**flank** *n* the fleshy part of the side from the ribs to the hip; the side of anything; the right or left side of a formation of troops. • *vt* to attack the flank of; to skirt the side of; to be situated at the side of.

**flannel** *n* a soft light cotton or woollen cloth; a small cloth for washing the face and hands; (*sl*) nonsense, equivocation; (*pl*) trousers of such cloth. • *vt* (*pt* **flannelled**) to wash with a flannel; (*inf*) to flatter.

**flannelette** *n* a soft cotton fabric.

**flap** *vi* (*pt* **flapped**) to move up and down, as wings; to sway loosely and noisily; to move or hang like a flap; (*inf*) to get into a fluster. • *n* the motion or noise of a flap; anything broad and flexible, either hinged or hanging loose; a light blow with a flat object; (*inf*) agitation, panic.

**flare** *vi* to burn with a sudden, bright, unsteady flame; to burst into emotion, esp anger; to widen out gradually. • *n* an unsteady flame; a sudden flash; a bright light used as a signal or illumination; a widened part or shape.

**flare-up** *n* a sudden burst of fire; (*inf*) a sudden burst of emotion.

**flash** *n* a sudden, brief light; a brief moment; a sudden brief display; (*TV, radio*) a sudden brief news item on an important event; (*photog*) a device producing a brief intense light; a sudden onrush of water. • *vi* to emit a sudden, brief light; to sparkle; to come or pass suddenly; (*sl*) to expose the genitals indecently. • *vt* to cause to flash; to send (news, etc) swiftly; (*inf*) to show off. • *adj* (*inf*) flashy.—**flasher** *n*.

**flashback** *n* an interruption in the continuity of a story, etc, by telling or showing an earlier episode.

**flashbulb** *n* a small bulb giving an intense light used in photography.

**flashlight** *n* a torch.

**flashy** *adj* (**flashier, flashiest**) pretentious; showy, gaudy.

**flask** *n* a slim-necked bottle; a vacuum flask.

**flat** *adj* (**flatter, flattest**) having a smooth level surface; lying spread out; broad, even, and thin; not fluctuating; (*tyre*) deflated; dull, tedious; (*drink*) not fizzy; (*battery*) drained of electric current. • *adv* in a flat manner or position; exactly; (*mus*) below true pitch. • *n* anything flat, esp a surface, part, or expanse; a flat tyre; a set of rooms on one floor of a building.—**flatly** *adv*.—**flatness** *n*.

**flatten** *vti* to make or become flat.

**flatter** *vt* to praise excessively or insincerely, esp to win favour; to display to advantage; to represent as more attractive, etc than reality; to gratify the vanity of; to encourage falsely.—**flatterer** *n*.—**flattery** *n*.

**flaunt** *vi* to move or behave ostentatiously; (*flag*) to wave in the wind. • *vt* to display.

**flavour, flavor** (*US*) *n* the taste of something in the mouth; a characteristic quality. • *vt* to give flavour to.

**flavouring, flavoring** (*US*) *n* any substance used to give flavour to food.

**flaw** *n* a defect; a crack. • *vti* to make or become flawed.—**flawless** *adj*.

**flax** *n* a blue-flowered plant cultivated for its fibre and seed; its fibre.

**flaxen** *adj* made of flax; pale yellow.

**flea** *n* a small wingless jumping bloodsucking insect.

**fledge** *vt* (*birds*) to rear until ready to fly; to cover or provide with feathers.

**fledgling** *n* a young bird just fledged; an inexperienced person, a trainee.

**flee** *vti* (*pt* **fled**) to run away from danger, etc; to pass away quickly, to disappear.

**fleece** *n* the woollen coat of sheep or similar animal. • *vt* to remove wool from; to defraud.—**fleecy** *adj*.

**fleet**[1] *n* a number of warships under one command; (*often with cap*) a country's navy; any group of cars, ships, buses, etc, under one control.

**fleet**[2] *adj* swift moving; nimble.—**fleetly** *adv*.—**fleetness** *n*.

**fleeting** *adj* brief, transient.

**flesh** *n* the soft substance of the body, esp the muscular tissue; the pulpy part of fruits and vegetables; meat; the body as distinct from the soul; all mankind; a yellowish-pink colour. • *vt* to give substance to (*usu with out*). —**fleshy** *adj*.

**flexible, flexile** *adj* easily bent; adaptable, versatile; docile.—**flexibly** *adv*. — **flexibility** *n*.

**flick** *n* a light stroke or blow; (*inf*) a cinema film. • *vt* to strike or propel with a flick; a flicking movement.

**flicker** *vi* to burn unsteadily, as a flame; to move quickly to and fro. • *n* a flickering moment of light or flame; a flickering movement.

**flier** *see* **flyer**.

**flight**[1] *n* the act, manner, or power of flying; distance flown; a group of creatures or things flying together; an aircraft scheduled to fly a certain trip; a trip by aircraft; a set of stairs, as between landings; a mental act of soaring beyond the ordinary; a set of feathers on a dart or arrow.

**flight**[2] *n* an act or instance of fleeing.

**flimsy** *adj* (**flimsier, flimsiest**) weak, insubstantial; light and thin; (*excuse etc*) unconvincing.—**flimsily** *adv*.—**flimsiness** *n*.

**flinch** *vi* to draw back, as from pain or fear; to wince.

**fling** *vb* (*pt* **flung**) *vt* to cast, throw aside, esp with force; to put or send suddenly or without warning. • *vi* to kick out violently; to move or rush quickly or impetuously. • *n* the act of flinging; a lively dance; a period of pleasurable indulgence.

**flint** *n* a very hard rock that produces sparks when struck with steel; an alloy used for producing a spark in lighters.

**flip**[1] *n* a drink made from any alcoholic beverage sweetened and mixed with beaten egg.

**flip**[2] *vb* (*pt* **flipped**) *vt* to toss with a jerk, to flick; to snap (a coin) in the air with the thumb; to turn or turn over. • *vi* to move jerkily; (*inf*) to burst into anger.

**flippant** *adj* impertinent; frivolous.—**flippancy** *n*.—**flippantly** *adv*.

**flirt** *vi* to make insincere amorous approaches; to trifle or toy (eg with an idea). • *n* a person who toys amorously with the opposite sex.—**flirtation** *n*.

**flit** *vi* (*pt* **flitted**) to move lightly and rapidly; to vacate (a premises) stealthily.—*also n*.

**float** *vi* to rest on the surface of or be suspended in a liquid; to move lightly; to wander aimlessly. • *vt* to cause to float; to put into circulation; to start up a business, esp by offering shares for sale. • *n* anything that floats; a cork or other device used on a fishing line to signal that the bait has been taken; a low flat vehicle decorated for exhibit in a parade; a small sum of money available for cash expenditures.

**flock**[1] *n* a group of certain animals as birds, sheep, etc, living and feeding together; a group of people or things. • *vi* to assemble or travel in a flock or crowd.

**flock**[2] *n* a tuft of wool or cotton fibre; woollen or cotton waste used for stuffing furniture.

**flog** *vt* (*pt* **flogged**) to beat harshly with a rod, stick or whip; (*sl*) to sell.— **flogging** *n*.

**flood** *n* an overflowing of water on an area normally dry; the rising of the tide; a great outpouring, as of words. • *vt* to cover or fill, as with a flood; to put too much water, fuel, etc on or in. • *vi* to gush out in a flood; to become flooded.

**floodlight** *n* a strong beam of light used to illuminate a stage, sports field, stadium, etc. • *vt* (*pt* **floodlit**) to illuminate with floodlights.

**floor** *n* the inside bottom surface of a room; the bottom surface of anything, as the ocean; a storey in a building; the area in a legislative assembly where the members debate; the lower limit, the base. • *vt* to provide with a floor; to knock down (a person) in a fight; (*inf*) to defeat; (*inf*) to shock, to confuse.

**floorboard** *n* one of the boards making up a floor.

**flop** *vi* (*pt* **flopped**) to sway or bounce loosely; to move in a heavy, clumsy or relaxed manner; (*inf*) to fail. • *n* a flopping movement; a collapse; (*inf*) a complete failure.

**floppy** *adj* (**floppier, floppiest**) limp, hanging loosely.—**floppiness** *n*.

**flora** *n* (*pl* **floras, florae**) the plants of a region or a period.

**floral** *adj* pertaining to flowers.

**florid** *adj* flowery; elaborate; (*complexion*) ruddy.

**florist** *n* a person who sells or grows flowers and ornamental plants.

**flotation** *n* the act or process of floating; a launching of a business venture.

**flounce**[1] *vi* to move in an emphatic or impatient manner.—*also n*.

**flounce**[2] *n* a frill of material sewn to the skirt of a dress. • *vt* to add flounces to.

**flounder**[1] *vi* to move awkwardly and with difficulty; to be clumsy in thinking or speaking.

**flounder**[2] *n* a small flatfish used as food.

**flour** *n* the finely ground powder of wheat or other grain. • *vt* to sprinkle with flour.—**floury** *adj*.

**flourish** *vi* (*plants*) to grow luxuriantly; to thrive, prosper; to live and work at a specified time. • *vt* to brandish dramatically. • *n* embellishment; a curve made by a bold stroke of a pen; a sweeping gesture; a musical fanfare.

**flout** *vt* to treat with contempt; to disobey openly.—**flouter** *n*.—**floutingly** *adv*.

**flow** *vi* (*liquids*) to move (as if) in a stream; (*tide*) to rise; to glide smoothly; (*conversation, etc*) to continue effortlessly; to be characterized by smooth and easy movement; to hang free or loosely; to be plentiful. • *n* a flowing; the rate of flow; anything that flows; the rising of the tide.

**flow chart** *n* a diagram representing the sequence of and relationships between different steps or procedures in a complex process, eg manufacturing.

**flower** *n* the seed-producing structure of a flowering plant, blossom; a plant cultivated for its blossoms; the best or finest part. • *vt* to cause to bear flowers. • *vi* to produce blossoms; to reach the best stage.

**flowery** *adj* full of or decorated with flowers; (*language*) full of elaborate expressions.

**flown** *see* **fly**.

**flu** n (inf) influenza.

**fluctuate** vi (prices, etc) to be continually varying in an irregular way.—**fluctuation** n.

**fluent** adj able to write and speak a foreign language with ease; articulate, speaking and writing easily and smoothly; graceful.—**fluency** n.—**fluently** adv.

**fluff** n soft, light down; a loose, soft mass, as of hair; (inf) a mistake, bungle. • vt to pat or shake until fluffy; (inf) to bungle.

**fluffy** adj (**fluffier, fluffiest**) like fluff; feathery.—**fluffiness** n.

**fluid** n a substance able to flow freely, as a liquid or gas does. • adj able to flow freely; able to change rapidly or easily.—**fluidity** n.

**fluke**[1] n a flatfish; a flattened parasitic worm.

**fluke**[2] n the part of an anchor that fastens in the sea bed, river bottom, etc; the barbed end of a harpoon; one of the lobes of a whale's tail.

**fluke**[3] n a stroke of luck.—**fluky** adj.

**flung** see **fling**.

**fluoride** n any of various compounds of fluorine.

**flurry** n a sudden gust of wind, rain, or snow; a sudden commotion. • vti to (cause to) become flustered.

**flush**[1] n a rapid flow, as of water; sudden, vigorous growth; a sudden excitement; a blush; a sudden feeling of heat, as in a fever. • vi to flow rapidly; to blush or glow; to be washed out by a sudden flow of water. • vt to wash out with a sudden flow of water; to cause to blush; to excite. • adj level or in one plane with another surface; (inf) abundant, well-supplied, esp with money.

**flush**[2] vt to make game birds fly away suddenly.

**flush**[3] n (poker, etc) a hand of cards all of the same suit.

**fluster** vti to make or become confused. • n agitation or confusion.

**flute** n an orchestral woodwind instrument in the form of a straight pipe (with finger holes and keys) held horizontally and played through a hole located near one end; a decorative groove. • vi to play or make sounds like a flute; to cut grooves in.

**flutter** vi (birds) to flap the wings; to wave about rapidly; (heart) to beat irregularly or spasmodically. • vt to cause to flutter. • n rapid, irregular motion; nervous excitement; commotion, confusion; (inf) a small bet.—**fluttery** adj.

**flux** n a continual flowing or changing; a substance used to help metals fuse together, as in soldering.

**fly**[1] n a two-winged insect; a natural or imitation fly attached to a fish-hook as bait.

**fly**[2] vb (pt **flew**, pp **flown**) vi to move through the air, esp on wings; to travel in an aircraft; to control an aircraft; to take flight, flee; to pass quickly; (inf) to depart quickly. • vt to cause to fly, as a kite; to escape, flee from; to transport by aircraft. • n a flap that hides buttons, a zip, etc on trousers; material forming the outer roof of a tent; a device for regulating machinery, a flywheel.

**fly**[3] adj (inf) sly, astute.

**flyer** n something that flies or moves very fast; a pilot.—also **flier**.

**flying** adj capable of flight; fleeing; fast-moving. • n the act of flying an aircraft, etc.

**flying saucer** n an unidentified flying disc-shaped object, purportedly from outer space.

**flying start** n a start in a race when the competitor is already moving at the starting line; a promising start.

**flyover** n a bridge that carries a road or railway over another; a fly-past.

**fly-past** *n* a processional flight of air-craft.

**flywheel** *n* a heavy wheel which stores energy by inertia, used to regulate machinery.

**foal** *n* the young of a horse or related animal. • *vti* to give birth to a foal.

**foam** *n* froth or fine bubbles on the surface of liquid; something like foam, as frothy saliva; a rigid or springy cellular mass made from liquid rubber, plastic, etc. • *vi* to cause or emit foam.—**foamy** *adj*.

**fob**[1] *n* the chain or ribbon for attaching a watch to a waistcoat; any object attached to a watch chain; a small pocket in a waistcoat for a watch.

**fob**[2] *vt* (*pt* **fobbed**) (*with* **off**) to cheat; to put off; to palm off (upon).

**focal** *adj* of or pertaining to a focus.

**focus** *n* (*pl* **focuses, foci**) a point where rays of light, heat, etc meet after being bent by a lens, curved mirror, etc; correct adjustment of the eye or lens to form a clear image; a centre of activity or interest. • *vt* (*pt* **focused** *or* **focussed**) to adjust the focus of; to bring into focus; to concentrate.

**fodder** *n* dried food for horses, etc.

**foe** *n* an enemy, an adversary.

**foetus** *see* **fetus**.

**fog** *n* (a state of poor visibility caused by) a large mass of water vapour condensed to fine particles just above the earth's surface; a state of mental confusion; (*photog*) cloudiness on a developed photograph. • *vti* (*pt* **fogged**) to make or become foggy.

**foggy** *adj* (**foggier, foggiest**) thick with fog; mentally confused; indistinct, opaque.—**fogginess** *n*.

**foible** *n* a slight weakness or failing; an idiosyncrasy.

**foil**[1] *vt* to defeat; to frustrate.

**foil**[2] *n* a very thin sheet of metal; anything that sets off or enhances another by contrast.

**foil**[3] *n* a long, thin blunted sword used for fencing.

**fold**[1] *vt* to cover by bending or doubling over so that one part covers another; to wrap up, envelop; to interlace (one's arms); to clasp (one's hands); to embrace; to incorporate (an ingredient) into a food mixture by gentle overturnings. • *vi* to become folded; to fail completely; to collapse, esp to go out of business. • *n* something folded, as a piece of cloth; a crease or hollow made by folding.

**fold**[2] *n* a pen for sheep; a group of people or institutions having a common belief, etc. • *vt* to pen in a fold.

**folder** *n* a folded cover or large envelope for holding loose papers.

**foliage** *n* leaves, as of a plant or tree.

**folk** *n* a people of a country or tribe; people in general, esp those of a particular area; relatives; folk music. • *adj* of or originating among ordinary people.

**folklore** *n* the traditional beliefs, legends, etc of a people.

**folk song** *n* a traditional song.

**follow** *vt* to go or come after; to pursue; to go along (a path, road, etc); to copy; to obey; to adopt, as an opinion; to watch fixedly; to focus the mind on; to understand the meaning of; to monitor the progress of; to come or occur after in time; to result from; (*with* **through**) to pursue (an aim) to a conclusion; (*with* **up**) to pursue a question, inquiry, etc, that has been started. • *vi* to go or come after another; to result; (*with* **on**) (*cricket*) to take a second innings immediately after a first; (*with* **through**) (*sport*) to continue a stroke or motion of a bat, club, etc after the ball has been struck.

**follower** *n* a disciple or adherent; a person who imitates another.

**following** n a body of adherents or believers. • adj next after; now to be stated.

**folly** n a lack of sense; a foolish act or idea; an extravagant and fanciful building which serves no practical purpose.

**fond** adj loving, affectionate; doting, indulgent; (with of) having a liking for. —**fondly** adv.— **fondness** n.

**fondle** vt to caress.

**font**[1] n a receptacle for baptismal water; a receptacle for holy water.

**font**[2] see **fount**[1].

**food** n any substance, esp a solid, taken in by a plant or animal to enable it to live and grow; anything that nourishes.

**foodstuff** n a substance used as food.

**fool** n a person lacking wisdom or common sense; (Middle Ages) a jester; a dupe; a cold dessert of whipped cream and fruit purée. • vt to deceive, make a fool of. • vi to act jokingly; to spend time idly; to tease or meddle with.—**foolery** n.

**foolhardy** adj foolishly bold; rash.— **foolhardiness** n.

**foolish** adj unwise; ridiculous; ill-judged.—**foolishly** adv.—**foolishness** n.

**foolproof** adj proof against failure; easy to understand; easy to use.

**foot** n (pl **feet**) the end part of the leg, on which one stands; anything resembling foot, as the lower part of a chair, table, etc; the lower part or edge of something, bottom; a measure of length equal to 12 inches (30.48 cm); the part of a garment that covers the foot; an attachment on a sewing machine that grips the fabric; a group of syllables serving as a unit of metre in verse. • vi to dance. • vt to walk, dance over or on; to pay the entire cost of (a bill).

**foot-and-mouth disease** n a contagious diasease of cattle.

**football** n a field game played with an inflated leather ball by two teams; the ball used.—**footballer** n.

**footbridge** n a narrow bridge for pedestrians.

**foothill** n a hill at the foot of higher hills.

**foothold** n a ledge, etc, for placing the foot when climbing, etc; a place from which further progress may be made.

**footing** n the basis upon which something rests; status, relationship; a foothold.

**footlights** npl a row of lights in front of a stage floor.

**footman** n a liveried servant.

**footnote** n a note or comment at the foot of a page.

**footpath** n a narrow path for pedestrians.

**footsore** adj having painful feet from excessive walking.

**footwear** n shoes and socks, etc.

**for** prep because of, as a result of; as the price of, or recompense of; in order to be, to serve as; appropriate to, or adapted to; in quest of; in the direction of; on behalf of; in place of; in favour of; with respect to; notwithstanding, in spite of; to the extent of; throughout the space of; during. • conj because.

**forage** n food for domestic animals, esp when taken by browsing or grazing; a search for provisions. • vi to search for food.—**forager** n.

**foray** n a sudden raid. • vti to plunder.

**forbade** see **forbid**.

**forbear** vb (pt **forbore**, pp **forborne**) vi to endure, to avoid. • vt to hold oneself back from.—**forbearance** n.

**forbid** vt (pt **forbad** or **forbade**, pp. **forbidden**) to command (a person) not to do something; to render impossible, prevent.

**forbidding** *adj* unfriendly, solemn, strict.—**forbiddingly** *adv*.

**force** *n* strength, power, effort; (*physics*) (the intensity of) an influence that causes movement of a body or other effects; a body of soldiers, police, etc prepared for action; effectiveness; violence, compulsion; legal or logical validity. • *vt* to compel or oblige by physical effort, superior strength, etc; to achieve by force; to press or drive against resistance; to produce with effort; to break open, penetrate; to impose, inflict; to cause (plants, animals) to grow faster than normal.

**forceful** *adj* powerful, effective.— **forcefully** *adv*.—**forcefulness** *n*.

**forceps** *n* an instrument for grasping and holding firmly, or exerting traction upon objects, esp by jewellers and surgeons.

**ford** *n* a shallow crossing place in a river, etc.—*also vt*.—**fordable** *adj*.

**fore** *adj* in front. • *n* the front. • *adv* in, at or towards the front. • *interj* (*golf*) a warning cry to anybody who may be hit by the ball.

**forearm**[1] *n* the arm between the elbow and the wrist.

**forearm**[2] *vt* to arm in advance.

**forecast** *vt* (*pt* **forecast** *or* **forecasted**) to predict (events, weather, etc) through rational analysis; to serve as a forecast of.—*also n*.

**forecourt** *n* an enclosed space in front of a building, as in a filling station.

**forefathers** *npl* ancestors.

**forefinger** *n* the finger next the thumb.

**forego**[1] *see* **forgo**.

**forego**[2] *vt* (*pt* **forewent**, *pp* **foregone**) to precede.

**foregone conclusion** *n* an inevitable result, easily predictable.

**foreground** *n* the part of a picture or view nearest the spectator's vision.

**forehead** *n* the part of the face above the eyes.

**foreign** *adj* of, in, or belonging to another country; involving other countries; alien in character; introduced from outside.

**foreigner** *n* a person from another country.

**foreman** *n* a person who supervises workers in a factory, etc; the spokesperson of a jury.—**forewoman** *nf*.

**foremost** *adj* first in importance; most advanced in rank or position.

**forensic** *adj* belonging to or used in courts of law.—**forensically** *adv*.

**forensic medicine** *n* the application of medical expertise to legal and criminal investigations.

**forerunner** *n* a person or thing that comes in advance of another; a portent.

**foresee** *vt* (*pt* **foresaw**, *pp* **foreseen**) to be aware of beforehand.

**foresight** *n* foreseeing; the power to foresee; provision for the future.

**forest** *n* a thick growth of trees, etc covering a large tract of land; something resembling a forest.

**forestall** *vt* to prevent by taking action beforehand; to anticipate.

**forestry** *n* the science of planting and cultivating forests.

**foretell** *vt* (*pt* **foretold**) to forecast, to predict.

**for ever, forever** *adv* for all future time; continually.

**foreword** *n* a preface to a book.

**forfeit** *n* something confiscated or given up as a penalty for a fault. • *vt* to lose or be penalized by forfeiture.—**forfeiture** *n*.

**forgave** *see* **forgive**.

**forge**[1] *n* (a workshop with) a furnace in which metals are heated and shaped. • *vt* to shape (metal) by heating and hammering; to counterfeit (eg a signature). • *vi* to commit forgery.

**forge**[2] *vt* to move steadily forward with effort.

**forgery** *n* fraudulently copying; a forged copy.

**forget** *vti* (*pt* **forgot**, *pp* **forgotten**) to be unable to remember; to overlook or neglect.

**forgetful** *adj* apt to forget, inattentive. —**forgetfully** *adv*.—**forgetfulness** *n*.

**forgive** *vt* (*pt* **forgave**, *pp* **forgiven**) to cease to feel resentment against (a person); to pardon. • *vi* to be merciful or forgiving.—**forgiveness** *n*.

**forgo** *vt* (*pt* **forwent**, *pp* **forgone**) to give up, abstain from.—*also* **forego**.

**fork** *n* a small, usu metal, instrument with two or more thin prongs set in a handle, used in eating and cooking; a pronged agricultural or gardening tool for digging, etc; anything that divides into prongs or branches; one of the branches into which a road or river divides; the point of separation. • *vi* to divide into branches; to follow a branch of a fork in a road, etc. • *vt* to form as a fork; to dig, lift, etc with a fork.

**fork-lift truck** *n* a vehicle with power-operated prongs for raising and lowering loads.

**form** *n* general structure; the figure of a person or animal; a mould; a particular mode, kind, type, etc; arrangement; a way of doing something requiring skill; a conventional procedure; a printed document with blanks to be filled in; a class in school; condition of mind or body; a chart giving information about racehorses; changed appearance of a word to show inflection; (*sl*) a criminal record. • *vt* to shape; to train; to develop (habits); to constitute. • *vi* to be formed.

**formal** *adj* in conformity with established rules or habits; regular; relating to outward appearance only; ceremonial; punctilious; stiff.—**formally** *adv*.

**format** *n* the size, form, shape in which books, etc are issued; the general style or presentation of something, eg a television programme; (*comput*) the arrangement of data on magnetic disk, etc for access and storage. • *vt* (*pt* **formatted**) to arrange in a particular form, esp for a computer.

**formation** *n* form of making or producing; that which is formed; structure; regular array or prearranged order.

**formative** *adj* pertaining to formation and development; shaping.

**former** *adj* of or occurring in a previous time; the first mentioned (of two). —**formerly** *adv*.

**formidable** *adj* causing fear or awe; difficult to defeat or overcome; difficult to handle.—**formidably** *adv*.

**formula** *n* (*pl* **formulas**, **formulae**) a set of symbols expressing the composition of a substance; a general expression in algebraic form for solving a problem; a prescribed form; a formal statement of doctrines; a list of ingredients, as for a prescription or recipe; a fixed method according to which something is to be done; a prescribed recipe for baby food.

**formulate** *vt* to express in a formula; to devise.—**formulation** *n*.

**forsake** *vt* (*pt* **forsook**, *pp* **forsaken**) to desert; to give up, renounce.

**fort** *n* a fortified place for military defence.

**forte**[1] *n* something at which a person excels.

**forte**[2] *adv* (*mus*) loudly.

**forth** *adv* forwards; onwards; out.

**forthcoming** *adj* about to appear; readily available; responsive.

**forthright** *adv* frank, direct, outspoken.—**forthrightness** *n*.

**fortification** *n* act or process or fortifying; a wall, barricade, etc built to defend a position.

**fortify** *vt* to strengthen physically, emotionally, etc; to strengthen against attack, as with forts; to support; (*wine, etc*) to add alcohol to; (*milk*) to add vitamins to.

**fortitude** *n* courage in adversity.

**fortnight** *n* a period of two weeks or fourteen consecutive days.

**fortnightly** *adj, adv* once a fortnight.

**fortress** *n* a strong fort or fortified town.

**fortuitous** *adj* happening by chance. — **fortuitously** *adv.*—**fortuitousness** *n.*—**fortuity** *n.*

**fortunate** *adj* having or occurring by good luck.—**fortunately** *adv.*

**fortune** *n* the supposed arbitrary power that determines events; luck; destiny; prosperity, success; vast wealth.

**fortune-teller** *n* a person who claims to foretell a person's future.

**forty** *n* four times ten, the symbol for this (40, XL, xl).—*also adj.*—**fortieth** *adj.*

**forum** *n* an assembly or meeting to discuss topics of public concern; a medium for public debate, as a magazine; the marketplace and centre of public affairs in ancient Rome.

**forward** *adj* at, toward, or of the front; advanced; onward; prompt; bold; presumptuous; of or for the future. • *vt* to promote; to send on. • *n* (*sport*) an attacking player in various games. • *adv* toward the front; ahead.—**forwardness** *n.*

**forwent** *see* **forgo.**

**fossil** *n* the petrified remains of an animal or vegetable preserved in rock; (*inf*) a thing or person regarded as outmoded or redundant. • *adj* of or like a fossil; dug from the earth.

**foster** *vt* to encourage; to bring up (a child that is not one's own).

**fought** *see* **fight.**

**foul** *adj* stinking, loathsome; extremely dirty; indecent; wicked; (*language*) obscene; (*weather*) stormy; (*sports*) against the rules. • *vt* to make filthy;

to dishonour; to obstruct; to entangle (a rope, etc); to make a foul against, as in a game. • *vi* to be or become fouled. • *n* (*sports*) a hit, blow, move, etc that is foul.—**foully** *adv.*

**found**[1] *see* **find.**

**found**[2] *vt* to bring into being; to establish (as an institution) often with provision for future maintenance.

**found**[3] *vt* to melt and pour (metal) into a mould to produce castings.

**foundation** *n* an endowment for an institution; such an institution; the base of a house, wall, etc; a first layer of cosmetic applied to the skin; an underlying principle, etc; a supporting undergarment, as a corset.

**founder**[1] *n* one who founds an institution, a benefactor.

**founder**[2] *n* a person who casts metal.

**founder**[3] *vi* (*ship*) to fill with water and sink; to collapse; to fail.

**foundry** *n* a workshop or factory where metal castings are produced.

**fount**[1] *n* a set of printing type or characters of one style and size.—*also* **font.**

**fount**[2] *n* a source.

**fountain** *n* a natural spring of water; a source; an artificial jet or flow of water; the basin where this flows; a reservoir, as for ink. • *vti* to (cause to) flow or spurt like a fountain.

**four** *n* one more than three; the symbol for this (4, IV, iv); the fourth in a series or set; something having four units as members (as a four-cylinder engine).—*also adj.*

**fourteen** *n, adj* four and ten; the symbol for this (14, XIV, xiv).—**fourteenth** *adj.*

**fourth** *adj* next after third. • *n* one of four equal parts of something.— **fourthly** *adv.*

**fowl** *n* any of the domestic birds used as food, as the chicken, etc; the flesh of these birds. • *vi* to hunt or snare wildfowl.—**fowling** *n*.—**fowler** *n*.

**fox** *n* any of various small, alert wild mammals of the dog family; the fur of the fox; a sly, crafty person. • *vt* to deceive by cunning. • *vi* (*inf*) to bemuse, puzzle.

**foyer** *n* an anteroom; an entrance hallway, as in a hotel or theatre.

**fraction** *n* a small part, amount, etc; (*math*) a quantity less than a whole, expressed as a decimal or with a numerator and denominator.—**fractional** *adj*.—**fractionally** *adv*.

**fracture** *n* the breaking of any hard material, esp a bone. • *vti* to break; to cause or suffer a fracture.

**fragile** *adj* easily broken; frail; delicate.—**fragilely** *adv*.—**fragility** *n*.

**fragment** *n* a piece broken off or detached; an incomplete portion. • *vti* to break or cause to break into fragments.

**fragmentary** *adj* consisting of fragments; incomplete.

**fragrance, fragrancy** *n* a pleasant scent, a perfume.

**fragrant** *adj* sweet-scented.—**fragrantly** *adv*.

**frail** *adj* physically or morally weak; fragile.

**frame** *vt* to form according to a pattern; to construct; to put into words; to enclose (a picture) in a border; (*sl*) to falsify evidence against (an innocent person). • *n* something composed of parts fitted together and united; the physical make-up of an animal, esp a human body; the framework of a house; the case enclosing a window, door, etc; an ornamental border, as round a picture; (*snooker*) a triangular mould for setting up balls before play; (*snooker*) a single game.—**framer** *n*.

**framework** *n* a structural frame; a basic structure; frame of reference.

**franchise** *n* the right to vote in public elections; authorization to sell the goods of a manufacturer in a particular area. • *vt* to grant a franchise.

**frank** *adj* free and direct in expressing oneself; honest, open. • *vt* to mark letters, etc with a mark denoting free postage. • *n* a mark indicating free postage.—**frankness** *n*.

**frantic** *adj* violently agitated; furious, wild.—**frantically** *adv*.

**fraternal** *adj* of or belonging to a brother or fraternity; friendly, brotherly.—**fraternally** *adv*.

**fraternity** *n* brotherly feeling; a society of people with common interests.

**fraternize** *vt* to associate in a friendly manner.—**fraternization** *n*.

**fraud** *n* deliberate deceit; an act of deception; (*inf*) a deceitful person; an impostor.

**fraudulent** *adj* deceiving or intending to deceive; obtained by deceit.—**fraudulence** *n*.—**fraudulently** *adv*.

**fraught** *adj* filled or loaded (with).

**fray**[1] *n* a fight, a brawl.

**fray**[2] *vti* (*fabric, etc*) to (cause to) wear away into threads, esp at the edge of; (*nerves, temper*) to make or become irritated or strained.

**freak** *n* an unusual happening; any abnormal animal, person, or plant; (*inf*) a person who dresses or acts in a notably unconventional manner; an ardent enthusiast.—**freakish** *adj*.

**freckle** *n* a small, brownish spot on the skin. • *vti* to make or become spotted with freckles.—**freckled, freckly** *adj*.

**free** *adj* (**freer, freest**) not under the control or power of another; having social and political liberty; independent; able to move in any direction; not burdened by obligations; not confined to the usual rules; not exact; generous; frank; with no cost or charge; exempt from taxes, duties, etc; clear of obstruction; not fastened. • *adv* without cost; in a free manner. • *vt* (*pt* **freed**) to set free; to clear of obstruction, etc.—**freely** *adv*.

**freedom** *n* being free; exemption from obligation; unrestricted use; a right or privilege.

**freelance** *n* a person who pursues a profession without long-term commitment to any employer (—*also* **freelancer**). • *vt* to work as a freelance.

**Freemason** *n* a member of the secretive fraternity (Free and Accepted Masons) dedicated to mutual aid.

**free trade** *n* trade based on the unrestricted international exchange of goods with tariffs used only as a source of revenue.—**freetrader** *n*.

**freeway** *n* in North America, a fast road, a motorway.

**freewheel** *n* a device for temporarily disconnecting and setting free the back wheel of a bicycle from the driving gear. • *vi* to ride a bicycle with the gear disconnected; to drive a car with the gear in neutral.—**freewheeler** *n*.

**free will** *n* voluntary choice or decision; freedom of human beings to make choices that are not determined by prior causes or by divine intervention.

**freeze** *vb* (*pt* **froze**, *pp* **frozen**) *vi* to be formed into, or become covered by ice; to become very cold; to be damaged or killed by cold; to become motionless; to be made speechless by strong emotion; to become formal and unfriendly. • *vt* to harden into ice; to convert from a liquid to a solid with cold; to make extremely cold; to act towards in a stiff and formal way; to act on usu destructively by frost; to anaesthetize by cold; to fix (prices, etc) at a given level by au-

thority; to make (funds, etc) unavailable to the owners by authority.

**freezer** *n* a container that freezes and preserves food for long periods.

**freezing point** *n* the temperature at which a liquid solidifies.

**freight** *n* the transport of goods by water, land, or air; the cost for this; the goods transported. • *vt* to load with freight; to send by freight.

**freighter** *n* a ship or aircraft carrying freight.

**French** *adj* of France, its people, culture, etc. • *n* the language of France.

**French fries, french fries** *npl* thin strips of potato fried in oil, etc, chips.

**French windows, French doors** *npl* a pair of floor-length casement windows in an outside wall, opening on to a patio, garden, etc.

**frenzy** *n* wild excitement; violent mental derangement.—**frenzied** *adj*.—**frenziedly** *adv*.

**frequency** *n* repeated occurrence; the number of occurrences, cycles, etc in a given period.

**frequent** *adj* coming or happening often. • *vi* to visit often; to resort to.—**frequently** *adv*.

**fresco** *n* (*pl* **frescos**, **frescoes**) a picture painted on walls covered with damp freshly laid plaster.

**fresh** *adj* recently made, grown, etc; not salted, pickled, etc; not spoiled; lively, not tired; not worn, soiled, faded, etc; new, recent; inexperienced; cool and refreshing; (*wind*) brisk; (*water*) not salt; (*inf*) presumptuous, impertinent.—**freshly** *adv*.—**freshness** *n*.

**freshen** *vi* to make or become fresh.—**freshener** *n*.

**freshwater** *adj* of a river; not sea-going.

**fret**[1] *vti* (*pt* **fretted**) to make or become worried or anxious; to wear away or roughen by rubbing.

**fret**[2] *n* a running design of interlacing small bars. • *vt* (*pt* **fretted**) to furnish with frets.

**fret**[3] *n* any of a series of metal ridges along the finger-board of a guitar, banjo, etc used as a guide for depressing the strings.

**friar** *n* a member of certain Roman Catholic religious orders.

**friction** *n* a rubbing of one object against another; conflict between differing opinions, ideas, etc; the resistance to motion of things that touch.—**frictional** *adj*.

**Friday** *n* the sixth day of the week.

**fridge** *n* (*inf*) a refrigerator.

**fried** *see* **fry**[1].

**friend** *n* a person whom one knows well and is fond of; an ally, supporter —**friendless** *adj*.—**friendship** *n*.

**friendly** *adj* (**friendlier, friendliest**) like a friend; kindly; favourable. • *n* a sporting game played for fun, not in competition.—**friendliness** *n*.

**frieze** *n* a decorative band along the top of the wall of a room.

**frigate** *n* a warship smaller than a destroyer used for escort, anti-submarine, and patrol duties.

**fright** *n* sudden fear; a shock; (*inf*) something unsightly or ridiculous in appearance.

**frighten** *vt* to terrify, to scare; to force by frightening.

**frightful** *adj* terrible, shocking; (*inf*) extreme, very bad.—**frightfully** *adv*.

**frigid** *adj* extremely cold; not warm or friendly; unresponsive sexually.—**frigidly** *adv*.—**frigidity** *n*.

**frill** *n* a piece of pleated or gathered fabric used for edging; something superfluous, an affectation. • *vt* to decorate with a frill or frills.—**frilled** *adj*.—**frilly** *adj*.

**fringe** *n* a decorative border of hanging threads; hair hanging over the forehead; an outer edge; a marginal or minor part. • *vt* to be or make a fringe for. • *adj* at the outer edge; additional; minor; unconventional.

**frisk** *vi* to leap playfully. • *vt* (*inf*) to search (a person) by feeling for concealed weapons, etc.

**frisky** *adj* (**friskier, friskiest**) lively, playful.—**friskiness** *n*.

**fritter**[1] *n* a slice of fruit or meat fried in batter.

**fritter**[2] *vt* (*with* **away**) to waste; to break into tiny pieces.

**frivolity** *n* a trifling act, thought, or action.

**frivolous** *adj* irresponsible; trifling; silly.—**frivolously** *adv*.

**fro** *adv* away from; backward.

**frock** *n* a dress.

**frog** *n* a small tailless web-footed jumping amphibian; a decorative loop used to fasten clothing; (*offensive*) a French person.

**frogman** *n* a person who wears rubber suit, flippers, oxygen supply, etc and is trained in working underwater.

**frolic** *n* a lively party or game; merriment, fun. • *vi* (*pt* **frolicked**) to play happily.

**from** *prep* beginning at, starting with; out of; originating with; out of the possibility or use of.

**front** *n* outward behaviour; (*inf*) an appearance of social standing; etc; the part facing forward; the first part; a forward or leading position; the promenade of a seaside resort; the advanced battle area in warfare; a person or group used to hide another's activity; an advancing mass of cold or warm air. • *adj* at, to, in, on, or of the front. • *vti* to face; to serve as a front (for).

**frontal** *adj* of or belonging to the front; of or pertaining to the forehead. • *n* a decorative covering for the front of an altar.

**frontier** *n* the border between two

countries; the limit of existing knowledge of a subject.

**frost** n temperature at or below freezing point; a coating of powdery ice particles; coldness of manner. • vt to cover (as if) with frost or frosting; to give a frost-like opaque surface to (glass).

**frostbite** n injury to a part of the body by exposure to cold.

**frosting** n icing.

**frosty** adj (**frostier, frostiest**) cold with frost; cold or reserved in manner.— **frostily** adv.—**frostiness** n.

**froth** n foam; foaming saliva; frivolity. —also vi.—**frothily** adv.—**frothy** adj.

**frown** vi to contract the brow as in anger or thought; (with **upon**) to regard with displeasure or disapproval.— also n.

**froze, frozen** see **freeze**.

**frugal** adj economical, thrifty; inexpensive, meagre.—**frugally** adv.— **frugality** n.

**fruit** n the seed-bearing part of any plant; the fleshy part of this used as food; the result or product of any action. • vti to bear or cause to bear fruit.

**fruitful** adj producing lots of fruit; productive.—**fruitfulness** n.

**fruition** n a coming to fulfilment, realization.

**fruit machine** n a coin-operated gambling machine, using symbols of fruit to indicate a winning combination.

**frustrate** vt to prevent from achieving a goal or gratifying a desire; to discourage, to irritate, to tire.—**frustration** n.

**fry**[1] vti (pt **fried**) to cook over direct heat in hot fat. • n a dish of things fried.

**fry**[2] n recently hatched fishes.

**f-stop** see **stop**.

**ft.** abbr = foot or feet.

**fuchsia** n any of a genus of decorative shrubs.

**fudge** n a soft sweet made of butter, milk, sugar, flavouring, etc. • vi to refuse to commit oneself; to cheat. • vt to fake; to fail to come to grips with.

**fuel** n material burned to supply heat and power, or as a source of nuclear energy; anything that serves to intensify strong feelings. • vti (pt **fuelled**) to supply with fuel.

**fugitive** n a person who flees. • adj fleeing, as from danger or justice; fleeting, transient.

**fugue** n a polyphonic musical composition with its theme taken up successively by different voices.—**fugal** adj.

**fulfil, fulfill** (US) vt (pt **fulfilled**) to carry out (a promise, etc); to achieve the completion of; to satisfy; to bring to an end, complete.—**fulfilment** n.

**full** adj having or holding all that can be contained; having eaten all one wants; having a great number (of); complete; having reached to greatest size, extent, etc. • n the greatest amount, extent etc. • adv completely, directly, exactly.

**fullback** n (football, rugby, hockey, etc) one of the defensive players at the back; the position held by this player.

**full-stop** n the punctuation mark (.) at the end of a sentence.—also **period**.

**full time** n the finish of a match.

**full-time** adj working or lasting the whole time.—**full-timer** n.

**fully** adv thoroughly, at least

**fumble** vi to grope about. • vt to handle clumsily; to say or act awkwardly; to fail to catch (a ball) cleanly.—also n.

**fume** n (usu pl) smoke, gas or vapour, esp if offensive or suffocating. • vi to give off fumes; to express anger.

**fumigate** vt to disinfect or exterminate

(pests, etc) using fumes.—**fumiga-tion** n.

**fun** n (what provides) amusement and enjoyment.

**function** n the activity characteristic of a person or thing; the specific purpose of a certain person or thing; an official ceremony or social entertainment. • vi to perform a function; to act, operate.

**functional** adj of a function or functions; practical, not ornamental.

**fund** n a supply that can be drawn upon; a sum of money set aside for a purpose; (pl) ready money. • vt to provide funds for.

**fundamental** adj basic; essential. • n that which serves as a groundwork; an essential.—**fundamentally** adv.

**funeral** n the ceremony associated with the burial or cremation of the dead; a procession accompanying a coffin to a burial.

**fungus** n (pl fungi, funguses) any of a major group of lower plants, as mildews, mushrooms, yeasts, etc, that lack chlorophyll and reproduce by spores.—**fungal** adj.

**funnel** n an implement, usually a cone with a wide top and tapering to a narrow tube, for pouring fluids, powders, into bottles, etc; a metal chimney for the escape of smoke, steam, etc. • vti (pt **funnelled**) to (cause) to pour through a funnel.

**funny** adj (**funnier, funniest**) causing laughter; puzzling; odd; (inf) unwell, queasy.—**funnily** adv.—**funniness** n.

**fur** n the short, soft, fine hair on the bodies of certain animals; their skins with the fur attached; a garment made of fur; a fabric made in imitation of fur; a fur-like coating, as on the tongue. • vti (pt **furred**) to cover or become covered with fur.

**furious** adj full of anger; intense, violent.—**furiously** adv.

**furlong** n 220 yards, one-eighth of a mile.

**furlough** n leave of absence from duty, esp for military personnel. • vt to grant a furlough to.

**furnace** n an enclosed chamber in which heat is produced to burn refuse, smelt ore, etc.

**furnish** vt to provide (a room, etc) with furniture; to equip with what is necessary; to supply.

**furnishings** npl furniture, carpets, etc.

**furniture** n the things in a room, etc that equip it for living, as chairs, etc.

**furrow** n the groove in the earth made by a plough; a groove or track resembling this; a wrinkle. • vti to make furrows in; to wrinkle.

**furry** adj (**furrier, furriest**) like, made of, or covered with, fur.

**further** adv at or to a greater distance or degree; in addition. • adj more distant, remote; additional. • vt to help forward, promote.

**furthermore** adv moreover, besides.

**furthest** adj at or to the greatest distance.

**furtive** adj stealthy; sly.—**furtively** adv. —**furtiveness** n.

**fury** n intense rage; a frenzy; a violently angry person.

**fuse** vti to join or become joined by melting; to (cause to) melt by the application of heat; to equip a plug, circuit, etc with a fuse; to (cause to) fail by blowing a fuse. • n a tube or wick filled with combustible material for setting off an explosive charge; a piece of thin wire that melts and breaks when an electric current exceeds a certain level.

**fuselage** n the body of an aircraft.

**fusible** adj able to be fused.—**fusibly** adv.

**fusion** n the act of melting, blending or fusing; a product of fusion; union, partnership; nuclear fusion.

**fuss** *n* excited activity, bustle; a nervous state; (*inf*) a quarrel; (*inf*) a showy display of approval. • *vi* to worry over trifles; to whine, as a baby.—**fusser** *n*.

**fussy** *adj* (**fussier, fussiest**) worrying over details; hard to please; fastidious; over-elaborate.—**fussily** *adv*.—**fussiness** *n*.

**futile** *adj* useless; ineffective.—**futility** *n*.

**future** *adj* that is to be; of or referring to time yet to come. • *n* the time to come; future events; likelihood of eventual success.

**futuristic** *adj* forward-looking in design, appearance, intention, etc.

**fuzzy** *adj* (**fuzzier, fuzziest**) like fuzz; fluffy; blurred.—**fuzzily** *adv*.—**fuzziness** *n*.

# G

**g** *abbr* = gallons(s); gram(s); gravity; acceleration due to gravity.

**gabble** *vti* to talk or utter rapidly or incoherently; to utter inarticulate or animal sounds.—**gabbler** *n*.

**gable** *n* the triangular upper part of a wall enclosed by the sloping ends of a pitched roof.—**gabled** *adj*.

**gadget** *n* a small, often ingenious, mechanical or electronic tool or device.

**gag** *n* something put over or into the mouth to prevent talking; any restraint of free speech; a joke. • *vb* (*pt* **gagged**) *vt* to cause to retch; to keep from speaking, as by stopping the mouth of. • *vi* to retch; to tell jokes.

**gaiety** *n* happiness, liveliness; colourful appearance.

**gaily** *adv* in a cheerful manner; with bright colours.

**gain** *vt* to obtain, earn, esp by effort; to win in a contest; to attract; to get as an addition (esp profit or advantage); to make an increase in; to reach. • *vi* to make progress; to increase in weight. • *n* an increase esp in profit or advantage; an acquisition.

**gainful** *adj* profitable.—**gainfully** *adv*.

**gainsay** *vt* (*pt* **gainsaid**) (*formal*) to dispute; to deny.

**gait** *n* a manner of walking or running; the sequence of footsteps made by a moving horse.

**gala** *n* a celebration, festival.

**galaxy** *n* any of the systems of stars in the universe; any splendid assemblage; (*with cap*) the galaxy containing the Earth's solar system; the Milky Way.

**gale** *n* a strong wind, specifically one between 39 to 46 mph; an outburst.

**gallant** *adj* dignified, stately; brave; noble; (*man*) polite and chivalrous to women.—**gallantly** *adv*.—**gallantry** *n*.

**gall bladder** *n* a membranous sac attached to the liver in which bile is stored.

**gallery** *n* a covered passage for walking; a long narrow outside balcony; a balcony running along the inside wall of a building; (the occupants of) an upper area of seating in a theatre; a long narrow room used for a special purpose, eg shooting practice; a room or building designed for the exhibition of works of art; the spectators at a golf tournament, tennis match, etc.

**galley** *n* a long, usu low, ship of ancient or medieval times, propelled by oars; the kitchen of a ship, aircraft; (*print*) a shallow tray for holding type; proofs printed from such type (—*also* **galley proof**).

**gallon** *n* a unit of liquid measure comprising 277.42 cubic inches (in US,

231 cubic inches); (*pl*) (*inf*) a large amount.

**gallop** *n* the fastest gait of a horse, etc; a succession of leaping strides; a fast pace. • *vti* to go or cause to go at a gallop; to move swiftly.

**gallows** *n* (*pl* **gallowses, gallows**) a wooden frame used for hanging criminals.

**gallstone** *n* a small solid mass in the gall bladder.

**gambit** *n* (*chess*) an opening in which a piece is sacrificed to gain an advantage; any action to gain an advantage.

**gamble** *vi* to play games of chance for money; to take a risk for some advantage. • *vt* to risk in gambling, to bet. • *n* a risky venture; a bet.— **gambler** *n*.

**game**[1] *n* any form of play, amusement; activity or sport involving competition; a scheme, a plan; wild birds or animals hunted for sport or food, the flesh of such animals. • *vi* to play for a stake. • *adj* (*inf*) brave, resolute; (*inf*) willing.—**gamely** *adv*.— **gameness** *n*.

**game**[2] *adj* (*limbs*) injured, crippled.

**gamekeeper** *n* a person who breeds and takes care of game birds and animals, as on an estate.

**gammon** *n* cured or smoked ham; meat from the hindquarters of a side of bacon.

**gander** *n* an adult male goose; (*inf*) a quick look.

**gang** *n* a group of persons, esp labourers, working together; a group of persons acting or associating together, esp for illegal purposes. • *vti* to form into or act as a gang.

**gangrene** *n* death of body tissue when the blood supply is obstructed.— **gangrenous** *adj*.

**gangster** *n* a member of a criminal gang.

**gangway** *n* a passageway, esp an opening in a ship's side for loading, etc; a gangplank.

**gaol, gaoler** *see* **jail, jailer**.

**gap** *n* a break or opening in something, as a wall or fence; an interruption in continuity, an interval; a mountain pass; a divergence, disparity. • *vt* (*pt* **gapped**) to make a gap in.—**gappy** *adj*.

**gape** *vi* to open the mouth wide; to stare in astonishment, esp with the mouth open; to open widely. • *n* the act of gaping; a wide opening.

**garage** *n* an enclosed shelter for motor vehicles; a place where motor vehicles are repaired and serviced, and fuel sold. • *vt* to put or keep in a garage.

**garbage** *n* food waste; unwanted or useless material; rubbish.

**garden** *n* an area of ground for growing herbs, fruits, flowers, or vegetables, usu attached to a house; a fertile, well-cultivated region; a public park or recreation area, usu laid-out with plants and trees. • *vi* to make, or work in, a garden.—**gardener** *n*.— **gardening** *n*.

**gargle** *vti* to rinse the throat by breathing air from the lungs through liquid held in the mouth. • *n* a liquid for this purpose; the sound made by gargling.

**gargoyle** *n* a grotesquely carved face or figure, usu acting as a spout to drain water from a gutter; a person with an ugly face.

**garish** *adj* crudely bright, gaudy.—**garishly** *adv*.

**garland** *n* a wreath of flowers or leaves worn or hung as decoration. • *vt* to decorate with a garland.

**garlic** *n* a bulbous herb cultivated for its compound bulbs used in cookery; its bulb.—**garlicky** *adj*.

**garment** *n* an item of clothing.

**garnish** *vt* to decorate; to decorate (food) with something that adds colour or flavour. • *n* something used to garnish food.—**garniture** *n*.

**garret** *n* an attic.

**garrison** *n* troops stationed at a fort; a fortified place with troops. • *vt* to station (troops) in (a fortified place) for its defence.

**garrulous** *adj* excessively talkative. — **garrulity** *n*.—**garrulous** *adv.*—**garrulousness** *n*.

**garter** *n* an elasticated band used to support a stocking or sock.

**gas** *n* (*pl* **gases**) an air-like substance with the capacity to expand indefinitely and not liquefy or solidify at ordinary temperatures; any mixture of flammable gases used for lighting or heating; any gas used as an anaesthetic; any poisonous substance dispersed in the air, as in war; (*inf*) empty talk; gasoline. • *vt* (*pt* **gassed**) to poison or disable with gas; (*inf*) to talk idly.

**gash** *n* a long, deep, open cut.—*also vt*.

**gasket** *n* a piece or ring of rubber, metal, etc sandwiched between metal surfaces to act as a seal.

**gas mask** *n* a protective breathing device worn over the face, which filters out poisonous gases.

**gasoline, gasolene** *n* petrol.

**gasp** *vi* to draw in the breath suddenly and audibly, as from shock; to struggle to catch the breath. • *vt* to utter breathlessly. • *n* the act of gasping.

**gastric** *adj* of, in, or near the stomach.

**gastronomy** *n* the art and science of good eating.—**gastronomic** *adj*.

**gate** *n* a movable structure controlling passage through an opening in a fence or wall; a gateway; a movable barrier; a structure controlling the flow of water, as in a canal; a device (as in a computer) that outputs a signal when specified input conditions are met; the total amount or number of paid admissions to a football match, etc. • *vt* to supply with a gate; to keep within the gates (of a university) as a punishment.

**gate-crasher** *n* a person who attends a party, etc without being invited.— **gatecrash** *vi*.

**gateway** *n* an opening for a gate; a means of entrance or exit.

**gather** *vt* to bring together in one place or group; to get gradually; to collect (as taxes); to harvest; to draw (parts) together; to pucker fabric by pulling a thread or stitching; to understand, infer. • *vi* to come together in a body; to cluster around a focus of attention; (*sore*) to swell and fill with pus.

**gathering** *n* the act of gathering or assembling together; an assembly; folds made in a garment by gathering.

**gauche** *adj* socially inept; graceless, tactless.—**gauchely** *adv*.

**gaudy** *adj* (**gaudier, gaudiest**) excessively ornamented; tastelessly bright. —**gaudily** *adv.*—**gaudiness** *n*.

**gauge, gage** (*US*) *n* measurement according to some standard or system; any device for measuring; the distance between rails of a railway; the size of the bore of a shotgun; the thickness of sheet metal, wire, etc. • *vt* to measure the size, amount, etc, of.—**gaugeable** *adj.*—**gauger** *n*.

**gaunt** *adj* excessively thin as from hunger or age; looking grim or forbidding.—**gauntness** *n*.

**gauntlet**[1] *n* a knight's armoured glove; a long glove, often with a flaring cuff.

**gauntlet**[2] *n* (*formerly*) a type of military punishment in which a victim was forced to run between two lines of men who struck him as he passed.

**gauze** *n* any very thin, loosely woven fabric, as of cotton or silk; a firm woven material of metal or plastic

filaments; a surgical dressing.—
**gauzy** adj.—**gauzily** adv.

**gave** see **give**.

**gawp** vi (inf) to stare stupidly.

**gay** adj joyous and lively; colourful;
homosexual.—**gayness** n.

**gaze** vi to look steadily. • n a steady
look.

**gazelle** n any of numerous small swift
Asian or African antelopes.

**gazump** vti to force up a price (esp of
a house) after a price has been
agreed. —**gazumper** n.

**GB** abbr = Great Britain.

**GCE** abbr = General Certificate of
Education.

**gear** n clothing; equipment, esp for
some task or activity; a toothed wheel
for meshing with another; (often pl)
a system of such gears meshed to
transmit motion; a specific adjustment of such a system; a part of a
mechanism with a specific function.
• vt to connect by or furnish with
gears; to adapt (one thing) to conform with another.

**gearbox** n a metal case enclosing a system of gears.

**gear lever** n a lever used to engage or
change gear, esp in a motor vehicle.

**geese** see **goose**.

**gelatin, gelatine** n a tasteless, odourless substance extracted by boiling
bones, hoofs, etc and used in food,
photographic film, medicines, etc.

**gelignite** n an explosive consisting of
nitroglycerin absorbed in a base of
wood pulp mixed with sodium or potassium nitrate.

**gem** n a precious stone, esp when cut
and polished for use as a jewel; a
person or thing regarded as extremely valuable or beloved.

**Gemini** n the third sign of the zodiac,
represented by the twins Castor and
Pollux, operative 21 May–20 June.

**gender** n the classification by which

words are grouped as feminine, masculine, or neuter; (inf) the sex of a
person.

**general** adj not local, special, or specialized; of or for a whole genus, relating to or covering all instances or
individuals of a class or group; widespread, common to many; not specific or precise; holding superior
rank, chief. • n something that involves or is applicable to the whole;
a commissioned officer above a lieutenant general; a leader, commander; the title of the head of some
religious orders.

**general election** n a national election
to choose parliamentary representatives in every constituency.

**generalize** vti to form general conclusions from specific instances; to talk
(about something) in general
terms.—**generalization** n.

**generally** adv widely; popularly; usually; not specifically.

**general practitioner** n a non-specialist
doctor who treats all types of ill-
nesses in the community.

**generate** vt to bring into existence; to
produce.

**generation** n the act or process of generating; a single succession in natural
descent; people of the same period;
production, as of electric current.

**generator** n one who or that which
generates; a machine that changes
mechanical energy to electrical energy.

**generosity** n the quality of being generous; liberality; munificence.

**generous** adj magnanimous; of a noble nature; willing to give or share;
large, ample.—**generously** adv.

**genetic** adj of or relating to the origin,
development or causes of some-
thing; of or relating to genes or ge-
netics.—**genetically** adv.

**genial** adj kindly, sympathetic and

cheerful in manner; mild, pleasantly warm.—**genially** adv.—**geniality** n.

**genitals, genitalia** npl the (external) sexual organs.

**genitive** adj (gram) of or belonging to the case of nouns, pronouns and adjectives expressing ownership or relation. • n the genitive case.

**genius** n (pl **geniuses**) a person possessing extraordinary intellectual power; (with **for**) natural ability.

**gent** n (inf) a gentleman.

**genteel** adj polite or well-bred; affectedly refined.—**genteelly** adv.

**gentle** adj belonging to a family of high social station; refined, courteous; generous; kind; kindly; patient; not harsh or rough.—**gently** adv.

**gentleman** n a man of good family and social standing; a courteous, gracious and honourable man; a polite term of address.—**gentlemanly** adj.

**gentry** n people of high social standing; (formerly) landed proprietors not belonging to the nobility.

**genuine** adj not fake or artificial, real; sincere.—**genuinely** adv.—**genuineness** n.

**geography** n the science of the physical nature of the earth, such as land and sea masses, climate, vegetation, etc, and their interaction with the human population; the physical features of a region.—**geographer** n.—**geographic, geographical** adj.—**geographically** adv.

**geology** n the science relating to the history and structure of the earth's crust, its rocks and fossils.—**geologist** n.—**geological** adj.—**geologically** adv.

**geometry** n the branch of mathematics dealing with the properties, measurement, and relationships of points, lines, planes, and solids.—**geometric, geometrical** adj.—**geometrically** adv.

**geranium** n a garden plant with red, pink or white flowers.

**germ** n a simple form of living matter capable of growth and development into an organism; any microscopic, disease-causing organism; an origin or foundation capable of growing and developing.

**German** adj of or relating to Germany, its people or their language. • n a native of Germany.

**German measles** n (used as sing) a mild contagious disease similar to measles.—also **rubella**.

**germinate** vti to start developing; to sprout, as from a seed.—**germination** n.—**germinator** n.

**gestate** vt to carry (young) in the womb during pregnancy; to develop (a plan, etc) gradually in the mind. —**gestation** n.

**gesticulate** vi to make expressive gestures, esp when speaking.—**gesticulation** n.

**gesture** n movement of part of the body to express or emphasize ideas, emotions, etc. • vi to make a gesture. —**gestural** adj.

**get** vb (pr p **getting**, pt **got**, pp **got** or **gotten**) vt to obtain, gain, win; to receive; to acquire; to go and bring; to catch; to persuade; to cause to be; to prepare; (inf) (with **have** or **has**) to be obliged to; to possess; (inf) to strike, kill, baffle; defeat, etc; (inf) to understand; (with **out of**) to avoid doing; (with **over**) to communicate effectively. • vi to come; to go; to arrive; to come to be; to manage or contrive; (with **at**) to reach; (inf) to imply; (inf) to criticize; (inf) to corrupt, bribe; (with **away**) to escape; (with **by**) (inf) to manage, to survive; (with **off**) to come off, down, or out of; to be acquitted; to depart; (with **on**) to go on or into; to put on; to proceed; to grow older; to manage;

to succeed; (*with* **on with**) to establish a friendly relationship; (*with* **out**) to go out or away; to take out; to disclose, publish; (*with* **over**) to recover from; to forget; (*with* **through**) to finish; to manage to survive; to succeed; (*with* **up**) to rise to one's feet; to get out of bed; (*inf*) to organize; (*inf*) to dress in a certain style; (*inf*) to be involved in (mischief, etc).

**getaway** *n* the act of escaping; a start in a race, etc.

**get-together** *n* (*inf*) an informal social gathering or meeting.

**get-up** *n* (*inf*) dress, costume.

**geyser** *n* a natural spring from which columns of boiling water and steam gush into the air at intervals; a water heater.

**ghastly** *adj* (**ghastlier, ghastliest**) terrifying, horrible; (*inf*) intensely disagreeable; pale, unwell looking.—**ghastliness** *n*.

**gherkin** *n* a small cucumber used for pickling.

**ghetto** *n* (*pl* **ghettos**) a section of a city in which members of a minority group live, esp because of social, legal or economic pressure.

**ghost** *n* the supposed disembodied spirit of a dead person, appearing as a shadowy apparition; a faint trace or suggestion; a false image in a photographic negative.—**ghostly** *adj*.—**ghostliness** *n*.

**giant** *n* a huge legendary being of great strength; a person or thing of great size, strength, intellect, etc. • *adj* incredibly large.—**giantess** *nf*.

**gibberish** *n* unintelligible talk, nonsense.

**gibe** *n* a taunt, sneer. • *vti* to jeer, scoff (at).—*also* **jibe**.

**giblets** *npl* the edible internal organs of a bird.

**giddy** *adj* (**giddier, giddiest**) frivolous, flighty; having a feeling of whirling around as if about to lose balance and fall; causing giddiness.—**giddily** *adv*.—**giddiness** *n*.

**gift** *n* something given; the act of giving; a natural ability. • *vt* to present with or as a gift.

**gifted** *adj* having great natural ability.

**gigantic** *adj* exceedingly large.—**gigantically** *adv*.

**giggle** *vi* to laugh in a nervous or silly manner. • *n* a laugh in this manner; (*inf*) a prank, a joke.—**giggler** *n*.

**gild** *vt* (*pt* **gilded** *or* **gilt**) to coat with gold leaf; to give a deceptively attractive appearance to.—**gilder** *n*—**gilding** *n*.

**gill**¹ *n* an organ, esp in fish, for breathing in water.

**gill**² *n* a liquid measure equal to a quarter of a pint.

**gills** *npl* the fold of skin below the beak of certain birds; one of the radiating plates under the cap of a mushroom; a person's cheeks or jowls.

**gilt**¹ *see* **gild**.

**gilt**² *n* gilding; a substance used for this.

**gimlet** *n* a small tool with a screw point for boring holes.

**gimmick** *n* a trick or device for attracting notice, advertising or promoting a person, product or service. —**gimmickry** *n*.—**gimmicky** *adj*.

**gin**¹ *n* an alcoholic spirit distilled from grain and flavoured with juniper berries.

**gin**² *n* a trap for catching small animals; a type of crane; a machine for separating seeds from raw cotton.

**ginger** *n* a tropical plant with fleshy roots used as a flavouring; spice prepared by drying and grinding; (*inf*) vigour; a reddish-brown.—**gingery** *adj*.

**ginger ale, ginger beer** *n* a carbonated soft drink flavoured with ginger.

**gingerbread** n a cake flavoured with ginger.

**gingerly** adv with care or caution. • adj cautious.

**gingham** n a cotton fabric with stripes or checks.

**gipsy** see **gypsy**.

**giraffe** n a large cud-chewing mammal of Africa, with very long legs and neck.

**girder** n a large steel beam for supporting joists, the framework of a building, etc.

**girdle** n a belt for the waist.

**girl** n a female child; a young woman; (inf) a woman of any age.—**girlhood** n.—**girlish** adj.

**girlfriend** n a female friend, esp with whom one is romantically involved.

**girth** n the thickness round something; a band put around the belly of a horse, etc to hold a saddle or pack.

**gist** n the principal point or essence of anything.

**give** vb (pt **gave**, pp **given**) vt to hand over as a present; to deliver; to hand over in or for payment; to pass (regards etc) along; to act as host or sponsor of; to supply; to yield; (advice) to offer; (punishment, etc) to inflict; to sacrifice; to perform; (with away) to make a gift of; to give (the bride) to the bridegroom; to sell cheaply; to reveal, betray; (with in) to deliver (a document, etc); (with off) to emit (fumes, etc); (with out) to discharge; to make public; to distribute; (with over) to devote time to a specific activity; to cease (an activity); (with up) to hand over; to renounce; to cease; to stop trying; to despair of; to devote wholly. • vi to bend, move, etc from force or pressure; (inf) to be happening. • n capacity or tendency to yield to force or strain; the quality or state of being springy; (with in) to submit; (with out) to become worn out; (with up) to surrender.

**give-away** n (inf) an unintentional revelation.

**glacier** n a large mass of snow and ice moving slowly down a mountain.

**glad** adj (**gladder**, **gladdest**) happy; causing joy; very willing; bright.—**gladly** adv.—**gladness** n.

**gladden** vti to make or become glad.

**gladiator** n (ancient Rome) a person trained to fight with men or beasts in a public arena.—**gladiatorial** adj.

**glamour, glamor** (US) n charm, allure; attractiveness, beauty.—**glamorous** adj.—**glamorously** adv.

**glance** vi to strike obliquely and go off at an angle; to flash; to look quickly. • n a glancing off; a flash; a quick look.—**glancingly** adv.

**gland** n an organ that separates substances from the blood and synthesizes them for further use in, or for elimination from, the body.—**glandular** adj.

**glare** n a harsh uncomfortably bright light, esp painfully bright sunlight; an angry or fierce stare. • vi to shine with a steady, dazzling light; to stare fiercely.

**glass** n a hard brittle substance, usu transparent; glassware, a glass article, as a drinking vessel; (pl) spectacles or binoculars; the amount held by a drinking glass. • adj of or made of glass. • vt to equip, enclose, or cover with glass.

**glasshouse** n a large greenhouse for the commercial cultivation of plants; (inf) a military prison.

**glassware** n objects made of glass, esp drinking vessels.

**glassy** adj (**glassier**, **glassiest**) resembling glass; smooth; expressionless, lifeless.—**glassily** adv.—**glassiness** n.

**glaze** *vt* to provide (windows etc) with glass; to give a hard glossy finish to (pottery, etc); to cover (foods, etc) with a glossy surface. • *vi* to become glassy or glossy. • *n* a glassy finish or coating.—**glazer** *n*.

**glazier** *n* a person who fits glass in windows.—**glaziery** *n*.

**gleam** *n* a subdued or moderate beam of light; a brief show of some quality or emotion, esp hope. • *vi* to emit or reflect a beam of light.

**glee** *n* joy and gaiety; delight; (*mus*) a song in parts for three or more male voices.—**gleeful** *adj*.—**gleefully** *adv*.

**glen** *n* a narrow valley.

**glib** *adj* (**glibber, glibbest**) speaking or spoken smoothly, to the point of insincerity; lacking depth and substance.—**glibly** *adv*.—**glibness** *n*.

**glide** *vti* to move smoothly and effortlessly; to descend in an aircraft or glider with little or no engine power. • *n* a gliding movement.

**glider** *n* an engineless aircraft carried along by air currents.

**gliding** *n* the sport of flying gliders.

**glimmer** *vi* to give a faint, flickering light; to appear faintly.—*also n*.

**glimpse** *n* a brief, momentary view. • *vt* to catch a glimpse of.

**glint** *n* a brief flash of light; a brief indication. • *vti* to (cause to) gleam brightly.

**glisten** *vi* to shine, as light reflected from a wet surface.

**glitter** *vi* to sparkle; (*usu with* **with**) to be brilliantly attractive. • *n* a sparkle; showiness, glamour; tiny pieces of sparkling material used for decoration.—**glittery** *adj*.

**gloaming** *n* twilight.

**gloat** *vi* to gaze or contemplate with wicked or malicious satisfaction.

**global** *adj* worldwide; comprehensive.—**globally** *adv*.

**globe** *n* anything spherical or almost spherical; the earth, or a model of it.

**gloom** *n* near darkness; deep sadness. • *vti* to look sullen or dejected; to make or become cloudy or murky.

**gloomy** *adj* (**gloomier, gloomiest**) almost dark, obscure; depressed, dejected.—**gloomily** *adv*.—**gloominess** *n*.

**glorify** *vt* to worship; to praise, to honour; to cause to appear more worthy, important, or splendid than in reality.—**glorification** *n*.

**glorious** *adj* having or deserving glory; conferring glory or renown; beautiful; delightful.—**gloriously** *adv*.

**glory** *n* great honour or fame, or its source; adoration; great splendour or beauty; heavenly bliss. • *vi* (*with* **in**) to exult, rejoice proudly.

**gloss**[1] *n* the lustre of a polished surface; a superficially attractive appearance. • *vt* to give a shiny surface to; (*with* **over**) to hide (an error, etc) or make seem right or inconsequential.

**gloss**[2] *n* an explanation of an unusual word (in the margin or between the lines of a text); a misleading explanation; a glossary. • *vt* to provide with glosses; to give a misleading sense of.

**glossary** *n* a list of specialized or technical words and their definitions.

**glossy** *adj* (**glossier, glossiest**) having a shiny or highly polished surface; superficial; (*magazines*) lavishly produced.—**glossily** *adv*.—**glossiness** *n*.

**glove** *n* a covering for the hand; a baseball player's mitt; a boxing glove. • *vt* to cover (as if) with a glove.

**glow** *vi* to shine (as if) with an intense heat; to emit a steady light without flames; to be full of life and enthusiasm; to flush or redden with emotion. • *n* a light emitted due to intense heat; a steady, even light without flames; a reddening of the complexion; warmth of emotion or feeling.

**glower** vi to scowl; to stare sullenly or angrily.—also n.—**gloweringly** adv.

**glucose** n a crystalline sugar occurring naturally in fruits, honey, etc.

**glue** n a sticky, viscous substance used as an adhesive. • vt (pr p **gluing**, pt **glued**) to join with glue.—**gluey** adj.

**glum** adj (**glummer**, **glummest**) sullen; gloomy.—**glumly** adv.—**glumness** n.

**glut** vt (pt **glutted**) to over-supply (the market). • n a surfeit, an excess of supply.

**glutton** n a person who eats and drinks to excess; a person who has a tremendous capacity for something (eg for work).—**gluttonous** adj.—**gluttony** n.

**gm** abbr = gram(s).

**gnarled** adj (tree trunks) full of knots; (hands) rough, knobbly; crabby in disposition.

**gnat** n any of various small, two-winged insects that bite or sting.

**gnaw** vti (pp **gnawed** or **gnawn**) to bite away bit by bit; to torment, as by constant pain.

**gnome** n (folklore) a dwarf who dwells in the earth and guards its treasure; a small statue of a gnome used as a garden decoration; a small and ugly person; (sl) an international banker or financier.

**go**¹ vb (pt **went**, pp **gone**) vi to move on a course; to proceed; to work properly; to act, sound, as specified; to result; to become; to be accepted or valid; to leave, to depart; to die; to be allotted or sold; to be able to pass (through); to fit (into); to be capable of being divided (into); to belong; (with **about**) to handle (a task, etc) efficiently; to undertake (duties, etc); (sailing) to change tack; (with **off**) to explode; to become stale; to fall asleep; to take place as planned; to cease to like; (with **slow**) to work at a slow rate as part of an industrial

dispute. • vt to travel along; (inf) to put up with. • n (pl **goes**) a success; (inf) a try; (inf) energy.

**go**² n a Japanese board game.

**goad** n a sharp-pointed stick for driving cattle, etc; any stimulus to action. • vt to drive (as if) with a goad; to irritate, nag persistently.

**go-ahead** n (inf) permission to proceed. • adj (inf) enterprising, ambitious.

**goal** n the place at which a race, trip, etc is ended; an objective; the place over or into which (the ball) must go to score in some games; the score made.

**goalkeeper** n a player who defends the goal.

**goat** n a mammal related to the sheep that has backward curving horns, a short tail, and usu straight hair; a lecherous man.

**gobble** vt to eat greedily; (often with up) to take, accept or read eagerly. • vi to make a gurgling noise, as a turkey.

**go-between** n a messenger, an intermediary.

**goblet** n a large drinking vessel with a base and stem but without a handle.

**goblin** n an evil or mischievous elf.

**god** n any of various beings conceived of as supernatural and immortal, esp a male deity; an idol; a person or thing deified; (with cap) in monotheistic religions, the creator and ruler of the universe.

**godchild** n (pl **godchildren**) the child a godparent sponsors.

**goddess** n a female god; a lovely woman.

**godfather** n a male godparent; the head of a Mafia crime family or other criminal organization.

**god-forsaken** adj desolate, wretched.

**godmother** n a female godparent.

**godparent** n a person who sponsors a

child, as at baptism, taking responsibility for its faith.

**godsend** *n* anything that comes unexpectedly when needed or desired.

**godson** *n* a male godchild.

**goggle** *vi* to stare with bulging eyes. • *npl* large spectacles fitting snugly against the face, to protect the eyes.

**going** *n* an act or instance of going, a departure; the state of the ground, eg for walking, etc; rate of progress. • *adj* that goes; commonly accepted; thriving; existing.

**gold** *n* a malleable yellow metallic element used esp for coins and jewellery; a precious metal; money, wealth; a yellow colour. • *adj* of, or like, gold.

**golden** *adj* made of or relating to gold; bright yellow; priceless; flourishing.

**golden rule** *n* a guiding principle.

**goldfish** *n* (*pl* **goldfish**) a small gold-coloured fish of the carp family, kept in ponds and aquariums.

**golf** *n* an outdoor game in which the player attempts to hit a small ball with clubs around a turfed course into a succession of holes in the smallest number of strokes.—**golfer** *n*.

**golf club** *n* a club with a wooden or metal head used in golf; a golf association or its premises.

**golf course, golf links** *n* a tract of land laid out for playing golf.

**gondola** *n* a long, narrow, black boat used on the canals of Venice; a cabin suspended under an airship or balloon; an enclosed car suspended from a cable used to transport passengers, esp skiers up a mountain; a display structure in a supermarket, etc.

**gone**[1] *see* **go**[1].

**gone**[2] *adj* departed; dead; lost; (*inf*) in an excited state; (*inf*) pregnant for a specified period.

**gong** *n* a disk-shaped percussion instrument struck with a usu padded hammer; (*sl*) a medal. • *vi* to sound a gong.

**good** *adj* (**better, best**) having the right or proper qualities; beneficial; valid; healthy or sound; virtuous, honourable; enjoyable, pleasant, etc; skilled; considerable. • *n* something good; benefit; something that has economic utility; (*with* **the**) good persons; (*pl*) personal property; commodities; (*pl*) the desired or required articles. • *adv* (*inf*) well; fully.

**goodbye** *interj* a concluding remark at parting; farewell.—*also n*.

**Good Friday** *n* the Friday before Easter, commemorating the Crucifixion of Christ.

**good-looking** *adj* handsome.

**goodness** *n* the state of being good; the good element in something; kindness; virtue. • *interj* an exclamation of surprise.

**goodwill** *n* benevolence; willingness; the established custom and reputation of a business.

**goose** *n* (*pl* **geese**) a large, long-necked, web-footed bird related to swans and ducks; its flesh as food; a female goose as distinguished from a gander; (*inf*) a foolish person.

**gooseberry** *n* the berry of a shrub related to the currant, used in jams, etc.

**goose bumps, goose pimples, goose flesh** *n* a roughening of the skin caused usu by cold or fear.

**gore**[1] *n* (clotted) blood from a wound.

**gore**[2] *n* a tapering section of material used to shape a garment, sail, etc.

**gore**[3] *vt* to pierce or wound as with a tusk or horns.

**gorge** *n* a ravine. • *vt* to swallow greedily; to glut. • *vi* to feed gluttonously.

**gorgeous** *adj* strikingly attractive; brilliantly coloured; *(inf)* magnificent.—**gorgeously** *adv.*—**gorgeousness** *n*.

**gorilla** *n* an anthropoid ape of western equatorial Africa related to the chimpanzee but much larger.

**gorse** *n* a spiny yellow-flowered European shrub.

**gory** *adj* (**gorier**, **goriest**) bloodthirsty; causing bloodshed; covered in blood.—**gorily** *adv.*—**goriness** *n*.

**go-slow** *n* a deliberate slowing of the work rate by employees as a form of industrial action.

**gospel** *n* the life and teachings of Christ contained in the first four books of the New Testament; *(with cap)* one of these books; anything proclaimed or accepted as the absolute truth.

**gossamer** *n* very fine cobwebs; any very light and flimsy material. • *adj* light as gossamer.

**gossip** *n* one who chatters idly about others; such talk. • *vi* to take part in or spread gossip.—**gossipy** *adj*.

**got, gotten** *see* **get**.

**gout** *n* a disease causing painful inflammation of the joints; esp of the great toe.—**gouty** *adj*.

**govern** *vti* to exercise authority over; to rule, to control; to influence the action of; to determine.

**governess** *n* a woman employed in a private home to teach children.

**government** *n* the exercise of authority over a state, organization, etc; a system of ruling, political administration, etc; those who direct the affairs of a state, etc.—**governmental** *adj*.

**governor** *n* a person appointed to govern a province, etc; the elected head of any state of the US; the director or head of a governing body of an organization or institution; *(sl)* an employer; a mechanical device for automatically controlling the speed of an engine.

**gown** *n* a loose outer garment, specifically a woman's formal dress, a nightgown, a long, flowing robe worn by clergymen, judges, university teachers, etc; a type of overall worn in the operating room.

**GP** *abbr* = general practitioner.

**grab** *vt* (*pt* **grabbed**) to take or grasp suddenly; to obtain unscrupulously; *(inf)* to catch the interest or attention of. • *n* a sudden clutch or attempt to grasp; a mechanical device for grasping and lifting objects.

**grace** *n* beauty or charm of form, movement, or expression; good will; favour; a delay granted for payment of an obligation; a short prayer of thanks for a meal. • *vt* to decorate; to dignify.

**graceful** *adj* having beauty of form, movement, or expression.—**gracefully** *adv.*—**gracefulness** *n*.

**gracious** *adj* having or showing kindness, courtesy, etc; compassionate; polite to supposed inferiors; marked by luxury, ease, etc. • *interj* an expression of surprise.—**graciously** *adv.*—**graciousness** *n*.

**gradation** *n* a series of systematic steps in rank, degree, etc; arranging in such stages; a single stage in a gradual progression; progressive change.

**grade** *n* a stage or step in a progression; a degree in a scale of quality, rank, etc; a group of people of the same rank, merit, etc; the degree of slope; a sloping part; a mark or rating in an examination, etc. • *vt* to arrange in grades; to give a grade to; to make level or evenly sloping.

**gradient** *n* a sloping road or railway; the degree of slope in a road, etc.

**gradual** *adj* taking place by degrees.—**gradually** *adv*.

**graduate** *n* a person who has completed a course of study at a school, college, etc; a receptacle marked with figures for measuring contents. • *adj* holding an academic degree or diploma; of or relating to studies beyond the first or bachelor's degree.

**graduation** *n* graduating or being graduated; the ceremony at which degrees are conferred by a college or university; an arranging or marking in grades or stages.

**graft** *n* a shoot or bud of one plant inserted into another, where it grows permanently; the transplanting of skin, bone, etc; the getting of money or advantage dishonestly.

**grain** *n* the seed of any cereal plant, as wheat, corn, etc; cereal plants; a tiny, solid particle, as of salt or sand; a unit of weight, 0.0648 gram; the arrangement of fibres, layers, etc of wood, leather, etc; the markings or texture due to this; natural disposition. • *vt* to form into grains; to paint in imitation of the grain of wood, etc. • *vi* to become granular.

**gram, gramme** *n* the basic unit of weight in the metric system, equal to one thousandth of a kilogram (one 28th of an ounce).

**grammar** *n* the study of the forms of words and their arrangement in sentences; a system of rules for speaking and writing a language; a grammar textbook; the use of language in speech or writing judged with regard to correctness of spelling, syntax, etc.

**grammatical** *adj* conforming to the rules of grammar.—**grammatically** *adv.*

**gramophone** *n* a record player, esp an old mechanical model with an acoustic horn.

**granary** *n* a building for storing grain.

**grand** *adj* higher in rank than others; most important; imposing in size, beauty, extent, etc; distinguished; illustrious; comprehensive; (*inf*) very good; delightful. • *n* a grand piano; (*inf*) a thousand pounds or dollars. —**grandly** *adv.*—**grandness** *n.*

**grandchild** *n* the child of a person's son or daughter.

**granddad** *n* (*inf*) grandfather; an old man.

**granddaughter** *n* the daughter of a person's son or daughter.

**grandfather** *n* the father of a person's father or mother.

**grandiose** *adj* having grandeur; imposing; pompous and showy.—**grandiosity** *n.*

**grandmother** *n* the mother of a person's father or mother.

**grand piano** *n* a large piano with a horizontal harp-shaped case.

**grandson** *n* the son of a person's son or daughter.

**grandstand** *n* the main structure for seating spectators at a sporting event.

**granite** *n* a hard, igneous rock consisting chiefly of feldspar and quartz; unyielding firmness of endurance.

**granny, grannie** *n* (*inf*) a grandmother; (*inf*) an old woman.

**grant** *vt* to consent to; to give or transfer by legal procedure; to admit as true. • *n* the act of granting; a thing granted, esp a gift for a particular purpose; a transfer of property by deed; the instrument by which such a transfer is made.

**granule** *n* a small grain or particle.

**grape** *n* a small round, juicy berry, growing in clusters on a vine; a dark purplish red.

**grapefruit** *n* a large, round, sour citrus fruit with a yellow rind.

**graph** *n* a diagram representing successive changes in the value of a variable quantity or quantities.—*also vt.*

**graphic, graphical** *adj* described in

realistic detail; pertaining to a graph, lettering, drawing, painting, etc.

**grapple** vt to seize or grip firmly. • vi to struggle hand-to-hand with; to deal or contend with. • n a grapnel; an act of grappling, a wrestle; a grip.

**grasp** vt to grip, as with the hand; to seize; to understand. • vi to try to clutch, seize; (with at) to take eagerly. • n a firm grip; power of seizing and holding; comprehension.

**grasping** adj greedy, avaricious.

**grass** n any of a large family of plants with jointed stems and long narrow leaves including cereals, bamboo, etc; such plants grown as lawn; pasture; (sl) marijuana; (sl) an informer. • vi to cover with grass; (sl) to inform, betray.

**grasshopper** n any of a group of plant-eating, winged insects with powerful hind legs for jumping.

**grassy** adj (**grassier**, **grassiest**) abounding in, covered with, or like, grass.—**grassiness** n.

**grate**[1] n a frame of metal bars for holding fuel in a fireplace; a fireplace; a grating.

**grate**[2] vt to grind into particles by scraping; to rub against (an object) or grind (the teeth) together with a harsh sound; to irritate. • vi to rub or rasp noisily; to cause irritation.

**grateful** adj appreciative; welcome. — **gratefully** adv.—**gratefulness** n.

**grater** n a metal implement with a jagged surface for grating food.

**gratify** vt to please; to indulge.—**gratification** n.

**grating**[1] n a open framework or lattice of bars placed across an opening.

**grating**[2] adj harsh; irritating.— **gratingly** adv.

**gratitude** n a being thankful for favours received.

**gratuity** n money given for a service, a tip.

**grave**[1] n a hole dug in the ground for burying the dead; any place of burial, a tomb.

**grave**[2] adj serious, important; harmful; solemn, sombre; (sound) low in pitch. • n an accent (') over a vowel. —**gravely** adv.

**gravel** n coarse sand with small rounded stones. • vt (pt **gravelled**) to cover, spread with gravel.

**gravestone** n a stone marking a grave, usu inscribed with the name and details of the deceased.

**graveyard** n a burial ground, cemetery.

**gravitate** vi to move or tend to move under the force of gravitation.

**gravity** n importance, esp seriousness; weight; the attraction of bodies toward the centre of the earth, the moon, or a planet.

**gravy** n the juice given off by meat in cooking; the sauce made from this juice; (sl) money easily obtained.

**graze**[1] vi to feed on growing grass or pasture. • vt to put (animals) to feed on growing grass or pasture.

**graze**[2] vt to touch lightly in passing; to scrape, scratch. • n an abrasion, esp on the skin, caused by scraping.

**grease** n melted animal fat; any thick, oily substance or lubricant. • vt to smear or lubricate with grease.

**greasy** adj (**greasier**, **greasiest**) covered with grease; full of grease; slippery; oily in manner.—**greasily** adv. —**greasiness** n.

**great** adj of much more than ordinary size, extent, etc; much above the average; intense; eminent; most important; more distant in a family relationship by one generation; (often with at) (inf) skilful; (inf) excellent; fine. • n (inf) a distinguished person.—**greatly** adv.—**greatness** n.

**greed** n excessive desire, esp for food or wealth.

**greedy** adj (**greedier**, **greediest**) wanting more than one needs or deserves; having too strong a desire for food and drink.—**greedily** adv.—**greediness** n.

**Greek** adj of Greece, its people, or its language. • n a native of Greece; the language used by Greeks; (inf) something unintelligible.

**green** adj of the colour green; covered with plants or foliage; environmentally conscious; having a sickly appearance; unripe; inexperienced, naive; not fully processed or treated; (inf) jealous. • n a colour between blue and yellow in the spectrum; the colour of growing grass; something of a green colour; (pl) green leafy vegetables, as spinach, etc; a grassy plot, esp the end of a golf fairway.—**greenish** adj.—**greeny** adj.—**greenly** adv.—**greenness** n.

**greengrocer** n a dealer in vegetables and fruit.—**greengrocery** n.

**greenhouse** n a heated building, mainly of glass, for growing plants.

**greet** vt to address with friendliness; to meet (a person, event, etc) in a specified way; to present itself to.

**greeting** n the act of welcoming with words or gestures; an expression of good wishes; (pl) a message of regards.

**gregarious** adj (animals) living in flocks and herds; (people) sociable, fond of company.—**gregariously** adv.

**grenade** n a small bomb thrown manually or projected (as by a rifle or special launcher).

**grew** see grow.

**grey, gray** (US) n any of a series of neutral colours ranging between black and white; something (as an animal, etc) of a grey colour. • adj grey in colour; having grey hair; darkish; dreary; vague, indeterminate.—**greyish** adj.—**greyness** n.

**greyhound** n any of a breed of tall and slender dogs noted for its great speed and keen sight.

**grid** n a gridiron, a grating; an electrode for controlling the flow of electrons in an electron tube; a network of squares on a map used for easy reference; a national network of transmission lines, pipes, etc for electricity, water, gas, etc.

**grief** n extreme sorrow caused as by a loss; deep distress.

**grievance** n a circumstance thought to be unjust and cause for complaint.

**grieve** vti to feel or cause to feel grief.

**grill** vt to cook by direct heat using a grill or gridiron; (inf) to question relentlessly. • n a device on a cooker that radiates heat downward for grilling; a gridiron; grilled food; a grille; a grillroom.

**grille, grill** n an open grating forming a screen.

**grillroom** n a restaurant that specializes in grilled food.

**grim** adj (**grimmer, grimmest**) hard and unyielding, stern; appearing harsh, forbidding; repellent, ghastly in character.—**grimly** adv.—**grimness** n.

**grimace** n a contortion of the face expressing pain, anguish, humour, etc.—also vi.

**grime** n soot or dirt, rubbed into a surface, as the skin. • vt to dirty, soil with grime.—**grimy** adj.—**griminess** n.

**grin** vi (pt **grinned**) to smile broadly as in amusement; to show the teeth in pain, scorn, etc. • n a broad smile.

**grind** vb (pt **ground**) vt to reduce to powder or fragments by crushing; to wear down, sharpen, or smooth by friction; to rub (teeth) harshly together; to oppress, tyrannize; to operate by a crank. • vi to be crushed, smoothed, or sharpened by grinding; to jar or grate; to work monotonously; to rotate the hips erotically. • n the act or sound of grinding; hard monotonous work.

**grip** n a secure grasp; the manner of

holding a bat, club, racket, etc; the power of grasping firmly; mental grasp; mastery; a handle; a small travelling bag. • vt (pt **gripped**) to take firmly and hold fast.

**gripe** vt to cause sharp pain in the bowels of; (sl) to annoy. • vi (sl) to complain.

**grisly** adj (**grislier, grisliest**) terrifying; ghastly; arousing horror.

**gristle** n cartilage, esp in meat.—**gristly** adv.

**grit** n rough particles, as of sand; firmness of spirit; stubborn courage. • vt (pt **gritted**) to clench or grind together (eg the teeth); to spread grit on (eg an icy road).

**groan** vi to utter a deep moan; to make a harsh sound (as of creaking) under sudden or prolonged strain.—also n.

**grocer** n a dealer in food and household supplies.

**groggy** adj (**groggier, groggiest**) (inf) weak and unsteady, usu through illness, exhaustion or alcohol.—**groggily** adv.—**grogginess** n.

**groin** n the fold marking the junction of the lower abdomen and the thighs; the location of the genitals.

**groom** n one employed to care for horses; a bridegroom. • vt to clean and care for (animals); to make neat and tidy; to train (a person) for a purpose.

**groove** n a long, narrow channel; a spiral track in a gramophone record for the stylus; a settled routine. • vt to make a groove in.

**grope** vi to search about blindly as in the dark; to search uncertainly for a solution to a problem. • vt to find by feeling; (sl) to fondle sexually. • n the act of groping.—**gropingly** adv.

**gross** adj fat and coarse-looking; flagrant, dense, thick; lacking in refinement; earthy; obscene; total, with no

deductions. • n (pl **grosses**) an overall total; (pl **gross**) twelve dozen. • vt to earn as total revenue.

**grotesque** adj distorted or fantastic in appearance, shape, etc; ridiculous; absurdly incongruous. • n a grotesque person or thing; a decorative device combining distorted plant, animal and human forms.—**grotesquely** adv.—**grotesqueness** n.

**grotto** n (pl **grottoes, grottos**) a cave, esp one with attractive features.

**ground** n the solid surface of the earth; soil; the background, as in design; the connection of an electrical conductor with the earth; (pl) a basis for belief, action, or argument; the area about and relating to a building; a tract of land; sediment. • vti to set on the ground; to run aground or cause to run aground; to base, found, or establish; to instruct in the first principles of; to prevent (aircraft) from flying.

**grounding** n basic general knowledge of a subject.

**groundsheet** n a waterproof sheet placed on the ground in a tent.

**groundwork** n foundation, basis.

**group** n a number of persons or things considered as a collective unit; a small musical band of players or singers; a number of companies under single ownership; two or more figures forming one artistic design. • vti to form into a group or groups.

**grouse**[1] n (pl **grouse**) a game bird; its flesh as food.

**grouse**[2] vi (inf) to complain.— **grouser** n.

**grove** n a small wood, generally without undergrowth.

**grovel** vi (pt **grovelled**) to lie and crawl in a prostrate position as a sign of respect, fear or humility. —**groveller** n.

**grow** vb (pt **grew**, pp **grown**) vi to come into being; to be produced naturally;

to develop, as a living thing; to increase in size, quantity, etc. • vt to cause or let grow; to raise, to cultivate. —**growable** adj.—**grower** n.

**growl** vi to make a rumbling, menacing sound such as an angry dog makes. • vt to express in a growling manner. • n a growling noise; a grumble.—**growler** n.

**growth** n the act or process of growing; progressive increase, development; something that grows or has grown; an abnormal formation of tissue, as a tumour.

**grub** vb (pt **grubbed**) vi to dig in the ground; to work hard. • vt to clear (ground) of roots; to uproot. • n the worm-like larva of a beetle; (sl) food.

**grubby** adj (**grubbier**, **grubbiest**) dirty, soiled.—**grubbiness** n.

**grudge** n a deep feeling of resentment or ill will. • vt to be reluctant to give or admit something.—**grudging** adj. —**grudgingly** adv.

**gruelling, grueling** (US) adj severely testing, exhausting.

**gruesome** adj causing horror or loathing.

**gruff** adj rough or surly; hoarse.— **gruffly** adv.—**gruffness** n.

**grumble** vti to mutter in discontent; to make a rumbling sound.—also n. —**grumbler** n.

**grumpy** adj (**grumpier**, **grumpiest**) bad-tempered, peevish.—**grumpily** adv.—**grumpiness** n.

**grunt** vi to make a gruff guttural sound like a pig; to say or speak in such a manner.—also n.

**guarantee** n a pledge or security for another's debt or obligation; a pledge to replace something substandard, etc; an assurance that something will be done as specified; something offered as a pledge or security; a guarantor. • vt to give a guarantee for; to promise.

**guarantor** n a person who gives a guaranty or guarantee.

**guard** vt to watch over and protect; to defend; to keep from escape or trouble; to restrain. • vi to keep watch (against); to act as a guard. • n defence; protection; a posture of readiness for defence; a device to protect against injury or loss; a person or group that guards; (boxing, fencing, cricket) a defensive attitude; an official in charge of a train.

**guarded** adj discreet; cautious.— **guardedly** adv.

**guardian** n a custodian; a person legally in charge of a minor or someone incapable of taking care of their own affairs.—**guardianship** n.

**guerrilla, guerilla** n a member of a small force of irregular soldiers, making surprise raids.—also adj.

**guess** vt to form an opinion of or state with little or no factual knowledge; to judge correctly by doing this; to think or suppose. • n an estimate based on guessing.—**guesser** n.

**guest** n a person entertained at the home, club, etc of another; any paying customer of a hotel, restaurant, etc; a performer appearing by special invitation.

**guesthouse** n a private home or boarding-house offering accommodation.

**guestroom** n a room kept for guests.

**guffaw** n a crude noisy laugh.—also vi.

**guidance** n leadership; advice or counsel.

**guide** vt to point out the way for; to lead; to direct the course of; to control. • n a person who leads or directs others; a person who shows and explains points of interest; something that provides a person with guiding information; a device controlling the motion of something; a book of basic instruction; (with cap) a member of the girls' organization equivalent to the Scouts.

**guidebook** *n* a book containing directions and information for tourists.

**guided missile** *n* a military missile whose course is controlled by radar or internal instruments, etc.

**guide dog** *n* a dog trained to guide people who are blind.

**guild** *n* a club, society; an association of people with common interests formed for mutual aid and protection, as craftsmen in the Middle Ages.

**guile** *n* craftiness, deceit.—**guileful** *adj*.—**guileless** *adj*.

**guillotine** *n* an instrument for beheading by a heavy blade descending between grooved posts; a device or machine for cutting paper; a rule for limiting time for discussion in a legislature.—*also vt.*

**guilt** *n* the fact of having done a wrong or committed an offence; a feeling of self-reproach from believing one has done a wrong.

**guiltless** *adj* innocent.

**guilty** *adj* (**guiltier**, **guiltiest**) having guilt; feeling or showing guilt.— **guiltily** *adv*.—**guiltiness** *n*.

**guinea** *n* a former English gold coin equal to 21 shillings (£1.05).

**guinea pig** *n* a rodent-like animal commonly kept as a pet, and often used in scientific experiments; a person or thing subject to an experiment.

**guise** *n* an external appearance, aspect; an assumed appearance, pretence.

**guitar** *n* a stringed musical instrument with a long, fretted neck, and a flat body, which is plucked with a plectrum or the fingers.—**guitarist** *n*.

**gulf** *n* a large area of ocean reaching into land; a wide, deep chasm; a vast separation.

**gull** *n* any of numerous long-winged web-footed sea birds.

**gullet** *n* the oesophagus; the throat.

**gullible** *adj* easily deceived.—**gullibility** *n*.—**gullibly** *adv*.

**gully** *n* a narrow trench cut by running water after rain; (*cricket*) a fielding position between the slips and point. • *vt* to make gullies in.

**gulp** *vt* to swallow hastily or greedily; to choke back as if swallowing. • *n* a gulping or swallowing; a mouthful.

**gum**[1] *n* the firm tissue that surrounds the teeth.

**gum**[2] *n* a sticky substance found in certain trees and plants; an adhesive; chewing gum. • *vb* (*pt* **gummed**) *vt* to coat or unite with gum. • *vi* to become sticky or clogged.

**gumboot** *n* a rubber, waterproof boot, a wellington.

**gumption** *n* (*inf*) shrewd practical common sense; initiative.

**gun** *n* a weapon with a metal tube from which a projectile is discharged by an explosive; the shooting of a gun as a signal or salute; anything like a gun. • *vb* (*pt* **gunned**) *vi* to shoot or hunt with a gun. • *vt* (*inf*) to shoot (a person); (*sl*) to advance the throttle of an engine.

**gunboat** *n* a small armed ship.

**gunman** *n* an armed gangster; a hired killer.

**gunner** *n* a soldier, etc who helps fire artillery; a naval warrant officer in charge of a ship's guns.

**gunpowder** *n* an explosive powder used in guns, for blasting, etc.

**gurgle** *vi* (*liquid*) to make a low bubbling sound; to utter with this sound.—*also n.*

**gush** *vi* to issue plentifully; to have a sudden flow; to talk or write effusively. • *vt* to cause to gush. • *n* a sudden outpouring.—**gushy** *adj*.

**gusset** *n* a small triangular piece of cloth inserted in a garment to strengthen or enlarge a part.

**gust** *n* a sudden brief rush of wind; a sudden outburst. • *vi* to blow in gusts. —**gusty** *adj*.—**gustily** *adv*.

**gusto** n great enjoyment, zest.

**gut** n (often pl) the bowels or the stomach; the intestine; tough cord made from animal intestines; (pl) (sl) daring; courage. • vt (pt **gutted**) to remove the intestines from; to destroy the interior of.

**gutter** n a channel for carrying off water, esp at a roadside or under the eaves of a roof; a channel or groove to direct something (as of a bowling alley); the lowest condition of human life. • adj marked by extreme vulgarity or indecency. • vt to provide with a gutter. • vi to flow in rivulets; (candle) to melt unevenly; (candle flame) to flutter.—**guttering** n.

**guttersnipe** n a dirty child who plays in the streets, esp slum areas.

**guttural** adj formed or pronounced in the throat; harsh-sounding.—**gutturally** adv.

**guy**[1] n a rope, chain, etc, for fixing or steadying anything. • vt to fix or steady with a guy.

**guy**[2] n an effigy of Guy Fawkes made from old clothes stuffed with newspapers, etc burnt on the anniversary of the Gunpowder Plot (5 November); (inf) a man or boy; (pl) (inf) men or women; a shabby person. • vt to tease.

**guzzle** vti to gulp down food or drink greedily.—**guzzler** n.

**gym** n (inf) a gymnasium.

**gymnasium** n a room or building equipped for physical training and sports.

**gymnast** n a person skilled in gymnastics.

**gymnastics** n (used as sing) training in exercises devised to strengthen the body; (pl) gymnastic exercises; (pl) feats of dexterity or agility.

**gynaecology, gynecology** (US) n the branch of medicine that deals with the diseases and disorders of the female reproductive system.—**gynaecological** adj.—**gynaecologist** n.

**gypsy** n (with cap) a member of a travelling people, orig from India, now spread throughout Europe and North America; a person who looks or lives like a Gypsy.—also **gipsy**.

**gyrate** vi to revolve; to whirl or spiral. —**gyration** n.—**gyratory** adj.

# H

**haberdasher** n a dealer in sewing accessories; in US, a dealer in men's clothing.—**haberdashery** n.

**habit** n a distinctive costume, as of a nun, etc; a thing done often and hence easily; a usual way of doing things; an addiction, esp to narcotics. • vt to clothe.

**habitual** adj having the nature of a habit; regular.—**habitually** adv.

**hack**[1] vt to cut or chop (at) violently; to clear (vegetation) by chopping; (comput) to gain illegal access to confidential data. • n a gash or notch; a harsh, dry cough.

**hack**[2] n a riding horse for hire; an old worn-out horse; a mediocre or unexceptional writer; a coach for hire; (inf) a taxicab. • vti to ride a horse cross-country. • adj banal, hackneyed.

**hackneyed** adj made trite or banal through overuse.

**had** see **have**.

**haddock** n (pl **haddock**) an important Atlantic food fish related to the cod.

**haemorrhage, hemorrhage** (US) n the escape of blood from a blood vessel; heavy bleeding. • vi to bleed heavily.

**haemorrhoids, hemorrhoids** (US) npl swollen or bleeding veins around the anus.—also **piles**.

**haggard** n adj having an exhausted, untidy look.

**haggle** vi to bargain; barter.—**haggler** n.

**hail**[1] vt to greet; to summon by shouting or signalling, as a taxi; to welcome with approval, to acclaim. • vi to originate from. • interj an exclamation of tribute, greeting, etc. • n a shout to gain attention; a distance within which one can be heard calling.—**hailer** n.

**hail**[2] n frozen raindrops; something, as abuse, bullets, etc, sent forcefully in rapid succession. • vti to pour down like hail.

**hailstone** n a pellet of hail.

**hair** n a threadlike growth from the skin of mammals; a mass of hairs, esp on the human head; a threadlike growth on a plant.

**haircut** n a shortening and styling of hair by cutting it; the style of cutting.

**hair-do** n a particular style of hair after cutting, etc.

**hairdresser** n a person who cuts, styles, colours, etc hair.

**hairpiece** n a wig or toupee; an additional piece of hair attached to a person's real hair.

**hairpin** n U-shaped pin used to hold hair in place.

**hairpin bend** n a sharply curving bend in a road, etc.

**hair-raising** adj terrifying, shocking.

**hairstyle** n the way in which hair is arranged.—**hairstylist** n.

**hairy** adj (**hairier, hairiest**) covered with hair; (inf) difficult, dangerous.—**hairiness** n.

**hake** n (pl **hake**) a marine food fish related to the cod.

**half** n (pl **halves**) either of two equal parts of something; (inf) a half-price ticket for a bus, etc; (inf) half a pint. • adj being a half; incomplete; partial. • adv to the extent of a half; (inf) partly.

**halfback** n (football, hockey) a player occupying a position between the forwards and the fullbacks; a player in this position in other sports.

**half-caste** n a person whose parents are of different races.

**half-hearted** adj with little interest, enthusiasm, etc.

**half hour** n 30 minutes; the point 30 minutes after the beginning of an hour.

**half-time** n (sport) an interval between two halves of a game.

**halfway** adj midway between two points, etc.

**halibut** n a large marine flatfish used as food.

**hall** n a public building with offices, etc; a large room for exhibits, gatherings, etc; the main house on a landed estate; a college building, esp a dining room; a vestibule at the entrance of a building; a hallway.

**hallmark** n a mark used on gold, silver or platinum articles to signify a standard of purity, weight, date of manufacture; a mark or symbol of high quality; a characteristic feature. • vt to stamp with a hallmark.

**hallo** see **hollo**.

**hallucination** n the apparent perception of sights, sounds, etc that are not actually present; something perceived in this manner.—**hallucinatory** adj.

**halo** n (pl **haloes, halos**) a circle of light, as around the sun; a symbolic ring of light around the head of a saint in pictures; the aura of glory surrounding an idealized person or thing.

**halt**[1] n a temporary interruption or cessation of progress; a minor station on a railway line. • vti to stop or come to a stop.

**halt**[2] *vi* to falter; to hesitate.—**halting** *adj*.

**halve** *vt* to divide equally into two; to reduce by half; (*golf*) to play one hole in the same number of strokes as one's opponent.

**halves** *see* **half**.

**ham** *n* the upper part of a pig's hind leg, salted, smoked, etc; the meat from this area; (*inf*) the back of the upper thigh; (*inf*) an actor who overacts; (*inf*) a licensed amateur radio operator. • *vt* (*pt* **hammed**) to speak or move in an exaggerated manner, to overact.

**hamburger** *n* ground beef; a cooked patty of such meat, often in a bread roll with pickle, etc.

**hamlet** *n* a very small village.

**hammer** *n* a tool for pounding, driving nails, etc, having a heavy head and a handle; a thing like this in shape or use, as the part of the gun that strikes the firing pin; a bone of the middle ear; a heavy metal ball attached to a wire thrown in athletic contests. • *vti* to strike repeatedly, as with a hammer; to drive, force, or shape, as with hammer blows; (*inf*) to defeat utterly.

**hammock** *n* a length of strong cloth or netting suspended by the ends and used as a bed.

**hamper**[1] *vt* to hinder; to interfere with; to encumber.

**hamper**[2] *n* a large, usu covered, basket for storing or transporting food and crockery, etc.

**hand** *n* the part of the arm below the wrist, used for grasping; a side or direction; possession or care; control; an active part; a promise to marry; skill; one having a special skill; handwriting; applause; help; a hired worker; a source; one of a ship's crew; anything like a hand, as a pointer on a clock; the breadth of a hand, four inches when measuring the height of a horse; the cards held by a player at one time; a round of card play; (*inf*) applause. • *adj* of, for, or controlled by the hand. • *vt* to give as with the hand; to help or conduct with the hand. • *vi* (*with* **on**) to pass to the next.

**handbag** *n* a woman's small bag for carrying personal items.

**handbook** *n* a book containing useful instructions.

**handcuff** *n* (*usu pl*) either of a pair of connected steel rings for shackling the wrists of a prisoner. • *vt* to manacle.

**handful** *n* as much as will fill the hand; a few; (*inf*) a person who is difficult to handle or control.

**handicap** *n* a mental or physical impairment; a contest in which difficulties are imposed on, or advantages given to, contestants to equalize their chances; such a difficulty or advantage; any hindrance. • *vt* (*pt* **handicapped**) to give a handicap to; to hinder.—**handicapper** *n*.

**handicraft** *n* a skill involving the hands, such as basketwork, pottery, etc; an item of pottery, etc made by hand.

**handkerchief** *n* a small cloth for blowing the nose, etc.

**handle** *vt* to touch, hold, or move with the hand; to manage or operate with the hands; to manage, deal with; to buy and sell (goods). • *vi* to react in a specified way. • *n* a part of anything designed to be held or grasped by the hand.—**handleable** *adj*.—**handling** *n*.

**handlebar** *n* (*often pl*) the curved metal bar with a grip at each end used to steer a bicycle, etc; a bushy moustache with curved ends.

**handmade** *adj* made by hand, carefully crafted.

**handsome** *adj* good-looking; dignified; generous; ample.—**handsomely** *adv*.—**handsomeness** *n*.

**handy** adj (**handier, handiest**) convenient, near; easy to use; skilled with the hands.—**handily** adv.—**handiness** n.

**handyman** n a person who does odd jobs.

**hang** vb (pt **hung**) vt to support from above, esp by a rope, chain, etc, to suspend; (door, etc) to attach by hinges to allow to swing freely; to decorate with pictures, or other suspended objects; (wallpaper) to stick to a wall; to exhibit (works of art); to prevent (a jury) from coming to a decision; (pt **hanged**) to put to execute or kill by suspending by the neck. • vi to be suspended, so as to dangle loosely; to fall or droop; (clothing, etc) to fall or flow in a certain direction; to lean, incline, or protrude; to depend; to remain in the air; to be in suspense; (pt **hanged**) to die by hanging; (with **about, around**) to loiter; (with **back**) to hesitate, be reluctant; (with **out**) to meet regularly at a particular place. • n the way in which anything hangs; (sl) a damn.

**hangar** n a shelter for aircraft.

**hanger** n a device on which something is hung.

**hanger-on** n a sycophantic follower.

**hang-glider** n an unpowered aircraft consisting of a metal frame over which a lightweight material is stretched, with a harness for the pilot suspended below.—**hang gliding** n.

**hangover** n the unpleasant after-effects of excessive consumption of alcohol; something surviving from an earlier time.

**hang-up** n an emotional preoccupation with something.

**hank** n a coiled or looped bundle of wool, rope, etc.

**hanker** vi (with **after, for**) to desire longingly.—**hankering** n.

**hanky, hankie** n (inf) a handkerchief.

**haphazard** adj not planned; random. • adv by chance.—**haphazardly** adv.

**happen** vi to take place; to be, occur, or come by chance.

**happening** n an occurrence; an improvization.

**happy** adj (**happier, happiest**) fortunate; having, expressing, or enjoying pleasure or contentment; pleased; appropriate, felicitous.—**happily** adv.—**happiness** n.

**happy-go-lucky** adj irresponsible; carefree.

**harass** vt to annoy, to irritate; to trouble (an enemy) by constant raids and attacks.—**harassment** n.

**harbour, harbor** (US) n a protected inlet for anchoring ships; any place of refuge. • vt to shelter or house; (grudge, etc) to keep in the mind secretly. • vi to take shelter.

**hard** adj firm, solid, not easily cut or punctured; difficult to comprehend; difficult to accomplish; difficult to bear, painful; severe, unfeeling, ungenerous; indisputable, intractable; (drugs) addictive and damaging to health; (weather) severe; (currency) stable in value; (news) definite, not speculative; (drink) very alcoholic; (water) having a high mineral content that prevents lathering with soap; (colour, sound) harsh. • adv with great effort or intensity; earnestly, with concentration; so as to cause hardness; with difficulty; with bitterness or grief; close, near by.—**hardness** n.

**hardback** n a book bound with a stiff cover.—also adj.

**hardboard** n a stiff board made of compressed wood chips.

**hard-boiled** adj (eggs) boiled until solid; (inf) unfeeling.

**hard cash** n payment in coins and notes as opposed to cheque, etc.

**harden** *vti* to make or become hard.—
**hardener** *n*.

**hardly** *adv* scarcely; barely; with difficulty; not to be expected.

**hard sell** *n* an aggressive selling technique.

**hardship** *n* something that causes suffering or privation.

**hard up** *adj* (*inf*) short of money.

**hardware** *n* articles made of metal as
tools, nails, etc; (*comput*) the mechanical and electronic components
that make up a computer system.

**hardy** *adj* (**hardier, hardiest**) bold,
resolute; robust; vigorous; able to
withstand exposure to physical or
emotional hardship.—**hardily** *adv*.—
**hardiness** *n*.

**hare** *n* any of various timid, swift, long-
eared mammals, resembling but
larger than the rabbit.

**harebrained** *adj* flighty; foolish.

**harelip** *n* a congenital deformity of the
upper lip in the form of a vertical fissure.

**harem, hareem** *n* the secluded part of
a Muslim household where the
women live; the women in a harem.

**harm** *n* hurt; damage; injury. • *vt*. to
inflict hurt, damage, or injury upon.

**harmful** *adj* hurtful.—**harmfully** *adv*.

**harmless** *adj* not likely to cause
harm.—**harmlessly** *adv*.—**harmless-
ness** *n*.

**harmonic** *adj* (*mus*) of or in harmony.
• *n* an overtone; (*pl*) the science of
musical sounds.

**harmonica** *n* a small wind instrument
that produces tones when air is
blown or sucked across a series of
metal reeds; a mouth-organ.

**harmonious** *adj* fitting together in an
orderly and pleasing manner; agreeing in ideas, interests, etc; melodious. —**harmoniously** *adv*.

**harmonium** *n* a keyboard musical instrument whose tones are produced
by thin metal reeds operated by foot
bellows.

**harmonize** *vi* to be in harmony; to sing
in harmony. • *vt* to make harmonious.—**harmonization** *n*.

**harmony** *n* a pleasing agreement of
parts in colour, size, etc; agreement
in action, ideas, etc; the pleasing combination of musical tones in a chord.

**harness** *n* the leather straps and metal
pieces by which a horse is fastened
to a vehicle, plough, etc; any similar
fastening or attachment, eg for a
parachute, hang-glider. • *vt* to put
a harness on; to control so as to use
the power of.

**harp** *n* a stringed musical instrument
played by plucking. • *vi* (*with on or*
**upon**) to talk persistently (on some
subject).—**harpist** *n*.

**harpoon** *n* a barbed spear with an attached line, for spearing whales,
etc.—*also vt.*

**harpsichord** *n* a musical instrument
resembling a grand piano whose
strings are plucked by a mechanism
rather than struck.

**harrow** *n* a heavy frame with spikes,
spring teeth, or disks for breaking
up and levelling ploughed ground.
• *vt* to draw a harrow over (land);
to cause mental distress to.—**har-
rowing** *adj*.

**harsh** *adj* unpleasantly rough; jarring
on the senses or feelings; rigorous;
cruel.—**harshly** *adv*.—**harshness** *n*.

**harvest** *n* (the season of) gathering in
the ripened crops; the yield of a particular crop; the reward or product
of any exertion or action. • *vti* to
gather in (a crop). • *vt* to win by
achievement. —**harvester** *n*.

**has** *see* **have**.

**hash**[1] *n* a chopped mixture of reheated
cooked meat and vegetables. • *vt* to
chop up (meat or vegetables) for
hash; to mix or mess up.

**hash**[2] n (inf) hashish.

**hashish** n resin derived from the leaves and shoots of the hemp plant, smoked or chewed as an intoxicant.

**haste** n quickness of motion.

**hasten** vt to accelerate; to cause to hurry. • vi to move or act with speed.

**hasty** adj (**hastier, hastiest**) done in a hurry; rash, precipitate.—**hastily** adv. —**hastiness** n.

**hat** n a covering for the head.

**hatch**[1] n a small door or opening (as on an aircraft or spaceship); an opening in the deck of a ship or in the floor or roof of a building; a lid for such an opening; a hatchway.

**hatch**[2] vt to produce (young) from the egg, esp by incubating; to devise (eg a plot). • vi to emerge from the egg; to incubate.

**hatch**[3] vt (drawing, engraving) to shade using closely spaced parallel lines or incisions.

**hatchback** n a sloping rear end on a car with a door; a car of this design.

**hatchet** n a small axe with a short handle.

**hate** vt to feel intense dislike for. • vi to feel hatred; to wish to avoid. • n a strong feeling of dislike or contempt; the person or thing hated.

**hateful** adj deserving or arousing hate.—**hatefully** adv.

**hatred** n intense dislike or enmity.

**hat trick** n (cricket) the taking of three wickets with three successive bowls; the scoring of three successive goals, points, etc in any game.

**haughty** adj (**haughtier, haughtiest**) having or expressing arrogance.— **haughtily** adv.—**haughtiness** n.

**haul** vti to move by pulling; to transport by truck, etc. • n the act of hauling; the amount gained, caught, etc at one time; the distance over which something is transported.

**haulage** n the transport of commodities; the charge for this.

**haulier** n a person or business that transports goods by road.

**haunch** n the part of the body around the hips; the leg and loin of a deer, sheep, etc.

**haunt** vt to visit often or continually; to recur repeatedly to. • vi to linger; to appear habitually as a ghost. • n a place often visited.

**have** vt (pres t **has**, pr p **having**, pt **had**) to have in one's possession; to possess as an attribute; to hold in the mind; to experience; to give birth to; to allow, or tolerate; to arrange or hold; to engage in; to cause, compel, or require to be; to to be obliged; (sl) to have sexual intercourse with; to be pregnant with; (inf) to hold at a disadvantage; (inf) to deceive; to accept or receive; to consume food, drink, etc; to show some quality; to perplex.

**haven** n a place where ships can safely anchor; a refuge.

**haversack** n a canvas bag similar to a knapsack but worn over one shoulder.

**havoc** n widespread destruction or disorder.

**hawk**[1] n any of numerous birds of prey; a person who advocates aggressive or intimidatory action.—**hawkish** adj.

**hawk**[2] vti to clear the throat (of) audibly.

**hawk**[3] vt to offer goods for sale, as in the street.

**hawker** n a person who goes about offering goods for sale.

**hay** n grass cut and dried for fodder.

**hay fever** n an allergic reaction to pollen causing irritation of the nose and eyes.

**haystack, hayrick** n a pile of stacked hay ready for storing.

**haywire** adj (inf) out of order; disorganized.

**hazard** n risk; danger; an obstacle on a golf course. • vt to risk.

**hazardous** adj dangerous; risky.

**haze** n a thin vapour of fog, smoke, etc in the air; slight vagueness of mind. • vti to make or become hazy.

**hazy** adj (**hazier, haziest**) misty; vague.—**hazily** adv.—**haziness** n.

**he** pron the male person or animal named before; a person (male or female). • n a male person or animal.

**head** n the part of an animal or human body containing the brain, eyes, ears, nose and mouth; the top part of anything; the foremost part; the chief person; (pl) a unit of counting; the striking part of a tool; mind; understanding; the topic of a chapter, etc; crisis, conclusion; pressure of water, steam, etc; the source of a river, etc; froth, as on beer. • adj at the head, top or front; coming from in front; chief, leading. • vt to command; to lead; to cause to go in a specified direction; to set out; to travel (in a particular direction); to strike (a football) with the head.—**headless** adj.

**headache** n a continuous pain in the head; (inf) a cause of worry or trouble.

**heading** n something forming the head, top, or front; the title, topic, etc of a chapter, etc; the direction in which a vehicle is moving.

**headland** n a promontory.

**headlight, headlamp** n a light at the front of a vehicle.

**headline** n printed lines at the top of a newspaper article giving the topic; a brief news summary. • vt to give featured billing or publicity to.

**headlong** adj with the head first; with uncontrolled speed or force; rashly.—also adv.

**headmaster, headmistress** n the principal of a school.

**head-on** adj with the head or front foremost; without compromise.—also adv.

**headquarters** n the centre of operations of one in command, as in an army; the main office in any organization.

**headrest** n a support for the head.

**headroom** n space overhead, as in a doorway or tunnel.

**headstrong** adj determined to do as one pleases.

**head waiter** n the head of the dining-room staff in a restaurant.

**headway** n forward motion; progress.

**headwind** n a wind blowing against the direction of a ship or aircraft.

**heady** adj (**headier, headiest**) (alcoholic drinks) intoxicating; invigorating, exciting; impetuous.—**headily** adv.—**headiness** n.

**heal** vti to make or become healthy; to cure; (wound, etc) to repair by natural processes.—**healer** n.

**health** n physical and mental well-being; freedom from disease, etc; the condition of body or mind; a wish for health and happiness, as in a toast.

**healthy** adj (**healthier, healthiest**) having or producing good health; beneficial; sound.—**healthily** adv.—**healthiness** n.

**heap** n a mass or pile of jumbled things; (pl) (inf) a large amount. • vt to throw in a heap; to pile high; to fill (a plate, etc) full or to overflowing.

**hear** vb (pt **heard**) vt to perceive by the ear; to listen to; to conduct a hearing of (a law case, etc); to be informed of; to learn. • vi to be able to hear sounds; (with **of** or **about**) to be told.—**hearer** n.

**hearing** n the sense by which sound is perceived by the ear; an opportunity to be heard; the distance over which something can be heard, earshot.

**hearing aid** *n* a small electronic amplifier worn behind the ear to improve hearing.

**hearsay** *n* rumour, gossip.

**hearse** *n* a vehicle for transporting a coffin to a funeral.

**heart** *n* the hollow, muscular organ that circulates the blood; the central, vital, or main part; the human heart as the centre of emotions, esp sympathy, courage, etc; a conventional design representing a heart; one of a suit of playing cards marked with such a symbol in red.

**heartache** *n* sorrow or grief.

**heart attack** *n* a sudden instance of abnormal heart functioning, esp coronary thrombosis.

**heartbeat** *n* the rhythmic contraction and dilation of the heart.

**heartbreak** *n* overwhelming sorrow or grief.—**heartbreaking** *adj*.—**heartbroken** *adj*.

**heartburn** *n* a burning sensation in the lower chest.

**heartfelt** *adj* sincere.

**hearth** *n* the floor of a fireplace and surrounding area; this as symbolic of house and home.

**heartily** *adv* vigorously, enthusiastically; sincerely.

**heartless** *adj* unfeeling.—**heartlessly** *adv*.—**heartlessness** *n*.

**hearty** *adj* (**heartier, heartiest**) warm and friendly; unrestrained, as laughter; strong and healthy; nourishing and plentiful.—**heartiness** *n*.

**heat** *n* energy produced by molecular agitation; the quality of being hot; the perception of hotness; hot weather or climate; strong feeling, esp anger, etc; a single bout, round, or trial in sports; the period of sexual excitement and readiness for mating in female animals; (*sl*) coercion.

• *vti* to make or become warm or hot; to make or become excited.

**heated** *adj* made hot; excited, impassioned.—**heatedly** *adv*.

**heater** *n* a device that provides heat; (*sl*) a gun.

**heath** *n* an area of uncultivated land with scrubby vegetation; any of various shrubby plants that thrive on sandy soil, eg heather.

**heathen** *n* (*pl* **heathens, heathen**) anyone not acknowledging the God of Christian, Jew, or Muslim belief; a person regarded as irreligious, uncivilized, etc.

**heather** *n* a common evergreen shrub of northern and alpine regions with small stalkless leaves and tiny usu purplish pink flowers.

**heating** *n* a system of providing heat, as central heating; the warmth provided.

**heat wave** *n* a prolonged period of hot weather.

**heave** *vb vt* to lift or move, esp with great effort; to utter (a sigh, etc) with effort; (*inf*) to throw. • *vi* to rise and fall rhythmically; to vomit; to pant; to gasp; to haul; (*pt* **hove**) (*with* **to**) (*ship*) to come to a stop. • *n* the act or effort of heaving.

**heaven** *n* (*usu pl*) the visible sky; (*sometimes cap*) the dwelling place of God and his angels where the blessed go after death; any place or state of great happiness; (*pl*) *interj* an exclamation of surprise.

**heavenly** *adj* of or relating to heaven or heavens; divine; (*inf*) excellent, delightful.—**heavenliness** *n*.

**heavy** *adj* (**heavier, heaviest**) hard to lift or carry; of more than the usual, expected, or defined weight; to an unusual extent; hard to do; stodgy, hard to digest; cloudy; (*industry*) using massive machinery to produce basic materials, as chemicals and steel; (*ground*) difficult to make fast progress on; clumsy; dull, serious. • *n* (*theatre*) a villain; (*sl*) a person hired to threaten violence, a thug.—**heavily** *adv*.—**heaviness** *n*.

**heavyweight** *n* a professional boxer weighing more than 175 pounds (79 kg) or wrestler weighing over 209 pounds (95 kg); (*inf*) a very influential or important individual.

**Hebrew** *n* a member of an ancient Semitic people; an Israelite; a Jew; the ancient Semitic language of the Hebrews; its modern form.—*also adj*.

**heckle** *vti* to harass (a speaker) with questions or taunts.—**heckler** *n*.

**hectic** *adj* involving intense excitement or activity.—**hectically** *adv*.

**he'd** = he had, he would.

**hedge** *n* a fence consisting of a dense line of bushes or small trees; a barrier or means of protection against something, esp financial loss; an evasive or noncommittal answer or statement. • *vt* to surround or enclose with a hedge; to place secondary bets as a precaution. • *vi* to avoid giving a direct answer in an argument or debate.

**hedgehog** *n* a small insectivorous mammal with sharp spines on the back.

**heed** *vt* to pay close attention (to). • *n* careful attention.—**heedful** *adj*.

**heedless** *adj* inattentive; thoughtless. —**heedlessly** *adv*.

**heel**[1] *n* the back part of the foot, under the ankle; the part covering or supporting the heel in stockings, socks, etc or shoes; a solid attachment forming the back of the sole of a shoe; (*inf*) a despicable person. • *vt* to furnish with a heel; to follow closely; (*inf*) to provide with money, etc. • *vi* to follow along at the heels of someone.

**heel**[2] *vti* to tilt or become tilted to one side, as a ship.

**hefty** *adj* (**heftier, heftiest**) (*inf*) heavy; large and strong; big.—**heftily** *adv*.—**heftiness** *n*.

**heifer** *n* a young cow that has not calved.

**height** *n* the topmost point; the highest limit; the distance from the bottom to the top; altitude; a relatively great distance above a given level; an eminence; a hill.

**heighten** *vti* to make or come higher or more intense.

**heir** *n* a person who inherits or is entitled to inherit another's property, title, etc.

**heiress** *n* a woman or girl who is an heir, esp to great wealth.

**heirloom** *n* any possession handed down from generation to generation.

**held** *see* **hold**[1].

**helicopter** *n* a kind of aircraft lifted and moved, or kept hovering, by large rotary blades mounted horizontally.

**hell** *n* (*Christianity*) the place of punishment of the wicked after death; the home of devils and demons; any place or state of supreme misery or discomfort; (*inf*) a cause of this. • *interj* (*inf*) an exclamation of anger, surprise, etc.

**he'll** = he will.

**hellish** *adj* of, pertaining to or resembling hell; very wicked; (*inf*) very unpleasant.

**hello** *interj* an expression of greeting. • *n* the act of saying "hello."—*also* **hallo, hullo**.

**helm** *n* the tiller or wheel used to steer a ship; a position of control or direction, authority.

**helmet** *n* protective headgear worn by soldiers, policemen, divers, etc.

**helmsman** *n* a person who steers.—**helmswoman** *nf*.

**help** *vt* to make things better or easier for; to aid; to assist; to remedy; to keep from; to serve or wait on. • *vi* to give aid; to be useful. • *n* the action of helping; aid; assistance; a remedy; a person that helps, esp a hired person. —**helper** *n*.

**helpful** *adj* giving help; useful.—**helpfully** *adv*.—**helpfulness** *n*.

**helping** *n* a single portion of food.

**helpless** *adj* unable to manage alone, dependent on others; weak and defenceless.—**helplessly** *adv*.—**helplessness** *n*.

**hem** *n* the edge of a garment, etc turned back and stitched or fixed. • *vt* (*pt* **hemmed**) to finish (a garment) with a hem; (*with* **in**) to enclose, confine.—**hemmer** *n*.

**hemisphere** *n* half of a sphere or globe; any of the halves (northern, southern, eastern, or western) of the earth.—**hemispherical** *adj*.

**hemp** *n* a widely cultivated Asian herb of the mulberry family; its fibre, used to mmke rope, sailcloth, etc; a narcotic drug obtained from different varieties of this plant (—*also* **cannabis, marijuana**).

**hen** *n* the female of many birds, esp the chicken.

**hence** *adv* from here; from this time; from this reason.

**henceforth, henceforward** *adv* from now on.

**henchman** *n* a trusted helper or follower.

**henpeck** *vt* to nag and domineer over (one's husband).—**henpecked** *adj*.

**her** *pron* the objective case of **she**. • *adj* of or belonging to her.

**herald** *n* a person who conveys news or messages; a forerunner, harbinger; (*Middle Ages*) an official at a tournament. • *vt* to usher in; to proclaim.

**heraldry** *n* the study of genealogies and coats of arms; ceremony; pomp. —**heraldic** *adj*.

**herb** *n* any seed plant whose stem withers away annually; any plant used as a medicine, seasoning, etc.—**herby** *adj*.

**herd** *n* a large number of animals, esp cattle, living and feeding together. • *vi* to assemble or move animals together. • *vt* to gather together and move as if a herd; to tend, as a herdsman.—**herder** *n*.

**here** *adv* at or in this place; to or into this place; now; on earth.

**hereafter** *adv* after this, in some future time or state. • *n* (*with* **the**) the future, life after death.

**hereby** *adv* by this means.

**hereditary** *adj* descending by inheritance; transmitted to offspring.

**heredity** *n* the transmission of genetic material that determines physical and mental characteristics from one generation to another.

**heresy** *n* a religious belief regarded as contrary to the orthodox doctrine of a church; any belief or opinion contrary to established or accepted theory.

**heretic** *n* a dissenter from an established belief or doctrine.—**heretical** *adj*.

**heritage** *n* something inherited at birth; anything deriving from the past or tradition; historical sites, traditions, practices, etc regarded as the valuable inheritance of contemporary society.

**hermetic** *adj* perfectly closed and airtight.—**hermetically** *adv*.

**hermit** *n* a person who lives in complete solitude, esp for religious reasons; a recluse.

**hernia** *n* the protrusion of an organ, esp part of the intestine, through an opening in the wall of the cavity in which it sits; a rupture.—**hernial** *adj*.

**hero** *n* (*pl* **heroes**) a person of exceptional bravery; a person admired for superior qualities and achievements; the central male character in a novel, play, etc.

**heroic** *adj* of or like a hero; of or about heroes and their deeds; daring, risky.—**heroically** *adv*.

**heroin** *n* a powerfully addictive drug derived from morphine.

**heroine** *n* a woman with the attributes of a hero; the leading female character in a novel, film or play.

**heroism** *n* the qualities or conduct of a hero.

**heron** *n* a slim long-necked wading bird.

**herring** *n* (*pl* **herrings, herring**) a small food fish.

**hers** *pron* something or someone belonging to her.

**herself** *pron* the reflexive form of **she** or **her**.

**he's** = he is; he has.

**hesitant** *adj* hesitating.—**hesitantly** *adv*.—**hesitancy** *n*.

**hesitate** *vi* to be slow in acting due to uncertainty or indecision; to be reluctant (to); to falter or stammer when speaking.—**hesitating** *adj*.—**hesitation** *n*.

**het-up** *adj* (*inf*) agitated, annoyed.

**hew** *vb* (*pp* **hewed** *or* **hewn**) *vt* to strike or cut with blows using an axe, etc; to shape with such blows. • *vi* to conform (to a rule, principle, etc).—**hewer** *n*.

**hexagon** *n* a polygon having six sides and six angles.—**hexagonal** *adj*.—**hexagonally** *adv*.

**heyday** *n* a period of greatest success, happiness, etc.

**hi** *interj* an exclamation of greeting.

**hibernate** *vi* to spend the winter in a dormant condition like deep sleep; to be inactive.—**hibernation** *n*.

**hiccup** *n* a sudden involuntary spasm of the diaphragm followed by inhalation and closure of the glottis producing a characteristic sound; (*inf*) a minor setback. • *vt* (*pt* **hiccuped** *or* **hiccupped**) to have hiccups.

**hide**[1] *vb* (*pt* **hid**, *pp* **hidden, hid**) *vt* to conceal, put out of sight; to keep secret; to screen or obscure from view. • *vi* to conceal oneself. • *n* a camouflaged place of concealment used by hunters, bird-watchers, etc.

**hide**[2] *n* the raw or dressed skin of an animal; (*inf*) the human skin.

**hideous** *adj* visually repulsive; horrifying.—**hideously** *adv*.

**hiding** *n* (*inf*) a thrashing.

**hierarchy** *n* a group of persons or things arranged in order of rank, grade, etc.—**hierarchical** *adj*.

**high** *adj* lofty, tall; extending upward a (specified) distance; situated at or done from a height; above others in rank, position, etc; greater in size, amount, cost, etc than usual; raised or acute in pitch; (*meat*) slightly bad; (*inf*) intoxicated; (*inf*) under the influence of drugs. • *adv* in or to a high degree, rank, etc. • *n* a high level, place, etc; an area of high barometric pressure; (*inf*) a euphoric condition induced by alcohol or drugs.

**highbrow** *n* (*inf*) an intellectual.—*also adj*.

**high-flyer, high-flier** *n* an ambitious person; a person of great ability in any profession.

**high-handed** *adj* overbearing.

**highjack** *see* hijack.

**highlight** *n* the lightest area of a painting, etc; the most interesting or important feature; (*pl*) lightening of areas of the hair using a bleach. • *vt* to bring to special attention; to give highlights to.

**highly** *adv* highly, very much; favourably; at a high level, wage, rank, etc.

**highness** *n* the state or quality of being high; (*with cap*) a title used in speaking to or of royalty.

**high-rise** *adj* (*building*) having multiple storeys.—*also n*.

**high school** *n* a secondary school.

**highway** *n* a public road; a main thoroughfare.

**hijack** *vt* to steal (goods in transit) by force; to force (an aircraft) to make an unscheduled flight. • *n* a hijacking.—*also* **highjack**.—**hijacker, highjacker** *n*.

**hike** *vi* to take a long walk. • *vt* (*inf*) to pull up. • *n* a long walk; a tramp.—**hiker** *n*.

**hilarious** *adj* highly amusing.—**hilariously** *adv*.—**hilarity** *n*.

**hill** *n* a natural rise of land lower than a mountain; a heap or mound; an slope in a road, etc.—**hilly** *adj*.

**hilt** *n* the handle of a sword, dagger, tool, etc.

**him** *pron* the objective case of **he**.

**himself** *pron* the reflexive or emphatic form of **he, him**.

**hind**[1] *adj* (**hinder, hindmost** *or* **hindermost**) situated at the back; rear.

**hind**[2] *n* (*pl* **hinds, hind**) a female deer.

**hinder** *vt* to keep back, or prevent the progress of. • *vi* to be an obstacle.—**hinderer** *n*. —**hinderingly** *adv*.

**hindrance** *n* the act of hindering; an obstacle, impediment.

**hinge** *n* a joint or flexible part on which a door, lid, etc turns; a natural joint, as of a clam; a small piece of gummed paper for sticking stamps in an album. • *vti* to attach or hang by a hinge; to depend.

**hint** *n* an indirect or subtle suggestion; a slight mention; a little piece of practical or helpful advice. • *vt* to suggest or indicate indirectly. • *vi* to give a hint.

**hip**[1] *n* either side of the body below the waist and above the thigh.

**hip**[2] *n* the fruit of the wild rose.

**hip**[3] *interj* used as part of a cheer (**hip, hip, hurrah**).

**hip**[4] *adj* (*sl*) stylish, up-to-date.

**hippopotamus** *n* (*pl* **hippopotamuses**) a large African water-loving mammal with thick dark skin, short legs, and a very large head and muzzle.

**hire** *vt* to pay for the services of (a person) or the use of (a thing). • *n* the payment for the temporary use of anything.—**hirer** *n*.

**hire-purchase** *n* a system by which a person takes possession of an article after paying a deposit and then becomes the owner only after payment of a series of instalments is completed.

**his** *poss pron* of or belonging to **him**.—*also adj*.

**hiss** *vi* to make a sound resembling a prolonged *s*; to show disapproval by hissing. • *vt* to say or indicate by hissing. • *n* the act or sound of hissing.

**historian** *n* a person who writes or studies history.

**historic** *adj* (potentially) important or famous in history.

**historical** *adj* belonging to or involving history or historical methods; concerning actual events as opposed to myth or legend; based on history.—**historically** *adv*.

**history** *n* a record or account of past events; the study, analysis of past events; past events in total; the past events or experiences of a specific person or thing; an unusual or significant past.

**hit** *vti* (*pt* **hit**) to come against (something) with force; to give a blow (to), to strike; to strike with a missile; to affect strongly; to arrive at; (*with* **on**) to discover by accident or unexpectedly. • *n* a blow that strikes its mark; a collision; a successful and popular song, book, etc; (*inf*) an underworld killing; (*sl*) a dose of a drug.

**hit-and-run** *n* a motor vehicle accident in which the driver leaves the scene without stopping or informing the authorities.

**hitch** *vt* to move, pull, etc with jerks; to fasten with a hook, knot, etc; to obtain a ride by hitchhiking. • *vi* to hitchhike. • *n* a tug; a hindrance, obstruction; a kind of knot used for temporary fastening; (*inf*) a ride obtained from hitchhiking.

**hitchhike** *vt* to travel by asking for free lifts from motorists along the way.—**hitchhiker** *n*.

**hive** *n* a shelter for a colony of bees; a beehive; the bees of a hive; a crowd of busy people; a place of great activity. • *vt* to gather (bees) into a hive. • *vi* to enter a hive; (*with* **off**) to separate from a group.

**HMS** *abbr* = Her (or His) Majesty's Ship.

**hoard** *n* an accumulation of food, money, etc stored away for future use. • *vti* to accumulate and store away.—**hoarder** *n*.

**hoarding** *n* a temporary screen of boards erected around a construction site; a large board used for advertising.

**hoarse** *adj* (*voice*) rough, as from a cold; (*person*) having a hoarse voice.—**hoarsely** *adv*.—**hoarseness** *n*.

**hoax** *n* a deception; a practical joke. • *vt* to deceive by a hoax.—**hoaxer** *n*.

**hob** *n* a ledge near a fireplace for keeping kettles, etc hot; a flat surface on a cooker incorporating hot plates or burners.

**hobble** *vi* to walk unsteadily, to limp. • *vt* to fasten the legs of (horses, etc) loosely together to prevent straying. • *n* a limp; a rope etc used to hobble a horse.

**hobby** *n* a spare-time activity carried out for personal amusement.

**hock**[1] *vt* (*sl*) to give something in security for a loan.

**hock**[2] *n* the joint bending backward on the hind leg of a horse, etc.

**hock**[3] *n* a variety of German white wine.

**hockey** *n* an outdoor game played by two teams of 11 players with a ball and clubs curved at one end; ice hockey.

**hoe** *n* a long-handled tool for weeding, loosening the earth, etc. • *vti* (*pr p* **hoeing**, *pt* **hoed**) to dig, weed, till, etc with a hoe.

**hog** *n* a castrated male pig raised for its meat; (*inf*) a selfish, greedy, or filthy person. • *vt* (*pt* **hogged**) to take more than one's due; to hoard greedily.

**hoist** *vt* to raise aloft, esp with a pulley, crane, etc. • *n* a hoisting; an apparatus for lifting.

**hold**[1] *vb* (*pt* **held**) *vt* to take and keep in one's possession; to grasp; to maintain in a certain position or condition; to retain; to contain; to own, to occupy; to support, sustain; to remain firm; to carry on, as a meeting; to regard; to believe, to consider; to bear or carry oneself; (*with* **back**) to withhold; to restrain; (*with* **down**) to restrain; (*inf*) to manage to retain one's job, etc; (*with* **forth**) to offer (eg an inducement); (*with* **off**) to keep apart; (*with* **up**) to delay; to hinder; to commit an armed robbery. • *vi* to go on being firm, loyal, etc; to remain unbroken or unyielding; to be true or valid; to continue; (*with* **back**) to refrain; (*with* **forth**) to speak at length; (*with* **off**) to wait, to refrain; (*with* **on**) to maintain a grip on; to persist; (*inf*) to keep a telephone line open. • *n* the act or manner of holding; grip; a dominating force on a person.—**holder** *n*.

**hold**[2] *n* the storage space in a ship or aircraft used for cargo.

**holdall** *n* a portable container for miscellaneous articles.

**holding** *n* (*often pl*) property, esp land, stocks and bonds.

**hold-up** *n* a delay; an armed robbery.

**hole** *n* a hollow place; a cavity; a pit; an animal's burrow; an aperture; a perforation; a small, squalid, dingy place; (*inf*) a difficult situation; (*golf*) a small cavity into which the ball is hit; the tee, the fairway, etc leading to this. • *vti* to make a hole in (something); to drive into a hole; (*with* **up**) to hibernate; (*inf*) to hide oneself.

**holey** *adj* full of holes.

**holiday** *n* a period away from work, school, etc for travel, rest or recreation; a day of freedom from work, etc, esp one set aside by law. • *vi* to spend a holiday..

**holiday-maker** *n* a person on holiday.

**holiness** *n* sanctity; (*with cap* ) the title of the Pope.

**hollow** *adj* having a cavity within or below; recessed, concave; empty or worthless. • *n* a hole, cavity; a depression, a valley. • *vti* to make or become hollow.—**hollowly** *adv.*

**holly** *n* an evergreen shrub with prickly leaves and red berries.

**holster** *n* a leather case attached to a belt for a pistol.

**holy** *adj* (**holier, holiest**) dedicated to religious use; without sin; deserving reverence.

**Holy Ghost** *n* the Holy Spirit.

**Holy Spirit** *n* the Third Person of the Trinity.

**homage** *n* a public demonstration of respect or honour towards someone or something.

**home** *n* the place where one lives; the city, etc where one was born or reared; a place thought of as home; a household and its affairs; an institution for the aged, orphans, etc. • *adj* of one's home or country; domestic. • *adv* at, to, or in the direction of home; to the point aimed at. • *vi* (*birds*) to return home; to be guided onto a target; to head for a destination; to send or go home.

**homeland** *n* the country where a person was born.

**homely** *adj* (**homelier, homeliest**) simple, everyday; crude; not good-looking.—**homeliness** *n.*

**home-made** *adj* made, or as if made, at home.

**homeopath** *n* a medical practitioner of homeopathy.—*also* **homoeopath, homeopathist, homoeopathist.**

**homeopathy** *n* the system of treating disease by small quantities of drugs that cause symptoms similar to those of the disease.—*also* **homoeopathy.** —**homeopathic, homoeopathic** *adj.* —**homeopathically, homoeopathically** *adv.*

**homesick** *adj* longing for home.— **homesickness** *n.*

**homeward** *adj* going towards home. • *adv* homewards.

**homework** *n* work, esp piecework, done at home; schoolwork to be done outside the classroom; preliminary study for a project.

**homicide** *n* the killing of a person by another; a person who kills another. —**homicidal** *adj.*

**homoeopath, homoeopathy** *see* **homeopath, homeopathy.**

**homogeneous** *adj* composed of parts that are of identical or a similar kind or nature; of uniform structure.— **homogeneity** *n.*

**homosexual** *adj* sexually attracted towards a person of the same sex. • *n* a homosexual person.—**homosexuality** *n.*

**honest** *adj* truthful; trustworthy; sincere or genuine; gained by fair means; frank, open.

**honestly** *adv* in an honest manner; really.

**honesty** *n* the quality of being honest; a plant that forms transparent seed pods.

**honey** *n* (*pl* **honeys**) a sweet sticky

yellowish substance that bees make as food from the nectar of flowers; sweetness; its colour; (*inf*) darling. • *adj* of, resembling honey; much loved.

**honeycomb** *n* the structure of six-sided wax cells made by bees to hold their honey, eggs, etc; anything arranged like this. • *vt* to fill with holes like a honeycomb.

**honeymoon** *n* the vacation spent together by a newly married couple.— *also vi.*—**honeymooner** *n*.

**honk** *n* (a sound like) the call of the wild goose; the sound made by an old-fashioned motor horn.—*also vti.*

**honorary** *adj* given as an honour; (*office*) voluntary, unpaid.

**honour, honor** (*US*) *n* high regard or respect; glory; fame; good reputation; integrity; chastity; high rank; distinction; (*with cap*) the title of certain officials, as judges; cards of the highest value in certain card games. • *vt* to respect greatly; to do or give something in honour of; to accept and pay (a cheque when due, etc).

**honourable, honorable** (*US*) *adj* worthy of being honoured; honest; upright; bringing honour; (*with cap*) a title of respect for certain officials, as Members of Parliament, when addressing each other.—**honourably** *adv*.

**hood**[1] *n* a loose covering to protect the head and back of the neck; any hood-like thing as the (folding) top of a car, etc; a car bonnet.

**hood**[2] *n* (*inf*) a hoodlum.

**hoodwink** *vt* to mislead by trickery.

**hoof** *n* (*pl* **hoofs, hooves**) the horny covering on the ends of the feet of certain animals, as horses, cows, etc.

**hook** *n* a piece of bent or curved metal to catch or hold anything; a fishhook; something shaped like a hook; a strike, blow, etc, in which a curving motion is involved. • *vt* to seize, fasten, hold, as with a hook; (*rugby*) to pass the ball backwards from a scrum.

**hooligan** *n* a lawless young person.— **hooliganism** *n*.

**hoop** *n* a circular band of metal or wood; an iron band for holding together the staves of barrels; anything like this, as a child's toy or ring in a hoop skirt. • *vt* to bind (as if) with hoops.

**hoot** *n* the sound that an owl makes; a similar sound, as made by a train whistle; a shout of scorn; (*inf*) laughter; (*inf*) an amusing person or thing. • *vi* to utter a hoot; to blow a whistle, etc. • *vt* to express (scorn) of (someone) by hooting.

**hooter** *n* something that hoots, such as a car horn; (*sl*) a nose.

**hooves** *see* **hoof**.

**hop**[1] *vi* (*pt* **hopped**) to jump up on one leg; to leap with all feet at once, as a frog, etc; (*inf*) to make a quick trip. • *n* a hopping movement; (*inf*) an informal dance; a trip, esp in an aircraft.

**hop**[2] *n* a climbing plant with small cone-shaped flowers; (*pl*) the dried ripe cones, used for flavouring beer.

**hope** *n* a feeling that what is wanted will happen; the object of this; a person or thing on which one may base some hope. • *vt* to want and expect. • *vi* to have hope (for).

**hopeful** *adj* filled with hope; inspiring hope or promise of success. • *n* a person who hopes to or looks likely to be a success.

**hopefully** *adv* in a hopeful manner; it is hoped.

**hopeless** *adj* without hope; offering no grounds for hope or promise of success; impossible to solve; (*inf*) incompetent.—**hopelessly** *adv*.— **hopelessness** *n*.

**horde** *n* a crowd or throng; a swarm.

**horizon** *n* the apparent line along which the earth and sky meet; the limit of a person's knowledge, interest, etc.

**horizontal** *adj* level; parallel to the plane of the horizon.—**horizontally** *adv*.

**hormone** *n* a product of living cells formed in one part of the organism and carried to another part, where it takes effect; a synthetic compound having the same purpose.—**hormonal** *adj*.

**horn** *n* a bony outgrowth on the head of certain animals; the hard substance of which this is made; any projection like a horn; a wind instrument, esp the French horn or trumpet; a device to sound a warning.

**horned** *adj* having horns.

**hornet** *n* a large wasp with a severe sting.

**horny** *adj* (**hornier, horniest**) like horn; hard; callous; (*sl*) sexually aroused.

**horoscope** *n* a chart of the signs and positions of planets, etc, by which astrologers profess to predict future events, esp in the life of an individual.

**horrible** *adj* arousing horror; (*inf*) very bad, unpleasant, etc.—**horribly** *adv*.

**horrid** *adj* terrible; horrible.—**horridly** *adv*.

**horrify** *vt* to fill with horror.

**horror** *n* the strong feeling caused by something frightful or shocking; strong dislike; a person, thing inspiring horror.

**hors-d'oeuvre** *n* an appetizer served at the beginning of a meal.

**horse** *n* four-legged, solid-hoofed herbivorous mammal with a flowing mane and a tail, domesticated for carrying loads or riders, etc; cavalry; a vaulting horse; a frame with legs to support something.

**horse chestnut** *n* a large tree with large palmate leaves and erect clusters of flowers.

**horseman** *n* a person skilled in the riding or care of horses.—**horsemanship** *n*.

**horsepower** *n* a unit for measuring the power of engines, etc, equal to 746 watts or 33,000 foot-pounds per minute.

**horseradish** *n* a tall herb of the mustard family; a sauce or relish made with its pungent root.

**horseshoe** *n* a flat U-shaped, protective metal plate nailed to a horse's hoof; anything shaped like this.

**horticulture** *n* the art or science of growing flowers, fruits, and vegetables.—**horticultural** *adj*.—**horticulturist** *n*.

**hose**[1] *n* a flexible tube used to convey fluids. • *vt* to spray with a hose.

**hose**[2] *n* (*pl* **hose**) stockings, socks, tights collectively.

**hosiery** *n* stockings; socks.

**hospitable** *adj* offering a generous welcome to guests or strangers; sociable.—**hospitably** *adv*.

**hospital** *n* an institution where the sick or injured are given medical treatment.

**hospitality** *n* the act, practice, or quality of being hospitable.

**host**[1] *n* a person who receives or entertains a stranger or guest at his house; an animal or plant on or in which another lives; a compere on a television or radio programme. • *vti* to act as a host (to a party, television programme, etc).

**host**[2] *n* a very large number of people or things.

**host**[3] *n* the wafer of bread used in the Eucharist or Holy Communion.

**hostage** *n* a person given or kept as security until certain conditions are met.

**hostel** *n* a lodging place for the home-less, travellers, or other groups.

**hostess** *n* a woman acting as a host; a woman who entertains guests at a nightclub, etc.

**hostile** *adj* of or being an enemy; un-friendly.—**hostilely** *adv*.

**hostility** *n* enmity, antagonism; (*pl*) deliberate acts of warfare.

**hot** *adj* (**hotter, hottest**) of high temperature; very warm; giving or feel-ing heat; causing a burning sensa-tion on the tongue; full of intense feeling; following closely; electrically charged; (*inf*) recent, new; (*inf*) ra-dioactive; (*inf*) stolen. • *adv* in a hot manner.—**hotly** *adv*.—**hotness** *n*.

**hot dog** *n* a sausage, esp a frankfurter, served in a long soft roll.

**hotel** *n* a commercial establishment providing lodging and meals for trav-ellers, etc.

**hotelier** *n* the owner or manager of a hotel.

**hothead** *n* an impetuous person.—**hot-headed** *adj*.

**hothouse** *n* a heated greenhouse for raising plants; an environment that encourages rapid growth.

**hotplate** *n* a heated surface for cook-ing or keeping food warm; a small portable heating device.

**hound** *n* a dog used in hunting; a con-temptible person. • *vt* to hunt or chase as with hounds; to urge on by harassment.—**hounder** *n*.

**hour** *n* a period of 60 minutes, a 24th part of a day; the time for a specific activity; the time; a special point in time; the distance covered in an hour; (*pl*) the customary period for work, etc.

**hourly** *adj* occurring every hour; done during an hour; frequent. • *adv* at every hour; frequently.

**house** *n* a building to live in, esp by one person or family; a household; a family or dynasty including relatives, ancestors and descendants; the au-dience in a theatre; a business firm; a legislative assembly. • *vt* to pro-vide accommodation or storage for; to cover, encase.

**house arrest** *n* detention in one's own house, as opposed to prison.

**houseboat** *n* a boat furnished and used as a home.

**housebreaker** *n* a burglar; a person employed to demolish buildings.—**housebreaking** *n*.

**household** *n* all those people living to-gether in the same house. • *adj* per-taining to running a house and fam-ily; domestic; familiar.

**housekeeper** *n* a person who runs a home, esp one hired to do so.

**housekeeping** *n* the daily running of a household; (*inf*) money used for do-mestic expenses; routine mainte-nance of equipment, records, etc in an organization.

**house warming** *n* a party given to cel-ebrate moving into a new house.

**housewife** *n* the woman who keeps house.—**housewifery** *n*.

**housework** *n* the cooking, cleaning, etc involved in running a home.

**housing** *n* houses collectively; the pro-vision of accommodation; a casing enclosing a piece of machinery, etc; a slot or groove in a piece of wood, etc to receive an insertion.

**housing estate** *n* accommodation, shops, leisure facilities, etc planned as a single unit.

**hovel** *n* a small miserable dwelling.

**hover** *vi* (*bird, etc*) to hang in the air stationary; to hang about, to linger.

**hovercraft** *n* a land or water vehicle that travels supported on a cushion of air.

**how** *adv* in what way or manner; by what means; to what extent; in what condition.

**howl** *vi* to utter the long, wailing cry

of wolves, dogs, etc; to utter a similar cry of anger, pain, etc; to shout or laugh in pain, amusement, etc. • *vt* to utter with a howl; to drive by howling. • *n* the wailing cry of a wolf, dog, etc; any similar sound.

**howler** *n* (*inf*) a stupid mistake.

**HP** *abbr* = hire purchase; horsepower; high pressure; Houses of Parliament.

**HQ** *abbr* = headquarters.

**hub** *n* the centre part of a wheel; a centre of activity.

**hubbub** *n* a confused noise of many voices; an uproar.

**huddle** *vti* to crowd together in a confined space; to curl (oneself) up. • *n* a confused crowd or heap.

**hue** *n* colour; a particular shade or tint of a colour.

**huff** *n* a state of smouldering resentment. • *vi* to blow; to puff.—**huffy** *adj*.—**huffily** *adv*.

**hug** *vb* (*pt* **hugged**) *vt* to hold or squeeze tightly with the arms; to cling to; to keep close to. • *vi* to embrace one another. • *n* a strong embrace.—**huggable** *adj*.

**huge** *adj* very large, enormous.—**hugely** *adv*. –**hugeness** *n*.

**hulk** *n* the body of a ship, esp if old and dismantled; a large, clumsy person or thing.

**hulking** *adj* unwieldy, bulky.

**hull** *n* the outer covering of a fruit or seed; the framework of a ship. • *vt* to remove the hulls of, to pierce the hull of ( a ship, etc).

**hullo** *see* **hello**.

**hum** *vb* (*pt* **hummed**) *vi* to make a low continuous vibrating sound; to hesitate in speaking and utter an inarticulate sound; (*inf*) to be lively, busy; (*sl*) to stink. • *vt* to sing with closed lips. • *n* a humming sound; a murmur; (*sl*) a stink.

**human** *adj* of or relating to human beings; having the qualities of humans as opposed to animals; kind, considerate. • *n* a human being.

**humane** *adj* kind, compassionate, merciful.—**humanely** *adv*.

**humanity** *n* the human race; the state or quality of being human or humane; philanthropy; kindness; (*pl*) the study of literature and the arts, as opposed to the sciences.

**humble** *adj* having a low estimation of one's abilities; modest, unpretentious; servile. • *vt* to lower in condition or rank; to humiliate.—**humbly** *adv*.—**humbleness** *n*.

**humbug** *n* fraud, sham, hoax; an insincere person; a peppermint-flavoured sweet. • *vt* (*pt* **humbugged**) to cheat or impose upon; to hoax.

**humdrum** *adj* dull, ordinary, boring.

**humid** *adj* (*air*) moist, damp.

**humidity** *n* (a measure of the amount of) dampness in the air.

**humiliate** *vt* to cause to feel humble; to lower the pride or dignity of.—**humiliation** *n*.

**humility** *n* the state of being humble.

**humorist** *n* a person who writes or speaks in a humorous manner.

**humorous** *adj* funny, amusing; causing laughter.—**humorously** *adv*.—**humorousness** *n*.

**humour, humor** (*US*) *n* the ability to appreciate or express what is funny, amusing, etc; the expression of this; temperament, disposition; state of mind; (*formerly*) any of the four fluids of the body (blood, phlegm, yellow and black bile) that were thought to determine temperament. • *vt* to indulge; to gratify by conforming to the wishes of.—**humourless** *adj*.

**hump** *n* a rounded protuberance; a fleshy lump on the back of an animal (as a camel or whale); a deformity causing curvature of the spine. • *vt* to hunch; to arch.

**humpback** *n* a hunchback.—**hump-backed** *adj*.

**hunch** *n* a hump; (*inf*) an intuitive feeling. • *vt* to arch into a hump. • *vi* to move forward jerkily.

**hunchback** *n* a person with curvature of the spine.

**hundred** *adj, n* ten times ten; the symbol for this (100, C, c); the hundredth in a series or set.

**hundredweight** *n* a unit of weight, equal to 112 pounds in Britain and 100 pounds in the US.

**hung** *see* **hang**.

**hunger** *n* (a feeling weak or empty from) a need for food; a strong desire. • *vi* to feel hunger; to have a strong desire (for).

**hungry** *adj* (**hungrier, hungriest**) desiring food; craving for something; greedy.—**hungrily** *adv*.

**hunt** *vti* to seek out to kill or capture (game) for food or sport; to search (for); to chase. • *n* a chase; a search; a party organized for hunting.

**hunter** *n* a person who hunts; a horse used in hunting.—**huntress** *nf*.

**hunting** *n* the art or practice of one who hunts; a pursuit; a search.

**hurdle** *n* a portable frame of bars for temporary fences or for jumping over by horses or runners; an obstacle. (*pl*) a race over hurdles.—**hurdler** *n*.

**hurl** *vt* to throw violently; to utter vehemently.—*also n*.

**hurrah** *interj* an exclamation of approval or joy.

**hurricane** *n* a violent tropical cyclone with winds of at least 74 miles per hour.

**hurried** *adj* performed with great haste.—**hurriedly** *adv*.

**hurry** *n* rush; urgency; eagerness to do, go, etc. • *vt* to cause to move or happen more quickly. • *vi* to move or act with haste.

**hurt** *vb* (*pt* **hurt**) *vt* to cause physical pain to; to injure, damage; to offend. • *vi* to feel pain; to cause pain.—**hurtful** *adj*.

**hurtle** *vti* to move or throw with great speed and force.

**husband** *n* a man to whom a woman is married. • *vt* to conserve; to manage economically.

**hush** *vti* to make or become silent. • *n* a silence or calm.

**husk** *n* the dry covering of certain fruits and seeds; any dry, rough, or useless covering. • *vt* to strip the husk from.

**husky**[1] *adj* (**huskier, huskiest**) (*voice*) hoarse; rough-sounding; hefty, strong.—**huskily** *adv*.—**huskiness** *n*.

**husky**[2] *n* an Arctic sled dog.

**hustle** *vt* to jostle or push roughly or hurriedly; to force hurriedly; (*sl*) to obtain by rough or illegal means. • *vi* to move hurriedly. • *n* an instance of hustling.—**hustler** *n*.

**hut** *n* a very plain or crude little house or cabin.

**hutch** *n* a pen or coop for small animals; a hut.

**hyacinth** *n* a plant of the lily family with spikes of bell-shaped flowers; the orange gemstone jacinth; a light violet to moderate purple.

**hyaena** *see* **hyena**.

**hybrid** *n* the offspring of two plants or animals of different species; a mongrel. • *adj* crossbred.

**hydrant** *n* a large pipe with a valve for drawing water from a main.

**hydraulic** *adj* operated by water or other liquid, esp by moving through pipes under pressure; of hydraulics.—**hydraulically** *adv*.

**hydraulics** *npl* (*used as sing*) the science dealing with the mechanical properties of liquids and their application in engineering.

**hydroelectricity** *n* electricity

generated by water power.—**hydro-electric** adj.

**hydrogen** n a flammable, colourless, odourless, tasteless, gaseous chemical element, the lightest substance known.

**hyena** n a nocturnal, carnivorous, scavenging mammal like a wolf.—also **hyaena**.

**hygiene** n the principles and practice of health and cleanliness.—**hygienic** adj.—**hygienically** adv.

**hymn** n a song of praise to God or other object of worship.

**hyphen** n a punctuation mark (-) used to join two syllables or words, or to divide words into parts. • vt to hyphenate.

**hypnosis** n (pl **hypnoses**) a relaxed state resembling sleep in which the mind responds to external suggestion.

**hypnotism** n the act of inducing hypnosis; the study and use of hypnosis. —**hypnotist** n.

**hypnotize** vt to put in a state of hypnosis; to fascinate.

**hypocrisy** n a falsely pretending to possess virtues, beliefs, etc; an example of this.—**hypocrite** n.—**hypocritical** adj.—**hypocritically** adv.

**hypothesis** n (pl **hypotheses**) something assumed for the purpose of argument; a theory to explain some fact that may or may not prove to be true; supposition; conjecture.

**hypothetical** adj based on hypothesis, conjectural.—**hypothetically** adv.

**hysteria** n a mental disorder marked by excitability, anxiety, imaginary organic disorders, etc; frenzied emotion or excitement.

**hysteric** n a hysterical person; (pl) fits of hysteria.

**hysterical** adj caused by hysteria; suffering from hysteria; (inf) extremely funny.—**hysterically** adv.

**I**

**I** pron the person who is speaking or writing, used in referring to himself or herself.

**ice** n water frozen solid; a sheet of this; a portion of ice cream or water ice; (sl) diamonds. • vti (often with **up** or **over**) to freeze; to cool with ice; to cover with icing.

**iceberg** n a great mass of mostly submerged ice floating in the sea.

**icebox** n a compartment in a refrigerator for making and storing ice; a refrigerator.

**ice cream** adj a sweet frozen food, made from flavoured milk or cream.

**ice hockey** n indoor or outdoor hockey played on ice by two teams of six skaters with curved sticks and a puck.

**icicle** n a hanging tapering length of ice formed when dripping water freezes.

**icing** n a semi-solid sugary mixture covering cakes, etc.

**icon** n an image; (Eastern Church) a sacred image, usu on a wooden panel.

**icy** adj (**icier, iciest**) full of, made of, or covered with ice; slippery or very cold; cold in manner.—**icily** adv.—**iciness** n.

**I'd** = I had, I should, I would.

**idea** n a mental impression of anything; a vague impression, notion; an opinion or belief; a scheme; a supposition; a person's conception of something; a significance or purpose.

**ideal** adj existing in the mind or as an idea; satisfying an ideal, perfect. • n the most perfect conception of anything; a person, thing regarded as perfect; a standard for attainment or imitation; an aim or principle.—**ideally** *adv*.

**identical** *adj* exactly the same; having the same origin.—**identically** *adv*.

**identification** *n* the act of identifying; the state of being identified; that which identifies.

**identify** *vt* to consider to be the same, equate; to establish the identity of; to associate closely; to regard (oneself) as similar to another.—**identifier** *n*.

**identity** *n* the state of being exactly alike; the distinguishing characteristics of a person, personality; the state of being the same as a specified person or thing.

**ideology** *n* the doctrines, beliefs or opinions of an individual, social class, political party, etc.—**ideological** *adj*.—**ideologist, ideologue** *n*.

**idiocy** *n* mental deficiency; stupidity, imbecility; something stupid, foolish.

**idiom** *n* an accepted phrase or expression with a different meaning from the literal; the usual way in which the words of a language are used to express thought; the dialect of a people, region, etc; the characteristic style of a school of art, literature, etc—**idiomatic** *adj*.—**idiomatically** *adv*.

**idiosyncrasy** *n* a type of behaviour or characteristic peculiar to a person or group; a quirk, eccentricity.—**idiosyncratic** *adj*.

**idiot** *n* a severely mentally retarded adult; (*inf*) a foolish or stupid person.

**idiotic** *adj* stupid; senseless.—**idiotically** *adv*.

**idle** *adj* not employed, unoccupied; not in use; averse to work; useless; worthless. • *vt* to waste or spend (time) in idleness. • *vi* to move slowly or aimlessly; (*engine*) to operate without transmitting power.—**idleness** *n*.—**idler** *n*.—**idly** *adv*.

**idol** *n* an image or object worshipped as a god; a person who is intensely loved, admired or honoured.

**idolize** *vt* to make an idol of, for worship; to love to excess.—**idolization** *n*.

**i.e.** *abbr* = *id est*, that is.

**if** *conj* on condition that; in the event that; supposing that; even though; whenever; whether.

**igloo** *n* an Eskimo house built of blocks of snow and ice.

**ignite** *vti* to set fire to; to catch fire; to burn or cause to burn.

**ignition** *n* an act or instance of igniting; the starting of an internal combustion engine; the mechanism that ignites an internal combustion engine.

**ignorant** *adj* lacking knowledge; uninformed, uneducated; resulting from or showing lack of knowledge.—**ignorance** *n*.—**ignorantly** *adv*.

**ignore** *vt* to disregard; to deliberately refuse to notice someone.

**ill** *adj* not in good health; harmful; bad; hostile; faulty; unfavourable. • *adv* badly, wrongly; hardly, with difficulty. • *n* trouble; harm; evil.

**I'll** = I shall, I will.

**ill-advised** *adj* unwise.

**ill at ease** *adj* uneasy, embarrassed.

**illegal** *adj* against the law.—**illegally** *adv*.—**illegality** *n*.

**illegible** *adj* impossible to read.—**illegibly** *adv*.—**illegibility** *n*.

**illegitimate** *adj* born of parents not married to each other; contrary to law, rules, or logic.—**illegitimately** *adv*.—**illegitimacy** *n*.

**illicit** *adj* improper; unlawful.—**illicitly** *adv*.

**illiterate** *adj* uneducated, esp not knowing how to read or write. • *n*

an illiterate person.—**illiterately**
*adv*.—**illiteracy** *n*.

**ill-natured** *adj* spiteful.

**illness** *n* a state of ill-health; sickness.

**illogical** *adj* not logical or reasonable.—**illogically** *adv*.—**illogicality** *n*.

**ill-treat** *vt* to treat unkindly, unfairly,
etc.—**ill-treatment** *n*.

**illuminate** *vt* to give light to; to light
up; to make clear; to inform; to decorate as with gold or lights.—**illumination** *n*.—**illuminative** *adj*.

**illusion** *n* a false idea or conception; an
unreal or misleading image or appearance.—**illusional, illusionary** *adj*.

**illusory, illusive** *adj* deceptive; based
on illusion.

**illustrate** *vt* to explain, as by examples;
to provide (books, etc) with explanatory pictures, charts, etc; to serve as
an example.—**illustrative** *adj*.—**illus-
trator** *n*.

**illustration** *n* the act of illustrating; the
state of being illustrated; an exam-
ple that explains or corroborates; a
picture or diagram in a book, etc.

**illustrious** *adj* distinguished, famous.
—**illustriousness** *n*.

**ill-will** *n* antagonism, hostility.

**I'm** = I am.

**image** *n* a representation of a person
or thing; the visual impression of
something in a lens, mirror, etc; a
copy; a likeness; a mental picture;
the concept of a person, product, etc
held by the public at large. • *vt* to
make a representation of; to reflect;
to imagine.

**imagery** *n* the work of the imagination;
mental pictures; figures of speech;
images in general or collectively.

**imaginary** *adj* existing only in the imagination.

**imagination** *n* the image-forming power
of the mind, or the power of the mind
that modifies the conceptions, esp
the higher form of this power exer-

cised in art and poetry; creative ability; resourcefulness in overcoming
practical difficulties, etc.

**imaginative** *adj* having or showing imagination; produced by imagina-
tion.—**imaginatively** *adv*.

**imagine** *vt* to form a mental image of;
to believe falsely; (*inf*) to suppose;
to guess. • *vi* to employ the imagination.

**imbalance** *n* a lack of balance, as in
proportion, emphasis, etc

**imbecile** *n* an adult with a mental age
of a three-to eight-year-old child; an
idiotic person. • *adj* stupid or foolish.—**imbecility** *n*.

**imitate** *vt* to try to follow as a pattern
or model; to mimic humorously, impersonate; to copy, reproduce.—**imi-
tator** *n*.

**imitation** *n* an act or instance of imitating; a copy; an act of mimicking
or impersonation.

**immaculate** *adj* spotless; flawless;
pure, morally unblemished.—**im-
maculately** *adv*.

**immaterial** *adj* spiritual as opposed to
physical; unimportant.

**immature** *adj* not mature.—**immaturity** *n*.

**immediate** *adj* acting or occurring
without delay; next, nearest, without
intervening agency; next in relationship; in close proximity, near to; directly concerning or touching a person or thing.—**immediacy** *n*.

**immediately** *adv* without delay; directly;
near, close by. • *conj* as soon as.

**immense** *adj* very large in size or extent; limitless; (*inf*) excellent.—**im-
mensely** *adv*.

**immerse** *vt* to plunge into a liquid; to
absorb or engross; to baptize by total submergence.—**immersible** *adj*.

**immersion heater** *n* an electric element
for heating liquids, esp water in a
domestic hot-water tank.

**immigrant** *n* a person who immigrates;

a person recently settled in a country but not born there.

**immigrate** *vi* to come into a new country, esp to settle permanently.—**immigration** *n*.—**immigratory** *adj*.

**imminent** *adj* about to happen; impending.—**imminence** *n*.—**imminently** *adv*.

**immobilize** *vt* to make immobile.—**immobilization** *n*.

**immoral** *adj* against accepted standards of proper behaviour; sexually degenerate; corrupt; wicked.—**immorally** *adv*.—**immorality** *n*.

**immortal** *adj* living for ever; enduring; having lasting fame. • *n* an immortal being or person; (*pl*) the gods of classical mythology.—**immortality** *n*.

**immortalize** *vt* to render immortal; to bestow lasting fame upon.—**immortalization** *n*.

**immune** *adj* not susceptible to a specified disease through inoculation or natural resistance; conferring immunity; exempt from a certain obligation, tax, duty, etc.

**immunize** *vt* to make immune, esp against infection.—**immunization** *n*.

**impact** *n* violent contact; a shocking effect; the force of a body colliding with another. • *vt* to force tightly together. • *vi* to hit with force.—**impaction** *n*.

**impair** *vt* to make worse, less, etc.—**impairment** *n*.

**impale** *vt* to fix on, or pierce through, with something pointed.—**impalement** *n*.

**impartial** *adj* not favouring one side more than another, unbiased.—**impartiality** *n*.—**impartially** *adv*.

**impassable** *adj* (*roads, etc*) incapable of being travelled through or over.—**impassability** *n*.—**impassably** *adv*.

**impatient** *adj* lacking patience; intolerant of delay, etc; restless.—**impatience** *n*.—**impatiently** *adv*.

**impeach** *vt* to question a person's

honesty; to try (a public official) on a charge of wrongdoing.—**impeachment** *n*.

**impeccable** *adj* without defect or error; faultless.—**impeccability** *n*.—**impeccably** *adv*.

**impede** *vt* to obstruct or hinder the progress of.

**impediment** *n* something that impedes; an obstruction; a physical defect, as a stammer that prevents fluency of speech.

**impend** *vi* to be imminent; to threaten.—**impending** *adj*.

**imperative** *adj* urgent, pressing; authoritative; obligatory; designating or of the mood of a verb that expresses a command, entreaty, etc. • *n* a command; (*gram*) the imperative mood of a verb.

**imperceptible** *adj* not able to be detected by the mind or senses; slight, minute, gradual.—**imperceptibility** *n*.—**imperceptibly** *adv*.

**imperfect** *adj* having faults, flaws, mistakes, etc; defective; incomplete; (*gram*) designating a verb tense that indicates a past action or state as incomplete or continuous. • (*gram*) an imperfect tense.

**imperfection** *n* the state or quality of being imperfect; a defect, fault.

**imperial** *adj* of an empire, emperor, or empress; majestic; of great size or superior quality; of the British non-metric system of weights and measures.—**imperially** *adv*.

**impersonal** *adj* not referring to any particular person; cold, unfeeling; not existing as a person; (*verb*) occurring only in the third person singular, usu with "it" as subject.—**impersonality** *n*.—**impersonally** *adv*.

**impersonate** *vt* to assume the role of another person as entertainment or for fraud.—**impersonation** *n*.—**impersonator** *n*.

**impertinent** *adj* impudent; insolent; irrelevant.—**impertinence** *n.*—**impertinently** *adv.*

**impervious** *adj* incapable of being penetrated, as by water; not readily receptive (to) or affected (by).

**impetuous** *adj* acting or done suddenly with impulsive energy.—**impetuosity** *n.*—**impetuously** *adv.*

**impetus** *n* the force with which a body moves against resistance; driving force or motive.

**impinge** *vi* (*with* **on, upon**) to have an impact; to encroach.—**impingement** *n.*

**implausible** *adj* not plausible.—**implausibility** *n.*—**implausibly** *adv.*

**implement** *n* something used in a given activity. • *vt* to carry out, put into effect.—**implementation** *n.*

**implicate** *vt* to show to have a part, esp in a crime; to imply.

**implication** *n* an implicating or being implicated; that which is implied; an inference not expressed but understood; deduction.

**implicit** *adj* implied rather than stated explicitly; unquestioning, absolute.—**implicitly** *adv.*

**implore** *vt* to request earnestly; to plead, entreat.—**imploringly** *adv.*

**imply** *vt* to hint, suggest indirectly; to indicate or involve as a consequence.

**impolite** *adj* not polite, rude.—**impolitely** *adv.*—**impoliteness** *n.*

**imponderable** *adj* not able to be weighed or measured. • *n* something difficult to measure or assess.

**import** *vt* to bring (goods) in from a foreign country for sale or use; to mean; to signify. • *vi* to be of importance, to matter. • *n* something imported; meaning; importance.—**importable** *adj.*—**importer** *n.*

**importance** *n* the quality of being important; a high place in public estimation; high self-esteem.

**important** *adj* having great significance or consequence; (*person*) having power, authority, etc.—**importantly** *adv.*

**impose** *vt* to put (a burden, tax, punishment) on or upon; to force (oneself) on others; to lay pages of type or film and secure them. • *vi* (*with* **on** *or* **upon**) to take advantage of; to cheat or defraud.

**imposing** *adj* impressive because of size, appearance, dignity, etc.—**imposingly** *adv.*

**impossibility** *n* the character of being impossible; that which cannot be, or be supposed to be, done.

**impossible** *adj* not capable of existing, being done, or happening; (*inf*) unendurable, outrageous.—**impossibly** *adv.*

**impostor, imposter** *n* a person who acts fraudulently by impersonating another.

**impotent** *adj* lacking in necessary strength, powerless; (*man*) unable to engage in sexual intercourse.—**impotence** *n.*—**impotently** *adv.*

**impound** *vt* to take legal possession of; to shut up (an animal) in a pound.

**impoverish** *vt* to make poor; to deprive of strength.—**impoverishment** *n.*

**impracticable** *adj* not able to be carried out, not feasible.—**impracticability** *n.*—**impracticably** *adv.*

**impractical** *adj* not practical; not competent in practical skills.—**impracticality** *n.*—**impractically** *adv.*

**imprecise** *adj* not precise; ill-defined.—**imprecisely** *adv.*—**imprecision** *n.*

**impregnable** *adj* secure against attack, unyielding.—**impregnability** *n.*—**impregnably** *adv.*

**impregnate** *vt* to cause to become pregnant, to fertilize; to saturate, soak (with); to pervade.—**impregnation** *n.*

**impresario** n the manager of an opera, a concert series, etc.

**impress**[1] vt to make a strong, usu favourable, impression on; to fix deeply in the mind; to stamp with a mark; to imprint. • n an imprint, a mark.

**impress**[2] vt to coerce into military service.—**impressment** n.

**impression** n the effect produced in the mind by an experience; a mark produced by imprinting; a vague idea, notion; the act of impressing or being impressed; a notable or strong influence on the mind or senses; the number of copies of a book printed at one go; an impersonation or act of mimicry.

**impressionable** n easily impressed or influenced.—**impressionability** n.—**impressionably** adv.

**impressive** adj tending to impress the mind or emotions; arousing wonder or admiration.—**impressiveness** n.

**imprison** vt to put in a prison; to confine, as in a prison.—**imprisonment** n.

**improbable** adj unlikely to be true or to happen.—**improbability** n.—**improbably** adv.

**impromptu** adj, adv unrehearsed, unprepared. • n something impromptu, as a speech.

**improper** adj lacking propriety, indecent; incorrect; not suitable or appropriate.—**improperly** adv.

**impropriety** n the quality of being improper; indecency; an improper act, etc.

**improve** vt to make or become better.—**improvable** adj.—**improver** n.

**improvement** n the act of improving or being improved; an alteration that improves or adds to the value of something.

**improvise** vti to compose, perform, recite, etc without preparation; to make or do with whatever is at hand.—**improvisation** n.—**improviser** n.

**impulse** n a sudden push or thrust; a stimulus transmitted through a nerve or a muscle; a sudden instinctive urge to act.

**impulsive** adj tending to act on impulse; forceful, impelling; acting momentarily.—**impulsively** adv.—**impulsiveness** n.

**impunity** n exemption or freedom from punishment or harm.

**impure** adj unclean; adulterated.

**impurity** n a being impure; an impure substance or constituent.

**in** prep inside; within; at; as contained by; during; at the end of; not beyond; affected by; being a member of; wearing; using; because of; into. • adv to or at a certain place; so as to be contained by a certain space, condition, etc; (games) batting, in play. • adj that is in power; inner; inside; gathered, counted, etc; (inf) currently smart, fashionable, etc.

**in.** abbr = inch(es).

**inability** n lack of ability.

**inaccessible** adj not accessible, unapproachable.—**inaccessibility** n.—**inaccessibly** adv.

**inaccurate** adj not accurate, imprecise.—**inaccuracy** n.—**inaccurately** adv.

**inactive** adj not active.—**inactively** adv.—**inactivity** n.

**inadequate** adj not adequate; not capable.— **inadequacy** n.—**inadequately** adv.

**inadmissible** adj not admissible, esp as evidence.—**inadmissibility** n.

**inadvertent** adj not attentive or observant, careless; due to oversight.—**inadvertence** n.—**inadvertency** n.—**inadvertently** adv.

**inadvisable** adj not advisable; inexpedient.—**inadvisably** adv.

**inane** *adj* lacking sense, silly.—**inanely** *adv*.—**inanity** *n*.

**inanimate** *adj* not animate; showing no signs of life; dull.—**inanimately** *adv*.—**inanimation** *n*.

**inappropriate** *adj* unsuitable.—**inappropriately** *adv*.—**inappropriateness** *n*.

**inarticulate** *adj* not expressed in words; incapable of being expressed in words; incapable of coherent or effective expression of ideas, feelings, etc.—**inarticulately** *adv*.

**inasmuch** *adv* in like degree; (*with* **as**) seeing that; because.

**inattentive** *adj* not attending; neglectful.—**inattention** *n*.

**inaudible** *adj* unable to be heard.—**inaudibility** *n*.—**inaudibly** *adv*.

**inaugural** *n* of or pertaining to an inauguration; a speech made at an inauguration.

**inaugurate** *vt* to admit ceremonially into office; to open (a building, etc) formally to the public; to cause to begin, initiate.—**inauguration** *n*.

**inborn** *adj* present from birth; hereditary.

**inbred** *adj* innate; produced by inbreeding.

**inbreed** *vti* (*pt* **inbred**) to breed by continual mating of individuals of the same or closely related stocks.

**Inc.** *abbr* = Incorporated.

**incapable** *adj* lacking capability; not able or fit to perform an activity.—**incapability** *n*.—**incapably** *adv*.

**incapacitate** *vt* to weaken, to disable; to make ineligible.—**incapacitation** *n*.

**incarnate** *adj* endowed with a human body; personified. • *vt* to give bodily form to; to be the type or embodiment of.—**incarnation** *n*.

**incendiary** *adj* pertaining to arson; (*bomb*) designed to start fires; tending to stir up or inflame. • *n* a person that sets fire to a building, etc maliciously, an arsonist; an incendiary substance (as in a bomb); a person who stirs up violence, etc.

**incense**[1] *vt* to make extremely angry.

**incense**[2] *n* a substance that gives off a fragrant odour when burned; the fumes so produced; any pleasant odour.

**incessant** *adj* never ceasing; continual, constant.—**incessantly** *adv*.

**incest** *n* sexual intercourse between persons too closely related to marry legally.

**inch** *n* a measure of length equal to one twelfth of a foot (2.54 cm); a very small distance or amount. • *vti* to move very slowly, or by degrees.

**incidence** *n* the degree or range of occurrence or effect.

**incidental** *adj* happening in connection with something more important; happening by chance. • *npl* miscellaneous items, minor expenses.

**incidentally** *adv* in passing, as an aside.

**incinerator** *n* a furnace for burning rubbish.

**incipient** *adj* beginning to be or appear; initial.—**incipience** *n*.

**incision** *n* incising; a cut made into something, esp by a surgeon into a body.

**incisive** *adj* keen, penetrating; decisive; biting.—**incisively** *adv*.—**incisiveness** *n*.

**incite** *vt* to urge to action; to rouse.—**incitement** *n*.

**inclination** *n* a propensity or disposition, esp a liking; a deviation from the horizontal or vertical; a slope; inclining or being inclined; a bending movement, a bow.

**incline** *vi* to lean, to slope; to be disposed towards an opinion or action. • *vt* to cause to bend (the head or body) forwards; to cause to deviate, esp from the horizontal or vertical. • *n* a slope.

**include** *vt* to enclose, contain; to comprise as part or a larger group, amount, etc.—**inclusion** *n*.

**inclusive** *adj* comprehensive; including the limits specified.—**inclusively** *adv*.

**incognito** *adj*, *adv* under an assumed name or identity. • *n* (*pl* **incognitos**) a person appearing or living incognito; the name assumed by such a person.—**incognita** *nf*.

**incoherent** *adj* lacking organization or clarity; inarticulate in speech or thought.—**incoherence** *n*.—**incoherently** *adv*.

**income** *n* the money etc received for labour or services, or from property, investments, etc.

**income tax** *n* a tax levied on the net income of a person or business.

**incoming** *adj* coming; accruing. • *n* the act of coming in; that which comes in; income.

**incompatible** *adj* not able to exist together in harmony; antagonistic; inconsistent.—**incompatibility** *n*.—**incompatibly** *adv*.

**incompetent** *adj* lacking the necessary ability, skill, etc. • *n* an incompetent person.—**incompetence** *n*.—**incompetently** *adv*.

**incomplete** *adj* unfinished; lacking a part or parts.—**incompletely** *adv*.—**incompleteness** *n*.

**incomprehensible** *adj* not to be understood or grasped by the mind; inconceivable.—**incomprehension** *n*.

**inconclusive** *adj* leading to no definite result; ineffective; inefficient.—**inconclusively** *adv*.—**inconclusiveness** *n*.

**incongruous** *adj* lacking harmony or agreement of parts; unsuitable; inappropriate.—**incongruity** *n*.—**incongruously** *adv*.

**inconsequential, inconsequent** *adj* not following logically; irrelevant.—**inconsequentially, inconsequently** *adv*.

**inconsiderate** *adj* uncaring about others; thoughtless.—**inconsiderately** *adv*.—**inconsiderateness, inconsideration** *n*.

**inconsistent** *adj* not compatible with other facts; contradictory; irregular, fickle.—**inconsistency** *n*.—**inconsistently** *adv*.

**inconspicuous** *adj* not conspicuous.—**inconspicuously** *adv*.—**inconspicuousness** *n*.

**inconstant** *adj* subject to change; unstable; variable; fickle; capricious.—**inconstancy** *n*.

**incontinent** *adj* unable to control the excretion of bodily wastes; lacking sexual restraint.—**incontinence** *n*.

**inconvenience** *n* want of convenience; unfitness; that which incommodes; disadvantage. • *vt* to put to inconvenience; to annoy.—**inconvenient** *adj*.

**incorrect** *adj* faulty; inaccurate; improper.—**incorrectly** *adv*.

**incorruptible** *adj* incapable of physical corruption, decay or dissolution; incapable of being bribed; not liable to moral perversion or contamination.—**incorruptibly** *adv*.

**increase** *vti* to make or become greater in size, quality, amount, etc. • *n* increasing or becoming increased; the result or amount by which something increases.—**increasingly** *adv*.

**incredible** *adj* unbelievable; (*inf*) wonderful.—**incredibly** *adv*.

**incredulous** *adj* not able or willing to accept as true; unbelieving.—**incredulity** *n*.—**incredulously** *adv*.

**increment** *n* (the amount of) an increase; an addition.—**incremental** *adj*.

**incriminate** *vt* to involve in or indicate as involved in a crime or fault.—**incrimination** *n*.—**incriminatory** *adj*.

**incubator** *n* an apparatus in which eggs are hatched by artificial heat; an apparatus for nurturing premature babies until they can survive unaided.

**incur** *vt* (*pt* **incurred**) to bring upon oneself (something undesirable).

**incurable** *adj* incapable of being cured; beyond the power of skill or medicine; lacking remedy; incorrigible. • *n* a person diseased beyond cure.—**incurably** *adv*.

**incursion** *n* an invasion or raid into another's territory, etc.

**indebted** *adj* in debt; owing gratitude.—**indebtedness** *n*.

**indecent** *adj* offending against accepted standards of decent behaviour.—**indecency** *n*.—**indecently** *adv*.

**indecision** *n* not able to make a decision; hesitation.

**indecisive** *adj* inconclusive; irresolute.—**indecisively** *adv*.—**indecisiveness** *n*.

**indeed** *adv* truly, certainly. • *interj* expressing irony, surprise, disbelief, etc.

**indefinable** *adj* that cannot be defined.—**indefinably** *adv*.

**indefinite** *adj* not certain, undecided; imprecise, vague; having no fixed limits.—**indefinitely** *adv*.—**indefiniteness** *n*.

**indelible** *adj* not able to be removed or erased; (*pen, ink, etc*) making an indelible mark.—**indelibly** *adv*.

**indemnify** *vt* to insure against loss, damage, etc; to repay (for damage, loss, etc).—**indemnification** *n*.

**indentation** *n* a being indented; a notch, cut, inlet, etc; a dent; a spacing in from the margin (—*also* **indention, indent**).

**independence** *n* the state of being independent.

**independent** *adj* freedom from the influence or control of others; self-governing; self-determined; not adhering to any political party; not connected with others; not depending on another for financial support. • *n* a person who is independent in thinking, action etc.—**independently** *adv*.

**indescribable** *adj* unable to be described; too beautiful, horrible, intense, etc for words.

**index** *n* (*pl* **indexes, indices**) an alphabetical list of names, subjects, items, etc mentioned in a printed book, usu listed alphabetically at the end of the text; a figure showing ratio or relative change, as of prices or wages; any indication or sign; a pointer or dial on an instrument; the exponent of a number. • *vt* to make an index of or for.—**indexer** *n*.

**index finger** *n* the forefinger.

**index-linked** *adj* (*salary, pension, etc*) linked directly to changes in the cost-of-living index.

**Indian** *n* a native of India; an American Indian, the original inhabitants of the continent of America.

**indicate** *vt* to point out; to show or demonstrate; to be a sign or symptom of; to state briefly, suggest.—**indication** *n*.

**indicative** *adj* serving as a sign (of); (*gram*) denoting the mood of the verb that affirms or denies.

**indicator** *n* a thing that indicates or points; a measuring device with a pointer, etc; an instrument showing the operating condition of a piece of machinery, etc; a device giving updated information, such as a departure board in a railway station or airport; a flashing light used to warn of a change in direction of a vehicle.

**indict** *vt* to charge with a crime; to accuse.

**indictable** *adj* subject to being indicted; making one liable to indictment.

**indictment** *n* a formal written statement framed by a prosecuting authority charging a person of a crime.

**indifferent** *adj* showing no concern, uninterested; unimportant; impartial; average; mediocre.—**indifference** *n*.—**indifferently** *adv*.

**indigenous** *adj* existing naturally in a particular country, region, or environment; native.

**indigestible** *adj* difficult or impossible to digest.—**indigestibility** *n*.

**indigestion** *n* a pain caused by difficulty in digesting food.

**indignant** *adj* expressing anger, esp at mean or unjust action.—**indignantly** *adv*.

**indignation** *n* anger at something regarded as unfair, wicked, etc.

**indignity** *n* humiliation; treatment making one feel degraded, undignified.

**indirect** *adj* not straight; roundabout; secondary; dishonest.—**indirectly** *adv*.

**indiscreet** *adj* not discreet; tactless.—**indiscreetly** *adv*.

**indiscretion** *n* an indiscreet act; rashness.

**indiscriminate** *adj* not making a careful choice; confused; random; making no distinctions.—**indiscriminately** *adv*.—**indiscrimination** *n*.

**indispensable** *adj* absolutely essential.—**indispensability** *n*.—**indispensably** *adv*.

**indisposed** *adj* ill or sick; reluctant; disinclined.

**indisputable** *adj* unquestionable; certain.—**indisputability** *n*.—**indisputably** *adv*.

**indistinct** *adj* not clearly marked; dim; not distinct.—**indistinctly** *adv*.—**indistinctness** *n*.

**individual** *adj* existing as a separate thing or being; of, by, for, or relating to a single person or thing. • *n* a single thing or being; a person.

**individualist** *n* a person who thinks or behaves with marked independence.—**individualism** *n*.—**individualistic** *adj*.

**individuality** *n* the condition of being individual; separate or distinct existence; distinctive character.

**indoctrinate** *vt* to systematically instruct in doctrines, ideas, beliefs, etc.—**indoctrination** *n*.

**indolent** *adj* idle; lazy.—**indolently** *adv*.—**indolence** *n*.

**indoor** *adj* done, used, or situated within a building.

**indoors** *adv* in or into a building.

**indubitable** *adj* not capable of being doubted.—**indubitably** *adv*.

**induce** *vt* to persuade; to bring on; to draw (a conclusion) from particular facts; to bring about (an electric or magnetic effect) in a body by placing it within a field of force.

**inducement** *n* something that induces; a stimulus; a motive.

**induction** *n* the act or an instance of inducting, eg into office; reasoning from particular premises to general conclusions; the inducing of an electric or magnetic effect by a field of force.—**inductive** *adj*.

**indulge** *vt* to satisfy (a desire); to gratify the wishes of; to humour. • *vi* to give way to one's desire.

**indulgence** *n* indulging or being indulged; a thing indulged in; a favour or privilege; (*RC Church*) a remission of punishment still due for a sin after the guilt has been forgiven.

**indulgent** *adj* indulging or characterized by indulgence; lenient.—**indulgently** *adv*.

**industrial** *adj* relating to or engaged in industry; used in industry; having many highly developed industries.—**industrially** *adv*.

**industrialist** *n* a person who owns or manages an industrial enterprise.

**industrialize** *vti* to make or become industrial.—**industrialization** *n*.

**industrious** *adj* hard-working.—**industriously** *adv*.—**industriousness** *n*.

**industry** *n* organized production or manufacture of goods; manufacturing enterprises collectively; a branch of commercial enterprise producing a particular product; any large-scale business activity; the owners and managers of industry; diligence.

**inebriated** *adj* drunken.—**inebriation** *n*.

**inedible** *adj* not fit to be eaten.

**ineffective** *adj* not effective.—**ineffectively** *adv*.

**ineffectual** *adj* not effectual; futile. —**ineffectually** *adv*.

**inefficiency** *n* the quality or condition of being inefficient; an instance of inefficiency or incompetence.

**inefficient** *adj* not efficient.—**inefficiently** *adv*.

**ineligible** *adj* not eligible.—**ineligibility** *n*.

**inept** *adj* unsuitable; unfit; foolish; awkward; clumsy.—**ineptitude** *n*.—**ineptly** *adv*.

**inequality** *n* lack of equality in size, status, etc; unevenness.

**inert** *adj* without power to move or to resist; inactive; dull; slow; with few or no active properties.—**inertly** *adv*.—**inertness** *n*.

**inertia** *n* (*physics*) the tendency of matter to remain at rest (or continue in a fixed direction) unless acted on by an outside force; disinclination to act.

**inestimable** *adj* not to be estimated; beyond measure or price; incalculable; invaluable.—**inestimably** *adv*.

**inevitable** *adj* sure to happen; unavoidable. • something that is inevitable.—**inevitability** *n*.—**inevitably** *adv*.

**inexact** *adj* not strictly true or correct.—**inexactitude** *n*.—**inexactly** *adv*.

**inexhaustible** *adj* not to be exhausted or spent; unfailing; unwearied.—**inexhaustibly** *adv*.

**inexorable** *adj* unable to be persuaded by persuasion or entreaty, relentless.—**inexorably** *adv*.

**inexpensive** *adj* cheap.—**inexpensively** *adv*.

**inexperience** *n* want of experience or of the knowledge that comes by experience.

**inexperienced** *adj* lacking experience; unpractised; unskilled; unversed.

**inexplicable** *adj* not to be explained, made plain, or intelligible; not to be interpreted or accounted for.—**inexplicably** *adv*.

**inextricable** *adj* that cannot be disentangled, solved, or escaped from.—**inextricably** *adv*.

**infallible** *adj* incapable of being wrong; dependable; reliable.—**infallibility** *n*.—**infallibly** *adv*.

**infamous** *adj* having a bad reputation; notorious; causing a bad reputation; scandalous.

**infamy** *n* ill fame; public disgrace; ignominy.

**infancy** *n* early childhood; the beginning or early existence of anything.

**infant** *n* a very young child; a baby.

**infantile** *adj* of infants; like an infant, babyish.

**infantry** *n* soldiers trained to fight on foot.

**infatuate** *vt* to inspire with intense, foolish, or short-lived passion.—**infatuated** *adj*.—**infatuation** *n*.

**infect** *vt* to contaminate with disease-causing microorganisms; to taint; to affect, esp so as to harm.—**infective** *adj*.

**infection** *n* an infecting or being infected; an infectious disease; a diseased condition.

**infectious** *adj* (*disease*) able to be transmitted; a disease caused by the spread of bacteria in the body, etc;

causing or transmitted by infection; tending to spread to others.

**infer** *vt* (*pt* **inferred**) to conclude by reasoning from facts or premises, to deduce; to accept as a fact or consequence.—**inferable, inferible** *adj*.

**inference** *n* an inferring; something inferred or deduced; a reasoning from premises to a conclusion.—**inferential** *adj*.

**inferior** *adj* lower in position, rank, degree, or quality. • *n* an inferior person.—**inferiority** *n*.

**inferiority complex** *n* (*psychol*) an acute sense of inferiority expressed by a lack of confidence or in exaggerated aggression.

**infernal** *adj* of hell; hellish; fiendish; (*inf*) irritating, detestable.—**infernally** *adv*.

**inferno** *n* (*pl* **infernos**) hell; intense heat; a devastating fire.

**infertile** *adj* not fertile.—**infertility** *n*.

**infest** *vt* to overrun in large numbers, usu so as to be harmful; to be parasitic in or on.—**infestation** *n*.

**infidelity** *n* unfaithfulness, esp in marriage.

**infighting** *n* (*boxing*) exchanging punches at close quarters; intense competition within an organization.—**infighter** *n*.

**infiltrate** *vti* to filter or pass gradually through or into; to permeate; to penetrate (enemy lines, etc) gradually or stealthily, eg as spies.—**infiltration** *n*.—**infiltrator** *n*.

**infinite** *adj* endless, limitless; very great; vast.—**infinitely** *adv*.

**infinitive** *n* (*gram*) the form of a verb without reference to person, number or tense.

**infinity** *n* the condition or quality of being infinite; an unlimited number, quantity, or time period.

**infirmary** *n* a hospital or place for the treatment of the sick.

**infirmity** *n* being infirm; a physical weakness.

**inflame** *vti* to arouse, excite, etc or to become aroused, excited, etc; to undergo or cause to undergo inflammation.

**inflammable** *adj* able to catch fire, flammable; easily excited.

**inflammation** *n* an inflaming or being inflamed; redness, pain, heat, and swelling in the body, due to injury or disease.

**inflate** *vti* to fill or become filled with air or gas; to puff up with pride; to increase beyond what is normal, esp the supply of money or credit.—**inflatable** *adj*.

**inflation** *n* an inflating or being inflated; an increase in the currency in circulation or a marked expansion of credit, resulting in a fall in currency value and a sharp rise in prices.

**inflexible** *adj* not flexible; stiff, rigid; fixed; unyielding.—**inflexibility** *n*.—**inflexibly** *adv*.

**inflict** *vt* to impose (pain, a penalty, etc) on a person or thing.—**infliction** *n*.

**influence** *n* the power to affect others; the power to produce effects by having wealth, position, ability, etc; a person with influence. • *vt* to have influence on.

**influential** *adj* having or exerting great influence.—**influentially** *adv*.

**influenza** *n* a contagious feverish virus disease marked by muscular pain and inflammation of the respiratory system.

**influx** *n* a sudden inflow of people or things to a place.

**inform** *vt* to provide knowledge of something to. • *vi* to give information to the police, etc, esp in accusing another.

**informal** *adj* not formal; not according to fixed rules or ceremony, etc; casual.—**informally** *adv*.

**informality** *n* the lack of regular, customary, or legal form; an informal act.

**information** *n* something told or facts learned; news; knowledge; data stored in or retrieved from a computer.

**informative** *adj* conveying information, instructive.

**informer** *n* a person who informs on another, esp to the police for a reward.

**infrared** *n* (*radiation*) having a wavelength longer than light but shorter than radio waves; of, pertaining to, or using such radiation.

**infrequent** *adj* seldom occurring; rare.—**infrequence, infrequency** *n*.

**infringe** *vt* to break or violate, esp an agreement or a law.—**infringement** *n*.

**infuriate** *vt* to enrage; to make furious.—**infuriating** *adj*.

**ingenious** *adj* clever, resourceful, etc; made or done in an original or clever way.—**ingeniously** *adv*.—**ingenuity** *n*.

**ingot** *n* a brick-shaped mass of cast metal, esp gold or silver.

**ingrained** *adj* (*habits, feelings, etc*) firmly established; (*dirt*) deeply embedded.—*also* **engrained**.

**ingratiate** *vt* to bring oneself into another's favour.

**ingratitude** *n* absence of gratitude; insensibility to kindness.

**ingredient** *n* something included in a mixture; a component.

**inhabit** *vt* to live in; to occupy; to reside.

**inhabitant** *n* a person or animal inhabiting a specified place.

**inhale** *vti* to breathe in.—**inhalation** *n*.

**inherit** *vt* to receive (property, a title, etc) under a will or by right of legal succession; to possess by genetic transmission. • *vi* to receive by inheritance; to succeed as heir.—**inheritor** *n*.

**inheritance** *n* the action of inheriting; something inherited.

**inhibit** *vt* to restrain; to prohibit.—**inhibiter** *n*.

**inhibition** *n* an inhibiting or being inhibited; a mental process that restrains or represses an action, emotion, or thought.

**inhospitable** *adj* not hospitable; affording no shelter; barren; cheerless.—**inhospitably** *adv*.—**inhospitality** *n*.

**inhuman** *adj* lacking in the human qualities of kindness, pity, etc; cruel, brutal, unfeeling; not human.

**inimitable** *adj* impossible to imitate; matchless.—**inimitably** *adv*.

**iniquity** *n* wickedness; great injustice.

**initial** *adj* of or at the beginning. • *n* the first letter of each word in a name; a large letter at the beginning of a chapter, etc. • *vt* (*pt* **initialled**) to sign with initials.—**initially** *adv*.

**initiate** *vt* to bring (something) into practice or use; to teach the fundamentals of a subject to; to admit as a member into a club, etc, esp with a secret ceremony. • *n* an initiated person.—**initiation** *n*.—**initiator** *n*.—**initiatory** *adj*.

**initiative** *n* the action of taking the first step; ability to originate new ideas or methods.

**inject** *vt* to force (a fluid) into a vein, tissue, etc, esp with a syringe; to introduce (a remark, quality, etc), to interject.

**injection** *n* an injecting; a substance that is injected.

**injure** *vt* to harm physically or mentally; to hurt, do wrong to.

**injury** *n* physical damage; harm.

**injustice** *n* the state or practice of being unfair; an unjust act.

**ink** *n* a coloured liquid used for writing, printing, etc; the dark protective secretion of an octopus, etc. • *vt* to cover, mark, or colour with ink.

**inkling** *n* a hint; a vague notion.

**inlaid** *see* **inlay.**

**inland** *adj* of or in the interior of a country. • *n* an inland region. • *adv* into or toward this region.

**in-law** *n* a relative by marriage.

**inlay** *vt* (*pt* **inlaid**) to decorate a surface by inserting pieces of metal, wood, etc. • *n* inlaid work; material inlaid.

**inlet** *n* a narrow strip of water extending into a body of land; an opening; a passage, pipe, etc for liquid to enter a machine, etc.

**inmate** *n* a person confined with others in a prison or institution.

**inn** *n* a small hotel; a restaurant or public house, esp in the countryside.

**innate** *adj* existing from birth; inherent; instinctive.—**innately** *adv.*

**inner** *adj* further within; inside, internal; private, exclusive. • *n* (*archery*) the innermost ring on a target.

**innocent** *adj* not guilty of a particular crime; free from sin; blameless; harmless; inoffensive; simple, credulous, naive. • *n* an innocent person, as a child.—**innocence** *n.*—**innocently** *adv.*

**innocuous** *adj* harmless.—**innocuously** *adv.*—**innocuousness** *n.*

**innovate** *vi* to introduce new methods, ideas, etc; to make changes.—**innovation** *n.*—**innovative, innovatory** *adv.*

**innuendo** *n* (*pl* **innuendoes, innuendos**) a hint or sly remark, usu derogatory; an insinuation.

**inoculate** *vt* to inject a serum or a vaccine into, esp in order to create immunity; to protect as if by inoculation.—**inoculation** *n.*

**inopportune** *adj* unseasonable; untimely.

**inordinate** *adj* excessive.— **inordinately** *adv.*

**inorganic** *adj* not having the structure or characteristics of living organisms; denoting a chemical compound not containing carbon.—**inorganically** *adv.*

**inpatient** *n* a patient being treated while remaining in hospital.

**input** *n* what is put in, as power into a machine, data into a computer, etc. • *vt* (*pt* **input** *or* **inputted**) to put in; to enter (data) into a computer.

**inquest** *n* a judicial inquiry held by a coroner, esp into a case of violent or unexplained death; (*inf*) any detailed inquiry or investigation.

**inquire** *vi* to request information about; (*usu with* **into**) to investigate. • *vt* to ask about.—*also* **enquire.**—**inquirer, enquirer** *n.*

**inquiry** *n* the act of inquiring; a search by questioning; an investigation; a question; research.—*also* **enquiry.**

**inquisitive** *adj* eager for knowledge; unnecessarily curious; prying.—**inquisitively** *adv.*—**inquisitiveness** *n.*

**inroad** *n* a raid into enemy territory; an encroachment or advance.

**insane** *adj* not sane, mentally ill; of or for insane people; very foolish.—**insanely** *adv.*

**insanitary** *adj* unclean, likely to cause infection or ill-health.

**insanity** *n* derangement of the mind or intellect; lunacy; madness.

**insatiable** *adj* not easily satisfied; greedy.—**insatiability** *n.*—**insatiably** *adv.*

**inscribe** *vt* to mark or engrave (words, etc) on (a surface); to add (a person's name) to a list; to dedicate (a book) to someone; to autograph; to fix in the mind.

**inscription** *n* an inscribing; words, etc, inscribed on a tomb, coin, etc.

**inscrutable** *adj* hard to understand, incomprehensible; enigmatic.—**inscrutability** *n.*—**inscrutably** *adv.*

**insect** *n* any of a class of small

arthropods with three pairs of legs, a head, thorax, and abdomen and two or four wings.

**insecticide** *n* a substance for killing insects.

**insecure** *adj* not safe; feeling anxiety; not dependable.—**insecurely** *adv*.

**insecurity** *n* the condition of being insecure; lack of confidence or sureness; instability; something insecure.

**insensible** *adj* unconscious; unaware; indifferent; imperceptible.—**insensibility** *n*.—**insensibly** *adv*.

**inseparable** *adj* not able to be separated; closely attached, as romantically.

**insert** *vt* to put or fit (something) into something else. • *n* something inserted.—**insertion** *n*.

**inshore** *adj, adv* near or towards the shore.

**inside** *n* the inner side, surface, or part; (*pl*: *inf*) the internal organs, stomach, bowels. • *adj* internal; known only to insiders; secret. • *adv* on or in the inside; within; indoors; (*sl*) in prison. • *prep* in or within.

**inside out** *adj* reversed; with the inner surface facing the outside.

**insider** *n* a person within a place or group; a person with access to confidential information.

**insidious** *adj* marked by slyness or treachery; more dangerous than seems evident.—**insidiously** *adv*.—**insidiousness** *n*.

**insight** *n* the ability to see and understand clearly the inner nature of things, esp by intuition; an instance of such understanding.—**insightful** *adj*.

**insignificant** *adj* having little or no importance; trivial; worthless; small, inadequate.—**insignificance** *n*.—**insignificantly** *adv*.

**insincere** *adj* not sincere; hypocritical.—**insincerely** *adv*.—**insincerity** *n*.

**insinuate** *vt* to introduce or work in slowly, indirectly, etc; to hint.—**insinuation** *n*.

**insipid** *adj* lacking any distinctive flavour; uninteresting, dull.—**insipidity** *n*.—**insipidly** *adv*.—**insipidness** *n*.

**insist** *vi* (*often with* **on** *or* **upon**) to take and maintain a stand. • *vt* to demand strongly; to declare firmly.

**insistent** *adj* insisting or demanding.—**insistence** *n*.—**insistently** *adv*.

**insolent** *adj* disrespectful; impudent, arrogant; rude.—**insolence** *n*.—**insolently** *adv*.

**insoluble** *adj* incapable of being dissolved; impossible to solve or explain.—**insolubility** *n*.—**insolubly** *adv*.

**insolvent** *adj* unable to pay one's debts; bankrupt.—**insolvency** *n*.

**insomnia** *n* abnormal inability to sleep.

**inspect** *vt* to look at carefully; to examine or review officially.—**inspection** *n*.

**inspector** *n* an official who inspects in order to ensure compliance with regulations, etc; a police officer ranking below a superintendent.—**inspectorate** *n*.

**inspiration** *n* an inspiring; any stimulus to creative thought; an inspired idea, action, etc.—**inspirational** *adj*.

**inspire** *vt* to stimulate, as to some creative effort; to motivate by divine influence; to arouse (a thought or feeling) in (someone); to cause.—**inspiring** *adj*.

**install, instal** *vt* (*pt* **installed**) to formally place in an office, rank, etc; to establish in a place; to settle in a position or state.—**installer** *n*.

**installation** *n* the act of installing or being installed; machinery, equipment, etc that has been installed.

**instalment, installment** (*US*) *n* a sum of money to be paid at regular specified times; any of several parts, as of a magazine story or television serial.

**instance** n an example; a step in proceeding; an occasion. • vt to give as an example.

**instant** adj immediate; (food) concentrated or precooked for quick preparation. • n a moment; a particular moment.

**instantly** adv immediately.

**instead** adv in place of the one mentioned.

**instep** n the upper part of the arch of the foot, between the ankle and the toes.

**instigate** vt to urge on, goad; to initiate.—**instigation** n.—**instigator** n.

**instil, instill** (US) vt (pt **instilled**) to put (an idea, etc) in or into (the mind) gradually.—**instillation** n.—**instilment, instillment** n.

**instinct** n the inborn tendency to behave in a way characteristic of a species; a natural or acquired tendency; a knack.

**instinctive, instinctual** adj of, relating to, or prompted by instinct.—**instinctively, instinctually** adv.

**institute** vt to organize, establish; to start, initiate. • n an organization for the promotion of science, art, etc; a school, college, or department of a university specializing in some field.

**institution** n an established law, custom, etc; an organization having a social, educational, or religious purpose; the building housing it; (inf) a long-established person or thing.

**instruct** vt to provide with information; to teach; to give instructions to; to authorize.—**instructor** n.—**instructress** nf.

**instruction** n an order, direction; the act or process of teaching or training; knowledge imparted; (comput) a command in a program to perform a particular operation; (pl) orders, directions; detailed guidance.—**instructional** adj.

**instructive** adj issuing or containing instructions; giving information, educational.—**instructively** adv.

**instrument** n a thing by means of which something is done; a tool or implement; any of various devices for indicating, measuring, controlling, etc; any of various devices producing musical sound; a formal document. • vt to orchestrate.

**instrumental** adj serving as a means of doing something; helpful; of, performed on, or written for a musical instrument or instruments.

**instrumentalist** n a person who plays a musical instrument.

**insubordinate** adj not submitting to authority; rebellious.—**insubordination** n.

**insufferable** adj intolerable; unbearable.—**insufferably** adv.

**insufficient** adj not sufficient.—**insufficiency** n.—**insufficiently** adv.

**insular** adj of or like an island or islanders; narrow-minded; illiberal.—**insularity** n.

**insulate** vt to set apart; to isolate; to cover with a nonconducting material in order to prevent the escape of electricity, heat, sound, etc.—**insulation** n.—**insulator** n.

**insulin** n a hormone that controls absorption of sugar by the body, secreted by islets of tissue in the pancreas.

**insult** vt to treat with indignity or contempt; to offend. • n an insulting remark or act.

**insuperable** adj unable to be overcome.—**insuperability** n.—**insuperably** adv.

**insurance** n insuring or being insured; a contract purchased to guarantee compensation for a specified loss by fire, death, etc; the amount for which something is insured; the business of insuring against loss.

**insure** *vt* to take out or issue insurance on; to ensure. • *vi* to contract to give or take insurance.—**insurer** *n*.

**insurrection** *adj* a rising or revolt against established authority.—**insurrectionist** *n*.

**intact** *adj* unimpaired; whole.

**intake** *n* the place in a pipe, etc where a liquid or gas is taken in; a thing or quantity taken in, as students, etc; the process of taking in.

**intangible** *adj* that cannot be touched, incorporeal; representing value but without material being, as good will; indefinable. • *n* something that is intangible.—**intangibility** *n*.—**intangibly** *adv*.

**integral** *adj* necessary for completeness; whole or complete; made up of parts forming a whole. • *n* the result of a mathematical integration.—**integrally** *adv*.

**integrate** *vti* to make whole or become complete; to bring (parts) together into a whole; to remove barriers imposing segregation upon (racial groups); to abolish segregation; (*math*) to find the integral of.—**integration** *n*.

**integrity** *n* honesty, sincerity; completeness, wholeness; an unimpaired condition.

**intellect** *n* the ability to reason or understand; high intelligence; a very intelligent person.

**intellectual** *adj* of, involving, or appealing to the intellect; requiring intelligence. • *n* an intellectual person.

**intelligence** *n* the ability to learn or understand; the ability to cope with a new situation; news or information; those engaged in gathering secret, esp military, information.

**intelligent** *adj* having or showing intelligence; clever, wise, etc.—**intelligently** *adv*.

**intelligible** *adj* able to be understood;

clear.—**intelligibility** *n*.—**intelligibly** *adv*.

**intemperate** *adj* indulging excessively in alcoholic drink; unrestrained; (*climate*) extreme.—**intemperance** *n*.—**intemperately** *adv*.

**intend** *vt* to mean, to signify; to propose, have in mind as an aim or purpose.

**intense** *adj* very strong, concentrated; passionate, emotional.—**intensely** *adv*.

**intensify** *vti* to make or become more intense.—**intensification** *n*.

**intensity** *n* the state or quality of being intense; density, as of a negative plate; the force or energy of any physical agent.

**intensive** *adj* of or characterized by intensity; thorough; denoting careful attention given to patients right after surgery, etc.—**intensively** *adv*.

**intent** *adj* firmly directed; having one's attention or purpose firmly fixed. • *n* intention; something intended; purpose or meaning.—**intently** *adv*.—**intentness** *n*.

**intention** *n* a determination to act in a specified way; anything intended.

**intentional** *adj* done purposely.—**intentionally** *adv*.

**inter** *vt* (*pt* **interred**) to bury.

**interact** *vi* to act upon each other.—**interaction** *n*.

**intercede** *vi* to intervene on another's behalf; to mediate.

**intercept** *vt* to stop or catch in its course. • *n* a point of intersection of two geometric figures; interception by an interceptor.—**interception** *n*.

**interchange** *vt* to give and receive one thing for another; to exchange, to put (each of two things) in the place of the other; to alternate. • *n* an interchanging; a junction on a motorway designed to prevent traffic intersecting.

**interchangeable** *adj* able to be interchanged.—**interchangeability** *n*.

**intercom** *n* (*inf*) a system of intercommunicating, as in an aircraft.

**interconnect** *vti* to connect by reciprocal links.—**interconnection** *n*.

**intercourse** *n* a connection by dealings or communication between individuals or groups; sexual intercourse, copulation.

**interest** *n* a feeling of curiosity about something; the power of causing this feeling; a share in, or a right to, something; anything in which one has a share; benefit; money paid for the use of money; the rate of such payment. • *vt* to excite the attention of; to cause to have a share in; to concern oneself with.

**interested** *adj* having or expressing an interest; affected by personal interest, not impartial.

**interesting** *n* engaging the attention.

**interfere** *vi* to clash; to come between; to intervene; to meddle; to obstruct.

**interference** *n* an interfering; (*radio, TV*) the interruption of reception by atmospherics or by unwanted signals.

**interim** *n* an intervening period of time. • *adj* provisional, temporary. • *adv* meanwhile.

**interior** *adj* situated within; inner; inland; private. • *n* the interior part, as of a room, country, etc.

**interjection** *n* an interjecting; an interruption; an exclamation.

**interlock** *vti* to lock or become locked together; to join with one another.

**interloper** *n* a person who meddles; an intruder.

**interlude** *n* anything that fills time between two events, as music between acts of a play.

**intermarry** *vi* (*different races, religions, etc*) to become connected by marriage; to marry within one's close family.—**intermarriage** *n*.

**intermediary** *n* a mediator. • *adj* acting as a mediator; intermediate.

**intermediate** *adj* in the middle; in between.

**intermission** *n* an interval of time between parts of a performance.

**intermittent** *adj* stopping and starting again at intervals; periodic.—**intermittently** *adv*.

**intern** *vt* to detain and confine within an area, esp during wartime.—**internment** *n*.

**internal** *adj* of or on the inside; of or inside the body; intrinsic; domestic.—**internally** *adv*.

**international** *adj* between or among nations; concerned with the relations between nations; for the use of all nations; of or for people in various nations. • *n* a sporting competition between teams from different countries; a member of an international team of players.—**internationally** *adv*.

**interplay** *n* the action of two things on each other, interaction.

**interpret** *vt* to explain; to translate; to construe; to give one's own conception of, as in a play or musical composition. • *vi* to translate between speakers of different languages.—**interpretation** *n*.

**interpreter** *n* a person who translates orally for persons speaking in different languages; (*comput*) a program that translates an instruction into machine code.

**interrogate** *vti* to question, esp formally.—**interrogation** *n*.—**interrogator** *n*.

**interrogative** *adj* asking a question. • *n* a word used in asking a question.—**interrogatively** *adv*.

**interrogatory** *adj* questioning.

**interrupt** *vt* to break into (a discussion, etc) or break in upon (a speaker, worker, etc); to make a break in the continuity of. • *vi* to interrupt an action, talk, etc.—**interrupter** *n*.—**interruption** *n*.

**intersect** *vti* to cut or divide by passing through or crossing; (*lines, roads, etc*) to meet and cross.

**intersection** *n* an intersecting; the place where two lines, roads, etc meet or cross.

**intersperse** *vt* to scatter or insert among other things; to diversify with other things scattered here and there.

**intertwine** *vti* to twine or twist closely together.

**interval** *n* a space between things; the time between events; (*mus*) the difference of pitch between two notes.

**intervene** *vi* to occur or come between; to occur between two events, etc; to come in to modify, settle, or hinder some action, etc.—**intervention** *n*.

**interview** *n* a meeting in which a person is asked about his or her views, etc, as by a newspaper or television reporter; a published account of this; a formal meeting at which a candidate for a job is questioned and assessed by a prospective employer. • *vt* to have an interview with.—**interviewer** *n*.

**intestate** *adj* having made no will. • *n* a person who dies intestate.—**intestacy** *n*.

**intestine** *n* the lower part of the alimentary canal between the stomach and the anus.—**intestinal** *adj*.

**intimacy** *n* close or confidential friendship; familiarity; sexual relations.

**intimate** *adj* most private or personal; very close or familiar, esp sexually; deep and thorough. • *n* an intimate friend. • *vt* to indicate; to make known; to hint or imply.—**intimately** *adv*.

**intimation** *n* the act of intimating; a notice, announcement.

**intimidate** *vt* to frighten; to discourage, silence, etc esp by threats.—**intimidation** *n*.

**into** *prep* to the interior or inner parts of; to the middle; to a particular condition; (*inf*) deeply interested or involved in.

**intolerable** *adj* unbearable.—**intolerably** *adv*.

**intolerance** *n* lack of toleration of the opinions or practices of others; inability to bear or endure.—**intolerant** *adj*.

**intonation** *n* intoning; variations in pitch of the speaking voice; an accent.

**intoxicate** *vt* to make drunken; to elate; to poison.

**intoxication** *n* drunkenness; great excitement; poisoning.

**intractable** *adj* unmanageable, uncontrollable; (*problem, illness, etc*) difficult to solve, alleviate, or cure.—**intractability** *n*.—**intractably** *adv*.

**intransigent** *adj* unwilling to compromise, irreconcilable.—**intransigence** *n*.

**intransitive** *adj* (*gram*) denoting a verb that does not take a direct object.—**intransitively** *adv*.

**intravenous** *adj* into a vein.—**intravenously** *adv*.

**intrepid** *adj* bold; fearless; brave.—**intrepidity** *n*.—**intrepidly** *adv*.

**intricate** *adj* difficult to understand; complex, complicated; involved, detailed.—**intricacy** *n*.—**intricately** *adv*.

**intrigue** *n* a secret or underhand plotting; a secret or underhanded plot or scheme; a secret love affair. • *vi* to carry on an intrigue. • *vt* to excite the interest or curiosity of.

**intrinsic** *adj* belonging to the real nature of a person or thing; inherent.—**intrinsically** *adv*.

**introduce** *vt* to make (a person) acquainted by name (with other persons); to bring into use or establish; to present (a bill, etc) for consideration or approval (by parliament, etc); to present a radio or television programme; to bring into or insert.

**introduction** *n* an introducing or being introduced; the presentation of one person to another; preliminary text in a book; a preliminary passage in a musical composition.

**introductory** *adj* serving as an introduction; preliminary.

**introspection** *n* examination of one's own mind and feelings, etc.—**introspective** *adj*.

**introvert** *n* a person who is more interested in his or her own thoughts, feelings, etc than in external objects or events. • *adj* characterized by introversion (—*also* **introverted**).—**introversion** *n*.

**intrude** *vti* to force (oneself) upon others unasked.—**intruder** *n*.

**intrusion** *n* the act or an instance of intruding; the forcible entry of molten rock into and between existing rocks.—**intrusively** *adv*.

**intuition** *n* a perceiving of the truth of something immediately without reasoning or analysis; a hunch, an insight.—**intuitively** *adv*.

**inundate** *vt* to cover as with a flood; to deluge.—**inundation** *n*.

**invade** *vt* to enter (a country) with hostile intentions; to encroach upon; to penetrate; to crowd into as if invading.—**invader** *n*.

**invalid**[1] *adj* not valid.

**invalid**[2] *n* a person who is ill or disabled. • *vt* to cause to become an invalid; to disable; to cause to retire from the armed forces because of ill-health or injury.

**invalidate** *vt* to render not valid; to deprive of legal force.—**invalidation** *n*.

**invaluable** *adj* too valuable to be measured in money.—**invaluably** *adv*.

**invariable** *adj* never changing; constant.—**invariably** *adv*.

**invasion** *n* the act of invading with military forces; an encroachment, intrusion.

**invective** *n* the use of violent or abusive language or writing.

**invent** *vt* to think up; to think out or produce (a new device, process, etc); to originate; to fabricate (a lie, etc).—**inventor** *n*.

**invention** *n* something invented; inventiveness.

**inventive** *adj* pertaining to invention; skilled in inventing.—**inventiveness** *n*.

**inventory** *n* an itemized list of goods, property, etc, as of a business; the store of such goods for such a listing; a list of the property of an individual or an estate. • *vt* to make an inventory of; to enter in an inventory.

**inverse** *adj* reversed in order or position; opposite, contrary. • *n* an inverse state or thing.—**inversely** *adv*.

**invert** *vt* to turn upside down or inside out; to reverse in order, position or relationship.

**invertebrate** *adj* without a backbone. • *n* an animal without a backbone.

**invest** *vt* to commit (money) to property, stocks and shares, etc for profit; to devote effort, time, etc on a particular activity; to install in office with ceremony; to furnish with power, authority, etc. • *vi* to invest money.

**investigate** *vti* to search (into); to inquire, examine.—**investigator** *n*.

**investigation** *n* the act of investigating; an inquiry; a search to uncover facts, etc.

**investiture** *n* the act or right of giving legal possession; the ceremony of investing a person with an office, robes, title, etc.

**investment** *n* the act of investing money productively; the amount invested; an activity in which time, effort or money has been invested.

**investor** *n* a person who invests money.

**inveterate** *adj* firmly established, ingrained; habitual.—**inveteracy** *n*.—**inveterately** *adv*.

**invidious** *adj* tending to provoke ill-will, resentment or envy; (*decisions, etc*) unfairly discriminating.—**invidiously** *adv*.—**invidiousness** *n*.

**invigorate** *vt* to fill with vigour and energy; to refresh.—**invigorating** *adj*.

**invincible** *adj* unconquerable.—**invincibility** *n*.—**invincibly** *adv*.

**inviolate** *adj* not violated; unbroken, unharmed.

**invisible** *adj* unable to be seen; hidden.—**invisibility** *n*.—**invisibly** *adv*.

**invitation** *n* a message used in inviting.

**invite** *vt* to ask to come somewhere or do something; to ask for; to give occasion for; to tempt; to entice. • *n* (*inf*) an invitation.

**inviting** *adj* attractive, enticing.—**invitingly** *adv*.

**invoice** *n* a list of goods dispatched, usu with particulars of their price and quantity. • *vt* to submit an invoice for or to.

**invoke** *vt* to call on (God, etc) for help, blessing, etc; to resort to (a law, etc) as pertinent; to implore.

**involuntary** *adj* not done by choice; not consciously controlled.—**involuntarily** *adv*.—**involuntariness** *n*.

**involve** *vt* to affect or include; to require; to occupy, to make busy; to complicate; to implicate.—**involvement** *n*.

**invulnerable** *adj* not capable of being wounded or hurt in any way.—**invulnerability** *n*.

**inward** *adj* situated within or directed to the inside; relating to or in the mind or spirit. • *adv* inwards.

**inwardly** *adv* within; in the mind or spirit; towards the inside or centre.

**inwards** *adv* towards the inside or interior; in the mind or spirit.

**iodine** *n* a nonmetallic element, found in seawater and seaweed, whose compounds are used in medicine and photography.

**iota** *n* the ninth letter of the Greek alphabet; a very small quantity; a jot.

**IOU** *n* a written note promising to pay a sum of money to the holder.

**IQ** *abbr* = Intelligence Quotient.

**irascible** *adj* easily angered; hot-tempered.—**irascibility** *n*.—**irascibly** *adv*.

**irate** *adj* enraged, furious.—**irately** *adv*.

**iris** *n* (*pl* **irises, irides**) the round, pigmented membrane surrounding the pupil of the eye; (*pl* **irises**) a perennial herbaceous plant with sword-shaped leaves and brightly coloured flowers.

**Irish** *adj* of Ireland or its people. • *n* the Celtic language of Ireland.

**irk** *vt* to annoy, irritate.

**irksome** *adj* tedious; tiresome.

**iron** *n* a metallic element, the most common of all metals; a tool, etc of this metal; a heavy implement with a heated flat underface for pressing cloth; (*pl*) shackles of iron; firm strength; power; any of certain golf clubs with angled metal heads. • *adj* of iron; like iron, strong and firm. • *vti* to press with a hot iron.

**ironic, ironical** *adj* of or using irony.—**ironically** *adv*.

**ironmonger** *n* a dealer in metal utensils, tools, etc; a hardware shop.—**ironmongery** *n*.

**ironworks** *n* a factory where iron is smelted, cast, or wrought.

**irony** *n* an expression in which the intended meaning of the words is the opposite of their usual sense; an event or result that is the opposite of what is expected.

**irrational** *adj* not rational, lacking the power of reason; senseless; unreasonable; absurd.—**irrationality** *n*.—**irrationally** *adv*.

**irreconcilable** *adj* not able to be brought into agreement; incompatible.—**irreconcilably** *adv*.

**irredeemable** *adj* not able to be redeemed.—**irredeemably** *adv*.

**irrefutable** *adj* unable to deny or disprove; indisputable.—**irrefutably** *adv*.

**irregular** *adj* not regular, straight or even; not conforming to the rules; imperfect; (*troops*) not part of the regular armed forces.—**irregularly** *adv*.

**irregularity** *n* departure from a rule, order or method; crookedness.

**irrelevant** *adj* not pertinent; not to the point.—**irrelevance** *n*.—**irrelevantly** *adv*.

**irreparable** *adj* that cannot be repaired, rectified or made good.—**irreparably** *adv*.

**irreplaceable** *adj* unable to be replaced.—**irreplaceability** *n*.

**irrepressible** *adj* unable to be controlled or restrained.—**irrepressibly** *adv*.

**irreproachable** *adj* blameless; faultless.—**irreproachably** *adv*.

**irresistible** *adj* not able to be resisted; overpowering; fascinating; very charming, alluring.—**irresistibly** *adv*.

**irresolute** *adj* lacking resolution, uncertain, hesitating.—**irresolutely** *adv*.—**irresoluteness** *n*.—**irresolution** *n*.

**irrespective** *adj* (*with* of) regardless.—**irrespectively** *adv*.

**irresponsible** *adj* not showing a proper sense of the consequences of one's actions; unable to bear responsibility.—**irresponsibility** *n*.—**irresponsibly** *adv*.

**irreverent** *adj* not reverent, disrespectful.—**irreverence** *n*.—**irreverently** *adv*.

**irrevocable** *adj* unable to be revoked, unalterable.

**irrigate** *vt* to supply (land) with water as by means of artificial ditches, pipes, etc; (*med*) to wash out (a cavity, wound, etc).—**irrigation** *n*.—**irrigator** *n*.

**irritable** *adj* easily annoyed, irritated, or provoked; (*med*) excessively sensitive to a stimulus.—**irritability** *n*.—**irritably** *adv*.

**irritate** *vt* to provoke to anger; to annoy; to make inflamed or sore.—**irritation** *n*.

**is** *see* be.

**Islam** *n* the Muslim religion, a monotheistic religion founded by Mohammed; the Muslim world.—**Islamic** *adj*.

**island** *n* a land mass smaller than a continent and surrounded by water; anything like this in position or isolation.

**islander** *n* a native or inhabitant of an island.

**isle** *n* an island, esp a small one.

**isn't** = is not.

**isolate** *vt* to set apart from others; to place alone; to quarantine a person or animal with a contagious disease; to separate a constituent substance from a compound.—**isolation** *n*.

**isotope** *n* any of two or more forms of an element having the same atomic number but different atomic weights.—**isotopic** *adj*.

**issue** *n* an outgoing; an outlet; a result; offspring; a point under dispute; a sending or giving out; all that is put forth at one time (an issue of bonds, a periodical, etc). • *vi* to go or flow out; to result (from) or end (in); to be published. • *vt* to let out; to discharge; to give or deal out, as supplies; to publish.

**isthmus** *n* (*pl* **isthmuses, isthmi**) a narrow strip of land having water at each side and connecting two larger bodies of land.

**it** *pron* the thing mentioned; the subject of an impersonal verb; a subject or object of indefinite sense in various constructions. • *n* the player, as in tag, who must catch another.

**Italian** *adj* of Italy or its people. • *n* a native of Italy; the Italian language.

**italic** *adj* denoting a type in which the letters slant upward to the right (*this is italic type*). • *n* (*usu pl*) italic type or handwriting.

**itch** *n* an irritating sensation on the surface of the skin causing a need to scratch; an insistent desire. • *vi* to have or feel an irritating sensation in the skin; to feel a restless desire.

**itchy** *adj* (**itchier, itchiest**) pertaining to or affected with an itch.—**itchiness** *n*.

**item** *n* an article; a unit; a separate thing; a bit of news or information; (*inf*) a couple having an affair.

**itemize** *vt* to specify the items of; to set down by items.—**itemization** *n*.

**itinerant** *adj* travelling from place to place. • *n* a traveller.

**itinerary** *n* a route; a record of a journey; a detailed plan of a journey.

**it'll** = it will, it shall.

**its** *poss pron* relating to or belonging to it.

**it's** = it is, it has.

**itself** *pron* the reflexive and emphatic form of **it**.

**ITV** *abbr* = Independent Television.

**ivory** *n* the hard, creamy-white substance forming the tusks of elephants, etc; any substance like ivory; creamy white. • *adj* of or like ivory; creamy white.

**ivy** *n* a climbing or creeping vine with a woody stem and evergreen leaves.

# J

**jab** *vti* (*pt* **jabbed**) to poke or thrust roughly; to punch with short, straight blows. • *n* a sudden thrust or stab; (*inf*) an injection with a hypodermic needle.

**jabber** *vti* to speak or say rapidly, incoherently, or foolishly. • *n* such talk.

**jack** *n* any of various mechanical or hydraulic devices used to lift something heavy; a playing card with a knave's picture on it, ranking below the queen; a small flag flown on a ship's bow as a signal or to show nationality; (*bowls*) a small white ball used as a target. • *vt* to raise by means of a jack.

**jacket** *n* a short coat; an outer covering, as the removable paper cover of a book.

**jackknife** *n* a pocket-knife; a dive in which the diver touches his feet with knees straight and then straightens out. • *vi* (*articulated lorry*) to lose control so that the trailer and cab swing against each other.

**jackpot** *n* the accumulated stakes in certain games, as poker.

**jade** *n* a hard, ornamental semiprecious stone; its light green colour.

**jaded** *adj* tired, exhausted; satiated.

**jagged** *adj* having sharp projecting points; notched or ragged.—**jaggedly** *adv*.

**jail** *n* a prison. • *vt* to send to or confine in prison.—*also* **gaol**.

**jailer** *n* a person in charge of prisoners in a jail.—*also* **gaoler**.

**jam**[1] *n* a preserve made from fruit boiled with sugar until thickened; (*inf*) something easy or desirable.

**jam**[2] *vb* (*pt* **jammed**) *vt* to press or

squeeze into a confined space; to crowd full with people or things; to cause (machinery) to become wedged and inoperable; to cause interference to a radio signal rendering it unintelligible. • *vi* to become stuck or blocked; (*sl*) to play in a jam session. • *n* a crowded mass or congestion in a confined space; a blockage caused by jamming; (*inf*) a difficult situation.

**jamb** *n* the straight vertical side post of a door, etc.

**jangle** *vi* to make a harsh or discordant sound, as bells. • *vt* to cause to jangle; to irritate.—*also n.*

**janitor** *n* a person who looks after a building, doing routine maintenance, etc.—**janitorial** *adj*.

**January** *n* the first month of the year, having 31 days.

**Japanese** *adj* of Japan, its people or language. • *n* the language of Japan.

**jar**¹ *vb* (*pt* **jarred**) *vi* to make a harsh, discordant noise; to have an irritating effect (on one); to vibrate from an impact; to clash. • *vt* to jolt. • *n* a grating sound; a vibration due to impact; a jolt.

**jar**² *n* a short cylindrical glass vessel with a wide mouth; (*inf*) a pint of beer.

**jargon** *n* the specialized or technical vocabulary of a science, profession, etc; obscure and usu pretentious language.

**jasmine** *n* any of a genus of climbing shrubs with fragrant white or yellow flowers.

**jaundice** *n* a condition characterized by yellowing of the skin, caused by excess of bile in the bloodstream; bitterness; resentment; prejudice.

**jaundiced** *adj* affected with jaundice; jealous, envious, disillusioned.

**jaunt** *n* a short journey, usu for pleasure. • *vi* to make such a journey.

**jaunty** *adj* (**jauntier, jauntiest**) sprightly or self-confident in manner.—**jauntily** *adv*.—**jauntiness** *n*.

**javelin** *n* a light spear, esp one thrown some distance in a contest.

**jaw** *n* one of the bones in which teeth are set; either of two movable parts that grasp or crush something, as in a vice; (*sl*) a friendly chat, gossip. • *vi* (*sl*) to talk boringly and at length.

**jaywalk** *vi* to walk across a street carelessly without obeying traffic rules or signals.—**jaywalker** *n*.

**jazz** *n* a general term for American popular music, characterized by syncopated rhythms and embracing ragtime, blues, swing, jive, and bebop; (*sl*) pretentious or nonsensical talk or actions. • *vt* (*sl*) (*with* **up**) to enliven or embellish.—**jazzy** *adj*.—**jazziness** *n*.

**jealous** *adj* apprehensive of or hostile towards someone thought of as a rival; envious of, resentful; anxiously vigilant or protective.—**jealously** *adv*.

**jealousy** *n* suspicious fear or watchfulness, esp the fear of being supplanted by a rival.

**jeans** *npl* trousers made from denim.

**jeep** *n* a small robust vehicle with heavy duty tyres and four-wheel drive for use on rough terrain, esp by the military.

**jeer** *vt* to laugh derisively. • *vi* to scoff (at). • *n* a jeering remark.

**jelly** *n* a soft, gelatinous food made from fruit syrup or meat juice; any substance like this.—**jellied** *adj*.

**jellyfish** *n* a sea creature with a nearly transparent body and long tentacles.

**jeopardize** *vt* to endanger, put at risk.

**jeopardy** *n* great danger or risk.

**jerk**¹ *n* a sudden sharp pull or twist; a sudden muscular contraction or reflex; (*inf*) a stupid person. • *vti* to move with a jerk; to pull sharply; to twitch.

**jerk**[2] *vt* to preserve (meat) by cutting it into long strips and drying it in the sun. • *n* jerked meat (—*also* **jerky**).

**jerkin** *n* a close-fitting sleeveless jacket.

**jerky** *adj* (**jerkier, jerkiest**) moving with jerks.—**jerkily** *adv*.—**jerkiness** *n*.

**jersey** *n* any plain machine-knitted fabric of natural or man-made fibres; a knitted sweater. • *adj* pertaining to the island of Jersey or its breed of cattle.

**jest** *n* a joke; a thing to be laughed at. • *vi* to jeer; to joke.

**jet**[1] *n* a hard, black, compact mineral that can be polished and is used in jewellery; a lustrous black.—**jet-black** *adj*.

**jet**[2] *n* a stream of liquid or gas suddenly emitted; a spout for emitting a jet; a jet-propelled aircraft. • *vti* (*pt* **jetted**) to gush out in a stream; (*inf*) to travel or convey by jet.

**jet engine** *n* an engine, such as a gas turbine, producing jet propulsion.

**jetsam** *n* cargo thrown overboard from a ship in distress to lighten it, esp such cargo when washed up on the shore.

**jettison** *vt* to abandon, to throw overboard.

**jetty** *n* a wharf; a small pier.

**Jew** *n* a person descended, or regarded as descended, from the ancient Hebrews; a person whose religion is Judaism.

**jewel** *n* a precious stone; a gem; a piece of jewellery; someone or something highly esteemed; a small gem used as a bearing in a watch.

**jeweller, jeweler** (*US*) *n* a person who makes, repairs or deals in jewellery, watches, etc.

**jewellery, jewelry**(*US*) *n* jewels such as rings, brooches, etc, worn for decoration.

**Jewish** *adj* of or like Jews.

**jib** *n* a triangular sail extending from the foremast in a ship; the projecting arm of a crane. • *vti* (*pt* **jibbed**) to pull (a sail) round to the other side; (*sail*) to swing round.

**jibe** *see* **gibe**.

**jiffy, jiff** *n* (*inf*) a very short time.

**jigsaw** *n* a saw with a narrow fine-toothed blade for cutting irregular shapes; a picture on wood or board cut into irregular pieces for re-assembling for amusement.

**jilt** *vt* to discard (a lover) unfeelingly, esp without warning.

**jingle** *n* a metallic tinkling sound like a bunch of keys being shaken together; a catchy verse or song with easy rhythm, simple rhymes, etc. • *vti* (to cause) to make a light tinkling sound.

**jinx** *n* (*inf*) someone or something thought to bring bad luck.

**jitter** *vi* (*inf*) to feel nervous or act nervously. • *npl* (*inf*) (*with* **the**) an uneasy nervous feeling; fidgets.

**job** *n* a piece of work done for pay; a task; a duty; the thing or material being worked on; work; employment; (*sl*) a criminal enterprise; (*inf*) a difficult task. • *adj* hired or done by the job. • *vti* (*pt* **jobbed**) to deal in (goods) as a jobber; to sub-let (work, etc).

**jobless** *adj* unemployed.

**jockey** *n* a person whose job is riding horses in races. • *vti* to act as a jockey; to manœuvre for a more advantageous position; to swindle or cheat.

**jocular** *adj* joking; full of jokes.—**jocularity** *n*.—**jocularly** *adv*.

**jog** *vb* (*pt* **jogged**) *vt* to give a slight shake or nudge to; to rouse, as the memory. • *vi* to move up and down with an unsteady motion; to run at a relaxed trot for exercise; (*horse*) to run at a jog-trot. • *n* a slight shake or push; a nudge; a slow walk or trot.—**jogger** *n*.

**join** *vti* to bring and come together (with); to connect; to unite; to become a part or member of (a club, etc); to participate (in a conversation, etc); (*with* up) to enlist in the armed forces; to unite, connect. • *n* a joining; a place of joining.

**joiner** *n* a carpenter who finishes interior woodwork; (*inf*) a person who is involved in many clubs and activities, etc.

**joint** *n* a place where, or way in which, two things are joined; any of the parts of a jointed whole; the parts where two bones move on one another in an animal; a division of an animal carcass made by a butcher; (*sl*) a cheap bar or restaurant; (*sl*) a gambling or drinking den; (*sl*) a cannabis cigarette. • *adj* common to two or more; sharing with another. • *vt* to connect by a joint or joints; to divide (an animal carcass) into parts for cooking.

**jointly** *adv* in common.

**joist** *n* any of the parallel beams supporting the floor-boards or the laths of a ceiling.

**joke** *n* something said or done to cause laughter; a thing done or said merely in fun; a person or thing to be laughed at. • *vi* to make jokes.

**joker** *n* a person who jokes; (*sl*) a person; an extra playing card made use of in certain games.

**jolly** *adj* (**jollier, jolliest**) merry; full of fun; delightful; (*inf*) enjoyable. • *vti* (*inf*) to try to make (a person) feel good; to make fun of (someone).

**jolt** *vt* to give a sudden shake or knock to; to move along jerkily; to surprise or shock suddenly. • *n* a sudden jar or knock; an emotional shock.

**jostle** *vti* to shake or knock roughly; to collide or come into contact (with); to elbow for position.—*also n*.

**jot** *n* a very small amount. • *vt* (*pt* **jotted**) to note (down) briefly.

**jotter** *n* a notebook.

**journal** *n* a daily record of happenings, as a diary; a newspaper or periodical; (*bookkeeping*) a book of original entry for recording transactions; that part of a shaft or axle that turns in a bearing.

**journalese** *n* a facile style of writing found in many magazines, newspapers, etc.

**journalism** *n* the work of gathering news for, or producing a newspaper, magazine or news broadcast.—**journalist** *n*.—**journalistic** *adj*.

**journey** *n* a travelling or going from one place to another; the distance covered when travelling. • *vi* to make a journey.

**jowl** *n* the lower jaw; (*usu pl*) the cheek; the loose flesh around the throat; the similar flesh in an animal, as a dewlap.

**joy** *n* intense happiness; something that causes this.—**joyless** *adj*.—**joylessly** *adv*.—**joylessness** *n*.

**joyful** *adj* filled with, expressing, or causing joy.—**joyfully** *adv*.—**joyfulness** *n*.

**joyous** *adj* joyful.—**joyously** *adv*.—**joyousness** *n*.

**joy-ride** *n* (*inf*) a car ride, often in a stolen vehicle and at reckless speed, just for pleasure.—**joy-rider** *n*.—**joy-riding** *n*.

**JP** *abbr* = Justice of the Peace.

**Jr.** *abbr* = Junior.

**jubilant** *adj* joyful and triumphant; elated; rejoicing.—**jubilation** *n*.

**jubilee** *n* a 50th or 25th anniversary; a time of rejoicing.

**judge** *n* a public official with authority to hear and decide cases in a court of law; a person chosen to settle a dispute or decide who wins; a person qualified to decide on the relative worth of anything. • *vti* to hear and pass judgment (on) in a court of law; to determine the winner of (a contest) or settle (a dispute); to form an opinion about; to criticize or censure; to suppose, think.

**judgment, judgement** *n* a judging; a deciding; a legal decision; an opinion; the ability to come to a wise decision; censure.

**judicial** *adj* of judges, courts, or their functions; jurisdiction; judges or courts collectively.—**judicially** *adv*.

**judicious** *adj* possessing or characterized by sound judgment.—**judiciously** *adv*.

**judo** *n* a Japanese system of unarmed combat, adapted as a competitive sport from jujitsu.

**jug** *n* a vessel for holding and pouring liquids, with a handle and curved lip; a pitcher; (*sl*) prison. • *vt* (*pt* **jugged**) to stew meat (esp hare) in an earthenware pot; (*sl*) to put into prison.—**jugful** *n*.

**juggernaut** *n* a terrible, irresistible force; a large heavy truck.

**juggle** *vi* to toss up balls, etc and keep them in the air. • *vt* to manipulate skilfully; to manipulate so as to deceive. • *n* a juggling.—**juggler** *n*.

**juice** *n* the liquid part of fruit, vegetables or meat; liquid secreted by a bodily organ; (*inf*) vitality; (*inf*) electric current; (*inf*) petrol.

**juicy** *adj* (**juicier, juiciest**) full of juice; (*inf*) very interesting; (*inf*) highly profitable.—**juicily** *adv*.—**juiciness** *n*.

**jukebox** *n* a coin-operated automatic record or CD player.

**July** *n* the seventh month of the year, having 31 days.

**jumble** *vt* (*often with* **up**) to mix together in a disordered mass. • *n* items mixed together in a confused mass; articles for a jumble sale.

**jumble sale** *n* a sale of second-hand clothes, books, etc to raise money for charity.

**jumbo** *n* (*pl* **jumbos**) something very large of its kind.

**jumbo jet** *n* a very large jet airliner.

**jump** *vi* to spring or leap from the ground, a height, etc; to jerk; (*often with* **at**) to act swiftly and eagerly; to pass suddenly, as to a new topic; to rise suddenly, as prices; (*sl*) to be lively. • *vt* to leap or pass over (something); to leap upon; to cause (prices, etc) to rise; to fail to turn up (for trial when out on bail); (*inf*) to attack suddenly; (*inf*) to react to prematurely; (*sl*) to leave suddenly. • *n* a jumping; a distance jumped; a sudden transition; an obstacle; a nervous start.

**jumper** *n* a knitted garment for the upper body; a sleeveless dress for wearing over a blouse, etc.

**jumpy** *adj* (**jumpier, jumpiest**) moving in jerks, etc; easily startled, apprehensive.—**jumpily** *adv*.—**jumpiness** *n*.

**junction** *n* a place or point where things join; a place where roads or railway lines, etc meet, link or cross each other.

**juncture** *n* a junction; a point of time; a crisis.

**June** *n* the sixth month of the year, having 30 days.

**jungle** *n* an area overgrown with dense tropical trees and other vegetation, etc; any scene of wild confusion, disorder, or of ruthless competition for survival.

**junior** *adj* younger in age; of more recent or lower status; of juniors. • *n* a person who is younger, of lower rank, etc; a young person employed in minor capacity in an office; a member of a junior school; (*inf*) (*with cap*) the younger son, in US often used after the name if the same as the father's.

**juniper** *n* an evergreen shrub that yields purple berries.

**junk**[1] *n* a flat-bottomed sailing vessel prevalent in the China Seas.

**junk**[2] *n* discarded useless objects; (*inf*) rubbish, trash; (*sl*) any narcotic drug, such as heroin. • *vt* (*inf*) to scrap.

**junk shop** *n* a shop selling miscellaneous second-hand goods.

**junta** *n* a group of people, esp military, who assume responsibility for the government of a country following a coup d'état or revolution.

**jurisdiction** *n* the right or authority to apply the law; the exercise of such authority; the limits of territory over which such authority extends.

**jurisprudence** *n* the science or philosophy of law; a division of law.—**jurisprudential** *adj*.

**juror** *n* a member of a jury; a person who takes an oath.

**jury** *n* a body of usu 12 people sworn to hear evidence and to deliver a verdict on a case; a committee or panel that decides winners in a contest.

**just** *adj* fair, impartial; deserved, merited; proper, exact; conforming strictly with the facts. • *adv* exactly; nearly; only; barely; a very short time ago; immediately; (*inf*) really; justly, equitably; by right.—**justly** *adv*.— **justness** *n*.

**justice** *n* justness, fairness; the use of authority to maintain what is just; the administration of law; a judge.

**jut** *vti* (*pt* **jutted**) to stick out; to project. • *n* a part that juts.

**juvenile** *adj* young; immature; of or for young persons. • *n* a young person.

**juxtapose** *vt* to place side by side.— **juxtaposition** *n*.

# K

**kaleidoscope** *n* a small tube containing bits of coloured glass reflected by mirrors to form symmetrical patterns as the tube is rotated; anything that constantly changes. —**kaleidoscopic** *adj*.

**kangaroo** *n* an Australian mammal with short forelegs and strong, large hind legs for jumping.

**karat** *see* **carat**.

**keel** *n* one of the main structural members of a ship extending along the bottom from stem to stern to which the frame is attached; any structure resembling this. • *vti* (to cause) to turn over.

**keen**[1] *adj* eager, enthusiastic; intellectually acute, shrewd; having a sharp point or fine edge; (*senses*) perceptive, penetrating; extremely cold and piercing; intense; (*prices*) very low so as to be competitive.—**keenly** *adv*.—**keenness** *n*.

**keen**[2] *n* a dirge or lament for the dead. • *vi* to lament the dead.

**keep** *vb* (*pt* **kept**) *vt* to celebrate, observe; to fulfil; to protect, guard; to take care of; to preserve; to provide for; to make regular entries in; to maintain in a specified state; to hold for the future; to hold and not let go. • *vi* to stay in a specified condition; to continue, go on; to refrain or restrain oneself; to stay fresh, not spoil. • *n* food and shelter; care and custody; the inner stronghold of a castle.

**keeper** *n* one who guards, watches, or takes care of persons or things.

**keeping** *n* care, charge; observance; agreement, conformity.

**keepsake** *n* something kept in memory of the giver.

**keg** *n* a small barrel.

**kennel** *n* a small shelter for a dog, a doghouse; (*often pl*) a place where dogs are bred or kept. • *vt* (*pt* **kennelled**) to keep in a kennel.

**kept** *see* **keep**.

**kerb** *n* a line of raised stone forming the edge of a pavement.—**kerbstone** *n*.

**kernel** *n* the inner edible part of a fruit or nut; the essential part of anything.

**kerosene, kerosine** *n* a fuel oil distilled from petroleum, paraffin.

**ketchup** *n* any of various thick sauces, esp one made from puréed tomato, for meat, fish, etc.—*also* **catchup, catsup**

**kettle** *n* a container with a handle and spout for boiling water.

**kettledrum** *n* a musical instrument consisting of a hollow metal body with a parchment head, the tension of which controls the pitch and is adjusted by screws.

**key**[1] *n* a device for locking and unlocking something; a thing that explains or solves, as the legend of a map, a code, etc; a controlling position, person, or thing; one of a set of parts or levers pressed in a keyboard or typewriter, etc; (*mus*) a system of related tones based on a keynote and forming a given scale; style or mood of expression; a roughened surface for improved adhesion of plaster, etc; an electric circuit breaker. • *vt* to furnish with a key; to bring into harmony. • *adj* controlling; important.

**key**[2] *n* a low island or reef.

**keyboard** *n* a set of keys in a piano, organ, computer, etc.

**keyhole** *n* an opening (in a lock) into which a key is inserted.

**keynote** *n* the basic note of a musical scale; the basic idea or ruling principle. • *vt* to give the keynote of; to give the keynote speech at.

**khaki** *adj* dull yellowish-brown. • *n* (*pl* **khakis**) strong, twilled cloth of this colour; (*often pl*) a khaki uniform or trousers.

**kick** *vt* to strike with the foot; to drive, force, etc as by kicking; to score (a goal, etc) by kicking. • *vi* to strike out with the foot; to recoil, as a gun; (*inf*) to complain; (*with off*) (*football*) to give the ball the first kick to start play; (*inf*) to start. • *n* an act or method of kicking; a sudden recoil; (*inf*) a thrill; (*inf*) an intoxicating effect.—**kicker** *n*.

**kickoff** *n* (*football*) a kick putting the ball into play; the beginning or start of proceedings, eg a discussion.

**kid** *n* a young goat; soft leather made from its skin; (*inf*) a child. • *vti* (*pt* **kidded**) (*inf*) to tease or fool playfully; (*goat*) to bring forth young.

**kidnap** *vt* (*pt* **kidnapped**) to seize and hold to ransom, as of a person.—**kidnapper** *n*.

**kidney** *n* (*pl* **kidneys**) either of a pair of glandular organs excreting waste products from the blood as urine; an animal's kidney used as food.

**kill** *vt* to cause the death of; to destroy; to neutralize (a colour); to spend (time) on trivial matters; to turn off (an engine, etc); (*inf*) to cause severe discomfort or pain to • *n* the act of killing; an animal or animals killed.—**killer** *n*.

**killing** *adj* (*inf*) tiring; very amusing; causing death, deadly. • *n* the act of killing, murder; (*inf*) a sudden (financial) success.

**kiln** *n* a furnace or large oven for baking or drying (lime, bricks, pottery, etc).

**kilo** *n* kilogram; kilometre.

**kilogram, kilogramme** *n* a unit of weight and mass, equal to 1000 grams or 2.2046 pounds.

**kilometre, kilometer** (*US*) *n* a unit of

length equal to 1000 metres or 0.62 mile.—**kilometric** *adj*.

**kilowatt** *n* a unit of electrical power, equal to 1000 watts.

**kilt** *n* a knee-length skirt made from tartan material pleated at the sides, worn as part of the Scottish Highland dress for men and women.

**kimono** *n* a loose Japanese robe.

**kin** *n* relatives; family.

**kind**[1] *n* sort; variety; class; a natural group or division; essential character.

**kind**[2] *adj* sympathetic; friendly; gentle; benevolent.—**kind-hearted** *adj*.—**kindness** *n*.

**kindergarten** *n* a class or school for very young children.

**kindle** *vt* to set on fire; to excite (feelings, interest, etc). • *vi* to catch fire; to become aroused or excited.

**kindly** *adj* (**kindlier, kindliest**) kind; gracious; agreeable; pleasant. • *adv* in a kindly manner; favourably.— **kindliness** *n*.

**kindred** *n* a person's family or relatives; family relationship; resemblance. • *adj* related; like, similar.

**kinetic** *adj* of or produced by movement.

**king** *n* the man who rules a country and its people; a man with the title of ruler, but with limited power to rule; man supreme in a certain sphere; something best in its class; the chief piece in chess; a playing card with a picture of a king on it, ranking above a queen; (*draughts*) a piece that has been crowned.

**kingdom** *n* a country headed by a king or queen; a realm, domain; any of the three divisions of the natural world: animal: vegetable, mineral.

**kingfisher** *n* a short-tailed diving bird that feeds chiefly on fish.

**king-size, king-sized** *adj* larger than standard size.

**kink** *n* a tight twist or curl in a piece of string, rope, hair, etc; a painful cramp in the neck, back, etc; an eccentricity of personality. • *vti* to form or cause to form a kink or kinks.

**kinky** *adj* (**kinkier, kinkiest**) full of kinks; (*inf*) eccentric; (*inf*) sexually bizarre.—**kinkily** *adv*.—**kinkiness** *n*.

**kiosk** *n* a small open structure used for selling newspapers, confectionery, etc; a public telephone booth.

**kipper** *n* a kippered herring, etc. • *vt* to cure (fish) by salting and drying or smoking.

**kiss** *vti* to touch with the lips as an expression of love, affection or in greeting; to touch the lips with those of another person as a sign of love or desire; to touch lightly. • *n* an act of kissing; a light, gentle touch.

**kit** *n* clothing and personal equipment, etc; tools and equipment for a specific purpose; a set of parts with instructions ready to be assembled. • *vt* (*pt* **kitted**) (*usu with* **out** *or* **up**) to provide with kit.

**kitbag** *n* a strong cylindrical bag carried over one shoulder used for holding kit, esp by military personnel.

**kitchen** *n* a place where food is prepared and cooked.

**kite** *n* a bird of prey with long narrow wings and a forked tail; a light frame covered with a thin covering for flying in the wind.

**kith** *n* friends and relations, now only in **kith and kin**.

**kitten** *n* a young cat; the young of other small mammals. • *vti* to give birth to kittens.

**kitty** *n* the stakes in a game of poker or other gambling game; a shared fund of money.

**kleptomania** *n* an uncontrollable impulse to steal.—**kleptomaniac** *n*.

**knack** *n* an ability to do something easily; a trick; a habit.

**knapsack** *n* a bag for carrying equipment or supplies on the back.

**knave** *n* (*formerly*) a tricky or dishonest man; the jack in a pack of playing cards.—**knavery** *n*.—**knavish** *adj*.

**knead** *vt* to squeeze and press together (dough, clay, etc) into a uniform lump with the hands; to make (bread, etc) by kneading; to squeeze and press with the hands.

**knee** *n* the joint between the thigh and the lower part of the human leg; anything shaped like a bent knee. • *vt* (*pt* **kneed**) to hit or touch with the knee.

**kneecap** *n* the small bone covering and protecting the front part of the knee-joint. • *vt* (*pt* **kneecapped**) to maim by shooting into the kneecap.—**kneecapping** *n*.

**kneel** *vi* (*pt* **knelt**) to go down on one's knee or knees; to remain in this position.

**knell** *n* the sound of a bell rung slowly and solemnly at a death or funeral; a warning of death, failure, etc. • *vi* (*bell*) to ring a knell; to summon, announce, etc (as if) by a knell.

**knelt** *see* **kneel**.

**knew** *see* **know**.

**knickers** *npl* an undergarment covering the lower body and having separate leg holes, worn by women and girls.

**knife** *n* (*pl* **knives**) a flat piece of steel, etc, with a sharp edge set in a handle, used to cut or as a weapon; a sharp blade forming part of a tool or machine. • *vt* to cut or stab with a knife.

**knight** *n* (*Middle Ages*) a medieval mounted soldier; a man who for some achievement is given honorary rank entitling him to use "Sir" before his given name; a chessman shaped like a horse's head. • *vt* to make (a man) a knight.—**knighthood** *n*.—**knightly** *adv*.

**knit** *vb* (*pt* **knitted** *or* **knit**) *vt* to form (fabric or a garment) by interlooping yarn using knitting needles or a machine; to cause (eg broken bones) to grow together; to link or join together closely; to draw (the brows) together. • *vi* to make knitted fabric from yarn by means of needles; to grow together; to become joined or united. • *n* a knitted garment or fabric.—**knitter** *n*.

**knitting** *n* work being knitted.

**knitting needle** *n* a long thin eyeless needle, usu made of plastic or steel, used in knitting.

**knitwear** *n* knitted clothing.

**knob** *n* a rounded lump or protuberance; a handle, usu round, of a door, drawer, etc.

**knock** *vi* to strike with a sharp blow; to rap on a door; to bump, collide; (*engine*) to make a thumping noise; (*with* **off**) (*inf*) to finish work. • *vt* to strike; (*inf*) to criticize; (*with* **about, around**) to wander around aimlessly; to treat roughly; (*with* **back**) (*inf*) to drink, swallow quickly; to reject, refuse; (*with* **down**) to indicate a sale at an auction; (*with* **down** *or* **off**) to hit so as to cause to fall; (*with* **off**) (*inf*) to complete hastily; (*inf*) to reduce in price; (*sl*) to steal; (*with* **out**) to make unconscious or exhausted; to eliminate in a knockout competition; (*inf*) to amaze. • *n* a knocking, a hit, a rap.

**knockdown** *adj* cheap; (*furniture*) easy to dismantle.

**knocker** *n* a device hinged against a door for use in knocking.

**knock-kneed** *adj* having inward-curving legs.

**knockout** *n* a punch or blow that produces unconsciousness; a contest in which competitors are eliminated at each round; (*inf*) an attractive or extremely impressive person or thing.

**knot** *n* a lump in a thread, etc formed by a tightened loop or tangling; a fastening made by tying lengths of rope, etc; an ornamental bow; a small group, cluster; a hard mass of wood where a branch grows out from a tree, which shows as a roundish, cross-grained piece in a board; a unit of speed of one nautical mile per hour; something that ties closely, esp the bond of marriage. • *vti* (*pt* **knotted**) to make or form a knot (in); to entangle or become entangled.

**knotty** *adj* (**knottier, knottiest**) full of knots; hard to solve; puzzling.

**know** *vt* (*pt* **knew**, *pp* **known**) to be well-informed about; to be aware of; to be acquainted with; to recognize or distinguish.

**know-how** *n* practical skill, experience.

**knowing** *adj* having knowledge; shrewd; clever; implying a secret understanding.—**knowingly** *adv*.

**knowledge** *n* what one knows; the body of facts, etc accumulated over time; fact of knowing; range of information or understanding; the act of knowing.

**knowledgeable, knowledgable** *adj* having knowledge or intelligence; well-informed.

**known** *see* **know**.

**knuckle** *n* a joint of the finger, esp at the roots of the fingers; the knee of an animal used as food. • *vi* (*with* **down**) (*inf*) to start to work hard; (*with* **under**) to yield, to give in.

**KO** *abbr* = knockout.

**Koran** *n* the sacred book of the Muslims.

**kW** *abbr* = kilowatt(s).

# L

**l** *abbr* = litre(s).

**lab** *n* (*inf*) laboratory.

**label** *n* a slip of paper, cloth, metal, etc attached to anything to provide information about its nature, contents, ownership, etc; a term of generalized classification. • *vt* (*pt* **labelled**) to attach a label to; to designate or classify (as).

**laboratory** *n* a room or building where scientific work and research is carried out.

**laborious** *adj* requiring much work; hard-working; laboured.—**laboriously** *adv*.—**laboriousness** *n*.

**labour, labor** (*US*) *n* work, physical or mental exertion; a specific task; all wage-earning workers; workers collectively; the process of childbirth. • *vi* to work; to work hard; to move with difficulty; to suffer (delusions, etc); to be in childbirth. • *vt* to develop in unnecessary detail.

**labour camp** *n* a penal colony where forced labour takes place.

**labourer, laborer** (*US*) *n* a person who labours, esp a person whose work requires strength rather than skill.

**labyrinth** *n* a structure containing winding passages through which it is hard to find one's way; a maze.—**labyrinthine** *adj*.

**lace** *n* a cord, etc used to draw together and fasten parts of a shoe, a corset, etc; a delicate ornamental fabric of openwork design using fine cotton, silk, etc. • *vt* to fasten with a lace or laces; to intertwine, weave; to fortify (a drink, etc) with a dash of spirits.

**lack** *n* the fact or state of not having any or not having enough; the thing that is needed. • *vti* to be deficient in or entirely without.

**lackadaisical** *adj* showing lack of energy or interest; listless.—**lackadaisically** *adv*.

**laconic** *adj* using few words; concise.—**laconically** *adv*.

**lacquer** *n* a glossy varnish. • *vt* to coat with lacquer, to make glossy.

**lad** *n* a boy; a young man; a fellow, chap.

**ladder** *n* a portable metal or wooden framework with rungs between two vertical supports for climbing up and down; something that resembles a ladder in form or use.

**laden** *adj* loaded with cargo; burdened.

**ladle** *n* a long-handled, cup-like spoon for scooping liquids; a device like a ladle in shape or use.

**lady** *n* a polite term for any woman; (*with cap*) a title of honour given to various ranks of women in the British peerage.

**ladybird** *n* a small, usu brightly-coloured beetle.

**ladylike** *adj* like or suitable for a lady; refined, polite.

**lag**[1] *vi* (*pt* **lagged**) to fall behind, hang back; to fail to keep pace in movement or development; to weaken in strength or intensity. • *n* a falling behind; a delay.

**lag**[2] *vt* (*pt* **lagged**) to insulate (pipes, etc) with lagging.

**lag**[3] *n* (*sl*) a convict; a term of imprisonment.

**lager** *n* a light beer that has been aged for a certain period.

**lagging** *n* insulating material used to lag pipes, boilers, etc.

**lagoon** *n* a shallow lake or pond, esp one connected with a larger body of water; the water enclosed by a circular coral reef.

**laid** *see* **lay**[2].

**laid back** *adj* relaxed, easy-going.

**lain** *see* **lie**[2].

**lair** *n* the dwelling or resting place of a wild animal; (*inf*) a secluded place, a retreat.

**laity** *n* laymen, as opposed to clergymen.

**lake**[1] *n* a large inland body of water.

**lake**[2] *n* a purplish-red pigment, originally made from lac.

**lamb** *n* a young sheep; its flesh as food; (*inf*) an innocent or gentle person. •

*vi* to give birth to a lamb; to tend (ewes) at lambing time.

**lame** *adj* disabled or crippled, esp in the feet or legs; stiff and painful; weak, ineffectual. • *vt* to make lame.—**lamely** *adv*.—**lameness** *n*.

**lament** *vti* to feel or express deep sorrow (for); to mourn. • *n* a lamenting; an elegy, dirge, etc mourning some loss or death.

**lamentable** *adj* distressing, deplorable.—**lamentably** *adv*.

**laminated** *adj* built in thin sheets or layers.

**lamp** *n* any device producing light, either by electricity, gas, or by burning oil, etc; a holder or base for such a device; any device for producing therapeutic rays.

**lampoon** *n* a piece of satirical writing attacking someone. • *vt* to ridicule maliciously in a lampoon.—**lampooner** *n*.—**lampoonery** *n*.—**lampoonist** *n*.

**lamppost** *n* a post supporting a street lamp.

**lance** *n* a long wooden spear with a sharp iron or steel head. • *vt* to pierce (as if) with a lance; to open a boil, etc with a lancet.

**land** *n* the solid part of the earth's surface; ground, soil, a country and its people; property in land. • *vt* to set (an aircraft) down on land or water; to put on shore from a ship; to bring to a particular place; to catch (a fish); to get or secure (a job, prize, etc); to deliver (a blow). • *vi* to go ashore from a ship; to come to port; to arrive at a specified place; to come to rest.

**landing** *n* the act of coming to shore or to the ground; the place where persons or goods are loaded or unloaded from a ship; a platform at the end of a flight of stairs.

**landing stage** *n* a platform for landing goods or people from a ship.

**landing strip** *n* an airstrip.

**landlady** *n* a woman who owns and rents property; a woman who owns and runs a boarding house, pub, etc.

**landlocked** *adj* surrounded by land.

**landlord** *n* a man who owns and rents property; a man who owns and runs a boarding house, pub, etc.

**landlubber** *n* a person who has had little experience of the sea.

**landmark** *n* any prominent feature of the landscape distinguishing a locality; an important event or turning point.

**landowner** *n* a person who owns land.

**landscape** *n* an expanse of natural scenery seen in one view; a picture of natural, inland scenery. • *vt* to make (a plot of ground) more attractive, as by adding lawns, bushes, trees, etc.

**landslide** *n* the sliding of a mass of soil or rocks down a slope; an overwhelming victory, esp in an election.

**lane** *n* a narrow road, path, etc; a path or strip specifically designated for ships, aircraft, cars, etc; one of the narrow strips dividing a running track, swimming pool, etc for athletes and swimmers; one of the narrow passages along which balls are bowled in a bowling alley.

**language** *n* human speech or the written symbols for speech; any means of communicating; a special set of symbols used for programming a computer; the speech of a particular nation, etc; the particular style of verbal expression characteristic of a person, group, profession, etc.

**languid** *adj* lacking energy or vitality; apathetic, not interested; drooping, sluggish.—**languidly** *adv*.—**languidness** *n*.

**languish** *vi* to lose strength and vitality; to pine; to suffer neglect or hardship; to assume a pleading or melancholic expression.

**lank** *adj* tall and thin; long and limp.—**lankly** *adv*.—**lankness** *n*.

**lanky** *adj* (**lankier, lankiest**) lean, tall, and ungainly.—**lankily** *adv*.—**lankiness** *n*.

**lantern** *n* a portable transparent case for holding a light; a structure with windows on top of a door or roof to provide light and ventilation; the light-chamber of a lighthouse.

**lap**[1] *vti* (*pt* **lapped**) to take in (liquid) with the tongue; (*waves*) to flow gently with a splashing sound.

**lap**[2] *n* the flat area from waist to knees formed by a person sitting; the part of the clothing covering this.

**lap**[3] *n* an overlapping; a part that overlaps; one complete circuit of a race track. • *vb* (*pt* **lapped**) *vt* to fold (over or on); to wrap. • *vi* to overlap; to extend over something in space or time.

**lapel** *n* a part of a suit, coat, jacket, etc folded back and continuous with the collar.—**lapelled** *adj*.

**lapse** *n* a small error; a decline or drop to a lower condition, degree, or state; a moral decline; a period of time elapsed; the termination of a legal right or privilege through disuse. • *vi* to depart from the usual or accepted standard, esp in morals; to pass out of existence or use; to become void or discontinued; (*time*) to slip away.

**larceny** *n* theft.—**larcenous** *adj*.

**lard** *n* melted and clarified pig fat. • *vt* to insert strips of bacon or pork fat (in meat) before cooking; to embellish.

**larder** *n* a room or cupboard where food is stored.

**large** *adj* great in size, amount, or number; bulky; big; spacious; bigger than others of its kind; operating on a big scale.—**largeness** *n*.

**largely** *adv* much, in great amounts; mainly, for the most part.

**lark**[1] *n* any of a family of songbirds.

**lark**[2] *n* a playful or amusing adventure; a harmless prank. • *vi* (*usu with* **about**) to have fun, frolic.

**larva** *n* (*pl* **larvae**) the immature form of many animals after emerging from an egg before transformation into the adult state, eg a caterpillar.—**larval** *adj*.

**laryngitis** *n* inflammation of the larynx.

**larynx** *n* (*pl* **larynges**, **larynxes**) the structure at the upper end of the windpipe, containing the vocal cords.

**lascivious** *adj* lecherous, lustful; arousing sexual desire.—**lasciviously** *adv*.—**lasciviousness** *n*.

**laser** *n* a device that produces an intense beam of coherent light or other electromagnetic radiation.

**lash** *vt* to strike forcefully (as if) with a lash; to fasten or secure with a cord, etc; to attack with criticism or ridicule. • *vi* to move quickly and violently; (*rain, waves, etc*) to beat violently against; (*with* **out**) to attack physically or verbally. • *n* the flexible part of a whip; an eyelash; a stroke (as if) with a whip.

**lass, lassie** *n* a young woman or girl.

**lasso** *n* (*pl* **lassoes**, **lassos**) a long rope or leather thong with a running noose for catching horses, cattle, etc. • *vt* (*pr p* **lassoing**, *pt* **lassoed**) to catch (as if) with a lasso.

**last**[1] *n* a shoemaker's model of the foot on which boots and shoes are made or repaired. • *vt* to shape with a last.

**last**[2] *vi* to remain in existence, use, etc; to endure. • *vt* to continue during; to be enough for.

**last**[3] *adj* being or coming after all the others in time or place; only remaining; the most recent; least likely; conclusive. • *adv* after all the others; most recently; finally. • *n* the one coming last.

**lasting** *adj* enduring.—**lastingly** *adv*.

**lastly** *adv* at the end, in the last place, finally.

**last-minute** *adj* at the last possible time when something can be done.

**latch** *n* a fastening for a door, gate, or window, esp a bar, etc that fits into a notch. • *vti* to fasten with a latch.

**latchkey** *n* the key of an outer door.

**late** *adj, adv* after the usual or expected time; at an advanced stage or age; near the end; far on in the day or evening; just prior to the present; deceased; not long past; until lately; out of office.—**lateness** *n*.

**lately** *adv* recently, in recent times.

**latent** *adj* existing but not yet visible or developed.—**latency** *n*.

**lateral** *adj* of, at, from, towards the side.—**laterally** *adv*.

**lath** *n* a thin narrow strip of wood used in constructing a framework for plaster, etc.

**lathe** *n* a machine that rotates wood, metal, etc for shaping.

**lather** *n* a foam made by soap or detergent mixed with water; frothy sweat; a state of excitement or agitation. • *vti* to cover with or form lather.

**Latin** *adj* of ancient Rome, its people, their language, etc; denoting or of the languages derived from Latin (Italian, Spanish, etc), the peoples who speak them, their countries, etc. • *n* a native or inhabitant of ancient Rome; the language of ancient Rome; a person, as a Spaniard or Italian, whose language is derived from Latin.

**latitude** *n* the distance from north or south of the equator, measured in degrees; a region with reference to this distance; extent; scope; freedom from restrictions on actions or opinions.—**latitudinal** *adj*.—**latitudinally** *adv*.

**latrine** *n* a lavatory, as in a military camp.

**latter** *adj* later; more recent; nearer the end; being the last mentioned of two.

**latterly** *adv* recently.

**lattice** *n* a network of crossed laths or bars.

**laudable** *adj* praiseworthy.

**laugh** *vi* to emit explosive inarticulate vocal sounds expressive of amusement, joy or derision. • *vt* to utter or express with laughter. • *n* the act or sound of laughing; (*inf*) an amusing person or thing.—**laughingly** *adv*.

**laughable** *adj* causing laughter; ridiculous.—**laughably** *adv*.

**laughing stock** *n* an object of ridicule.

**laughter** *n* the act or sound of laughing.

**launch**[1] *vt* to throw, hurl or propel forward; to cause (a vessel) to slide into the water; (*rocket, missile*) to set off; to put into action; to put a new product onto the market. • *vi* to involve oneself enthusiastically. • *n* the act or occasion of launching.

**launch**[2] *n* an open, or partly enclosed, motor boat.

**launching pad, launch pad** *n* a platform from which a spacecraft is launched.

**launder** *vti* to wash and iron clothes. • *vt* to legitimize (money) obtained from criminal activity by passing it through foreign banks, or investing in legitimate businesses, etc.

**launderette, laundrette** *n* an establishment equipped with coin-operated washing machines and driers for public use.

**laundry** *n* a place where clothes are washed and ironed; clothes sent to be washed and ironed.

**laureate** *adj* crowned with laurel leaves as a mark of honour. • *n* a poet laureate.

**laurel** *n* an evergreen shrub with large, glossy leaves; the leaves used by the ancient Greeks as a symbol of achievement.

**lava** *n* molten rock flowing from a volcano; the solid substance formed as this cools.

**lavatory** *n* a sanitary device for the disposal of faeces and urine; a room equipped with this, a toilet.

**lavender** *n* the fragrant flowers of a perennial shrub dried and used in sachets; a pale purple.

**lavish** *vt* to give or spend freely. • *adj* abundant, profuse; generous; extravagant.—**lavishly** *adv*.—**lavishness** *n*.

**law** *n* all the rules of conduct in an organized community as upheld by authority; any one of such rules; obedience to such rules; the study of such rules, jurisprudence; the seeking of justice in courts under such rules; the profession of lawyers, judges, etc; (*inf*) the police; a sequence of events occurring with unvarying uniformity under the same conditions; any rule expected to be observed.

**law-abiding** *adj* obeying the law.

**lawbreaker** *n* a person who violates the law.

**lawful** *adj* in conformity with the law; recognized by law.—**lawfully** *adv*.

**lawless** *adj* not regulated by law; not in conformity with law, illegal.—**lawlessly** *adv*.—**lawlessness** *n*.

**lawn**[1] *n* a fine sheer cloth of linen or cotton.

**lawn**[2] *n* land covered with closely cut grass, esp around a house.

**lawn mower** *n* a hand-propelled or power-driven machine to cut lawn grass.

**lawn tennis** *n* tennis played on a grass court.

**lawsuit** *n* a suit between private parties in a law court.

**lawyer** *n* a person whose profession is advising others in matters of law or representing them in a court of law.

**lax** *adj* slack, loose; not tight; not strict or exact.—**laxly** *adv.*—**laxness** *n.*

**laxative** *n* a substance that promotes emptying of the bowels.—*also adj.*

**laxity** *n* the state or quality of being lax, laxness.

**lay¹** *see* **lie².**

**lay²** *vt* (*pt* **laid**) to put down; to allay or suppress; to place in a resting position; to place or set; to place in a correct position; to produce (an egg); (*sl*) to have sexual intercourse with; to devise; to present or assert; to stake a bet; (*with* **off**) to suspend from work temporarily or permanently; (*with* **on**) to supply; (*with* **out**) to plan in detail; to arrange for display; to prepare (a corpse) for viewing; (*inf*) to spend money, esp lavishly. • *vi* (*inf*) to leave (a person or thing) alone. • *n* a way or position in which something is situated; (*sl*) an act of sexual intercourse; a sexual partner.

**lay³** *n* a simple narrative poem, esp as intended to be sung; a ballad.

**lay⁴** *adj* of or pertaining to those who are not members of the clergy; not belonging to a profession.

**layabout** *n* a loafer, lazy person.

**lay-by** *n* a place where motorists can stop at the side of a road without obstructing other traffic.

**layer** *n* a single thickness, fold, etc. • *vi* to separate into layers; to form by superimposing layers.

**layman** *n* a person who is not a member of the clergy; a non-specialist, someone who does not possess professional knowledge.

**layout** *n* the manner in which anything is laid out, esp arrangement of text and pictures on the pages of a newspaper or magazine, etc; the thing laid out.

**laze** *vti* to idle or loaf.

**lazy** *adj* (**lazier, laziest**) disinclined to work or exertion; encouraging or causing indolence; sluggishly moving.—**lazily** *adv.*—**laziness** *n.*

**lb** *abbr* = pound.

**lead¹** *vb* (*pt* **led**) *vt* to show the way, esp by going first; to direct or guide on a course; to direct by influence; to be head of (an expedition, orchestra, etc); to be ahead of in a contest; to live, spend (one's life). • *vi* to show the way, as by going first; (*with* **to**) to tend in a certain direction; to be or go first. • *n* the role of a leader; first place; the amount or distance ahead; anything that leads, as a clue; the leading role in a play, etc; the right of playing first in cards or the card played.

**lead²** *n* a heavy, soft, bluish-grey, metallic element; a weight for sounding depths at sea, etc; bullets; a stick of graphite, used in pencils; (*print*) a thin strip of metal used to space lines of type. • *adj* of or containing lead. • *vt* (*pt* **leaded**) to cover, weight, or space out with lead.

**leaden** *adj* made of lead; very heavy; dull grey; gloomy.

**leader** *n* the person who goes first; the principal first violin-player in an orchestra; the director of an orchestra; the inspiration or head of a movement, such as a political party; a person whose example is followed, a leading article in a newspaper.

**leadership** *n* the act of leading; the ability to be a leader; the leaders of an organization or movement collectively.

**leading¹** *adj* capable of guiding or influencing; principal; in first position.

**leading²** *n* a covering of lead; (*print*) the body of a type, larger than the size, giving space.

**leaf** *n* (*pl* **leaves**) any of the flat, thin (usu green) parts growing from the stem of a plant; a sheet of paper; a very thin sheet of metal; a hinged or removable part of a table top. • *vi* to bear leaves; (*with* **through**) to turn the pages of.

**leaflet** *n* a small or young leaf; a sheet of printed information (often folded), esp advertising matter distributed free. • *vi* to distribute leaflets (to).

**league**¹ *n* an association of nations, groups, etc for promoting common interests; an association of sports clubs that organizes matches between members; any class or category. • *vti* to form into a league.

**league**² *n* (*formerly*) a varying measure of distance, averaging about three miles (5km).

**leak** *n* a crack or hole through which liquid or gas may accidentally pass; the liquid or gas passing through such an opening; confidential information made public deliberately or accidentally. • *vi* to (let) escape though an opening; to disclose information surreptitiously.

**lean**¹ *adj* thin, with little flesh or fat; spare; meagre. • *n* meat with little or no fat.—**leanness** *n*.

**lean**² *vb* (*pt* **leaned** *or* **leant**) *vi* to bend or slant from an upright position; to rest supported (on or against); to rely or depend for help (on). • *vt* to cause to lean.

**leaning** *n* inclination, tendency.

**leap** *vb* (*pt* **leaped** *or* **leapt**) *vi* to jump; (*with* **at**) to accept something offered eagerly. • *vt* to pass over by a jump; to cause to leap. • *n* an act of leaping; bound; space passed by leaping; an abrupt transition.

**leapfrog** *n* a game in which one player vaults over another's bent back. • *vi* (*pt* **leapfrogged**) to vault in this manner; to advance in alternate jumps.

**leap year** *n* a year with an extra day (29 February) occurring every fourth year.

**learn** *vti* (*pt* **learnt** *or* **learned**) to gain knowledge of or skill in; to memorize; to become aware of, realize.—**learner** *n*.

**learned** *adj* having learning; erudite; acquired by study, experience, etc.—**learnedly** *adv*.

**learning** *n* a gaining of knowledge; the acquiring of knowledge or skill through study.

**lease** *n* a contract by which an owner lets land, property, etc to another person for a specified period. • *vt* to grant by or hold under lease.

**leash** *n* a cord, strap, etc by which a dog or animal is held in check. • *vt* to hold or restrain on a leash.

**least** *adj* smallest in size, degree, etc; slightest. • *adv* to the smallest degree. • *n* the smallest in amount.

**leather** *n* material made from the skin of an animal prepared by removing the hair and tanning; something made of leather. • *vt* to cover with leather; to thrash.

**leave**¹ *n* permission to do something; official authorization to be absent; the period covered by this.

**leave**² *vb* (*pt* **left**) *vt* to depart from; to cause or allow to remain in a specified state; to cause to remain behind; to refrain from consuming or dealing with; to have remaining at death, to bequeath; to have as a remainder; to allow to stay or or continue doing without interference; to entrust or commit to another; to abandon. • *vi* to depart.

**lecherous** *adj* characterized by or encouraging lechery.

**lectern** *n* a reading stand in a church; any similar reading support.

**lecture** *n* an informative talk to a class, etc; a lengthy reprimand. • *vti* to give a lecture (to); to reprimand.—**lecturer** *n*.

**led** *see* **lead**¹.

**ledge** *n* a narrow horizontal surface resembling a shelf projecting from a wall, rock face, etc; an underwater ridge of rocks; a rock layer containing ore.

**ledger** *n* a book in which a record of debits, credits, etc is kept.

**lee** *n* a shelter; the side or part away from the wind.

**leech** *n* a blood-sucking worm; a person who clings to or exploits another.

**leek** *n* a vegetable that resembles a greatly elongated green onion.

**leer** *n* a sly, oblique or lascivious look.—*also vi.*

**leeway** *n* the distance a ship or aircraft has strayed sideways of its course; freedom of action as regards expenditure of time, money, etc.

**left**[1] *see* **leave**[2].

**left**[2] *adj* of or on the side that is towards the west when one faces north; worn on the left hand, foot, etc. • *n* the left side; (*often cap*) of or relating to the left in politics; the left hand; (*boxing*) a blow with the left hand.

**left-hand** *adj* of or towards the left side of a person or thing; for use by the left hand.

**left-handed** *adj* using the left hand in preference to the right; done or made for use with the left hand; ambiguous, backhanded. • *adv* with the left hand.

**left luggage office** *n* a temporary repository for luggage at a railway station, etc.—*also* **checkroom**.

**leftovers** *npl* unused portions of something, esp uneaten food.

**left-wing** *adj* of or relating to the liberal faction of a political party, organization, etc.—**left-winger** *n.*

**leg** *n* one of the limbs on which humans and animals support themselves and walk; the part of a garment covering the leg; anything shaped or used like a leg; a branch or limb of a forked object; a section, as of a trip; any of a series of games or matches in a competition.

**legacy** *n* money, property, etc left to someone in a will; something passed on by an ancestor or remaining from the past.

**legal** *adj* of or based on law; permitted by law; of or for lawyers.—**legally** *adv.*

**legalize** *vt* to make lawful.—**legalization** *n.*

**legation** *n* a diplomatic minister and staff; the headquarters of a diplomatic minister.

**legend** *n* a story handed down from the past; a notable person or the stories of his or her exploits; an inscription on a coin, etc; a caption; an explanation of the symbols used on a map.

**legendary** *adj* of, based on, or presented in legends; famous, notorious.

**leggings** *npl* protective outer coverings for the lower legs; a leg-hugging fashion garment for women.

**legible** *adj* able to be read.—**legibly** *adv.*—**legibility** *n.*

**legion** *n* an infantry unit of the ancient Roman army; a large body of soldiers; a large number, a multitude.

**legislate** *vi* to make or pass laws. • *vt* to bring about by legislation.

**legislation** *n* the act or process of lawmaking; the laws themselves.

**legislative** *adj* of legislation or a legislature; having the power to make laws.

**legislator** *n* a member of a legislative body.

**legislature** *n* the body of people who have the power of making laws.

**legitimate** *adj* lawful; reasonable, justifiable; conforming to accepted rules, standards, etc; (*child*) born of parents married to each other.—**legitimacy** *n.*—**legitimately** *adv.*

**leisure** *n* ease, relaxation, esp freedom from employment or duties. • *adj* free and unoccupied.—**leisured** *adj*.

**leisurely** *adj* relaxed, without hurry.—**leisureliness** *n*.

**lemon** *n* (a tree bearing) a small yellow oval fruit with an acid pulp; pale yellow; (*sl*) a person or thing considered disappointing or useless.—**lemony** *adj*.

**lemonade** *n* a lemon-flavoured drink.

**lend** *vb* (*pt* **lent**) *vt* to give the use of something temporarily in expectation of its return; to provide (money) at interest; to give, impart. • *vi* to make loans.—**lender** *n*.

**length** *n* the extent of something from end to end, usu the longest dimension; a specified distance or period of time; something of a certain length taken from a larger piece; a long expanse; (*often pl*) the degree of effort put into some action.

**lengthen** *vti* to make or become longer.

**lengthways, lengthwise** *adv* in the direction of the length.

**lengthy** *adj* (**lengthier, lengthiest**) long, esp too long.—**lengthily** *adv*.—**lengthiness** *n*.

**lenient** *adj* not harsh or severe; merciful.—**leniency** *n*.—**leniently** *adv*.

**lens** *n* a curved piece of transparent glass, plastic, etc used in optical instruments to form an image; any device used to focus electromagnetic rays, sound waves, etc; a similar transparent part of the eye that focuses light rays on the retina.

**Lent** *n* the forty weekdays from Ash Wednesday to Easter, observed by Christians as a period of fasting and penitence.—**Lenten** *adj*.

**lentil** *n* any of several leguminous plants with edible seeds; their seed used for food.

**Leo** *n* (*astrol*) the 5th sign of the zodiac, in astrology operative 22 July–21 August; (*astron*) the Lion, a constellation in the northern hemisphere.

**leopard** *n* a large tawny feline with black spots found in Africa and Asia.—*also* **panther**.

**leotard** *n* a skintight one-piece garment worn by dancers and others engaged in strenuous exercise.

**leper** *n* a person with leprosy.

**leprosy** *n* a chronic infectious bacterial disease of the skin, often resulting in disfigurement.—**leprous** *adj*.

**lesbian** *n* a female homosexual. • *adj* of or characteristic of lesbians.—**lesbianism** *n*.

**less** *adj* not so much, not so great, etc; fewer; smaller. • *adv* to a smaller extent. • *n* a smaller amount. • *prep* minus.

**lessen** *vti* to make or become less.

**lesson** *n* something to be learned or studied; something that has been learned or studied; a unit of learning or teaching; (*pl*) a course of instruction; a selection from the Bible, read as a part of a church service.

**lest** *conj* in order, or for fear, that not; that.

**let**[1] *n* a stoppage; (*tennis*) a minor obstruction of the ball that requires a point to be replayed.

**let**[2] *vb* (*pr p* **letting**, *pt* **let**) *vt* to allow, permit; to rent; to assign (a contract); to cause to run out, as blood; as an auxiliary in giving suggestions or commands (*let us go*); (*with* **down**) to lower; to deflate; to disappoint; to untie; to lengthen; (*with* **off**) to allow to leave (a ship, etc); to fire (a gun) or explode (a bomb); to release; to deal leniently with; (*with* **out**) to release; to reveal; to rent out; to make a garment larger; (*with* **up**) to relax; to cease. • *vi* to be rented; (*with* **on**) (*inf*) to pretend; (*inf*) to indicate one's awareness (of a secret, etc). • *n* the letting of property or accommodation.

**let-down** *n* a disappointment.

**lethal** *adj* deadly.—**lethality** *n*.—**lethally** *adv*.

**lethargy** *n* an abnormal drowsiness; sluggishness; apathy.—**lethargic** *adj*.—**lethargically** *adv*.

**letter** *n* a symbol representing a phonetic value in a written language; a character of the alphabet; a written or printed message; (*pl*) literature; learning; knowledge; literal meaning. • *vt* to mark with letters.

**letter bomb** *n* an explosive device concealed in an envelope and sent through the post.

**letter box** *n* a slit in the doorway of a house or building through which letters are delivered; a postbox.

**lettering** *n* the act or process of inscribing with letters; letters collectively; a title; an inscription.

**lettuce** *n* a plant with succulent leaves used in salads.

**leukaemia, leukemia** (*US*) *n* a chronic disease characterized by an abnormal increase in the number of white blood cells in body tissues and the blood.

**level** *n* a horizontal line or plane; a position in a scale of values; a flat area or surface; an instrument for determining the horizontal. • *adj* horizontal; having a flat surface; at the same height, rank, position, etc; steady. • *vti* (*pt* **levelled**) to make or become level; to demolish; to raise and aim (a gun, criticism, etc).—**levelly** *adv*.—**leveller** *n*.

**level crossing** *n* a place where a road and railway or two railway lines cross at the same level.

**level-headed** *adj* having an even temper and sound judgment.

**lever** *n* a bar used for prising or moving

something; a means to an end; a device consisting of a bar turning about a fixed point; any device used in the same way, eg to operate machinery. • *vt* to raise or move (as with) a lever.

**leverage** *n* the action of a lever; the mechanical advantage gained by the use of a lever; power, influence.

**levity** *n* excessive frivolity; lack of necessary seriousness.

**levy** *vt* to collect by force or authority, as a tax, fine, etc; an amount levied; to enrol or conscript troops; to prepare for or wage war. • *n* a levying; the amount levied.

**lewd** *adj* indecent; lustful; obscene.—**lewdly** *adv*.—**lewdness** *n*.

**liability** *n* a being liable; something for which one is liable; (*inf*) a handicap, disadvantage; (*pl*) debts, obligations, disadvantages.

**liable** *adj* legally bound or responsible; subject to; likely (to).

**liaison** *n* intercommunication as between units of a military force; an illicit love affair; a thickening for sauces, soups, etc, as egg yolks or cream.

**liar** *n* a person who tells lies.

**libel** *n* any written or printed matter tending to injure a person's reputation unjustly; (*inf*) any defamatory or damaging assertion about a person. • *vt* (*pt* **libelled**) to utter or publish a libel against.—**libellous** *adj*.

**liberal** *adj* ample, abundant; not literal or strict; tolerant; (*education*) contributing to a general broadening of the mind, non-specialist; favouring reform or progress. • *n* a person who favours reform or progress.—**liberally** *adv*.

**liberate** *vt* to set free from foreign occupation, slavery, etc.—**liberation** *n*.—**liberator** *n*.

**liberty** *n* freedom from slavery,

captivity, etc; the right to do as one pleases, freedom; a particular right, freedom, etc granted by authority; an impertinent attitude; authorized leave granted to a sailor.

**Libra** *n* (*astrol*) the 7th sign of the zodiac, operative 24 September–23 October; a constellation represented as a pair of scales.

**librarian** *n* a person in charge of a library or trained in librarianship.

**library** *n* a collection of books, tapes, records, photographs, etc for reference or borrowing; a room, building or institution containing such a collection; (*comput*) a set of, usu general purpose, programs or subroutines for use in programming.

**libretto** *n* (*pl* **librettos, libretti**) the text to which an opera, oratorio, etc is set.—**librettist** *n*.

**lice** *see* **louse**.

**licence, license** (*US*) *n* a formal or legal permission to do something specified; a document granting such permission; freedom to deviate from rule, practice, etc; excessive freedom, an abuse of liberty.

**license** *vt* to grant a licence to or for; to permit.

**licentious** *adj* morally unrestrained; lascivious.—**licentiousness** *n*.

**lichen** *n* any of various small plants consisting of an alga and a fungus living in symbiotic association, growing on stones, trees, etc.

**lick** *vt* to draw the tongue over, esp to taste or clean; (*flames, etc*) to flicker around or touch lightly; (*inf*) to thrash; (*inf*) to defeat. • *n* a licking with the tongue; (*inf*) a sharp blow; (*inf*) a short, rapid burst of activity.

**lid** *n* a removable cover as for a box, etc; an eyelid.—**lidded** *adj*.

**lido** *n* an open-air swimming pool and recreational complex for public use.

**lie**[1] *n* an untrue statement made with intent to deceive; something that deceives or misleads. • *vi* (*pr p* **lying**, *pt* **lied**) to speak untruthfully with an intention to deceive; to create a false impression.

**lie**[2] *vi* (*pr p* **lying**, *pt* **lay**, *pp* **lain**) to be or put oneself in a reclining or horizontal position; to rest on a support in a horizontal position; to be in a specified condition; to be situated; to exist. • *n* the way in which something is situated.

**lieutenant** *n* a commissioned army officer ranking below a captain; a naval officer next below a lieutenant commander; a deputy, a chief assistant to a superior.—**lieutenancy** *n*.

**life** *n* (*pl* **lives**) that property of plants and animals (ending at death) that enables them to use food, grow, reproduce, etc; the state of having this property; living things collectively; the time a person or thing exists; one's manner of living; one's animate existence; vigour, liveliness; (*inf*) a life sentence; a biography. • *adj* of animate being; lifelong; using a living model; of or relating to or provided by life insurance.

**lifebelt** *n* an inflatable ring to support a person in the water; a safety belt.

**lifeboat** *n* a small rescue boat carried by a ship; a specially designed and equipped rescue vessel that helps those in distress along the coastline.

**lifeguard** *n* an expert swimmer employed to prevent drownings.

**life jacket** *n* a sleeveless jacket or vest of buoyant material to keep a person afloat.

**lifeless** *adj* dead; unconscious; dull.—**lifelessly** *adv*.—**lifelessness** *n*.

**lifelike** *adj* resembling a real life person or thing.

**lifeline** *n* a rope for raising or lowering a diver; a rope for rescuing a person, eg as attached to a lifebelt; a vitally important channel of communication or transport.

**lifelong** *adj* lasting one's whole life.

**life preserver** *n* a club used as a weapon of self-defence; a lifebelt or life jacket.

**lifetime** *n* the length of time that a person lives or something lasts.

**lift** *vt* to bring to a higher position, raise; to raise in rank, condition, etc; (*sl*) to steal; to revoke. • *vi* to exert oneself in raising something; to rise; to go up; (*fog, etc*) to disperse; (*with off*) (*rocket, etc*) to take off. • *n* act or fact of lifting; distance through which a thing is lifted; elevation of mood, etc; elevated position or carriage; a ride in the direction in which one is going; help of any kind; a cage or platform for moving something from one level to another (—*also elevator*); upward air pressure maintaining an aircraft in flight.

**liftoff** *n* the vertical thrust of a spacecraft, etc at launching; the time of this.

**ligament** *n* a band of tissue connecting bones; a unifying bond.

**light**[1] *n* the agent of illumination that stimulates the sense of sight; electromagnetic radiation such as ultraviolet, infrared or X-rays; brightness, illumination; a source of light, as the sun, a lamp, etc; daylight; a thing used to ignite something; a window; knowledge, enlightenment; aspect or appearance. • *adj* having light; bright; pale in colour. • *adv* palely. • *vt* (*pt* lit *or* lighted) to ignite; to cause to give off light; to furnish with light; to brighten, animate.

**light**[2] *adj* having little weight; not heavy; less than usual in weight, amount, force, etc; of little importance; easy to bear; easy to digest; happy; dizzy, giddy; not serious; moderate; moving with ease;

producing small products. • *adv* lightly. • *vi* (*pt* lighted *or* lit) to come to rest after travelling through the air; to dismount, to alight; to come or happen on or upon; to strike suddenly, as a blow.—**lightly** *adv*.—**lightness** *n*.

**lighten**[1] *vti* to make or become light or lighter; to shine, flash.

**lighten**[2] *vti* to make or become lighter in weight; to make or become more cheerful; to mitigate.

**lighter**[1] *n* a small device that produces a naked flame to light cigarettes.

**lighter**[2] *n* a large barge used in loading or unloading larger ships.

**light-headed** *adj* dizzy; delirious.

**light-hearted** *adj* carefree.

**lighthouse** *n* a tower with a bright light to guide ships.

**lighting** *n* the process of giving light; equipment for illuminating a stage, television set, etc; the distribution of light on an object, as in a work of art.

**lightning** *n* a discharge or flash of electricity in the sky. • *adv* fast, sudden.

**lightning conductor, lightning rod** *n* a metal rod placed high on a building and grounded to divert lightning from the structure.

**lightweight** *adj* of less than average weight; trivial, unimportant. • *n* a person or thing of less than average weight; a professional boxer weighing 130–135 pounds (59–61 kg); a person of little importance or influence.

**light year** *n* the distance light travels in one year.

**like**[1] *adj* having the same characteristics; similar; equal. • *adv* (*inf*) likely. • *prep* similar to; characteristic of; in the mood for; indicative of; as for example. • *conj* (*inf*) as; as if. • *n* an equal; counterpart.

**like**[2] *vt* to be pleased with; to wish. • *vi* to be so inclined.

**likelihood** *n* probability.

**likely** *adj* (**likelier, likeliest**) reasonably to be expected; suitable; showing promise of success.• *adv* probably.—**likeliness** *n*.

**like-minded** *adj* sharing the same tastes, ideas, etc.

**liken** *vt* to compare.

**likewise** *adv* the same; also.

**liking** *n* fondness; affection; preference.

**lilac** *n* a shrub with large clusters of tiny, fragrant flowers; a pale purple. • *adj* lilac coloured.

**lily** *n* a bulbous plant having typically trumpet-shaped flowers; its flower.

**lily of the valley** *n* a small plant of the lily family with white bell-shaped flowers.

**limb** *n* a projecting appendage of an animal body, as an arm, leg, or wing; a large branch of a tree; a participating member, agent; an arm of a cross.

**limber**[1] *adj* flexible, able to bend the body easily. • *vti* to make or become limber.

**limber**[2] *n* the detachable wheeled section of a gun carriage.

**limbo**[1] *n* (*pl* **limbos**) (*Christianity*) the abode after death assigned to unbaptized souls; a place for lost, unwanted, or neglected persons or things; an intermediate stage or condition between extremes.

**limbo**[2] *n* (*pl* **limbos**) a West Indian dance that involves bending over backwards and passing under a horizontal bar that is progressively lowered.

**lime**[1] *n* a white calcium compound used for making cement and in agriculture. • *vt* to treat or cover with lime.

**lime**[2] *n* a small yellowish-green fruit with a juicy, sour pulp; the tree that bears it; its colour.

**lime**[3] *n* the linden tree.

**limelight** *n* intense publicity; a type of lamp, formerly used in stage lighting, in which lime was heated to produce a brilliant flame.

**limerick** *n* a type of humorous verse consisting of five lines.

**limestone** *n* a type of rock composed mainly of calcium carbonate.

**limit** *n* a boundary; (*pl*) bounds; the greatest amount allowed; (*inf*) as much as one can tolerate. • *vt* to set a limit to; to restrict.

**limitation** *n* the act of limiting or being limited; a hindrance to ability or achievement.

**limited** *adj* confined within bounds; lacking imagination or originality.

**limousine** *n* a large luxury car.

**limp**[1] *vi* to walk with or as with a lame leg. • *n* a lameness in walking.

**limp**[2] *adj* not firm; lethargic; wilted; flexible.—**limply** *adv*.—**limpness** *n*.

**limpet** *n* a mollusc with a low conical shell that clings to rocks.

**line**[1] *vt* to put, or serve as, a lining in.

**line**[2] *n* a length of cord, rope, or wire; a cord for measuring, making level; a system of conducting fluid, electricity, etc; a thin threadlike mark; anything resembling such a mark, as a wrinkle; edge, limit, boundary; border, outline, contour; a row of persons or things, as printed letters across a page; a succession of persons, lineage; a connected series of things; the course a moving thing takes; a course of conduct, actions, etc; a whole system of transportation; a person's trade or occupation; a field of experience or interest; (*inf*) glib, persuasive talk; a verse; the forward combat position in warfare; fortifications, trenches or other defences used in war; a stock of goods; a piece of information; a short letter, note; (*pl*) all the speeches of a character in a play. • *vt* to mark with lines; to form a line along; to cover with lines; to arrange in a line. • *vi* to align.

**linear** *adj* of, made of, or using a line or lines; narrow and long; in relation to length only.—**linearity** *n*.

**linen** *n* thread or cloth made of flax; household articles (sheets, cloths, etc) made of linen or cotton cloth.

**liner** *n* a large passenger ship or aircraft travelling a regular route.

**linesman** *n* an official in certain games who assists the referee in deciding when the ball is out of play, etc.

**line-up** *n* an arrangement of persons or things in a line, eg for inspection.

**linger** *vi* to stay a long time; to delay departure; to dawdle or loiter; to dwell on in the mind; to remain alive though on the point of death.

**lingo** *n* (*pl* **lingoes**) (*inf*) a dialect, jargon, etc.

**linguist** *n* a person who is skilled in speaking foreign languages.

**linguistic** *adj* of or pertaining to language or linguistics.—**linguistically** *adv*.

**linguistics** *n* (*used as sing*) the science of language.

**lining** *n* a material used to cover the inner surface of a garment, etc; any material covering an inner surface.

**link** *n* a single loop or ring of a chain; something resembling a loop or ring or connecting piece; a person or thing acting as a connection, as in a communication system, machine or organization. • *vti* to connect or become connected.

**links** *npl* (*also used as sing*) flat sandy soil; a golf course, esp by the sea.

**link-up** *n* a linking together.

**linoleum** *n* a floor covering of coarse fabric backing with a smooth, hard decorative coating.

**lint** *n* scraped and softened linen used to dress wounds; fluff.

**lintel** *n* the horizontal crosspiece spanning a doorway or window.

**lion** *n* a large, flesh-eating feline mammal with a shaggy mane in the adult male; a person of great courage or strength.—**lioness** *nf*.

**lip** *n* either of the two fleshy flaps that surround the mouth; anything like a lip, as the rim of a jug; (*sl*) insolent talk. • *vt* (*pt* **lipped**) to touch with the lips; to kiss; to utter.

**lip service** *n* support expressed but not acted upon.

**lipstick** *n* a small stick of cosmetic for colouring the lips; the cosmetic itself.

**liqueur** *n* a sweet and variously flavoured alcoholic drink.

**liquid** *n* a substance that, unlike a gas, does not expand indefinitely and, unlike a solid, flows readily. • *adj* in liquid form; clear; limpid; flowing smoothly and musically, as verse; (*assets*) readily convertible into cash.—**liquidity** *n*.

**liquidate** *vt* to settle the accounts of; to close a (bankrupt) business and distribute its assets among its creditors; to convert into cash; to eliminate, kill.—**liquidation** *n*.—**liquidator** *n*.

**liquidize** *vt* to make liquid.

**liquor** *n* an alcoholic drink; any liquid, esp that in which food has been cooked.

**liquorice, licorice** (*US*) *n* a black extract made from the root of a European plant, used in medicine and confectionery; a liquorice-flavoured sweet.

**lisp** *vi* to substitute the sounds *th* (as in *thin*) for *s* or *th* (as in *then*) for *z*; a speech defect or habit involving such pronunciation; to utter imperfectly. • *vt* to speak or utter with a lisp.—*also n.*

**list**[1] *n* a series of names, numbers,

words, etc written or printed in order. • *vt* to make a list of; to enter in a directory, etc.

**list**[2] *vti* to tilt to one side, as a ship. • *n* such a tilting.

**listen** *vi* to try to hear; to pay attention, take heed; (*with* **in**) to overhear a conversation, eg on the telephone; to tune into a radio broadcast; to eavesdrop.

**listener** *n* a person who listens; a person listening to a radio broadcast.

**listless** *adj* lacking energy or enthusiasm because of illness, dejection, etc; languid.—**listlessly** *adv.*—**listlessness** *n*.

**lit** *see* **light**[1], **light**[2].

**litany** *n* a type of prayer in which petitions to God are recited by a priest and elicit set responses by the congregation; any tedious or automatic recital.

**literacy** *n* the ability to read and write.

**literal** *adj* in accordance with the exact meaning of a word or text; in a basic or strict sense; prosaic, unimaginative; real.—**literally** *adv*.

**literary** *adj* of or dealing with literature; knowing much about literature.

**literate** *adj* able to read and write; educated.—*also n*.

**literature** *n* the writings of a period or of a country, esp those valued for their excellence; of style or form; all the books and articles on a subject; (*inf*) any printed matter.

**lithe** *adj* supple, flexible.

**litigate** *vti* to bring or contest in a lawsuit.—**litigation** *n*.

**litre, liter** (*US*) *n* a measure of liquid capacity in the metric system, equivalent to 1.76 pints.

**litter** *n* rubbish scattered about; young animals produced at one time; straw, hay, etc used as bedding for animals; a stretcher for carrying a sick or wounded person. • *vt* to make untidy; to scatter about carelessly.

**little** *adj* not great or big, small in size, amount, degree, etc; short in duration; small in importance or power; narrow-minded. • *n* small in amount, degree, etc. • *adv* less, least, slightly; not much; not in the least.

**liturgy** *n* the prescribed form of service of a church.—**liturgical** *adj.*—**liturgically** *adv*.

**live**[1] *vi* to have life; to remain alive; to endure; to pass life in a specified manner; to enjoy a full life; to reside. • *vt* to carry out in one's life; to spend; pass.

**live**[2] *adj* having life; of the living state or living beings; of present interest; still burning; unexploded; carrying electric current; broadcast during the actual performance.

**livelihood** *n* employment; a means of living.

**lively** *adj* (**livelier, liveliest**) full of life; spirited; exciting; vivid; keen. • *adv* in a lively manner.—**liveliness** *n*.

**liver** *n* the largest glandular organ in vertebrate animals, which secretes bile, etc and is important in metabolism; the liver of an animal used as food; a reddish-brown colour.

**livery** *n* an identifying uniform, as that worn by a servant.

**lives** *see* **life**.

**livestock** *n* (farm) animals raised for use or sale.

**livid** *adj* (*skin*) discoloured, as from bruising; greyish in colour; (*inf*) extremely angry.

**living** *adj* having life; still in use; true to life, vivid; of life, for living in. • *n* a being alive; livelihood; manner of existence.

**living room** *n* a room in a house used for general entertainment and relaxation.

**living wage** *n* a wage sufficient to maintain a reasonable standard of comfort.

**lizard** *n* a reptile with a slender body, four legs, and a tapering tail.

**llama** *n* a South American animal, related to the camel, used for carrying loads and as a source of wool.

**load** *n* an amount carried at one time; something borne with difficulty; a burden; (*often pl*) (*inf*) a great amount. • *vt* to put into or upon; to burden; to oppress; to supply in large quantities; to alter, as by adding a weight to dice or an adulterant to alcoholic drink; to put a charge of ammunition into (a firearm); to put film into (a camera); (*comput*) to install a program in memory. • *vi* to take on a load.

**loaded** *adj* (*sl*) having plenty of money; drunk; under the influence of drugs.

**loaf**[1] *n* (*pl* **loaves**) a mass of bread of regular shape and standard weight; food shaped like this; (*sl*) the head.

**loaf**[2] *vi* to pass time in idleness.—**loafer** *n*.

**loam** *n* rich and fertile soil.—**loamy** *adj*.

**loan** *n* the act of lending; something lent, esp money. • *vti* to lend.

**loath** *adj* unwilling.—*also* **loth**.

**loathe** *vt* to dislike intensely; to detest.—**loathing** *n*.

**lobby** *n* an entrance hall of a public building; a person or group that tries to influence legislators. • *vti* to try to influence (legislators) to support a particular cause or take certain action.

**lobe** *n* a rounded projection, as the lower end of the ear; any of the divisions of the lungs or brain.

**lobster** *n* any of a family of edible sea crustaceans with four pairs of legs and a pair of large pincers.

**local** *adj* of or belonging to a particular place; serving the needs of a specific district; of or for a particular part of the body. • *n* an inhabitant of a specific place; (*inf*) a pub serving a particular district.—**locally** *adv*.

**locality** *n* a neighbourhood or a district; a particular scene, position, or place; the fact or condition of having a location in space and time.

**locate** *vt* to determine or indicate the position of something; to set in or assign to a particular position.

**location** *n* a specific position or place; a locating or being located; a place outside a studio where a film is (partly) shot; (*comput*) an area in memory where a single item of data is stored.

**loch** *n* (*Scot*) a lake.

**lock**[1] *n* a fastening device on doors, etc, operated by a key or combination; part of a canal, dock, etc in which the level of the water can be changed by the operation of gates; the part of a gun by which the charge is fired; a controlling hold, as used in wrestling. • *vt* to fasten with a lock; to shut; to fit, link; to jam together so as to make immovable. • *vi* to become locked; to interlock.

**lock**[2] *n* a curl of hair; a tuft of wool, etc.

**locker** *n* a small cupboard, chest, etc that can be locked, esp one for storing possessions in a public place.

**locket** *n* a small ornamental case, usu holding a lock of hair, photograph or other memento, hung from the neck.

**lockjaw** *n* tetanus.

**locomotive** *n* an electric, steam, or diesel engine on wheels, designed to move a railway train. • *adj* of locomotion.

**locust** *n* a type of large grasshopper often travelling in swarms and destroying crops; a type of hardwooded leguminous tree.

**lodge** *n* a small house at the entrance to a park or stately home; a country house for seasonal leisure activities;

a resort hotel or motel; the local chapter or hall of a fraternal society; a beaver's lair. • *vt* to house temporarily; to shoot, thrust, etc firmly (in); to bring before legal authorities; to confer upon. • *vi* to live in a place for a time; to live as a paying guest; to come to rest and stick firmly (in).

**lodger** *n* a person who lives in a rented room in another's home.

**lodging** *n* a temporary residence; (*pl*) accommodation rented in another's house.

**loft** *n* a space under a roof; a storage area under the roof of a barn or stable; a gallery in a church or hall. • *vt* to send into a high curve.

**lofty** *adj* (**loftier, loftiest**) (*objects*) of a great height, elevated; (*person*) noble, haughty, superior in manner.—**loftily** *adv*.—**loftiness** *n*.

**log** *n* a section of a felled tree; a device for ascertaining the speed of a ship; a record of speed, progress, etc, esp one kept on a ship's voyage or aircraft's flight. • *vb* (*pt* **logged**) *vt* to record in a log; to sail or fly (a specified distance). • *vi* (*with* **on, off**) (*comput*) to establish or disestablish communication with a mainframe computer from a remote terminal in a multi-user system.—**logger** *n*.

**logbook** *n* an official record of a ship's or aircraft's voyage or flight; an official document containing details of a vehicle's registration.

**logic** *n* correct reasoning, or the science of this; way of reasoning; what is expected by the working of cause and effect.—**logician** *n*.

**logical** *adj* conforming to the rules of logic; capable of reasoning according to logic.—**logically** *adv*.—**logicality** *n*.

**logistics** *n* (*used as sing*) the science of the organization, transport and supply of military forces; the planning and organization of any complex activity.—**logistic** *adj*.

**loin** *n* (*usu pl*) the lower part of the back between the hipbones and the ribs; the front part of the hindquarters of an animal used for food.

**loiter** *vi* to linger or stand about aimlessly.—**loiterer** *n*.

**loll** *vi* to lean or recline in a lazy manner, to lounge; (*tongue*) to hang loosely.

**lollipop** *n* a flat boiled sweet at the end of a stick.

**lone** *adj* by oneself; isolated; without companions, solitary.

**lonely** *adj* (**lonelier, loneliest**) isolated; unhappy at being alone; (*places*) remote, rarely visited.

**loner** *n* a person who avoids the company of others.

**long**[1] *adj* measuring much in space or time; having a greater than usual length, quantity, etc; tedious, slow; far-reaching; well-supplied. • *adv* for a long time; from start to finish; at a remote time.

**long**[2] *vi* to desire earnestly, esp for something not likely to be attained.

**long-distance** *adj* travelling or communicating over long distances.

**longhand** *n* ordinary handwriting, as opposed to shorthand.

**longing** *n* an intense desire.

**longitude** *n* distance east or west of the prime meridian, expressed in degrees or time.

**long jump** *n* an athletic event consisting of a horizontal running jump.

**long-playing** *adj* of or relating to an LP record.

**long-range** *adj* reaching over a long distance or period of time.

**long-sighted** *adj* only seeing distant objects clearly.

**long-standing** *adj* having continued for a long time.

**long-suffering** *adj* enduring pain, provocation, etc patiently.

**long-term** *adj* of or extending over a long time.

**long wave** *n* a radio wave of a frequency less than 300 kHz.

**long-winded** *adj* speaking or writing at great length; tiresome.

**loo** *n* (*inf*) a lavatory.

**look** *vi* to try to see; to see; to search; to appear, seem; to be facing in a specified direction; (*with* **in**) to pay a brief visit; (*with* **up**) to improve in prospects. • *vt* to direct one's eyes on; to have an appearance befitting. • *n* the act of looking; a gaze, glance; appearance; aspect; (*with* **after**) to take care of; (*with* **over**) to examine; (*with* **up**) to research (for information, etc) in book; to visit.

**look-alike** *n* a person that looks like another.

**lookout** *n* a place for keeping watch; a person assigned to watch.

**loom**[1] *n* a machine or frame for weaving yarn or thread. • *vt* to weave on a loom.

**loom**[2] *vi* to come into view indistinctly and often threateningly; to come ominously close, as an impending event.

**loop** *n* a figure made by a curved line crossing itself; a similar rounded shape in cord, rope, etc crossed on itself; anything forming this figure; (*comput*) a set of instructions in a program that are executed repeatedly; an intrauterine contraceptive device; a segment of film or magnetic tape. • *vt* to make a loop of; to fasten with a loop. • *vi* to form a loop or loops.

**loophole** *n* a means of evading an obligation, etc; a slit in a wall for looking or shooting through.

**loose** *adj* free from confinement or restraint; not firmly fastened; not tight or compact; not precise; inexact; (*inf*) relaxed. • *vt* to release; to unfasten; to untie; to detach; (*bullet*) to discharge. • *vi* to become loose.—**loosely** *adv*.—**looseness** *n*.

**loosen** *vti* to make or become loose or looser.

**loot** *n* goods taken during warfare, civil unrest, etc; (*sl*) money. • *vti* to plunder, pillage.—**looter** *n*.

**lop** *vt* (*pt* **lopped**) to sever the branches or twigs from a tree; to cut off or out as superfluous.

**lopsided** *adj* having one side larger in weight, height, or size than the other; badly balanced.

**lord** *n* a ruler, master or monarch; a male member of the nobility; (*with cap and* **the**) God; a form of address used to certain peers, bishops and judges.

**lordly** *adj* (**lordlier**, **lordliest**) noble; haughty; arrogant.

**lordship** *n* the rank or authority of a lord; rule, dominion; (*with* **his** *or* **your**) a title used in speaking of or to a lord.

**lore** *n* knowledge; learning, esp of a traditional nature; a particular body of tradition.

**lorry** *n* a large motor vehicle for transporting heavy loads, a truck.

**lose** *vb* (*pt* **lost**) *vt* to have taken from one by death, accident, removal, etc; to be unable to find; to fail to keep, as one's temper; to fail to see, hear, or understand; to fail to have, get, etc; to fail to win; to cause the loss of; to wander from (one's way, etc); to squander. • *vi* to suffer (a) loss.—**loser** *n*.

**loss** *n* a losing or being lost; the damage, trouble caused by losing; the person, thing, or amount lost.

**lost** *adj* no longer possessed; missing; not won; destroyed or ruined; having wandered astray; wasted.

**lot** *n* an object, such as a straw, slip of paper, etc drawn from others at random to reach a decision by chance; the decision thus arrived at; one's share by lot; fortune; a plot of ground; a group of persons or things; an item or set of items put up for auction; (*often pl*) (*inf*) a great amount; much; (*inf*) sort.

**loth** *see* **loath**.

**lotion** *n* a liquid for cosmetic or external medical use.

**lottery** *n* a system of raising money by selling numbered tickets that offer the chance of winning a prize; an enterprise, etc which may or may not succeed.

**loud** *adj* characterized by or producing great noise; emphatic; (*inf*) obtrusive or flashy.—**loudly** *adv*.—**loudness** *n*.

**loudspeaker** *n* a device for converting electrical energy into sound.

**lounge** *vi* to move, sit, lie, etc in a relaxed way; to spend time idly. • *n* a room with comfortable furniture for sitting, as a waiting room at an airport, etc; a comfortable sitting room in a hotel or private house.

**louse** *n* (*pl* **lice**) any of various small wingless insects that are parasitic on humans and animals; any similar but unrelated insects that are parasitic on plants; (*inf*) (*pl* **louses**) a mean, contemptible person.

**lousy** *adj* (**lousier, lousiest**) infested with lice; (*sl*) disgusting, of poor quality, or inferior; (*sl*) well supplied (with).

**lout** *n* a clumsy, rude person.—**loutish** *adj*.

**lovable, loveable** *adj* easy to love or feel affection for.

**love** *n* a strong liking for someone or something; a passionate affection for another person; the object of such affection; (*tennis*) a score of zero. • *vti* to feel love (for).

**love affair** *n* a romantic or sexual relationship between two people.

**lovely** *adj* (**lovelier, loveliest**) beautiful; (*inf*) highly enjoyable.—**loveliness** *n*.

**lover** *n* a person in love with another person; a person, esp a man, having an extramarital sexual relationship; (*pl*) a couple in love with each other; someone who loves a specific person or thing.

**loving** *adj* affectionate.—**lovingly** *adv*.

**low**[1] *n* the sound a cow makes, a moo. • *vi* to make this sound.

**low**[2] *adj* not high or tall; below the normal level; less in size, degree, amount, etc, than usual; deep in pitch; depressed in spirits; humble, of low rank; vulgar, coarse; not loud. • *adv* in or to a low degree, level, etc. • *n* a low level, degree, etc; a region of low barometric pressure.

**loyal** *adj* firm in allegiance to a person, cause, country, party, etc, faithful; demonstrating unswerving allegiance.—**loyally** *adv*.—**loyalty** *n*.

**lozenge** *n* a four-sided diamond-shaped figure; a cough drop, sweet, etc, originally diamond-shaped.

**LP** *n* a long-playing record, usu 12 inches (30.5 cm) in diameter and played at a speed of 33.33 revolutions per minute.

**Ltd** *abbr* = limited liability (used by private companies only).

**lubricant** *n* a substance that lubricates.

**lubricate** *vt* to coat or treat (machinery, etc) with oil or grease to lessen friction; to make smooth, slippery, or greasy. • *vi* to act as a lubricant.—**lubrication** *n*.—**lubricator** *n*.

**lucid** *adj* easily understood; sane.—**lucidly** *adv*.—**lucidity** *n*.

**luck** *n* chance; good fortune.

**lucky** *adj* (**luckier, luckiest**) having or bringing good luck.—**luckily** *adv*.

**lucrative** *adj* producing wealth or profit; profitable.—**lucrativeness** *n*.

**ludicrous** adj absurd, laughable.—**ludicrously** adv.

**lug**[1] vt (pt **lugged**) to pull or drag along with effort.

**lug**[2] n an ear-like projection by which a thing is held or supported.

**luggage** n the suitcases and other baggage containing the possessions of a traveller.

**lukewarm** adj barely warm, tepid; lacking enthusiasm.

**lull** vt to soothe, to calm; to calm the suspicions of, esp by deception. • n a short period of calm.

**lullaby** n a song to lull children to sleep.

**lumbago** n rheumatic pain in the lower back.

**lumber**[1] n timber, logs, beams, boards, etc, roughly cut and prepared for use; articles of unused household furniture that are stored away; any useless articles. • vi to cut down timber and saw it into lumber. • vt to clutter with lumber; to heap in disorder.

**lumber**[2] vi to move heavily or clumsily.

**lumberjack** n a person employed to fell trees and transport and prepare timber.

**luminous** adj emitting light; glowing in the dark, clear, easily understood.

**lump** n a small, compact mass of something, usu without definite shape; an abnormal swelling; a dull or stupid person. • adj in a lump or lumps. • vt to treat or deal with in a mass. • vi to become lumpy.

**lumpy** adj (**lumpier**, **lumpiest**) filled or covered with lumps.—**lumpily** adv.—**lumpiness** n.

**lunacy** n insanity; utter folly.

**lunar** adj of or like the moon.

**lunatic** adj insane; utterly foolish. • n an insane person.

**lunch** n a light meal, esp between breakfast and dinner. • vi to eat lunch.

**luncheon** n lunch, esp a formal lunch.

**luncheon voucher** n a voucher, issued to an employee in addition to pay, that can be exchanged for food in certain restaurants.

**lung** n either of the two sponge-like breathing organs in the chest of vertebrates.

**lunge** n a sudden forceful thrust, as with a sword; a sudden plunge forward. • vti to move, or cause to move, with a lunge.

**lurch** vi to lean or pitch suddenly to the side.—also n.

**lure** n something that attracts, tempts or entices; a brightly coloured fishing bait; a device used to recall a trained hawk; a decoy for wild animals. • vt to entice, attract, or tempt.

**lurid** adj vivid, glaring; shocking; sensational.—**luridly** adv.—**luridness** n.

**lurk** vi to lie hidden in wait; to loiter furtively.

**luscious** adj delicious; richly sweet; delighting any of the senses.—**lusciously** adv.—**lusciousness** n.

**lush**[1] adj tender and juicy; of or showing abundant growth.—**lushly** adv.—**lushness** n.

**lush**[2] n (sl) an alcoholic.

**lust** n strong sexual desire (for); an intense longing for something. • vi to feel lust.—**lustful** adj.—**lustfully** adv.

**lustre, luster** (US) n gloss; sheen; brightness; radiance; brilliant beauty or fame; glory.—**lustrous** adj.

**lusty** adj (**lustier**, **lustiest**) strong; vigorous; healthy.—**lustily** adv.—**lustiness** n.

**lute** n an old-fashioned stringed instrument.

**luxuriant** adj profuse, abundant; ornate; fertile.—**luxuriance** n.

**luxurious** adj constituting luxury; indulging in luxury; rich, comfortable.—**luxuriously** adv.—**luxuriousness** n.

**luxury** *n* indulgence and pleasure in sumptuous and expensive food, accommodation, clothes, etc; (*often pl*) something that is costly and enjoyable but not indispensable. • *adj* relating to or supplying luxury.

**lying** *see* **lie**[1], **lie**[2].

**lynch** *vt* to murder (an accused person) by mob action, without lawful trial, as by hanging.

**lynx** *n* (*pl* **lynxes, lynx**) a wild feline of Europe and North America with spotted fur.

**lyre** *n* an ancient musical instrument of the harp family.

**lyric** *adj* denoting or of poetry expressing the writer's emotion; of, or having a high voice with a light, flexible quality. • *n* a lyric poem; (*pl*) the words of a popular song.

**lyrical** *adj* lyric; (*inf*) expressing rapture or enthusiasm.

# M

**m** *abbr* = metre(s); mile(s); million(s).

**MA** *abbr* = Master of Arts; Massachusetts.

**mac, mack** *n* (*inf*) mackintosh.

**macaroni** *n* pasta in the form of tubes.

**mace**[1] *n* a staff used as a symbol of authority by certain institutions.

**mace**[2] *n* an aromatic spice made from the external covering of the nutmeg.

**machine** *n* a structure of fixed and moving parts, for doing useful work; an organization functioning like a machine; the controlling group in a political party; a device, as the lever, etc that transmits, or changes the application of energy. • *vt* to shape or finish by machine-operated tools. • *adj* of machines; done by machinery.

**machine gun** *n* an automatic gun, firing a rapid stream of bullets.—*also vt.*

**machinery** *n* machines collectively; the parts of a machine; the framework for keeping something going.

**machinist** *n* one who makes, repairs, or operates machinery.

**mackerel** *n* (*pl* **mackerel, mackerels**) a common oily food fish.

**mackintosh, macintosh** *n* a waterproof raincoat.

**mad** *adj* (**madder, maddest**) insane; frantic; foolish and rash; infatuated; (*inf*) angry.

**madam** *n* a polite term of address to a woman; a woman in charge of a brothel; (*inf*) a precocious little girl.

**madden** *vti* to make or become insane, angry, or wildly excited.—**maddening** *adj.*—**maddeningly** *adv.*

**made** *see* **make**

**made-to-measure** *adj* (*garment*) made according to the customers individual measurements or requirements.

**madly** *adv* in an insane manner; at great speed, force; (*inf*) excessively.

**madman** *n* an insane person.—**madwoman** *nf.*

**madness** *n* insanity; foolishness; excitability.

**magazine** *n* a military store; a space where explosives are stored, as in a fort; a supply chamber, as in a camera, a rifle, etc; a periodical publication containing articles, fiction, photographs, etc.

**magenta** *n* a purplish-red dye; purplish red.—*also adj.*

**maggot** *n* a wormlike larva, as of the housefly.—**maggoty** *adj.*

**magic** *n* the use of charms, spells, etc to supposedly influence events by supernatural means; any mysterious power; the art of producing illusions by sleight of hand, etc. • *adj* of or relating to magic; possessing supposedly supernatural powers; (*inf*) wonderful. • *vt* (*pt* **magicked**) to influence, produce or take (away) by or as if by magic.—**magical** *adj*.—**magically** *adv*.

**magician** *n* one skilled in magic; a conjurer.

**magistrate** *n* a public officer empowered to administer the law.

**magnanimous** *adj* noble and generous in conduct or spirit, not petty.— **magnanimously** *adv*.

**magnate** *n* a very wealthy or influential person.

**magnet** *n* any piece of iron or steel that has the property of attracting iron; anything that attracts.

**magnetic** *adj* of magnetism or a magnet; producing or acting by magnetism; having the ability to attract or charm people.—**magnetically** *adv*.

**magnetism** *n* the property, quality, or condition of being magnetic; the force to which this is due; personal charm.

**magnification** *n* magnifying or being magnified; the degree of enlargement of something by a lens, microscope, etc.

**magnificent** *adj* splendid, stately or sumptuous in appearance; superb, of very high quality.—**magnificence** *n*.—**magnificently** *adv*.

**magnify** *vt* to exaggerate; to increase the apparent size of (an object) as (with) a lens.—**magnifier** *n*.

**magnitude** *n* greatness of size, extent, etc; importance; (*astron*) the apparent brightness of a star.

**magnolia** *n* a spring-flowering shrub or tree with evergreen or deciduous leaves and showy flowers.

**magpie** *n* a black and white bird of the crow family; a person who chatters; an acquisitive person.

**mahogany** *n* the hard, reddish-brown wood of a tropical tree; a reddish-brown colour.

**maid** *n* a maiden; a woman servant.

**maiden** *n* a girl or young unmarried woman. • *adj* unmarried or virgin; untried; first; (*cricket*) (*over*) without runs.—**maidenhood** *n*.—**maidenliness** *n*.—**maidenly** *adv*.

**maiden name** *n* the surname of a woman before marriage.

**mail**[1] *n* a body armour made of small metal rings or links.

**mail**[2] *n* letters, packages, etc transported and delivered by the post office; a postal system. • *vt* to send by mail.

**mail order** *n* an order for goods to be sent by post.

**maim** *vt* to cripple; to mutilate.

**main** *adj* chief in size, importance, etc; principal. • *n* (*often pl but used a sing*) a principal pipe in a distribution system for water, gas, etc; the essential point.

**mainland** *n* the principal land mass of a continent, as distinguished from nearby islands.

**maintain** *vt* to preserve; to support, to sustain; to keep in good condition; to affirm.—**maintainable** *adj*.

**maintenance** *n* upkeep; (*financial*) support, esp of a spouse after a divorce.

**maisonette** *n* a small house; self-contained living quarters, usu on two floors with its own entrance, as part of a larger house.

**maize** *n* corn; a light yellow colour.

**majestic** *adj* dignified; imposing.— **majestically** *adv*.

**majesty** *n* grandeur; (*with cap*) a title used in speaking to or of a sovereign.

**major** *adj* greater in size, importance, amount, etc; (*surgery*) very serious, life-threatening; (*mus*) higher than the corresponding minor by half a tone. • *vi* to specialize (in a field of study). • *n* in US, an officer rank-ing just above a captain, in UK, a lieutenant-colonel; (*mus*) a major key, chord or scale.

**majority** *n* the greater number or part of; the excess of the larger number of votes cast for a candidate in an election; full legal age; the military rank of a major.

**make** *vb* (*pt* **made**) *vt* to cause to ex-ist, occur, or appear; to build, cre-ate, produce, manufacture, etc; to prepare for use; to amount to; to have the qualities of; to acquire, earn; to understand; to do, execute; to cause or force; to arrive at, reach; (*with* **believe**) to imagine, pretend; (*with* **good**) to make up for, pay compen-sation; (*with* **out**) to write out; to complete (a form, etc) in writing; to attempt to understand; to discern, identify; (*with* **up**) to invent, fabri-cate, esp to deceive; to prepare; to make complete; to put together; to settle differences between. • *vi* (*with* **do**) to manage with what is available; (*with* **for**) to go in the di-rection of; to bring about; (*with* **good**) to become successful or wealthy; (*with* **off**) to leave in haste; (*with* **out**) to pretend; to fare, manage; (*with* **up**) to become reconciled; to compensate for; to put on make-up for the stage. • *n* style, brand, or origin; manner of production.—**maker** *n*.

**make-believe** *adj* imagined, pre-tended.—*also n.*

**makeshift** *adj* being a temporary sub-stitute.—*also n.*

**make-up** *n* the cosmetics, etc used by an actor; cosmetics generally; the way something is put together, com-position; nature, disposition.

**making** *n* the act or process of mak-ing, creation; (*pl*) earnings; (*pl*) po-tential; (*pl*) (*sl*) the materials for roll-ing a cigarette.

**maladjusted** *adj* poorly adjusted, esp

to the social environment.—**malad-justment** *n*.

**malaise** *n* a feeling of discomfort or of uneasiness.

**malaria** *n* an infectious disease caused by mosquito bites, and characterized by recurring attacks of fevers and chills.—**malarial** *adj*.

**male** *adj* denoting or of the sex that fertilizes the ovum; of, like, or suit-able for men and boys; masculine. • *n* a male person, animal or plant.

**malevolent** *adj* ill-disposed towards others; spiteful, malicious.—**ma-levolence** *n*.—**malevolently** *adv*.

**malfunction** *n* faulty functioning. • *vi* to function wrongly.

**malice** *n* active ill will, intention to inflict injury upon another.—**malicious** *adj*.—**maliciously** *adv*.—**maliciousness** *n*.

**malign** *adj* harmful; evil. • *vt* to slan-der; to defame.—**malignity** *n*.—**malignly** *adv*.

**malignant** *adj* having a wish to harm others; injurious; (*disease*) rapidly spreading, resistant to treatment, esp of a tumour.—**malignancy** *n*.—**malignantly** *adv*.

**malinger** *vi* to feign illness in order to evade work, duty.—**malingerer** *n*.

**malleable** *adj* pliable; capable of be-ing shaped.—**malleability** *n*.

**mallet** *n* a small, usu wooden-headed, short-handled hammer; a long-han-dled version for striking the ball in the games of polo and croquet.

**malnutrition** *n* lack of nutrition.

**malpractice** *n* professional miscon-duct, esp by a medical practitioner.

**malt** *n* a cereal grain, such as barley, which is soaked and dried and used in brewing; (*inf*) malt liquor, malt whisky.—**malty** *adj*.

**mammal** *n* any member of a class of warm-blooded vertebrates that suckle their young with milk.—**mam-malian** *adj*.

**mammoth** *n* an extinct elephant with long, curved tusks. • *adj* enormous.

**man** *n* (*pl* **men**) a human being, esp an adult male; the human race; an adult male with manly qualities, eg courage, virility; a male servant; an individual person; a person with specific qualities for a task, etc; an ordinary soldier, as opposed to an officer; a member of a team, etc; a piece in games such as chess, draughts, etc; a husband. • *vt* (*pt* **manned**) to provide with men for work, defence, etc.

**manage** *vt* to control the movement or behaviour of; to have charge of; to direct; to succeed in accomplishing. • *vi* to carry on business; to contrive to get along.—**manageable** *adj*.

**management** *n* those carrying out the administration of a business; the managers collectively; the technique of managing or controlling.

**manager** *n* a person who manages a company, organization, etc; an agent who looks after the business affairs of an actor, writer, etc; a person who organizes the training of a sports team; a person who manages efficiently.—**managerial** *adj*.—**managerially** *adv*.

**manageress** *n* a woman who manages a business, shop, etc.

**managing** *adj* administering; controlling; having authority.

**mandarin** *n* (*formerly*) a high-ranking bureaucrat of the Chinese empire; any high-ranking official, esp one given to pedantic sometimes obscure public pronouncements; (*with cap*) the Beijing dialect that is the official pronunciation of the Chinese language; the fruit of a small spiny Chinese tree that has been developed in cultivation (—*also* **tangerine**).

**mandate** *n* an order or command; the authority to act on the behalf of another, esp the will of constituents ex-

pressed to their representatives in legislatures. • *vt* to entrust by mandate.

**mandatory** *adj* compulsory.

**mandolin, mandoline** *n* a stringed instrument similar to a lute, with four or five pairs of strings.

**mane** *n* long hair that grows on the back of the neck of the horse, lion, etc.

**manful** *adj* showing courage and resolution.—**manfully** *adv*.

**mangle**[1] *vt* to crush, mutilate; to spoil, ruin.

**mangle**[2] *n* a machine for drying and pressing sheets, etc between rollers. • *vt* to smooth through a mangle.

**mango** *n* (*pl* **mangoes**) a yellow-red fleshy tropical fruit with a firm central stone.

**mangy** *adj* (**mangier, mangiest**) having mange; scruffy, shabby.—**manginess** *n*.

**manhandle** *vt* to handle roughly; to move by human force.

**manhole** *n* a hole through which one can enter a sewer, drain, etc.

**manhood** *n* the state or time of being a man; virility; courage, etc.

**manhunt** *n* a hunt for a fugitive.—**manhunter** *n*.

**mania** *n* a mental disorder displaying sometimes violent behaviour and great excitement; great excitement or enthusiasm; a craze.

**maniac** *n* a madman; a person with wild behaviour; a person with great enthusiasm for something.—**maniacal** *adj*.

**manicure** *n* trimming, polishing etc of fingernails.—*also vt*.—**manicurist** *n*.

**manifest** *adj* obvious, clearly evident. • *vt* to make clear; to display, to reveal. • *n* a list of a ship's or aircraft's cargo; a list of passengers on an aircraft.—**manifestation** *n*.—**manifestly** *adv*.

**manifesto** *n* (*pl* **manifestoes, manifestos**) a public printed declaration of intent and policy issued by a government or political party.

**manipulate** vt to work or handle skilfully; to manage shrewdly or artfully, often in an unfair way.—**manipulation** n.—**manipulative** adj.—**manipulator** n.

**mankind** n the human race.

**manly** adj (**manlier, manliest**) appropriate in character to a man; strong; virile.—**manliness** n.

**man-made** adj manufactured or created by man; artificial, synthetic.

**manner** n a method of way of doing something; behaviour; type or kind; habit; (pl) polite social behaviour.—**mannerly** adj.

**mannerism** n an idiosyncracy.

**manoeuvre, maneuver** (US) n a planned and controlled movement of troops, warships, etc; a skilful or shrewd move; a stratagem. • vti to perform or cause to perform manoeuvres; to manage or plan skilfully; to move, get, make, etc by some scheme.—**manoeuvrable** adj.,

**manor** n a landed estate; the main house on such an estate; (sl) a police district.—**manorial** adj.

**manpower** n power furnish ed by human strength; the collective availability for work of people in a given area.

**mansion** n a large, imposing house.

**manslaughter** n the killing of a human being by another, esp when unlawful but without malice.

**mantel** n the facing above a fireplace; the shelf above a fireplace.—*also* **mantelpiece, mantelshelf**.

**manual** adj of the hands; operated, done, or used by the hand; involving physical skill or hard work rather than the mind. • n a handy book for use as a guide, reference, etc; a book of instructions.—**manually** adv.

**manufacture** vt to make, esp on a large scale, using machinery; to invent, fabricate. • n the production of goods by manufacturing.—**manufacturer** n.

**manure** n animal dung used to fertilize soil. • vt to spread manure on.

**manuscript** n a book or document that is handwritten or typewritten as opposed to printed; an author's original handwritten or typewritten copy as submitted to a publisher before typesetting and printing.

**many** adj numerous. • n a large number of persons or things.

**map** n a representation of all or part of the earth's surface, showing either natural features as continents and seas, etc or man-made features as roads, railroads etc. • vt (pt **mapped**) to make a map of.

**maple** n a tree with two-winged fruits, grown for shade, wood, or sap; its hard light-coloured wood; the flavour of the syrup or sugar made from the sap of the sugar maple.

**mar** vt (pt **marred**) to blemish, to spoil, to impair.

**marathon** n a foot race of 26 miles, 385 yards (42.195 km); any endurance contest.

**maraud** vi to roam in search of plunder.—**marauder** n.—**marauding** adj.

**marble** n a hard limestone rock that takes a high polish; a block or work of art made of marble; a little ball of stone, glass, etc; (pl) a children's game played with such balls; (pl) (sl) wits. • adj of or like marble.

**March** n the third month of the year having 31 days.

**march** vi to walk with regular steps, as in military formation; to advance steadily. • vt to make a person or group march. • n a steady advance; a regular, steady step; the distance covered in marching; a piece of music for marching.

**mare** *n* a mature female horse, mule, donkey.

**margarine** *n* a butter substitute made from vegetable and animal fats, etc.

**margin** *n* a border, edge; the blank border of a printed or written page; an amount beyond what is needed; provision for increase, error, etc; (*commerce*) the difference between cost and selling price.

**marginal** *adj* written in the margin; situated at the margin or border; close to the lower limit of acceptability; very slight, insignificant; (*British politics*) denoting a constituency where the sitting MP has only a small majority. • *n* a marginal constituency.—**marginally** *adv*.

**marigold** *n* a plant with a yellow or orange flower.

**marijuana, marihuana** *n* a narcotic obtained by smoking the dried flowers and leaves of the hemp plant.—*also* **cannabis, pot.**

**marina** *n* a small harbour with docks, services, etc for pleasure craft.

**marine** *adj* of, in, near, or relating to the sea; maritime; nautical; naval. • *n* a soldier trained for service on land or sea; naval or merchant ships.

**marital** *adj* of marriage, matrimonial.

**maritime** *adj* on, near, or living near the sea; of navigation, shipping, etc.

**mark**[1] *n* a spot, scratch, etc on a surface; a distinguishing sign or characteristic; a cross made instead of a signature; a printed or written symbol, as a punctuation mark; a brand or label on an article showing the maker, etc; an indication of some quality, character, etc; a grade for academic work; a standard of quality; impression, influence, etc; a target; (*sl*) a potential victim for a swindle. • *vt* to make a mark or marks on; to identify as by a mark; to show plainly; to heed; to grade, rate; (*Brit football*) to stay close to an opponent so as to hinder his play.

**mark**[2] *n* the basic monetary unit of Germany.

**marked** *adj* having a mark or marks; noticeable; obvious.—**markedly** *adv*.

**marker** *n* one that marks; something used for marking.

**market** *n* a meeting of people for buying and selling merchandise; a space or building in which a market is held; the chance to sell or buy; demand for (goods, etc); a region where goods can be sold; a section of the community offering demand for goods. • *vti* to offer for sale; to sell, buy domestic provisions.—**marketability** *n*.—**marketable** *adj*.

**marketing** *n* act of buying or selling; all the processes involved in moving goods from the producer to the consumer.

**marksman** *n* one who is skilled at shooting.—**marksmanship** *n*.

**marmalade** *n* a jam-like preserve made from oranges, sugar and water.

**maroon**[1] *n* a dark brownish red (—*also adj*); a type of distress rocket.

**maroon**[2] *vt* to abandon alone, esp on a desolate island; to leave helpless and alone.

**marquee** *n* a large tent used for entertainment; a canopy over an entrance, as to a theatre.

**marquess** *n* (*UK*) a title of nobility ranking between a duke and an earl.

**marquis** *n* (*Europe*) a nobleman equivalent in rank to a British marquess.

**marriage** *n* the legal contract by which a woman and man become wife and husband; a wedding, either religious or civil; a close union.—**marriageable** *adj*.

**marrow** *n* the fatty tissue in the cavities of bones; the best part or essence of anything; a widely grown green fruit eaten as a vegetable.

**marry** vt to join as wife and husband; to take in marriage; to unite. • vi to get married.

**marsh** n an area of boggy, poorly drained land.—**marshiness** n.—**marshy** adj.

**marshal** n in some armies, a general officer of the highest rank; an official in charge of ceremonies, parades, etc. • vt (pt **marshalled**) (ideas, troops) to arrange in order; to guide.

**martial** adj warlike; military.—**martially** adv.

**martial law** n rule by military authorities over civilians, as during a war or political emergency.

**martyr** n a person tortured for a belief or cause; a person who suffers from an illness. • vt to kill as a martyr; to make a martyr of.—**martyrdom** n.

**marvel** n anything wonderful; a miracle. • vti (pt **marvelled**) to become filled with wonder, surprise, etc.—**marvellous** adj.

**Marxism** n the theory and practice developed by Karl Marx and Friedrich Engels advocating public ownership of the means of production and the dictatorship of the proletariat until the establishment of a classless society.—**Marxist** adj, n.

**marzipan** n a paste made from ground almonds, sugar and egg white, used to coat cakes or make confectionery.

**mascara** n a cosmetic for darkening the eyelashes.

**mascot** n a person, animal or thing thought to bring good luck.

**masculine** adj having characteristics of or appropriate to the male sex; (gram) of the male gender.—**masculinity** n.

**mask** n a covering to conceal or protect the face; a moulded likeness of the face; anything that conceals or disguises; a respirator placed over the nose and mouth to aid or prevent inhalation of a gas; (surgery) a protective gauze placed over the nose and mouth to prevent the spread of germs; (photog) a screen used to cover part of a sensitive surface to prevent exposure by light. • vt to cover or conceal as with a mask; to disguise one's intentions or character.—**masked** adj.

**mason** n a person skilled in working or building with stone; (with cap) a Freemason.

**masonry** n stonework.

**masquerade** n a ball or party at which fancy dress and masks are worn; a pretence, false show. • vi to take part in a masquerade; to pretend to be what one is not.—**masquerader** n.

**mass** n a quantity of matter of indefinite shape and size; a large quantity or number; bulk; size; the main part; (physics) the property of a body expressed as a measure of the amount of material contained in it; (pl) the common people, esp the lower social classes; (with cap) The celebration of the Eucharist. • adj of or for the masses or for a large number. • vti to gather or form into a mass.

**massacre** n the cruel and indiscriminate killing of many people or animals. • vt to kill in large numbers.

**massage** n a kneading and rubbing of the muscles to stimulate the circulation of the blood. • vt to give a massage to.

**masseur** n a man who gives a massage professionally.—**masseuse** nf.

**massive** adj big, solid, or heavy; large and imposing; relatively large in comparison to normal; extensive.—**massively** adv.—**massiveness** n.

**mass media** npl newspapers, radio, television, and other means of communication with large numbers of people.

**mast** *n* a tall vertical pole used to support the sails on a ship; a vertical pole from which a flag is flown; a tall structure supporting a television or radio aerial.

**master** *n* a man who rules others or has control over something, esp the head of a household; an employer; an owner of an animal or slave; the captain of a merchant ship; a male teacher in a private school; an expert craftsman; a writer or painter regarded as great; an original from which a copy can be made, esp a phonograph record or magnetic tape; (*with cap*) a title for a boy; one holding an advanced academic degree. • *adj* being a master; chief; main; controlling. • *vt* to be for become master of; (*in art, etc*) to become expert.

**masterly** *adj* expert; skilful.— **masterliness** *n*.

**mastermind** *n* a very clever person, esp one who plans or directs a project. • *vt* to be the mastermind of.

**masterpiece** *n* a work done with extraordinary skill; the greatest work of a person or group.

**mastery** *n* control as by a master; victory; expertise.

**masturbate** *vi* to manually stimulate one's sexual organs to achieve orgasm without sexual intercourse.— **masturbation** *n*.

**mat**[1] *n* a piece of material of woven fibres, etc, used for protection, as under a vase, etc, or on the floor; a thick pad used in wrestling, gymnastics, etc; anything interwoven or tangled into a thick mass. • *vti* (*pt* **matted**) to cover as with a mat; to interweave or tangle into a thick mass.

**mat**[2] *see* **matt**.

**match**[1] *n* a thin strip of wood or cardboard tipped with a chemical that ignites under friction.

**match**[2] *n* any person or thing equal or similar to another; two persons or things that go well together; a contest or game; a mating or marriage. • *vt* to join in marriage; to put in opposition (with, against); to be equal or similar to; (*one thing*) to suit to another. • *vi* to be equal, similar, suitable, etc.

**matchbox** *n* a small box for holding matches.

**matchless** *adj* unequalled.— **matchlessly** *adv*.

**mate**[1] *n* an associate or colleague; (*inf*) a friend; one of a matched pair; a marriage partner; the male or female of paired animals; an officer of a merchant ship, ranking below the master. • *vti* to join as a pair; to couple in marriage or sexual union.

**mate**[2] *vt* to checkmate.

**material** *adj* of, derived from, or composed of matter, physical; of the body or bodily needs, comfort, etc, not spiritual; important, essential, etc. • *n* what a thing is, or may be made of; elements or parts; cloth, fabric; (*pl*) tools, etc needed to make or do something; a person regarded as fit for a particular task, position, etc.

**materialize** *vt* to give material form to. • *vi* to become fact; to make an unexpected appearance.—**materialization** *n*.

**maternal** *adj* of, like, or from a mother; related through the mother's side of the family.—**maternally** *adv*.

**maternity** *n* motherhood; motherliness. • *adj* relating to pregnancy.

**math** *n* (*inf*) mathematics.

**mathematical, mathematic** *adj* of, like or concerned with mathematics; exact and precise.—**mathematically** *adv*.

**mathematics** *n* (*used as sing*) the

science dealing with quantities, forms, space, etc and their relationships by the use of numbers and symbols; (*sing or pl*) the mathematical operations or processes used in a particular problem, discipline, etc.—**mathematician** *n*.

**maths** *n* (*used as sing or pl*) (*inf*) mathematics.

**matinée** *n* an afternoon performance of a play, etc.

**matriarch** *n* a woman who heads or rules her family or tribe.—**matriarchal** *adj*.

**matriculate** *vti* to enrol, esp as a student.—**matriculation** *n*.

**matrimony** *n* the act or rite of marriage; the married state.—**matrimonial** *adj*.—**matrimonially** *adv*.

**matron** *n* a wife or widow, esp one of mature appearance and manner; a woman in charge of domestic and nursing arrangements in a school, hospital or other institution.—**matronly** *adv*.

**matt** *adj* without lustre, dull.—*also* **mat**.

**matter** *n* what a thing is made of; material; whatever occupies space and is perceptible to the senses; any specified substance; content of thought or expression; a quantity; a thing or affair; significance; trouble, difficulty; pus. • *vi* to be of importance.

**matter-of-fact** *adj* relating to facts, not opinions, imagination, etc.

**matting** *n* a coarse material, such as woven straw or hemp, used for making mats.

**mattress** *n* a casing of strong cloth filled with cotton, foam rubber, coiled springs, etc, used on a bed.

**mature** *adj* mentally and physically well-developed, grown-up; (*fruit, cheese, etc*) ripe; (*bill*) due; (*plan*) completely worked out. • *vti* to

make or become mature; to become due.—**maturely** *adv*.—**matureness** *n*.

**maturity** *n* the state of being mature; full development; the date a loan becomes due.

**maudlin** *adj* foolishly sentimental; tearfully drunk.

**maul** *vt* to bruise or lacerate; to paw.

**mausoleum** *n* a large tomb.

**mauve** *n* any of several shades of pale purple. • *adj* of this colour.

**mawkish** *adj* maudlin; insipid.—**mawkishly** *adv*.—**mawkishness** *n*.

**max.** *abbr* = maximum.

**maxim** *n* a concise rule of conduct; a precept.

**maximum** *n* (*pl* **maxima, maximums**) the greatest quantity, number, etc. • *adj* highest; greatest possible reached.

**May** *n* the fifth month of the year having 31 days.

**may** *vb aux* (*past* **might**) *expressing* possibility; permission; wish or hope.

**maybe** *adv* perhaps.

**Mayday** *n* the international radio-telephone signal indicating a ship or aircraft in distress.

**May Day** *n* the first day of May, celebrated as a traditional spring festival; observed in many countries as a labour holiday.

**mayhem** *n* violent destruction, confusion.

**mayonnaise** *n* a salad dressing made from egg yolks whisked with oil and lemon juice or vinegar.

**mayor** *n* the chief administrative officer of a municipality.

**mayoress** *n* the wife of a mayor; a female mayor.

**maze** *n* a confusing, intricate network of pathways; a confused state.

**me** *pers pron* the objective case of I.

**meadow** *n* a piece of land where grass is grown for hay; low, level, moist grassland.

**meagre, meager** (*US*) *adj* thin, emaciated; lacking in quality or quantity.—**meagrely** *adv*.—**meagreness** *n*.

**meal**[1] *n* any of the times for eating, as lunch, dinner, etc; the food served at such a time.

**meal**[2] *n* any coarsely ground edible grain; any substance similarly ground.—**mealiness** *n*.—**mealy** *adj*.

**mealy-mouthed** *adj* not outspoken and blunt; euphemistic; devious in speech.

**mean**[1] *adj* selfish, ungenerous; despicable; shabby; bad-tempered; (*sl*) difficult; (*sl*) expert.—**meanly** *adv*.—**meanness** *n*.

**mean**[2] *adj* halfway between extremes; average. • *n* what is between extremes.

**mean**[3] *vb* (*pt* **meant**) *vt* to have in mind; to intend; to intend to express; to signify. • *vi* to have a (specified) degree of importance, effect, etc.

**meander** *n* a winding path esp a labyrinth; a winding of a stream or river. • *vi* (*river*) to wind; to wander aimlessly.—**meandering** *adj*.

**meaning** *n* sense; significance; import. • *adj* significant.—**meaningful** *adj*.—**meaningless** *adj*.

**meant** *see* **mean**[1].

**meantime, meanwhile** *adv* in or during the intervening time; at the same time. • *n* the intervening time.

**measles** *n* (*used as sing*) an acute, contagious viral disease, characterized by small red spots on the skin.

**measly** *adj* (**measlier, measliest**) (*inf*) slight, worthless; having measles.

**measure** *n* the extent, dimension, capacity, etc of anything; a determining of this, measurement; a unit of measurement; any standard of valuation; an instrument for measuring; a definite quantity measured out; a course of action; a statute, law; a rhythmical unit. • *vt* to find out the extent, dimensions etc of, esp by a standard; to mark off by measuring; to be a measure of. • *vi* to be of specified measurements.—**measurable** *adj*.—**measurably** *adv*.

**measured** *adj* set or marked off by a standard; rhythmical, regular; carefully planned or considered.

**measurement** *n* a measuring or being measured; an extent or quantity determined by measuring; a system of measuring or of measures.

**meat** *n* animal flesh; food as opposed to drink; the essence of something.

**meaty** *adj* (**meatier, meatiest**) full of meat; full of substance.

**mechanic** *n* a person skilled in maintaining or operating machines, cars, etc.

**mechanical** *adj* of or using machinery or tools; produced or operated by machinery; done as if by a machine, lacking thought or emotion; of the science of mechanics.—**mechanically** *adv*.

**mechanics** *n* (*used as sing*) the science of motion and the action of forces on bodies; knowledge of machinery; (*pl*) the technical aspects of something.

**mechanism** *n* the working parts of a machine; any system of interrelated parts; any physical or mental process by which a result is produced.

**mechanize** *vt* to make mechanical; to equip with machinery or motor vehicles.—**mechanization** *n*.—**mechanized** *adj*.

**medal** *n* a small, flat piece of inscribed metal, commemorating some event or person or awarded for some distinction.

**medallion** *n* a large medal; a design, portrait, etc shaped like a medal; a medal worn on a chain around the neck.

**medallist, medalist** (*US*) *n* one awarded a medal.

**meddle** *vi* to interfere in another's affairs.—**meddler** *n.*—**meddlesome** *adj.*

**media** *see* **medium.**

**mediaeval** *see* **medieval.**

**mediate** *vt* to intervene (in a dispute); to bring about agreement. • *vi* to be in an intermediate position; to be an intermediary.—**mediation** *n.*—**mediator** *n.*

**medical** *adj* relating to the practice or study of medicine. • *n* (*inf*) a medical examination.—**medically** *adv.*

**medicine** *n* any substance used to treat or prevent disease; the science of preventing, treating or curing disease.—**medicinal** *adj.*—**medicinally** *adv.*

**medieval** *adj* of or like the Middle Ages.—also **mediaeval.**

**mediocre** *adj* average; ordinary; inferior.—**mediocrity** *n.*

**meditate** *vi* to think deeply; to reflect.—**meditative** *adj.*

**meditation** *n* the act of meditating; contemplation of spiritual or religious matters.

**Mediterranean** *n* the Mediterranean Sea. • *adj* of, or relating to (the area around) the Mediterranean Sea; denoting a subdivision of the Caucasian race characterized by a slender build and dark complexion; (*climate*) marked by hot, dry summers and warm, wet winters.

**medium** *n* (*pl* **media, mediums**) the middle state or condition; a substance for transmitting an effect; any intervening means, instrument, or agency; (*pl* **media**) a means of communicating information (eg newspapers, television, radio); (*pl* **mediums**) a person claiming to act as an intermediary between the living and the dead. • *adj* midway; average.

**medley** *n* (*pl* **medleys**) a miscellany; a musical piece made up of various tunes or passages.

**meek** *adj* patient, long-suffering; submissive.—**meekly** *adv.*—**meekness** *n.*

**meet** *vb* (*pt* **met**) *vt* to encounter, to come together; to make the acquaintance of; to contend with, deal with; to experience; to be perceived by (the eye, etc); (*demand, etc*) to satisfy; (*bill, etc*) to pay. • *vi* to come into contact with; to be introduced. • *n* a meeting to hunt or for an athletics competition.

**meeting** *n* a coming together; a gathering.

**megaphone** *n* a device to amplify and direct the voice.

**melancholy** *n* gloominess or depression; sadness. • *adj* sad; depressed.—**melancholia** *n.*—**melancholic** *adj.*

**mellow** *adj* (*fruit*) sweet and ripe; (*wine*) matured; (*colour, light, sound*) soft, not harsh; kind-hearted and understanding. • *vti* to soften through age; to mature.—**mellowness** *n.*

**melodrama** *n* a play, film, etc filled with overdramatic emotion and action; drama of this genre; sensational events or emotions.—**melodramatic** *adj.*—**melodramatically** *adv.*

**melody** *n* a tune; a pleasing series of sounds.—**melodic** *adj.*—**melodious** *adj.*

**melon** *n* the large juicy many-seeded fruit of trailing plants, as the watermelon, cantaloupe.

**melt** *vti* (*pp* **melted** *or* **molten**) to make or become liquid; to dissolve; to fade or disappear; to soften or be softened emotionally.—**melting** *adj.*—**meltingly** *adv.*

**meltdown** *n* the melting of the fuel core of a nuclear reactor; the drastic collapse of almost anything.

**melting point** *n* the temperature at which a solid melts.

**member** *n* a person belonging to a society or club; a part of a body, such as a limb; a representative in a legislative body; a distinct part of a complex whole.

**membership** *n* the state of being a member; the number of members of a body; the members collectively.

**membrane** *n* a thin pliable sheet or film; the fibrous tissue that covers or lines animal organs.—**membranous, membranaceous** *adj*.

**memento** *n* (*pl* **mementos, mementoes**) a reminder, esp a souvenir.

**memo** *n* (*pl* **memos**) a memorandum.

**memoir** *n* an historical account based on personal experience; (*pl*) an autobiographical record.

**memorable** *adj* worth remembering; easy to remember.—**memorably** *adv*.

**memorandum** *n* (*pl* **memorandums**) an informal written communication as within an office; (*pl* **memoranda**) a note to help the memory.

**memorial** *adj* serving to preserve the memory of the dead. • *n* a remembrance; a monument.

**memorize** *vt* to learn by heart, to commit to memory.—**memorization** *n*.

**memory** *n* the process of retaining and reproducing past thoughts and sensations; the sum of things remembered; an individual recollection; commemoration; remembrance; the part of a computer that stores information (—*also* **store**).

**men** *see* **man**.

**menace** *n* a threat; (*inf*) a nuisance. • *vt* to threaten.—**menacing** *adj*.—**menacingly** *adv*.

**menagerie** *n* a place where wild animals are kept for exhibition; a collection of wild animals.

**mend** *vt* to repair; (*manners, etc*) to reform, improve. • *vi* to become better. • *n* the act of mending; a repaired area in a garment, etc.

**menial** *adj* consisting of work of little skill; servile. • *n* a domestic servant; a servile person.

**meningitis** *n* inflammation of the membranes enveloping the brain or spinal cord.

**menopause** *n* the time of life during which a woman's menstrual cycle ceases permanently.—**menopausal** *adj*.

**menstruation** *n* the monthly discharge of blood from the uterus.—**menstrual** *adj*.—**menstruate** *vi*.

**mental** *adj* of, or relating to the mind; occurring or performed in the mind; having a psychiatric disorder; (*inf*) crazy, stupid.—**mentally** *adv*.

**mentality** *n* intellectual power; disposition, character.

**mention** *n* a brief reference to something in speech or writing; an official recognition or citation. • *vt* to refer to briefly; to remark; to honour officially.—**mentionable** *adj*.

**menu** *n* the list of dishes served in a restaurant; a list of options on a computer display.

**mercantile** *adj* of merchants or trade.

**mercenary** *adj* working or done for money only. • *n* a soldier hired to fight for a foreign army.

**merchandise** *n* commercial goods. • *vti* to sell, trade.

**merchant** *n* a trader; a retailer; (*sl*) a person fond of a particular activity.

**merchant navy** *n* commercial shipping.

**merciful** *adj* compassionate, humane.—**mercifulness** *n*.

**merciless** *adj* cruel, pitiless; without mercy.—**mercilessly** *adv*.—**mercilessness** *n*.

**mercury** *n* a heavy silvery liquid metallic element used in thermometers etc.

**mercy** *n* clemency; compassion; kindness; pity.

**mere** *adj* nothing more than; simple, unmixed.

**merely** *adv* simply; solely.

**merge** *vti* to blend or cause to fuse together gradually; to (cause to) combine, unite.

**merger** *n* a combining together, esp of two or more commercial organizations.

**meridian** *n* the imaginary circle on the surface of the earth passing through the north and south poles.

**meringue** *n* a mixture of egg whites beaten with sugar and baked; a small cake or shell made from this, usu filled with cream.

**merit** *n* excellence; worth; (*pl*) (*of a case*) rights and wrongs; a deserving act. • *vt* to be worthy of, to deserve.—**meritorious** *adj*.

**mermaid** *n* (*legend*) a woman with a fish's tale.

**merry** *adj* (**merrier, merriest**) cheerful; causing laughter; lively; (*inf*) slightly drunk.—**merrily** *adv*.—**merriment** *n*.

**merry-go-round** *n* a revolving platform of hobbyhorses, etc, a carousel, a roundabout.

**mesh** *n* an opening between cords of a net, wires of a screen, etc; a net; a network; a snare; (*geared wheels, etc*) engagement. • *vt* to entangle, ensnare. • *vi* to become entangled or interlocked.

**mesmerize** *vt* to hypnotize; to fascinate.

**mess** *n* a state of disorder or untidiness, esp if dirty; a muddle; an unsightly or disagreeable mixture; a portion of soft and pulpy or semi-liquid food; a building where service personnel dine; a communal meal. • *vti* to make a mess (of), bungle; to eat in company; to potter (about).

**message** *n* any spoken, written, or other form of communication; the chief idea that the writer, artist, etc seeks to communicate in a work.

**messenger** *n* a person who carries a message.

**messy** *adj* (**messier, messiest**) dirty; confused; untidy.—**messily** *adv*.—**messiness** *n*.

**met** *see* **meet**.

**metabolism** *n* the total processes in living organisms by which tissue is formed, energy produced and waste products eliminated.—**metabolic** *adj*.

**metal** *n* any of a class of chemical elements which are often lustrous, ductile solids, and are good conductors of heat, electricity, etc, such as gold, iron, copper, etc; any alloy of such elements as brass, bronze, etc; anything consisting of metal.—**metalled** *adj*.

**metallic** *adj* of, relating to, or made of metal; similar to metal.

**metallurgy** *n* the science of separating metals from their ores and preparing them for use by smelting, refining, etc.—**metallurgical** *adj*.—**metallurgist** *n*.

**metamorphosis** *n* (*pl* **metamorphoses**) a complete change of form, structure, substance, character, appearance, etc; transformation; the marked change in some animals at a stage in their growth, eg chrysalis to butterfly.—**metamorphic** *adj*.—**metamorphose** *vi*.

**metaphor** *n* a figure of speech in which a word or phrase is used for another of which it is an image.—**metaphorical** *adj*.—**metaphorically** *adv*.

**metaphysics** *n* (*used as sing*) the branch of philosophy that seeks to explain the nature of being and reality; speculative philosophy in general.—**metaphysical** *adj*.

**mete** *vt* to allot; to portion (out).

**meteor** *n* a small particle of matter which travels at great speed through space and becomes luminous through friction as it enters the earth's atmosphere; a shooting star.

**meter** *n* a device for measuring and recording a quantity of gas, water, time, etc supplied; a parking meter. • *vt* to measure using a meter.

**method** *n* the mode or procedure of accomplishing something; orderliness of thought; an orderly arrangement or system.

**methodical** *adj* orderly, systematic.— **methodically** *adv*.

**methylated spirit** *n* a form of alcohol, adulterated to render it undrinkable, used as a solvent.

**meticulous** *adj* very precise about small details.- **meticulously** *adv*.— **meticulousness** *n*.

**metre**[1], **meter** (*US*) *n* rhythmic pattern in verse, the measured arrangement of syllables according to stress; rhythmic pattern in music.

**metre**[2], **meter** (*US*) *n* the basic unit of length in the metric system, consisting of 100 centimetres and equal to 39.37 inches.

**metric** *adj* based on the metre as a standard of measurement; of, relating to, or using the metric system.

**metrical** *adj* of, relating to, or composed in rhythmic metre.

**metrication** *n* conversion of an existent system of units into the metric system.

**metric system** *n* a decimal system of weights and measures based on the metre, litre and kilogram.

**metronome** *n* an instrument that beats musical tempo.

**metropolis** *n* the main city, often a capital of a country, state, etc; any large and important city.—**metropolitan** *adj*.

**mettle** *n* courage, spirit.

**mew** *vi* (*cat*) to emit a high-pitched cry.

**mezzanine** *n* an intermediate storey between others; a theatre balcony.

**mice** *see* **mouse**.

**microbe** *n* a microscopic organism, esp a disease-causing bacterium.

**microfilm** *n* film on which documents, etc, are recorded in reduced scale. • *vt* to record on microfilm.

**microphone** *n* an instrument for transforming sound waves into electric signals, esp for transmission, or recording.—*also* **mike**.

**microscope** *n* an optical instrument for making magnified images of minute objects by means of a lens or lenses.

**microscopic** *adj* of, with, like, a microscope; visible only through a microscope; very small.—**microscopically** *adv*.

**mid** *adj* middle. • *prep* amid.

**midday** *n* the middle of the day, noon.

**middle** *adj* halfway between two given points, times, etc; intermediate; central. • *n* the point halfway between two extremes; something intermediate; the waist.

**middle age** *n* the time between youth and old age.—**middle-aged** *adj*.

**Middle Ages** *npl* the period of European history between about Ad 500 and 1500.

**middle class** *n* the class between the lower and upper classes, mostly composed of professional and business people.—**middle-class** *adj*.

**middleman** *n* a dealer between producer and consumer; an intermediary.

**middling** *adj* of medium quality, size, etc; second-rate. • *adv* moderately.

**midge** *n* a small gnat-like insect with a painful bite.

**midget** *n* a very small person, a dwarf; something small of its kind.—*also* *adj*.

**midnight** *n* twelve o'clock at night.

**midriff** *n* the middle part of the torso between the abdomen and the chest.

**midst** n middle. • prep amidst, among.

**midway** adv halfway.

**midwife** n a person trained to assist women before, during, and after childbirth.—**midwifery** n.

**might**[1] see **may**.

**might**[2] n power, bodily strength.

**mightn't** = might not.

**mighty** adj (**mightier, mightiest**) powerful, strong; massive; (inf) very.—**mightily** adv.—**mightiness** n.

**migraine** n an intense, periodic headache, usu limited to one side of the head.

**migrant** n a person or animal that moves from one region or country to another; an itinerant agricultural labourer. • adj migrating.

**migrate** vi to settle in another country or region; (birds, animals) to move to another region with the change in season.—**migration** n.—**migratory** adj.

**mike** see **microphone**.

**mild** adj (temper) gentle; (weather) temperate; bland; feeble.—**mildly** adv.—**mildness** n.

**mildew** n a fungus that attacks some plants or appears on damp cloth, etc as a whitish coating. • vti to affect or be affected with mildew.—**mildewy** adj.

**mile** n a unit of linear measure equal to 5,280 feet (1.61 km); the nautical mile is 6,075 feet (1.85 km).

**mileage** n total miles travelled; an allowance per mile for travelling expenses; the average number of miles that can be travelled, as per litre of fuel.

**milestone** n a stone marking the number of miles to a place; an important event in life, history, etc.

**milieu** n (pl **milieus, milieux**) environment, esp social setting.

**militant** adj ready to fight, esp for some cause; combative.—also n.—**militancy** n.—**militantly** adv.

**military** adj relating to soldiers or to war; warlike. • n the armed forces.

**militia** n an army composed of civilians called out in time of emergency.

**milk** n a white nutritious liquid secreted by female mammals for feeding their young. • vt to draw milk from; to extract money, etc, from; to exploit.—**milkiness** n.—**milky** adj.

**milkman** n a person who delivers milk to homes.

**mill** n an apparatus for grinding by crushing between rough surfaces; a building where grain is ground into flour; a factory. • vt to produce or grind in a mill; (coins) to put a raised edge on. • vi to move around confusedly.—**miller** n.

**millennium** n (pl **millennia, millenniums**) a period of a thousand years.—**millennial** adj.

**millet** n a cereal grass used for grain and fodder.

**milli-** prefix a thousandth part.

**millimetre, millimeter** (US) n a thousandth (0.001) of a metre.

**milliner** n a designer or seller of women's hats.—**millinery** n.

**million** n a thousand thousands, the number one followed by six zeros: 1,000,000; (inf) a very large number.—**millionth** adj.

**millionaire** n a person who owns at least a million of money; one who is extremely rich.

**millstone** n a stone used for grinding corn; a heavy burden.

**mime** n a theatrical technique using action without words; a mimic. • vi act or express using gestures alone; (singers, musicians) to perform as if singing or playing live to what is actually a prerecorded piece of music.

**mimic** n a person who imitates, esp an actor skilled in mimicry. • adj related to mimicry; make-believe; sham. • *(pt* **mimicked)** to imitate or ridicule.

**mimicry** *n* practice, art, or way of mimicking.

**min.** *abbr* = minimum; minute(s).

**minaret** *n* a high, slender tower on a mosque from which the call to prayer is made.

**mince** *vt* to chop or cut up into small pieces; to diminish or moderate one's words. • *vi* to speak or walk with affected daintiness.—**mincing** *adj.*—**mincingly** *adv.*

**mincemeat** *n* a mixture of chopped apples, raisins, etc used as a pie filling.

**mind** *n* the faculty responsible for intellect, thought, feelings, speech; memory; intellect; reason; opinion; sanity. • *vt* to object to, take offence to; to pay attention to; to obey; to take care of; to be careful about; to care about. • *vi* to pay attention; to be obedient; to be careful; to object.

**mindful** *adj* heedful, not forgetful.—**mindfully** *adv.*

**mindless** *adj* unthinking, stupid; requiring little intellectual effort.—**mindlessly** *adv.*

**mine**[1] *poss pron* belonging to me.

**mine**[2] *n* an excavation from which minerals are dug; an explosive device concealed in the water or ground to destroy enemy ships, personnel, or vehicles that pass over or near them; a rich supply or source. • *vt* to excavate; to lay explosive mines in an area. • *vi* to dig or work a mine.

**mine detector** *n* a device for indicating the whereabouts of explosive mines.

**minefield** *n* an area sown with explosive mines; a situation containing hidden problems.

**miner** *n* a person who works in a mine.

**mineral** *n* an inorganic substance, found naturally in the earth; any substance neither vegetable nor animal. • *adj* relating to or containing minerals.

**mineralogy** *n* the science of minerals.—**mineralogical** *adj.*—**mineralogically** *adv.*—**mineralogist** *n.*

**mineral water** *n* water containing mineral salts or gases, often with medicinal properties.

**minesweeper** *n* a ship for clearing away explosive mines.—**minesweeping** *n.*

**mingle** *vti* to mix; to combine.

**miniature** *adj* minute, on a small scale. • *n* a painting or reproduction on a very small scale.

**minibus** *n* a small bus for carrying up to twelve passengers.

**minimal** *adj* very minute; least possible.—**minimally** *adv.*

**minimize** *vt* to reduce to or estimate at a minimum.—**minimization** *n.*

**minimum** *n* (*pl* **minima, minimums**) the least possible amount; the lowest degree or point reached.

**mining** *n* the act, process, or industry of excavating from the earth; (*mil*) the laying of explosive mines.

**minister** *n* a clergyman serving a church; an official heading a government department; a diplomat. • *vi* to serve as a minister in a church; to give help (to).—**ministerial** *adj.*—**ministerially** *adv.*

**ministry** *n* the act of ministering; the clergy; the profession of a clergyman; a government department headed by a minister; the building housing a government department.

**mink** *n* any of several carnivorous weasel-like mammals valued for its durable soft fur.

**minnow** *n* a small, slender freshwater fish.

**minor** *adj* lesser in size, importance, degree, extent, etc; (*mus*) lower than the corresponding major by a semitone. • *n* a person under full legal age.

**minority** *n* the smaller part or number; a political or racial group smaller than the majority group; the state of being under age.

**minstrel** *n* a travelling entertainer and musician, esp in the Middle Ages.

**mint**[1] *n* the place where money is coined; a large amount of money; a source of supply. • *adj* unused, in perfect condition. • *vt* (*coins*) to imprint; to invent.

**mint**[2] *n* an aromatic plant whose leaves are used for flavouring.

**minuet** *n* (the music for) a slow, graceful dance in triple time.

**minus** *prep* less; (*inf*) without. • *adj* involving subtraction; negative; less than. • *n* a sign (-), indicating subtraction or negative quantity.

**minute**[1] *n* the sixtieth part of an hour or a degree; a moment; (*pl*) an official record of a meeting. • *vt* to record or summarize the proceedings (of).

**minute**[2] *adj* tiny; detailed; exact.—**minutely** *adv*.—**minuteness** *n*.

**miracle** *n* an extraordinary event attributed to the supernatural; an unusual or astounding event; a remarkable example of something.—**miraculous** *adj*.—**miraculously** *adv*.

**mirage** *n* an optical illusion in which a distant object or expanse of water seems to be nearby, caused by light reflection from hot air; anything illusory or fanciful.

**mirror** *n* a smooth surface that reflects images; a faithful depiction. • *vt* (*pt* **mirrored**) to reflect or depict faithfully.

**mirth** *n* merriment, esp with laughter.—**mirthful** *adj*.—**mirthless** *adj*.

**mis-** *prefix* wrong(ly); bad(ly); no, not.

**misadventure** *n* an unlucky accident; bad luck.

**misanthrope, misanthropist** *n* a person who hates or distrusts mankind.—**misanthropic** *adj*.—**misanthropically** *adv*.—**misanthropy** *n*.

**misapprehension** *n* misunderstanding.

**misappropriate** *vt* to appropriate wrongly or dishonestly; to embezzle.—**misappropriation** *n*.

**misbehave** *vi* to behave badly.—**misbehaviour** *n*.

**miscalculate** *vti* to calculate wrongly.—**miscalculation** *n*.

**miscarriage** *n* the spontaneous expulsion of a foetus prematurely; mismanagement or failure.

**miscellaneous** *adj* consisting of various kinds; mixed.—**miscellaneously** *adv*.

**miscellany** *n* a mixed collection; a book comprising miscellaneous writings, etc.

**mischief** *n* wayward behaviour; damage.

**mischievous** *adj* harmful, prankish.—**mischievously** *adv*.—**mischievousness** *n*.

**misconception** *n* a mistaken idea.

**misconduct** *n* dishonest management; improper behaviour.—*also vt*.

**misconstrue** *vt* to misinterpret.—**misconstruction** *n*.

**misdemeanour, misdemeanor** (*US*) *n* (*law*) a minor offence, a misdeed.

**miser** *n* a greedy, stingy person who hoards money for its own sake.—**miserliness** *n*.—**miserly** *adj*.

**miserable** *adj* wretched; unhappy; causing misery; bad, inadequate; pitiable.—**miserableness** *n*.—**miserably** *adv*.

**misery** *n* extreme pain, unhappiness, or poverty; a cause of suffering.

**misfire** *vi* (*engine, etc*) to fail to ignite, start; to fail to succeed.—*also n*.

**misfit** *n* something that fits badly; a maladjusted person.—*also vti*.

**misfortune** *n* ill luck; trouble; a mishap.

**misgiving** *n* a feeling of misapprehension, mistrust.

**misguided** *adj* foolish; mistaken.

**mishap** *n* an unfortunate accident.

**misinform** *vt* to supply with wrong information.—**misinformation** *n*.

**misjudge** *vt* to judge wrongly, to form a wrong opinion.—**misjudgment, misjudgement** *n*.

**mislay** *vt* (*pt* **mislaid**) to lose something temporarily; to put down or install improperly.

**mislead** *vt* (*pt* **misled**) to deceive; to give wrong information to; to lead into wrongdoing.

**misleading** *adj* deceptive; confusing.

**misnomer** *n* an incorrect or unsuitable name or description.

**misplace** *vt* to put in a wrong place; (*trust, etc*) to place unwisely.—**misplacement** *n*.

**misprint** *vt* to print incorrectly. • *n* an error in printing.

**misrepresent** *vt* to represent falsely; to give an untrue idea of.—**misrepresentation** *n*.—**misrepresentative** *adj*.

**miss**[1] *n* (*pl* **misses**) a girl; (*with cap*) a title used before the surname of an unmarried woman or girl.

**miss**[2] *vt* to fail to reach, hit, find, meet, hear; to omit; to fail to take advantage of; to regret or discover the absence or loss of. • *vi* to fail to hit; to fail to be successful; to misfire, as an engine. • *n* a failure to hit, reach, obtain, etc.

**missal** *n* a book containing the prayers for Mass.

**misshapen** *adj* badly shaped; deformed.

**missile** *n* an object, as a rock, spear, rocket, etc, to be thrown, fired, or launched.

**missing** *adj* absent; lost.

**mission** *n* a group of people sent by a church, government, etc to carry out a special duty or task; the sending of an aircraft or spacecraft on a special assignment; a vocation.

**missionary** *n* a person who tries to convert unbelievers to his/her religious faith.—*also adj*.

**misspent** *adj* wasted, frittered away.

**mist** *n* a large mass of water vapour, less dense than a fog; something that dims or obscures. • *vti* to cover or be covered, as with mist.—**mistily** *adv*.—**mistiness** *n*.—**misty** *adj*.

**mistake** *vb* (*pt* **mistook**, *pp* **mistaken**) • *vt* to misunderstand; to misinterpret. • *vi* to make a mistake. • *n* a wrong idea, answer, etc; an error of judgment; a blunder; a misunderstanding.—**mistakable, mistakeable** *adj*.

**mistaken** *adj* erroneous, ill-judged.—**mistakenly** *adv*.

**mister** *n* (*inf*) sir; (*with cap*) the title used before a man's surname.

**mistletoe** *n* an evergreen parasitic plant with white berries used as a Christmas decoration.

**mistreat** *vt* to treat wrongly or badly.—**mistreatment** *n*.

**mistress** *n* a woman who is head of a household; a woman with whom a man is having a prolonged affair; a female schoolteacher; (*with cap*) the title used before a married woman's surname.

**mistrust** *n* lack of trust. • *vti* to doubt; to suspect.—**mistrustful** *adj*. —**mistrustfully** *adv*

**misunderstand** *vt* (*pt* **misunderstood**) to fail to understand correctly.—**misunderstood** *adj*.

**misunderstanding** *n* a mistake as to sense; a quarrel or disagreement.

**misuse** *vt* to use for the wrong purpose or in the wrong way; to ill-treat, abuse. • *n* improper or incorrect use.

**mitigate** *vti* to become or make less severe.—**mitigable** *adj*.—**mitigating** *adj*.—**mitigation** *n*.

**mitre, miter** (*US*) *n* the headdress of a bishop; a diagonal joint between two pieces of wood to form a corner. • *vt* to join with a mitre corner.

**mitt** *n* a glove covering the hand but only the base of the fingers; (*sl*) a hand; a boxing glove; a baseball glove.

**mitten** *n* a glove with a thumb but no separate fingers.

**mix** *vt* to blend together in a single mass; to make by blending ingredients, as a cake; to combine; (*with* up) to make into a mixture; to make disordered; to confuse or mistake. • *vi* to be mixed or blended; to get along together. • *n* a mixture.

**mixed** *adj* blended; made up of different parts, classes, races, etc; confused.

**mixed-up** *adj* (*inf*) perplexed, mentally confused.

**mixer** *n* a device that blends or mixes; a person considered in terms of their ability (good or bad) to get on with others; a soft drink added to an alcoholic beverage.

**mixture** *n* the process of mixing; a blend made by mixing.

**mix-up** *n* a mistake; confusion, muddle; (*inf*) a fight.

**moan** *n* a low mournful sound as of sorrow or pain. • *vti* to utter a moan; to complain.—**moaner** *n*.

**moat** *n* a deep ditch surrounding a fortification or castle, usu filled with water.

**mob** *n* a disorderly or riotous crowd; a contemptuous term for the masses; (*sl*) a gang of criminals. • *vt* (*pt* **mobbed**) to attack in a disorderly group; to surround.

**mobile** *adj* movable, not fixed; easily changing; characterized by ease in change of social status; capable of moving freely and quickly; (*inf*) having transport. • *n* a suspended structure of wood, metal, etc with parts that move in air currents.—**mobility** *n*.

**moccasin** *n* a flat shoe based on Amerindian footwear; any soft, flexible shoe resembling this.

**mock** *vt* to imitate or ridicule; to behave with scorn; to defy; (*with* up) to make a model of. • *n* ridicule; an object of scorn. • *adj* false, sham, counterfeit.—**mocking** *n*, *adj*.—**mockingly** *adv*.

**mockery** *n* derision, ridicule, or contempt; imitation, esp derisive; someone or something that is mocked; an inadequate person, thing, or action.

**mock-up** *n* a full-scale working model of a machine, etc.

**MOD** *abbr* = Ministry of Defence.

**mod cons** *npl* (*inf*) modern conveniences.

**mode** *n* a way of acting, doing or existing; a style or fashion; form; (*mus*) any of the scales used in composition; (*statistics*) the predominant item in a series of items; (*gram*) mood.—**modal** *adj*.—**modality** *n*.

**model** *n* a pattern; an ideal; a standard worth imitating; a representation on a smaller scale, usu three-dimensional; a person who sits for an artist or photographer; a person who displays clothes by wearing them. • *adj* serving as a model; representative of others of the same style. • *vb* (*pt* **modelled**) *vt* (*with* **after, on**) to create by following a model; to display clothes by wearing. • *vi* to serve as a model for an artist, etc.—**modeller** *n*.—**modelling** *n*.

**moderate** *vti* to make or become moderate; to preside over. • *adj* having reasonable limits; avoiding extremes; mild, calm; of medium quality, amount, etc. • *n* a person who holds moderate views.—**moderately** *adv.*—**moderation** *n.*

**modern** *adj* of the present or recent times, contemporary; up-to-date.—**modernity** *n.*

**modernize** *vti* to make or become modern.—**modernization** *n.*

**modest** *adj* moderate; having a humble opinion of oneself; unpretentious.—**modestly** *adv.*—**modesty** *n.*

**modicum** *n* a small quantity.

**modify** *vt* to lessen the severity of; to change or alter slightly; (*gram*) to limit in meaning, to qualify.—**modifiable** *adj.*—**modification** *n.*—**modifier** *n.*

**module** *n* a unit of measurement; a self-contained unit, esp in a spacecraft.—**modular** *adj.*

**mohair** *n* the long, fine hair of the Angora goat; the silk cloth made from it.

**moist** *adj* damp; slightly wet.—**moistly** *adv.*—**moistness** *n.*

**moisten** *vti* to make or become moist.

**moisture** *n* liquid in a diffused, absorbed, or condensed state.

**moisturize** *vt* (*skin, air, etc*) to add moisture to.—**moisturizer** *n.*

**molar** *n* a back tooth, used for grinding food.

**molasses** *n* (*used as sing*) the thick brown sugar that is produced during the refining of sugar; treacle.

**mole**[1] *n* a spot on the skin, usu dark-coloured and raised.

**mole**[2] *n* a small burrowing insectivore with soft dark fur; a spy within an organization.

**mole**[3] *n* a large breakwater.

**mole**[4] *n* the basic SI unit of substance.

**molecule** *n* the simplest unit of a substance, retaining the chemical properties of that substance; a small particle.—**molecular** *adj.*

**molest** *vt* to annoy; to attack or assault, esp sexually.—**molestation** *n.*—**molester** *n.*

**mollusc, mollusk** (*US*) *n* an invertebrate animal usu enclosed in a shell, as oysters, etc.

**molten** *adj* melted by heat.

**moment** *n* an indefinitely brief period of time; a definite point in time; a brief time of importance.

**momentary** *adj* lasting only for a moment.

**momentous** *adj* very important.—**momentously** *adv.*

**momentum** *n* (*pl* **momenta**, **momentums**) the impetus of a moving object, equal to the product of its mass and its velocity.

**monarch** *n* a sovereign who rules by hereditary right.—**monarchic** *adj.*—**monarchical** *adj.*

**monarchy** *n* a government headed by a monarch; a kingdom.

**monastery** *n* the residence of a group of monks, or nuns.

**monastic** *adj* of monks or monasteries. • *n* a monk; a recluse.—**monastically** *adv.*—**monasticism** *n.*

**Monday** *n* the second day of the week.

**monetary** *adj* of the coinage or currency of a country; of or relating to money.

**money** *n* (*pl* **moneys, monies**) coins or paper notes authorized by a government as a medium of exchange; property; wealth.

**mongrel** *n* an animal or plant of mixed or unknown breed, esp a dog.—*also adj.*

**monitor** *n* a student chosen to help the teacher; any device for regulating the performance of a machine, aircraft, etc; a screen for viewing the image being produced by a television camera; a display screen connected to a computer. • *vti* (*TV or radio transmissions, etc*) to observe or listen to for political or technical reasons; to watch or check on; to regulate or control, a machine, etc.—**monitory** adj.

**monk** n a male member of a religious order living in a monastery.

**monkey** n (pl **monkeys**) any of the primates except man and the lemurs, esp the smaller, long-tailed primates; a mischievous child; (sl) £500 or $500. • vi (inf) to play, trifle, or meddle.

**monkey nut** n a peanut.

**monkey wrench** n a large wrench with an adjustable jaw.

**mono-** prefix alone, sole, single.

**monochrome** n a painting, drawing, or print in a single colour.

**monocle** n a single eyeglass held in place by the face muscles.

**monogram** n the embroidered or printed initials of one's name on clothing, stationery, etc.—**monogrammed** adj.

**monologue, monolog** n a long speech; a soliloquy, a skit, etc for one actor only.

**monopolize** vt to get, have, or exploit a monopoly of; to get full control of.—**monopolization** n.

**monopoly** n exclusive control in dealing in a particular commodity or supplying a service; exclusive use or possession; that which is exclusively controlled; such control granted by a government.—**monopolist** n.—**monopolistic** adj.

**monosyllable** n a word of one syllable.—**monosyllabic** adj.

**monotone** n an utterance or musical tone without a change in pitch; a tiresome sameness of style, colour, etc.—**monotonous** adj.—**monotonously** adv.—**monotony** n.

**monsoon** n a seasonal wind of southern Asia; the rainy season.

**monster** n any greatly malformed plant or animal; an imaginary beast; a very wicked person; a very large animal or thing. • adj very large, huge.—**monstrosity** n.

**monstrous** adj abnormally developed; enormous; horrible.—**monstrously** adv.

**montage** n a rapid sequence of film shots, often superimposed; the art or technique of assembling various elements, esp pictures or photographs; such an assemblage.

**month** n any of the twelve divisions of the year; a calendar month.

**monthly** adj continuing for a month; done, happening, payable, etc, every month. • n a monthly periodical. • adv once a month; every month.

**monument** n an obelisk, statue or building that commemorates a person or an event; an exceptional example.

**monumental** adj of, like, or serving as a monument; colossal; lasting.—**monumentally** adv.

**mood** n a temporary state of mind or temper; a gloomy feeling; a predominant feeling or spirit; (gram) that form of a verb indicating mode of action; (mus) mode.

**moody** adj (**moodier, moodiest**) gloomy; temperamental.—**moodily** adv.—**moodiness** n.

**moon** n the natural satellite that revolves around the earth and shines by reflected sunlight; any natural satellite of another planet; something shaped like the moon. • vi to behave in an idle or abstracted way.

**moonbeam** n a ray of moonlight.

**moonlight** n the light of the moon. • vi (inf) to have a secondary (usu nighttime) job.

**moonlit** adj lit by the moon.

**moor**[1] n a tract of open wasteland, usu covered with heather and often marshy.

**moor**[2] vti (a ship) to secure or be secured by cable or anchor.

**mooring** *n* the act of mooring; the place where a ship is moored; (*pl*) the lines, cables, etc by which a ship is moored.

**moose** *n* (*pl* **moose**) the largest member of the deer family, native to North America.

**moot** *adj* debatable; hypothetical. • *vt* to propose for discussion.

**mop** *n* a rag, sponge, etc fixed to a handle for washing floors or dishes; a thick or tangled head of hair. • *vt* (*pt* **mopped**) to wash with a mop.

**mope** *vi* to be gloomy and apathetic.— **mopey** *adj*.

**moped** *n* a light, motor-assisted bicycle.

**moral** *adj* of or relating to character and human behaviour, particularly as regards right and wrong; virtuous, esp in sexual conduct; capable of distinguishing right from wrong; probable, although not certain; psychological, emotional. • *n* a moral lesson taught by a fable, event, etc; (*pl*) principles; ethics. —**moralist** *n*.— **moralistic** *adj*.—**morally** *adv*.

**morale** *n* moral or mental condition with respect to courage, discipline, confidence, etc.

**morality** *n* virtue; moral principles; a particular system of moral principles.

**morass** *n* a bog, marsh.

**morbid** *adj* diseased, resulting as from a diseased state of mind; gruesome.—**morbidly** *adv*.—**morbidness** *n*.

**more** *adj* (*superl* **most**) greater; further; additional(—*also compar of* **many, much**). • *adv* to a greater extent or degree; again; further.

**moreover** *adv* in addition to what has been said before; besides.

**morgue** *n* a place where the bodies of unknown dead or those dead of unknown causes are temporarily kept

prior to burial; a collection of reference materials, eg newspaper clippings.

**morning** *n* the part of the day from midnight or dawn until noon; the early part of anything.

**moron** *n* an adult mentally equal to a 8 to 12-year-old child; (*inf*) a very stupid person.—**moronic** *adj*.

**morose** *adj* sullen, surly; gloomy.— **morosely** *adv*.—**moroseness** *n*.

**morphine** *n* an alkaloid derived from opium, used as an anaesthetic and sedative.

**Morse code** *n* a code in which letters are represented by dots and dashes or long and short sounds, and are transmitted by visual or audible signals.

**morsel** *n* a small quantity of food; a small piece of anything.

**mortal** *adj* subject to death; causing death, fatal; hostile; very intense. • *n* a human being.—**mortally** *adv*.

**mortality** *n* state of being mortal; death on a large scale, as from war; number or frequency of deaths in a given period relative to population.

**mortar** *n* a mixture of cement or lime with sand and water used in building; an artillery piece that fires shells at low velocities and high trajectories; a bowl in which substances are pounded with a pestle.

**mortgage** *n* a transfer of rights to a piece of property usu as security for the payment of a loan or debt that becomes void when the debt is paid.—*also vt*.

**mortify** *vti* to subdue by repression or penance; to humiliate or shame; to become gangrenous.—**mortification** *n*.

**mortuary** *n* a place of temporary storage for dead bodies.

**mosaic** *n* a surface decoration made by inlaying small pieces (of glass, stone, etc) to form figures or patterns; a design made in mosaic.—*also adj*.

**Moslem** *see* **Muslim**.

**mosque** *n* a place of worship for Muslims.

**mosquito** *n* (*pl* **mosquitoes**) a small two-winged bloodsucking insect.

**moss** *n* a very small green plant that grows in clusters on rocks, moist ground, etc.—**mossy** *adj*.

**most** *adj* (*compar* **more**) greatest in number; greatest in amount or degree; in the greatest number of instances (—*also superl of* **many**, **much**). • *adv* in or to the greatest degree or extent. • *n* the greatest amount or degree; (*with pl*) the greatest number (of).

**mostly** *adv* for the most part; mainly, usually.

**MOT** *abbr* = Ministry of Transport.

**motel** *n* an hotel for motorists with adjacent parking.

**moth** *n* a four-winged chiefly night-flying insect related to the butterfly.

**mothball** *n* a small ball of camphor or naphthalene used to protect stored clothes from moths.

**moth-eaten** *adj* eaten into by moths; dilapidated; outmoded.

**mother** *n* a female who has given birth to offspring; an origin or source. • *adj* of or like a mother; native. • *vt* to be the mother of or a mother to.—**motherhood** *n*.

**mother-in-law** *n* the mother of one's spouse.

**motherly** *adj* of, proper to a mother; like a mother.—**motherliness** *n*.

**mother-of-pearl** *n* the iridescent lining of the shell of the pearl oyster.

**motif** *see* **motive**.

**motion** *n* activity, movement; a formal suggestion made in a meeting, law court, or legislative assembly; evacuation of the bowels. • *vti* to signal or direct by a gesture.

**motionless** *adj* not moving, still.

**motion picture** *n* a film, movie.

**motive** *n* something (as a need or desire) that causes a person to act; a recurrent theme in a musical composition (—*also* **motif**). • *adj* moving to action; of or relating to motion.

**motley** *adj* multicoloured; composed of diverse elements.

**motor** *n* anything that produces motion; a machine for converting electrical energy into mechanical energy; a motor car. • *adj* producing motion; of or powered by a motor; of, by or for motor vehicles; of or involving muscular movements. • *vi* to travel by car.

**motorbike** *n* a motorcycle.

**motorboat** *n* a boat propelled by an engine or motor.

**motorcycle** *n* a two-wheeled motor vehicle.—**motorcyclist** *n*.

**motorist** *n* a person who drives a car.

**motor scooter** *n* a small-wheeled motorcycle with an enclosed engine.

**motorway** *n* a road with controlled access for fast-moving traffic.—*also* **freeway** *n*.

**mottled** *adj* marked with blotches of various colours.

**motto** *n* (*pl* **mottoes, mottos**) a short saying adopted as a maxim or ideal.

**mould**[1], **mold** (*US*) *n* a fungus producing a furry growth on the surface of organic matter. • *vi* to become mouldy.—**mouldiness** *n*.—**mouldy** *adj*.

**mould**[2], **mold** (*US*) *n* a hollow form in which something is cast; a pattern; something made in a mould; distinctive character. • *vt* to make in or on a mould; to form, shape, guide.

**moult, molt** (*US*) *vi* to shed hair, skin, horns, etc prior to replacement of new growth.—*also n*.

**mound** *n* an artificial bank of earth or stones; a heap or bank of earth. • *vt* to form into a mound.

**mount**[1] *n* a high hill.

**mount**[2] *vi* to increase. • *vt* to climb, ascend; to get up on (a horse, platform, etc); to provide with horses; (*a jewel*) to fix on a support; (*a picture*) to frame. • *n* a horse for riding; (*for a picture*) a backing.

**mountain** *n* a land mass higher than a hill; a vast number or quantity. • *adj* of or in mountains.

**mountaineer** *n* one who climbs mountains.

**mountaineering** *n* the technique of climbing mountains.

**mountainous** *adj* having many mountains; very high; huge.

**mourn** *vti* (*someone dead*) to grieve for; (*something regrettable*) to feel or express sorrow for.—**mourner** *n*.

**mournful** *adj* expressing grief or sorrow; causing sorrow.—**mournfully** *adv*.

**mourning** *adj* grieving. • *n* the expression of grief; dark clothes worn by mourners.

**mouse** *n* (*pl* **mice**) a small rodent with a pointed snout, long body and slender tail; a timid person; a hand-held device used to position the cursor and control software on a computer screen.

**moustache, mustache** (*US*) *n* the hair on the upper lip.

**mousy, mousey** *adj* (**mousier, mousiest**) mouse-like; grey-brown in colour; quiet, stealthy; timid, retiring.

**mouth** *n* (*pl* **mouths**) the opening in the head through which food is eaten, sound uttered or words spoken; the lips; opening, entrance, as of a bottle, etc. • *vt* to say, esp insincerely; to form words with the mouth without uttering sound. • *vi* to utter pompously; to grimace.

**mouthful** *n* as much (food) as fills the mouth; a word or phrase that is difficult to say correctly; (*sl*) a pertinent remark.

**mouth organ** *n* a harmonica.

**mouthwatering** *adj* appetizing; tasty.

**movable, moveable** *adj* that may be moved. • *npl* personal property.

**move** *vt* to shift or change place; to set in motion; to rouse the emotions; to put (a motion) formally. • *vi* to go from one place to another; to walk, to carry oneself; to change place; to evacuate the bowels; to propose a motion as in a meeting; to change residence; (*chess, draughts, etc*) to change the position of a piece on the board. • *n* the act of moving; a movement, esp in board games; one's turn to move; a premeditated action.—**mover** *n*.

**movement** *n* act of moving; the moving part of a machine, esp a clock; the policy and activities of a group; a trend, eg in prices; a division of a musical work; tempo.

**movie** *n* a cinema film, motion picture; (*pl*) the showing of a motion picture; the motion-picture medium or industry.

**moving** *adj* arousing the emotions; changing position; causing motion.—**movingly** *adv*.

**mow** *vti* (*pt* **mowed** *or* **mown**) (*grass, etc*) to cut from with a sickle or lawn mower; (*with* **down**) to cause to fall like cut grass.—**mower** *n*.

**MP** *abbr* = Member of Parliament.

**mpg** *abbr* = miles per gallon.

**mph** *abbr* = miles per hour.

**Mr** *n* (*pl* **Messrs**) used as a title before a man's name or an office he holds.

**Mrs** *n* used as a title before a married woman's name.

**Ms** *n* the title used before a woman's name instead of Miss or Mrs.

**much** *adj* (*compar* **more**, *superl* **most**)

plenty. • *adv* considerably; to a great extent.

**muck** *n* moist manure; black earth with decaying matter; mud, dirt, filth. • *vt* to spread manure; to make dirty; (*with* **out**) to clear of muck. • *vi* to move or load muck; (*with* **about, around**) to engage in useless activity.—**muckiness** *n*.—**mucky** *adj*.

**mucus** *n* the slimy secretion that keeps mucous membranes moist.

**mud** *n* soft, wet earth.

**muddle** *vt* to confuse; to mix up. • *n* confusion, mess.

**muddy** *adj* (**muddier, muddiest**) like or covered with mud; not bright or clear; confused. • *vti* to make or become dirty or unclear.—**muddily** *adv*.—**muddiness** *n*.

**mudguard** *n* a screen on a wheel to catch mud splashes.

**muff**[1] *n* a warm soft fur cover for warming the hands.

**muff**[2] *n* a bungling performance; failure to hold a ball when trying to catch it. • *vti* to bungle.

**muffin** *n* baked yeast roll.

**muffle** *vt* to wrap up for warmth or to hide; (*sound*) to deaden by wrapping up.

**muffler** *n* a long scarf; any means of deadening sound; the silencer of a motor vehicle.

**mug** *n* a cylindrical drinking cup, usu of metal or earthenware; its contents; (*sl*) the face; (*sl*) a fool. • *vb* (*pt* **mugged**) *vt* to assault, usu with intent to rob.

**muggy** *adj* (**muggier, muggiest**) (*weather*) warm, damp and close.

**mule**[1] *n* the offspring of a male donkey and a female horse; a machine for spinning cotton; an obstinate person.—**mulish** *adj*.—**mulishly** *adv*.—**mulishness** *n*.

**mule**[2] *n* a slipper without a heel.

**mull**[1] *vti* (*inf*) to ponder (over).

**mull**[2] *vt* (*wine, etc*) to heat, sweeten and spice.—**mulled** *adj*.

**mult-, multi-** *prefix* much, many.

**multiple** *adj* of many parts; manifold; various; complex. • *n* (*math*) a number exactly divisible by another.

**multiple sclerosis** *n* a disease of the nervous system with loss of muscular coordination, etc.

**multiplication** *n* the act of multiplying; the process of repeatedly adding a quantity to itself a certain number of times, or any other process which has the same result.

**multiply** *vti* to increase in number, degree, etc; to find the product (of) by multiplication.

**multitude** *n* a large number (of people).—**multitudinous** *adj*.

**mum**[1], **mummy** *n* (*inf*) mother.

**mum**[2] *adj* silent, not speaking.

**mumble** *vti* to speak indistinctly, mutter. • *n* a mumbled utterance.—**mumbler** *n*.—**mumbling** *adj*.

**mummy**[1] *see* **mum**[1].

**mummy**[2] *n* a carefully preserved dead body, esp an embalmed corpse of ancient Egypt.—**mummification** *n*.—**mummify** *vt*.

**mumps** *npl* (*used as sing or pl*) an acute contagious virus disease characterized by swelling of the salivary glands.

**munch** *vti* to chew steadily.

**mundane** *adj* routine, everyday; banal; worldly.—**mundanely** *adv*.

**municipal** *adj* of or concerning a city, town, etc or its local government.—**municipally** *adv*.

**municipality** *n* a city or town having corporate status and powers of self-government; the governing body of a municipality.

**munitions** *npl* war supplies, esp weapons and ammunition.

**mural** *adj* relating to a wall. • *n* a

picture or design painted directly onto a wall.

**murder** *n* the intentional and unlawful killing of one person by another; (*inf*) something unusually difficult or dangerous to do or deal with.— *also vt*.—**murderer** *n*.—**murderous** *adj*.—**murderously** *adv*.

**murky** *adj* (**murkier, murkiest**) dark, gloomy; darkly vague or obscure.— **murkily** *adv*.—**murkiness** *n*.

**murmur** *n* a continuous low, indistinct sound; a mumbled complaint; (*med*) an abnormal sound made by the heart. • *vti* to make a murmur; to say in a murmur.—**murmurous** *adj*.

**muscle** *n* fibrous tissue that contracts and relaxes, producing bodily movement; strength; brawn; power. • *vi* (*inf*) to force one's way (in).—**muscular** *adj*.—**muscularity** *n*.—**muscularly** *adv*.

**muse** *vti* to ponder, meditate.—**musing** *adj*.

**museum** *n* a building for exhibiting objects of artistic, historic or scientific interest.

**mushroom** *n* a fleshy fungus with a capped stalk, some varieties of which are edible. • *vi* to gather mushrooms; to spread rapidly, to increase.

**music** *n* the art of combining tones into a composition having structure and continuity; vocal or instrumental sounds having rhythm, melody or harmony; an agreeable sound.

**musical** *adj* of or relating to music or musicians; having the pleasant tonal qualities of music; having an interest in or talent for music. • *n* a play or film incorporating dialogue, singing and dancing.—**musically** *adv*.

**musician** *n* one skilled in music, esp a performer.

**Muslim** *n* an adherent of Islam.—*also adj*.

**muslin** *n* a fine cotton cloth.

**mussel** *n* an edible marine bivalve shellfish.

**must** *aux vb expressing*: necessity; probability; certainty. • *n* (*inf*) something that must be done, had, etc.

**mustard** *n* the powdered seeds of the mustard plant used as a condiment; a brownish-yellow colour; (*sl*) zest.

**muster** *vt* to assemble or call together, as troops for inspection or duty; to gather. • *vi* to be assembled, as troops. • *n* gathering; review; assembly.

**musty** *adj* (**mustier, mustiest**) mouldy, damp; stale.

**mute** *adj* silent; dumb; (*colour*) subdued. • *n* a person who is unable to speak; a device that softens the sound of a musical instrument. • *vt* to lessen the sound of a musical instrument.—**mutely** *adv*.—**muteness** *n*.

**mutilate** *vt* to maim; to damage by removing an essential part of.—**mutilation** *n*.—**mutilator** *n*.

**mutiny** *vi* to revolt against authority in military service.—*also n*.—**mutineer** *n*.—**mutinous** *adj*.—**mutinously** *adv*.

**mutter** *vti* to utter in a low tone or indistinctly; to grumble.—**muttering** *n*.

**mutton** *n* the edible flesh of sheep.

**mutual** *adj* given and received in equal amount; having the same feelings one for the other; shared in common.—**mutuality** *n*.—**mutually** *adv*.

**muzzle** *n* the projecting nose or mouth of an animal; a strap fitted over the jaws to prevent biting; the open end of a gun barrel. • *vt* to put a muzzle on; to silence or gag.

**my** *poss adj* of or belonging to me.

**myself** *pron* emphatic and reflexive form of I; in my normal state.

**mystery** *n* something unexplained and secret; a story about a secret crime, etc; secrecy.—**mysterious** *adj*.—**mysteriously** *adv*.

**mystic** *adj* having a meaning beyond normal human understanding; magical. • *n* one who seeks direct knowledge of God or spiritual truths by self-surrender.—**mysticism** *n*.

**mystify** *vt* to bewilder, confuse.—**mystification** *n*.

**myth** *n* a fable; a fictitious event; a traditional story of gods and heroes, taken to be true.—**mythical** *adj*.—**mythically** *adv*.

**mythology** *n* myths collectively; the study of myths.—**mythological** *adj*.—**mythologist** *n*.

# N

**nab** *vt* (*pt* **nabbed**) (*sl*) to catch, arrest.

**nag**[1] *vti* (*pt* **nagged**) to scold constantly; to harass; to be felt persistently. • *n* a person who nags.

**nag**[2] (*inf*) a horse.

**nail** *n* a horny plate covering the end of a human finger or toe; a thin pointed metal spike for driving into wood as a fastening or hanging device. • *vt* to fasten with nails; to fix, secure; (*inf*) to catch or hit; (*inf*) to arrest.

**naive, naïve** *adj* inexperienced; unsophisticated; (*argument*) simple.—**naively, naïvely** *adv*.—**naivety, naiveté, naïveté** *n*.

**naked** *adj* bare, without clothes; without a covering; without addition or ornament; (*eye*) without optical aid.—**nakedness** *n*.

**name** *n* a word or term by which a person or thing is called; a title; reputation; authority. • *vt* to give a name to; to call by name; to designate; to appoint to an office; (*a date, price, etc*) to specify.

**name-dropping** *n* the practice of mentioning the names of famous or important people as if they were friends, in order to impress others.—**name-dropper** *n*.

**nameless** *adj* without a name; obscure; anonymous; unnamed; indefinable; too distressing or horrifying to be described.

**namely** *adv* that is to say.

**namesake** *n* a person or thing with the same name as another.

**nanny, nannie** *n* a child's nurse; (*inf*) a grandmother.

**nap**[1] *n* a short sleep, doze. • *vi* (*pt* **napped**) to take a nap.

**nap**[2] *n* a hairy surface on cloth or leather; such a surface.

**napalm** *n* a substance added to petrol to form a jelly-like compound used in firebombs and flame-throwers. • *vt* to attack or burn with napalm.

**nape** *n* the back of the neck.

**napkin** *n* a square of cloth or paper for wiping fingers or mouth or protecting clothes at table, a serviette; a nappy.

**nappy** *n* a piece of absorbent material wrapped around a baby to absorb or retain its excreta.—*also* **diaper, napkin**.

**narcotic** *adj* inducing sleep. • *n* a drug, often addictive, used to relieve pain and induce sleep.

**narrate** *vt* (*a story*) to tell, relate; to give an account of; (*film, TV*) to provide a spoken commentary for.—**narration** *n*.—**narrator** *n*.

**narrative** *n* a spoken or written account of a sequence of events, experiences, etc; the art or process of narration.—*also adj*.

**narrow** *adj* small in width; limited; with little margin; (*views*) prejudiced or bigoted. • *n* (*usu pl*) the narrow part of a pass, street, or channel. • *vti* to make or grow narrow; to decrease; to contract.—**narrowly** *adv*.—**narrowness** *n*.

**narrow-minded** *adj* prejudiced, bigoted; illiberal.—**narrow-mindedness** *n*.

**nasal** *adj* of the nose; sounded through the nose. • *n* a sound made through the nose.—**nasally** *adv*.

**nasty** *adj* (*pl* **nastier, nastiest**) unpleasant; offensive; ill-natured; disagreeable; (*problem*) hard to deal with; (*illness*) serious or dangerous.—**nastily** *adv*.—**nastiness** *n*.

**nation** *n* people of common territory, descent, culture, language, or history; people united under a single government.

**national** *adj* of a nation; common to a whole nation, general. • *n* a citizen or subject of a specific country.—**nationally** *adv*.

**nationalism** *n* patriotic sentiments, principles, etc; a policy of national independence or self-government; fanatical patriotism, chauvinism.—**nationalist** *n*.—**nationalistic** *adj*.

**nationality** *n* the status of belonging to a nation by birth or naturalization; a nation or national group.

**nationalize** *vt* to make national; to convert into public or government property.—**nationalization** *n*.

**native** *adj* inborn; natural to a person; innate; (*language, etc*) of one's place of birth; relating to the indigenous inhabitants of a country or area; occurring naturally. • *n* a person born in the place indicated; a local inhabitant; an indigenous plant or animal; an indigenous inhabitant, esp a non-White under colonial rule.

**natter** *vi* (*inf*) to chat, talk aimlessly.—*also n*.

**natural** *adj* of or produced by nature; not artificial; innate, not acquired; true to nature; lifelike; normal; at ease; (*mus*) not flat or sharp. • *n* (*inf*) a person or thing considered to have a natural aptitude (for) or to be

an obvious choice (for); (*inf*) a certainty; (*mus*) a natural note or a sign indicating one.—**naturalness** *n*.

**natural history** *n* the study of nature, esp the animal, mineral and vegetable world.

**naturalism** *n* (*arts*) the theory or practice of describing nature, character, etc, in realistic detail.—**naturalistic** *adj*.

**naturalist** *n* a person who studies natural history; a person who advocates or practises naturalism.

**naturalize** *vt* to confer citizenship upon (a person of foreign birth); (*plants*) to become established in a different climate. • *vi* to become established as if native.—**naturalization** *n*.

**naturally** *adv* in a natural manner, by nature; of course.

**natural selection** *see* **selection**.

**nature** *n* the phenomena of physical life not dominated by man; the entire material world as a whole, or forces observable in it; the essential character of anything; the innate character of a person, temperament; kind, class; vital force or functions; natural scenery.

**naught** *see* **nought**.

**naughty** *adj* (**naughtier, naughtiest**) mischievous or disobedient; titillating.—**naughtily** *adv*.—**naughtiness** *n*.

**nausea** *n* a desire to vomit; disgust.

**nauseate** *vti* to arouse feelings of disgust; to feel nausea or revulsion.—**nauseating** *adj*.

**nautical** *adj* of ships, sailors, or navigation.

**nautical mile** *see* **mile**.

**naval** *adj* of the navy; of ships.

**nave** *n* the central space of a church, distinct from the chancel and aisles.

**navel** *n* the small scar in the abdomen caused by severance of the umbilical cord; a central point.

**navigable** *adj* (rivers, seas) that can be sailed upon or steered through.—**navigability** *n*.

**navigate** *vti* to steer or direct a ship, aircraft, etc; to travel through or over (*water, air, etc*) in a ship or aircraft; to find a way through, over, etc, and to keep to a course.—**navigator** *n*.

**navigation** *n* the act, art or science of navigating; the method of calculating the position of a ship, aircraft, etc.

**navvy** *n* a labourer, esp one who works on roads or railways.

**navy** *n* (*often* with cap) the warships of a nation; a nation's entire sea force, including ships, men, stores, etc; navy blue.

**navy blue** *n* an almost black blue.

**near** *adj* close, not distant in space or time; closely related, intimate; approximate, (*escape, etc*) narrow. • *adv* to or at a little distance; close by; almost. • *prep* close to. • *vti* to approach; to draw close to.—**nearness** *n*.

**nearby** *adj* neighbouring; close by in position.

**nearly** *adv* almost, closely.

**near-sighted** *adj* short-sighted, myopic.—**near-sightedness** *n*.

**neat** *adj* clean and tidy; skilful; efficiently done; well made; (*alcoholic drink*) undiluted; (*sl*) nice, pleasing, etc.—**neatly** *adv*.—**neatness** *n*.

**nebulous** *adj* indistinct; formless.

**necessarily** *adv* as a natural consequence.

**necessary** *adj* indispensable; required; inevitable. • *n* something necessary; (*pl*) essential needs.

**necessitate** *vt* to make necessary; to compel.

**necessity** *n* a prerequisite; something that cannot be done without; compulsion; need.

**neck** *n* the part of the body that connects the head and shoulders; that part of a garment nearest the neck; a neck-like part, esp a narrow strip of land; the narrowest part of a bottle; a strait. • *vti* (*sl*) to kiss and caress.

**necklace** *n* a string or band, often of precious stones, beads, or pearls, worn around the neck.

**née, nee** *adj* (*literally*) born: indicating the maiden name of a married woman.

**need** *n* necessity; a lack of something; a requirement; poverty. • *vt* to have a need for; to require; to be obliged.

**needle** *n* a small pointed piece of steel for sewing; a larger pointed rod for knitting or crocheting; a stylus; the pointer of a compass, gauge, etc; the thin, short leaf of the pine, spruce, etc; the sharp, slender metal tube at the end of a hypodermic syringe. • *vt* to goad, prod, or tease.

**needless** *adj* not needed, unnecessary; uncalled for, pointless.—**needlessly** *adv*.—**needlessness** *n*.

**needy** *adj* (**needier, neediest**) in need, very poor.

**negation** *n* a negative statement, denial; the opposite or absence of something; a contradiction.

**negative** *adj* expressing or meaning denial or refusal; lacking positive attributes; (*math*) denoting a quantity less than zero, or one to be subtracted; (*photog*) reversing the light and shade of the original subject, or having the colours replaced by complementary ones; (*elect*) of the charge carried by electrons; producing such a charge. • *n* a negative word, reply, etc; refusal; something that is the opposite or negation of something else; (*in debate, etc*) the side that votes or argues for the opposition; (*photog*) a negative image on transparent film or a plate.

• *vt* to refuse assent, contradict; to veto.—**negatively** *adv*.

**neglect** *vt* to pay little or no attention to; to disregard; to leave uncared for; to fail to do something. • *n* disregard; lack of attention or care.

**negligée, negligee** *n* a woman's loosely fitting dressing gown.

**negligence** *n* lack of attention or care; an act of carelessness; a carelessly easy manner.—**negligent** *adj*.—**negligently** *adv*.

**negligible** *adj* that need not be regarded; unimportant; trifling.

**negotiable** *adj* able to be legally negotiated; (*bills, drafts, etc*) transferable.—**negotiability** *n*.

**negotiate** *vti* to discuss, bargain in order to reach an agreement or settlement; to settle by agreement; (*fin*) to obtain or give money value for (a bill); (*obstacle, etc*) to overcome.—**negotiation** *n* —**negotiator** *n*.

**Negro** *n* (*pl* **Negroes**) a member of the dark-skinned, indigenous peoples of Africa; a member of the Negroid group; a person with some Negro ancestors.—*also adj*.—**Negress** *nf*.

**neighbour, neighbor** (*US*) *n* a person who lives near another; a person or thing situated next to another; a fellow human being.

**neighbourhood, neighborhood** (*US*) *n* a particular community, area, or district; the people in an area.

**neighbouring, neighboring** (*US*) *adj* adjoining, nearby.

**neighbourly, neighborly** (*US*) *adj* characteristic of a neighbour, friendly.—*also adv*.—**neighbourliness** *n*.

**neither** *adj, pron* not one or the other (of two); not either. • *conj* not either; also not.

**neon** *n* an inert gaseous element that gives off a bright orange glow, used in lighting and advertisements.

**nephew** *n* the son of a brother or sister.

**nerve** *n* any of the fibres or bundles of fibres that transmit impulses of sensation or of movement between the brain and spinal cord and all parts of the body; courage, coolness in danger; (*inf*) audacity, boldness; (*pl*) nervousness, anxiety. • *vt* to give strength, courage, or vigour to.

**nerve-racking, nerve-wracking** *adj* straining the nerves, stressful.

**nervous** *adj* excitable, highly strung; anxious, apprehensive; affecting or acting on the nerves or nervous system.

**nervous breakdown** *n* a (usu temporary) period of mental illness resulting from severe emotional strain or anxiety.

**nest** *n* a structure or place where birds, fish, mice, etc, lay eggs or give birth to young; a place where young are nurtured; a swarm or brood; a lair; a cosy place; a set of boxes, tables, etc of different sizes, designed to fit together. • *vi* to make or occupy a nest.

**nestle** *vti* to rest snugly; to lie snugly, as in a nest; to lie sheltered or half-hidden.

**net**[1] *n* an openwork material of string, rope, or twine knotted into meshes; a piece of this used to catch fish, to divide a tennis court, etc; a snare. • *vti* (*pt* **netted**) to snare or enclose as with a net; to hit (a ball) into a net or goal.

**net**[2], **nett** *adj* clear of deductions, allowances or charges. • *n* a net amount, price, weight, profit, etc. • *vt* to clear as a profit.

**netball** *n* a game for two teams of seven players, in which points are scored by putting a ball through an elevated horizontal ring.

**netting** *n* netted fabric.

**nettle** *n* a wild plant with stinging hairs.
• *vt* to irritate, annoy.

**network** *n* an arrangement of intersecting lines; a group of people who co-operate with each other; a chain of interconnected operations, computers, etc; (*radio, TV*) a group of broadcasting stations connected to transmit the same programme simultaneously. • *vt* to broadcast on a network; (*comput*) to interconnect systems so that information, software, and peripheral devices, such as printers, can be shared.

**neurosis** *n* (*pl* **neuroses**) a mental disorder with symptoms such as anxiety and phobia.

**neurotic** *adj* suffering from neurosis; highly strung; of or acting upon the nerves. • *n* someone with neurosis.

**neuter** *adj* (*gram*) of gender, neither masculine nor feminine; (*biol*) having no sex organs; having undeveloped sex organs in the adult. • *n* a neuter person, word, plant, or animal. • *vt* to castrate or spay.

**neutral** *adj* nonaligned; not taking sides with either party in a dispute or war; having no distinctive characteristics; (*colour*) dull; (*chem*) neither acid nor alkaline; (*physics*) having zero charge. • *n* a neutral state, person, or colour; a position of a gear mechanism in which power is not transmitted.—**neutrality** *n*.

**never** *adv* at no time, not ever; not at all; in no case; (*inf*) surely not.

**nevertheless** *adv* all the same, notwithstanding; in spite of, however.

**new** *adj* recently made, discovered, or invented; seen, known, or used for the first time; different, changed; recently grown, fresh; unused; unaccustomed; unfamiliar; recently begun. • *adv* again; newly; recently.

**newborn** *adj* newly born; reborn.

**newcomer** *n* a recent arrival.

**newly** *adv* recently, lately.

**new moon** *n* the moon when first visible as a crescent.

**news** *npl* current events; recent happenings; the mass media's coverage of such events; a programme of news on television or radio; information not known before.

**newsagent, newsdealer** *n* a retailer of newspapers, magazines, etc.

**newsflash** *n* an important news item broadcast separately and often interrupting other programmes.

**newspaper** *n* a printed periodical containing news published daily or weekly.

**New Year's (Day)** *n* the first day of a new year; 1 January, a legal holiday in many countries.

**next** *adj* nearest; immediately preceding or following; adjacent. • *adv* in the nearest time, place, rank, etc; on the first subsequent occasion.

**next of kin** *n* the nearest relative of a person.

**NHS** *abbr* = National Health Service.

**nib** *n* a pen point.

**nibble** *vti* to take small bites at (food, etc); to bite (at) lightly and intermittently.—**nibbler** *n*.

**nice** *adj* pleasant, attractive, kind, good, etc; particular, fastidious; delicately sensitive.—**nicely** *adv*.—**niceness** *n*.

**niche** *n* a shallow recess in a wall for a statue, etc; a place, use, or work for which a person or thing is best suited.

**nick** *n* a small cut, chip, etc, made on a surface; (*slang*) a police station, prison. • *vt* to make a nick in; to wound superficially; (*sl*) to steal; (*sl*) to arrest.

**nickel** *n* a silvery-white metallic element used in alloys and plating; a US or Canadian coin worth five cents.

**nickname** *n* a substitute name, often

descriptive, given in fun; a familiar form of a proper name. • *vt* to give as a nickname.

**nicotine** *n* a poisonous alkaloid present in tobacco.

**niece** *n* the daughter of a brother or sister.

**niggling** *adj* finicky, fussy; petty; gnawing, irritating.

**night** *n* the period of darkness from sunset to sunrise; nightfall; a specified or appointed evening.

**nightcap** *n* a cap worn in bed; (*inf*) an alcoholic drink taken just before going to bed.

**nightclub** *n* a place of entertainment for drinking, dancing, etc, at night.

**nightdress** *n* a loose garment worn in bed by women and girls.

**nightfall** *n* the close of the day.

**nightie, nighty** *n* (*inf*) a nightdress, nightgown.

**nightingale** *n* a songbird celebrated for its musical song at night.

**nightlife** *n* social entertainment at night, esp in towns.

**nightly** *adj*, *adv* done or happening by night or every night.

**nightmare** *n* a frightening dream; any horrible experience.—**nightmarish** *adj*.

**night school** *n* an educational institution where classes are held in the evening.

**night-time** *n* night.

**night watchman** *n* the person who guards a building at night.

**nil** *n* nothing.

**nimble** *adj* agile; quick.—**nimbly** *adv*.

**nine** *adj*, *n* one more than eight. • *n* the symbol for this (9, IX, ix); the ninth in a series or set; something having nine units as members.

**nineteen** *adj*, *n* one more than eighteen. • *n* the symbol for this (19, XIX, xix).—**nineteenth** *adj*.

**ninety** *adj*, *n* nine times ten. • *n* the

symbol for this (90, XC, xc); (*in pl*) **nineties**; the numbers from 90 to 99; the same numbers in a life or century.—**ninetieth** *adj*.

**ninth** *adj*, *n* next after eighth; one of nine equal parts of a thing.

**nip**[1] *vt* (*pt* **nipped**) to pinch, pinch off; to squeeze between two surfaces; (*dog*) to give a small bite; to prevent the growth of; (*plants*) to have a harmful effect on because of cold. • *n* a pinch; a sharp squeeze; a bite; severe frost or biting coldness.

**nip**[2] *n* a small drink of spirits. • *vti* to drink in nips.

**nipple** *n* the small protuberance on a breast or udder through which the milk passes, a teat; a teat-like rubber part on the cap of a baby's bottle; a projection resembling a nipple.

**nippy** *adj* (**nippier, nippiest**) (*inf*) quick, nimble; (*weather*) frosty; (*motor car*) small but powerful.

**nitrogen** *n* a gaseous element forming nearly 78 per cent of air.

**No, no**[1] *abbr* = number.

**no**[2] *adv* (*used to express denial or disagreement*) not so, not at all, by no amount. • *adj* not any; not a; not one; none; not at all; by no means. • *n* (*pl* **noes, nos**) a denial; a refusal; a negative vote or voter.

**nobility** *n* nobleness of character, mind, birth, or rank; the class of people of noble birth.

**noble** *adj* famous or renowned; excellent in quality or character; of high rank or birth. • *n* a person of high rank in society.—**nobleman** *n*.—**nobly** *adv*.

**nobody** *n* a person of no importance. • *pron* no person.

**nod** *vti* (*pt* **nodded**) to incline the head quickly, esp in agreement or greeting; to let the head drop, be drowsy; to indicate by a nod; (*with* **off**) (*inf*) to fall asleep. • *n* a quick bob of the head; a sign of assent or command.

**noise** *n* a sound, esp a loud, disturbing or unpleasant one; a din; unwanted fluctuations in a transmitted signal; (*pl*) conventional sounds, words, etc made in reaction, such as sympathy. • *vt* to make public.

**noisy** *adj* (**noisier, noisiest**) making much noise; turbulent, clamorous.—**noisily** *adv*.—**noisiness** *n*.

**nomad** *n* one of a people or tribe who move in search of pasture; a wanderer.—**nomadic** *adj*.

**no-man's-land** *n* an unclaimed piece of land; a strip of land, esp between armies, borders; an ambiguous area, subject, etc.

**nominal** *adj* of or like a name; existing in name only; having minimal real worth, token.—**nominally** *adv*.

**nominate** *vt* to appoint to an office or position; (*candidate*) to propose for election.—**nominator** *n*.

**nomination** *n* the act or right of nominating; the state of being nominated.

**nominee** *n* a person who is nominated.

**non-** *prefix* not, reversing the meaning of a word.

**nonchalant** *adj* calm; cool, unconcerned, indifferent.—**nonchalance** *n*.—**nonchalantly** *adv*.

**noncommittal** *adj* not revealing one's opinion.—**noncommittally** *adv*.

**nondescript** *adj* hard to classify, indeterminate; lacking individual characteristics. • *n* a nondescript person or thing.

**none** *pron* no one; not anyone; (*pl verb*) not any; no one. • *adv* not at all.

**nonentity** *n* a person or thing of no significance.

**nonflammable** *adj* not easily set on fire.

**nonplus** *vt* (*pt* **nonplussed**) to cause to be so perplexed that one cannot, go, speak, act further.

**nonsense** *n* words, actions, etc, that are absurd and have no meaning.—*also adj*.—**nonsensical** *adj*.

**nonstop** *adj* (*train, plane, etc*) not making any intermediate stops; not ceasing. • *adv* without stopping or pausing.

**noodle**[1] *n* (*often pl*) pasta formed into a strip.

**noodle**[2] *n* (*inf*) a foolish person; (*sl*) the head.

**nook** *n* a secluded corner, a retreat; a recess.

**noon** *n* midday; twelve o'clock in the day.

**nor** *conj* and not; not either.

**norm** *n* a standard or model, esp the standard of achievement of a large group.—**normative** *adj*.

**normal** *adj* regular; usual; stable mentally. • *n* anything normal; the usual state, amount, etc.—**normalcy** *n*.—**normality** *n*.—**normally** *adv*.

**north** *n* one of the four points of the compass, opposite the sun at noon, to the right of a person facing the sunset; the direction in which a compass needle points; (*often with cap*) the northern part of one's country or the earth. • *adj* in, of, or towards the north; from the north. • *adv* in or towards the north.

**northeast** *adj*, *n* (of) the direction midway between north and east.

**northern** *adj* of or in the north.

**northward** *adj* towards or in the north.—*also adv*.—**northwards** *adv*.

**northwest** *adj*, *n* (of) the direction midway between north and west.

**Norwegian** *adj*, *n* (of or relating to) the language, people, etc, of Norway.

**nose** *n* the part of the face above the mouth, used for breathing and smelling, having two nostrils; the sense of smell; anything like a nose in shape or position. • *vt* to discover as by smell; to nuzzle; to push (away, etc) with the front forward. • *vi* to sniff for; to inch forwards; to pry.

**nose dive** *n* a swift downward plunge of an aircraft, nose first; any sudden sharp drop, as in prices.—*also vi.*

**nosey** *see* **nosy**.

**nostalgia** *n* yearning for past times or places.

**nostalgic** *adj* feeling or expressing nostalgia; longing for one's youth.— **nostalgically** *adv*.

**nostril** *n* one of the two external openings of the nose for breathing and smelling.

**nosy** *adj* (**nosier, nosiest**) (*inf*) inquisitive, snooping.—**nosily** *adv*.—**nosiness** *n*.—*also* **nosey**.

**not** *adv expressing* denial, refusal, or negation.

**notable** *adj* worthy of being noted or remembered; remarkable, eminent. • *n* an eminent or famous person.— **notably** *adv*.

**notch** *n* a V-shaped cut in an edge or surface; (*inf*) a step, degree; a narrow pass with steep sides. • *vt* to cut notches in.

**note** *n* a brief summary or record, written down for future reference; a memorandum; a short letter; notice, attention; an explanation or comment on the text of a book; a musical sound of a particular pitch; a sign representing such a sound; a piano or organ key; the vocal sound of a bird. • *vt* to notice, observe; to write down; to annotate.

**notebook** *n* a book with blank pages for writing in.

**noted** *adj* celebrated, well-known.

**notepaper** *n* paper for writing letters.

**nothing** *n* no thing; not anything; nothingness; a zero; a trifle; a person or thing of no importance or value. • *adv* in no way, not at all.

**notice** *n* an announcement; a warning; a placard giving information; a short article about a book, play, etc; attention, heed; a formal warning of intention to end an agreement at a certain time. • *vt* to observe; to remark upon. • *vi* to be aware of.

**noticeable** *adj* easily noticed or seen.— **noticeably** *adv*.

**notice board** *n* a board on which notices, bulletins, etc, are pinned for public information.

**notify** *vt* to inform; to report, give notice of.

**notion** *n* a general idea; an opinion; a whim;.

**notorious** *adj* widely known, esp unfavourably.—**notoriously** *adv*.

**notwithstanding** *prep* in spite of. • *adv* nevertheless. • *conj* although.

**nougat** *n* a chewy sweet consisting of sugar paste with nuts.

**nought** *n* nothing; a zero.—*also* **naught**.

**noun** *n* (*gram*) a word that names a person, a living being, an object, action etc; a substantive.

**nourish** *vt* to feed; to encourage the growth of; to raise, bring up.

**nourishing** *adj* containing nourishment; health-giving; beneficial.

**nourishment** *n* food; the act of nourishing.

**novel** *n* a relatively long prose narrative that is usually fictitious and in the form of a story. • *adj* new and unusual.

**novelist** *n* a writer of novels.

**novelty** *n* a novel thing or occurrence; a new or unusual thing; (*pl*) cheap, small objects for sale.

**November** *n* the eleventh month, having 30 days.

**novice** *n* a person on probation in a religious order before taking final vows; a beginner.

**now** *adv* at the present time; by this time; at once; nowadays. • *conj* since; seeing that. • *n* the present time. • *adj* of the present time.

**nowadays** *adv* in these days; at the present time.

**nowhere** *adv* not in, at, or to anywhere.

**nozzle** *n* the spout at the end of a hose, pipe, etc.

**nuance** *n* a subtle difference in meaning, colour, etc.

**nuclear** *adj* of or relating to a nucleus; using nuclear energy; having nuclear weapons.

**nuclear energy** *n* energy released as a result of nuclear fission or fusion.

**nuclear fission** *n* the splitting of a nucleus of an atom either spontaneously or by bombarding it with particles.

**nuclear fusion** *n* the combining of two nuclei into a heavier nucleus, releasing energy in the process.

**nuclear power** *n* electrical or motive power produced by a nuclear reactor.

**nuclear reactor** *n* a device in which nuclear fission is maintained and harnessed to produce energy.

**nucleus** *n* (*pl* **nuclei, nucleuses**) the central part of core around which something may develop, or be grouped or concentrated; the centrally positively charged portion of an atom; the part of an animal or plant cell containing genetic material.

**nude** *adj* naked; bare; undressed. • *n* a naked human figure, esp in a work of art; the state of being nude.—**nudity** *n*.

**nudge** *vt* to touch gently with the elbow to attract attention or urge into action; to push slightly.—*also n*.

**nuisance** *n* a person or thing that annoys or causes trouble.

**null** *adj* without legal force; invalid.

**nullify** *vt* to make null, to cancel out.—**nullification** *n*.

**numb** *adj* deadened; having no feeling (due to cold, shock, etc). • *vt* to make numb.—**numbness** *n*.

**number** *n* a symbol or word indicating how many; a numeral identifying a person or thing by its position in a series; a single issue of a magazine; a song or piece of music, esp as an item in a performance; (*inf*) an object singled out; a total of persons or things; (*gram*) the form of a word indicating singular or plural; a telephone number; (*pl*) arithmetic; (*pl*) numerical superiority. • *vti* to count; to give a number to; to include or be included as one of a group; to limit the number of; to total.

**numberplate** *n* a plate on the front or rear of a motor vehicle that displays its registration number.

**numeral** *n* a symbol or group of symbols used to express a number (eg two = 2 or II, etc).

**numerical, numeric** *adj* of or relating to numbers; expressed in numbers.

**numerous** *adj* many, consisting of many items.

**nun** *n* a woman belonging to a religious order.

**nurse** *n* a person trained to care for the sick, injured or aged; a person who looks after another person's child or children. • *vt* to tend, to care for; (*baby*) to feed at the breast; (*hatred*) to foster; to tend with an eye to the future.

**nursery** *n* a room set aside for children; a place where children may be left in temporary care; a place where young trees and plants are raised for transplanting.

**nursery rhyme** *n* a short traditional poem or song for children.

**nursery school** *n* a school for young children, usu under five.

**nursery slope** *n* a gently inclined slope for novice skiers.

**nursing** *n* the profession of a nurse.

**nursing home** *n* an establishment

providing care for convalescent, chronically ill, or disabled people.

**nut** *n* a kernel (sometimes edible) enclosed in a hard shell; a usu metallic threaded block screwed on the end of a bolt; (*sl*) a mad person; (*sl*) a devotee, fan.

**nutcracker** *n* (usu *pl*) a tool for cracking nuts; a bird with speckled plumage.

**nutmeg** *n* the aromatic kernel produced by a tree, grated and used as a spice.

**nutrition** *n* the act or process by which plants and animals take in and assimilate food in their systems; the study of the human diet.—**nutritional** *adj*.

**nutritious** *adj* efficient as food; health-giving, nourishing.

**nylon** *n* any of numerous strong, tough, elastic, synthetic materials used esp in plastics and textiles; (*pl*) stockings made of nylon.

# O

**oaf** *n* (*pl* **oafs**) a loutish or stupid person.—**oafish** *adj*.—**oafishness** *n*.

**oak** *n* a tree with a hard durable wood, having acorns as fruits.

**OAP** *abbr* = old age pensioner.

**oar** *n* a pole with a flat blade for rowing a boat; an oarsman.

**oasis** *n* (*pl* **oases**) a fertile place in a desert; a refuge.

**oath** *n* a solemn declaration to a god or a higher authority that one will speak the truth or keep a promise; a swear word; a blasphemous expression.

**oatmeal** *n* ground oats; a porridge of this; a pale greyish-brown colour.

**oats** *npl* a cereal grass widely cultivated for its edible grain; the seeds.

**obedience** *n* the condition of being obedient; observance of orders, instructions, etc; respect for authority.

**obedient** *adj* obeying; compliant; submissive to authority, dutiful.—**obediently** *adv*.

**obelisk** *n* a four-sided tapering pillar usu with a pyramidal top.

**obey** *vti* to carry out (orders, instructions); to comply (with); to submit (to).

**obituary** *n* an announcement of a person's death, often with a short biography.

**object** *n* something that can be recognized by the senses; a person or thing towards which action, feeling, etc, is directed; a purpose or aim; (*gram*) a noun or part of a sentence governed by a transitive verb or a preposition. • *vti* to state or raise an objection; to oppose; to disapprove.—**objector** *n*.

**objection** *n* the act of objecting; a ground for, or expression of, disapproval.

**objectionable** *adj* causing an objection; disagreeable.—**objectionably** *adv*.

**objective** *adj* relating to an object; not influenced by opinions or feelings; impartial; having an independent existence of its own, real; (*gram*) of, or appropriate to an object governed by a verb or a preposition. • *n* the thing or placed aimed at; (*gram*) the objective case.—**objectively** *adv*.—**objectivity** *n*.

**obligation** *n* the act of obligating; a moral or legal requirement; a debt; a favour; a commitment to pay a certain amount of money; the amount owed.

**obligatory** *adj* binding, not optional; compulsory.

**oblige** *vt* to compel by moral, legal, or

physical force; (*person*) to make grateful for some favour; to do a favour for.

**obliging** *adj* ready to do favours, agreeable.—**obligingly** *adv*.

**oblique** *adj* slanting, at an angle; diverging from the straight; indirect, allusive. • *n* an oblique line.—**obliquely** *adv*.

**obliterate** *vt* to wipe out, to erase, to destroy.—**obliteration** *n*.

**oblivion** *n* a state of forgetting or being forgotten; a state of mental withdrawal.

**oblivious** *adj* forgetful, unheeding; unaware (of).

**oblong** *adj* rectangular. • *n* any oblong figure.

**obnoxious** *adj* objectionable; highly offensive.—**obnoxiously** *adv*.—**obnoxiousness** *n*.

**oboe** *n* an orchestral woodwind instrument having a mouthpiece with a double reed.—**oboist** *n*.

**obscene** *adj* indecent, lewd; offensive to a moral or social standard.—**obscenely** *adv*.

**obscenity** *n* the state or quality of being obscene; an obscene act, word, etc.

**obscure** *adj* not clear; dim; indistinct; remote, secret; not easily understood; inconspicuous; unimportant, humble. • *vt* to make unclear, to confuse; to hide.—**obscurely** *adv*.

**obscurity** *n* the state or quality of being obscure; an obscure thing or person.

**obsequious** *adj* subservient; fawning.—**obsequiously** *adv*.

**observance** *n* the observing of a rule, duty, law, etc; a ceremony or religious rite.

**observant** *adj* watchful; attentive, mindful.—**observantly** *adv*.

**observation** *n* the act or faculty of observing; a comment or remark; careful noting of the symptoms of a patient, movements of a suspect, etc prior to diagnosis, analysis or interpretation.

**observatory** *n* a building for astronomical observation; an institution whose primary purpose is making such observations.

**observe** *vt* to notice; to perceive; (*a law, etc*) to keep to or adhere to; to arrive at as a conclusion; to examine scientifically. • *vi* to take notice; to make a comment (on).—**observable** *adj*.

**observer** *n* a person who observes; a delegate who attends a formal meeting but may not take part; an expert analyst and commentator in a particular field.

**obsess** *vt* to possess or haunt the mind of; to preoccupy.—**obsessive** *adj, n*.—**obsessively** *adv*.

**obsession** *n* a fixed idea, often associated with mental illness; a persistent idea or preoccupation; the condition of obsessing or being obsessed.

**obsolescent** *adj* becoming obsolete, going out of date.—**obsolescence** *n*.

**obsolete** *adj* disused, out of date.

**obstacle** *n* anything that hinders something; an obstruction.

**obstacle race** *n* a race in which the competitors negotiate various obstacles.

**obstetrics** *n* (*used as sing*) the branch of medicine concerned with the care and treatment of women during pregnancy and childbirth.—**obstetric** *adj*.—**obstetrician** *n*.

**obstinate** *adj* stubborn, self-willed; intractable; persistent.—**obstinacy** *n*.—**obstinately** *adv*.

**obstreperous** *adj* unruly, turbulent, noisy.

**obstruct** *vt* to block with an obstacle; to impede; to prevent, hinder; to keep (light, etc) from.

**obstruction** *n* that which obstructs; the

act or an example of obstructing; a hindrance, obstacle.

**obstructive** *adj* tending to obstruct; preventing, hindering.— **obstructively** *adv*.

**obtain** *vt* to get, to acquire, to gain. • *vi* to be prevalent, hold good.— **obtainable** *adj*.

**obtrusive** *adj* apt to obtrude, pushy; protruding, sticking out.—**obtrusively** *adv*.—**obtrusiveness** *n*.

**obtuse** *adj* mentally slow; not pointed; dull, stupid; (*geom*) greater than a right angle.—**obtusely** *adv*.—**obtuseness** *n*.

**obviate** *vt* to make unnecessary; (*danger*, *difficulty*) to prevent, clear away.

**obvious** *adj* easily seen or understood; evident.—**obviously** *adv*.—**obviousness** *n*.

**occasion** *n* a special occurrence or event; a time when something happens; an opportunity; reason or grounds; a subsidiary cause. • *vt* to cause; to bring about.

**occasional** *adj* infrequent, not continuous; intermittent; produced for an occasion; (*a cause*) incidental.

**occupation** *n* the act of occupying; the state of being occupied; employment or profession; a pursuit.—**occupational** *adj*.

**occupy** *vt* to live in; (*room*, *office*) to take up or fill; (*a position*) to hold; to engross (one's mind); (*city*, *etc*) to take possession of.—**occupier** *n*.

**occur** *vi* (*pt* **occurred**) to happen; to exist; to come into the mind of.

**occurrence** *n* a happening, an incident, an event; the act or fact of occurring.

**ocean** *n* a large stretch of sea, esp one of the earth's five oceans; a huge quantity or expanse.

**ochre, ocher** (*US*) *n* a yellow to orange-coloured clay used as a pigment.

**o'clock** *adv* indicating the hour; indicating a relative direction or position, twelve o'clock being directly ahead or above.

**octave** *n* (*mus*) the eighth full tone above or below a given tone, the interval of eight degrees between a tone and either of its octaves, or the series of tones within this interval.

**October** *n* the tenth month of the year, having 31 days.

**octopus** *n* (*pl* **octopuses**) a mollusc having a soft body and eight tentacles covered with suckers.

**odd** *adj* eccentric; peculiar; occasional; not divisible by two; with the other of the pair missing; extra or left over. • *npl* probability; balance of advantage in favour of one against another; excess of one number over another, esp in betting; likelihood; disagreement; strife; miscellaneous articles, scraps.—**oddly** *adv*.—**oddness** *n*.

**oddity** *n* the state of being odd; an odd thing or person; peculiarity.

**oddment** *n* an odd piece left over, esp of fabric.

**ode** *n* a lyric poem marked by lofty feeling and dignified style.

**odious** *adj* causing hatred or offence; disgusting.—**odiously** *adv*.—**odiousness** *n*.

**odour, odor** (*US*) *n* smell; scent; aroma; a characteristic or predominant quality.

**odourless, odorless** (*US*) *adj* without odour.

**of** *prep* from; belonging or relating to; concerning; among; by; during; owing to.

**off** *adv* away, from; detached, gone; unavailable; disconnected; out of condition; entirely. • *prep* away from; not on. • *adj* distant; no longer operating; cancelled; (*food or drink*) having gone bad; on the right-hand side; (*runners*, *etc*) having started a race.

**offal** *n* the entrails of an animal eaten as food.

**off-colour** *adj* unwell; risqué.

**offence, offense** (*US*) *n* an illegal action, crime; a sin; an affront, insult; a cause of displeasure or anger.

**offend** *vt* to affront, displease; to insult. • *vi* to break a law.—**offender** *n*.

**offensive** *adj* causing offence; repulsive, disagreeable; insulting; aggressive. • *n* an attack; a forceful campaign for a cause, etc.—**offensively** *adv*.—**offensiveness** *n*.

**offer** *vt* to present for acceptance or rejection; to show willingness (to do something); to present for consideration; to bid; (*a prayer*) to say. • *vi* to present itself; to declare oneself willing. • *n* something offered; a bid or proposal.

**offering** *n* a gift, present; a sacrifice.

**offhand** *adv* impromptu; without thinking. • *adj* inconsiderate; curt, brusque; unceremonious.

**office** *n* a room or building where business is carried out; the people there; (*with cap*) the location, staff, of authority of a Government department, etc; a task or function; a position of authority; a duty; a religious ceremony, rite.

**officer** *n* an official; a person holding a position of authority in a government, business, club, military services, etc; a policeman.

**official** *adj* of an office or its tenure; properly authorized; formal. • *n* a person who holds a public office.—**officially** *adv*.

**officious** *adj* interfering, meddlesome; offering unwanted advice.—**officiously** *adv*.—**officiousness** *n*.

**offing** *n* the near or foreseeable future.

**off-licence** *n* a licence to sell alcohol for consumption off the premises; a place so licensed.

**off-peak** *adj* denoting use of a service, etc, in a period of lesser demand.

**offset** *vt* (*pr p* **offsetting**, *pt* **offset**) to compensate for, counterbalance. • *n* compensation; a method of printing in which an image is transferred from a plate to a rubber surface and then to paper; a sloping ledge on the face of a wall.

**offshore** *adv* at sea some distance from the shore.

**offside** *adj, adv* illegally in advance of the ball.

**offspring** *n* a child, progeny; a result.

**offstage** *adj, adv* out of sight of the audience; behind the scenes.

**often** *adv* many times, frequently.

**ogle** *vti* to gape at; to make eyes at; to look at lustfully.

**oil** *n* a greasy, combustible liquid substance obtained from animal, vegetable, or mineral matter; petroleum; an oil painting; (*pl*) paint mixed by grinding a pigment in oil. • *vt* to smear with oil, lubricate.

**oilcan** *n* a container with a long spout for releasing oil for lubricating in individual drops.

**oilfield** *n* an area on land or under the sea that produces petroleum.

**oil painting** *n* a painting in oils; the art of painting in oils; (*inf*) a good-looking person.

**oilskin** *n* fabric made waterproof by treatment with oil; a waterproof garment of oilskin or a plastic-coated fabric.

**oil slick** *n* a mass of oil floating on the surface of water.

**oil well** *n* a well from which petroleum is extracted.

**oily** *adj* (**oilier, oiliest**) like or covered with oil; greasy; too suave or smooth, unctuous.—**oiliness** *n*.

**ointment** *n* a fatty substance used on the skin for healing or cosmetic purposes; a salve.

**OK, okay** *adj*, *adv* (*inf*) all right; correct(ly). • *n* (*pl* **OK's, okays**) approval.

**old** *adj* aged; elderly, not young; having lived or existed for a long time; long used, not new; former; of the past, not modern; experienced; worn out; of long standing.

**old-fashioned** *adj* out of date; in a fashion of an older time.

**olive** *n* an evergreen tree cultivated for its edible hard-stoned fruit and oil; its fruit; a yellow-green colour. • *adj* of a yellow-green colour.

**olive oil** *n* an edible yellow oil obtained from the fruit of the olive by pressing.

**Olympic Games, Olympics** *n* (*used as sing or pl*) an ancient athletic contest revived in 1896 as an international meeting held every four years in a different country.

**omelette, omelet** (*US*) *n* eggs beaten and cooked flat in a pan.

**omen** *n* a sign or warning of impending happiness or disaster.

**ominous** *adj* relating to an omen; foreboding evil; threatening.—**ominously** *adv*.

**omission** *n* something that has been left out or neglected; the act of omitting.

**omit** *vt* (*pt* **omitted**) to leave out; to neglect to do, leave undone.

**omni-** *prefix* all; universally.

**on** *prep* in contact with the upper surface of; supported by, attached to, or covering; directed toward; at the time of; concerning, about; using as a basis, condition or principle; immediately after; (*sl*) using; addicted to. • *adv* (so as to be) covering or in contact with something; forward; (*device*) switched on; continuously in progress; due to take place; (*actor*) on stage; on duty. • *adj* (*cricket*) designating the part of the field on the batsman's side in front of the wicket. • *n* (*cricket*) the on side.

**once** *adv* on one occasion only; formerly; at some time. • *conj* as soon as. • *n* one time.

**oncoming** *adj* approaching.

**one** *adj* single; undivided, united; the same; a certain unspecified (time, etc). • *n* the first and lowest cardinal number; an individual thing or person; (*inf*) a drink; (*inf*) a joke. • *pron* an indefinite person, used to apply to many people; someone.

**oneself** *pron reflex form of* one.

**one-way** *adj* (*traffic*) restricted to one direction; requiring no reciprocal action or obligation.

**ongoing** *adj* progressing, continuing.

**onion** *n* an edible bulb with a pungent taste and odour.

**onlooker** *n* a spectator.

**only** *adj* alone of its kind; single, sole. • *adv* solely, merely; just; not more than. • *conj* except that, but.

**onset** *n* a beginning; an assault, attack.

**onslaught** *n* a fierce attack.

**onto** *prep* to a position on.

**onus** *n* responsibility, duty; burden.

**onward** *adj* advancing, forward. • *adv* onwards.

**onwards** *adv* to the front, ahead, forward.

**onyx** *n* a limestone similar to marble with layers of colour.

**ooze** *vti* to flow or leak out slowly; to seep; to exude. • *n* soft mud or slime.

**opal** *n* a white or bluish stone with a play of iridescent colours.

**opaque** *adj* not letting light through; neither transparent nor translucent.—**opaquely** *adv*.—**opaqueness** *n*.

**open** *adj* not closed; accessible; uncovered, unprotected; not fenced; free from trees; spread out, unfolded; public; lacking reserve; (*a* *person*) forthcoming; generous; readily understood; liable (to); unrestricted; (*syllable*) ending with a vowel; (*consonant*) made without stopping the stream of breath. • *vti* to make or become accessible; to unfasten; to begin; to expand, unfold; to come into view. • *n* a wide space; (*sport*) a competition that any player can enter.—**openness** *n*.

**opening** *n* a gap, aperture; a beginning; a chance; a job opportunity. • *adj* initial.

**openly** *adv* frankly; publicly.

**open-minded** *adj* unprejudiced.— **open-mindedness** *n*.

**opera** *n* a dramatic work represented through music and song; plural form of **opus**.

**operate** *vi* to work, to function; to produce a desired effect; to carry out a surgical operation. • *vt* (*a machine*) to work or control; to carry on, run.

**operatic** *adj* of or relating to opera; exaggerated, overacting.

**operation** *n* a method of operating; a procedure; a military action; a surgical procedure.

**operational** *adj* of or relating to an operation; functioning; ready for use; involved in military activity.—**operationally** *adv*.

**operative** *adj* functioning; in force, effective; of, by surgery. • *n* a mechanic; a secret agent; a private detective.

**operator** *n* a person who operates or works a machine, esp a telephone switchboard; a person who owns or runs a business; a person who manipulates.

**operetta** *n* a short or light opera.

**opinion** *n* a belief that is not based on proof; judgment; estimation, evaluation; a formal expert judgment; professional advice.

**opinionated** *adj* unduly confident in one's opinions, dogmatic.

**opium** *n* a narcotic drug produced from an annual Eurasian poppy.

**opponent** *n* a person who opposes another; an adversary, antagonist. • *adj* opposing.

**opportune** *adj* well-timed; convenient.—**opportunely** *adv*.

**opportunist** *n* a person who forms or adapts his or her views or principles to benefit from opportunities; to seize opportunities as they may arise.—**opportunism** *n*.

**opportunity** *n* chance; a favourable combination of circumstances.

**oppose** *vt* to put in front of or in the way of; to place in opposition; to resist; to fight against; to balance against.—**opposer** *n*.

**opposite** *adj* placed on opposed sides of; face to face; diametrically different; contrary. • *n* a person or thing that is opposite; an antithesis. • *prep*, *adv* across from.

**opposition** *n* the act of opposing or the condition of being opposed; resistance; antithesis; hostility; a political party opposing the government; (*astron*) the diametrically opposite position of two heavenly bodies, when 180 degrees apart.

**oppress** *vt* to treat unjustly; to subjugate; to weigh down in the mind.— **oppressor** *n*.

**oppression** *n* the act of oppressing; the state of being oppressed; persecution; physical or mental distress.

**oppressive** *adj* tyrannical; burdensome; (*weather*) sultry, close.—**oppressively** *adv*.—**oppressiveness** *n*.

**opt** *vi* to choose or to exercise an option.

**optical** *adj* of or relating to the eye or light; optic; aiding or correcting vision; visual.—**optically** *adv*.

**optician** *n* a person who makes or sells optical aids.

**optimism** *n* a tendency to take the most

cheerful view of things; hopefulness; the belief that good must ultimately prevail.—**optimist** *n*.—**optimistic** *adj*.—**optimistically** *adv*.

**optimum** *n* the best, most favourable condition.—*also adj*.

**option** *n* the act of choosing; the power to choose; a choice; the right to buy, sell or lease at a fixed price within a specified time.

**optional** *adj* left to choice; not compulsory.— **optionally** *adv*.

**opulent** *adj* wealthy; luxuriant.—**opulence** *n*.

**opus** (*pl* **opuses, opera**) an artistic or literary work; a musical composition.

**or** *conj denoting* an alternative; the last in a series of choices.

**oracle** *n* a place in ancient Greece where a deity was consulted; the response given (often ambiguous); a wise adviser; sage advice.—**oracular** *adj*.

**oral** *adj* of the mouth; (*drugs*) taken by mouth; spoken, not written. • *n* a spoken examination.—**orally** *adv*.

**orange** *n* a round, reddish-yellow, juicy, edible citrus fruit; the tree bearing it; its colour. • *adj* orange-coloured.

**oration** *n* a formal or public speech.

**orator** *n* an eloquent public speaker.

**oratorio** *n* (*pl* **oratorios**) a sacred story set to music for voices and instruments.

**orb** *n* a sphere or globe; an ornamental sphere surmounted by a cross, esp as carried by a sovereign at a coronation.

**orbit** *n* (*astron*) a curved path along which a planet or satellite moves; a field of action or influence; the eye socket; (*physics*) the path of an electron around the nucleus of an atom. • *vti* to put (a satellite, etc) into orbit; to circle round.—**orbital** *adj*.

**orchard** *n* an area of land planted with fruit trees.

**orchestra** *n* a group of musicians playing together under a conductor; their instruments; the space (or pit) in a theatre where they sit; the stalls of a theatre.—**orchestral** *adj*.

**orchid** *n* a plant with unusually shaped flowers in brilliant colours comprising three petals of uneven size.

**ordain** *vti* to confer holy orders upon; to appoint; to decree; to order, to command.

**ordeal** *n* a severe trial or test; an exacting experience.

**order** *n* arrangement; method; relative position; sequence; an undisturbed condition; tidiness; rules of procedure; an efficient state; a class, group, or sort; a religious fraternity; a style of architecture; an honour or decoration; an instruction or command; a rule or regulation; a state or condition, esp with regard to functioning; a request to supply something; the goods supplied; (*zool*) divisions between class and family or genus. • *vti* to put or keep (things) in order; to arrange; to command; to request (something) to be supplied.

**orderly** *adj* in good order; well-behaved; methodical. • *n* a hospital attendant; a soldier attending an officer.—**orderliness** *n*.

**ordinal** *adj* showing position in a series. • *n* an ordinal number.

**ordinary** *adj* normal, usual; common; plain, unexceptional.—**ordinarily** *adv*.

**ordination** *n* the act of ordaining or being ordained; admission to the ministry.

**ore** *n* a substance from which minerals can be extracted.

**organ** *n* a usu large and complex musical wind instrument with pipes, stops, and a keyboard; a part of an animal or plant that performs a vital or natural function; the means by which anything is done; a medium of information or opinion, a periodical.

**organic** *adj* of or relating to bodily organs; (disease) affecting a bodily organ; of, or derived from, living organisms; systematically arranged; structural; (*chem*) of the class of compounds that are formed from carbon; (vegetables, etc) grown without the use of artificial fertilizers or pesticides.—**organically** *adv*.

**organism** *n* an animal or plant, any living thing; an organized body.

**organist** *n* a person who plays an organ.

**organization** *n* the act or process of organizing; the state of being organized; arrangement, structure; an organized body or association.

**organize** *vt* to arrange in an orderly way; to establish; to institute; to persuade to join a cause, group, etc; to arrange for.—**organizer** *n*.

**orgasm** *n* the climax of sexual excitement.—**orgasmic** *adj*.

**orgy** *n* a wild party or gathering of people, with excessive drinking and indiscriminate sexual activity; over-indulgence in any activity.

**Orient** *n* the East, or Asia, esp the Far East.

**orient, orientate** *vti* to adjust (oneself) to a particular situation; to arrange in a direction, esp in relation to the points of the compass; to face or turn in a particular direction.

**oriental** *adj* of the Orient, its people or languages.

**orifice** *n* an opening or mouth of a cavity.

**origin** *n* the source or beginning of anything; ancestry or parentage.

**original** *adj* relating to the origin or beginning; earliest, primitive; novel; unusual; inventive, creative. • *n* an original work, as of art or literature;

something from which copies are made; a creative person; an eccentric.—**originality** *n*.—**originally** *adv*.

**originate** *vti* to initiate or begin; to bring or come into being.—**origination** *n*.—**originator** *n*.

**ornament** *n* anything that enhances the appearance of a person or thing; a small decorative object. • *vt* to adorn, to decorate with ornaments.

**ornamental** *adj* serving as an ornament; decorative, not useful.—**ornamentally** *adv*.

**ornate** *adj* richly adorned; (*style*) highly elaborate.—**ornately** *adv*.—**ornateness** *n*.

**ornithology** *n* the study of birds.—**ornithological** *adj*.—**ornithologist** *n*.

**orphan** *n* a child whose parents are dead. • *vt* to cause to become an orphan.—*also adj*.

**orphanage** *n* a residential institution for the care of orphans.

**orthodox** *adj* conforming with established behaviour or opinions; not heretical; generally accepted, conventional; (*with cap*) of or relating to a conservative political or religious group.

**orthopaedics, orthopedics** (*US*) *n* the study and surgical treatment of bone and joint disorders.—**orthopaedic** *adj*.—**orthopaedist** *n*.

**oscillate** *vi* to swing back and forth as a pendulum; to waver, vacillate between extremes of opinion, etc.—**oscillation** *n*.

**ostensible** *adj* apparent; seeming; pretended.—**ostensibly** *adv*.

**ostentation** *n* a showy, pretentious display.—**ostentatious** *adj*.—**ostentatiously** *adv*.

**osteopathy** *n* the treatment of disease by manipulation of the bones and muscles, often as an adjunct to medical and surgical measures.—**osteopath** *n*.

**ostracize** *vt* to exclude, banish from a group, society, etc.—**ostracism** *n*.

**ostrich** *n* a large, flightless, swift-running African bird.

**other** *adj* second; remaining; different; additional. • *pron* the other one; some other one.

**otherwise** *adv* if not, or else; differently.

**otter** *n* a fish-eating mammal with smooth fur and a flat tail.

**ought** *aux vb* expressing obligation or duty; to be bound, to be obliged (to).

**ounce** *n* a unit of weight, equal to one sixteenth of a pound or 28.34 grams; one sixteenth of a pint, one fluid ounce.

**our** *poss adj*, *pron* relating or belonging to us.

**ours** *pron* belonging to us.

**ourselves** *pron* emphatic and reflexive form of we.

**oust** *vt* to eject, expel, esp by underhand means; to remove forcibly.

**out** *adv* not in; outside; in the open air; to the full extent; beyond bounds; no longer holding office; ruled out, no longer considered; loudly and clearly; no longer included (in a game, fashion, etc); in error; on strike; at an end; extinguished; into the open; published; revealed; (*radio conversation*) transmission ends. • *prep* out of; out through; outside. • *adj* external; outward. • *n* an exit; means of escape.

**outboard** *adj* (*engine*) outside a ship, etc. • *n* an engine attached to the outside of a boat.

**outbreak** *n* a sudden eruption (of disease, strife, etc).

**outburst** *n* a bursting out; a spurt; an explosion of anger, etc.

**outcast** *n* a person who is rejected by society.

**outclass** *vt* to surpass or excel greatly.

**outcome** *n* the result, consequence.

**outcry** *n* protest; uproar.

**outdo** *vt* (*pt* **outdid**, *pp* **outdone**) to surpass, to do more than, to excel.

**outdoor** *adj* existing, taking place, or used in the open air.

**outdoors** *adv* in or into the open air; out of doors. • *n* the open air, outside world.

**outer** *adj* further out or away.

**outer space** *n* any region of space beyond the earth's atmosphere.

**outfit** *n* the equipment used in an activity; clothes worn together, an ensemble; a group of people associated in an activity. • *vt* (*pt* **outfitted**) to provide with an outfit or equipment.

**outfitter** *n* a supplier of equipment or clothes.

**outgoing** *adj* departing; retiring; sociable, forthcoming. • *n* an outlay; (*pl*) expenditure.

**outing** *n* a pleasure trip; an excursion.

**outlandish** *adj* unconventional; strange; fantastic.

**outlaw** *vt* to declare illegal. • *n* an outlawed person; a habitual or notorious criminal.

**outlay** *n* a spending (of money); expenditure.

**outlet** *n* an opening or release; a means of expression; a market for goods or services.

**outline** *n* a profile; a general indication; a rough sketch or draft.—*also vt*.

**outlive** *vt* to live longer than, outlast; to live through; to survive.

**outlook** *n* mental attitude; view; prospect.

**outlying** *adj* detached; remote, distant.

**outmoded** *adj* old-fashioned.

**outpatient** *n* a person treated at, but not resident in, a hospital.

**outpost** *n* (*mil*) a post or detachment at a distance from a main force.

**output** *n* the quantity (of goods, etc) produced, esp over a given period;

information delivered by a computer, esp to a printer; (*elect*) the useful voltage, current, or power delivered.—*also vt.*

**outrage** *n* an extremely vicious or violent act; a grave insult or offence; great anger, etc, aroused by this.—*also vt.*—**outrageous** *adj*.

**outright** *adj* complete, downright, direct. • *adv* at once; without restrictions.

**outset** *n* the start, beginning.

**outside** *n* the outer part or surface, the exterior. • *adj* outer; outdoor; (*chance, etc*) slight. • *adv* on or to the outside. • *prep* on or to the exterior of; beyond.

**outsider** *n* a person or thing not included in a set, group, etc, a nonmember; a contestant not thought to have a chance in a race.

**outsize** *adj* of a larger than usual size.

**outskirts** *npl* districts remote from the centre, as of a city.

**outspoken** *adj* candid in speech, frank, blunt.

**outstanding** *adj* excellent; distinguished, prominent; unpaid; unresolved, still to be done.

**outward** *adj* directed towards the outside; external; clearly apparent. • *adv* outwards.

**outwardly** *adv* externally.

**outweigh** *vt* to count for more than, to exceed in value, weight, or importance.

**outwit** *vt* (*pt* **outwitted**) to get the better of, defeat, by wit or cunning.

**oval** *adj* egg-shaped; elliptical. • *n* anything oval.

**ovary** *n* one of the two female reproductive organs producing eggs.—**ovarian** *adj*.

**ovation** *n* enthusiastic applause or public welcome.

**oven** *n* an enclosed, heated compartment for baking or drying.

**over** *prep* higher than; on top of; across; to the other side of; above; more than; concerning. • *adv* above; across; in every part; completed; from beginning to end; up and down; in addition; too. • *adj* upper; excessive; surplus; finished; remaining. • *n* (*cricket*) the number of balls bowled before changing ends.

**over-** *prefix* in excess, too much; above.

**overact** *vti* to act in an exaggerated manner, to overdo a part.

**overall** *adj* including everything. • *adv* as a whole; generally. • *n* a loose protective garment; (*pl*) a one-piece protective garment covering body and legs.

**overawe** *vt* to restrain by awe, to daunt.

**overbalance** *vti* to fall over; to upset; to outweigh. • *n* a surplus.

**overbearing** *adj* domineering; overriding.

**overboard** *adv* over the side of a ship, etc; (*inf*) to extremes of enthusiasm.

**overcast** *adj* clouded over.

**overcharge** *vt* (*battery*) to overload; to fill to excess; to demand too high a price (from). • *n* an excessive or exorbitant charge or load.

**overcoat** *n* a warm, heavy topcoat.

**overcome** *vti* (*pt* **overcame**, *pp* **overcome**) to get the better of, to prevail; to render helpless or powerless, as by tears, laughter, emotion, etc; to be victorious; to surmount obstacles, etc.

**overdo** *vt* (*pt* **overdid**, *pp* **overdone**) to do to excess; to overact; to cook (food) too much.—**overdone** *adj*.

**overdose** *n* an excessive dose —*also vti.*

**overdraft** *n* an overdrawing, an amount overdrawn, at a bank.

**overdraw** *vti* (*pt* **overdrew**, *pp* **overdrawn**) to draw in excess of a credit balance; to exaggerate in describing; to make an overdraft.

**overestimate** *vt* to set too high an estimate on or for.—*also n*.

**overflow** *vti* (*pp* **overflown**) to flow over, to flood; to exceed the bounds (of); to abound (with emotion, etc). • *n* that which overflows; surplus, excess; an outlet for surplus water, etc.

**overgrown** *adj* grown beyond the normal size; rank; ungainly.

**overhaul** *vt* to examine for, or make, repairs; to overtake.—*also n*.

**overhead** *adj*, *adv* above the head; in the sky. • *n* (often *pl*) the general, continuing costs of a business, as of rent, light, etc.

**overhear** *vt* (*pt* **overheard**) to hear without the knowledge of the speaker.

**overjoyed** *adj* highly delighted.

**overland** *adj*, *adv* by, on, or across land.

**overlap** *vt* (*pt* **overlapped**) to extend over (a thing or each other) so as to coincide in part.—*also n*.

**overload** *vt* to put too great a burden on; (*elect*) to charge with too much current.

**overlook** *vt* to fail to notice; to look at from above; to excuse.

**overnight** *adv* for the night; in the course of the night; suddenly. • *adj* done in the night; lasting the night; sudden.

**overpass** *n* a road crossing another road, path, etc, at a higher level; the upper level of such a crossing.

**overpower** *vt* to overcome by superior force, to subdue; to overwhelm.

**overpowering** *adj* overwhelming; compelling; unbearable.

**overrate** *vt* to value or assess too highly.

**override** *vt* (*pt* **overrode**, *pp* **overridden**) to ride over; to nullify; to prevail.

**overrule** *vt* to set aside by higher authority; to prevail over.

**overseas** *adj*, *adv* across or beyond the sea; abroad.

**overshadow** *vt* to throw a shadow over; to appear more prominent or important than.

**overshoot** *vt* (*pt* **overshot**) to shoot or send beyond (a target, etc); (*aircraft*) to fly or taxi beyond the end of a runway when landing or taking off.—*also n*.

**oversight** *n* a careless mistake or omission; supervision.

**oversleep** *vi* (*pt* **overslept**) to sleep beyond the intended time.

**overspill** *vi* (*pt* **overspilt** *or* **overspilled**) to spill over, overflow. • *n* that which overspills; excess.—*also adj*.

**overt** *adj* openly done, unconcealed; (*law*) done with evident intent, deliberate.—**overtly** *adv*.

**overtake** *vt* (*pt* **overtook**, *pp* **overtaken**) to catch up with and pass; to come upon suddenly.

**overthrow** *vt* (*pt* **overthrew**, *pp* **overthrown**) to throw over, overturn; (*government*, *etc*) to bring down by force.—*also n*.

**overtime** *adv* beyond regular working hours. • *n* extra time worked; payment for this.

**overtone** *n* an additional subtle meaning; an implicit quality; (*mus*) a harmonic; the colour of light reflected (as by a paint).

**overture** *n* an initiating of negotiations; a formal offer, proposal; (*mus*) an instrumental introduction to an opera, etc.

**overturn** *vti* to upset, turn over; to overthrow.

**overweight** *adj* weighing more than the proper amount. • *n* excess weight.

**overwhelm** *vt* to overcome totally; to submerge; to crush; to overpower with emotion.

**overwhelming** *adj* irresistible; uncontrollable; vast; vastly superior; extreme.

**overwork** *vti* to work or use too hard or too long.

**overwrought** *adj* over-excited; too elaborate.

**owe** *vti* to be in debt; to be obliged to pay; to feel the need to give, do, etc, as because of gratitude.

**owing** *adj* due, to be paid; owed; (*with to*) because of, on account of.

**owl** *n* a nocturnal bird of prey with a large head and eyes; a person of nocturnal habits, solemn appearance, etc.—**owlish** *adj*.

**own**[1] *vti* to possess; to acknowledge, admit; to confess to.

**own**[2] *adj* belonging to oneself or itself, often used reflexively (*my own, their own*).

**owner** *n* one who owns, a possessor, a proprietor.—**ownership** *n*.

**ox** *n* (*pl* **oxen**) a cud-chewing mammal of the cattle family; a castrated bull.

**oxide** *n* a compound of oxygen with another element.

**oxtail** *n* the tail of an ox, esp skinned and used for stews, soups, etc.

**oxygen** *n* a colourless, odourless, tasteless, highly reactive gaseous element forming part of air, water, etc, and essential to life and combustion.

**oxygen mask** *n* an apparatus worn over the nose and mouth through which oxygen passes from a storage tank.

**oxygen tent** *n* a canopy over a hospital bed, etc, within which a supply of oxygen is maintained.

**oyster** *n* an edible marine bivalve shellfish.

**oz** *abbr* = ounce(s).

**ozone** *n* a condensed form of oxygen; (*inf*) bracing seaside air.

**ozone layer** *n* a layer of ozone in the upper atmosphere that absorbs ultraviolet rays from the sun.

# P

**p** *abbr* = page; penny, pence.

**p.a.** *abbr* = per annum.

**pace** *n* a single step; the measure of a single stride; speed of movement. • *vti* to measure by paces; to walk up and down; to determine the pace in a race; to walk with regular steps.—**pacer** *n*.

**pacemaker** *n* a person who sets the pace in a race; an electronic device inserted in the heart, used to regulate heartbeat.

**pacify** *vt* to soothe; to calm; to restore peace to.—**pacification** *n*.

**pack** *n* a load or bundle (esp one carried on the back); a set of playing cards; a group or mass; a number of wild animals living together; an organized troop (as of Cub Scouts); a compact mass (as of snow); a small package used as a container for goods for sale. • *vt* to put together in a bundle or pack; (*suitcase*) to fill; to crowd; to press tightly so as to prevent leakage; to carry in a pack; to send (off); (*sl: gun, etc*) to carry; (*sl: punch*) to deliver with force. • *vi* (*snow, ice*) to form into a hard mass; to assemble one's belongings in suitcases or boxes. • *adj* used for carrying packs, loads, etc.—**packer** *n*.

**package** *n* a parcel, a wrapped bundle; several items, arrangements, etc offered as a unit. • *vt* to make a parcel of; to group together several items, etc.

**packet** *n* a small box or package; (*sl*) a considerable sum; a vessel carrying mail, etc, between one port and another.

**pack ice** *n* sea ice formed into a mass by the crushing together of floes, etc.

**packing** *n* material for protecting packed goods or for making airtight or watertight; the act of filling a suitcase, box, etc.

**pact** *n* an agreement or treaty.

**pad**[1] *n* the dull sound of a footstep. • *vi* (*pt* **padded**) to walk, esp with a soft step.

**pad**[2] *n* a piece of a soft material or stuffing; several sheets of paper glued together at one edge; the cushioned thickening of an animal's sole; a piece of folded absorbent material used as a surgical dressing; a flat concrete surface; (*sl*) one's own home or room. • *vt* (*pt* **padded**) to stuff with soft material; to fill with irrelevant information.

**padding** *n* stuffing; anything unimportant or false added to achieve length or amount.

**paddle**[1] *vi* to wade about or play in shallow water.

**paddle**[2] *n* a short oar with a wide blade at one or both ends; a implement shaped like this, used to hit, beat or stir. • *vti* (*canoe, etc*) to propel by a paddle; to beat as with a paddle; to spank.

**paddock** *n* an enclosed field in which horses are exercised.

**paddy** *n* threshed unmilled rice; a rice field.

**padlock** *n* a detachable lock used to fasten doors etc. • *vt* to secure with a padlock.

**padre** *n* (*sl*) a priest or chaplain.

**paediatrics, pediatrics** (*US*) *n* the branch of medicine dealing with children and their diseases.—**paediatric** *adj*.—**paediatrician** *n*.

**pagan** *n* a heathen; a person who has no religion.—*also adj*.—**paganism** *n*.

**page**[1] *n* a boy attendant at a formal function (as a wedding); a uniformed boy employed to run errands. • *vt* to summon by messenger, loudspeaker, etc.

**page**[2] *n* a sheet of paper in a book, newspaper etc. • *vt* (*a book*) to number the pages of.—*also* **paginate**.

**pageant** *n* a spectacular procession or parade; representation in costume of historical events; a mere show.—*also adj*.—**pageantry** *n*.

**pageboy** *n* a page; a medium-length hairstyle with ends of hair turned under.

**paid** *see* **pay**.

**pail** *n* a bucket.

**pain** *n* physical or mental suffering; hurting; (*pl*) trouble, exertion. • *vt* to cause distress to.

**pained** *adj* hurt, offended.

**painful** *adj* giving pain, distressing.—**painfully** *adv*.—**painfulness** *n*.

**painkiller** *n* (*inf*) a medicine that relieves pain.

**painless** *adj* without pain.—**painlessly** *adv*.

**painstaking** *adj* very careful, laborious.—**painstakingly** *adv*.

**paint** *vt* (*a picture*) to make using oil pigments, etc; to depict with paints; to cover or decorate with paint; to describe. • *vi* to make a picture. • *n* a colouring pigment; a dried coat of paint.

**painter**[1] *n* a person who paints, esp an artist.

**painter**[2] *n* a bow rope for tying up a boat.

**painting** *n* the act or art of applying paint; a painted picture.

**pair** *n* a set of two things that are equal, suited, or used together; any two persons or animals regarded as a unit. • *vti* to form a pair (of); to mate.

**pal** *n* a close friend.—**pally** *adj*.

**palace** *n* the official residence of a sovereign, president or bishop; a large stately house or public building.

**palatable** *adj* (*taste*) pleasant; (*fig*)

pleasant or acceptable.—**palatably**
*adv.*

**palate** *n* the roof of the mouth; taste;
mental relish.

**pale**[1] *n* a fence stake; a boundary; (*her*)
a vertical stripe in the middle of a
shield.

**pale**[2] *adj* (*complexion*) with less colour than usual; (*colour, light*) faint,
wan, dim.. • *vti* to make or become
pale.—**paleness** *n*.

**palette** *n* a small, wooden board on
which coloured paints are mixed.

**pall**[1] *n* a heavy cloth over a coffin; (*of
smoke*) a mantle.

**pall**[2] *vi* to become boring; to become
satiated.

**pallet**[1] *n* a portable platform for lifting
and stacking goods.

**pallet**[2] *n* a straw bed.

**pallid** *adj* wan, pale.—**pallidness** *n*.

**palm**[1] *n* the underside of the hand between fingers and wrist. • *vt* to conceal in or touch with the palm; (*with
off*) to pass off by fraud, foist.

**palm**[2] *n* a tropical branchless tree with
fan-shaped leaves; a symbol of victory.

**Palm Sunday** *n* the Sunday before
Easter.

**palpable** *adj* tangible; easily perceived,
obvious.—**palpably** *adj*.

**paltry** *adj* almost worthless; trifling.—
**paltrily** *adv*.—**paltriness** *n*.

**pamper** *vt* to overindulge; to coddle,
spoil.

**pamphlet** *n* a thin, unbound booklet; a
brochure.

**pan**[1] *n* a wide metal container, a saucepan; (*of scales*) a tray; the bowl of a
lavatory. • *vi* (*pt* **panned**) (*with* out)
(*inf*) to turn out, esp to turn out well;
to succeed.

**pan**[2] *vt* (*pt* **panned**) to wash gold-bear-
ing gravel in a pan; (*inf*) to dispar-
age, find fault with.

**pan**[3] *vti* (*pt* **panned**) (*film camera*) to
move horizontally to follow an object
or provide a panoramic view.—*also n*.

**panacea** *n* a cure-all, universal remedy.

**pancake** *n* a round, thin cake made
from batter and cooked on a grid-
dle; a thing shaped thus. • *vi* (*aircraft*) to descend vertically in a level
position.

**panda** *n* a large black and white bear-
like herbivore.

**pandemonium** *n* uproar; chaos.

**pander** *n* a pimp. • *vi* (*somebody's
desires or weaknesses*) to gratify.

**pane** *n* a sheet of glass in a frame of a
window, door, etc.—**paned** *adj*.

**panel** *n* a usu rectangular section or
division forming part of a wall, door,
etc; a board for instruments or controls; a lengthwise strip in a skirt,
etc; a group of selected persons for
judging, discussing, etc. • *vt* (*pt*
**panelled**) to decorate with panels.

**panelling, paneling** (*US*) *n* panels collectively; sheets of wood, plastic, etc,
used for panels.

**pang** *n* a sudden sharp pain or feeling.

**panic** *n* a sudden overpowering fright
or terror.—*also adj*. • *vti* (*pt* **pan-
icked**) to affect or be affected with
panic.—**panicky** *adj*.

**pannier** *n* a large basket for carrying
loads on the back of an animal or the
shoulders of a person; a bag or case
slung over the rear wheel of a bicycle or motorcycle.

**panorama** *n* a complete view in all directions; a comprehensive presentation of a subject; a constantly changing scene.—**panoramic** *adj*.

**pansy** *n* a garden flower of the violet
family, with velvety petals; (*sl*) an effeminate boy or man.

**pant** *vi* to breathe noisily, gasp; to yearn
(for or after something). • *vt* to
speak while gasping.

**panther** *n* a leopard, esp black; a cougar or jaguar.

**panties** *npl* (*inf*) short underpants.

**pantomime** *n* a Christmas theatrical entertainment with music and jokes; a drama without words, using only actions and gestures; mime. • *vti* to mime.

**pantry** *n* a small room or cupboard for storing cooking ingredients and utensils, etc.

**pants** *npl* trousers; underpants.

**panty hose** *n* tights.

**papacy** *n* the office or authority of the pope; papal system of government.

**papal** *adj* of the pope or the papacy.

**paper** *n* the thin, flexible material made from pulped rags, wood, etc which is used to write on, wrap in, or cover walls; a single sheet of this; an official document; a newspaper; an essay or lecture; a set of examination questions; (*pl*) personal documents. • *adj* like or made of paper. • *vt* to cover with wallpaper.—**papery** *adj*.

**paperback** *n* a book bound in a flexible paper cover.

**paperweight** *n* a small heavy object for keeping papers in place.

**paperwork** *n* clerical work of any kind.

**papier-mâché** *n* a substance made of paper pulp mixed with size, glue, etc, and moulded into various objects when moist.

**paprika** *n* a mild red condiment ground from the fruit of certain peppers.

**par** *n* the standard or normal level; the established value of a currency in foreign-exchange rates; the face value of stocks, shares, etc; (*golf*) the score for a hole by a perfect player; equality.

**parable** *n* a short story using everyday events to illustrate a religious or moral point.

**parachute** *n* a fabric umbrella-like canopy used to retard speed of fall from an aircraft. • *vti* to drop, descend by parachute.—**parachutist** *n*.

**parade** *n* a ceremonial procession; an assembly of troops for review; ostentatious display; public walk, promenade. • *vti* to march or walk through, as for display; to show off; to assemble in military order.

**paradise** *n* heaven; (*Bible*) the Garden of Eden; any place of perfection.

**paradox** *n* a self-contradictory statement that may be true; an opinion that conflicts with common beliefs; something with seeming contradictory qualities or phases.—**paradoxical** *adj*.—**paradoxically** *adv*.

**paraffin** *n* a distilled oil used as fuel.

**paragraph** *n* a subdivision in a piece of writing used to separate ideas, marked by the beginning of a new line; a brief mention in a newspaper. • *vt* to divide into paragraphs.

**parallel** *adj* equidistant at every point and extended in the same direction; side by side; never intersecting; similar, corresponding. • *n* a parallel line, surface, etc; a likeness, counterpart; comparison; a line of latitude. • *vt* (*pt* **paralleled**) to make or be parallel; to compare.

**paralyse, paralyze** (*US*) *vt* to affect with paralysis; to bring to a stop.—**paralytic** *adj, n*.

**paralysis** *n* (*pl* **paralyses**) a partial or complete loss of voluntary muscle function or sensation in any part of the body; a condition of helpless inactivity.

**paramount** *adj* of great importance.

**paranoia** *n* a mental illness characterized by delusions of grandeur and persecution; (*inf*) unfounded fear, suspicion.—**paranoid** *adj, n*.—**paranoiac** *adj, n*.

**paraphernalia** *npl* personal belongings;

accessories; (*law*) what a wife possesses in her own right.

**paraphrase** *n* expression of a passage in other words in order to clarify meaning. • *vt* to restate.

**parasite** *n* an organism that lives on and feeds off another without rendering any service in return; a person who sponges off another.—**parasitic** *adj*.—**parasitically** *adv*.

**paratroops** *npl* troops dropped by parachute into the enemy area.—**paratrooper** *n*.

**parcel** *n* a tract or plot of land; a wrapped bundle; a package; a collection or group of persons, animals, or things. • *vt* (*pt* **parcelled**) to wrap up into a parcel; (*with* **out**) to apportion.

**parch** *vti* to make or become hot and dry, thirsty; to scorch, roast.—**parched** *adj*.

**parchment** *n* the skin of a sheep, etc prepared as a writing material; paper like parchment.

**pardon** *vt* to forgive; to excuse; to release from penalty. • *n* forgiveness; remission of penalty.—**pardonable** *adj*.

**parent** *n* a father or a mother; an organism producing another; a source.—**parental** *adj*.—**parenthood** *n*.

**parenthesis** *n* (*pl* **parentheses**) an explanatory comment in a sentence contained within brackets and set in a sentence, independently of grammatical sequence; the brackets themselves ().—**parenthetical** *adj*.

**parish** *n* an ecclesiastical area in the charge of one clergyman; the congregation of a church.

**parishioner** *n* an inhabitant of a parish.

**parity** *n* equality; equality of value at a given ratio between different kinds of money, etc; being at par.

**park** *n* land kept as a game preserve or recreation area; a piece of ground in an urban area kept for ornament or recreation; an enclosed stadium, esp for ball games; a large enclosed piece of ground attached to a country house. • *vti* (*vehicle*) to leave in a certain place temporarily; (*vehicle*) to manoeuvre into a parking space.

**parking lot** *n* a car park.

**parking meter** *n* a coin-operated machine that registers the purchase of parking time for a motor vehicle.

**parliament** *n* a legislative assembly made up of representatives of a nation or part of a nation.—**parliamentarian** *n*.

**parliamentary** *adj* of, used in, or enacted by a parliament; conforming to the rules of a parliament; having a parliament.

**parlour, parlor** (*US*) *n* a room in a house used primarily for conversation or receiving guests; a room or a shop used for business.

**parochial** *adj* of or relating to a parish; narrow; provincial in outlook.—**parochialism** *n*.

**parody** *n* a satirical or humorous imitation of a literary or musical work or style. • *vt* to make a parody of.—**parodist** *n*.

**parole** *n* word of honour; the release of a prisoner before his sentence has expired, on condition of future good behaviour. • *vt* to release on parole.

**parquet** *n* an inlaid hard wood flooring; the stalls of a theatre.

**parrot** *n* a tropical or subtropical bird with brilliant plumage and the ability to mimic human speech; one who repeats another's words without understanding. • *vt* to repeat mechanically.

**parry** *vt* to ward off, turn aside. • *n* a defensive movement in fencing.

**parsley** *n* a bright green herb used to flavour or garnish some foods.

**parsnip** *n* a long tapered root used as a vegetable.

**parson** *n* a priest of a parish, vicar; (*inf*) any clergyman.

**part** *n* a section; a portion (of a whole); an essential, separable component of a piece of equipment or a machine; the role of an actor in a play; a written copy of his/her words; (*mus*) one of the melodies of a harmony; the music for it; duty, share; one of the sides in a conflict; a parting of the hair; (*pl*) qualities, talent. • *vt* to separate; to comb the hair so as to leave a parting. • *vi* to become separated; to go different ways.

**partial** *adj* incomplete; biased, prejudiced; (*with* **to**) having a liking or preference for.—**partiality** *n*.—**partially** *adv*.

**participate** *vi* to join in or take part with others (in some activity).—**participant** *n*.

**participation** *n* the act of participating; the state of being related to a larger whole.

**participle** *n* (*gram*) a verb form used as an adjective.—**participial** *adj*.

**particle** *n* a tiny portion of matter; a speck; a very small part; (*gram*) a word that cannot be used alone, a prefix, a suffix.

**particular** *adj* referring or belonging to a specific person or thing; distinct; exceptional; careful; fastidious. • *n* a detail, single item; (*pl*) detailed information.

**particularly** *adv* very; especially; in detail.

**parting** *n* a departure; a breaking or separating; a dividing line in combing hair. • *adj* departing, esp dying; separating; dividing.

**partisan** *n* a strong supporter of a person, party, or cause.—*also adj*.—**partisanship** *n*.

**partition** *n* division into parts; that which divides into separate parts; a dividing wall between rooms. • *vt* to divide.

**partly** *adv* in part; to some extent.

**partner** *n* one of two or more persons jointly owning a business who share the risks and profits; one of a pair who dance or play a game together; either member of a married or non-married couple. • *vt* to be a partner (in or of).

**partridge** *n* a stout-bodied game bird of the grouse family.

**part-time** *adj* working fewer than the full number of hours.—**part time** *adv*.—**part-timer** *n*.

**party** *n* a group of people united for political or other purpose; a social gathering; a person involved in a contract or lawsuit; a small company, detachment; a person consenting, accessory; (*inf*) an individual. • *vi* to attend social parties. • *vt* to give a party for. • *adj* of or for a party.

**pass** *vb* (*pt* **passed**) *vi* to go past; to go beyond or exceed; to move from one place or state to another; (*time*) to elapse; to go; to die; to happen; (*with* **for**) to be considered as; (*in exam*) to be successful; (*cards*) to decline to make a bid; (*law*) to be approved by a legislative assembly. • *vt* to go past, through, over, etc; (*time*) to spend; to omit; (*law*) to enact; (*judgment*) to pronounce; to excrete; (*in test, etc*) to gain the required marks; to approve. • *n* a narrow passage or road; a permit; (*in a test, etc*) success; transfer of (a ball) to another player; a gesture of the hand; (*inf*) an uninvited sexual approach.

**passable** *adj* fairly good, tolerable; (*a river, etc*) that can be crossed.—**passably** *adv*.

**passage** *n* act or right of passing; transit; transition; a corridor; a channel;

a route or crossing; a lapse of time; a piece of text or music.

**passenger** *n* a traveller in a public or private conveyance; one who does not pull his/her weight.

**passer-by** *n* (*pl* **passers-by**) one who happens to pass or go by.

**passing** *adj* transient; casual. • *n* departure, death.

**passion** *n* compelling emotion, such as love, hate, envy; ardent love, esp sexual desire; (*with cap*) the suffering of Christ on the cross; the object of any strong desire.

**passionate** *adj* moved by, showing, strong emotion or desire; intense; sensual.—**passionately** *adv*.

**passive** *adj* acted upon, not acting; submissive; (*gram*) denoting the voice of a verb whose subject receives the action.—**passively** *adv*.—**passiveness** *n*.—**passivity** *n*.

**passport** *n* an official document giving the owner the right to travel abroad; something that secures admission or acceptance.

**password** *n* a secret term by which a person is recognized and allowed to pass; any means of admission; a sequence of characters required to access a computer system.

**past** *adj* completed; ended; in time already elapsed. • *adv* by. • *prep* beyond (in time, place, or amount). • *n* time that has gone by; the history of a person, group, etc; a personal background that is hidden or questionable.

**pasta** *n* the flour paste from which spaghetti, noodles, etc is made; any dish of cooked pasta.

**paste** *n* a soft plastic mixture; flour and water forming dough or adhesive; a fine glass used for artificial gems. • *vt* to attach with paste; (*sl*) to beat, thrash.

**pastel** *n* a substance made of chalk,

used for drawing; a drawing made with such; a soft, pale colour. • *adj* delicately coloured.

**pasteurize** *vt* (*milk, etc*) to sterilize by heat or radiation to destroy harmful organisms.—**pasteurization** *n*.

**pastille** *n* an aromatic or medicated lozenge.

**pastime** *n* a hobby; recreation, diversion.

**pastoral** *adj* of shepherds or rural life; pertaining to spiritual care, esp of a congregation.—**pastorally** *adv*.

**pastry** *n* dough made of flour, water, and fat used for making pies, tarts, etc; (*pl*) baked goods.

**pasture** *n* land covered with grass for grazing livestock; the grass growing on it. • *vt* (*cattle, etc*) to put out to graze in a pasture.—**pasturage** *n*.

**pasty**[1] *n* meat, etc enclosed in pastry and baked; a turnover.

**pasty**[2] *adj* (**pastier, pastiest**) like paste; pallid and unhealthy in appearance.

**pat**[1] *vti* (*pt* **patted**) to strike gently with the palm of the hand or a flat object; to shape or apply by patting. • *n* a light tap, usu with the palm of the hand; a light sound; a small lump of shaped butter.

**pat**[2] *adj* apt; exact; glib.—*also adv*.

**patch** *n* a piece of cloth used for mending; a scrap of material; a shield for an injured eye; a black spot of silk, etc worn on the face; an irregular spot on a surface; a plot of ground; a bandage; an area or spot. • *vt* to repair with a patch; to piece together; to mend in a makeshift way.

**patchwork** *n* needlework made of pieces sewn together; something made of various bits.

**patchy** *adj* (**patchier, patchiest**) irregular; uneven; covered with patches.—**patchily** *adv*.—**patchiness** *n*.

**pâté** *n* a spread made of liver, herbs, etc.

**patent** *adj* plain; apparent; open to public inspection; protected by a patent. • *n* a government document, granting the exclusive right to produce and sell an invention, etc for a certain time; the right so granted; the thing protected by such a right. • *vt* to secure a patent for.

**patent leather** *n* leather with a hard, glossy finish.

**paternal** *adj* fatherly in disposition; related through the father.—**paternally** *adv*.

**paternity** *n* fatherhood; origin or descent from a father.

**path** *n* a way worn by footsteps; a track for people on foot; a direction; a course of conduct.

**pathetic** *adj* inspiring pity; (*sl*) uninteresting, inadequate.—**pathetically** *adv*.

**pathologist** *n* a medical specialist who diagnoses by interpreting the changes in tissue and body fluid caused by a disease.

**pathology** *n* the branch of medicine that deals with the nature of disease, esp its functional and structural effects; any abnormal variation from a sound condition.—**pathological** *adj*.—**pathologically** *adv*.

**pathway** *n* a path; (*chem*) a sequence of enzyme-catalyzed reactions.

**patience** *n* the capacity to endure or wait calmly; a card game for one.

**patient** *adj* even-tempered; able to wait or endure calmly; persevering. • *n* a person receiving medical, dental, etc treatment.—**patiently** *adv*.

**patio** *n* (*pl* **patios**) an inner courtyard open to the sky; a paved area adjoining a house, for outdoor lounging, dining, etc.

**patriot** *n* one who strongly supports and serves his or her country.—**patriotic** *adj*.—**patriotically** *adv*.—**patriotism** *n*.

**patrol** *vti* (*pt* **patrolled**) to walk around a building or area in order to watch, guard, inspect. • *n* the act of going the rounds; a unit of persons or vehicles employed for reconnaissance, security, or combat; a subdivision of a Scout or Guide group.

**patron** *n* a regular client or customer; a person who sponsors and supports the arts, charities, etc; a protector.

**patronage** *n* the support given or custom brought by a patron; clientele; business; trade; the power to grant political favours; such favours.

**patronize** *vt* to treat with condescension; to sponsor or support; to be a regular customer of.—**patronizing** *adj*.—**patronizingly** *adv*.

**patter**[1] *vi* to make quick tapping sounds, as if by striking something; to run with light steps. • *n* the sound of tapping or quick steps.

**patter**[2] *vi* to talk rapidly and glibly. • *vt* to repeat speech, to gabble. • *n* glib speech; chatter; lingo.

**pattern** *n* a decorative arrangement; a model to be copied; instructions to be followed to make something; a regular way of acting or doing; a predictable route, movement, etc. • *vt* to make or do in imitation of a pattern.—**patterned** *adj*.

**paunch** *n* the belly; esp a potbelly

**pauper** *n* a very poor person; (*formerly*) a person dependent on charity.—**pauperism** *n*.

**pause** *n* a temporary stop, esp in speech, action or music. • *vi* to cease in action temporarily, wait; to hesitate.

**pave** *vt* (*a road, etc*) to cover with concrete to provide a hard level surface.—**paving** *n*.

**pavement** *n* flat slabs, tiles, etc, forming a surface; a paved path adjacent to a road for pedestrians.

**pavilion** *n* a building at a sports ground

used by players; a temporary building for exhibitions; a domed tent.

**paw** n a foot of a mammal with claws;
(sl) a hand. • vti to touch, dig, hit,
etc with paws; to maul; to handle
clumsily or roughly.

**pawn**[1] n the piece of lowest value in
chess; a person used to advance another's purpose.

**pawn**[2] vt to deposit an article as security for a loan; to wager or risk. • n
a thing pawned; the state of being
given as a pawn.

**pawnbroker** n a person licensed to lend
money at interest on personal property left with him as security.

**pay** vti (pt **paid**) to give (money) to in
payment for a debt, goods or serv-
ices; to give in compensation; to yield
a profit; to bear a cost; to suffer a
penalty; (homage, attention) to give.
• n payment for services or goods;
salary, wages.—**paying** adj.—**payer** n.

**payable** adj that must be paid, due; to
be paid on a specified date.

**payee** n one to whom money is paid.

**payment** n the act of paying; amount
paid; reward.

**payroll** n a list of employees and their
wages; the actual money for paying
wages.

**pc** abbr = per cent; postcard.

**pea** n the edible, round, green seed of
a climbing leguminous annual plant.

**peace** n tranquillity, stillness; freedom
from contention, violence or war; a
treaty that ends a war.

**peaceable** adj inclined to peace.—
**peaceably** adv.

**peaceful** adj having peace; tranquil;
quiet.—**peacefully** adv.—**peaceful-
ness** n.

**peach** n a round, sweet, juicy, downy-
skinned stone-fruit; the tree bearing it; a yellowish pink colour; (sl) a
well-liked person or thing.

**peacock** n a male bird with a large

brilliantly coloured fan-like tail (nf
**peahen**); a man who is a show-off.

**peak** n the summit of a mountain; the
highest point; the pointed end of
anything; maximum value; the eye-
shade of a cap, visor. • vti (politician, actor, etc) to reach or cause to
reach the height of power, popularity; (prices) to reach and stay at the
highest level.

**peal** n a reverberating sound as of
thunder, laughter, bells, etc; a set of
bells, the changes rung on them.
• vti to sound in peals, ring out.

**peanut** n a leguminous plant with underground pods containing edible
seeds; the pod or any of its seeds;
(pl: sl) a trifling sum.

**peanut butter** n a food paste made by
grinding roasted peanuts.

**pear** n a common juicy fruit of tapering oval shape; the tree bearing it.

**pearl** n the lustrous white round gem
produced by oysters; mother-of-
pearl; anything resembling a pearl
intrinsically or physically; one that is
choice and precious; a bluish medium grey.—**pearly** adj.

**peasant** n an agricultural labourer.

**peat** n decayed vegetable matter from
bogs, which is dried and cut into
blocks for fuel or used as a fertilizer.—**peaty** adj.

**pebble** n a small rounded stone; an irregular, grainy surface.—**pebbled**
adj.—**pebbly** adj.

**peck** vt to strike with the beak or a
pointed object; to pick at one's food;
(inf) to kiss lightly; to nag.—also n.

**peckish** adj (sl) hungry.

**peculiar** adj belonging exclusively (to);
special; distinct; characteristic;
strange.—**peculiarly** adv.

**peculiarity** n an idiosyncrasy; a characteristic; an oddity.

**pecuniary** adj of or consisting of
money.

**pedal** *n* a lever operated by the foot.
• *vt* (*pt* **pedalled**) to operate, propel by pressing pedals with the foot.

**pedant** *n* a person who attaches too much importance to insignificant details.—**pedantic** *adj.*—**pedantically** *adv.*

**peddle** *vt* to go from place to place selling small goods; (*drugs*) to sell.

**pedestal** *n* the base that supports a column, statue, etc.

**pedestrian** *adj* on foot; dull, commonplace. • *n* a person who walks.

**pedigree** *n* a line of descent of an animal; a recorded purity of breed of an individual; a genealogy; lineage; derivation.—*also adj.*

**pedlar** *n* a peddler.

**peek** *vi* to look quickly or furtively.—*also n.*

**peel** *vt* to remove skin or rind from; to bare. • *vi* to flake off, as skin or paint. • *n* rind, esp that of fruit and vegetables.—**peeling** *n.*

**peep**[1] *vi* to make shrill noises as a young bird. • *n* a peeping sound.

**peep**[2] *vi* to look hastily or furtively; to look through a slit or narrow opening; to be just showing. • *n* a furtive or hurried glance, a glimpse; (*of day*) the first appearance.

**peer**[1] *vi* to look closely; to look with difficulty; to peep out.

**peer**[2] *n* an equal in rank, ability, etc; a nobleman.—**peeress** *nf.*

**peerage** *n* the rank or title of a peer; peers collectively; a book with a list of peers.

**peeved** *adj* annoyed, resentful.

**peevish** *adj* fretful, irritable.—**peevishly** *adv.*—**peevishness** *n.*

**peg** *n* a tapered piece (of wood) for securing or hanging things on, for marking position, or for adjusting the strings of an instrument; a predetermined level at which (a price) is fixed; (*a fact or opinion*) used as a

support, pretext, or reason; (*mus*) one of the movable parts for tuning the string of an instrument. • *vti* (*pt* **pegged**) to fasten or mark with a peg; (*a price*) to keep steady; to work steadily, persevere.

**pejorative** *adj* disparaging, derogatory.—**pejoratively** *adv.*

**Pekingese, Pekinese** *n* a breed of small dog with long, silky hair, short legs, and a pug nose.

**pelican** *n* a large fish-eating waterbird with an expandable pouched bill.

**pellet** *n* a small ball, a pill; a piece of shot.

**pelmet** *n* a canopy for a window frame to hide rods, etc; a valance.

**pelt**[1] *vt* to throw missiles, or words, at. • *vi* (*rain*) to fall heavily; to hurry, rush. • *n* a rush.

**pelt**[2] *n* a usu undressed skin of an animal with its hair, wool, or fur.

**pelvis** *n* the bony cavity that joins the lower limbs to the body; the bones forming this.—**pelvic** *adj.*

**pen**[1] *n* an implement used with ink for writing or drawing. • *vt* (*pt* **penned**) to write, compose.

**pen**[2] *n* a small enclosure for cattle, poultry, etc; a small place of confinement. • *vt* (*pt* **penned**) to enclose in a pen, shut up.

**penal** *adj* relating to, liable to, or prescribing punishment; punitive.—**penally** *adv.*

**penalize** *vt* to impose a penalty; to put under a disadvantage.—**penalization** *n.*

**penalty** *n* a punishment attached to an offence; suffering or loss as a result of one's own mistake; a disadvantage imposed for breaking a rule as in football; a fine.

**penance** *n* voluntary suffering to atone for a sin; a sacramental rite consisting of confession, absolution, and penance.

**pence** see **penny**.

**pencil** n a pointed rod-shaped instrument with a core of graphite or crayon for writing, drawing, etc; a set of convergent light rays or straight lines; a fine paintbrush. • vt (pt **pencilled**) to write, draw, or colour with a pencil; (with **in**) to commit tentatively.

**pendant, pendent** n a hanging ornament; a complement or match. • adj (usu **pendent**) hanging; projecting; undecided.

**pending** adj undecided; unfinished; imminent. • prep during; until, awaiting.

**pendulum** n a weight suspended from a fixed point so as to swing freely; such a device used to regulate the movement of a clock; something that swings to and fro.

**penetrate** vti to thrust, force a way into or through something; to pierce; to permeate; to understand.—**penetrable** adj.—**penetrability** n.

**penetrating** adj acute, discerning; (voice) easily heard through other sounds.

**penetration** n the capability, act, or action of penetrating; acute insight.

**pen friend** n a friend made and kept through exchanging letters.

**penguin** n a flightless, marine bird with black and white plumage, usu found in the Antarctic.

**penicillin** n an antibiotic produced synthetically from moulds.

**peninsula** n a piece of land almost surrounded by sea.—**peninsular** adj.

**penis** n the male copulative organ in mammals and humans.

**penitent** adj feeling regret for sin, repentant, contrite. • n a person who atones for sin.—**penitence** n.—**penitently** adv.

**penitentiary** n a state or federal prison in the US.

**penknife** n a small knife, usually with one folding blade, that fits into the pocket.

**pennant** n a long tapering flag used for identifying vessels and for signalling; such a flag symbolizing a championship.

**penniless** adj having no money; poor.

**penny** n (pl **pence** denoting sum, **pennies** denoting separate coins) a bronze coin of the UK worth one hundredth of a pound; (formerly) a bronze coin worth one twelfth of a shilling, or one two hundred and fortieth of a pound; a US or Canadian cent.

**pension** n a periodic payment to a person beyond retirement age, or widowed, or disabled; a periodic payment in consideration of past services. • vt to grant a pension to; (with **off**) to dismiss or retire from service with a pension.—**pensionable** adj.

**pensioner** n a person who receives a pension; a senior citizen.

**pensive** adj thoughtful, musing; wistful, melancholic.—**pensively** adv.—**pensiveness** n.

**pentagon** n (geom) a polygon with five sides; (with cap) the US military leadership.—**pentagonal** adj.

**Pentecost** n a Christian festival on the seventh Sunday after Easter; Whit Sunday.

**penthouse** n an apartment on the flat roof or in the top floor of a building.

**pent-up** adj (emotion) repressed, confined.

**penultimate** adj last but one.

**people** n the body of enfranchised citizens of a state; a person's family, relatives; the persons of a certain place, group, or class; persons considered indefinitely; human beings; (pl) all the persons of a racial or ethnic group, typically having a common language, institutions, homes, and folkways. • *vt* to populate with people.

**pep** *n* (*inf*) energy, vigour.

**pepper** *n* a sharp, hot condiment made from the fruit of various plants; the fruit of the pepper plant, which can be red, yellow, or green, sweet or hot, and is eaten as a vegetable. • *vt* to sprinkle or flavour with pepper; to hit with small shot; to pelt; to beat.

**peppermint** *n* a pungent and aromatic mint; its oil used for flavouring; a sweet flavoured with peppermint.

**pep talk** *n* (*inf*) a vigorous talk made with the intention of arousing enthusiasm, increasing confidence, etc.

**per** *prep* for or in each; through, by, by means of; (*inf*) according to.

**per annum** *adv* yearly; each year.

**perceive** *vt* to become aware of, apprehend, through the senses; to recognize.

**per cent** *adv* in, for each hundred; (*inf*) percentage.

**percentage** *n* rate per hundred parts; a proportion; (*inf*) profit, gain.

**perceptible** *adj* able to be perceived; discernible.—**perceptibility** *n*.—**perceptibly** *adv*.

**perception** *n* the act or faculty of perceiving; discernment; insight; a way of perceiving, view.

**perceptive** *adj* able to perceive; observant.—**perceptively** *adv*.—**perceptiveness** *n*.

**perch**[1] *n* (*pl* **perch**) a spiny-finned chiefly freshwater edible fish.

**perch**[2] *n* a pole on which birds roost or alight; an elevated seat or position. • *vti* to alight, rest, on a perch; to balance (oneself) on; to set in a high position.

**percolator** *n* a coffee pot in which boiling water is forced through coffee grounds.

**percussion** *n* impact, collision; shock, sound, caused by this; (*med*) tapping the body to discover the condition of an organ by the sounds; musical instruments played by striking with sticks or hammers, eg cymbals, drums, etc.—**percussionist** *n*.—**percussive** *adj*.

**peremptory** *adj* urgent; absolute; dogmatic; dictatorial.—**peremptorily** *adv*.—**peremptoriness** *n*.

**perennial** *adj* perpetual; lasting throughout the year. • *n* (*bot*) a plant lasting more than two years.—**perennially** *adv*.

**perfect** *adj* faultless; exact; excellent; complete. • *n* (*gram*) a verb form expressing completed action or designating a present state that is the result of an action in the past. • *vt* to improve; to finish; to make fully accomplished in anything.—**perfectly** *adv*.

**perfection** *n* the act of perfecting; the quality or condition of being perfect; great excellence; faultlessness; the highest degree; a perfect person or thing.

**perfectionist** *n* one who demands the highest standard; one who holds that moral perfection may be attained in this world.—**perfectionism** *n*.

**perforate** *vt* to pierce; to make a hole or row of holes, by boring through.

**perforation** *n* the act of perforating; the condition of being perforated; a hole; a row of holes to facilitate tearing.

**perform** *vti* to carry out, do; to put into effect; to act; to execute; to act before an audience; to play a musical instrument.—**performing** *adj*.

**performance** *n* the act of performing; a dramatic production; an act or action.

**performer** *n* a person who performs, esp one who entertains an audience.

**perfume** *n* a pleasing odour; fragrance; a mixture containing fragrant essential oils and a fixative. • *vt* to scent; to put perfume on.

**perfunctory** *adj* superficial, hasty; done merely as a matter of form, half-hearted; done carelessly; indifferent.—**perfunctorily** *adv*.

**perhaps** *adv* possibly, maybe.

**peril** *n* danger, jeopardy; risk, hazard.

**perilous** *adj* dangerous.— **perilously** *adv*.

**perimeter** *n* a boundary around an area; (*math*) the curve or line bounding a closed figure, its length.

**period** *n* a portion of time; menstruation; an interval of time as in an academic day, playing time in a game, etc; an age or era in history, epoch; a stage in life; (*gram*) a full stop (.); (*astron*) a planet's time of revolution. • *interj* an exclamation used for emphasis.

**periodic** *adj* relating to a period; recurring at regular intervals, cyclic; intermittent.—**periodically** *adv*.

**periodical** *adj* periodic. • *n* a magazine, etc issued at regular intervals.

**peripheral** *adj* incidental, superficial; relating to a periphery.

**periphery** *n* the outer surface or boundary of an area; the outside surface of anything.

**periscope** *n* a device with mirrors that enables the viewer to see objects above or around an obstacle or above water, as from a submarine.

**perish** *vi* to be destroyed or ruined; to die, esp violently.

**perishable** *adj* (*food*) liable to spoil or decay. • *n* something perishable, esp food.—**perishability** *n*.

**perjure** *vt* to commit perjury, swear falsely.

**perjury** *n* (*law*) the crime of giving false witness under oath, swearing to what is untrue.

**perk** *n* (*inf*) a privilege, gain or profit incidental to regular wages; a tip, gratuity.

**perk up** *vti* to recover self-confidence; to become lively or cheerful; to prick up, as of a dog's ears; to smarten, trim.—**perky** *adj*.

**perm** *vt* (*inf*) (*hair*) to give a permanent wave. —*also n*.

**permanence** *n* the condition or quality of being permanent.

**permanent** *adj* lasting, or intended to last, indefinitely. • *n* a straightening or curling of hair by use of chemicals or heat lasting through many washings.—**permanently** *adv*.

**permeate** *vti* to fill every part of, saturate; to pervade, be diffused (through); to pass through by osmosis.—**permeable** *adj*.—**permeability** *n*.

**permissible** *adj* allowable.

**permission** *n* authorization; consent.

**permissive** *adj* allowing permission; lenient; sexually indulgent.—**permissively** *adv*.—**permissiveness** *n*.

**permit** *vti* (*pt* permitted) to allow to be done; to authorize; to give opportunity. • *n* a licence.

**permutation** *n* any radical alteration; a change in the order of a series; any of the total number of groupings within a group; an ordered arrangement of a set of objects.

**pernicious** *adj* destructive; very harmful.—**perniciously** *adv*.—**perniciousness** *n*.

**perpendicular** *adj* upright, vertical; (*geom*) at right angles (to).—*also n*.

**perpetrate** *vt* (*something evil, criminal, etc*) to do; (*a blunder, etc*) to commit.—**perpetration** *n*.—**perpetrator** *n*.

**perpetual** *adj* continuous; everlasting; (*plant*) blooming continuously throughout the season.—**perpetually** *adv*.

**perpetuity** *n* endless duration, eternity; perpetual continuance; an annuity payable forever.

**perplex** *vt* to puzzle, bewilder, confuse; to complicate.—**perplexity** *n*.

**persecute** *vt* to harass, oppress, esp for reasons of race, religion, etc; to worry persistently.—**persecution** *n*.—**persecutor** *n*.

**persevere** *vi* to persist, maintain effort in face of difficulties.—**perseverance, perseveringly** *adv*.

**persist** *vi* to continue in spite of obstacles or opposition; to persevere; to last.—**persistence** *n*.—**persistency** *n*.

**persistent** *adj* persevering; stubborn.—**persistently** *adv*.

**person** *n* a human being, individual; the body (including clothing) of a human being; (*in a play*) a character; one who is recognized by law as the subject of rights and duties; (*gram*) one of the three classes of personal pronouns and verb forms, referring to the person(s) speaking, spoken to, or spoken of.

**personable** *adj* pleasing in personality and appearance.

**personal** *adj* concerning a person's private affairs, or his/her character, habits, body, etc; done in person; (*law*) of property that is movable; (*gram*) denoting person.

**personality** *n* one's individual characteristics; excellence or distinction of social and personal traits; a person with such qualities; a celebrity.

**personally** *adv* in person; in one's own opinion; as though directed to oneself.

**personify** *vt* to think of, represent, as a person; to typify.—**personification** *n*.

**personnel** *n* the employees of an organization or company; the department that hires them.

**perspective** *n* objectivity; the art of drawing so as to give an impression of relative distance or solidity; a picture so drawn; relation, proportion, between parts of a subject; vista, prospect.—*also adj*.

**perspire** *vi* to sweat.—**perspiration** *n*.

**persuade** *vt* to convince; to induce by argument, reasoning, advice, etc.

**persuasion** *n* the act of persuading; a conviction or opinion; a system of religious beliefs; a group adhering to such a system.

**persuasive** *adj* able to persuade; influencing the mind or emotions.—**persuasively** *adv*.—**persuasiveness** *n*.

**pert** *adj* impudent, cheeky; sprightly.—**pertly** *adv*.

**pertinent** *adj* relevant; to the point.—**pertinence** *n*.—**pertinently** *adv*.

**perturb** *vt* to trouble; to agitate.

**perusal** *n* a careful reading.

**pervade** *vt* to permeate or spread through; to be rife among.—**pervasive** *adj*.

**perverse** *adj* deviating from right or truth; persisting in error; wayward; contrary.—**perversely** *adv*.—**perverseness** *n*.—**perversity** *n*.

**perversion** *n* an abnormal way of obtaining sexual gratification, eg sadism; a perverted form or usage of something.

**pervert** *vt* to corrupt; to misuse; to distort. • *n* a person who is sexually perverted.

**pessimism** *n* a tendency to see in the world what is bad rather than good; a negative outlook that always expects the worst.—**pessimist** *n*.—**pessimistic** *adj*.

**pest** *n* anything destructive, esp a plant or animal detrimental to man as rats, flies, weeds, etc; a person who pesters or annoys.

**pester** *vt* to annoy or irritate persistently.

**pesticide** *n* any chemical for killing pests.

**pestle** *n* a usu club-shaped tool for pounding or grinding substances in a mortar. • *vt* to beat, pound, or pulverize with a pestle.

**pet** *n* a domesticated animal kept as a companion; a person treated as a favourite. • *adj* kept as a pet; spoiled, indulged; favourite; particular. • *vti* (*pt* **petted**) to stroke or pat gently; to caress; (*inf*) to kiss, embrace, etc in making love.

**petal** *n* any of the leaf-like parts of a flower's corolla.—**petalled, petaled** *adj*.

**peter out** *vi* to come to an end; to dwindle to nothing.

**petite** *adj* (*woman*) small and trim in figure.

**petition** *n* a formal application or entreaty to an authority; a written demand for action by a government, etc, signed by a number of people. • *vti* to present a petition to; to ask humbly.—**petitionary** *adj*.—**petitioner** *n*.—**petitioning** *n*.

**petrol** *n* a liquid fuel or solvent distilled from petroleum.

**petroleum** *n* a crude oil occurring naturally in certain rock strata and distilled to yield petrol, paraffin, etc.

**petticoat** *n* an underskirt; a slip; (*inf*) woman.

**petty** *adj* (**pettier, pettiest**) trivial; small-minded; minor.—**pettily** *adv*.—**pettiness** *n*.

**petty officer** *n* a non-commissioned officer in the navy.

**petulant** *adj* showing impatience or irritation; bad-humoured.—**petulance** *n*.—**petulantly** *adv*.

**pew** *n* a wooden, bench-like seat in a church, often enclosed; (*sl*) a chair.

**pewter** *n* an alloy of tin and lead with a silvery-grey colour; dishes, etc, made of pewter.

**phantom** *n* a spectre or apparition. • *adj* illusionary.

**pharmacist** *n* one licensed to practise pharmacy.

**pharmacy** *n* the preparation and dispensing of drugs and medicines; a pharmacist's shop, a drug store.

**phase** *n* an amount of the moon's or a planet's surface illuminated at a given time; a characteristic period in a regularly recurring sequence of events or stage in a development. • *vt* to do by stages or gradually; (*with* **out**) (*making, using, etc*) to stop gradually.

**PhD** *abbr* = Doctor of Philosophy.

**pheasant** *n* a richly coloured game bird.

**phenomenon** *n* (*pl* **phenomena, phenomenons**) anything perceived by the senses as a fact; a fact or event that can be scientifically described; a remarkable thing or person.

**phial** *n* a small glass bottle; a vial.

**philanthropy** *n* love of mankind, esp as demonstrated by benevolent or charitable actions.—**philanthropic** *adj*.—**philanthropically** *adv*.—**philanthropist** *n*.

**philately** *n* the study and collecting of postage and imprinted stamps; stamp collecting.—**philatelic** *adj*.—**philatelist** *n*.

**philosopher** *n* a person who studies philosophy; a person who acts calmly and rationally.

**philosophical** *adj* of, relating to, or according to philosophy; serene; temperate; resigned.—**philosophically** *adv*.

**philosophy** *n* the study of the principles underlying conduct, thought, and the nature of the universe; general principles of a field of knowledge; a particular system of ethics; composure; calmness.

**phlegm** *n* a thick mucus discharged from the throat, as during a cold; sluggishness; apathy.

**phlegmatic** *adj* unemotional, composed; sluggish.

**phobia** *n* an irrational, excessive, and persistent fear of some thing or situation.—**phobic** *adj*.

**phone** *n*, *vti* (*inf*) (to) telephone.

**phonetics** *npl* (*used as sing*) the science concerned with pronunciation and the representation of speech sounds.

**phonograph** *n* a gramophone or record player.

**phony, phoney** *adj* (**phonier, phoniest**) (*inf*) not genuine. • *n* a fake; an insincere person.

**phosphate** *n* a compound of phosphorus.

**phosphorus** *n* a metalloid element; a phosphorescent substance or body, esp one that glows in the dark.

**photo** *see* **photograph**.

**photo-** *prefix* = light; a photographic process.

**photocopy** *n* a photographic reproduction of written or printed work. • *vt* to copy in this way.—**photocopier** *n*.

**photogenic** *adj* likely to look attractive in photographs; (*biol*) generating light.—**photogenically** *adv*.

**photograph** *n* an image produced by photography.—*also* **photo**.

**photography** *n* the art or process of recording images permanently and visibly by the chemical action of light on sensitive material, producing prints, slides or film.—**photographer** *n*.—**photographic** *adj*.—**photographically** *adv*.

**phrase** *n* a group of words that does not contain a finite verb but which expresses a single idea by itself; a pointed saying; a high-flown expression; (*mus*) a short, distinct musical passage. • *vt* to express orally, put in words; (*mus*) to divide into melodic phrases.

**phrase book** *n* a book containing idiomatic expressions of a foreign language and their translations.

**physical** *adj* relating to the world of matter and energy, the human body, or natural science. • *n* a general medical examination.—**physically** *adv*.

**physician** *n* a doctor of medicine.

**physicist** *n* a specialist in physics.

**physics** *n* the branch of science concerned with matter and energy and their interactions in the fields of mechanics, acoustics, optics, heat, electricity, magnetism, radiation, atomic structure and nuclear phenomena; the physical processes and phenomena of a particular system.

**physiology** *n* the science of the functioning and processes of living organisms.—**physiological** *adj*.—**physiologically** *adv*.—**physiologist** *n*.

**physiotherapy** *n* the treatment of disorders and disease by physical and mechanical means (as massage, exercise, water, heat, etc).—**physiotherapist** *n*.

**physique** *n* bodily structure and appearance; build.

**pianist** *n* a person who plays the piano.

**piano** *n* (*pl* **pianos**) a large stringed keyboard instrument in which each key operates a felt-covered hammer that strikes a corresponding steel wire or wires.

**piccolo** *n* (*pl* **piccolos**) a small shrill flute.

**pick** *n* a heavy tool with a shaft and pointed crossbar for breaking ground; a tool for picking, such as a toothpick or icepick; a plectrum; right of selection; choice; best (of). • *vti* to break up or remove with a pick; to pluck at; to nibble (at), eat fussily; to contrive; to choose; (*fruit, etc*) to gather; to steal from a pocket; (*lock*) to force open; (*with* **up**) to lift; to acquire; to call for; to recover; (*inf*) to make the acquaintance of casually; to learn gradually; to resume; to give a lift to; to increase speed.

**pickaxe, pickax** (*US*) *n* a pick.

**picket** *n* a pointed stake; a patrol or group of men selected for a special duty; a person posted by strikes outside a place of work to persuade others not to enter. • *vt* (*pt* **picketed**) to tether to a picket; to post as a military picket; to place pickets, or serve as a picket (at a factory, etc).

**pickle** *n* vegetables preserved in vinegar; (*inf*) a plight, mess. • *vt* to preserve in vinegar.

**pickpocket** *n* a person who steals from pockets.

**pick-up** *n* the act of picking up; a person or thing picked up; (*elect*) a device for picking up current; the power to accelerate rapidly; the balanced arm of a record player; a light truck with an enclosed cab and open body.

**picnic** *n* a usu informal meal taken on an excursion and eaten outdoors; an outdoor snack; the food so eaten; an easy or agreeable task. • *vi* (*pt* **picnicked**) to have a picnic.—**picnicker** *n*.

**pictorial** *adj* relating to pictures, painting, or drawing; containing pictures; expressed in pictures; graphic.—**pictorially** *adv*.

**picture** *n* drawing, painting, photography, or other visual representation; a scene; an impression or mental image; a vivid description; a cinema film. • *vt* to portray, describe in a picture; to visualize.

**picturesque** *adj* striking, vivid, usually pleasing; making an effective picture.—**picturesquely** *adv*.

**pidgin** *n* a jargon for trade purposes, using words and grammar from two or more different languages.

**pie** *n* a baked dish of fruit, meat, etc, with an under or upper crust of pastry, or both.

**piebald** *adj* covered with patches of two colours. • *n* a piebald horse, etc.

**piece** *n* a distinct part of anything; a single object; a literary, dramatic, artistic, or musical composition; (*sl*) a firearm; a man in chess or draughts; an opinion, view; a short distance. • *vt* to fit together, join.

**piecemeal** *adv* gradually; bit by bit.

**piecework** *n* work paid for according to the quantity produced.

**pier** *n* a structure supporting the spans of a bridge; a structure built out over water and supported by pillars, used as a landing place, promenade, etc; a heavy column used to support weight.

**pierce** *vt* to cut or make a hole through; to force a way into; (*fig*) to touch or move. • *vi* to penetrate.

**piercing** *adj* penetrating; keen; (*cold, pain*) acute.—**piercingly** *adv*.

**piety** *n* religious devoutness; the characteristic of being pious.

**pig** *n* a domesticated animal with a broad snout and fat body raised for food; a swine; a greedy or filthy person; an oblong casting of metal poured from the smelting furnace; (*sl*) a policeman. • *vi* (*pt* **pigged**) (*sow*) to give birth; (*inf*) to live in squalor.—**piggish** *adj*.

**pigeon** *n* a bird with a small head and a heavy body; (*inf*) an object of special concern.

**pigeonhole** *n* a small compartment for filing papers, etc; a category usu failing to reflect actual complexities. • *vt* to file, classify; to put aside for consideration, shelve.

**pigeon-toed** *adj* having the toes turned in.

**piggy bank** *n* a container for coins shaped like a pig.

**pigheaded** *adj* stupidly stubborn.

**piglet** *n* a young pig.

**pigment** *n* paint; a naturally occurring substance used for colouring.—**pigmentation** *n*.

**pigmy** *see* **pygmy.**

**pigsty** *n* a pen for pigs; a dirty hovel.

**pigtail** *n* a tight braid of hair.

**pike** *n* a sharp point or spike; the top of a spear; a long-snouted fish, important as a food and game fish.

**pilchard** *n* a fish of the herring family.

**pile**[1] *n* a heap or mound of objects; a large amount; a lofty building; a pyre; (*sl*) a fortune. • *vt* (*with* **up, on**) to heap or stack; to load; to accumulate. • *vi* to become heaped up; (*with* **up, out, on**) to move confusedly in a mass.

**pile**[2] *n* a vertical beam driven into (the ground) as a foundation for a building, etc. • *vt* to support with piles; to drive piles into.

**pile**[3] *n* the nap of a fabric or carpet; soft, fine fur or wool.

**pile**[4] *n* a haemorrhoid.

**pile-up** *n* an accumulation of tasks, etc; (*inf*) a collision of several vehicles.

**pilgrim** *n* a person who makes a pilgrimage.

**pilgrimage** *n* a journey to a holy place as an act of devotion; any long journey; a life's journey.

**pill** *n* medicine in round balls or tablet form; (*with cap*) an oral contraceptive.

**pillage** *n* looting, plunder. • *vti* to plunder, esp during war.—**pillager** *n*.

**pillar** *n* a slender, vertical structure used as a support or ornament; a column; a strong supporter of a cause.

**pillar box** *n* a red box for receiving letters for mailing, often columnar.

**pillion** *n* a seat behind the driver for a passenger on a motorcycle, etc.

**pillory** *n* (*formerly*) stocks in which criminals were put as punishment. • *vt* to expose to public scorn and ridicule.

**pillow** *n* a cushion that supports the head during sleep; something that supports to equalize or distribute pressure. • *vti* to rest on, serve as, a pillow.

**pillowcase, pillowslip** *n* a removable cover for a pillow.

**pilot** *n* a person who operates an aircraft; one who directs ships in and out of harbour; a guide; a television show produced as a sample of a proposed series. • *vt* to direct the course of, act as pilot; to lead or guide.

**pilot light** *n* a burning gas flame used to light a larger jet; an electric indicator light.

**pimp** *n* a prostitute's agent.—*also vt*.

**pimple** *n* a small, raised, inflamed swelling of the skin.—**pimpled, pimply** *adj*.

**pin** *n* a piece of metal or wood used to fasten things together; a small piece of pointed wire with a head; an ornament or badge with a pin or clasp for fastening to clothing; (*bowling*) one of the clubs at which the ball is rolled. • *vt* (*pt* **pinned**) to fasten with a pin; to hold, fix; (*with* **down**) to get (someone) to commit himself or herself as to plans, etc; (*a fact, etc*) to establish.

**pinafore** *n* a sleeveless garment worn over a dress, blouse, etc.

**pincers** *npl* a tool with two handles and jaws used for gripping and drawing out nails, etc; a grasping claw, as of a crab.

**pinch** *vti* to squeeze or compress painfully; to press between the fingers; to nip; (*sl*) to steal; (*sl*) to arrest. • *n* a squeeze or nip; what can be taken up between the finger and thumb, a small amount; a time of stress; an emergency.

**pine**[1] *n* an evergreen coniferous tree with long needles and well-formed cones; a tree of the pine family; its wood.

**pine**[2] *vi* to languish, waste away through longing or mental stress; (*with* for) to yearn.

**pineapple** *n* a tropical plant; its juicy, fleshy, yellow fruit.

**ping** *n* a high-pitched ringing sound. • *vti* to strike with a ping, emit a ping.

**ping-pong** *n* a name for table tennis; (*with caps*) a trade name for table tennis equipment.

**pink**[1] *n* a garden plant, including carnation, with a fragrant flower; a pale red colour; a huntsman's red coat; the highest type. • *adj* pink-coloured; (*inf*) radical in political views.

**pink**[2] *vt* to stab, pierce; (*cloth, etc*) to cut a zigzag edge on; to perforate with pinking shears.

**pink**[3] *vi* (*engine*) to make a metallic noise like knocking.

**pinnacle** *n* a slender tower crowning a roof, etc; a rocky peak of a mountain; the highest point, climax.

**pinpoint** *vt* to locate or identify very exactly.

**pinstripe** *n* a very narrow stripe in suit fabrics, etc.

**pint** *n* a liquid measure equal to half a quart or one eighth of a gallon; (*inf*) a drink of beer.

**pin-up** *n* (*sl*) a photograph of a naked or partially naked person; a person who has been so photographed; a photograph of a famous person.

**pioneer** *n* a person who initiates or explores new areas of enterprise, research, etc.—*also vti*.

**pious** *adj* devout; religious; sanctimonious.—**piously** *adv*.

**pip** *n* the seed in a fleshy fruit, eg apple, orange.

**pipe** *n* a tube of wood, metal etc for making musical sounds; (*pl*) the bagpipes; a stem with a bowl for smoking tobacco; a long tube or hollow body for conveying water, gas, etc. • *vt* to play on a pipe; (*gas, water, etc*) to convey by pipe; to lead, summon with the sound of a pipe(s); to trim with piping.

**pipeline** *n* a pipe (often underground) used to convey oil, gas, etc; a direct channel for information; the processes through which supplies pass from source to user.

**piper** *n* a person who plays a pipe, esp bagpipes.

**piping** *n* a length of pipe, pipes collectively; a tube-like fold of material used to trim seams; a strip of icing, cream, for decorating cakes, etc; the art of playing a pipe or bagpipes; a high-pitched sound. • *adj* making a high-pitched sound.

**piping hot** *adj* very hot.

**pique** *n* resentment, ill-feeling. • *vt* to cause resentment in; to offend.

**piracy** *n* robbery at sea; the hijacking of a ship or aircraft; infringement of copyright; unauthorized use of patented work.

**pirate** *n* a person who commits robbery at sea; a hijacker; one who infringes copyright. • *vti* to take by piracy; to publish or reproduce in violation of a copyright.

**pirouette** *n* a spin on the toes in ballet.—*also vi.*

**Pisces** *n* the Fishes, in astrology the twelfth sign of the zodiac, operative from 19 February - 20 March.

**pistol** *n* a small, short-barrelled handgun.

**piston** *n* a disc that slides to and fro in a close-fitting cylinder, as in engines, pumps.

**pit** *n* a deep hole in the earth; a (coal) mine; a scooped-out place for burning something; a sunken or depressed area below the adjacent floor area; a space at the front of the stage for the orchestra; the area in a securities or commodities exchange in which members do the trading; the scar left by smallpox, etc; the stone of a fruit; a place where racing cars refuel. • *vti* (*pt* **pitted**) to set in competition; to mark or become marked with pits; to make a pit stop.

**pitch**[1] *vti* (*tent, etc*) to erect by driving pegs, stakes, etc, into the ground; to set the level of; (*mus*) to set in key; to express in a style; to throw, hurl, to fall heavily, plunge, esp forward. • *n* a throw; height, intensity; a musical tone; a place where a street trader or performer works; distance between threads (of a screw); amount of slope; a sound wave frequency; a sports field; (*cricket*) the area between the wickets; sales talk.

**pitch**[2] *n* the black, sticky substance from distillation of tar, etc; any of various bituminous substances. • *vt* to smear with pitch.

**pitch-black** *adj* black, or extremely dark.

**pitch-dark** *adj* completely dark.

**pitcher** *n* a large water jug; (*baseball*) the player who pitches the ball.

**pitchfork** *n* a long-handled fork for tossing hay, etc. • *vt* to lift with this; to thrust suddenly or willy-nilly into.

**piteous** *adj* arousing pity; heart-rending.—**piteously** *adv*.

**pitfall** *n* concealed danger; unexpected difficulty.

**pith** *n* the soft tissue inside the rind of citrus fruits; the gist, essence; importance.

**pithy** *adj* (**pithier, pithiest**) like or full of pith; concise and full of meaning.—**pithily** *adv*.—**pithiness** *n*.

**pitiable** *adj* deserving pity, lamentable, wretched.—**pitiably** *adv*.

**pitiful** *adj* causing pity, touching; contemptible, paltry.—**pitifully** *adv*.

**pitiless** *adj* without pity, ruthless.—**pitilessly** *adv*.—**pitilessness** *n*.

**pittance** *n* a very small quantity or allowance of money.

**pity** *n* sympathy with the distress of others; a cause of grief; a regrettable fact. • *vt* to feel pity for.

**pivot** *n* a pin on which a part turns, fulcrum; a key person upon whom progress depends; a cardinal point or factor. • *vt* (*pt* **pivoted**) to turn or hinge (on) a pivot; to attach by a pivot. • *vi* to run on, or as if on, a pivot.—**pivotal** *adj*.

**pixy, pixie** *n* a fairy or elf.

**placard** *n* a poster or notice for public display.

**placate** *vt* to appease; to pacify.—**placatory** *adj*.

**place** *n* a locality, spot; a town or village; a building, residence; a short street, a square; space, room; a particular point, part, position, etc; the part of space occupied by a person or thing; a position or job; a seat; rank, precedence; a finishing position in a race. • *vt* to put; to put in a particular place; to find a place or seat for; to identify; to estimate; to rank; (*order*) to request material from a supplier. • *vi* to finish second or among the first three in a race.

**place mat** *n* a small mat serving as an individual table cover for a person at a meal.

**placid** *adj* calm, tranquil.—**placidity, placidness** *n*.—**placidly** *adv*.

**plagiarize** *vt* to appropriate writings from another author.—**plagiarism** *n*.—**plagiarist** *n*.

**plague** *n* a highly contagious and deadly disease; (*inf*) a person who is a nuisance. • *vt* to afflict with a plague; (*inf*) to annoy, harass.

**plaice** *n* (*pl* **plaice**) any of various flatfishes, esp a flounder.

**plaid** *n* a long wide piece of woollen cloth used as a cloak in Highland dress; cloth with a tartan or chequered pattern.

**plain** *adj* level, flat; understandable; straightforward; manifest, obvious; blunt; unadorned; not elaborate; not coloured or patterned; not beautiful; ugly; pure; unmixed. • *n* a large tract of level country.

**plain clothes** *n* ordinary clothes, not uniform, as worn by a policeman on duty.—*also adj.*

**plainly** *adv* clearly, intelligibly.

**plaintiff** *n* (*law*) a person who brings a civil action against another.

**plait** *n* intertwined strands of hair, straw, etc; a pigtail.—*also vti.*

**plan** *n* a scheme or idea; a drawing to scale of a building; a diagram, map; any outline or sketch. • *vti* (*pt* **planned**) to make a plan of; to design; to arrange beforehand, intend; to make plans.

**plane**¹ *n* a tall tree with large broad leaves.

**plane**² *n* a tool with a steel blade for smoothing level wooden surfaces. • *vt* to smooth with a plane.

**plane**³ *n* any level or flat surface; a level of attainment; one of the main supporting surfaces of an aeroplane; an aeroplane. • *adj* flat or level. • *vi* to fly while keeping the wings motionless; to skim across the surface of water; to travel by aeroplane.

**planet** *n* a celestial body that orbits the sun or other star.

**plank** *n* a long, broad, thick board; one of the policies forming the platform of a political party. • *vt* to cover with planks.

**plankton** *n* the microscopic organisms that float on seas, lakes, etc.

**plant** *n* a living organism with cellulose cell walls, which synthesizes its food from carbon dioxide, water and light; a soft-stemmed organism of this kind, as distinguished from a tree or shrub; the machinery, buildings, etc of a factory, etc; (*sl*) an act of planting; (*sl*) something or someone planted. • *vt* (*seeds, cuttings*) to put into the ground to grow; to place firmly in position; to found or establish; (*sl*) to conceal something in another's possession in order to implicate.

**plantation** *n* a large cultivated planting of trees; an estate where tea, rubber, cotton, etc, is grown, cultivated by local labour.

**plaque** *n* an ornamental tablet or disc attached to or inserted in a surface; a film of mucus on the teeth that harbours bacteria.

**plasma** *n* the colourless liquid part of blood, milk, or lymph; a collection of charged particles resembling gas but conducting electricity and affected by a magnetic field.

**plaster** *n* an adhesive dressing for cuts; a mixture of sand, lime and water that sets hard and is used for covering walls and ceilings. • *vt* to cover as with plaster; to apply like a plaster; to make lie smooth and flat; to load to excess.—**plasterer** *n*.

**plastered** *adj* (*sl*) intoxicated.

**plaster of Paris** *n* gypsum and water made into a quick-setting paste.

**plastic** *adj* able to be moulded; pliant; made of plastic; (*art*) relating to modelling or moulding. • *n* any of various nonmetallic compounds, synthetically produced, that can be moulded, cast, squeezed, drawn, or laminated into objects, films, or filaments.

**plastic surgery** *n* surgery to repair deformed or destroyed parts of the body.

**plate** *n* a flat sheet of metal on which an engraving is cut; an illustration printed from it; a full-page illustration separate from text; a sheet of metal photographically prepared with text, etc, for printing from; a sheet of glass with sensitized film used as a photographic negative; a trophy as prize at a race; a coating of metal on another metal; utensils plated in silver or gold; plated ware; a flat shallow dish from which food is eaten; a helping of food; the part of a denture that fits the palate; (*inf*) a denture. • *vt* (*a metal*) to coat with a thin film of another metal; to cover with metal plates.

**plateau** *n* (*pl* **plateaux, plateaus**) a flat, elevated area of land; a stable period; a graphic representation showing this.

**plate glass** *n* rolled, ground, and polished sheet glass.

**platform** *n* a raised floor for speakers, musicians, etc; a stage; a place or opportunity for public discussion; the raised area next to a railway track where passengers board trains; a statement of political aims.

**platinum** *n* a valuable, silvery-white metal used for jewellery, etc.

**platitude** *n* a dull truism; a commonplace remark.

**platoon** *n* a military unit consisting of two or more sections.

**platter** *n* an oval flat serving dish.

**plausible** *adj* apparently truthful or reasonable.—**plausibility** *n*.—**plausibly** *adv*.

**play** *vi* to amuse oneself (with toys, games, etc); to act carelessly or trifle (with somebody's feelings); to gamble; to act on the stage or perform a musical instrument; (*light*) to flicker, shimmer; (*water*) to discharge or direct on. • *vt* to participate in a sport; to be somebody's opponent in a game; to perform a dramatic production; (*instrument*) to produce music on; (*hose*) to direct; (*fish*) to give line to; to bet on. • *n*

fun, amusement; the playing of, or manner of playing, a game; the duration of a game; a literary work for performance by actors; gambling; scope, freedom to move.—**playful** *adj*.—**playfully** *adv*.—**playfulness** *n*.

**player** *n* a person who plays a specified game or instrument; an actor.

**playground** *n* an area outdoors for children's recreation.

**playgroup** *n* an organized, regular meeting for the shared supervision of children at play.

**playing card** *n* one of a set of 52 cards used for playing games, each card having an identical pattern on one side and its own symbol on the reverse.

**playing field** *n* a place for playing sport.

**playpen** *n* a portable usu collapsible enclosure in which a young child may be left to play safely.

**plaything** *n* a toy; a thing or person treated as a toy.

**playwright** *n* a writer of plays.

**plea** *n* (*law*) an answer to a charge, made by the accused person; a request; an entreaty.

**plead** *vti* (*pt* **pleaded, plead** *or* **pled**) to beg, implore; to give as an excuse; to answer (guilty or not guilty) to a charge; to argue (a law case).

**pleasant** *adj* agreeable; pleasing.—**pleasantly** *adv*.—**pleasantness** *n*.

**pleasantry** *n* a polite or amusing remark.

**please** *vti* to satisfy; to give pleasure to; to be willing; to have the wish. • *adv* as a word to express politeness or emphasis in a request; an expression of polite affirmation.—**pleasing** *adj*.—**pleasingly** *adv*.

**pleasure** *n* enjoyment, recreation; gratification of the senses; preference.—**pleasurable** *adj*.—**pleasurably** *adv*.

**pleat** *n* a double fold of cloth, etc

pressed or stitched in place.—*also vt.*

**plebiscite** *n* a direct vote of the electorate on a political issue such as annexation, independent nationhood, etc.

**plectrum** *n* a thin piece of metal, etc for plucking the strings of a guitar, etc.

**pledge** *n* a solemn promise; security for payment of a debt; a token or sign; a toast. • *vt* to give as security; to pawn; to bind by solemn promise; to drink a toast to.

**plentiful** *adj* abundant, copious.

**plenty** *n* an abundance; more than enough; a great number. • *adv* (*sl*) quite.

**pleurisy** *n* inflammation of the membranes enclosing the lung.

**pliable** *adj* easily bent or moulded; easily influenced.—**pliability** *n.*

**pliers** *npl* a tool with hinged arms and jaws for cutting, shaping wire.

**plight**[1] *n* a dangerous situation; a predicament.

**plight**[2] *vt* to pledge, vow solemnly.—*also n.*

**plod** *vi* (*pt* **plodded**) to walk heavily and slowly, to trudge; to work or study slowly and laboriously.—**plodder** *n.*

**plough, plow** (*US*) *n* a farm implement for turning up soil; any implement like this, as a snowplough. • *vt* to cut and turn up with a plough; to make a furrow (in), to wrinkle; to force a way through; to work at laboriously; (*with* **into**) to run into; (*with* **back**) to reinvest; (*sl*) to fail an examination.—**ploughman** *n.*

**plover** *n* a wading bird with a short tail and a bill like a pigeon's.

**ploy** *n* a tactic or manoeuvre to outwit an opponent; an occupation or job; an escapade.

**pluck** *vt* to pull off or at; to snatch; to strip off feathers; (*fruit, flowers, etc*) to pick; (*person*) to remove from one situation in life and transfer to another. • *vi* to make a sharp pull or twitch. • *n* a pull or tug; heart, courage; dogged resolution.

**plucky** *adj* (**pluckier, pluckiest**) brave, spirited.—**pluckily** *adv.*—**pluckiness** *n.*

**plug** *n* a stopper used for filling a hole; a device for connecting an appliance to an electricity supply; a cake of tobacco; a kind of fishing lure; (*inf*) a free advertisement usu incorporated in other matter. • *vti* (*pt* **plugged**) to stop up with a plug; (*sl*) to shoot or punch; (*inf*) to seek to advertise by frequent repetition; (*inf*) to work doggedly.

**plum** *n* an oval smooth-skinned sweet stone-fruit; a tree bearing it; a reddish-purple colour; a choice thing.

**plumb** *n* a lead weight attached to a line, for determining depth or verticality; any of various weights. • *adj* perfectly vertical. • *adv* vertically; in a direct manner; (*inf*) entirely. • *vt* to test by a plumb; to examine minutely and critically; to weight with lead; to seal with lead; to supply with or install as plumbing. • *vi* to work as a plumber.

**plumber** *n* a person who installs and repairs water or gas pipes.

**plumbing** *n* the system of pipes used in water or gas supply, or drainage; the plumber's craft.

**plume** *n* a large or ornamental bird's feather; a feathery ornament or thing; something resembling a feather in structure or density. • *vt* (*feathers*) to preen; to adorn with feathers; to indulge (oneself) with an obvious display of self-satisfaction.

**plummet** *n* a plumb. • *vi* (*pt* **plummeted**) to fall in a perpendicular manner; to drop sharply and abruptly.

**plump**[1] *adj* rounded, chubby. • *vti* to make or become plump; to swell.— **plumpness** *n*.

**plump**[2] *vti* to fall, drop or sink, or come into contact suddenly and heavily; (*someone, something*) to favour or give support. • *n* a sudden drop or plunge or the sound of this. • *adv* straight down, straight ahead; abruptly; bluntly.

**plunder** *vt* to steal goods by force, to loot. • *n* plundering; booty. —**plunderer** *n*.

**plunge** *vti* to immerse, dive suddenly; to penetrate quickly; to hurl oneself or rush; (*horse*) to start violently forward.

**plural** *adj* more than one; consisting of o r containing mor e than one kind or class. • *n* (*gram*) the form referring to more than one person or thing.

**plus** *prep* added to; in addition to. • *adj* indicating addition; positive. • *n* the sign (+) indicating a value greater than zero; an advantage or benefit; an extra.

**plush** *n* a velvet-like fabric with a nap. • *adj* made of plush; (*inf*) luxurious.

**ply**[1] *vti* to work at diligently and energetically; to wield; to subject to persistently; (*goods*) to sell; to go to and fro, run regularly; to keep busy.

**ply**[2] *n* a layer or thickness, as of cloth, plywood, etc; any of the twisted strands in a yarn, etc. • *vt* to twist together.

**plywood** *n* a construction material consisting of several thin layers of wood glued together.

**PM** *abbr* = prime minister.

**p.m.** *abbr* = post meridiem.

**pneumatic** *adj* concerning wind, air, or gases; operated by or filled with compressed air.

**pneumonia** *n* acute inflammation of the lungs.

**PO** *abbr* = post office; petty officer.

**poach**[1] *vt* to cook (an egg without its shell, fish, etc) in or over boiling water.

**poach**[2] *vti* to catch game or fish illegally; to trespass for this purpose; to encroach on, usurp another's rights, etc; to steal another's idea, employee, etc.—**poacher** *n*.—**poaching** *n*.

**pocket** *n* a small bag or pouch, esp in a garment, for carrying small articles; an isolated or enclosed area; a deposit (as of gold, water, or gas). • *adj* small enough to put in a pocket. • *vt* to put in one's pocket, to steal; (*ball*) to put in a pocket; to envelop, to enclose; (*money*) to take dishonestly; to suppress.—**pocketful** *adj*.

**pocketbook** *n* a wallet; a woman's purse; monetary resources; a small esp paperback book.

**pocketknife** *n* a penknife.

**pocket money** *n* money for occasional expenses; a child's allowance.

**pod** *n* a dry fruit or seed vessel, as of peas, beans, etc; a protective container or housing; a detachable compartment on a spacecraft. • *vi* (*pt* **podded**) to remove the pod from.

**podgy** *adj* (**podgier, podgiest**) short and fat, squat.

**poem** *n* an arrangement of words, esp in metre, often rhymed, in a style more imaginative than ordinary speech; a poetic thing.

**poet** *n* the writer of a poem; a person with imaginative power and a sense of beauty.

**poetic, poetical** *adj* of poets or poetry; written in verse; imaginative, romantic, like poetry.—**poetically** *adv*.

**poet laureate** *n* (*pl* **poets laureate**) the official poet of a nation, appointed to write poems celebrating national events, etc.

**poetry** *n* the art of writing poems; poems collectively; poetic quality or spirit.

**poignant** *adj* piercing; incisive; deeply moving.—**poignantly** *adv.*

**point** *n* a dot or tiny mark used in writing or printing (eg a decimal point, a full stop); a location; a place in a cycle, course, or scale; a unit in scoring or judging; the sharp end of a knife or pin; a moment of time; one of thirty-two divisions of the compass; a fundamental reason or aim; the tip; a physical characteristic; a railway switch; a unit of size in printing equal to one seventy-second of an inch; a unit used in quoting the prices of stocks, bonds and commodities; a headland or cape. • *vti* to give point to; to sharpen; to aim (at); to extend the finger (at or to); to indicate something; to call attention (to).

**point-blank** *adj* aimed straight at a mark; direct, blunt.—*also adv.*

**pointed** *adj* having a point; pertinent; aimed at a particular person or group; conspicuous.—**pointedly** *adv.*

**pointer** *n* a rod or needle for pointing; an indicator; a breed of hunting dogs.

**pointless** *adj* without a point; irrelevant, aimless.—**pointlessly** *adv.*

**poise** *vt* to balance; to hold supported without motion; (*the head*) to hold in a particular way; to put into readiness. • *vi* to become drawn up into readiness; to hover. • *n* a balanced state; self-possessed assurance of manner; gracious tact; bearing, carriage.—**poised** *adj.*

**poison** *n* a substance that through its chemical action usu destroys or injures an organism; any corrupt influence; an object of aversion or abhorrence. • *vt* to administer poison in order to kill or injure; to put poison into; to influence wrongfully.—**poisoner** *n.*—**poisonous** *adj.*—**poisonously** *adv.*

**poke** *vt* to thrust (at), jab or prod; (*hole, etc*) to make by poking; (*sl*) to hit. • *vi* to jab (at); to pry or search (about or around). • *n* a jab; a prod or nudge; a thrust.

**poker**[1] *n* a metal rod for poking or stirring fire.

**poker**[2] *n* a card game in which a player bets that the value of his hand is higher than that of the hands held by others.

**poker face** *n* an expressionless face, concealing a person's thoughts or feelings.—**poker-faced** *adj.*

**poky** *adj* (**pokier, pokiest**) small and uncomfortable.

**polar** *adj* of or near the North or South Pole; of a pole; having positive and negative electricity; directly opposite.

**polar bear** *n* a large creamy-white bear that inhabits arctic regions.

**polarize** *vt* (*light waves*) to cause to vibrate in a definite pattern; to give physical polarity to; to break up into opposing factions; to concentrate.—**polarization** *n.*

**pole**[1] *n* a long slender piece of wood, metal, etc; a flagstaff. • *vt* to propel, support with a pole.

**pole**[2] *n* either end of an axis, esp of the earth; either of two opposed forces, parts, etc, as the ends of a magnet, terminals of a battery, etc; either of two opposed principles.

**polemic** *n* a controversy or argument over doctrine; (*pl*) art of controversy.—**polemical** *adj.*

**pole vault** *n* a field event in which competitors jump over a high bar using a long flexible pole.

**police** *n* the governmental department for keeping order, detecting crime, law enforcement, etc; the members of such a department; any similar organization. • *vt* to control, protect, etc with police or a similar force.

**policeman** *n* a member of a police force.—**policewoman** *nf*.

**policy**[1] *n* a written insurance contract.

**policy**[2] *n* political wisdom, statecraft; a course of action selected from among alternatives; a high-level overall plan embracing the general principles and aims of an organization, esp a government.

**polish** *vti* to make or become smooth and shiny by rubbing (with a cloth and polish); (*fig*) to give elegance or culture to; (*with* **off**) (*inf: meal, job, etc*) to finish completely. • *n* smoothness; elegance of manner; a finish or gloss; a substance, such as wax, used to polish.—**polisher** *n*.

**polished** *adj* accomplished; smoothly or professionally done or performed; (*of rice*) having had the husk removed.

**polite** *adj* courteous; well-bred; refined.—**politely** *adv*.—**politeness** *n*.

**political** *adj* relating to politics or government; characteristic of political parties or politicians.—**politically** *adv*.

**politician** *n* a person engaged in politics, often used with implications of seeking personal or partisan gain, scheming, etc.

**politics** *npl* the science and art of government; political activities, beliefs or affairs; factional scheming for power.

**polka** *n* a lively dance; the music for this.

**polka dot** *n* any of a pattern of small round dots on cloth.

**poll** *n* a counting, listing, etc of persons, esp of voters; the number of votes recorded; an opinion survey; (*pl*) a place where votes are cast. • *vti* to receive the votes (of); to cast a vote; to canvass or question in a poll.

**pollen** *n* the yellow dust, containing male spores, that is formed in the anthers of flowers.

**pollination** *n* the transfer of pollen from the anthers of a flower to the stigma, esp by insects.— **pollinate** *vti*.

**pollute** *vt* to contaminate with harmful substances; to make corrupt; to profane —**polluter** *n*.

**pollution** *n* the act of polluting; the state of being polluted; contamination by chemicals, noise, etc.

**polo** *n* a game played on horseback by two teams, using a wooden ball and long-handled mallets.

**polo neck** *n* a high collar turned over at the top; a sweater with such a collar.

**polyester** *n* any of a number of synthetic polymeric resins used for adhesives, plastics, and textiles.

**polygamy** *n* the practice of being married to more than one person at a time.—**polygamist** *n*.—**polygamous** *adj*.

**polytechnic** *n* a college that provides instruction in many applied sciences and technical subjects.

**polythene, polyethylene** *n* a light, plastic, multipurpose material.

**pomegranate** *n* an edible fruit with many seeds; the widely cultivated tropical tree bearing it.

**pommel** *n* the rounded, upward-projecting front part of a saddle; a knob on the hilt of a sword. • *vt* to pummel.

**pomp** *n* stately ceremony; ostentation.

**pompous** *adj* stately; self-important.—**pompously** *adv*.—**pomposity** *n*.—**pompousness** *n*.

**pond** *n* a body of standing water smaller than a lake.

**ponder** *vti* to think deeply; to consider carefully.

**ponderous** *adj* heavy; awkward; dull; lifeless.—**ponderously** *adv*.

**pontiff** *n* the Pope; a bishop.

**pontificate** *vi* to speak sententiously, pompously or dogmatically; to officiate at a pontifical mass.

**pontoon**[1] *n* a boat or cylindrical float forming a support for a bridge.

**pontoon**[2] *n* a gambling game with cards in which players try to obtain points better than the banker's but not more than 21.—*also* **blackjack**.

**pony** *n* a small horse, a bronco, mustang, etc of the western US.

**pony tail** *n* a style of arranging hair to resemble a pony's tail.

**poodle** *n* a breed of dog with a solid-coloured curly coat of many colours and sizes.

**pool**[1] *n* a small pond; a puddle; a small collection of liquid; a tank for swimming.

**pool**[2] *n* a game of billiards played on a table with six pockets; a combination of resources, funds, supplies, people, etc for some common purpose; the parties forming such a combination. • *vti* to contribute to a common fund, to share.

**poor** *adj* having little money, needy; deserving pity, unfortunate; deficient; disappointing; inferior. • *n* those who have little.—**poorness** *n*.

**poorly** *adv* insufficiently, badly. • *adj* not in good health.

**pop**[1] *n* a short, explosive sound, a shot; any carbonated, nonalcoholic beverage. • *vti* (*pt* **popped**) to make or cause a pop; to shoot; to go or come quickly (in, out, up); (*corn, maize*) to roast until it pops; to put suddenly; (*eyes*) to bulge.

**pop**[2] *adj* in a popular modern style. • *n* pop music; pop art; pop culture.

**pop**[3] *n* (*inf*) father; (*inf*) a name used to address an old man.

**popcorn** *n* a kind of corn or maize, which when heated pops or puffs up.

**pope** *n* bishop of Rome, head of the RC Church.

**poplar** *n* a slender, quick-growing tree of the willow family.

**poplin** *n* a sturdy corded fabric.

**poppy** *n* an annual or perennial plant with showy flowers; a strong reddish colour.

**populace** *n* the common people; the masses; all the people in a country, region, etc.

**popular** *adj* of the people; well liked; pleasing to many people; easy to understand.—**popularly** *adv*.

**popularity** *n* the condition or quality of being popular.

**popularize** *vt* to make popular; to make generally accepted or understood.—**popularization** *n*.

**population** *n* all the inhabitants or the number of people in an area.

**populous** *adj* densely inhabited.

**porcelain** *n* a hard, white, translucent variety of ceramic ware.—*also adj*.

**porch** *n* a covered entrance to a building; an open or enclosed gallery or room on the outside of a building.

**porcupine** *n* a large rodent covered with protective quills.

**pore**[1] *n* a tiny opening, as in the skin, plant leaves, stem, etc, for absorbing and discharging fluids.

**pore**[2] *vti* to look with steady attention; to study closely.

**pork** *n* the flesh of a pig used as food.

**pornography** *n* writings, pictures, films, etc, intended primarily to arouse sexual desire.—**pornographic** *adj*.—**pornographer** *n*.

**porous** *adj* having pores; able to absorb air and fluids, etc.—**porousness** *n*.

**porpoise** *n* any of several small whales, esp a black blunt-nosed whale of the north Atlantic and Pacific; any of several bottle-nosed dolphins.

**porridge** *n* a thick food, usu made by

boiling oats or oatmeal in water or milk.

**port**[1] *n* a harbour; a town with a harbour where ships load and unload cargo; airport; a place where goods may be cleared through customs.

**port**[2] *n* a porthole; an opening, as in a valve face, for the passage of steam, etc; a hole in an armoured vehicle for firing a weapon; a circuit in a computer for inputting or outputting data.

**port**[3] *n* the left of an aircraft or ship looking forward.—*also adj*.

**port**[4] *n* a strong, sweet, fortified dark red wine.

**portable** *adj* capable of being carried or moved about easily.—**portability** *n*.

**portal** *n* an impressive gate or doorway.

**portcullis** *n* a grating that can be lowered to bar entrance to a castle.

**portent** *n* an omen, warning.

**porter**[1] *n* a doorman or gatekeeper.

**porter**[2] *n* a person who carries luggage, etc, for hire at a station, airport, etc; a railway attendant for passengers; a dark brown beer.

**porthole** *n* an opening (as a window) with a cover or closure esp in the side of a ship or aircraft; a port through which to shoot; an opening for intake or exhaust of a fluid.

**portico** *n* (*pl* **porticooo, porticos**) a covered walkway with columns supporting the roof.

**portion** *n* a part, a share, esp an allotted part; a helping of food; destiny. • *vt* to share out.

**portly** *adj* (**portlier, portliest**) dignified; stout.

**portrait** *n* a painting, photograph, etc, of a person, esp of the face; (*of person*) a likeness; a vivid description.

**portray** *vt* to make a portrait of; to depict in words; to play the part of in a play, film, etc.— **portrayal** *n*.

**pose** *n* a position or attitude, esp one held for an artist or photographer; an attitude deliberately adopted for effect. • *vti* to propound, assert; to assume an attitude for effect; to sit for a painting, photograph; to set oneself up (as).

**posh** *adj* (*inf*) elegant; fashionable.

**position** *n* place, situation; a position occupied; posture; a job; state of affairs; point of view. • *vt* to place or locate.

**positive** *adj* affirmative; definite; sure; marked by presence, not absence, of qualities; expressed clearly, or in a confident manner; constructive; empirical; (*elect*) charged with positive electricity; (*math*) greater than zero, plus; (*gram*) of adjective or adverb, denoting the simple form; (*photog*) having light, shade, colour as in the original. • *n* a positive quality or quantity; a photographic print made from a negative.

**posse** *n* a body of people summoned by a sheriff to assist in keeping the peace, etc.

**possess** *vt* to own, have, keep; to dominate or control the mind of.

**possession** *n* ownership; something possessed; (*pl*) property.

**possessive** *adj* of or indicating possession; (*gram*) denoting a case, form or construction expressing possession; having an excessive desire to possess or dominate.—**possessively** *adv*.

**possibility** *n* the state of being possible; a possible occurrence, a contingency.

**possible** *adj* that may be or may happen; feasible, practicable; (*inf*) tolerable.—**possibly** *adv*.

**post**[1] *n* a piece of wood, metal, etc, set upright to support a building, sign, etc; the starting point of a race. • *vt* (*poster, etc*) to put up; to announce by posting notices; (*name*) to put on a posted or published list.

**post**[2] *n* a fixed position, esp where a sentry or group of soldiers is stationed; a position or job; a trading post; a settlement. • *vt* to station in a given place.

**post**[3] *n* the official conveyance of letters and parcels, mail; letters, parcels, etc, so conveyed; collection or delivery of post, mail. • *vt* to send a letter or parcel; to keep informed.—**postal** *adj*.

**postage** *n* the charge for sending a letter, etc, as represented by stamps.

**postcard** *n* a card, usu decorative, for sending messages by post.

**postdate** *vt* to write a future date on a letter or cheque.

**poster** *n* a usu decorative or ornamental printed sheet for advertising.

**poste restante** *n* the department of a post office that will hold mail until it is called for.

**posterity** *n* future generations; all of a person's descendants.

**postgraduate** *n* a person pursuing study after obtaining a university degree.—*also adj*.

**posthumous** *adj* (*child*) born after its father's death; (*award, etc*) given after one's death.—**posthumously** *adv*.

**postman** *n* a person who collects or delivers mail.

**postmark** *n* the post office mark cancelling the stamp on a letter by showing the date, place of posting.

**postmaster** *n* the manager of a post office.

**postmortem** *n* an examination of a corpse to determine the cause of death; an autopsy.—*also adj*.

**post office** *n* the building where postage stamps are sold and other postal business conducted; (*with caps*) a government department handling the transmission of mail.

**postpone** *vt* to put off, delay to a future date.—**postponement** *n*.

**postscript** *n* (*abbr* **PS**) a note added to a letter after completion.

**postulate** *vt* to assume to be true; to demand or claim. • *n* a position taken as self-evident; (*math*) an unproved assumption taken as basic; an axiom.—**postulation** *n*.

**posture** *n* a pose; a body position; an attitude of mind; an official stand or position. • *vti* to pose in a particular way; to assume a pose.

**posy** *n* a small bunch of flowers.

**pot**[1] *n* a deep, round cooking vessel; an earthenware or plastic container for plants; a framework for catching fish or lobster; (*inf*) a large amount (as of money); (*inf*) all the money bet at a single time. • *vb* (*pt* **potted**) *vt* to put or preserve in a pot. • *vi* to take a pot shot, shoot.

**pot**[2] *n* (*sl*) cannabis.

**potash** *n* potassium carbonate.

**potato** *n* (*pl* **potatoes**) a starchy, oval tuber eaten as a vegetable.

**potency** *n* the quality or condition of being potent; power; strength.

**potent** *adj* powerful; influential; intoxicating; (*a male*) able to have sexual intercourse.—**potently** *adv*.

**potential** *adj* possible, but not yet actual. • *n* the unrealized ability to do something.—**potentiality** *n*.—**potentially** *adv*.

**pothole** *n* a hole worn in a road by traffic; (*geol*) a deep hole or cave in rock caused by the action of water.

**potholing** *n* an activity involving the exploration of deep underground caves.—**potholer** *n*.

**potion** *n* a mixture of liquids, such as poison.

**pot shot** *n* a random or easy shot.

**potter**[1] *vi* to busy oneself idly; to spend time. —*also* **putter**.

**potter**[2] *n* a person who makes earthenware vessels.

**pottery** *n* earthenware vessels; a workshop where such articles are made.

**potty**[1] *adj* (**pottier, pottiest**) (*inf*) slightly crazy; trivial, petty.

**potty**[2] *n* (*inf*) a chamber pot.

**pouch** *n* a small bag or sack; a bag for mail; a sacklike structure, as that on the abdomen of a kangaroo, etc, for carrying young.

**poultice** *n* a hot moist dressing applied to a sore part of the body.

**poultry** *n* domesticated birds kept for meat or eggs.

**pounce** *vi* to swoop or spring suddenly (upon) in order to seize; to make a sudden assault or approach.—*also n*.

**pound**[1] *n* a unit of weight equal to 16 ounces (*abbr* **lb**); a unit of money in the UK and other countries, symbol £.

**pound**[2] *vt* to beat into a powder or a pulp; to hit hard. • *vi* to deliver heavy blows repeatedly (at or on); to move with heavy steps; to throb; (*with* away) to work hard and continuously.

**pound**[3] *n* a municipal enclosure for stray animals; a depot for holding impounded personal property, eg cars, until claimed; a place or condition of confinement.

**pour** *vti* to cause to flow in a stream; to flow continuously; to rain heavily; to serve tea or coffee. —**pourer** *n*.

**pout** *vti* to push out (the lips); to look sulky. • *n* a thrusting out of the lips; (*pl*) a fit of pique.

**poverty** *n* the condition of being poor; scarcity.

**powder** *n* any substance in tiny, loose particles; a specific kind of powder, esp for medicinal or cosmetic use; fine dry light snow. • *vti* to sprinkle or cover with powder; to reduce to powder.

**powdery** *adj* like powder; easily crumbled.

**power** *n* ability to do something; political, social or financial control or force; a person or state with influence over others; legal force or authority; physical force; a source of energy; (*math*) the result of continued multiplication of a quantity by itself a specified number of times. • *adj* operated by electricity, a fuel engine, etc; served by an auxiliary system that reduces effort; carrying electricity. • *vt* to supply with a source of power.—**powered** *adj*.

**powerful** *adj* mighty; strong; influential.—**powerfully** *adv*.

**powerless** *adj* without power; helpless; feeble.—**powerlessly** *adv*.—**powerlessness** *n*.

**power station, power plant** *n* a building where electric power is generated.

**powwow** *n* an American Indian ceremony (as for victory in war); (*inf*) any conference or get-together. • *vi* to confer, chat.

**pox** *n* a virus disease marked by pustules; (*arch*) smallpox; syphilis; a plague; a curse.

**practicable** *adj* able to be practised; possible, feasible.—**practicability** *n*.

**practical** *adj* concerned with action, not theory; workable; suitable; trained by practice; virtual, in effect.

**practical joke** *n* a prank intended to embarrass or to cause discomfort.

**practically** *adv* in a practical manner; virtually.

**practice** *n* action; habit, custom; repetition and exercise to gain skill; the exercise of a profession.

**practise, practice** (*US*) *vti* to repeat an exercise to acquire skill; to put into practice; to do habitually or frequently; (*profession*) to work at.

**practitioner** *n* a person who practises a profession.

**pragmatic** *adj* practical; testing the validity of all concepts by their practical results.—**pragmatically** *adv*.

**prairie** *n* a large area of level or rolling land predominantly in grass; a dry treeless plateau.

**praise** *vt* to express approval of, to commend; to glorify, to worship. • *vi* to express praise. • *n* commendation; glorification.—**praiseworthy** *adj*.

**pram** *n* a four-wheeled carriage for a baby.

**prance** *vi* (*horse*) to spring on the hind legs, bound; (*person*) to walk or ride in a showy manner; to swagger.— *also n*.

**prank** *n* a mischievous trick or joke; a ludicrous act.

**prattle** *vti* to talk in a childish manner; to babble. • *n* empty chatter.

**prawn** *n* an edible marine shrimp-like crustacean.

**pray** *vti* to offer prayers to God; to implore.

**prayer** *n* supplication, entreaty, praise or thanks to God; the form of this; the act of praying; (*pl*) devotional services; something prayed for.

**preach** *vi* to advocate in an earnest or moralizing way. • *vt* to deliver a sermon; (*patience, etc*) to advocate.— **preacher** *n*.

**preamble** *n* an introductory part to a document, speech, or story, stating its purpose.

**precarious** *adj* dependent on chance; insecure; dangerous.—**precariously** *adv*.—**precariousness** *n*.

**precaution** *n* a preventive measure; care taken beforehand; careful foresight.—**precautionary** *adj*.

**precede** *vti* to be, come or go before in time, place, order, rank, or importance.

**precedence** *n* priority; the right of higher rank.

**precedent** *n* a previous and parallel case serving as an example; (*law*) a decision, etc, serving as a rule.

**preceding** *adj* coming or going before; former.

**precept** *n* a rule of moral conduct; a maxim; an order issued by a legally constituted authority to a subordinate.

**precinct** *n* (usu *pl*) an enclosure between buildings, walls, etc; a limited area; an urban area where traffic is prohibited; (*pl*) environs; in US, a police district or a subdivision of a voting ward.

**precious** *adj* of great cost or value; beloved; very fastidious; affected; thoroughgoing. • *adv* (*sl*) very.— **preciousness** *n*.

**precipice** *n* a cliff or overhanging rock face.

**precipitate** *vti* to throw from a height; to cause to happen suddenly or too soon; (*chem*) to separate out; to rain; to fall as rain, snow, dew, etc.—**precipitately** *adv*.

**precipitation** *n* the act of precipitating; undue haste; rain, snow, etc; the amount of this.

**precipitous** *adj* of or like a precipice; sheer, steep.—**precipitously** *adv*.

**precis, précis** *n* (*pl* **precis, précis**) a summary or abstract.—*also vt*.

**precise** *adj* clearly defined, exact; accurate; punctilious; particular.—**precisely** *adv*.

**preclude** *vt* to rule out in advance; to make impossible.—**preclusion** *n*.— **preclusive** *adj*.

**precocious** *adj* prematurely ripe or developed.—**precociously** *adv*.

**preconceive** *vt* to form an idea or opinion of before actual experience.

**precondition** *n* a requirement that must be met beforehand, a prerequisite. • *vt* (*organism, patient*) to prepare to behave or react in a certain way under certain conditions.

**precursor** *n* a predecessor; a substance from which another substance is formed.—**precursory** *adj*.

**predator** n a person who preys, plunders or devours; a carnivorous animal.

**predatory** adj living on prey, of or relating to a predator; characterized by hunting or plundering.

**predecessor** n a former holder of a position or office; an ancestor.

**predestine** vt to foreordain; to destine beforehand.

**predicament** n a difficult or embarrassing situation.

**predicate** vt to state as a quality or attribute; to base (on facts, conditions etc). • n (gram) that which is stated about the subject.

**predict** vt to foretell; to state (what one believes will happen).—**predictable** adj.—**predictably** adv.

**prediction** n the act of predicting; that which is predicted; a forecast or prophecy.

**predominant** adj ruling over, controlling; influencing.—**predominance** n.

**predominantly** adv mainly.

**predominate** vt to rule over; to have influence or control over; to prevail; to be greater in number, intensity, etc.

**pre-eminent** adj distinguished above others; outstanding.—**pre-eminence** n,—**pre-eminently** adv.

**pre-empt** vt to take action to check other action beforehand; to gain the right to buy (public land) by settling on it; to seize before anyone else can; (scheduled TV, radio programme) to replace; (in bridge) to bid highly to exclude bids from opponents.—**pre-emption** n.—**pre-emptive** adj.

**preen** vti (birds) to clean and trim the feathers; to congratulate (oneself) for achievement; to groom (oneself); to gloat.

**prefab** n (inf) a prefabricated building.

**preface** n an introduction or preliminary explanation; a foreword or introduction to a book; a preamble. • vt to serve as a preface; to introduce.

**prefect** n a person placed in authority over others; a student monitor in a school; in some countries, an administrative official.

**prefer** vt (pt preferred) to like better; to promote, advance; to put before (a court) for consideration.

**preferable** adj deserving preference; superior; more desirable.—**preferably** adv.

**preference** n the act of preferring, choosing, or favouring one above another; that which is chosen or preferred; prior right; advantage given to one person, country, etc, over others.

**preferential** adj giving or receiving preference.—**preferentially** adv.

**prefix** vt to put at the beginning of or before; to put as an introduction. • n a syllable or group of syllables placed at the beginning of a word, affecting its meaning.

**pregnant** adj having a foetus in the womb; significant, meaningful; imaginative; filled (with) or rich (in).—**pregnancy** n.

**prehistoric** adj of the period before written records began.—**prehistory** n.

**prejudge** vt to pass judgment on before a trial; to form a premature opinion.—**prejudgment, prejudgement** n.

**prejudice** n a judgment or opinion made without adequate knowledge; bias; intolerance or hatred of other races, etc; (law) injury or disadvantage due to another's action. • vt to affect or injure through prejudice.—**prejudiced** adj.

**preliminary** adj preparatory; introductory. • n an event preceding another; a preliminary step or measure; (in school) a preparatory examination.

**prelude** n an introductory act or event; an event preceding another of greater importance; (mus) a movement which acts as an introduction.—also vt.

**premarital** adj (sex) taking place before marriage.

**premature** adj occurring before the expected or normal time; too early, hasty.—**prematurely** adv.—**prematureness, prematurity** n.

**premier** adj principal; first. • n the head of a government, a prime minister.—**premiership** n.

**premiere** n the first public performance of a play, film, etc. • vt to give a premiere of. • vi to have a first performance; to appear for the first time as a star performer.

**premise** n a proposition on which reasoning is based; something assumed or taken for granted; (pl) a piece of land and its buildings. • vt to state as an introduction; to postulate; to base on certain assumptions.

**premium** n a reward, esp an inducement to buy; a periodical payment for insurance; excess over an original price; something given free or at a reduced price with a purchase; a high value or value in excess of expectation. • adj (goods) high quality.

**premonition** n a foreboding; a feeling of something about to happen.

**preoccupied** adj absent-minded, lost in thought; (with **with**) having one's attention completely taken up by.

**prep** abbr = preparatory school.

**preparation** n the act of preparing; a preparatory measure; something prepared, as a medicine, cosmetic, etc.

**preparatory** adj serving to prepare; introductory. • adv by way of preparation; in a preparatory manner.

**preparatory school** n a private school that prepares students for an advanced school or college.

**prepare** vt to make ready in advance; to fit out, equip; to cook; to instruct, teach; to put together. • vi to make oneself ready.

**prepared** adj subjected to a special process or treatment.

**preponderate** vi to be greater in number, amount, influence, etc; to predominate, prevail; to weigh more.—**preponderance** n.—**preponderant** adj.

**preposition** n a word used before a noun or pronoun to show its relation to another part of the sentence.—**prepositional** adj.

**preposterous** adj ridiculous; laughable; absurd.—**preposterously** adv.—**preposterousness** n.

**prerequisite** n a condition, etc, that must be fulfilled prior to something else. • adj required beforehand.

**prerogative** n a privilege or right accorded through office or hereditary rank.

**presbytery** n a ruling body in presbyterian churches consisting of the ministers and representative elders from congregations within a district; the house of a Roman Catholic priest.

**prescribe** vt to designate; to ordain; (rules) to lay down; (medicine, treatment) to order, advise.

**prescription** n act of prescribing; (med) a written instruction to a pharmacist for the preparation of a drug; (law) establishment of a right or title through long use.

**presence** n being present; immediate surroundings; personal appearance and bearing; impressive bearing, personality, etc; something (as a spirit) felt or believed to be present.

**presence of mind** n readiness of resource in an emergency, etc; the ability to say the right thing.

**present**[1] *adj* being at the specified place; existing or happening now; (*gram*) denoting action or state now or action that is always true. • *n* the time being; now; the present tense.

**present**[2] *n* a gift.

**present**[3] *vt* to introduce someone, esp socially; (*a play, etc*) to bring before the public, exhibit; to make a gift or award; to show; to perform; (*law*) to lay a charge before a court; (*weapon*) to point in a particular direction. • *vi* to present a weapon; to become manifest; to come forward as a patient.

**presentable** *adj* of decent appearance; fit to go into company.

**presentation** *n* act of presenting; a display or exhibition; style of presenting; something offered or given; a description or persuasive account; (*med*) the position of a fetus in the uterus.

**presently** *adv* in a short while, soon.

**preservation** *n* the act of preserving or securing; a state of being preserved or repaired.

**preservative** *adj* preserving. • *n* something that preserves or has the power of preserving, esp an additive.

**preserve** *vt* to keep safe from danger; to protect; (*food*) to can, pickle, or prepare for future use; to keep or reserve for personal or special use. • *vi* to make preserves; to raise and protect game for sport. • *n* (*usu pl*) fruit preserved by cooking in sugar; an area restricted for the protection of natural resources, esp one used for regulated hunting, etc; something regarded as reserved for certain persons.

**preside** *vi* to take the chair or hold the position of authority; to take control or exercise authority.

**president** *n* the head of state of a republic; the highest officer of a company, club, etc.—**presidency** *n*.—**presidential** *adj*.

**press** *vt* to act on with steady force or weight; to push against, squeeze, compress, etc; (*clothes, etc*) to iron; to embrace closely; to force, compel; to entreat; to emphasize; to trouble; to urge on; (*record*) to make from a matrix. • *vi* to weigh down; to crowd closely; to go forward with determination. • *n* pressure, urgency, etc; a crowd; a machine for crushing, stamping, etc; a machine for printing; a printing or publishing establishment; the gathering and distribution of news and those who perform these functions; newspapers collectively; any of various pressure devices; an upright closet for storing clothes.

**press conference** *n* a group interview given to members of the press by a politician, celebrity, etc.

**pressing** *adj* urgent; calling for immediate attention; importunate. • *n* a number of records made at one time from a master.

**pressure** *n* the act of pressing; a compelling force; a moral force; compression; urgency; constraint; (*physics*) force per unit of area. • *vt* to pressurize.

**pressure group** *n* a group of people organized to alert public opinion, legislators, etc, to a particular area of interest.

**pressurize** *vt* to keep nearly normal atmospheric pressure inside an aeroplane, etc, as at high altitudes; to exert pressure on; to attempt to compel, press.

**prestige** *n* standing in the eyes of people; commanding position in people's minds.

**prestigious** *adj* imparting prestige or distinction.

**presumably** *adv* as may be presumed.

**presume** *vt* to take for granted, suppose. • *vi* to assume to be true; to act without permission; to take liberties; (*with* **on, upon**) to take advantage of.

**presumption** *n* a supposition; a thing presumed; a strong probability; effrontery.

**presumptuous** *adj* tending to presume; bold; forward.—**presumptuously** *adv*.—**presumptuousness** *n*.

**presuppose** *vt* to assume beforehand; to involve as a necessary prior condition.—**presupposition** *n*.

**pretence, pretense** (*US*) *n* the act of pretending; a hypocritical show; a fraud, a sham.

**pretend** *vti* to claim, represent, or assert falsely; to feign, make believe; to lay claim (to).

**pretentious** *adj* claiming great importance; ostentatious.—**pretentiously** *adv*.—**pretentiousness** *n*.

**pretext** *n* a pretended reason to conceal a true one; an excuse.

**pretty** *adj* (**prettier, prettiest**) attractive in a dainty, graceful way. • *adv* (*inf*) fairly, moderately.—**prettily** *adv*.—**prettiness** *n*.

**prevail** *vi* to overcome; to predominate; to be customary or in force.

**prevailing** *adj* generally accepted, widespread; predominant.

**prevalent** *adj* current; predominant; widely practised or experienced.—**prevalence** *n*.

**prevent** *vt* to keep from happening; to hinder.—**preventable, preventible** *adj*.—**prevention** *n*.

**preventive, preventative** *adj* serving to prevent, precautionary. • *n* something used to prevent disease.

**preview** *n* an advance, restricted showing, as of a film; a showing of scenes from a film to advertise it. • *vt* to view or show in advance of public presentation; to give a preliminary survey.

**previous** *adj* coming before in time or order; prior, former.—**previously** *adv*.

**prey** *n* an animal killed for food by another; a victim. • *vi* (*with* **on, upon**) to seize and devour prey; (*person*) to victimize; to weigh heavily on the mind.

**price** *n* the amount, usu in money, paid for anything; the cost of obtaining some benefit; value, worth. • *vt* to set the price of something; to estimate a price; to deprive by raising prices excessively.

**priceless** *adj* very expensive; invaluable; (*inf*) very amusing, odd, or absurd.

**prick** *n* a sharp point; a puncture or piercing made by a sharp point; the wound or sensation inflicted; a qualm (of conscience); (*inf*) penis; (*offensive*) a spiteful person usu with authority. • *vti* to affect with anguish, grief, or remorse; to pierce slightly; to cause a sharp pain to; to goad, spur; (*the ears*) to erect; (*with* **out**) to transfer seedlings.

**prickle** *n* a thorn, spine or bristle; a pricking sensation. • *vti* to feel or cause to feel a pricking sensation.

**prickly** *adj* having prickles; tingling; irritable.—**prickliness** *n*.

**prickly heat** *n* a skin eruption caused by inflammation of the sweat glands.

**pride** *n* feeling of self-worth or esteem; excessive self-esteem; conceit; a sense of one's own importance; a feeling of elation due to success; the cause of this; splendour; a herd (of lions). • *vti* to be proud of; to take credit for.

**priest** *n* in various churches, a person authorized to perform sacred rites; an Anglican, Eastern Orthodox, or Roman Catholic clergyman ranking

below a bishop.—**priestliness** n.—
**priestly** adj.

**priestess** n a priest who is a woman; a
woman regarded as a leader (as of a
movement).

**priesthood** n the office of priest;
priests collectively.

**prig** n a smug, self-righteous person.—**priggish** adj.

**prim** adj (**primmer, primmest**) proper,
formal and precise in manner; demure.—**primly** adv.—**primness** n.

**primarily** adv mainly.

**primary** adj first; earliest; original; first
in order of time; chief; elementary.
• n a person or thing that is highest
in rank, importance, etc; in US, a
preliminary election at which candidates are chosen for the final election.

**primary school** n a school for children
up to the age of 11 or 12.

**primate** n an archbishop or the highest ranking bishop in a province, etc;
any of the highest order of mammals,
including man.

**prime**[1] adj first in rank, importance,
or quality; chief; (math) of a number,
divisible only by itself and 1. • n the
best time; the height of perfection;
full maturity; full health and
strength.

**prime**[2] vt to prepare or make something ready; to pour liquid into (a
pump) or powder into (a firearm);
to paint on a primer.

**prime minister** n the head of the government in a parliamentary democracy.

**primer**[1] n a simple book for teaching;
a small introductory book on a subject.

**primer**[2] n a detonating device; a first
coat of paint or oil.

**primeval** adj of the first age of the
world; primitive.

**primitive** adj of the beginning or the

earliest times; crude; simple; basic.
• n a primitive person or thing.—
**primitively** adv.

**primrose** n a perennial plant with pale
yellow flowers.

**prince** n the son of a sovereign; a ruler
ranking below a king; the head of a
principality; any pre-eminent person.

**princess** n a daughter of a sovereign;
the wife of a prince; one outstanding in a specified respect.

**principal** adj first in rank or importance; chief. • n a principal person;
a person who organizes; the head of
a college or school; the leading player
in a ballet, opera, etc; (law) the person who commits a crime; a person
for whom another acts as agent; a
capital sum lent or invested; a main
beam or rafter.

**principality** n the position of responsibility of a principal; the rank and territory of a prince.

**principally** adv mainly.

**principle** n a basic truth; a law or doctrine used as a basis for others; a
moral code of conduct; a chemical
constituent with a characteristic
quality; a scientific law explaining a
natural action; the method of a
thing's working.

**print** vti to stamp (a mark, letter, etc)
on a surface; to produce (on paper,
etc) the impressions of inked type,
etc; to produce (a book, etc); to write
in letters resembling printed ones;
to make (a photographic print). • n
a mark made on a surface by pressure; the impression of letters, designs, etc, made from inked type, a
plate, or block; an impression made
by a photomechanical process; a
photographic copy, esp from a negative.

**printer** n a person engaged in printing; a machine for printing from; a
device that produces printout.

**printing** *n* the activity, skill, or business of producing printed matter; a style of writing using capital letters; the total number of books, etc, printed at one time.

**printout** *n* a printed record produced automatically (as by a computer).

**prior** *adj* previous; taking precedence (as in importance). • *n* the superior ranking below an abbot in a monastery; the head of a house or group of houses in a religious community.— **prioress** *nf*.

**priority** *n* precedence in rank, time, or place; preference; something requiring specified attention.

**priory** *n* a religious house under a prior or prioress.

**prise** *vt* to force (open, up) with a lever, etc.

**prism** *n* (*geom*) a solid whose ends are similar, equal, and parallel plane figures and whose sides are parallelograms; a transparent body of this form usu with triangular ends used for dispersing or reflecting light.— **prismatic** *adj*.

**prison** *n* a building used to house convicted criminals for punishment and suspects remanded in custody while awaiting trial; a jail.

**prisoner** *n* a person held in prison or under arrest; a captive; a person confined by a restraint.

**pristine** *adj* pure; in an original, unspoiled condition.

**privacy** *n* being private; seclusion; secrecy; one's private life.

**private** *adj* of or concerning a particular person or group; not open to or controlled by the public; for an individual person; not holding public office; secret. • *n* (*pl*) the genitals; an enlisted man of the lowest military rank in the army.— **privately** *adv*.

**privet** *n* a white-flowered evergreen shrub used for hedges.

**privilege** *n* a right or special benefit enjoyed by a person or a small group; a prerogative. • *vt* to bestow a privilege on.

**privileged** *adj* having or enjoying privileges; not subject to disclosure in a court of law.

**privy** *adj* private; having access to confidential information. • *n* a lavatory, esp one outside; (*law*) a person with an interest in an action.

**prize** *n* an award won in competition or a lottery; a reward given for merit; a thing worth striving for. • *adj* given as, rewarded by, a prize. • *vt* to value highly.

**prizefight** *n* a professional boxing match.—**prizefighter** *n*.

**pro**[1] *adv, prep* in favour of. • *n* (*pl* **pros**) an argument for a proposal or motion.

**pro**[2] *adj, n* professional.

**probability** *n* that which is probable; likelihood; (*math*) the ratio of the chances in favour of an event to the total number.

**probable** *adj* likely; to be expected.

**probation** *n* testing of character or skill; release from prison under supervision by a probation officer; the state or period of being on probation.—**probationary** *adj*.

**probe** *n* a flexible surgical instrument for exploring a wound; a device, as an unmanned spacecraft, used to obtain information about an environment; an investigation. • *vt* to explore with a probe; to examine closely; to investigate.

**probity** *n* honesty, integrity, uprightness.

**problem** *n* a question for solution; a person, thing or matter difficult to cope with; a puzzle; (*math*) a proposition stating something to be done; an intricate unsettled question.

**problematic, problematical** *adj*

presenting a problem; questionable; uncertain.

**procedure** *n* an established mode of conducting business, esp in law or in a meeting; a practice; a prescribed or traditional course; a step taken as part of an established order of steps.—**procedural** *adj*.

**proceed** *vi* to go on, esp after stopping; to come from; to continue; to carry on; to issue; to take action; to go to law.

**proceeding** *n* an advance or going forward; (*pl*) steps, action, in a lawsuit; (*pl*) published records of a society, etc.

**proceeds** *npl* the total amount of money brought in; the net amount received.

**process** *n* a course or state of going on; a series of events or actions; a method of operation; forward movement; (*law*) a court summons; the whole course of proceedings in a legal action. • *vt* to handle something following set procedures; (*food, etc*) to prepare by a special process; (*law*) to take action; (*film*) to develop.

**procession** *n* a group of people in marching in order, as in a parade.

**proclaim** *vt* to announce publicly and officially; to tell openly; to praise.

**proclamation** *n* the act of proclaiming; an official notice to the public.

**procrastinate** *vti* to defer action, to delay.—**procrastination** *n*.

**procreate** *vt* to bring into being, to engender offspring. —**procreation** *n*.

**procure** *vt* to obtain by effort; to get and make available for promiscuous sexual intercourse; to bring about. • *vi* to procure women.—**procurement** *n*.

**prod** *vt* (*pt* **prodded**) to poke or jab, as with a pointed stick; to rouse into activity. • *n* the action of prodding; a sharp object; a stimulus.

**prodigal** *adj* wasteful; extravagant; open-handed. • *n* a wastrel; a person who squanders money.

**prodigious** *adj* enormous, vast; amazing.—**prodigiously** *adv*.

**prodigy** *n* an extraordinary person, thing or act; a gifted child.

**produce** *vt* to bring about; to bring forward, show; to yield; to cause; to manufacture, make; to give birth to; (*play, film*) to put before the public. • *vi* to yield something. • *n* that which is produced, esp agricultural products.

**producer** *n* someone who produces, esp a farmer or manufacturer; a person who finances or supervises the putting on of a play or making of a film; an apparatus or plant for making gas.

**product** *n* a thing produced by nature, industry or art; a result; an outgrowth; (*math*) the number obtained by multiplying two or more numbers together.

**production** *n* the act of producing; a thing produced; a work presented on the stage or screen or over the air.

**productive** *adj* producing or capable of producing; fertile.—**productively** *adv*.—**productiveness** *n*.

**productivity** *n* the state of being productive, the ratio of the output of a manufacturing business to the input of materials, labour, etc.

**profane** *adj* secular, not sacred; showing no respect for sacred things; irreverent; blasphemous; not possessing esoteric or expert knowledge. • *vt* to desecrate; to debase by a wrong, unworthy or vulgar use.—**profanely** *adv*.

**profess** *vt* to affirm publicly, declare; to claim to be expert in; to declare in words or appearance only.

**profession** *n* an act of professing; avowal, esp of religious belief; an occupation requiring specialized knowledge and often long and intensive academic preparation; the people engaged in this; affirmation; entry into a religious order.

**professional** *adj* of or following a profession; conforming to the technical or ethical standards of a profession; earning a livelihood in an activity or field often engaged in by amateurs; having a specified occupation as a permanent career; engaged in by persons receiving financial return; pursuing a line of conduct as though it were a profession.—*also n.*—**professionally** *adv*.

**professor** *n* a faculty member of the highest academic rank at a university; a teacher at a university, college, etc.—**professorial** *adj*.—**professorship** *n*.

**proficient** *adj* skilled, competent.—**proficiency** *n.*—**proficiently** *adv*.

**profile** *n* a side view of the head as in a portrait, drawing, etc; a biographical sketch; a graph representing a person's abilities. • *vt* to represent in profile; to produce (as by writing, drawing, etc) a profile of.

**profit** *n* gain; the excess of returns over expenditure; the compensation to entrepreneurs resulting from the assumption of risk; (*pl*) the excess returns from a business; advantage, benefit. • *vti* to be of advantage (to), benefit; to gain.

**profitable** *adj* yielding profit, lucrative; beneficial; useful.—**profitability** *n.*—**profitably** *adv*.

**profiteer** *vi* to make exorbitant profits, esp in wartime.—*also n.*—**profiteering** *n*.

**profound** *adj* at great depth; intellectually deep; abstruse, mysterious.—**profoundly** *adv*.

**profuse** *adj* abundant; generous; extravagant.—**profusely** *adv.*—**profuseness** *n*.

**profusion** *n* an abundance.

**progeny** *n* offspring; descendants; outcome.

**program** *n* a sequence of instructions fed into a computer. • *vti* (*pt* **programmed** *or* **programed**) to feed a program into a computer; to write a program.

**programme, program** (*US*) *n* a printed list containing details of a ceremony, of the actors in a play, etc; a scheduled radio or television broadcast; a curriculum or syllabus for a course of study; a plan or schedule. • *vt* (*pt* **programmed**) to prepare a plan or schedule.

**progress** *n* a movement forwards or onwards, advance; satisfactory growth or development; a tour from place to place in stages. • *vi* to move forward, advance; to improve. • *vt* (*project*) to take to completion.

**progression** *n* progress; advancement by degrees; (*math*) a series of numbers, each differing from the succeeding according to a fixed law; (*mus*) a regular succession of chords.

**progressive** *adj* advancing, improving; proceeding by degrees; continuously increasing; aiming at reforms. • *n* a person who believes in moderate political change, esp social improvement by government action.—**progressively** *adv.*—**progressiveness** *n*.

**prohibit** *vt* to forbid by law; to prevent.—**prohibitory** *adj*.

**prohibition** *n* the act of forbidding; an order that forbids; a legal ban on the manufacture and sale of alcoholic drinks.—**prohibitionist** *n*.

**prohibitive** *adj* forbidding; so high as to prevent purchase, use, etc, of something.—**prohibitively** *adv*.

**project** *n* a plan, scheme; an undertaking; a task carried out by students, etc, involving research. • *vt* to throw forward; (*light, shadow, etc*) to produce an outline of on a distance surface; to make objective or externalize; (*one's voice*) to make heard at a distance; (*feeling, etc*) to attribute to another; to imagine; to estimate, plan, or figure for the future. • *vi* to jut out; to come across vividly; to make oneself heard clearly.

**projectile** *n* a missile; something propelled by force. • *adj* throwing forward; capable of being thrown forward.

**projection** *n* the act of projecting or the condition of being projected; a thing projecting; the representation on a plane surface of part of the earth's surface; a projected image; an estimate of future possibilities based on a current trend; a mental image externalized; an unconscious attribution to another of one's own feelings and motives.

**projector** *n* an instrument that projects images from transparencies or film; an instrument that projects rays of light; a person who promotes enterprises.

**proletariat** *n* the lowest social or economic class of a community; wage earners; the industrial working class.—**proletarian** *adj*.

**proliferate** *vi* to grow or reproduce rapidly.—**proliferation** *n*.

**prolific** *adj* producing abundantly; fruitful.

**prologue, prolog** (*US*) *n* the introductory lines of a play, speech, or poem; an introductory event.

**prolong** *vt* to extend or lengthen in space or time; to spin out.

**prom** *n* a promenade; a dance.

**promenade** *n* an esplanade; a ball or dance.; a leisurely walk. • *vti* to take a promenade (along, through).

**prominence** *n* the state of being prominent; a projection; relative importance; celebrity, fame.

**prominent** *adj* jutting, projecting; standing out, conspicuous; widely and favourably known; distinguished.—**prominently** *adv*.

**promiscuous** *adj* indiscriminate, esp in sexual liaisons.—**promiscuity** *n*.—**promiscuously** *adv*.—**promiscuousness** *n*.

**promise** *n* a pledge; an undertaking to do or not to do something; an indication, as of a successful future. • *vti* to pledge; to undertake; to give reason to expect.

**promising** *adj* likely to turn out well; hopeful.

**promontory** *n* a peak of high land that juts out into a body of water.

**promote** *vt* to encourage; to advocate; to raise to a higher rank; (*employee, student*) to advance from one grade to the next higher grade; (*product*) to encourage sales by advertising, publicity, or discounting.

**promoter** *n* a person who promotes, esp one who organizes and finances a sporting event or pop concert; a substance that increases the activity of a catalyst.

**promotion** *n* an elevation in position or rank; the furtherance of the sale of merchandise through advertising, publicity, or discounting.—**promotional** *adj*.

**prompt** *adj* without delay; quick to respond; immediate; of or relating to prompting actors. • *vt* to urge; to inspire; (*actor*) to remind of forgotten words, etc (as in a play). • *n* something that reminds; a time limit for payment of an account; the contract by which this time is fixed.—**promptly** *adv*.

**prompter** *n* one that prompts, esp a person who sits offstage and reminds actors of forgotten lines.

**promptness** *n* alacrity in action or decision; quickness; punctuality.

**prone** *adj* face downwards; lying flat, prostrate; inclined or disposed (to).—**proneness** *n*.

**prong** *n* a spike of a fork or other forked object.—**pronged** *adj*.

**pronoun** *n* a word used to represent a noun (eg *I, he, she, it*).

**pronounce** *vt* to utter, articulate; to speak officially, pass (judgment); to declare formally.—**pronounceable** *adj*.

**pronounced** *adj* marked, noticeable.

**pronouncement** *n* a formal announcement, declaration; a confident assertion.

**pronunciation** *n* articulation; the way a word is pronounced.

**proof** *n* evidence that establishes the truth; the fact, act, or process of validating; test; demonstration; a sample from type, etc, for correction; a trial print from a photographic negative; the relative strength of an alcoholic liquor. • *adj* resistant; impervious, impenetrable. • *vt* to make proof against (water).

**prop**[1] *vt* (*pt* **propped**) to support by placing something under or against. • *n* a rigid support; a thing or person giving support.

**prop**[2] *see* **property**.

**prop**[3] *abbr* = propeller.

**propaganda** *n* the organized spread of ideas, doctrines, etc, to promote a cause; the ideas, etc, so spread.—**propagandist** *n, adj*.

**propel** *vt* (*pt* **propelled**) to drive or move forward.—**propellant, propellent** *n*.

**propeller** *n* a mechanism to impart drive; a device having two or more blades in a revolving hub for propelling a ship or aircraft.

**propensity** *n* a natural inclination; disposition, tendency.

**proper** *adj* own, individual, peculiar; appropriate, fit; correct, conventional; decent, respectable; in the most restricted sense; (*sl*) thorough.

**properly** *adv* in the right way; justifiably; (*sl*) thoroughly.

**property** *n* a quality or attribute; a distinctive feature or characteristic; one's possessions; real estate, land; a movable article used in a stage setting (—*also* **prop**).

**prophecy** *n* a message of divine will and purpose; prediction.

**prophesy** *vti* to predict with assurance or on the basis of mystic knowledge; to foretell.

**prophet** *n* a religious leader regarded as, or claiming to be, divinely inspired; one who predicts the future.— **prophetess** *nf*.

**prophetic, prophetical** *adj* of a prophet or prophecy; prophesying events.—**prophetically** *adv*.

**proportion** *n* the relationship between things in size, quantity, or degree; ratio; symmetry, balance; comparative part or share; (*math*) the equality of two ratios; a share or quota; (*pl*) dimensions. • *vt* to put in proper relation with something else; to make proportionate (to).

**proportional** *adj* of proportion; aiming at due proportion; proportionate.—**proportionality** *n*.—**proportionally** *adv*.

**proportionate** *adj* in due proportion, corresponding in amount. • *vt* to make proportionate.—**proportionately** *adv*.

**proposal** *n* a scheme, plan, or suggestion; an offer of marriage.

**propose** *vt* to present for consideration; to suggest; to intend; to announce the drinking of a toast to; (*person*) to nominate; to move as a resolution. • *vi* to make an offer (of marriage).—**proposer** *n*.

**proposition** *n* a proposal for consideration; a plan; a request for sexual intercourse; (*inf*) a proposed deal, as in business; (*inf*) an undertaking to be dealt with; (*math*) a problem to be solved.

**proprietor** *n* an owner.—**proprietress** *nf.*—**proprietorial** *adj.*

**propulsion** *n* the act of propelling; something that propels.

**prosaic** *adj* commonplace, matter-of-fact, dull.—**prosaically** *adv.*

**prose** *n* ordinary language without metre. • *adj* in prose; humdrum, dull.

**prosecute** *vt* to bring legal action against; to pursue. • *vi* to institute and carry on a legal suit or prosecution.

**prosecution** *n* the act of prosecuting, esp by law; the prosecuting party in a legal case.

**prosecutor** *n* a person who prosecutes, esp in a criminal court.

**prospect** *n* a wide view, a vista; (*pl*) measure of future success; future outlook; expectation; a likely customer, candidate, etc. • *vti* to explore or search (for).—**prospector** *n*.

**prospective** *adj* likely; anticipated, expected.

**prospectus** *n* a printed statement of the features of a new work, enterprise, etc; something (as a condition or statement) that forecasts the course or nature of a situation.

**prosper** *vi* to thrive; to flourish; to succeed.

**prosperity** *n* success; wealth.—**prosperous** *adj.*—**prosperously** *adv.*

**prostitute** *n* a person who has sexual intercourse for money; (*fig*) one who deliberately debases his or her talents (as for money). • *vt* to offer indiscriminately for sexual intercourse, esp for money; to devote to corrupt or unworthy purposes.

**prostrate** *adj* lying face downwards; helpless; overcome; lying prone or supine. • *vt* to throw oneself down; to lie flat; to humble oneself.—**prostration** *n*.

**protagonist** *n* the main character in a drama, novel, etc; a supporter of a cause.

**protect** *vt* to defend from danger or harm; to guard; to maintain the status and integrity of, esp through financial guarantees; to foster or shield from infringement or restriction; to restrict competition through tariffs and trade controls.—**protector** *n*.

**protection** *n* the act of protecting; the condition of being protected; something that protects; shelter; defence; patronage; the taxing of competing imports to foster home industry; the advocacy or theory of this (—*also* **protectionism**); immunity from prosecution or attack obtained by the payment of money.

**protective** *adj* serving to protect, defend, shelter.—**protectively** *adv.*

**protégé** *n* a person guided and helped in his career by another person.—**protégée** *nf*.

**protein** *n* a complex organic compound containing nitrogen that is an essential constituent of food.

**protest** *vi* to object to; to remonstrate. • *vt* to assert or affirm; to execute or have executed a formal protest against; to make a statement or gesture in objection to. • *n* public dissent; an objection; a complaint; a formal statement of objection.—**protestation** *n*.—**protester** *n*.

**Protestant** *n* a member or adherent of one of the Christian churches deriving from the Reformation; a Christian not of the Orthodox or Roman Catholic Church, who adheres to the principles of the Reformation.—**Protestantism** *n*.

**protocol** *n* a note, minute or draft of an agreement or transaction; the ceremonial etiquette accepted as correct in official dealings, as between heads of state or diplomatic officials; the formatting of data in an electronic communications system; the plan of a scientific experiment or treatment.

**proton** *n* an elementary particle in the nucleus of all atoms, carrying a unit positive charge of electricity.

**prototype** *n* an original model or type from which copies are made.

**protracted** *adj* extended, prolonged; long-drawn-out.—**protractedly** *adv*.

**protrude** *vti* to thrust outwards or forwards; to obtrude; to jut out, project.—**protrusive** *adj*.

**protuberance** *n* a swelling, prominence.—**protuberant** *adj*.

**proud** *adj* having too high an opinion of oneself; arrogant, haughty; having proper self-respect; satisfied with one's achievements.—**proudly** *adv*.

**prove** *vti* (*pt* **proved** *or* **proven**) to try out, test, by experiment; to establish or demonstrate as true using accepted procedures; to show (oneself) to be worthy or capable; to turn out (to be), esp after trial or test; to rise.

**proverb** *n* a short traditional saying expressing a truth or moral instruction; an adage.

**proverbial** *adj* of or like, a proverb; generally known.—**proverbially** *adv*.

**provide** *vti* to arrange for; to supply; to prepare; to afford (an opportunity); to make provision for (financially).—**provider** *n*.

**provided, providing** *conj* on condition (that).

**providence** *n* foresight, prudence; God's care and protection.

**province** *n* an administrative district or division of a country; the jurisdiction of an archbishop; (*pl*) the parts of a country removed from the main cities; a department of knowledge or activity.

**provincial** *adj* of a province or provinces; having the way, speech, etc of a certain province; country-like; rustic; unsophisticated. • *n* an inhabitant of the provinces or country areas; a person lacking sophistication.—**provincially** *adv*.

**provision** *n* a requirement; something provided for the future; a stipulation, condition; (*pl*) supplies of food, stores. • *vt* to supply with stores.

**provisional** *adj* temporary; conditional.—**provisionally** *adv*.

**proviso** *n* (*pl* **provisos, provisoes**) a condition, stipulation; a limiting clause in an agreement, etc.

**provocation** *n* the act of provoking or inciting; a cause of anger, resentment, etc.

**provocative** *adj* intentionally provoking, esp to anger or sexual desire; (*remark*) stimulating argument or discussion.—**provocatively** *adv*.

**provoke** *vt* to anger, infuriate; to incite, to arouse; to give rise to; to irritate, exasperate.

**prow** *n* the forward part of a ship, bow.

**prowess** *n* bravery, gallantry; skill.

**prowl** *vi* to move stealthily, esp in search of prey.—*also n*.

**prowler** *n* one that moves stealthily, esp an opportunist thief.

**proximity** *n* nearness in place, time, series, etc.

**proxy** *n* the authority to vote or act for another; a person so authorized.—*also adj*.

**prudence** *n* the quality of being prudent; caution; discretion; common sense.

**prudent** *adj* cautious; sensible; managing carefully; circumspect.—**prudently** *adv*.

**prune**[1] *n* a dried plum.

**prune**[2] *vti* (*plant*) to remove dead or living parts from; to cut away what is unwanted or superfluous.

**pry** *vi* to snoop into other people's affairs; to inquire impertinently.

**PS** *abbr* = postscript.

**psalm** *n* a sacred song or hymn, esp one from the Book of Psalms in the Bible.

**pseudo** *adj* false, pretended.

**pseudonym** *n* a false named adopted as by an author.—**pseudonymous** *adj*.

**psyche** *n* the spirit, soul; the mind, esp as a functional entity governing the total organism and its interactions with the environment.

**psychiatry** *n* the branch of medicine dealing with disorders of the mind, including psychoses and neuroses.—**psychiatric** *adj*.—**psychiatrist** *n*.

**psychic, psychical** *adj* of the soul or spirit; of the mind; having sensitivity to, or contact with, forces that cannot be explained by natural laws. • *n* a person apparently sensitive to nonphysical forces; a medium; psychic phenomena.

**psychoanalysis** *n* a method of treating neuroses, phobias, and some other mental disorders by analysing emotional conflicts, repressions, etc.—**psychoanalyse** *vt*.—**psychoanalyst** *n*.

**psychology** *n* the science that studies the human mind and behaviour; mental state.—**psychological** *adj*.—**psychologically** *adv*.—**psychologist** *n*.

**psychopath** *n* a person suffering from a mental disorder that results in antisocial behaviour and lack of guilt.—**psychopathic** *adj*.

**PTO** *abbr* = please turn over.

**pub** *n* a public house, an inn.

**puberty** *n* the stage at which the reproductive organs become functional.

**public** *adj* of, for, or by the people generally; performed in front of people; for the use of all people; open or known to all; acting officially for the people. • *n* the people in general; a particular section of the people, such as an audience, body of readers, etc; open observation.—**publicly** *adv*.

**publication** *n* public notification; the printing and distribution of books, magazines, etc; something published as a periodical, book, etc.

**public house** *n* a tavern or bar licensed to sell alcoholic drinks; an inn.

**publicity** *n* any information or action that brings a person or cause to public notice; work concerned with such promotional matter; notice by the public.

**public relations** *n* relations with the general public of a company, institution, etc, as through publicity.

**public school** *n* a school maintained by public money and supervised by local authorities; in England, a private secondary school, usu boarding.

**publish** *vt* to make generally known; to announce formally; (*book*) to issue for sale to the public. • *vi* to put out an edition; to have one's work accepted for publication.

**publisher** *n* a person or company that prints and issues books, magazines, etc.

**publishing** *n* the business of the production and distribution of books, magazines, recordings, etc.

**puce** *n, adj* (a) purplish brown.

**puck** *n* a hard rubber disc used in ice hockey.

**pucker** *vti* to draw together in creases, to wrinkle. • *n* a wrinkle or fold.

**pudding** *n* a dessert; a steamed or baked dessert; a suet pie.

**puddle** *n* a small pool of water, esp stagnant, spilled, or muddy water.

**puerile** *adj* juvenile; childish.

**puff** *n* a sudden short blast or gust; an exhalation of air or smoke; a light pastry; a pad for applying powder; a flattering notice, advertisement. • *vti* to emit a puff; to breathe hard, pant; to put out of breath; to praise with exaggeration; to swell; to blow, smoke, etc, with puffs.

**puffin** *n* a sea bird that has a short neck and a brightly coloured laterally compressed bill.

**puffy** *adj* (**puffier, puffiest**) inflated, swollen; panting.—**puffily** *adv*.

**pugnacious** *adj* fond of fighting, belligerent.—**pugnaciousness** *n*.—**pugnacity** *n*.

**pull** *vt* to tug at; to pluck; to move or draw towards oneself; to drag; to rip; to tear; (*muscle*) to strain; (*inf*) to carry out, perform; (*inf*) to restrain; (*inf: gun, etc*) to draw out; (*inf*) to attract. • *vi* to carry out the action of pulling something; to be capable of being pulled; to move (away, ahead, etc). • *n* the act of pulling or being pulled; a tug; a device for pulling; (*inf*) influence; (*inf*) drawing power.

**pulley** *n* (*pl* **pulleys**) a wheel with a grooved rim for a cord, etc, used to raise weights by downward pull or change of direction of the pull; a group of these used to increase applied force; a wheel driven by a belt.

**pullover** *n* a buttonless garment with or without sleeves pulled on over the head.

**pulp** *n* a soft, moist, sticky mass; the soft, juicy part of a fruit or soft pith of a plant stem; ground-up, moistened fibres of wood, rags, etc, used to make paper; a book or magazine printed on cheap paper and often dealing with sensational material. • *vti* to make or become pulp or pulpy; to produce or reproduce (written matter) in pulp form.—**pulpiness** *n*.—**pulpy** *adj*.

**pulpit** *n* a raised enclosed platform, esp in a church, from which a clergyman preaches; preachers as a group.

**pulsate** *vi* to beat or throb rhythmically; to vibrate, quiver.—**pulsation** *n*.

**pulse**[1] *n* a rhythmic beat or throb, as of the heart; a place where this is felt; an underlying opinion or sentiment or an indication of it; a short radio signal. • *vti* to throb, pulsate.

**pulse**[2] *n* the edible seeds of several leguminous plants, such as beans, peas and lentils; the plants producing them.

**pulverize** *vti* to reduce to a fine powder; to demolish, smash; to crumble.—**pulverization** *n*.

**puma** *n* a large tawny American animal of the cat family, a cougar or mountain lion.

**pummel** *vt* (*pt* **pummelled**) to strike repeatedly with the fists, to thump.

**pump**[1] *n* a device that forces a liquid or gas into, or draws it out of, something. • *vti* to move (fluids) with a pump; to remove water, etc, from; to drive air into with a pump; to draw out, move up and down, pour forth, etc, as a pump does; (*inf*) to obtain information through questioning. • **pump**[2] *n* a light low shoe or slipper; a rubber-soled shoe.

**pumpkin** *n* a large, round, orange fruit of the gourd family widely cultivated as food.

**pun** *n* a play on words of the same sound but different meanings, usu humorous.—*also vi*.

**punch**[1] *vt* to strike with the fist; to prod or poke; to stamp, perforate with a tool; (*cattle*) to herd. • *n* a blow with the fist; (*inf*) vigour; a machine or tool for punching.

**punch**[2] *n* a hot, sweet drink made with fruit juices, often mixed with wine or spirits.

**punctual** *adj* being on time; prompt.—**punctuality** *n*.—**punctually** *adv*.

**punctuate** vt to use certain standardized marks in (written matter) to clarify meaning; to interrupt; to emphasize. • vi to use punctuation marks.

**punctuation** n the act of punctuating; the state of being punctuated; a system of punctuation.

**puncture** n a small hole made by a sharp object; the deflation of a tyre caused by a puncture. • vt to make useless or ineffective as if by a puncture; to deflate. • vi to become punctured.

**pundit** n a learned person; an expert; a critic, esp a columnist.

**pungent** adj having an acrid smell or a sharp taste; caustic; bitter.—**pungency** n.—**pungently** adv.

**punish** vt to subject a person to a penalty for a crime or misdemeanour; to chastise; to handle roughly.

**punishable** adj liable to legal punishment.

**punishment** n a penalty for a crime or misdemeanour; rough treatment; the act of punishing or being punished.

**punt**[1] n a long flat-bottomed square-ended river boat usu propelled with a pole. • vti to propel or convey in a punt.

**punt**[2] vt to kick a dropped ball before it reaches the ground. • n such a kick.

**puny** adj (**punier, puniest**) of inferior size, strength, or importance; feeble.

**pup** n a young dog, a puppy; a young fox, seal, rat, etc. • vi (pt **pupped**) to give birth to pups.

**pupil**[1] n a child or young person taught under the supervision of a teacher or tutor; a person who has been taught or influenced by a famous or distinguished person.

**pupil**[2] n the round, dark opening in the centre of the iris of the eye through which light passes.

**puppet** n a doll moved by strings attached to its limbs or by a hand inserted in its body; a person controlled by another.—also adj.—**puppeteer** n.—**puppetry** n.

**puppy** n a young domestic dog less than a year old.

**purchase** vt to buy; to obtain by effort or suffering. • n the act of purchasing; an object bought; leverage for raising or moving loads; means of achieving advantage.—**purchaser** n.

**pure** adj clean; not contaminated; not mixed; chaste, innocent; free from taint or defilement; mere; that and that only; abstract and theoretical; (mus) not discordant, perfectly in tune.—**pureness** n.

**purge** vt to cleanse, purify; (nation, party, etc) to rid of troublesome people, to clear (oneself) of a charge; to clear out the bowels of. • n the act or process of purging; a purgative; the removal of persons believed to be disloyal from an organization, esp a political party.

**purify** vti to make or become pure; to cleanse; to make ceremonially clean; to free from harmful matter.—**purification** n.—**purifier** n.

**purist** n someone who is a stickler for correctness in language, style, etc.

**puritan** adj a person who is extremely strict in religion or morals; (with cap) an extreme Protestant of Elizabethan or Stuart times.—also adj.—**puritanic, puritanical** adj.

**purity** n the state of being pure.

**purl** vt to knit a stitch by drawing its base loop from front to back of the fabric.—also n.

**purple** n a dark, bluish red; crimson cloth or clothing, esp as a former emblem of royalty. • adj purple-coloured; royal; (writing style) over-elaborate.

**purport** vt to claim to be true; to imply; to be intended to seem. • n significance; apparent meaning.

**purpose** n objective; intention; aim;

function; resolution, determination.
• *vti* to intend, design.

**purposeful** *adj* determined, resolute;
intentional.—**purposefully** *adv*.—
**purposefulness** *n*.

**purr** *vi* (*cat*) to make a low, murmuring sound of pleasure.—**purring** *n*.

**purse** *n* a small pouch or bag for
money; finances, money; a sum of
money for a present or a prize; a
handbag. • *vt* to pucker, wrinkle up.

**purser** *n* an officer on a passenger ship
in charge of accounts, tickets, etc; an
airline official responsible for the
comfort and welfare of passengers.

**pursue** *vt* to follow; to chase; to strive
for; to seek to attain; to engage in; to
proceed with. • *vi* to follow in order to capture.—**pursuer** *n*.

**pursuit** *n* the act of pursuing; an occupation; a pastime.

**pus** *n* a yellowish fluid produced by
infected sores.

**push** *vti* to exert pressure so as to
move; to press against or forward; to
impel forward, shove; to urge the
use, sale, etc, of; (*inf*) to approach
an age; (*inf*) to sell drugs illegally; to
make an effort. • *n* a thrust, shove;
an effort; an advance against opposition; (*inf*) energy and drive.

**pushchair** *n* a wheeled metal and canvas chair for a small child.

**pushover** *n* (*inf*) something easily
done, as a victory over an opposing
team; (*inf*) a person easily taken advantage of.

**pushy** *adj* (**pushier, pushiest**) (*inf*) assertive; forceful; aggressively ambitious.—**pushily** *adv*.—**pushiness** *n*.

**puss, pussy** *n* an informal name for a
cat.

**put** *vti* (*pr p* **putting**, *pt* **put**) to place,
set; to cast, throw; to apply, direct;
to bring into a specified state; to add
(to); to subject to; to submit; to estimate; to stake; to express; to

translate; to propose; (*a weight*) to
hurl. • *adj* fixed.

**putrid** *adj* rotten or decayed and foul-
smelling.

**putt** *vti* (*golf*) to hit (a ball) with a
putter. • *n* in golf, a stroke to make
the ball roll into the hole.

**putter** *n* (*golf*) a straight-faced club
used in putting.

**putty** *n* a soft, plastic mixture of powdered chalk and linseed oil used to
fill small cracks, fix glass in window
frames, etc.

**puzzle** *vt* to bewilder; to perplex. • *vi*
to be perplexed; to exercise one's
mind, as over a problem. • *n* bewilderment; a difficult problem; a toy
or problem for testing skill or ingenuity; a conundrum.

**puzzling** *adj* perplexing, bewildering,
inexplicable.

**pygmy** *n* an undersized person.—*also*
**pigmy**.

**pyjamas, pajamas** (*US*) *npl* a loosely
fitting sleeping suit of jacket and
trousers.

**pylon** *n* a tower-like structure supporting electric power lines.

**pyramid** *n* (*geom*) a solid figure having a polygon as base, and whose
sides are triangles sharing a common vertex; a huge structure of this
shape, as a royal tomb of ancient
Egypt; an immaterial structure built
on a broad supporting base and nar-
rowing gradually to an apex.

**python** *n* a large, nonpoisonous snake
that kills by constriction.

# Q

**quack**[1] *n* the cry of a duck. • *vi* to
make a sound like a duck.

**quack**[2] *n* an untrained person who
practises medicine fraudulently; one

who pretends to have knowledge he does not have.—*also adj.*

**quad** *n* quadrangle; quadruplet.

**quadrangle** *n* (*geom*) a plane figure with four sides and four angles, a rectangle; a court enclosed by buildings.—**quadrangular** *adj.*

**quadruped** *n* a four-footed animal.—**quadrupedal** *adj.*

**quadruple** *adj* four times as much or as many; made up of or consisting or four; having four divisions or parts. • *vti* to make or become four times as many.

**quadruplet** *n* one of four children born at birth.

**quagmire** *n* soft, wet ground; a difficult situation.

**quail**[1] *vi* to cower, to shrink back with fear.

**quail**[2] *n* a small American game bird.

**quaint** *adj* attractive or pleasant in an odd or old-fashioned style.—**quaintly** *adv.*—**quaintness** *n.*

**quake** *vi* to tremble or shiver, esp with fear or cold; to quiver. • *n* a shaking or tremor; (*inf*) an earthquake.

**Quaker** *n* a popular name for a member of the Society of Friends, a religious sect advocating peace and simplicity.—**Quakerism** *n.*

**qualification** *n* qualifying; a thing that qualifies; a quality or acquirement that makes a person fit for a post, etc; modification; limitation; (*pl*) academic achievements.

**qualify** *vti* to restrict; to describe; to moderate; to modify, limit; to make or become capable or suitable; to fulfil conditions; to pass a final examination; (*gram*) to limit the meaning of.

**qualitative** *adj* of or depending on quality; determining the nature, not the quality, of components.—**qualitatively** *adv.*

**quality** *n* a characteristic or attribute;

degree of excellence; high standard. • *adj* of high quality.

**qualm** *n* a doubt; a misgiving; a scruple; a sudden feeling of faintness or nausea.

**quandary** *n* a predicament; a dilemma.

**quantitative, quantitive** *adj* capable of being measured; relating to size or amount.—**quantitatively, quantitively** *adv.*

**quantity** *n* an amount that can be measured, counted or weighed; a large amount; the property by which a thing can be measured; a number or symbol expressing this property.

**quarantine** *n* a period of isolation imposed to prevent the spread of disease; the time or place of this. • *vt* to put or keep in quarantine.

**quarrel** *n* an argument; an angry dispute; a cause of dispute. • *vi* (*pt* **quarrelled**) to argue violently; to fall out (with); to find fault (with).

**quarrelsome** *adj* contentious; apt to quarrel.

**quarry**[1] *n* an excavation for the extraction of stone, slate, etc; a place from which stone is excavated; a source of information, etc. • *vti* to excavate (from) a quarry; to research.

**quarry**[2] *n* a hunted animal, prey.

**quart** *n* a liquid measure equal to a quarter of a gallon or two pints; a dry measure equal to two pints.

**quarter** *n* a fourth of something; one fourth of a year; one fourth of an hour; (in US) 25 cents, or a coin of this value; any leg of a four-legged animal with the adjoining parts; a particular district or section; (*pl*) lodgings; a particular source; an unspecified person or group; a compass point other than the cardinal points; mercy; (*her*) any of four quadrants of a shield. • *vti* to share or divide into four; to provide with lodgings; to lodge; to range over (an area) in search (of). • *adj* constituting a quarter.

**quarterfinal** *n* one of four matches held before the semifinals in a tournament.—*also adj.*

**quarterly** *adj* occurring, issued, or spaced at three-month intervals; (*her*) divided into quarters. • *adv* once every three months; (*her*) in quarters. • *n* a publication issued four times a year.

**quartermaster** *n* (*mil*) an officer in charge of stores; (*naut*) a petty officer in charge of steering, etc.

**quartet, quartette** *n* a set or group of four; a piece of music composed for four instruments or voices; a group of four instrumentalists or voices.

**quartz** *n* a crystalline mineral, a form of silica, usu colourless and transparent.

**quash** *vt* (*rebellion etc*) to put down; to suppress; to make void.

**quasi** *adv* seemingly; as if. • *prefix* almost, apparently.

**quaver** *vi* to tremble, vibrate; to speak or sing with a quivering voice. • *n* a trembling sound or note; (*mus*) a note having half the duration of a crotchet, an eighth note.—**quavery** *adj.*

**quay** *n* a loading wharf or landing place for vessels.

**queasy** *adj* (**queasier, queasiest**) nauseous; easily upset; over-scrupulous.—**queasily** *adv.*—**queasiness** *n.*

**queen** *n* a female sovereign and head of state; the wife or widow of a king; a woman considered pre-eminent; the egg-laying female of bees, wasps, etc; a playing card with a picture of a queen; (*chess*) the most powerful piece; (*sl*) a male homosexual, esp one who ostentatiously takes a feminine role. • *vi* (*with* it) to act like a queen, esp to put on airs. • *vt* (a pawn) to promote to a queen in chess.—**queenly** *adj.*

**queen mother** *n* a queen dowager who is the mother of a ruling sovereign.

**queer** *adj* strange, odd, curious; (*inf*) eccentric; (*sl*) homosexual. • *n* a (male) homosexual. • *vt* (*sl*) to spoil the success of.—**queerness** *n.*

**quell** *vt* to suppress; to allay.

**quench** *vt* (*thirst*) to satisfy or slake; (*fire*) to put out, extinguish; (*steel*) to cool; to suppress.—**quenchable** *adj.*

**query** *n* a question; a question mark; doubt. • *vti* to question; to doubt the accuracy of.

**quest** *n* a search, seeking, esp involving a journey. • *vti* to search (about) for, seek.—**quester** *n.*—**questingly** *adv.*

**question** *n* an interrogative sentence; an inquiry; a problem; a doubtful or controversial point; a subject of debate before an assembly; a part of a test or examination. • *vti* to ask questions (of); to interrogate intensively; to dispute; to subject to analysis.—**questioner** *n.*

**questionable** *adj* doubtful; not clearly true or honest.—**questionably** *adv.*

**question mark** *n* a punctuation mark (?) used at the end of a sentence to indicate a question, or to express doubt about something; something unknown.

**questionnaire** *n* a series of questions designed to collect statistical information; a survey made by the use of questionnaire.

**queue** *n* a line of people, vehicles, etc awaiting a turn. • *vi* (*pr p* **queuing**, *pt* **queued**) to wait in turn.

**quibble** *n* a minor objection or criticism. • *vi* to argue about trifling matters.

**quick** *adj* rapid, speedy; nimble; prompt; responsive; alert; eager to learn. • *adv* in a quick manner. • *n* the sensitive flesh below a fingernail

or toenail; the inmost sensibilities.—
**quickly** adv.—**quickness** n.

**quicken** vti to speed up or accelerate;
to make alive; to come to life; to invigorate.

**quicksand** n loose wet sand easily
yielding to pressure in which persons, animals, etc may be swallowed
up.

**quickstep** n a ballroom dance in quick
time; its music.

**quick-witted** adj mentally alert; quick
in repartee.—**quick-wittedness** n.

**quid** n (sl) a pound (sterling).

**quiet** adj silent, not noisy; still, not
moving; gentle, not boisterous; unobtrusive, not showy; placid, calm;
monotonous, uneventful; undisturbed. • n stillness, peace, repose;
an undisturbed state. • vti to quieten.—**quietly** adv.—**quietness** n.

**quieten** vti to make or become quiet;
to calm, soothe.

**quill** n the hollow stem of a feather;
anything made of this, as a pen; a
stiff, hollow spine of a hedgehog or
porcupine.

**quilt** n a thick, warm bedcover; a bed-
spread; a coverlet of two cloths sewn
together with padding between.
• vti to stitch together like a quilt;
to make a quilt. **quilter** n.—**quilting**
n.

**quin** n a quintuplet.

**quinine** n a bitter crystalline alkaloid
used in medicine; one of its salts
used esp as an antimalarial and a bitter tonic.

**quintet, quintette** n a set or group of
five; a piece of music composed for
five instruments or voices; a group
of five instrumentalists or voices.

**quintuple** adj fivefold; having five divisions or parts; five times as much
or as many. • vti to multiply by five.
• n a number five times greater than
another.

**quintuplet** n one of five offspring produced at one birth.

**quip** n a witty remark; a gibe. • vt (pt
**quipped**) to make a clever or sarcastic remark.

**quirk** n an unexpected turn or twist; a
peculiarity of character or mannerism.—**quirky** adj.—**quirkiness** n.

**quit** vti (pt **quitted** or **quit**) to leave; to
stop or cease; to resign; to free from
obligation; to admit defeat. • adj
free from; released from.

**quite** adv completely; somewhat,
fairly; really.

**quits** adj even; on equal terms by payment or revenge.

**quiver**[1] vi to shake; to tremble, shiver.
• n a shiver, vibration.—**quivery** adj.

**quiver**[2] n a case for holding arrows.

**quiz** n (pl **quizzes**) a form of entertainment where players are asked ques-
tions of general knowledge; a short
written or oral test. • vt (pt **quizzed**)
to interrogate; to make fun of.

**quizzical** adj humorous and questioning.—**quizzically** adv.

**quoit** n a ring of metal, plastic, etc
thrown in quoits; (pl) a game in
which rings are thrown at or over a
peg.

**quorum** n the minimum number that
must be present at a meeting or assembly to make its proceedings valid.

**quota** n a proportional share; a prescribed amount; a part to be contributed.

**quotation** n the act of quoting; the
words quoted; an estimated price.

**quotation mark** n a punctuation mark
used to indicate the beginning (' or
") and the end (' or ") of a quoted
passage.

**quote** vt to cite; to refer to; to repeat
the words of a novel, play, poem,
speech, etc exactly; to adduce by way
of authority; to set off by quotation
marks; to state the price of

(something). • *n* (*inf*) something quoted; a quotation mark.—**quotable** *adj*.

# R

**rabbi** *n* (*pl* **rabbis**) the religious and spiritual leader of a Jewish congregation.

**rabbit** *n* a small burrowing mammal of the hare family with long ears, a short tail, and long hind legs; their flesh as food; their fur.

**rabble** *n* a disorderly crowd, a mob; the common herd.

**rabid** *adj* infected with rabies; raging; fanatical.

**rabies** *n* an acute, infectious, viral disease transmitted by the bite of an infected animal.

**raccoon** *n* a small nocturnal carnivore of North America that lives in trees; its yellowish grey fur.

**race**[1] *n* any of the divisions of humankind distinguished esp by colour of skin; any geographical, national, or tribal ethnic grouping; a subspecies of plants or animals; distinctive flavour or taste.

**race**[2] *n* a contest of speed; a rapid current of water. • *vi* to run at top speed or out of control; to compete in a race; (*engine*) to run without a working load. • *vt* to cause to race; to contest against.

**racecourse, racetrack** (*US*) *n* a track over which races are run, esp an oval track for racing horses.

**racehorse** *n* a horse bred and trained for racing.

**racial** *adj* of or relating to any of the divisions of humankind distinguished by colour, etc.

**racialism, racism** *n* a belief in the superiority of some races over others; prejudice against or hatred of other races; discriminating behaviour towards people of another race.—**racist** *n*.

**rack** *n* a frame for holding or displaying articles; an instrument for torture by stretching; the triangular frame for setting up balls in snooker; a toothed bar to engage with the teeth of a wheel; extreme pain or anxiety. • *vt* (*person*) to stretch on a rack; to arrange in or on a rack; to torture, torment; to move parts of machinery with a toothed rack.

**racket**[1] *n* a bat strung with nylon, for playing tennis, etc. (*pl*) a game for two or four players played in a four-walled court (—*also* **racquet**).

**racket**[2] *n* noisy confusion; din; an obtaining of money illegally; any fraudulent business.

**racy** *adj* lively, spirited; risqué.—**racily** *adv*.

**radar** *n* a system or device for detecting objects such as aircraft by using the reflection of radio waves.

**radiance** *n* the condition of being radiant; brilliant light; dazzling beauty.

**radiant** *adj* shining; beaming with happiness; sending out rays; transmitted by radiation.—**radiantly** *adv*.

**radiate** *vt* (*light*, *heat*, *etc*) to emit in rays; (*happiness*, *love*, *etc*) to give forth. • *vi* to spread out as if from a centre; to shine; to emit rays.

**radiation** *n* radiant particles emitted as energy; rays emitted in nuclear decay; (*med*) treatment using a radioactive substance.

**radiator** *n* an apparatus for heating a room; a cooling device for a vehicle engine.

**radical** *adj* of or relating to the root or origin; fundamental; favouring basic change. • *n* a person who advocates fundamental political or social change.—**radicalism** *n*.

**radio** *n* the transmission of sounds or signals by electromagnetic waves through space, without wires, to a receiving set; such a set; broadcasting by radio as an industry, etc. • *adj* of, using, used in, or sent by radio. • *vti* to transmit, or communicate with, by radio.

**radio-** *prefix* radial; radio; using radiant energy.

**radioactive** *adj* giving off radiant energy in the form of particles or rays caused by the disintegration of atomic nuclei.—**radioactivity** *n*.

**radiography** *n* the production of X-rays for use in medicine, industry, etc.—**radiographer** *n*.

**radiology** *n* a branch of medicine concerned with the use of radiant energy (as X-rays and radium) in the diagnosis and treatment of disease.—**radiologist** *n*.

**radish** *n* a pungent root eaten raw as a salad vegetable.

**radium** *n* a highly radioactive metallic element.

**radius** *n* (*pl* **radii** *or* **radiuses**) (*geom*) a straight line joining the centre of a circle or sphere to its circumference; a thing like this, a spoke; a sphere of activity; (*anat*) the thicker of the two bones of the forearm.

**raffia** *n* a kind of palm; fibre from its leaves used in basket-making, etc.

**raffle** *n* a lottery with prizes. • *vt* to offer as a prize in a raffle.

**raft** *n* a platform of logs, planks, etc strapped together to float on water.

**rafter** *n* one of the inclined, parallel beams that support a roof.

**rag** *n* a torn or waste scrap of cloth; a shred; (*inf*) a sensationalist newspaper; (*pl*) tattered or shabby clothing.

**ragbag** *n* a bag for scraps; a miscellaneous collection, jumble.

**rage** *n* violent anger; passion; frenzy; fashion, craze. • *vi* to behave with violent anger; to storm; to spread rapidly; to be prevalent.

**ragged** *adj* jagged; uneven; irregular; worn into rags; tattered.—**raggedly** *adv*.—**raggedness** *n*.

**raid** *n* a sudden attack to assault or seize. • *vt* to make a raid on; to steal from.—**raider** *n*.

**rail**[1] *n* a horizontal bar from one post to another, as in a fence, etc; one of a pair of parallel steel lines forming a track; a railway, railroad.

**rail**[2] *vi* to speak angrily.

**railing** *n* a fence of rails and posts; rails collectively.

**railroad** *n* a railway. • *vt* to force unduly; (*bill, etc*) to push forward fast; to imprison hastily, esp unjustly.

**railway, railroad** (*US*) *n* a track of parallel steel rails along which carriages are drawn by locomotive engines; a complete system of such tracks.

**rain** *n* water that falls from the clouds in the form of drops; a shower; a large quantity of anything falling like rain; (*pl*) the rainy season in the tropics. • *vti* (*of rain*) to fall; to fall like rain; (*rain, etc*) to pour down.

**rainbow** *n* the arc containing the colours of the spectrum formed in the sky by the sun's rays in falling rain or mist. • *adj* many-coloured.

**raincoat** *n* a waterproof coat.

**rainfall** *n* a fall of rain; the amount of rain that falls on a given area in a specified time.

**rainproof** *adj* rain-resisting.

**rainy** *adj* (**rainier, rainiest**) full of rain; wet.

**raise** *vt* to elevate; to lift up; to set or place upright; to stir up, rouse; to increase in size, amount, degree, intensity, etc; to breed, bring up; (*question, etc*) to put forward; to collect or levy; (*siege*) to abandon. • *n* a rise in wages.

**raisin** *n* a sweet, dried grape.

**raja, rajah** *n* an Indian or Malay prince or ruler; an Indian title.

**rake**[1] *n* a tool with a row of teeth and a handle for gathering, scraping or smoothing. • *vt* to scrape, gather as with a rake; to sweep with gaze or gunshot; (*with* **in**: *money, etc*) to gather a great amount rapidly; (*with* **up**: *past misdemeanours, etc*) to bring to light.

**rake**[2] *n* the incline or slope of a mast, stern, etc.

**rake**[3] *n* a dissolute man.

**rakish** *adj* jaunty, dashing; dissolute. —**rakishly** *adv*.—**rakishness** *n*.

**rally** *vti* to bring or come together; to recover strength, revive; to take part in a rally. • *n* a large assembly of people; a recovery; (*tennis*) a lengthy exchange of shots; a competitive test of driving and navigational skills.

**ram** *n* a male sheep; a battering device; a piston; (*with cap*) Aries, the first sign of the zodiac. • *vt* (*pt* **rammed**) to force or drive; to crash; to cram; to thrust violently.

**ramble** *vi* to wander or stroll about for pleasure; (*plant*) to straggle; to write or talk aimlessly. • *n* a leisurely walk in the countryside.

**rambler** *n* a person who rambles; a climbing rose.

**rambling** *adj* spread out, straggling; circuitous; disconnected; disjointed. • *n* the act of walking for pleasure.

**ramification** *n* a branching out; an offshoot; a consequence.

**ramp** *n* a sloping walk or runway joining different levels; a wheeled staircase for boarding a plane; a sloping runway for launching boats, as from trailers.

**rampage** *n* angry or violent behaviour. • *vi* to rush about in an angry or violent manner.

**rampant** *adj* dominant; luxuriant; unrestrained; violent; rife, prevalent; (*her*) (of a lion) standing on its hind legs.

**rampart** *n* an embankment surrounding a fortification; a protective wall.

**ramshackle** *adj* dilapidated.

**ran** *see* **run**.

**ranch** *n* a large farm for raising cattle, horses, or sheep; a style of house with all the rooms on one floor. • *vi* to own, manage, or work on a ranch.—**rancher** *n*.

**rancid** *adj* having an unpleasant smell and taste, as stale fats or oil.—**rancidity, rancidness** *n*.

**rancour, rancor** (*US*) *n* bitter hate or spite.—**rancorous** *adj*.—**rancorously** *adv*.

**random** *adj* haphazard; left to chance.

**randy** *adj* (**randier, randiest**) (*sl*) lustful, sexually aroused.

**rang** *see* **ring**[2].

**range** *n* a row; a series of mountains, etc; scope, compass; the distance a vehicle, etc can travel without refuelling; the distance a bullet, etc can travel, or from gun to target; fluctuation; a large open area for grazing livestock; a place for testing rockets in flight; a place for shooting or golf practice; a cooking stove. • *vt* to place in order or a row; to establish the range of; (*livestock*) to graze on a range. • *vi* to be situated in a line; to rank or classify; (*gun*) to point or aim; to vary (inside limits).

**ranger** *n* a forest or park warden.

**rank**[1] *n* a line of objects; a line of soldiers standing abreast; high standing or position; status; (*pl*) ordinary members of the armed forces. • *vti* to arrange in a line; to have a specific position in an organization or on a scale; (*with* **with**) to be counted among.

**rank**[2] *adj* growing uncontrollably; utter, flagrant; offensive in odour or flavour.

**rank and file** *n* ordinary soldiers; ordinary members, as distinguished from their leaders.

**rankle** *vi* to fester; to cause continuous resentment or irritation.

**ransack** *vt* to plunder; to search thoroughly.

**ransom** *n* the release of a captured person or thing; the price paid for this. • *vt* to secure release of by payment.

**rant** *vi* to speak loudly or violently; to preach noisily. • *n* loud, pompous talk.

**rap** *n* a sharp blow; a knock; (*inf*) talk, conversation; (*sl*) arrest for a crime; (*sl*) a song that is rapped. • *vti* (*pt* **rapped**) to strike lightly or sharply; to knock; (*sl*) to criticize sharply; (*with* **out**) to utter abruptly; (*sl*) to speak a song accompanied by an insistent electronic rhythm.

**rape**[1] *n* the act of forcing a woman to have sexual intercourse against her will; a plundering. • *vti* to commit rape (upon).—**rapist** *n*.

**rape**[2] *n* a bright yellow plant of the mustard family grown for its leaves and oily seeds.

**rapid** *adj* at great speed; fast; sudden; steep. • *npl* a part of a river where the current flows swiftly.—**rapidity** *n*.—**rapidly** *adv*.

**rapport** *n* a sympathetic relationship; accord.

**rapture** *n* the state of being carried away with love, joy, etc; intense delight, ecstasy.—**rapturous** *adj*.—**rapturously** *adv*.

**rare**[1] *adj* unusual; seldom seen; exceptionally good; (*gas*) of low density, thin. *adv*.—**rareness** *n*.

**rare**[2] *adj* not completely cooked, partly raw; underdone.

**rarefy** *vti* to make or become less dense; to thin out; to expand without the addition of matter; to make

more spiritual or refined.—**rarefied** *adj*.

**rarely** *adv* almost never; exceptionally, unusually.

**rarity** *n* rareness; a rare person or thing.

**rascal** *n* a rogue; a villain; a mischievous person.

**rase** *see* **raze**.

**rash**[1] *adj* reckless; impetuous.—**rashly** *adv*.—**rashness** *n*.

**rash**[2] *n* a skin eruption of spots, etc.

**rasher** *n* a thin slice of bacon or ham.

**rasp** *n* a coarse file; a grating sound. • *vt* to scrape with a rasp. • *vi* to produce a grating sound.—**rasping** *n*.

**raspberry** *n* a shrub with white flowers and red berry-like fruits; the fruit produced; (*inf*) a sound of dislike or derision.

**rat** *n* a long-tailed rodent similar to a mouse but larger; (*sl*) a sneaky, contemptible person. • *vi* (*pt* **ratted**) to hunt or catch rats; to betray or inform on someone.

**ratchet** *n* a device with a toothed wheel that moves in one direction only.

**rate** *n* the amount, degree, etc of something in relation to units of something else; price, esp per unit; degree. • *vt* to fix the value of; to rank; to regard or consider; (*sl*) to think highly of. • *vi* to have value or status.

**rather** *adv* more willingly; preferably; somewhat; more accurately; on the contrary; (*inf*) yes, certainly.

**ratify** *vt* to approve formally; to confirm.

**rating** *n* an assessment; an evaluation, an appraisal, as of credit worthiness; classification by grade, as of military personnel; (*radio*, *TV*) the relative popularity of a programme according to sample polls.

**ratio** *n* the number of times one thing

contains another; the quantitative relationship between two classes of objects; proportion.

**ration** *n* (*food*, *petrol*) a fixed amount or portion; (*pl*) food supply. • *vt* to supply with rations; (*food*, *petrol*) to restrict the supply of.

**rational** *adj* of or based on reason; reasonable; sane.—**rationally** *adv*.

**rationale** *n* the reason for a course of action; an explanation of principles.

**rationalize** *vti* to make rational; to justify one's reasons for an action; to cut down on personnel or equipment; to substitute a natural for a supernatural explanation.—**rationalization** *n*.

**rat race** *n* continual hectic competitive activity.

**rattle** *vi* to clatter. • *vt* to make a series of sharp, quick noises; to clatter; to recite rapidly; to chatter; (*inf*) to disconcert, fluster. • *n* a rattling sound; a baby's toy that makes a rattling sound; a voluble talker; the rings on the tail of a rattlesnake.

**rattlesnake** *n* a venomous American snake with a rattle in its tail.

**raucous** *adj* hoarse and harsh-sounding; loud and rowdy.

**ravage** *vt* to ruin, destroy; to plunder, lay waste. • *n* destruction; ruin; (*pl*) the effects of this.

**rave** *vi* to speak wildly or as if delirious; (*inf*) to enthuse. • *n* enthusiastic praise.—**raving** *adj*.

**raven** *n* a large crow-like bird with glossy black feathers. • *adj* of the colour or sheen of a raven.

**ravenous** *adj* very hungry; greedy.—**ravenously** *adv*.

**ravine** *n* a deep, narrow gorge, a large gully.

**ravioli** *n* small cases of pasta filled with highly seasoned chopped meat or vegetables.

**ravish** *vt* to violate; to rape; to captivate.

**ravishing** *adj* charming, captivating.

**raw** *adj* uncooked; unrefined; in a natural state, crude; untrained, inexperienced; sore, skinned; damp, chilly; (*inf*) harsh or unfair.—**rawness** *n*.

**raw material** *n* something out of which a finished article is made; something with a potential for development, improvement, etc.

**ray**[1] *n* a beam of light that comes from a bright source; any of several lines radiating from a centre; a beam of radiant energy, radioactive particles, etc; a tiny amount.

**ray**[2] *n* any of various fishes with a flattened body and the eyes on the upper surface.

**rayon** *n* a textile fibre made from a cellulose solution; a fabric of such fibres.

**raze** *vt* to demolish; to erase; to level to the ground.—*also* **rase**.

**razor** *n* a sharp-edged instrument for shaving.

**Rd** *abbr* = road.

**re** *prep* concerning, with reference to.

**reach** *vti* to arrive at; to extend as far as; to make contact with; to pass, hand over; to attain, realize; to stretch out the hand; to extend in influence, space, etc; to carry, as sight, sound, etc; to try to get. • *n* the act or power of reaching; extent; mental range; scope; a continuous extent, esp of water.

**react** *vi* to act in response to a person or stimulus; to have a mutual or reverse effect; to revolt; (*chem*) to undergo a chemical reaction.

**reaction** *n* an action in response to a stimulus; a revulsion of feeling; exhaustion after excitement, etc; opposition to new ideas; (*chem*) an action set up by one substance in another.

**reactionary** *adj*, *n* (a person) opposed to political or social change.

**reactor** *n* a person or substance that undergoes a reaction; (*chem*) a vessel in which a reaction occurs; a nuclear reactor.

**read** *vti* (*pt* **read**) to understand something written; to speak aloud (from a book); to study by reading; to interpret, divine; to register, as a gauge; to foretell; (of a computer) to obtain (information) from; (*sl*) to hear and understand (a radio communication, etc); (*with* **about, of**) to learn by reading; to be phrased in certain words. • *adj* well-informed.

**reader** *n* a person who reads; one who reads aloud to others; a proofreader; a person who evaluates manuscripts; a textbook, esp on reading; a unit that scans material for computation or storage; a senior lecturer.

**readership** *n* all the readers of a certain publication, author, etc.

**readily** *adv* in a ready manner; willingly, easily.

**reading** *n* the act of one who reads; any material to be read; the amount measured by a barometer, meter, etc; a particular interpretation of a play, etc.

**ready** *adj* (**readier, readiest**) prepared; fit for use; willing; inclined, apt; prompt, quick; handy. • *n* the state of being ready, esp the position of a firearm aimed for firing; (*sl*) money. • *vt* to make ready.—**readiness** *n*.

**ready-made** *adj* made in standard sizes, not to measure.

**real** *adj* existing, actual, not imaginary; true, genuine, not artificial; (*law*) immovable, consisting of land or houses. • *adv* (*sl*) very; really.

**real estate** *n* property; land.

**realism** *n* practical outlook; (*art, literature*) the ability to represent things as they really are; (*philos*) the doctrine that the physical world has an objective existence.—**realist** *n*.

**realistic** *adj* matter-of-fact, not visionary; lifelike; of or relating to realism.—**realistically** *adv*.

**reality** *n* the fact or condition of being real; an actual fact or thing; truth.

**realize** *vt* to become fully aware of; (*ambition, etc*) to make happen; to cause to appear real; to convert into money, be sold for.—**realization** *n*.

**really** *adv* in fact, in reality; positively, very. • *interj* indeed.

**realm** *n* a kingdom, country; domain, region; sphere.

**ream** *n* a quantity of paper varying from 480 to 516 sheets; (*pl: inf*) a great amount.

**reap** *vti* to harvest; to gain (a benefit).

**rear**[1] *n* the back part or position, esp of an army; (*sl*) the rump. • *adj* of, at, or in the rear.

**rear**[2] *vt* to raise; (*children*) to bring up; to educate, nourish, etc. • *vi* (*horse*) to stand on the hind legs.

**reason** *n* motive or justification (of an action or belief); the mental power to draw conclusions and determine truth; a cause; moderation; sanity; intelligence. • *vti* to think logically (about); to analyse; to argue or infer.

**reasonable** *adj* able to reason or listen to reason; rational; sensible; not expensive; moderate, fair.—**reasonableness** *n*.—**reasonably** *adv*.

**reassure** *vt* to hearten; to give confidence to; to free from anxiety.—**reassurance** *n*.

**rebate** *n* a refund of part of an amount paid; discount.

**rebel** *n* a person who refuses to conform with convention. • *vi* (*pt* **rebelled**) to rise up against authority; to dissent.—**rebellion** *n*.—**rebellious** *adj*.

**rebound** *vi* to spring back after impact; to bounce back; to recover. • *n* a recoil; an emotional reaction.

**rebuff** *vt* to snub, repulse; to refuse unexpectedly.—*also n.*

**rebuke** *vt* to reprimand, chide. • *n* censure, a reprimand.

**rebut** *vt* (*pt* **rebutted**) to disprove or refute by argument, etc.—**rebuttal** *n.*

**recall** *vt* to call back; to bring back to mind, remember; to revoke. • *n* remembrance; a summons to return; the removal from office by popular vote.

**recant** *vti* to repudiate or retract a former opinion, declaration, or belief.—**recantation** *n.*

**recap** *vti* (*pt* **recapped**) to recapitulate. • *n* (*inf*) recapitulation.

**recapitulate** *vt* to state again, to summarize.—**recapitulation** *n.*

**recapture** *vt* to capture again; (*a lost feeling, etc*) to discover anew, regain. • *n* the act of recapturing; a thing or feeling recaptured.

**recce** *n* (*sl*) reconnaissance. • *vti* (*pt* **recced** *or* **recceed**) (*sl*) to reconnoitre.

**recede** *vi* to move back; to withdraw, retreat; to slope backwards; to grow less; to decline in value.

**receding** *adj* sloping backwards; disappearing from view; (*hair*) ceasing to grow at the temples.

**receipt** *n* the act of receiving; a written proof of this; (*pl*) amount received from business. • *vt* to acknowledge and mark as paid; to write a receipt for.

**receive** *vt* to acquire, to be given; to experience, to be subjected to; to admit, to allow; to greet on arrival; to accept as true; (*stolen goods*) to take in; to transfer electrical signals. • *vi* to be a recipient; to convert radio waves into perceptible signals.

**receiver** *n* a person who receives; equipment that receives electronic signals, esp on a telephone; (*law*) a person appointed to manage or hold

in trust property in bankruptcy or pending a lawsuit.

**recent** *adj* happening lately, fresh; not long established, modern.—**recently** *adv.*

**receptacle** *n* a container.

**reception** *n* the act of receiving or being received; a welcome; a social gathering; a response, reaction; the quality of the sound or image produced by a radio or TV set.

**receptionist** *n* a person employed to receive visitors to an office, hotel, etc.

**receptive** *adj* able or quick to take in ideas or impressions.

**recess** *n* a temporary halting of work, a vacation; a hidden or inner place; an alcove or niche. • *vti* to place in a recess; to form a recess in; to take a recess.

**recipe** *n* a list of ingredients and directions for preparing food; a method for achieving an end.

**recipient** *n* a person who receives.

**reciprocal** *adj* done by each to the other; mutual; complementary; interchangeable; (*gram*) expressing a mutual relationship. • *n* (*math*) an expression so related to another that their product is 1.—**reciprocally** *adv.*—**reciprocity** *n.*

**reciprocate** *vti* to give in return; to repay; (*mech*) to move alternately backwards and forwards.—**reciprocating** *adj.*—**reciprocation** *n.*

**recital** *n* the act of reciting; a detailed account, narrative; a statement of facts; (*mus*) a performance given by an individual musician.

**recite** *vti* to repeat aloud from memory; to recount, enumerate; to repeat (a lesson).

**reckless** *adj* rash, careless, incautious.—**recklessly** *adv.*—**recklessness** *n.*

**reckon** *vti* to count; to regard or consider; to think; to calculate; (*with* **with**) to take into account.

**reckoning** *n* a calculation; the settlement of an account.

**reclaim** *vt* to recover, win back from a wild state or vice; (*wasteland*) to convert into land fit for cultivation; (*plastics, etc*) to obtain from waste materials.—**reclaimable** *adj.*—**reclamation** *n.*

**recline** *vti* to cause or permit to lean or bend backwards; to lie down on the back or side.—**reclinable** *adj.*

**recluse** *n* a person who lives in solitude; a hermit.

**recognition** *n* the act of recognizing; identification; acknowledgment, admission.

**recognize** *vt* to know again, identify; to greet; to acknowledge formally; to accept, admit.—**recognizable** *adj.*

**recoil** *vti* to spring back, kick, as a gun; to shrink or flinch. • *n* the act of recoiling, a rebound.

**recollect** *vti* to recall; to remind (oneself) of something temporarily forgotten; to call something to mind.

**recollection** *n* the act of recalling to mind; a memory, impression; something remembered; tranquillity of mind; religious contemplation.

**recommend** *vt* to counsel or advise; to commend or praise; to introduce favourably.—**recommendable** *adj.*—**recommendation** *n.*

**recompense** *n* to reward or pay an equivalent; to compensate. • *n* reward; repayment; compensation.

**reconcile** *vt* to re-establish friendly relations; to bring to agreement; to make compatible; to resolve; to settle; to make resigned (to); (*financial account*) to check with another account for accuracy.—**reconcilable** *adj.*—**reconciliation** *n.*

**recondition** *vt* to repair and restore to good working order.

**reconnaissance** *n* a survey of an area, esp for obtaining military information about an enemy.

**reconnoitre, reconnoiter** (*US*) *vti* to make a reconnaisance (of).

**reconsider** *vt* to consider afresh, review; to modify.—**reconsideration** *n.*

**reconstruct** *vt* to build again; to build up, as from remains, an image of the original; to supply missing parts by conjecture.—**reconstruction** *n.*

**record** *vti* to preserve evidence of; to write down; to chart; to register, enrol; to register permanently by mechanical means; (*sound or visual images*) to register on a disc, tape, etc for later reproduction; to celebrate. • *n* a written account; a register; a report of proceedings; the known facts about anything or anyone; an outstanding performance or achievement that surpasses others previously recorded; a grooved vinyl disc for playing on a record player; (*comput*) data in machine-readable form.

**recorder** *n* an official who keeps records; a machine or device that records; a tape recorder; a wind instrument of the flute family.

**recording** *n* what is recorded, as on a disc or tape; the record.

**record player** *n* an instrument for playing records through a loudspeaker.

**recount** *vt* to narrate the details of, to tell.

**re-count** *vt* to count again. • *n* a second counting of votes.

**recoup** *vti* to make good (financial losses); to regain; to make up for something lost.

**recourse** *n* a resort for help or protection when in danger; that to which one turns when seeking help.

**recover** *vti* to regain after losing; to reclaim; to regain health or after losing emotional control.—**recoverable** *adj.*

**re-cover** vt to put a new cover on.

**recovery** n the act or process of recovering; the condition of having recovered; reclamation; restoration; a retrieval of a capsule, etc after a space flight.

**re-create** vt to create over again, esp mentally.

**recreation** n relaxation of the body or mind; a sport, pastime or amusement.—**recreational** adj.

**recruit** n a soldier newly enlisted; a member newly joined; a beginner. • vti to enlist; to increase or maintain the numbers of; to restore, refresh.—**recruitment** n.

**rectangle** n a four-sided geometric figure with all its angles right angles.—**rectangular** adj.

**rectify** vt to put right, correct; to amend; (chem) to refine by repeated distillation; (elect) to convert to direct current.—**rectifiable** adj.

**rector** n in some churches, a clergyman in charge of a parish; the head of certain schools, colleges, etc.

**rectory** n the house of a minister or priest.

**recuperate** vti to get well again; to recover (losses, etc).—**recuperation** n.

**recur** vi (pt **recurred**) to be repeated in thought, talk, etc; to occur again or at intervals.—**recurrence** n.—**recurrent** adj.

**red** adj (**redder, reddest**) of the colour of blood; politically left-wing. • n the colour of blood; any red pigment; a communist.

**red carpet** n a strip of red carpet for dignitaries to walk on; a grand or impressive welcome or entertainment.

**Red Cross** n a red cross on a white ground, the symbol of the International Red Cross, a society for the relief of suffering in time of war and disaster.

**red currant** n a cultivated red clustered fruit.

**redden** vti to make or become red; to blush.

**reddish** adj tinged with red.—**reddishness** n.

**redeem** vt to recover by payment; to regain; to deliver from sin; to pay off; to restore to favour; to make amends for.—**redeemable** adj.—**redeemer** n.

**redeploy** vt (troops, workers) to assign to new positions or activities.—**redeployment** n.

**red-handed** adj caught in the act of committing a crime.

**redhead** n a person having red hair.—**redheaded** adj.

**red herring** n a herring cured to a dark brown colour; something that diverts attention from the real issue.

**red-hot** adj glowing with heat; extremely hot; very excited, angry, etc; very new.

**redirect** vt to change the direction or course of; to readdress.—**redirection** n.

**red light** n a warning signal, a cautionary sign; a deterrent.—also adj.

**redolent** adj having a strong scent, fragrant; reminiscent (of).—**redolence** n.

**redouble** vti to double again; to make or become twice as much.

**redress** vt to put right, adjust; to compensate, make up for. • n remedy; compensation.

**red tape** n rigid adherence to bureaucratic routine and regulations, causing delay.

**reduce** vt to diminish or make smaller in size, amount, extent, or number; to lower in price; to simplify; to make thin; to subdue; to bring or convert (to another state or form).—**reducible** adj.—**reduction** n.

**redundant** adj surplus to requirements; (person) deprived of one's job as being no longer necessary; (*words*) unnecessary to the meaning, excessive.—**redundancy** *n*.

**reed** *n* a tall grass found in marshes; a thin piece of cane in the mouthpiece of a musical instrument; a person or thing too weak to rely on; one easily swayed or overcome.

**reef** *n* a ridge of rocks, sand, or coral in water; a hazardous obstruction; a vein of ore.

**reek** *n* a strong smell. • *vi* to give off smoke, fumes or a strong or offensive smell.

**reel**[1] *n* a winding device; a spool or bobbin; thread wound on this; a length of film, about 300m (1,000ft). • *vt* to wind on to a reel; (*with* **in**) to draw in (fish, etc) by means of a reel; (*with* **off**) to tell, write, etc, with fluency; (*with* **out**) to unwind from a reel.

**reel**[2] *vi* to stagger or sway about; to be dizzy or in a whirl. • *n* a staggering motion.

**reel**[3] *n* a lively Scottish or Irish dance; the music for it. • *vi* to dance a reel.

**ref.** *abbr* = with reference to.

**refectory** *n* the dining hall of a monastery, college, etc.

**refer** *vti* (*pt* **referred**) to attribute, assign (to); (*with* **to**) to direct, have recourse (to); to relate to; to mention or allude to; to direct attention (to).—**referable** *adj*.

**referee** *n* an arbitrator; an umpire; a judge.

**reference** *n* the act of referring; a mention or allusion; a testimonial; a person who gives a testimonial; a direction to a passage in a book; a passage referred to.

**reference book** *n* a book for reference rather than general reading, eg a yearbook, directory.

**referendum** *n* (*pl* **referenda, referendums**) the submission of an issue directly to the vote of the electorate, a plebiscite.

**refill** *vt* to fill again. • *n* a replacement pack for an empty permanent container; a providing again.

**refine** *vti* to purify; to make free from impurities or coarseness; to make or become cultured.

**refined** *adj* polished, cultured; affected.

**refinement** *n* fineness of manners or taste; an improvement; a fine distinction.

**refinery** *n* a plant where raw materials, eg sugar, oil, are refined.

**reflect** *vt* (*light*, *heat*, *etc*) to throw back; to bend aside or back; to show an image of, as a mirror; to express. • *vi* to reproduce to the eye or mind; to mirror; to meditate; (*with* **upon**) to ponder; (*with* **on**) to discredit, disparage.

**reflection, reflexion** *n* a reflecting back, turning aside; the action of changing direction when a ray strikes and is thrown back; reflected heat, light or colour; a reflected image; meditation, thought; reconsideration; reproach.

**reflector** *n* a disc, instrument, strip or other surface that reflects light or heat.

**reflex** *n* an involuntary response to a stimulus. • *adj* (*angle*) of more than 180 degrees; (*camera*) with a full-size viewfinder using the main lens.

**reflexive** *adj* (*pron*, *verb*) referring back to the subject.—**reflexively** *adv*.

**reform** *vti* to improve; to make or become better by the removal of faults; to amend; to abolish abuse. • *n* improvement or transformation, esp of an institution; removal of social ills.—**reformed** *adj*.

**reformer** *n* a person who advocates or works for reform; an apparatus for changing molecular structure.

**refrain**[1] *vi* to abstain (from).

**refrain**[2] *n* recurring words in a song or poem; a chorus.

**refresh** *vt* to revive; to give new energy to; to make cool; to take a drink.

**refresher** *n* something that refreshes, esp a drink; a reminder; a training course to renew one's skill or knowledge.

**refreshment** *n* the act of refreshing; a restorative; (*pl*) food and drink; a light meal.

**refrigerator** *n* something that refrigerates; a chamber for keeping food, etc, cool; an apparatus for cooling.

**refuel** *vti* (*pt* **refuelled**) to supply with or take on fresh fuel.

**refuge** *n* a protection or shelter from danger; a retreat, sanctuary.

**refugee** *n* a person who flees to another country to escape political or religious persecution.

**refund** *vti* to repay; to reimburse. • *n* a refunding or the amount refunded.

**refusal** *n* the act or process of refusing; the choice of refusing or accepting.

**refurbish** *vt* to renovate or re-equip.— **refurbishment** *n*.

**refuse**[1] *n* rubbish, garbage, waste.

**refuse**[2] *vt* to decline, reject; to withhold, deny. • *vi* (*horse*) to decline to jump.

**refute** *vt* to rebut; to disprove.—**refutable** *adj*.—**refutably** *adv*.—**refutation** *n*.

**regain** *vt* to get back, recover; to reach again.

**regal** *adj* royal; relating to a king or queen.

**regalia** *npl* royal badges or prerogatives; the badges of an order, office, or membership; finery.

**regard** *vt* to gaze at, observe; to hold in respect; to consider; to heed, take into account. • *n* a look; attention; reference; respect, esteem; (*pl*) good wishes, greetings.

**regarding** *prep* with reference to, about.

**regardless** *adj* having no regard to. • *adv* (*inf*) in spite of everything; without heeding the cost, consequences, etc.

**regatta** *n* a meeting for yacht or boat races.

**regency** *n* the status or authority of a regent; rule by a regent; (*with cap*) in British history, the period 1810-20.

**regent** *n* a person who rules or administers a country during the sovereign's minority, absence, or incapacity; a member of a governing board (as of a university).

**regime** *n* a political or ruling system.

**regiment** *n* a military unit, smaller than a division, consisting usu of a number of battalions. • *vt* to organize in a strict manner; to subject to order or conformity.—**regimental** *adj*.

**regimentation** *n* the act of regimenting; excessive orderliness.

**region** *n* a large, indefinite part of the earth's surface; one of the zones into which the atmosphere is divided; an administrative area of a country; a part of the body.—**regional** *adj*.

**register** *n* an official list; a written record, as for attendance; the book containing such a record or list; a tone of voice; a variety of language appropriate to a subject or occasion; (*comput*) a device in which data can be stored and operated on; (*print*) exact alignment; a device for indicating speed, etc; a plate regulating draught. • *vti* to record; to enter in or sign a register; to correspond exactly; to entrust a letter to the post with special precautions for safety; to express emotion facially; to make or convey an impression.

**registered** *adj* recorded officially; qualified formally or officially.

**registrar** *n* a person who keeps records, esp one in an educational institution in charge of student records; a hospital doctor below a specialist in rank.

**registration** *n* the act of registering; the condition of having registered.

**registry** *n* registration; a place where records are kept; an official record book.

**registry office** *n* an office where civil marriages are held, and births and deaths recorded.

**regret** *vt* (*pt* **regretted**) to feel sorrow, grief, or loss; to remember with longing; (*with* **that**) to repent of. • *n* disappointment; sorrow; grief; (*pl*) polite refusal.—**regretful** *adj*.—**regretfully** *adv*.

**regrettable** *adj* to be regretted; deserving blame.—**regrettably** *adv*.

**regular** *adj* normal, habitual, not casual; at fixed intervals; according to rule, custom, or practice; uniform, consistent; symmetrical; fully qualified; belonging to a standing army; (*inf*) thorough, complete; (*inf*) pleasant, friendly. • *n* a professional soldier; (*inf*) a person who attends regularly.—**regularity** *n*.—**regularly** *adv*.

**regulate** *vt* to control according to a rule; to cause to conform to a standard or needs; to adjust so as to put in good order.—**regulatory** *adj*.

**regulation** *n* the act of regulating; a being regulated; a prescribed rule, decree. • *adj* normal, standard.

**rehabilitate** *vt* (*prisoner etc*) to help adapt to society after a stay in an institution; to put back in good condition; to restore to rights or privileges; (*sick person etc*) to help to adjust to normal conditions after illness.—**rehabilitation** *n*.

**rehash** *n* old materials put in a new form. • *vt* to dish up again.

**rehearse** *vti* to practise repeatedly before public performance; to recount, narrate in detail.—**rehearsal** *n*.

**reign** *n* the rule of a sovereign; the period of this; influence; domination. • *vi* to rule; to prevail.

**reimburse** *vt* to repay; to refund (for expense or loss).—**reimbursable** *adj*.—**reimbursement** *n*.

**rein** *n* the strap of a bridle for guiding or restraining a horse; (*pl*) a means of control or restraint. • *vt* to control with the rein; to restrain.

**reincarnation** *n* the incarnation of the soul after death in another body.—**reincarnate** *adj*, *vt*.

**reindeer** *n* a large deer with branched antlers found in northern regions.

**reinforce** *vt* (*army etc*) to strengthen with fresh troops; (*a material*) to add to the strength of.—**reinforcement** *n*.

**reinstate** *vt* to restore to a former position, rank, or condition.—**reinstatement** *n*.

**reiterate** *vt* to repeat; to say or do again or many times.—**reiteration** *n*.

**reject** *vt* to throw away, to discard; to refuse to accept, to decline; to rebuff. • *n* a thing or person rejected.—**rejection** *n*.

**rejoice** *vi* to feel joyful or happy.

**rejuvenate** *vt* to give youthful vigour to.—**rejuvenation** *n*.

**relapse** *vi* to fall back into a worse state after improvement; to return to a former vice. • *n* the recurrence of illness after apparent recovery.

**relate** *vt* to narrate, recount; to show a connection. • *vi* to have a formal relationship (with).

**related** *adj* connected, allied; akin.

**relation** *n* the way in which one thing stands in respect to another, footing; reference, regard; connection by blood or marriage; a relative; a narration, a narrative; (*pl*) the connections between or among persons, nations, etc; (*pl*) one's family and in-laws.

**relationship** *n* the tie or degree of kin-ship or intimacy; affinity; (*inf*) an affair.

**relative** *adj* having or expressing a re-lation; corresponding; pertinent; comparative, conditional; respec-tive; meaningful only in relation-ship; (*gram*) referring to a previous noun, clause, etc. • *n* a person re-lated by blood or marriage.—**rela-tively** *adv*.

**relax** *vti* to slacken; to make or become less severe or strict; to make (the muscles) less rigid; to take a rest.

**relaxation** *n* the act of relaxing; the condition of being relaxed; recrea-tion.

**relay** *n* a team of fresh horses, men, etc to relieve others; a race between teams, each member of which goes a part of the distance; (*elect*) a de-vice for enabling a weak current to control others; a relayed broadcast. • *vt* (*pt* **relayed**) (*news, etc*) to spread in stages; to broadcast sig-nals.

**release** *vt* to set free; to let go; to re-linquish; (*film, etc*) to issue for pub-lic exhibition; (*information*) to make available; (*law*) to make over to an-other. • *n* a releasing, as from prison, work, etc; a device to hold or release a mechanism; a news item, etc, released to the public; (*law*) a written surrender of a claim.

**relegate** *vt* to move to an inferior po-sition; to demote; to banish.—**rel-egation** *n*.

**relent** *vi* to soften in attitude; to be-come less harsh or severe.

**relentless** *adj* pitiless; unremitting.

**relevant** *adj* applying to the matter in hand, pertinent; to the point.—**rel-evance** *n*.—**relevancy** *n*.

**reliable** *adj* dependable, trustwor-thy.—**reliability** *n*.—**reliably** *adv*.

**relic** *n* an object, fragment, or custom that has survived from the past; part of a saint's body or belongings; (*pl*) remains of the dead.

**relief** *n* the sensation following the eas-ing or lifting of discomfort or stress; release from a duty by another per-son; a person who takes the place of another on duty; that which relieves; aid; assistance to the needy or vic-tims of a disaster; the projection of a carved design from its ground; dis-tinctness, vividness. • *adj* providing relief in disasters etc.

**relieve** *vt* to bring relief or assistance to; to release from obligation or duty; to ease; (*with* **oneself**) to empty the bladder or bowels. • *vi* to give re-lief; to break the monotony of; to bring into relief, to stand out.

**religion** *n* a belief in God or gods; a system of worship and faith; a for-malized expression of belief.

**relinquish** *vt* to give up; to renounce or surrender.—**relinquishment** *n*.

**relish** *n* an appetizing flavour; a dis-tinctive taste; enjoyment of food or an experience; a spicy accompani-ment to food; gusto, zest. • *vt* to like the flavour of; to enjoy, appreciate.

**reluctant** *adj* unwilling, loath; offering resistance.—**reluctance** *n*.—**reluc-tantly** *adv*.

**rely** *vi* to depend on; to trust.

**remain** *vi* to stay behind or in the same place; to continue to be; to survive, to last; to be left over. • *npl* anything left after use; a corpse.

**remainder** *n* what is left, the rest; (*math*) the result of subtraction, the quantity left over after division; (*books*) unsold stock; (*law*) the re-sidual interest in an estate.

**remand** *vt* to send back into custody for further evidence.—*also n*.

**remark** *vti* to notice; to observe; to pass a comment (upon). • *n* a brief comment.

**remarkable** *adj* unusual; extraordinary; worthy of comment.—**remarkably** *adv*.

**remedial** *adj* providing a remedy; correcting; relating to the teaching of people with learning difficulties.

**remedy** *n* a medicine or any means to cure a disease; anything that puts something else to rights. • *vt* to cure; to put right.

**remember** *vti* to recall; to bear in mind; to mention (a person) to another as sending regards; to exercise or have the power of memory.

**remembrance** *n* a reminiscence; a greeting or gift recalling or expressing friendship or affection; the extent of memory; an honouring of the dead or a past event.

**remind** *vt* to cause to remember.

**reminder** *n* a thing that reminds, esp a letter from a creditor.

**reminisce** *vi* to think, talk, or write about past events.

**reminiscence** *n* the recalling of a past experience; (*pl*) memoirs.

**reminiscent** *adj* reminding, suggestive (of); recalling the past.

**remission** *n* the act of remitting; the reduction in length of a prison term; the lessening of the symptoms of a disease; pardon, forgiveness.

**remit** *vti* (*pt* **remitted**) to forgive; to refrain from inflicting (a punishment) or exacting (a debt); to abate, moderate; to send payment (by post); (*law*) to refer to a lower court for reconsideration. • *n* the act of referring; an area of authority.

**remittance** *n* the sending of money or a payment (by post); the payment or money sent.

**remnant** *n* a small remaining fragment or number; an oddment or scrap; a trace; an unsold or unused end of piece goods.

**remorse** *n* regret and guilt for a misdemeanour; compassion.—**remorseful** *adj*.—**remorsefully** *adv*.

**remorseless** *adj* ruthless, cruel; relentless.—**remorselessly** *adv*.—**remorselessness** *n*.

**remote** *adj* far apart or distant in time or place; out of the way; not closely related; secluded; aloof; vague, faint.—**remotely** *adv*.

**remote control** *n* the control of a device or activity from a distance, usu by means of an electric circuit or the making or breaking of radio waves.

**removal** *n* the act of removing; a change of home or office; dismissal.

**remove** *vti* to take away and put elsewhere; to dismiss, as from office; to get rid of; to kill; to go away. • *n* a stage in gradation; a degree in relationship.—**removable** *adj*.

**remunerate** *vt* to pay for a service; to reward.—**remuneration** *n*.

**rend** *vti* (*pt* **rent**) to tear, to wrench (apart); to be torn apart.

**render** *vt* (*payments, accounts, etc*) to submit, as for approval; to give back; to pay back; to perform; to represent as by drawing; to translate, interpret; to cause to be; (*fat*) to melt down.

**rendering** *n* interpretation, translation.

**rendezvous** *n* (*pl* **rendezvous**) an arranged meeting; a place to meet; a popular haunt; the process of bringing two spacecraft together. • *vi* to meet by appointment.

**renegade** *n* a deserter; a person who is faithless to a principle, party, religion, or cause.

**renew** *vti* to restore to freshness or vigour; to begin again; to make or get anew; to replace; to grant or obtain an extension of.—**renewable** *adj*.—**renewal** *n*.

**renounce** *vt* to abandon formally; to give up; to disown.

**renovate** *vt* to renew; to restore to good condition; to do up, repair.—**renovation** *n*.—**renovator** *n*.

**renown** *n* fame, celebrity.

**renowned** *adj* famous, illustrious.

**rent**[1] *see* **rend**.

**rent**[2] *n* regular payment to another for the use of a house, machinery, etc.
• *vti* to occupy as a tenant; to hire; to let for rent.

**rental** *n* an amount paid or received as rent; a house, car, etc, for rent; an act of renting; a business that rents something.

**renunciation** *n* the act of renouncing; formal abandonment; repudiation.

**rep** *abbr* = representative; repertory.

**repair** *vt* to mend; to restore to good working order; to make amends for.
• *n* the act of repairing; a place repaired; condition as to soundness.

**repartee** *n* a witty reply; skill in making such replies.

**repay** *vt* (*pt* **repaid**) to pay back; to refund.—**repayable** *adj*.—**repayment** *n*.

**repeal** *vt* to annul, to rescind; to revoke.—*also n*.

**repeat** *vti* to say, write, or do again; to reiterate; to recite after another or from memory; to reproduce; to recur. • *n* a repetition, encore; anything said or done again, as a rebroadcast of a TV programme; (*mus*) a passage to be repeated; the sign for this.—**repeatable** *adj*.

**repeatedly** *adv* many times, over and over again.

**repel** *vt* (*pt* **repelled**) to drive back; to beat off, repulse; to reject; to hold off; to cause distaste; (*water, dirt*) to be resistant to.

**repellent** *adj* distasteful, unattractive; capable of repelling. • *n* a substance that repels, esp a spray for protection against insects.

**repent** *vi* to wish one had not done something; to feel remorse or regret (for); to regret and change from evil ways.—**repentance** *n*.—**repentant** *adj*.

**repercussion** *n* a rebound; a reverberation; a far-reaching, often indirect reaction to an event.

**repertoire** *n* the stock of plays, songs, etc, that a company, singer, etc, can perform.

**repertory** *n* a repertoire; the system of alternating several plays through a season with a permanent acting group.

**repetition** *n* the act of repeating; something repeated, a copy.—**repetitive** *adj*.

**replace** *vt* to put back; to take the place of, to substitute for; to supersede.—**replaceable** *adj*.—**replacement** *n*.

**replenish** *vt* to stock again, refill.—**replenishment** *n*.

**replete** *adj* filled, well provided; stuffed, gorged.

**replica** *n* an exact copy; a reproduction.

**reply** *vti* to answer, respond; to give as an answer. • *n* an answer.

**report** *vti* to give an account of; to tell as news; to take down and describe for publication; to make a formal statement of; to complain about or against; to inform against; to present oneself (for duty). • *n* an account of facts; the formal statement of the findings of an investigation; a newspaper, radio or TV account of an event; a rumour; a sharp, loud noise, as of a gun.

**reporter** *n* a person who gathers and reports news for a newspaper, radio or TV; a person authorized to make statements concerning law decisions or legislative proceedings.

**reprehensible** *adj* blameworthy, culpable.

**represent** *vt* to portray; to describe; to

typify; to stand for, symbolize; to point out; to perform on the stage; to act as an agent for; to deputize for; to serve as a specimen, example, etc, of.—**representable** adj.

**representation** n the act of representing or being represented, as in a parliamentary assembly; a portrait, reproduction; (pl) a presentation of claims, protests, views, etc.

**representative** adj typical; portraying; consisting of or based on representation of the electorate by delegates. • n an example or type; a person who acts for another; a delegate, agent, salesman, etc.

**repress** vt to suppress, restrain; (emotions) to keep under control; to exclude involuntarily from the conscious mind.—**repression** n.—**repressive** adj.

**reprieve** vt to postpone or commute the punishment of; to give respite to.—also n.

**reprimand** n a formal rebuke. • vt to reprove formally.

**reprisal** n an act of retaliation for an injury done.

**reproach** vt to accuse of a fault; to blame. • n a rebuke; a source of shame or disgrace.—**reproachful** adj.

**reproduce** vti to make a copy, duplicate, or likeness of; to produce offspring; to multiply.

**reproduction** n the act of reproducing; the process by which plants and animals breed; a copy or likeness; a representation.—**reproductive** adj.

**reprove** vt to rebuke, censure.—**reprovingly** adv.

**reptile** n any of a class of cold-blooded, air-breathing vertebrates with horny scales or plates; a grovelling or despised person.—**reptilian** adj.

**republic** n a government in which the people elect the head of state and in which the people and their elected representatives have supreme power; a country governed in this way.

**republican** adj of, characteristic of, or supporting a republic. • n an advocate of republican government; (with cap) a member of the US Republican party.—**republicanism** n.

**repudiate** vt to reject, disown; to refuse to acknowledge or pay; to deny.—**repudiation** n.

**repugnant** adj distasteful, offensive; contradictory; incompatible.—**repugnance** n.

**repulse** vt to drive back; to repel; to reject. • n a rebuff, rejection; a defeat, check.

**repulsion** n a feeling of disgust; aversion; (physics) the tendency of bodies to repel each other.

**repulsive** adj disgusting; detestable; exercising repulsion.—**repulsively** adv.

**reputable** adj of good repute, respectable.—**reputably** adv.

**reputation** n the estimation in which a person or thing is held; good name, honour.

**repute** vt to consider to be, to deem. • n reputation.

**reputed** adj generally reported; supposed.

**reputedly** adv in common estimation; by repute.

**request** n an asking for something; a petition; a demand; the thing asked for. • vt to ask for earnestly.

**requiem** n a mass for the dead; music for this.

**require** vt to demand; to need, call for; to order, command.

**requirement** n a need or want; an essential condition.

**requisite** adj needed; essential, indispensable. • n something required or indispensable.

**requisition** *n* a formal request, demand, or order, as for military supplies; the taking over of private property, etc for military use. • *vt* to order; to take by requisition.

**rescind** *vt* to annul, cancel.

**rescue** *vt* to save (a person, thing) from captivity, danger, or harm; to free forcibly from legal custody.—*also n.*—**rescuer** *n*.

**research** *n* a diligent search; a systematic and careful investigation of a particular subject; a scientific study. • *vi* to carry out an investigation; to study.—**researcher** *n*.

**resemble** *vt* to be like, to have a similarity to.—**resemblance** *n*.

**resent** *vt* to be indignant about; to begrudge; to take badly.—**resentful** *adj*.—**resentfully** *adv*.—**resentment** *n*.

**reservation** *n* the act of reserving; (*of tickets, accommodation, etc*) a holding until called for; a limitation or proviso; (*pl*) doubt, scepticism; land set aside for a special purpose.

**reserve** *vt* to hold back for future use; to retain; to have set aside; (*tickets, hotel room, etc*) to book. • *n* something put aside for future use; land set aside for wild animals; (*sport*) a substitute; (*mil*) a force supplementary to a regular army; a restriction or qualification; reticence of feelings; caution.—**reservable** *adj*.

**reserved** *adj* set apart, booked; uncommunicative, lacking cordiality.—**reservedly** *adv*.

**reservoir** *n* a tank or artificial lake for storing water; an extra supply or store.

**reside** *vi* to live in a place permanently; to be vested or present in.

**residence** *n* the act of living in a place; the period of residing; the house where one lives permanently; the status of a legal resident; a building used as a home.

**residential** *adj* of or relating to residence; used for private homes.

**residue** *n* a remainder; a part left over; what is left of an estate after payment of debts and legacies.

**resign** *vti* to give up (employment, etc); to relinquish; to yield to; to reconcile (oneself).

**resignation** *n* the resigning of office, etc; the written proof of this; patient endurance.

**resigned** *adj* submissive, acquiescent; accepting the inevitable.

**resilient** *adj* elastic, springing back; buoyant; (*person*) capable of carrying on after suffering hardship.—**resilience** *n*.—**resiliently** *adv*.

**resin** *n* a sticky substance exuded in the sap of trees and plants and used in medicines, varnishes, etc; a similar synthetic substance used in plastics.—**resinous** *adj*.

**resist** *vti* to fight against; to be proof against; to oppose or withstand.

**resistance** *n* the act of resisting; the power to resist, as to ward off disease; opposition, esp to an occupying force; hindrance; (*elect*) non-conductivity, opposition to a steady current.

**resolute** *adj* determined; firm of purpose, steadfast.—**resolutely** *adv*.—**resoluteness** *n*.

**resolution** *n* the act of resolving or the state of being resolved; determination; a fixed intention; the formal decision or opinion of a meeting; analysis, disintegration; (*med*) the dispersion of a tumour, etc; the picture definition in a TV.

**resolve** *vt* to break into component parts, dissolve; to convert or be converted (into); to analyse; to determine, make up one's mind; to solve, settle; to vote by resolution; to dispel (doubt); to explain; to conclude; (*med: tumour*) to disperse. • *n* a fixed intention; resolution; courage.

**resonant** adj ringing; resounding, echoing.

**resort** n a popular holiday location; a source of help, support, etc; recourse. • vi to have recourse to; to turn (to) for help, etc.

**resound** vti to echo; to reverberate; to go on sounding; to be much talked of; to spread (fame).

**resounding** adj echoing; notable; thorough.

**resource** n source of help; an expedient; the ability to cope with a situation; a means of diversion; (pl) wealth; assets; raw materials.

**resourceful** adj able to cope in difficult situations; ingenious.—**resourcefulness** n.

**respect** n esteem; consideration; regard; (pl) good wishes; reference; relation. • vt to feel or show esteem or regard to; to treat considerately.

**respectable** adj worthy of esteem; well-behaved; proper, correct, well-conducted; of moderate quality or size.—**respectability** n.—**respectably** adv.

**respective** adj proper to each, several.

**respectively** adv in the indicated order.

**respiration** n the act or process of breathing.

**respite** n a temporary delay; a period of rest or relief; a reprieve.

**resplendent** adj dazzling, shining brilliantly; magnificent.

**respond** vti to answer; to reply; to show a favourable reaction; to be answerable; (with to) to react.

**response** n an answer; a reaction to stimulation.

**responsibility** n being responsible; a moral obligation or duty; a charge or trust; a thing one is responsible for.

**responsible** adj having control (over); (with for) accountable (for); capable of rational conduct; trustworthy; involving responsibility.—**responsibly** adv.

**responsive** adj responding; sensitive to influence or stimulus; sympathetic.

**rest**[1] n stillness, sleep; inactivity; the state of not moving; relaxation; tranquillity; a support or prop; a pause in music, etc; a place of quiet. • vti to take a rest; to give rest to; to be still; to lie down; to relax; to be fixed (on); to lean, support or be supported; to put one's trust (in).

**rest**[2] n the remainder; the others. • vi to remain.

**restaurant** n a place where meals can be bought and eaten.

**restful** adj peaceful.—**restfully** adv.—**restfulness** n.

**rest home** n an old people's home; a convalescent home.

**restitution** n the restoring of something to its owner; a reimbursement, as for loss.

**restive** adj impatient; fidgety.

**restless** adj unsettled; agitated.—**restlessly** adv.—**restlessness** n.

**restoration** n the act of restoring; reconstruction; renovation; (with cap) the re-establishment of the monarchy in Britain in 1660 under Charles II.

**restore** vt to give or put back; to re-establish; to repair; to renovate; to bring back to the original condition.—**restorer** n.

**restrain** vt to hold back; to restrict; (person) to deprive of freedom.

**restrained** adj moderate; self-controlled; without exuberance.

**restraint** n the ability to hold back; something that restrains; control of emotions, impulses, etc.

**restrict** vt to keep within limits, circumscribe.

**restricted** adj affected by restriction; limited; not generally available.

**restriction** *n* restraint; limitation; a limiting regulation.—**restrictive** *adj*.

**rest room** *n* a room equipped with toilets, washbowls, etc for the use of the public.

**result** *vi* to have as a consequence; to terminate in. • *n* a consequence; an outcome; a value obtained by mathematical calculation; (*sport*) the final score; (*pl*) a desired effect.

**resume** *vti* to begin again; to continue after a stop or pause; to proceed after interruption.—**resumption** *n*.

**resurgence** *n* a revival; a renewal of activity.—**resurgent** *adj*.

**resurrection** *n* a revival; a rising from the dead; (*with cap*) the rising of Christ from the dead.

**resuscitate** *vti* to revive when apparently dead or unconscious.—**resuscitation** *n*.

**retail** *n* selling directly to the consumer in small quantities. • *adv* at a retail price. • *vti* to sell or be sold by retail.—*also adj*.—**retailer** *n*.—**retailing** *n*.

**retain** *vt* to keep possession of; to keep in the mind, to remember; to keep in place, support; to hire the services of.

**retainer** *n* that which returns; (*formerly*) a servant to a family, a dependant; a fee to retain the services of.

**retaliate** *vti* to revenge oneself, usu by returning like for like; to strike back; to cast back (an accusation).—**retaliation** *n*.—**retaliatory** *adj*.

**retarded** *adj* slow in physical or mental development.

**retch** *vi* to heave as if to vomit.

**rethink** *vt* (*pt* **rethought**) to consider or think about again, esp with a change in mind.

**reticent** *adj* reserved in speech; uncommunicative.—**reticence** *n*.

**retina** *n* (*pl* **retinas, retinae**) the innermost part of the eye, on which the image is formed.

**retinue** *n* a body of attendants.

**retire** *vi* to give up one's work when pensionable age is reached; to withdraw; to retreat; to go to bed. • *vt* (*troops*) to withdraw from use; to compel to retire from a position, work, etc.—**retirement** *n*.

**retiring** *adj* unobtrusive; shy.

**retort** *vi* to reply sharply or wittily. • *n* a sharp or witty reply; a vessel with a funnel bent downwards used in distilling; a receptacle used in making gas and steel.

**retract** *vti* to draw in or back; to withdraw (a statement, opinion, etc); to recant.—**retractable** *adj*.—**retraction** *n*.

**retreat** *vi* to withdraw, retire; to recede. • *n* a withdrawal, esp of troops; a sign for retiring; a quiet or secluded place, refuge; seclusion for religious devotion.

**retrial** *n* a second trial.

**retribution** *n* deserved reward; something given or exacted in compensation, esp punishment.

**retrieve** *vt* to recover; to revive; (*a loss*) to make good; (*comput*) to obtain information from data stored in a computer. • *vi* (*dogs*) to retrieve game.—**retrievable** *adj*.—**retrieval** *n*.

**retriever** *n* any of several breeds of dogs capable of being trained for retrieving.

**retrospect** *n* a looking back; a mental review of the past.—**retrospection** *n*.

**return** *vi* to come or go back; to reply; to recur. • *vt* to give or send back; to repay; to yield; to answer; to elect. • *n* something returned; a recurrence; recompense; (*pl*) yield, revenue; a form for computing (income) tax.

**reunion** *n* a meeting following separation; a social gathering of former colleagues.

**reunite** *vt* to unite again; to reconcile. • *vi* to become reunited.

**rev** *vt* (*pt* **revved**) (*inf*) (*with* **up**) to increase the speed of an engine. • *n* revolution per minute.

**revamp** *vt* to renovate, to rework, re-model; to transform. • *n* the process of revamping; something revamped.

**reveal** *vt* (*something hidden or secret*) to make known; to expose; to make visible.

**reveille** *n* a morning bugle call to wake soldiers.

**revel** *vi* (*pt* **revelled**) (*with* **in**) to take pleasure or delight in; to make merry. • *n* (*pl*) merrymaking; entertainment.—**reveller** *n*.—**revelry** *n*.

**revelation** *n* the act of revealing; the disclosure of something secret; a communication from God to man; an illuminating experience.

**revenge** *vt* to inflict punishment in return for; to satisfy oneself by retaliation; to avenge. • *n* the act of revenging; retaliation; a vindictive feeling.—**revenger** *n*.

**revengeful** *adj* keen for revenge; vindictive.

**revenue** *n* the total income produced by taxation; gross income from a business or investment.

**reverberate** *vi* to rebound, recoil; to be reflected in; to resound, to echo.—**reverberation** *n*.

**reverence** *n* profound respect; devotion; a gesture of respect (such as a bow). • *vt* to hold in respect.

**reverent** *adj* feeling or expressing reverence.—**reverently** *adv*.

**reverie** *n* a daydream; (*mus*) a dreamy piece.—*also* **revery**.

**reversal** *n* the act or process of reversing.

**reverse** *vti* to turn in the opposite direction; to turn outside in, upside down, etc; to move backwards; (*law*)

to revoke or annul. • *n* the contrary or opposite of something; the back, esp of a coin; a setback; a mechanism for reversing. • *adj* opposite, contrary; causing movement in the opposite direction.

**reversion** *n* return to a former condition or type; right to future possession.—**reversionary** *adj*.

**revert** *vi* to go back (to a former state); to take up again (a former subject); (*biol*) to return to a former or primitive type; (*law*) to go back to a former owner or his heirs.—**revertible** *adj*.

**review** *n* an evaluation; a survey; a reconsideration; a critical assessment; a periodical containing critical essays; an official inspection of ships or troops. • *vt* to re-examine; to inspect formally; to write an assessment of.

**reviewer** *n* a person who writes a review, esp for a newspaper, a critic.

**revise** *vt* to correct and amend; to prepare a new, improved version of; to study again (for an examination).—**revision** *n*.

**revival** *n* the act of reviving; recovery from a neglected or depressed state; renewed performance (of a play); renewed interest in; religious awakening

**revive** *vti* to return to life; to make active again; to take up again.—**reviver** *n*.

**revoke** *vt* to cancel; to rescind. • *vi* (*cards*) to fail to follow suit.—**revocable** *adj*.—**revocation** *n*.

**revolt** *vt* to rebel; to overturn; to shock. • *vi* to feel great disgust. • *n* rebellion; uprising; loathing.

**revolting** *adj* extremely offensive.—**revoltingly** *adv*.

**revolution** *n* the act of revolting; a motion round a centre or axis; a single completion of an orbit or rotation; a great change; an overthrow of a government, social system, etc.

**revolutionary** *adj* of, advocating revolution; radically new. • *n* a person who takes part in or favours revolution.

**revolutionize** *vt* to cause a complete change in.

**revolve** *vt* to travel or cause to travel in a circle or orbit; to rotate.

**revolver** *n* a handgun with a magazine that revolves to reload.

**revue** *n* a musical show with skits, dances, etc, often satirizing recent events.

**revulsion** *n* disgust; aversion; a sudden change or reversal of feeling.

**reward** *n* something that is given in return for something done; money offered, as for the capture of a criminal. • *vt* to give a reward.

**rewarding** *adj* (*experience, activity, etc*) pleasing, profitable.

**rewrite** *vt* to write again; to revise. • *n* something rewritten; revision.

**rhapsody** *n* an enthusiastic speech or writing; (*mus*) an irregular instrumental composition of an epic, heroic or national character.

**rhetoric** *n* the art of effective speaking and writing; skill in using speech; insincere language.

**rhetorical** *adj* of or relating to rhetoric; high-flown, bombastic. —**rhetorically** *adv*.

**rheumatic** *adj* of, relating to or suffering from rheumatism. • *n* a person who has rheumatism.

**rheumatism** *n* a disorder causing pain in muscles and joints.

**rhinoceros** *n* (*pl* **rhinoceroses, rhinoceros**) a large, thick-skinned mammal with one or two horns on the nose.—*also* **rhino**.

**rhododendron** *n* an evergreen shrub with large flowers.

**rhubarb** *n* a plant with large leaves and edible (when cooked) pink stalks; (*inf*) a noisy quarrel.

**rhyme** *n* the repetition of sounds usu at the ends of lines in verse; such poetry or verse; a word corresponding with another in end sound. • *vti* to form a rhyme (with); to put into rhyme.

**rhythm** *n* a regular recurrence of beat, accent or silence in the flow of sound, esp of words and music; a measured flow.—**rhythmic, rhythmical** *adj*.—**rhythmically** *adv*.

**rib** *n* one of the curved bones of the chest attached to the spine; any rib-like structure; a leaf vein; a vein of an insect's wing; a ridge or raised strip, as of knitting; a ridge of a mountain. • *vt* (*pt* **ribbed**) to provide with ribs; to form vertical ridges in knitting; (*inf*) to tease or ridicule.

**ribald** *adj* irreverent; humorously vulgar.

**ribbon** *n* silk, satin, velvet, etc, woven into a narrow band; a piece of this; a strip of cloth, etc, inked for use, as in a typewriter; (*pl*) torn shreds.

**rice** *n* an annual cereal grass cultivated in warm climates; its starchy food grain.

**rich** *adj* having much money, wealthy; abounding in natural resources, fertile; costly, fine; (*food*) sweet or oily, highly flavoured; deep in colour; (*inf*) full of humour. • *n* wealthy people collectively; (*pl* **riches**) wealth, abundance.—**richly** *adv*.—**richness** *n*.

**rickets** *n* a children's disease marked by softening of the bones, caused by vitamin D deficiency.

**rickety** *adj* shaky, unsteady.

**rickshaw** *n* a light, two-wheeled man-drawn vehicle, orig used in Japan.

**ricochet** *vi* (*pt* **ricocheted** or **ricochetted**) (*bullet*) to rebound or skip along ground or water. • *n* a rebound or glancing off; (*bullet*) a hit made after ricocheting.

**rid** vt (pt **rid** or **ridded**) to free from; to dispose (of).

**riddance** n clearance; disposal.

**ridden**[1] see **ride**.

**ridden**[2] adj oppressed by; full of.

**riddle**[1] n a puzzling question; an enigma; a mysterious person or thing.

**riddle**[2] n a coarse sieve. • vt to sieve or sift; to perforate with holes; to spread through, permeate.

**ride** vb (pt **rode**, pp **ridden**) vti to be carried along or travel in a vehicle or on an animal, bicycle, etc; to be supported or move on the water; to lie at anchor; to travel over a surface; to move on the body; (inf) to continue undisturbed. • vt (horse, bicycle etc); to sit on and control; to oppress, dominate; (inf) to torment. • n a trip or journey in a vehicle or on horseback, on a bicycle, etc; a thing to ride at a fairground.

**rider** n a person who rides; an addition to a document, amending a clause; an additional statement; something used to move along another piece.

**ridge** n a narrow crest or top; the ploughed earth thrown up between the furrows; a line where two slopes meet; (of land etc) a raised strip or elevation; a range of hills. • vti to form into ridges, wrinkle.—**ridged** adj.

**ridicule** n mockery, derision. • vt to make fun of, to mock.

**ridiculous** adj deserving ridicule; preposterous, silly.—**ridiculously** adv.—**ridiculousness** n.

**rife** adj widespread; prevalent.

**riffraff** n disreputable persons; refuse, rubbish.

**rifle**[1] n a shoulder gun with a spirally grooved bore.

**rifle**[2] vti to steal; to look through (a person's papers or belongings).

**rift** n a split; a cleft; a fissure. • vti to split.

**rig** vt (pt **rigged**) (naut) to equip with sails and tackle; to set up in working order; to manipulate fraudulently. • n the way sails, etc, are rigged; equipment or gear for a special purpose; a type of truck.

**rigging** n the ropes for supporting masts and sails; (in theatre) a network of ropes and pulleys to support and maintain scenery.

**right** adj correct, true; just or good; appropriate; fit, recovered; opposite to left; conservative; designating the side meant to be seen. • adv straight; directly; completely, exactly; correctly, properly; to or on the right side. • n that which is just or correct; truth; fairness; justice; privilege; just or legal claim; (pl) the correct condition. • vti to set or become upright; to correct; to redress.—**rightness** n.

**right angle** n an angle of 90 degrees.

**righteous** adj moral, virtuous.—**righteously** adv.—**righteousness** n.

**rightful** adj legitimate; having a just claim.—**rightfully** adv.—**rightfulness** n.

**right-hand** adj of or towards the right side of a person or thing; for use by the right hand.

**right-handed** adj using the right hand; done or made for use with the right hand. • adv with the right hand.

**right-hand man** n an important and supportive assistant.

**rightly** adv in truth; in the right; with good reason; properly.

**right-of-way** n a public path over private ground; the right to use this; precedence over other traffic.

**right-wing** adj of or relating to the conservative faction of a political party, organization, etc.—**right-winger** n.

**rigid** adj stiff, inflexible; severe,

strict.—**rigidity** n.—**rigidly** adv.—**rigidness** n.

**rigmarole** n nonsense; a foolishly involved procedure.

**rigour, rigor** (US) n harsh inflexibility; severity; strictness.—**rigorous** adj.

**rim** n a border or raised edge, esp of something circular; the outer part of a wheel. • vt (pt **rimmed**) to supply or surround with a rim; to form a rim.

**rimless** adj lacking a rim; (glasses) without a frame.

**rind** n crust; peel; bark.

**ring**[1] n a circular band, esp of metal, worn on the finger, in the ear, etc; a hollow circle; a round enclosure; an arena for boxing, etc; a group of people engaged in secret or criminal activity to control a market, etc. • vt (pt **ringed**) to encircle, surround; to fit with a ring.

**ring**[2] vti (pt **rang** or **rung**) to emit a bell-like sound; to resound; to peal; to sound a bell; to telephone; (with **up**) to total and record esp by means of a cash register; to achieve. • n a ringing sound; a resonant note; a set of church bells.

**ringlet** n a curling lock of hair.

**rink** n an expanse of ice for skating; a smooth floor for roller skating; an alley for bowling.

**rinse** vt to wash lightly; to flush under clean water to remove soap. • n the act of rinsing; a preparation for tinting the hair.

**riot** n violent public disorder; uproar; unrestrained profusion; (inf) something very funny. • vi to participate in a riot.—**rioter** n.—**rioting** n.

**riotous** adj tumultuous, disorderly; luxurious, wanton.—**riotously** adv.—**riotousness** n.

**rip** vti (pt **ripped**) to cut or tear apart roughly; to split; (with **off**, **out**) to remove in a violent or rough manner; (inf) to rush, speed; (with **into**) to attack, esp verbally. • n a tear; a split.

**rip cord** n a cord for releasing a parachute.

**ripe** adj ready to be eaten or harvested; fully developed; mature.—**ripely** adv.—**ripeness** n.

**ripen** vt to grow or make ripe.

**ripple** n a little wave on the surface of water; the sound of this. • vti to have or form little waves on the surface (of).

**rise** vi (pt **rose**, pp **risen**) to get up; to stand up; to ascend; to increase in value or size; to swell; to revolt; to be provoked; to originate; to tower; to slope up; (voice) to reach a higher pitch; to ascend from the grave; (fish) to come to the surface. • n an ascent; origin; an increase in price, salary, etc; an upward slope.

**risk** n chance of loss or injury; hazard; danger, peril. • vt to expose to possible danger or loss; to take the chance of.

**risky** adj (**riskier, riskiest**) dangerous.

**risqué** adj verging on indecency; slightly offensive.

**rissole** n a fried cake of minced meat, egg, and breadcrumbs.

**rite** n a ceremonial practice or procedure, esp religious.

**ritual** adj relating to rites or ceremonies. • n a fixed (religious) ceremony.—**ritually** adv.

**rival** n one of two or more people, organizations or teams competing with each other for the same goal. • adj competing; having comparable merit or claim. • vt (pt **rivalled**) to strive to equal or excel; to be comparable to; to compete.

**rivalry** n emulation; competition.

**river** n a large natural stream of fresh water flowing into an ocean, lake, etc; a copious flow.

**riverbed** *n* the channel formed by a river.

**riverside** *n* the bank of a river.

**rivet** *n* a short, metal bolt for holding metal plates together. • *vt* (*pt* **riveted**) to join with rivets; to fix one's eyes upon immovably; to engross one's attention.—**riveter** *n*.

**Riviera** *n* the coast of the northern Mediterranean from southeast France to northwest Italy.

**road** *n* a surfaced track for travelling on; a highway; a street; a way or route; an anchorage for ships.

**road block** *n* a barrier erected across a road to halt traffic.

**road hog** *n* a car driver who obstructs other vehicles by encroaching on the others' traffic lane.

**roadside** *n* the border of a road.—*also adj*.

**roadway** *n* the strip of land over which a road passes; the main part of a road, used by vehicles.

**roadworthy** *adj* (*vehicle*) fit for the road.—**roadworthiness** *n*.

**roam** *vti* to wander about, to travel.

**roar** *vti* to make a loud, full, growling sound, as a lion, wind, fire, the sea; to utter loudly, as in a rage; to bellow; to guffaw.—*also n*.

**roaring** *adj* boisterous, noisy; brisk.

**roast** *vti* (*meat, etc*) to cook with little or no moisture, as in an oven; (*coffee, etc*) to process by exposure to heat; to expose to great heat; (*inf*) to criticize severely; to undergo roasting. • *n* roasted meat; a cut of meat for roasting; a picnic at which food is roasted.

**rob** *vb* (*pt* **robbed**) *vt* to seize forcibly; to steal from; to plunder. • *vi* to commit robbery.—**robber** *n*.

**robbery** *n* theft from a person by intimidation or by violence.

**robe** *n* a long flowing outer garment; the official dress of a judge, academic, etc; a bathrobe or dressing gown; a covering or wrap; (*pl*) ceremonial vestments. • *vti* to put on or dress in robes.

**robin** *n* a songbird with a dull red breast.

**robot** *n* a mechanical device that acts in a seemingly human way; a mechanism guided by automatic controls.

**robust** *adj* strong, sturdy; vigorous.—**robustly** *adv*.—**robustness** *n*.

**rock**[1] *n* a large stone or boulder; a person or thing providing foundation or support; (*geol*) a natural mineral deposit including sand, clay, etc; a hard sweet; (*inf*) a diamond, ice.

**rock**[2] *vti* to move to and fro, or from side to side; to sway strongly; to shake. • *n* a rocking motion; rock and roll.

**rock and roll** *n* popular music that incorporates country and blues elements and is usu played with a heavily accented beat.

**rock bottom** *n* the lowest or most fundamental part or level. • *adj* very lowest.

**rocker** *n* a rocking chair; a curved support on which a cradle, etc rocks.

**rockery, rock garden** *n* a garden among rocks for alpine plants.

**rocket** *n* any device driven forward by gases escaping through a rear vent. • *vi* to move in or like a rocket; to soar.

**rocking chair** *n* a chair mounted on rockers.

**rocking horse** *n* a toy horse fixed on rockers or springs.

**rocky** *adj* (**rockier, rockiest**) having many rocks; like rock; rugged, hard; shaky, unstable.

**rod** *n* a stick; a thin bar of metal or wood; a staff of office; a wand; a fishing rod; (*sl*) a pistol.

**rode** *see* **ride**.

**rodent** *n* any of several relatively small

gnawing animals with two strong front teeth.

**rodeo** n (pl **rodeos**) the rounding up of cattle; a display of cowboy skill.

**roe**[1] n the eggs or sperm of fish.

**roe**[2] n a small reddish brown deer (— also **roe deer**); the female red deer.

**rogue** n a scoundrel; a rascal; a mischievous person; a wild animal that lives apart from the herd.—**roguish** adj.—**roguishly** adv.

**role** n a part in a film or play taken by an actor; a function.

**roll** n a scroll; anything wound into cylindrical form; a list or register; a turned-over edge; a rolling movement; a small cake of bread; a trill of some birds; an undulation; the sound of thunder; the beating of drumsticks. • vi to move by turning over or from side to side; to move like a wheel; to curl; to move in like waves; to flow. • vt to cause to roll; to turn on its axis; to move on wheels; to press with a roller; (dice) to throw; to beat rapidly, as a drum.

**roll call** n the reading aloud of a list of names to check attendance.

**rolled gold** n a thin coating of gold attached to another metal by passing through heavy rollers.

**roller** n a revolving cylinder used for spreading paint, flattening surfaces; a large wave; (sl) a Rolls Royce car.

**roller skate** n a four-wheeled skate strapped on to shoes.—**roller skating** n.

**rolling pin** n a wooden, plastic or stone cylinder for rolling out pastry.

**rolling stock** n all the vehicles of a railway.

**Roman** adj of or relating to the city of Rome or its ancient empire, or the Latin alphabet; Roman Catholic. • n an inhabitant or citizen of Rome; a Roman Catholic.

**Roman Catholic** adj belonging to the Christian church that is headed by the Pope.—also n.

**romance** n a prose narrative; a medieval tale of chivalry; a series of unusual adventures; a novel dealing with this; an atmosphere of awe or wonder; a love story; a love affair; a picturesque falsehood. • vi to write romantic fiction; to exaggerate.

**Roman numerals** npl the letters I, V, X, L, C, D and M used to represent numbers in the manner of the ancient Romans.

**romantic** adj of or given to romance; strange and picturesque; imaginative; (art, etc) preferring passion and imagination to proportion and finish.—**romantically** adv.

**romp** vi to play boisterously. • n a noisy game; a frolic; an easy win.

**rompers** npl a child's one-piece garment; a jumpsuit.

**roof** n (pl **roofs**) the upper covering of a building; the top of a vehicle; an upper limit. • vt to provide with a roof, to cover.

**roofing** n materials for a roof.

**rook**[1] n a crow-like bird.

**rook**[2] n (chess) a piece with the power to move horizontally or vertically; a castle.

**room** n space; unoccupied space; adequate space; a division of a house, a chamber; scope or opportunity; those in a room; (pl) lodgings. • vi to lodge.

**roommate** n a person with whom one shares a room or rooms.

**roomy** adj (**roomier, roomiest**) having ample space; wide.—**roominess** n.

**roost** n a bird's perch or sleeping-place; a place for resting. • vi to rest or sleep on a roost; to settle down.

**rooster** n an adult male domestic fowl, a cockerel.

**root**[1] n the part of a plant, usu underground, that anchors the plant, draws water from the soil, etc; the embedded part of a tooth, a hair, etc; a supporting or essential part; an origin or source; (*math*) the factor of a quantity which multiplied by itself gives the quantity; (*mus*) the fundamental note of a chord; (*pl*) plants with edible roots. • *vti* to take root; to become established; (*with out*) to tear up, to eradicate.

**root**² *vti* to dig up with the snout; to search about, rummage; (*with* for) (*inf*) to encourage a team by cheering.

**rope** *n* a thick cord or thin cable made of twisted fibres or wires; a string or row of things braided or threaded together; a thickening in a liquid. • *vt* to tie, bind, divide or enclose with a rope; to lasso; (*liquid*) to become ropy.—**ropy** *adj*.

**rosary** *n* a string of beads for keeping count of prayers; a series of prayers.

**rose**¹ *see* **rise**.

**rose**² *n* a prickly-stemmed plant with fragrant flowers of many delicate colours; its flower; a rosette; a perforated nozzle; a pinkish red or purplish red.

**rosé** *n* a pink wine made from skinless red grapes or by mixing white and red wine.

**rosemary** *n* a fragrant shrubby mint used in cookery and perfumery.

**rosette** *n* a rose-shaped bunch of ribbon; a carving, etc, in the shape of a rose.

**roster** *n* a list or roll, as of military personnel; a list of duties.

**rostrum** *n* (*pl* **rostrums, rostra**) a platform or stage for public speaking.

**rosy** *adj* (**rosier, rosiest**) of the colour of roses; having pink, healthy cheeks; optimistic, hopeful.—**rosily** *adv*.—**rosiness** *n*.

**rot** *vti* (*pt* **rotted**) to decompose; to decay; to become degenerate. • *n* decay; corruption; several different

diseases affecting timber or sheep; (*inf*) nonsense.

**rota** *n* a turn in succession; a list or roster of duties.

**rotary** *adj* revolving; turning like a wheel.

**rotate** *vti* to turn around an axis like a wheel; to follow a sequence.

**rotation** *n* the action of rotating; a regular succession, as of crops to avoid exhausting the soil.

**rotor** *n* a rotating part of a machine or engine.

**rotten** *adj* decayed, decomposed; corrupt; (*inf*) bad, nasty.—**rottenness** *n*.

**rotund** *adj* rounded; spherical; plump.

**rouble** *n* a coin and monetary unit of Russia.

**rouge** *n* a red cosmetic for colouring the cheeks; a red powder for polishing jewellery, etc. • *vti* to colour (the face) with rouge.

**rough** *adj* uneven; not smooth; ill-mannered; violent; rude, unpolished; shaggy; coarse in texture; unrefined; violent, boisterous; stormy; wild; harsh, discordant; crude, unfinished; approximate; (*inf*) difficult. • *n* rough ground; (*golf*) any part of a course with grass, etc, left uncut; a first sketch. • *vt* to make rough; to sketch roughly. • *adv* in a rough manner.—**roughly** *adv*.—**roughness** *n*.

**roulette** *n* a gambling game played with a revolving disc and a ball; a toothed wheel for making perforations.

**round** *adj* circular, spherical, or cylindrical in form; curved; plump; (*math*) expressed to the nearest ten, hundred, etc, not fractional; considerable; candid; (*style*) flowing, balanced; (*vowel*) pronounced with rounded lips. • *adv* circularly; on all sides; from one side to another; in a ring; by indirect way; through a recurring period of time; in circumference; in a roundabout way; about; near; here and there; with a rotating movement; in the opposite direction; around. • *prep* encircling; on every side of; in the vicinity of; in a circuit through; around. • *n* anything round; a circuit; (*of shots*) a volley; a unit of ammunition; a series or sequence; a turn; (*golf*) a circuit of a course; a stage of a contest; (*mus*) a kind of canon. • *vt* to make or become round or plump; (*math*) to express as a round number; to complete; to go or pass around. • *vi* to make a circuit; to turn; to reverse direction.—**roundly** *adv*.—**roundness** *n*.

**roundabout** *adj* indirect, circuitous. • *n* a circuitous route; a merry-go-round; a crossroad where traffic circulates around a traffic island.

**rounded** *adj* curved or round; flowing, not angular.

**round trip** *n* a journey to a place and back again.

**roundup** *n* a driving together of livestock; (*inf*) the detention of several prisoners; a summary, as of news.

**rouse** *vti* to provoke; to stir up; to awaken; to wake up; to become active.

**rousing** *adj* stirring; vigorous.

**rout**[1] *n* a noisy crowd, a rabble; a disorderly retreat. • *vt* to defeat and put to flight.

**rout**[2] *vti* to grub up, as a pig; to search haphazardly; to make a furrow in (as wood or metal); to cause to emerge, esp from bed; to come up with; to uncover.

**route** *n* a course to be taken; the roads travelled on a journey. • *vt* to plan the route of; to send (by a specified route).

**routine** *n* a procedure that is regular and unvarying; a sequence of set movements, as in a dance, skating, etc.—*also adj*.

**row**[1] *n* a line of persons or things; a line of seats (in a theatre, etc).

**row**[2] *vti* to propel with oars; to transport by rowing. • *n* an act or instance of rowing.—**rower** *n*.

**row**[3] *n* a noisy quarrel or dispute; a scolding; noise, disturbance. • *vi* to quarrel; to scold.

**rowdy** *adj* (**rowdier**, **rowdiest**) rough and noisy, disorderly. • *n* a rowdy person, a hooligan.—**rowdiness**, **rowdyism** *n*.

**royal** *adj* relating to or fit for a king or queen; regal; under the patronage of a king or queen; founded by a king or queen; of a kingdom, its government, etc. • *n* a type of topsail; a stag with a head of twelve points; (*inf*) a member of a royal family.—**royally** *adv*.

**royalist** *n* a person who advocates monarchy.

**royalty** *n* the rank or power of a king or queen; a royal person or persons; a share of the proceeds from a patent, book, song, etc, paid to the owner, author, etc.

**rpm** *abbr* = revolutions per minute.

**RSVP** *abbr* = répondez s'il vous plaît.

**rub** *vti* (*pt* **rubbed**) to move (a hand, cloth, etc) over the surface of with pressure; to wipe, scour; to clean or polish; (*with* **away**, **off**, **out**) to remove or erase by friction; to chafe, grate; to fret; to take a rubbing of; (*with* **along**) to manage somehow; (*with* **down**) to rub vigorously with a towel; to smooth down. • *n* the act or process of rubbing; a drawback, difficulty.

**rubber**[1] *n* an elastic substance made synthetically or from the sap of various tropical plants; an eraser.

**rubber**[2] *n* a group of three games at whist, bridge, etc; the deciding game.

**rubber-stamp** *vt* (*inf*) to give automatic approval without investigation.

**rubbish** *n* refuse; garbage, trash; nonsense. • *vt* (*inf*) to criticize.—**rubbishy** *adj*.

**rubble** *n* rough broken stone or rock; builders' rubbish.

**ruby** *n* a deep red, transparent, valuable precious stone. • *adj* of the colour of a ruby.

**rucksack** *n* a bag worn on the back by hikers.

**rudder** *n* a flat vertical piece of wood or metal hinged to the stern of a ship or boat or the rear of an aircraft to steer by; a guiding principle.

**ruddy** *adj* (**ruddier, ruddiest**) reddish pink; (*complexion*) of a healthy, red colour.

**rude** *adj* uncivil, ill-mannered; uncultured, coarse; harsh, brutal; crude, roughly made; in a natural state, primitive; vigorous, hearty.—**rudely** *adv*.—**rudeness** *n*.

**rudiment** *n* a first stage; a first slight beginning of something; an imperfectly developed organ; (*pl*) elements, first principles.

**rudimentary** *adj* elementary; imperfectly developed or represented only by a vestige.

**rueful** *adj* regretful; dejected; showing good-humoured self-pity.—**ruefully** *adv*.

**ruff** *n* a pleated collar or frill worn round the neck; a fringe of feathers or fur round the neck of a bird or animal.

**ruffian** *n* a brutal lawless person; a villain.

**ruffle** *vti* to disturb the smoothness of, to disarrange; to irritate; to agitate; to upset; to swagger about; to be quarrelsome; to flutter. • *n* pleated material used as a trim; a frill; a bird's ruff; a dispute, a quarrel.

**rug** *n* a thick heavy fabric used as a floor covering; a thick woollen wrap or coverlet.

**rugby** *n* a football game for two teams of 15 players played with an oval ball.

**rugged** *adj* rocky; rough, uneven; strong; stern; robust.—**ruggedly** *adv*.—**ruggedness** *n*.

**ruin** *n* destruction; downfall, wrecked state; the cause of this; a loss of fortune; (*pl*) the remains of something destroyed, decayed, etc. • *vti* to destroy; to spoil; to bankrupt; to come to ruin.

**ruinous** *adj* in ruins; causing ruin, disastrous.

**rule** *n* a straight-edged instrument for drawing lines and measuring; government; the exercise of authority; a regulation, an order; a principle, a standard; habitual practice; the code of a religious order; a straight line. • *vti* to govern, to exercise authority over; to manage; to draw (lines) with a ruler; (*with* **out**) to exclude, to eliminate; to make impossible.

**ruler** *n* a person who governs; a strip of wood, metal, etc, with a straight edge, used in drawing lines, measuring, etc.

**ruling** *adj* governing; reigning; dominant. • *n* an authoritative pronouncement.

**rum** *n* a spirit made from sugar cane.

**rumble** *vti* to make a low heavy rolling noise; to move with such a sound; (*sl*) to see through, find out. • *n* the dull deep vibrating noise of thunder, etc.

**rummage** *n* odds and ends; a search by ransacking. • *vti* to search thoroughly; to ransack; to fish (out).

**rummage sale** *n* a jumble sale.

**rumour, rumor** (*US*) *n* hearsay, gossip; common talk not based on definite knowledge; an unconfirmed report, story. • *vt* to report by way of rumour.

**rump** *n* the hindquarters of an animal's body; the buttocks; the back end.

**rumpus** *n* a commotion; a din.

**run** *vb* (*pt* **ran**) *vi* to go by moving the legs faster than in walking; to hurry; to flee; to flow; to operate; to be valid; to compete in a race, election, etc; (*colours*), to merge. • *vt* (*a car, etc*) to drive; (*a business, etc*) to manage; (*a story*) to publish in a newspaper; (*temperature*) to suffer from a fever; (*with* **out**) to exhaust a supply; (*inf*) to desert; (*with* **over**) (*vehicle*) to knock down a person or animal; to overflow; to exceed a limit; to rehearse quickly; (*with* **up**) to incur or amass. • *n* an act of running; a trip; a flow; a series; prevalence; a trend; an enclosure for chickens, etc; free and unrestricted access to all parts; (*in tights, etc*) a ladder.

**runaway** *n* a person or animal that has run away.

**rundown** *n* a summary.

**run-down** *adj* dilapidated.

**rung**[1] *see* **ring**[2].

**rung**[2] *n* the step of a ladder; the crossbar of a chair.

**runner** *n* an athlete; a person who runs; a smuggler; a groove or strip on which something glides.

**runner bean** *n* a climbing plant that produces long green edible pods.

**runner-up** *n* (*pl* **runners-up**) the competitor who finishes second in a race, contest, etc.

**running** *n* the act of moving swiftly; that which runs or flows; a racing, managing, etc. • *adj* moving swiftly; kept for a race; being in motion; continuous; discharing pus. • *adv* in succession.

**runny** *adj* (**runnier, runniest**) tending to flow.

**run-of-the-mill** *adj* average, mediocre.

**runt** *n* an unusually small animal, esp the smallest of a litter of pigs; a person of small stature.

**runway** *n* a landing strip for aircraft.

**rupture** *n* a breach; a severance, quarrel; the act of bursting or breaking; hernia. • *vti* to cause or suffer a rupture.

**rural** *adj* relating to the country or agriculture.—**rurally** *adv*.

**ruse** *n* a trick, deception.

**rush**[1] *vti* to move, push, drive, etc, swiftly or impetuously; to make a sudden attack (on); to do with unusual haste; to hurry. • *adj* marked by or needing extra speed or urgency. • *n* a sudden surge; a sudden demand; a press, as of business, requiring unusual haste; an unedited film print.

**rush**[2] *n* a marsh plant; its slender pithy stem; a worthless thing.

**rush hour** *n* the time at the beginning and end of the working day when traffic is at its heaviest.

**rusk** *n* a sweet or plain bread sliced and rebaked until dry and crisp.

**rust** *n* a reddish oxide coating formed on iron or steel when exposed to moisture; a reddish brown colour; a red mould on plants; the fungus causing this. • *vti* to form rust (on); to deteriorate, as through disuse.

**rustle** *n* a crisp, rubbing sound as of dry leaves, paper, etc. • *vti* to make or move with a rustle; to hustle; to steal (cattle); (*with* **up**) (*inf*) to collect or get together.

**rusty** *adj* (**rustier, rustiest**) coated with rust; rust-coloured, faded; out of practice; antiquated.—**rustiness** *n*.

**rut**[1] *n* a track worn by wheels; an undeviating mechanical routine. • *vt* (*pt* **rutted**) to mark with ruts.

**rut**[2] *n* the seasonal period of sexual excitement in certain male animals, eg deer. • *vi* (*pt* **rutted**) (*deer, etc*) to be in rut.

**ruthless** *adj* cruel; merciless.—**ruthlessly** *adv*.—**ruthlessness** *n*.

**rye** *n* a hardy annual grass; its grain,

used for making flour and whiskey; a whiskey made from rye.

# S

**sabbath** *n* a day of rest and worship observed on a Saturday by Jews, Sunday by Christians and Friday by Muslims.

**sabbatical** *n* a year's leave from a teaching post, often paid, for research or travel.

**sabotage** *n* deliberate damage of machinery, or disruption of public services, by enemy agents, disgruntled employees, etc, to prevent their effective operation. • *vt* to practise sabotage on; to spoil, disrupt.

**saccharin** *n* a non-fattening sugar substitute.

**saccharine** *adj* containing sugar; excessively sweet.

**sack**[1] *n* a large bag made of coarse cloth used as a container; the contents of this; a loose-fitting dress or coat; (*sl: with* **the**) dismissal. • *vt* to put into sacks; (*sl*) to dismiss.

**sack**[2] *n* the plunder or destruction of a place. • *vt* to plunder or loot.

**sacking** *n* the coarse cloth used for sacks; the storming and plundering of a place.

**sacrament** *n* a religious ceremony forming outward and visible sign of inward and spiritual grace, esp baptism and the Eucharist; the consecrated elements in the Eucharist, esp the bread; a sacred symbol or pledge.—**sacramental** *adj*.

**sacred** *adj* regarded as holy; consecrated to a god or God; connected with religion; worthy of or regarded with reverence, sacrosanct.

**sacrifice** *n* the act of offering ceremonially to a deity; the slaughter of an animal (or person) to please a deity; the surrender of something valuable for the sake of something more important; loss without return; something sacrificed, an offering. • *vt* to slaughter or give up as a sacrifice; to give up for a higher good; to sell at a loss.—**sacrificial** *adj*.

**sacrilege** *n* violation of anything holy or sacred.

**sacrosanct** *adj* inviolable; very holy.

**sad** *adj* (**sadder, saddest**) expressing grief or unhappiness; sorrowful; deplorable.—**sadly** *adv*.—**sadness** *n*.

**sadden** *vti* to make or become sad.

**saddle** *n* a seat, usu of leather, for a rider on a horse, bicycle, etc; a ridge connecting two mountain peaks; a joint of mutton or venison consisting of the two loins. • *vt* to put a saddle on; to burden, encumber.

**saddlebag** *n* a bag hung from the saddle of a horse or bicycle.

**sadism** *n* sexual pleasure obtained from inflicting cruelty upon another; extreme cruelty.—**sadist** *n*.—**sadistic** *adj*.

**safari** *n* (*pl* **safaris**) a journey or hunting expedition.

**safe** *adj* unhurt; out of danger; reliable; secure; involving no risk; trustworthy; giving protection; prudent; sure; incapable of doing harm. • *n* a locking metal box or compartment for valuables.—**safely** *adv*.

**safeguard** *n* anything that protects against injury or danger; a proviso against foreseen risks. • *vt* to protect.

**safekeeping** *n* the act or process of keeping safely; protection.

**safety** *n* freedom from danger; the state of being safe.

**safety belt** *n* a belt worn by a person working at a great height to prevent falling; a seatbelt in a car.

**safety pin** *n* a pin with a guard to cover the point.

**saffron** *n* a crocus whose bright yellow

stigmas are used as a food colouring and flavouring; an orange-yellow colour.

**sag** *vi* (*pt* **sagged**) to droop downwards in the middle; to sink or hang down unevenly under pressure.

**sage**[1] *adj* wise through reflection and experience. • *n* a person of profound wisdom.—**sagely** *adv*.

**sage**[2] *n* a herb with leaves used for flavouring food; sagebrush.

**Sagittarius** *n* the Archer, ninth sign of the zodiac; in astrology, operative 22 November - 20 December .

**sago** *n* a type of Asian palm; its starchy pith used in puddings.

**said** *see* **say**.

**sail** *n* a piece of canvas used to catch the wind to propel or steer a vessel; sails collectively; anything like a sail; an arm of a windmill; a voyage in a sailing vessel. • *vt* to navigate a vessel; to manage (a vessel). • *vi* to be moved by sails; to travel by water; to glide or pass smoothly; to walk in a stately manner.

**sailing** *n* the act of sailing; the motion or direction of a ship, etc on water; a departure from a port.

**sailing boat, sailboat** (*US*) *n* a boat that is propelled by a sail or sails.

**sailor** *n* a person who sails; one of a ship's crew.

**saint** *n* a person who is very patient, charitable, etc; a person who is canonized by the Roman Catholic church.—**sainthood** *n*.

**sake** *n* behalf; purpose; benefit; interest.

**salad** *n* a dish, usu cold, of vegetables, fruits, meat, eggs, etc; lettuce, etc, used for this.

**salad dressing** *n* a cooked or uncooked sauce of oil, vinegar, spices, etc, to put on a salad.

**salary** *n* fixed, regular payment for non-manual work, usu paid monthly.

**sale** *n* the act of selling; the exchange of goods or services for money; the market or opportunity of selling; an auction; the disposal of goods at reduced prices; the period of this.

**saleroom, salesroom** *n* a place where goods are displayed for sale; an auction room.

**salesman** *n* a person who sells either in a given territory or in a shop.—**saleswoman** *nf*.

**salient** *adj* projecting outwards; conspicuous; noteworthy; leaping, gushing.

**saliva** *n* the liquid secreted by glands in the mouth that aids digestion.—**salivary** *adj*.

**sallow** *adj* (*complexion*) an unhealthy yellow colour, a pale brown colour.—**sallowness** *n*.

**salmon** *n* (*pl* **salmon**) a large silvery edible fish that lives in salt water and spawns in fresh water; salmon pink.

**saloon** *n* a large reception room; a large cabin for the social use of a ship's passengers; a four-seater car with a boot; a place where alcoholic drinks are sold and consumed.

**salt** *n* a white crystalline substance (sodium chloride) used as a seasoning or preservative; piquancy, wit; (*chem*) a compound of an acid and a base; (*pl*) mineral salt as an aperient. • *adj* containing or tasting of salt; preserved with salt; pungent. • *vt* to flavour, pickle or sprinkle with salt; to give flavour or piquancy to (as a story); (*with* **away**) to hoard; to keep for the future.—**salty** *adj*.

**salt cellar** *n* a vessel for salt at the table; a saltshaker.

**salutary** *adj* beneficial, wholesome.—**salutarily** *adv*.—**salutariness** *n*.

**salute** *n* a gesture of respect or greeting; (*mil*) a motion of the right hand to the head, or of a rifle; a discharge of guns, etc, as a military mark of honour. • *vti* to make a salute (to); to greet; to kiss; to praise or honour.

**salvage** *n* the rescuing of a ship or property from loss at sea, by fire, etc; the reward paid for this; the thing salvaged; waste material intended for further use. • *vt* to save from loss or danger.

**salvation** *n* the act of saving or the state of being saved; in Christianity, the deliverance from evil; a means of preservation.

**salvo** *n* (**salvoes, salvos**) a firing of several guns or missiles simultaneously; a sudden burst; a spirited verbal attack.

**same** *adj* identical; exactly similar; unchanged; uniform, monotonous; previously mentioned. • *pron* the same person or thing. • *adv* in like manner.

**sample** *n* a specimen; a small part representative of the whole; an instance. • *vt* (*food, drink*) to taste a small quantity of; to test by taking a sample.

**sanatorium, sanitarium** (*US*) *n* (*pl* **sanatoriums, sanitariums**) an establishment for the treatment of convalescents or the chronically ill.— *also*

**sanctimonious** *adj* pretending to be holy; hypocritically pious or righteous.—**sanctimoniously** *adv*.

**sanction** *n* express permission, authorization; a binding influence; a penalty by which a law is enforced, esp a prohibition on trade with a country that has violated international law. • *vt* to permit; to give authority.

**sanctity** *n* the condition of being holy or sacred.

**sanctuary** *n* a sacred place; the part of a church around the altar; a place where one is free from arrest or violence, an asylum; a refuge; an animal reserve.

**sand** *n* very fine rock particles; (*pl*) a desert; a sandy beach. • *vt* to smooth or polish with sand or sandpaper; to sprinkle with sand.

**sandal** *n* a shoe consisting of a sole strapped to the foot; a low slipper or shoe.

**sandpaper** *n* a paper coated on one side with sand or another abrasive, used to smooth or polish. • *vt* to rub with sandpaper.

**sandstone** *n* a sedimentary rock of compacted sand.

**sandwich** *n* two slices of bread with meat, cheese, or other filling between; anything in a sandwich-like arrangement. • *vt* to place between two things or two layers; to make such a place for.

**sandy** *adj* (**sandier, sandiest**) of, like, or sprinkled with sand; yellowish grey.—**sandiness** *n*.

**sane** *adj* mentally sound, not mad; reasonable, sensible.—**sanely** *adv*.—**saneness** *n*.

**sang** *see* **sing**.

**sanguine** *adj* confident, hopeful; blood-red; (*complexion*) ruddy.

**sanitary** *adj* relating to the promotion and protection of health; relating to the supply of water, drainage, and sewage disposal; hygienic.

**sanitary towel** *n* an absorbent pad worn externally during menstruation.

**sanitation** *n* the science and practice of achieving hygienic conditions; drainage and disposal of sewage.

**sanity** *n* the condition of being sane; mental health.

**sank** *see* **sink**.

**Santa Claus** *n* a legendary fat, white-bearded old man who brings presents to children at Christmas.— *also* **Father Christmas**.

**sap** *n* the vital juice of plants; energy and health; (*inf*) a fool. • *vt* (*pt* **sapped**) to drain of sap; to exhaust the energy of; to weaken or undermine.

**sapling** *n* a young tree; a youth.

**sapphire** *n* a transparent blue precious stone; a deep pure blue.—*also adj*.

**sarcasm** *n* a scornful or ironic remark; the use of this.—**sarcastic** *adj*.—**sarcastically** *adv*.

**sardine** *n* a small, edible seafish.

**sash**[1] *n* a band of satin or ribbon worn around the waist or over the shoulder, often as a badge of honour.

**sash**[2] *n* a frame for holding the glass of a window, esp one that slides vertically.

**sat** *see* **sit**.

**Satan** *n* the devil, the adversary of God.—**satanic** *adj*.

**satchel** *n* a bag with shoulder straps for carrying school books, etc.

**satellite** *n* a planet orbiting another; a man-made object orbiting the earth, moon, etc, to gather scientific information or for communication; a nation economically dependent on a more powerful one.

**satin** *n* a fabric of woven silk with a smooth, shiny surface on one side. • *adj* of or resembling satin.

**satire** *n* a literary work in which folly or evil in people's behaviour are held up to ridicule; trenchant wit, sarcasm.—**satirical** *adj*.—**satirically** *adv*.

**satisfaction** *n* the act of satisfying or the condition of being satisfied; that which satisfies; comfort; atonement; reparation.

**satisfactory** *adj* giving satisfaction; adequate; acceptable; convincing.—**satisfactorily** *adv*.—**satisfactoriness** *n*.

**satisfy** *vi* to be enough for; to fulfil the needs or desires of. • *vt* to give enough to; (*hunger, desire etc*.) to appease; to please; to gratify; to comply with; (*creditor*) to discharge, to pay in full; to convince; to make reparation to; (*guilt, etc*) to atone for.

**saturate** *vt* to soak thoroughly; to fill completely.

**Saturday** *n* the seventh and last day of the week.

**sauce** *n* a liquid or dressing served with food to enhance ·its flavour; stewed or preserved fruit eaten with other food or as a dessert; (*inf*) impudence. • *vt* to season with sauce; to make piquant; (*sl*) to cheek.

**saucepan** *n* a deep cooking pan with a handle and lid.

**saucer** *n* a round shallow dish placed under a cup; a shallow depression; a thing shaped like a saucer.

**saucy** *adj* (**saucier, sauciest**) rude, impertinent; sprightly.—**saucily** *adv*.—**sauciness** *n*.

**saunter** *vi* to walk in a leisurely or idle way. • *n* a stroll.

**sausage** *n* minced seasoned meat, esp pork, packed into animal gut or other casing.

**savage** *adj* fierce; wild; untamed; uncivilized; ferocious; primitive. • *n* a member of a primitive society; a brutal, fierce person or animal.—**savagely** *adv*.—**savageness** *n*.

**savagery** *n* the state of being a savage; an act of violence or cruelty; an uncivilized state.

**save** *vt* to rescue from harm or danger; to keep, to accumulate; to set aside for future use; to avoid the necessity of; (*energy etc*) to prevent waste of; (*theol*) to deliver from sin. • *vi* to avoid waste, expense, etc; to economize; to store up money or goods; (*sports*) to keep an opponent from scoring or winning. • *n* (*sports*) the act of preventing one's opponent from scoring. • *conj*, *prep* except, but.

**saving** *adj* thrifty, economical; (*clause*) containing a reservation; redeeming. • *n* what is saved; (*pl*) money saved for future use. • *prep* except; with apology to.

**savings bank** *n* a bank receiving small deposits and holding them in interest-bearing accounts.

**saviour, savior** (*US*) *n* a person who saves another from harm or danger; (*with cap*) Jesus Christ.

**savour, savor** (*US*) *n* the flavour or smell of something; a distinctive quality. • *vti* to season; to enjoy; to have a specified taste or smell; to smack (of); to appreciate critically.

**savoury, savory** (*US*) *adj* having a good taste or smell; spicy, not sweet; reputable. • *n* a savoury dish at the beginning or end of dinner; (*pl*) snacks served with drinks.—**savouriness** *n*.

**saw**[1] *see* **see**[1]

**saw**[2] *n* a tool with a toothed edge for cutting wood, etc. • *vti* (*pt* **sawed**, *pp* **sawn**) to cut or shape with a saw; to use a saw; to make a to-and-fro motion.

**sawdust** *n* fine particles of wood caused by sawing.

**sawmill** *n* a mill where timber is cut into logs or planks.

**sawn** *see* **saw**[2].

**saxophone** *n* a brass wind instrument with a single reed and about twenty finger-keys.

**say** *vb* (*pt* **said**) *vt* to speak, to utter; to state in words; to affirm, declare; to recite; to estimate; to assume. • *vi* to tell; to express in words. • *n* the right or opportunity to speak; a share in a decision.

**saying** *n* a common remark; a proverb or adage.

**scab** *n* a dry crust on a wound or sore; a plant disease characterized by crustaceous spots; a worker who refuses to join a strike or who replaces a striking worker.—**scabby** *adj*.

**scaffold** *n* a raised platform for the execution of a criminal; capital punishment; scaffolding.

**scaffolding** *n* a temporary framework of wood and metal for use by workmen constructing a building, etc; materials for a scaffold.

**scald** *vt* to burn with hot liquid or steam; to heat almost to boiling point; to immerse in boiling water (to sterilize). • *n* an injury caused by hot liquid or steam.

**scale**[1] *n* (*pl*) a machine or instrument for weighing; one of the pans or the tray of a set of scales; (*pl with cap*) Libra, the seventh sign of the zodiac. • *vti* to weigh in a set of scales; to have a specified weight on a set of scales.

**scale**[2] *n* one of the thin plates covering a fish or reptile; a flake (of dry skin); an incrustation on teeth, etc. • *vti* to remove the scales from; to flake off.

**scale**[3] *n* a graduated measure; an instrument so marked; (*math*) the basis for a numerical system, 10 being that in general use; (*mus*) a series of tones from the keynote to its octave, in order of pitch; the proportion that a map, etc, bears to what it represents; a series of degrees classified by size, amount, etc; relative scope or size. • *vt* (*wall*) to go up or over; (*model*) to make or draw to scale; to increase or decrease in size.

**scallop** *n* an edible shellfish with two fluted, fan-shaped shells; one of a series of curves in an edging. • *vt* to cut into scallops.—**scalloped** *adj*.

**scalp** *n* the skin covering the skull, usu covered with hair. • *vti* to cut the scalp from; to criticize sharply; (*inf*) (*tickets, etc*) to buy and resell at higher prices.

**scalpel** *n* a short, thin, very sharp knife used esp for surgery.

**scamper** *vi* to run away quickly or playfully. • *n* a brisk or playful run or movement.

**scan** *vb* (*pt* **scanned**) *vt* (*page etc*) to look through quickly; to scrutinize; (*med*) to examine with a radiological device; (*TV*) to pass an electronic beam over; (*radar*) to detect with an electronic beam; (*poem*) to conform to a rhythmical pattern; to check for recorded data by means of a mechanical or electronic device; (*human body*) to make a scan of in a scanner. • *vi* to analyse the pattern of verse. • *n* the act of scanning or an instance of being scanned.

**scandal** *n* a disgraceful event or action; talk arising from immoral behaviour; a feeling of moral outrage; the thing or person causing this; disgrace; malicious gossip.

**scandalize** *vt* to shock the moral feelings of; to defame.

**scandalous** *adj* causing scandal; shameful; spreading slander.

**Scandinavia** *n* the region comprising Norway, Sweden, and Denmark, and sometimes Iceland.—**Scandinavian** *adj*.

**scant** *adj* limited; meagre; insufficient; scanty; grudging.

**scanty** *adj* (**scantier, scantiest**) barely adequate; insufficient; small.—**scantily** *adv*.—**scantiness** *n*.

**scapegoat** *n* a person who bears the blame for others; one who is the object of irrational hostility.

**scar**[1] *n* a mark left after the healing of a wound or sore; a blemish resulting from damage or wear. • *vti* (*pt* **scarred**) to mark with or form a scar.

**scar**[2] *n* a protruding or isolated rock; a precipitous crag; a rocky part of a hillside.

**scarce** *adj* not in abundance; hard to find; rare.—**scarceness** *n*.

**scarcely** *adv* hardly, only just; probably not or certainly not.

**scarcity** *n* the state of being scarce; a dearth, deficiency.

**scare** *vti* to startle; to frighten or become frightened; to drive away by frightening. • *n* a sudden fear; a period of general fear; a false alarm.

**scarecrow** *n* a wooden figure dressed in clothes for scaring birds from crops; a thin or tattered person; something frightening but harmless.

**scaremonger** *n* a person who causes fear or panic by spreading rumours; an alarmist.

**scarf** *n* (*pl* **scarves**) a rectangular or square piece of cloth worn around the neck, shoulders or head for warmth or decoration.

**scarlet** *n* a bright red with a tinge of orange; scarlet cloth or clothes. • *adj* scarlet coloured; immoral or sinful.

**scarlet fever** *n* an acute contagious disease marked by a sore throat, fever, and a scarlet rash.

**scathing** *adj* bitterly critical; cutting, withering.—**scathingly** *adv*.

**scatter** *vti* to throw loosely about; to sprinkle; to dissipate; to put or take to flight; to disperse; to occur at random. • *n* a scattering or sprinkling.

**scatterbrain** *n* a frivolous, heedless person.—**scatterbrained** *adj*.

**scattered** *adj* dispersed widely, spaced out; straggling.

**scavenge** *vi* to gather things discarded by others; (*animal*) to eat decaying matter.—**scavenger** *n*.

**scene** *n* the place in which anything occurs; the place in which the action of a play or a story occurs; a section of a play, a division of an act; the stage of a theatre; a painted screen, etc, used on this; an unseemly display of strong emotion; a landscape; surroundings; a place of action; (*inf*) an area of interest or activity (eg *the music scene*).

**scenery** *n* painted screens, etc, used to represent places, as in a play, film, etc; an aspect of a landscape, esp of beautiful or impressive countryside.

**scenic** *adj* relating to natural scenery; picturesque; of or used on the stage.—**scenically** *adv*.

**scent** *n* a perfume; an odour left by an animal, by which it can be tracked; the sense of smell; a line of pursuit or discovery. • *vt* to recognize by the sense of smell; to track by smell; to impart an odour to, to perfume; to get wind of, to detect.

**scented** *adj* perfumed.

**sceptic, skeptic** (*US*) *n* a person who questions opinions generally accepted; a person who doubts religious doctrines, an agnostic; an adherent of scepticism.

**sceptical, skeptical** (*US*) *adj* doubting; questioning.—**sceptically** *adv*.

**scepticism, skepticism** (*US*) *n* an attitude of questioning criticism, doubt; (*philos*) the doctrine that absolute knowledge is unattainable.

**sceptre, scepter** (*US*) *n* the staff of office held by a monarch on a ceremonial occasion; sovereignty.

**schedule** *n* a timetable; a list, inventory or tabulated statement; a timed plan for a project. • *vt* to make a schedule; to plan.

**scheme** *n* a plan; a project; a systematic arrangement; a diagram; an underhand plot. • *vti* to devise or plot.—**schemer** *n*.

**scheming** *adj* cunning; intriguing.

**schism** *n* a division or separation into two parties, esp of a church; the sin of this; discord, disharmony.

**schizophrenia** *n* a mental disorder characterized by withdrawal from reality and deterioration of the personality; the presence of mutually contradictory qualities or parts.—**schizophrenic** *adj*, *n*.

**scholar** *n* a pupil, a student; a learned person; the holder of a scholarship.

**scholarly** *adj* learned, erudite, academic.

**scholarship** *n* an annual grant to a scholar or student, usu won by competitive examination; learning, academic achievement.

**school**[1] *n* a shoal of porpoises, whales, or other aquatic animals of one kind swimming together.

**school**[2] *n* an educational establishment; its teachers and students; a regular session of teaching; formal education, schooling; a particular division of a university; a place or means of discipline; a group of thinkers, artists, writers, holding similar principles. • *vt* to train; to teach; to control or discipline.

**schoolboy** *n* a boy who attends school.

**schoolgirl** *n* a girl who attends school.

**schooling** *n* instruction in school.

**schoolmaster** *n* a man who teaches in school.

**schoolmistress** *n* a woman who teaches in school.

**schoolteacher** *n* a person who teaches in school.

**schooner** *n* a sailing ship with two or more masts rigged with fore-and-aft sails; a large drinking glass for sherry or beer.

**sciatica** *n* pain along the sciatic nerve, esp in the back of the thigh; (*loosely*) pain in the lower back or adjacent parts.

**science** *n* knowledge gained by systematic experimentation and analysis, and the formulation of general principles; a branch of this; skill or technique.

**science fiction** *n* highly imaginative fiction typically involving actual or projected scientific phenomena.

**scientific** *adj* of or concerned with science; based on or using the principles and methods of science; systematic and exact; having or showing expert skill.—**scientifically** *adv*.

**scientist** *n* a specialist in a branch of science, as in chemistry, etc.

**scintillating** *adj* sparkling; amusing.

**scissor** *vt* to cut with scissors, to clip. • *npl* a tool for cutting paper, hair, etc, consisting of two fastened pivoted blades whose edges slide past each other; a gymnastic feat in which the leg movements resemble the opening and closing of scissors.

**scoff**[1] *vti* to jeer (at) or mock. • *n* an expression or object of derision; mocking words, a taunt.

**scoff**[2] *vt* (*sl*) to eat quickly and greedily.

**scold** *vi* to reprove angrily; to tell off.

**scone** *n* a small, round cake made from flour and fat which is baked and spread with butter, etc.

**scoop** *n* a small shovel-like utensil as for taking up flour, ice cream, etc; the bucket of a dredge, etc; the act of scooping or the amount scooped up at one time; (*inf*) a piece of exclusive news; (*inf*) the advantage gained in being the first to publish or broadcast this. • *vt* to shovel, lift or hollow out with a scoop; (*inf*) to obtain as a scoop; (*inf: rival newspaper etc*) to forestall with a news item.

**scooter** *n* a child's two-wheeled vehicle with a footboard and steering handle; a motor scooter.

**scope** *n* the opportunity to use one's abilities; extent; range;.an instrument for viewing.

**scorch** *vti* to burn or be burned on the surface; to wither from over-exposure to heat; to singe; (*inf*) to drive or cycle furiously.

**scorcher** *n* (*inf*) a very hot day.

**scorching** *adj* (*inf: weather*) very hot; scathing.

**score** *n* the total number of points made in a game or examination; a notch or scratch; a line indicating deletion or position; a group of twenty; a written copy of a musical composition showing the different parts; the music composed for a film; a grievance for settling; a reason or motive; (*inf*) the real facts; a bill or reckoning; (*pl*) an indefinite, large number. • *vt* to mark with cuts; (*mus*) to arrange in a score, to orchestrate; to gain or record points, as in a game; to evaluate in testing. • *vi* to make points, as in a game; to keep the score of a game; to gain an advantage, a success, etc; (*sl*) to be successful in seduction.—**scorer** *n*.

**scorn** *n* extreme contempt or disdain; the object of this. • *vt* to treat with contempt, to despise; to reject or refuse as unworthy.—**scornful** *adj*.—**scornfully** *adv*.

**Scorpio** *n* the eighth sign of the zodiac in astrology, operative from 23 October–21 November.

**scorpion** *n* a small, tropical, insect-like animal with pincers and a jointed tail with a poisonous sting.

**Scot** *n* a native or inhabitant of Scotland; a member of a Celtic people from Ireland that settled in northern Britain in the 5th and 6th centuries.

**Scotch** *n* whisky made in Scotland.

**scotch** *vt* (*a rumour*) to stamp out.

**Scots** *adj* of or pertaining to Scotland, its law, money, and people, and the Scots language. • *n* the dialect of English developed in Lowland Scotland.

**Scottish** *adj* of or relating to Scotland and its people.

**scoundrel** *n* a rascal; a dishonest person.

**scour**[1] *vt* to clean by rubbing with an abrasive cloth; to flush out with a current of water; to purge. • *n* the act or process of scouring; a place scoured by running water; scouring action; damage done by scouring.

**scour**[2] *vt* to hasten over or along, to range over, esp in search or pursuit.

**scourge** *n* a whip; a means of inflicting punishment; a person who harasses and causes widespread and great affliction; a pest. • *vt* to flog; to punish harshly.

**scout** *n* a person, plane, etc, sent to observe the enemy's strength, etc; a person employed to find new talent or survey a competitor, etc; (*with cap*) a member of the Scouting Association, an organization for young people. • *vti* to reconnoitre; to go in search of (something).

**scowl** *n* a contraction of the brows in an angry or threatening manner; a sullen expression. • *vi* to make a scowl; to look sullen.

**scraggy** *adj* (**scraggier, scraggiest**) thin and bony, gaunt.

**scram** *vi* (*pt* **scrammed**) (*sl*) to get out, to go away at once.

**scramble** *vi* to move or climb hastily on all fours; to scuffle or struggle for something; to move with urgency or panic. • *vt* to mix haphazardly; to stir (slightly beaten eggs) while cooking; (*transmitted signals*) to make unintelligible in transit. • *n* a hard climb or advance; a disorderly struggle; a rapid emergency take-off of fighter planes; a motorcycle rally over rough ground.—**scrambler** *n*.

**scrap**[1] *n* a small piece; a fragment of discarded material; (*pl*) bits of food. • *adj* in the form of pieces, leftovers, etc; used and discarded. • *vt* (*pt* **scrapped**) to discard; to make into scraps.

**scrap**[2] *n* (*inf*) a fight or quarrel.—*also vi*.

**scrapbook** *n* a book for pasting clippings, etc, in.

**scrape** *vt* to rub with a sharp or abrasive object so as to clean, smooth or remove; to eke out or to be economical; to amass in small portions; to draw along with a grating or vibration; to get narrowly past, to graze; to draw back the foot in making a bow. • *n* the act of scraping; a grating sound; an abrasion, scratch; an awkward predicament.

**scraper** *n* an instrument for scraping; a grating or edge for scraping mud from boots.

**scrapheap** *n* a pile of discarded material or things.

**scrappy** *adj* (**scrappier, scrappiest**) disjointed; fragmentary; full of gaps.—**scrappiness** *n*.

**scratch** *vt* to mark with a sharp point; to scrape with the nails or claws; to rub to relieve an itch; to chafe; to write awkwardly; (*writing etc*) to strike out; to withdraw from a race, etc. • *vi* to use nails or claws to tear or dig. • *n* the act of scratching; a mark or sound made by this; a slight injury; a starting line for a race; a scribble. • *adj* taken at random, haphazard, impromptu; without a handicap.

**scrawl** *n* careless or illegible handwriting; a scribble. • *vti* to draw or write carelessly.

**scrawny** *adj* (**scrawnier, scrawniest**) skinny; bony.

**scream** *vti* to utter a piercing cry, as of pain, fear, etc; to shout; to shriek. • *n* a sharp, piercing cry; (*inf*) a very funny person or thing.

**scree** *n* loose shifting stones; a slope covered with these.

**screech** *n* a harsh, high-pitched cry. • *vti* to utter a screech, to shriek.

**screen** *n* a movable partition or framework to conceal, divide, or protect; a shelter or shield from heat, danger or view; an electronic display (as in a television set, computer terminal, etc); a surface on which films, slides, etc are projected; the motion picture industry; a coarse wire mesh over a window or door to keep out insects; a sieve. • *vt* to conceal or shelter; to grade by passing through a screen; to separate according to skill, etc; (*a film*) to show on a screen.

**screening** *n* a showing of a film; a metal or plastic mesh, as for window screens; the refuse matter after sieving.

**screw** *n* a metal cylinder or cone with a spiral thread around it for fastening things by being turned; any spiral thing like this; a twist or turn of a screw; a twist of paper; pressure; a propeller with revolving blades on a shaft. • *vt* to fasten, tighten etc with a screw; to oppress; to extort, to cheat out of something due; (*sl, vulg*) to have sexual intercourse with; (*with* up) to gather (courage, etc). • *vi* to go together or come apart by being turned like a screw; to twist or turn with a writhing movement; (*sl, vulg*) to have sexual intercourse; (*with* up) to bungle.

**screwdriver** *n* a tool like a blunt chisel for turning screws; a drink of vodka and orange juice.

**screwy** *adj* (*sl*) (**screwier, screwiest**) eccentric, odd.

**scribble** *vti* to draw or write hastily or carelessly, to scrawl; to be a writer. • *n* hasty writing, a scrawl.—**scribbler** *n*.

**script** *n* handwriting; a style of writing; the text of a stage play, screenplay or broadcast; a plan of action; (*print*) type that resembles handwriting. • *vt* to write a script (for).

**scriptural** *adj* of or based on the Bible or Scripture.

**scripture** *n* any sacred writing; (*with cap, often pl*) the Jewish Bible or Old Testament; the Christian Bible or Old and New Testaments. • *adj* contained in or quoted from the Bible.

**scriptwriter** *n* a writer of screenplays for films, TV, etc; a screenwriter — **scriptwriting** *n*.

**scroll** *n* a roll of parchment or paper with writing on it; an ornament like this; (*her*) a ribbon with a motto; a list. • *vti* (*comput*) to move text across a screen; to decorate with scrolls.

**scrounge** *vti* (*inf*) to seek or obtain (something) for nothing.— **scrounger** *n*.

**scrub**[1] *n* an arid area of stunted trees and shrubs; such vegetation; anything small or mean. • *adj* small, stunted, inferior, etc.

**scrub**[2] *vti* (*pt* **scrubbed**) to clean vigorously, to scour; to rub hard; (*inf*) to remove, to cancel. • *n* the act of scrubbing.

**scruff** *n* the back of the neck, the nape.

**scruffy** *adj* (**scruffier, scruffiest**) shabby; unkempt.—**scruffily** *adv*.— **scruffiness** *n*.

**scrum** *n* a scrummage.

**scrummage** *n* (*Rugby football*) a play consisting of a tussle between rival forwards in a compact mass for possession of the ball. • *vi* to form a scrum(mage).

**scruple** *n* (*usu pl*) a moral principle or belief causing one to doubt or hesitate about a course of action. • *vti* to hesitate owing to scruples.

**scrupulous** *adj* careful; conscientious; thorough.—**scrupulously** *adv*.— **scrupulousness** *n*.

**scrutinize** *vti* to look closely at, to examine narrowly; to make a scrutiny.

**scrutiny** *n* a careful examination; a critical gaze; an official inspection of votes cast in an election.

**scuff** *vti* to drag the feet, to shuffle; to wear or mark the surface of by doing this.

**scuffle** *n* a confused fight; the sound of shuffling. • *vi* to fight confusedly; to move by shuffling.

**scullery** *n* a room for storage or kitchen work, such as washing dishes, etc.

**sculptor** *n* a person skilled in sculpture.

**sculpture** *n* the art of carving wood or forming clay, stone, etc, into figures, statues, etc; a three-dimensional work of art; a sculptor's work. • *vt* to carve, adorn or portray with sculptures; to shape, mould or form like sculpture.—**sculptural** *adj*.

**scum** *n* a thin layer of impurities on top of a liquid; refuse; despicable people.

**scurrilous** *adj* abusive; grossly offensive.

**scurry** *vi* (*pt* **scurried**) to hurry with quick, short steps, to scamper. • *n* a bustle; a flurry (as of snow).

**scurvy** *n* a disease caused by a deficiency of vitamin C. • *adj* base; contemptible.

**scuttle**[1] *vi* to run quickly; to hurry away. • *n* a short swift run; a hurried pace.

**scuttle**[2] *n* a bucket with a lip for storing coal.

**scuttle**[3] *n* (*naut*) a hatchway, a hole with a cover in a ship's deck or side. • *vt* to sink a ship by making holes in it.

**scythe** *n* a two-handed implement with a large curved blade for cutting grass, etc. • *vti* to cut with a scythe; to mow down.

**sea** *n* the ocean; a section of this; a vast expanse of water; a heavy wave, the swell of the ocean; something like the sea in size; the seafaring life. • *adj* marine, of the sea.

**seaboard** *n, adj* (land) bordering on the sea.

**sea breeze** *n* a wind that blows from the sea to the land.

**seafood** *n* edible fish or shellfish from the sea.

**sea front** *n* the waterfront of a seaside place.

**seagoing** *adj* (*ship*) made for use on the open sea.

**seagull** *n* a gull.

**seal**[1] *n* an engraved stamp for impressing wax, lead, etc; wax, lead, etc, so impressed; that which authenticates or pledges; a device for closing or securing tightly. • *vt* to fix a seal to; to close tightly or securely; to shut up; to mark as settled, to confirm.

**seal**[2] *n* an aquatic mammal with four webbed flippers; the fur of some seals; a dark brown. • *vi* to hunt seals.

**sealant** *n* a thing that seals, as wax, etc; a substance for stopping a leak, making watertight, etc.

**sealer** *n* a person or ship whose business is hunting seals.

**sea level** *n* the level of the surface of the sea in relation to the land.

**sea lion** *n* a large seal of the Pacific Ocean that has a roar and, in the male, a mane.

**seam** *n* the line where two pieces of cloth are stitched together; (*geol*) a stratum of coal, oil, etc, between thicker ones; a line or wrinkle. • *vt* to join with a seam; to furrow.

**seaman** *n* a sailor; a naval rank.

**seamy** *adj* (**seamier, seamiest**) unpleasant or sordid.

**seance, séance** *n* a meeting of spiritualists to try to communicate with the dead.

**seaplane** *n* an aeroplane with floats that allow it to take off from and land on water.

**seaport** *n* a port, harbour or town accessible to oceangoing ships.

**search** *vi* to look around to find

something; to explore. • *vt* to examine or inspect closely; to probe into. • *n* the act of searching; an investigation; a quest.—**searcher** *n*.

**searching** *adj* keen, piercing; examining thoroughly.—**searchingly** *adv*.

**searchlight** *n* a powerful ray of light projected by an apparatus on a swivel; the apparatus.

**search warrant** *n* a legal document that authorizes a police search.

**seashore** *n* land beside the sea or between high and low water marks; the beach.

**seasick** *adj* affected with nausea brought on by the motion of a ship.

**seaside** *n* seashore.

**season** *n* one of the four equal parts into which the year is divided: spring, summer, autumn, or winter; a period of time; a time when something is plentiful or in use; a suitable time; (*inf*) a season ticket. • *vt* (*food*) to flavour by adding salt, spices, etc; to make mature or experienced; (*wood*) to dry until ready for use. • *vi* to become experienced.

**seasonal** *adj* of or relating to a particular season.

**seasoning** *n* salt, spices, etc, used to enhance the flavour of food; the process of making something fit for use.

**season ticket** *n* a ticket or set of tickets valid for a number of concerts, games, journeys, etc, during a specified period.

**seat** *n* a piece of furniture for sitting on, such as a chair, bench, etc; the part of a chair on which one sits; the buttocks, the part of the trousers covering them; a way of sitting (on a horse, etc); the chief location, or centre; a part at or forming a base; the right to sit as a member; a parliamentary constituency; a large country house. • *vt* to place on a seat; to provide with seats; to settle.

**seatbelt** *n* an anchored strap worn in a car or aeroplane to secure a person to a seat.

**seaweed** *n* a mass of plants growing in or under water; a sea plant, esp a marine alga.

**seaworthy** *adj* fit to go to sea; able to withstand sea water, watertight.

**sec.** *abbr* = second.

**secluded** *adj* private; sheltered; kept from contact with other people.

**seclusion** *n* the state of being secluded; privacy, solitude.

**second** *adj* next after first; alternate; another of the same kind; next below the first in rank, value, etc. • *n* a person or thing coming second; another; an article of merchandise not of first quality; an aid or assistant, as to a boxer, duellist; the gear after low gear; one sixtieth of a minute of time or of an angular degree; (*pl*) (*inf*) another helping of food. • *adv* in the second place, group, etc. • *vt* to act as a second (to); (*a motion, resolution, etc*) to support; (*mil*) to place on temporary service elsewhere.

**secondary** *adj* subordinate; second in rank or importance; in the second stage; derived, not primary; relating to secondary school. • *n* that which is secondary; a delegate, a deputy.—**secondarily** *adv*.

**secondary school** *n* a school between elementary or primary school and college or university.

**second class** *n* the class next to the first in a classification. • *adj* (second-class) relating to a second class; inferior, mediocre; (*seating, accommodation*) next in price and quality to first class; (*mail*) less expensive and handled more slowly (than first class).

**second-hand** *adj* bought after use by another; derived, not original.—*also adv.*

**secondly** *adv* in the second place.

**second-rate** *adj* of inferior quality.

**second thought** *n* a change in thought or decision after consideration.

**secrecy** *n* the state of being secret; the ability to keep secret.

**secret** *adj* not made public; concealed from others; hidden; private; remote. • *n* something hidden; a mystery; a hidden cause.—**secretly** *adv*.

**secretariat** *n* an administrative office or staff, as in a government.

**secretary** *n* a person employed to deal with correspondence, filing, telephone calls of another or of an association; the head of a state department.—**secretarial** *adj*.

**secretive** *adj* given to secrecy; uncommunicative, reticent.—**secretively** *adv*.—**secretiveness** *n*.

**sect** *n* a religious denomination; a group of people united by a common interest or belief; a faction.

**section** *n* the act of cutting; a severed or separable part; a division; a distinct portion; a slice; a representation of anything cut through to show its interior; (*geom*) the cutting of a solid by a plane; a plane figure formed by this. • *vti* to cut or separate into sections; to represent in sections; to become separated or cut into parts.

**sector** *n* (*geom*) a space enclosed by two radii of a circle and the arc they cut off; a distinctive part (as of an economy); a subdivision; (*mil*) an area of activity .

**secular** *adj* having no connection with religion or the church; worldly.

**secularize** *vt* to change from religious to civil use or control.—**secularization** *n*.

**secure** *adj* free from danger, safe; stable; firmly held or fixed; confident, assured (of); reliable. • *vt* to make safe; to fasten firmly; to protect; to

confine; to fortify; to guarantee; to gain possession of.—**securely** *adv*.

**security** *n* the state of being secure; a financial guarantee, surety; a pledge for repayment, etc; a protection or safeguard; a certificate of shares or bonds.

**sedate**[1] *adj* calm; composed; serious and unemotional.—**sedately** *adv*.—**sedateness** *n*.

**sedate**[2] *vti* to calm or become calm by the administration of a sedative.

**sedation** *n* the act of calming or the condition of being calmed, esp by sedatives; the administration of sedatives to calm a patient.

**sedative** *n* a drug with a soothing, calming effect. • *adj* having a soothing, calming effect.

**sediment** *n* matter that settles at the bottom of a liquid; (*geol*) matter deposited by water or wind.—**sedimentary** *adj*.

**seduce** *vt* to lead astray; to corrupt; to entice into unlawful sexual intercourse.—**seducer** *n*.

**seduction** *n* the act of seducing; temptations; attraction.

**seductive** *adj* tending to seduce; enticing, alluring.—**seductively** *adv*.

**see**[1] *vt* (*pt* **saw**, *pp* **seen**) to perceive with the eyes; to observe; to grasp with intelligence; to ascertain; to take care (that); to accompany; to visit to meet; to consult; (*guests*) to receive. • *vi* to have the faculty of sight; to make inquiry; to consider, to reflect; to understand.

**see**[2] *n* the diocese of a bishop.

**seed** *n* the small, hard part (ovule) of a plant from which a new plant grows; such seeds collectively; the source of anything; sperm or semen; descendants; (*tennis*) a seeded tournament player. • *vti* to sow (seed); to produce or shed seed; to remove seeds from; (*tennis*) to arrange (a tournament) so that the best players cannot meet until later rounds.

**seedling** *n* a young plant raised from seed, not from a cutting; a young tree before it is a sapling.

**seedy** *adj* (**seedier, seediest**) full of seeds; out of sorts, indisposed; shabby; rundown.—**seedily** *adv*.— **seediness** *n*.

**seeing** *n* vision, sight. • *adj* having sight; observant. • *conj* in view of the fact that; since.

**seek** *vti* (*pt* **sought**) to search for; to try to find, obtain, or achieve; to resort to; (*with* **to**) to try to, to endeavour; (*with* **out**) to try to secure the society of.—**seeker** *n*.

**seem** *vi* to appear (to be); to give the impression of; to appear to oneself.

**seen** *see* **see**[1].

**seep** *vi* to ooze gently, to leak through.

**seer** *n* a person who sees visions, a prophet.

**seesaw** *n* a plank balanced across a central support so that it is tilted up and down by a person sitting on each end; an up-and-down movement like this; vacillation. • *vi* to move up and down; to fluctuate. • *adj, adv* alternately rising and falling.

**seethe** *vi* to be very angry inwardly; to swarm (with people).

**segment** *n* a section; a portion; one of the two parts of a circle or sphere when a line is drawn through it. • *vti* to cut or separate into segments.

**segregate** *vti* to set apart from others, to isolate; to separate racial or minority groups.

**seize** *vt* to grasp; to capture; to take hold of suddenly or forcibly; to attack or afflict suddenly. • *vi* (*machinery*) to become jammed.— **seizable** *adj*.

**seizure** *n* the act of seizing; what is seized; a sudden attack of illness, an apoplectic stroke.

**seldom** *adv* not often, rarely.

**select** *vti* to choose or pick out. • *adj* excellent; choice; limited (eg in membership); exclusive.

**selection** *n* the act of selecting; what is or are selected; the process by which certain animals or plants survive while others are eliminated.— *also* **natural selection**.

**selective** *adj* having the power of selection; highly specific in activity or effect.

**self** *n* (*pl* **selves**) the identity, character, etc, of any person or thing; one's own person as distinct from all others; one's own interests or advantage. • *adj* (*colour*) matching, uniform.

**self-** *prefix* of itself or oneself; by, for, in relation to, itself or oneself; automatic.

**self-assured** *adj* confident.—**self-assurance** *n*.

**self-catering** *adj* catering for oneself.

**self-centred, self-centered** (*US*) *adj* preoccupied with one's own affairs.—**self-centredness** *n*.

**self-coloured, self-colored** (*US*) *adj* of a single colour.

**self-confident** *adj* sure of one's own powers.—**self-confidence** *n*.

**self-conscious** *adj* embarrassed or awkward in the presence of others, ill at ease.—**self-consciousness** *n*.

**self-contained** *adj* complete in itself; showing self-control; uncommunicative.

**self-control** *n* control of one's emotions, desires, etc, by the will.—**self-controlled** *adj*.

**self-defence, self-defense** (*US*) *n* the act of defending oneself; (*law*) a plea for the justification for the use of force.

**self-employed** *adj* earning one's living in one's own business or profession, not employed by another; working freelance.

**self-evident** *adj* evident without proof or explanation.—**self-evidence** *n*.

**self-indulgence** *n* undue gratification of one's desires, appetites, or whims.—**self-indulgent** *adj*.

**self-interest** *n* regard to one's own advantage.

**selfish** *adj* chiefly concerned with oneself; lacking consideration for others.—**selfishly** *adv*.—**selfishness** *n*.

**selfless** *adj* with no thought of self, unselfish.—**selflessness** *n*.

**self-portrait** *n* an artist or author's painting or account of himself or herself.

**self-possessed** *adj* cool and collected.

**self-reliant** *adj* relying on one's own powers; confident.—**self-reliance** *n*.

**self-respect** *n* proper respect for oneself, one's standing and dignity.—**self-respecting** *adj*.

**self-righteous** *adj* thinking oneself better than others; priggish.—**self-righteousness** *n*.

**self-sacrifice** *n* the sacrifice of one's own interests, welfare, etc, to secure that of others.

**self-satisfied** *adj* smugly conceited.

**self-service** *adj* serving oneself in a cafe, shop, filling station, etc.

**self-sufficient** *adj* independent; supporting oneself (eg in growing food) without the help of others.—**self-sufficiency** *n*.

**sell** *vb* (*pt* **sold**) *vt* to exchange (goods, services, etc) for money or other equivalent; to offer for sale; to promote; to deal in. • *vi* (*with* **off**) to clear out (stock) at bargain prices; (*with* **out**) to sell off, to betray for money or reward; (*inf*) to disappoint, to trick; to make sales; to attract buyers. • *n* an act or instance of selling; (*inf*) a disappointment, a trick, a fraud.—**seller** *n*.

**sellout** *n* a show, game, etc, for which all the tickets are sold; (*inf*) a betrayal.

**semaphore** *n* a system of visual signalling using the operator's arms, flags, etc; a signalling device consisting of a post with movable arms.

**semen** *n* the fluid that carries sperm in men and male animals.

**semi-** *prefix* half; not fully; twice in a (specified period).

**semibreve** *n* (*mus*) a note equal to two minims.

**semicircle** *n* half of a circle.—**semicircular** *adj*.

**semicolon** *n* the punctuation mark (;) of intermediate value between a comma and a full stop.

**semiconscious** *adj* not fully conscious.—**semiconsciousness** *n*.

**semi-detached** *adj* (*house*) with another joined to it on one side.—*also* *n*.

**semifinal** *adj*, *n* (the match or round) before the final in a knockout tournament.—**semifinalist** *n*.

**seminar** *n* a group of students engaged in study or research under supervision; any group meeting to pool and disuss ideas.

**semiquaver** *n* (*mus*) half a quaver.

**semiskilled** *adj* partly skilled or trained.

**semitone** *n* (*mus*) an interval equal to half a tone.

**semolina** *n* coarse particles of grain left after the sifting of wheat.

**senate** *n* a legislative or governing body; (*with cap*) the upper branch of a two-body legislature in France, the US, etc; the governing body of some universities.

**senator** *n* a member of a senate.—**senatorial** *adj*.

**send** *vti* (*pt* **sent**) to cause or enable to go; to have conveyed, to dispatch (a message or messenger); to cause to move, to propel; to grant; to cause to be; (*sl*) to move (a person) to ecstasy; (*with* **down**) to expel from university; (*with* **for**) to order to be brought, to summon; (*with* **up**) (*inf*) to send to prison; to imitate or make fun of.—**sender** *n*.

**send-off** *n* a friendly demonstration at a departure; a start given to someone or something.

**senile** *adj* of or relating to old age; weakened, esp mentally, by old age.—**senility** *n*.

**senior** *adj* higher in rank; of or for seniors; longer in service; older (when used to distinguish between father and son with the same first name). • *n* one's elder or superior in standing; a person of advanced age; a student in the last year of college or high school.

**seniority** *n* the condition of being senior; status, priority, etc, in a given job.

**sensation** *n* awareness due to stimulation of the senses; an effect on the senses; a thrill; a state of excited interest; the cause of this.

**sensational** *adj* of or relating to sensation; exciting violent emotions; melodramatic.—**sensationally** *adv*.

**sensationalism** *n* the use of sensational writing, language, etc; the doctrine that all knowledge is obtained from sense impressions.—**sensationalist** *n*.

**sense** *n* one of the five human and animal faculties by which objects are perceived: sight, hearing, smell, taste, and touch; awareness; moral discernment; soundness of judgment; meaning, intelligibility; (*pl*) conscious awareness. • *vt* to perceive; to become aware of; to understand; to detect.

**senseless** *adj* stupid, foolish; meaningless, purposeless; unconscious.—**senselessly** *adv*.—**senselessness** *n*.

**sensibility** *n* the capacity to feel; oversensitiveness; susceptibility; (*pl*) sensitive awareness or feelings.

**sensible** *adj* having good sense or judgment; reasonable; practical; perceptible by the senses, appreciable; conscious (of); sensitive.—**sensibleness** *n*.—**sensibly** *adv*.

**sensitive** *adj* having the power of sensation; feeling readily and acutely, keenly perceptive; (*skin*) delicate, easily irritated; (*wound etc*) still in a painful condition; easily hurt or shocked, tender, touchy; highly responsive to slight changes; sensory; (*photog*) reacting to light.—**sensitively** *adj*.—**sensitiveness** *n*.

**sensitivity** *n* (*pl* **sensitivities**) the condition of being sensitive; awareness of changes or differences; responsiveness to stimuli or feelings, esp to excess.

**sensual** *adj* bodily, relating to the senses rather than the mind; arousing sexual desire.—**sensuality** *n*.—**sensually** *adv*.

**sensuous** *adj* giving pleasure to the mind or body through the senses.—**sensuously** *adv*.—**sensuousness** *n*.

**sent** *see* **send**.

**sentence** *n* a court judgment; the punishment imposed; (*gram*) a series of words conveying a complete thought. • *vt* (*a convicted person*) to pronounce punishment upon; to condemn (to).

**sentiment** *n* a feeling, awareness, or emotion; the thought behind something; an attitude of mind; a tendency to be swayed by feeling rather than reason; an exaggerated emotion.

**sentimental** *adj* of or arising from feelings; foolishly emotional; nostalgic.

**sentry** *n* a soldier on guard to give warning of danger and to prevent unauthorized access.

**separate** *vt* to divide or part; to sever; to set or keep apart; to sort into different sizes. • *vi* to go different ways; to cease to live together as man and wife. • *adj* divided; distinct, individual; not shared. • *n (pl)* articles of clothing designed to be interchangeable with others to form various outfits.—**separately** *adv*.

**separation** *n* the act of separating or the state of being separate; a formal arrangement of husband and wife to live apart.

**September** *n* the ninth month of the year, having 30 days.

**septic** *adj* infected by micro-organisms; causing or caused by putrefaction.

**sequel** *n* something that follows, the succeeding part; a consequence; the continuation of a story begun in an earlier literary work, film, etc.

**sequence** *n* order of succession; a series of succeeding things; a single, uninterrupted episode, as in a film.

**sequin** *n* a shiny round piece of metal or foil sewn on clothes for decoration.

**serenade** *n* music sung or played at night beneath a person's window, esp by a lover. • *vt* to entertain with a serenade.

**serene** *adj* calm; untroubled; tranquil; clear and unclouded; (*with cap*) honoured (used as part of certain royal titles).—**serenely** *adv*.—**serenity** *n*.

**sergeant** *n* a noncommissioned officer ranking above a corporal in the army, air force, and marine corps; a police officer.

**serial** *adj* of or forming a series; published, shown or broadcast by instalments at regular intervals. • *n* a story presented in regular instalments with a connected plot.

**series** *n sing, pl* a succession of items or events; a succession of things connected by some likeness; a sequence, a set; a radio or television serial whose episodes have self-contained plots; a set of books issued by one publisher; (*math*) a progression of numbers or quantities according to a certain law.

**serious** *adj* grave, solemn, not frivolous; meaning what one says, sincere, earnest; requiring close attention or thought; important; critical.—**seriously** *adv*.—**seriousness** *n*.

**sermon** *n* a speech on religion or morals, esp by a clergyman; a long, serious talk of reproof, esp a tedious one.

**serrated** *adj* having an edge notched like the teeth of a saw.

**serum** *n* (*pl* **serums, sera**) the watery part of bodily fluid, esp liquid that separates out from the blood when it coagulates; such fluid taken from the blood of an animal immune to a disease, used as an antitoxin.

**servant** *n* a personal or domestic attendant; one in the service of another.

**serve** *vt* to work for; to do military or naval service (for); to be useful to; to meet the needs (of), to suffice; (*a customer*) to wait upon; (*food, etc*) to hand round; (*a sentence*) to undergo; to be a soldier, sailor, etc; (*of a male animal*) to copulate with; (*law*) to deliver (a summons, etc); (*naut*) to bind (a rope) with thin cord to prevent fraying; (*tennis*) to put (the ball) into play. • *vi* to be employed as a servant; to be enough. • *n* the act of serving in tennis, etc.

**service** *n* the act of serving; the state of being a servant; domestic employment; a department of state employ; the people engaged in it; military employment or duty; work done for others; use, assistance; attendance in a hotel, etc; a facility providing a regular supply of trains, etc; a set of dishes; any religious ceremony; an overhaul of a vehicle; (*tennis*) the act

or manner of seving; (*pl*) friendly help or professional aid; a system of providing a utility, as water, gas, etc.
• *vt* to provide with assistance; to overhaul.

**serviceable** *adj* useful; durable.— **serviceably** *adv*.—**serviceableness** *n*.

**serviceman** *n* a member of the armed services; a person whose work is repairing something.—**servicewoman** *nf*.

**serviette** *n* a small napkin.

**servile** *adj* of or like a slave; subservient; submissive; menial.

**session** *n* the meeting of a court, legislature, etc; a series of such meetings; a period of these; a period of study, classes, etc; a university year; a period of time passed in an activity.

**set** *vb* (*pr p* **setting**, *pt* **set**) vt to put in a specified place, condition, etc; (*trap for animals*) to fix; (*clock etc*) to adjust; (*table*) to arrange for a meal; (*hair*) to fix in a desired style; (*bone*)to put into normal position, etc; to make settled, rigid, or fixed; (*gems*) to mount; to direct; to furnish (an example) for others; to fit (words to music or music to words); (*type*) to arrange for printing. • *vi* to become firm, hard or fixed; to begin to move (out, forth, off, etc); (*sun*) to sink below the horizon; (*with* **in**) to stitch (a sleeve) within a garment; to become established; (*with* **off**) to show up by contrast; to set in motion; to cause to explode; (*with* **on**) to urge (as a dog) to attack or pursue; to go on, advance; (*with* **up**) to erect; to establish, to found; (*with* **upon**) to attack, usu with violence. • *adj* fixed, established; intentional; rigid, firm; obstinate; ready. • *n* a number of persons or things classed or belonging together; a group, a clique; the way in which a thing is set; direction; the scenery for a play, film, etc; assembled equipment for radio or television reception, etc; (*math*) the totality of points, numbers, or objects that satisfy a given condition; (*tennis*) a series of games forming a unit of a match; a rooted cutting of a plant ready for transplanting; a badger's burrow (—*also* **sett**).

**setback** *n* misfortune; a reversal.

**settee** *n* a sofa for two people.

**setting** *n* a background, scene, surroundings, environment; a mounting, as for a gem; the music for a song, etc.

**settle** *vti* to put in order; to pay (an account); to clarify; to decide, to come to an agreement; to make or become quiet or calm; to make or become firm; to establish or become established in a place, business, home, etc; to colonize (a country); to take up residence; to come to rest; (*dregs*) to fall to the bottom; to stabilize; to make or become comfortable (for resting); (*bird*) to alight; to bestow legally for life.

**settlement** *n* the act of settling; a sum settled, esp on a woman at her marriage; an arrangement; a small village; a newly established colony; subsidence (of buildings).

**settler** *n* a person who settles; an early colonist.

**set-up** *n* the plan, makeup, etc, of equipment used in an organization; the details of a situation, plan, etc; (*inf*) a contest, etc, arranged to result in an easy win.

**seven** *adj, n* one more than six. • *n* the symbol for this (7, VII, vii); the seventh in a series or set; something having seven units as members.

**seventeen** *adj, n* one more than sixteen. • *n* the symbol for this (17, XVII, xvii).—**seventeenth** *adj*.

**seventh** *adj, n* next after sixth; one of seven equal parts of a thing. • *n* (*mus*) an interval of seven diatonic degrees; the leading note.

**seventy** *adj, n* seven times ten. • *n* the symbol for this (70, LXX, lxx); (in *pl*) **seventies** (70s) the numbers for 70 to 79; the same numbers in a life or century.—**seventieth** *adj*.

**sever** *vti* to separate, to divide into parts; to break off.—**severance** *n*.

**several** *adj* more than two but not very many; various; separate, distinct; respective. • *pron* (*with pl vb*) a few. • *n* (*with pl vb*) a small number (of).

**severe** *adj* harsh, not lenient; very strict; stern; censorious; exacting, difficult; violent, not slight; (*illness*) critical; (*art*) plain, not florid.—**severely** *adv*.—**severity** *n*.

**sew** *vti* (*pt* **sewed**, *pp* **sewn** *or* **sewed**) to join or stitch together with needle and thread; to make, mend, etc, by sewing; (*with* **up**) to get full control of; (*inf*) to make sure of success in.—**sewing** *n*.

**sewage** *n* waste matter carried away in a sewer.

**sewer**[1] *n* one who sews.

**sewer**[2] *n* an underground pipe or drain for carrying off liquid waste matter, etc; a main drain.

**sewing machine** *n* a machine for sewing or stitching usu driven by an electric motor.

**sex** *n* the characteristics that distinguish male and female organisms on the basis of their reproductive function; either of the two categories (male and female) so distinguished; males or females collectively; the state of being male or female; the attraction between the sexes; (*inf*) sexual intercourse.

**sexual** *adj* of sex or the sexes; having sex.—**sexually** *adj*.

**sexy** *adj* (**sexier, sexiest**) (*inf*) exciting, or intending to excite, sexual desire.

**shabby** *adj* (**shabbier, shabbiest**) (*clothes*) threadbare, worn, or dirty; run-down, dilapidated; (*act, trick*) mean, shameful.—**shabbily** *adv*.—**shabbiness** *n*.

**shack** *n* a small, crudely built house or cabin; a shanty.

**shackle** *n* a metal fastening, usu in pairs, for the wrists or ankles of a prisoner; a staple; anything that restrains freedom; (*pl*) fetters. • *vt* to fasten or join by a shackle; to hamper, to impede.

**shade** *n* relative darkness; dimness; the darker parts of anything; shadow; a shield or screen protecting from bright light; a ghost; a place sheltered from the sun; degree of darkness of a colour, esp when made by the addition of black; a minute difference; a blind; (*pl*) the darkness of approaching night; (*pl: sl*) sunglasses. • *vti* to screen from light; to overshadow; to make dark; to pass by degrees into another colour; to change slightly or by degrees.

**shadow** *n* a patch of shade; darkness, obscurity; the dark parts of a painting, etc; shelter, protection; the dark shape of an object produced on a surface by intercepted light; an inseparable companion; a person (as a detective, etc) who shadows; an unsubstantial thing, a phantom; a mere remnant, a slight trace; gloom, affliction. • *vt* to cast a shadow over; to cloud; to follow and watch, esp in secret. • *adj* having an indistinct pattern or darker section; (*opposition party*) matching a function or position of the party in power.

**shadowy** *adj* full of shadows; dim, indistinct; unsubstantial.

**shady** *adj* (**shadier, shadiest**) giving or

full of shade; sheltered from the sun; (*inf*) of doubtful honesty, disreputable.

**shaft** *n* a straight rod, a pole; a stem, a shank; the main part of a column; an arrow or spear, or its stem; anything hurled like a missile; a ray of light, a stroke of lightning; a revolving rod for transmitting power, an axle; one of the poles between which a horse is harnessed; a hole giving access to a mine; a vertical opening through a building, as for a lift; a critical remark or attack; (*sl*) harsh or unfair treatment.

**shaggy** *adj* (**shaggier, shaggiest**) (*hair, fur, etc*) long and unkempt; rough; untidy.—**shagginess** *n*.

**shake** *vti* (*pt* **shook**, *pp* **shaken**) to move to and fro with quick short motions, to agitate; to tremble or vibrate; to jar or jolt; to brandish; to make or become unsteady; to weaken; to unsettle; to unnerve or become unnerved; to clasp (another's hand) as in greeting; (*with* **down**) to cause to subside by shaking; to obtain makeshift accommodation; (*sl*) to extort money from; (*with* **off**) to get rid of; (*with* **out**) to empty by shaking; to spread (a sail); (*with* **up**) to shake together, to mix; to upset. • *n* the act of shaking or being shaken; a jolt; a shock; a milkshake; (*inf*) a deal; (*pl inf*) a convulsive trembling.

**shake-up** *n* an extensive reorganization.

**shaky** *adj* (**shakier, shakiest**) unsteady; infirm; unreliable.—**shakily** *adv*.—**shakiness** *n*.

**shale** *n* a kind of clay rock like slate but softer.

**shall** *vb aux* (*pt* **should**) used formally to express the future in the 1st person and determination, obligation or necessity in the 2nd and 3rd person. The more common form is **will**.

**shallow** *adj* having little depth; superficial, trivial. • *n* a shallow area in otherwise deep water.—**shallowness** *n*.

**sham** *n* a pretence; a person or thing that is a fraud. • *adj* counterfeit; fake.

**shambles** *npl* a scene of great disorder.

**shame** *n* a painful emotion arising from guilt or impropriety; modesty; disgrace, dishonour; the cause of this; (*sl*) a piece of unfairness. • *vti* to cause to feel shame; to bring disgrace on; to force by shame (into); to humiliate by showing superior qualities.

**shamefaced** *adj* bashful or modest; sheepish; showing shame; ashamed.

**shameful** *adj* disgraceful; outrageous.

**shameless** *adj* immodest; impudent, brazen.

**shampoo** *n* a liquid cleansing agent for washing the hair; the process of washing the hair or a carpet, etc. • *vt* to wash with shampoo.

**shamrock** *n* a three-leaved cloverlike plant, the national emblem of Ireland.

**shandy** *n* beer diluted with a non-alcoholic drink (as lemonade).

**shanty**[1] *n* a crude hut built from corrugated iron or cardboard.

**shanty**[2] *n* a rhythmic working song sung by sailors.

**shape** *n* the external appearance, outline or contour of a thing; a figure; a definite form; an orderly arrangement; a mould or pattern; (*inf*) condition. • *vt* to give shape to; to form; to model, to mould; to determine; (*with* **up**) to develop to a definite or satisfactory form.

**shapeless** *adj* lacking definite form; baggy.—**shapelessness** *n*.

**shapely** *adj* (**shapelier, shapeliest**) well-proportioned.—**shapeliness** *n*.

**share** *n* an allotted portion, a part; one of the parts into which a company's capital stock is divided, entitling the holder to a share of profits. • *vti* to distribute, to apportion (out); to have or experience in common with others; to divide into portions; to contribute or receive a share of; to use jointly.

**shareholder** *n* a holder of shares in a property, esp a company.

**shark** *n* a large voracious marine fish; an extortioner, a swindler; (*sl*) an expert in a given activity.

**sharp** *adj* having a keen edge or fine point; pointed, not rounded; clear-cut; distinct; intense, piercing; cutting, severe; keen, biting; clever, artful; alert, mentally acute; (*mus*) raised a semitone in pitch; out of tune by being too high; (*sl*) smartly dressed. • *adv* punctually; quickly; (*mus*) above the right pitch. • *n* (*mus*) a note that is a semitone higher than the note denoted by the same letter; the symbol for this (≠).—**sharply** *adv.*—**sharpness** *n*.

**sharpen** *vti* to make or become sharp or sharper.

**sharpener** *n* something that sharpens.

**shatter** *vti* to reduce to fragments suddenly; to smash; to damage or be damaged severely.

**shave** *vti* to remove facial or body hair with a razor; to cut away thin slices, to pare; to miss narrowly, to graze. • *n* the act or process of shaving; a narrow escape or miss; a paring.

**shaven** *adj* shaved.

**shaver** *n* one who shaves; an instrument for shaving, esp an electrical one.

**shaving** *n* the act of using a razor or scraping; a thin slice of wood, metal, etc, shaved off.

**shawl** *n* a large square or oblong cloth worn as a covering for the head or shoulders or as a wrapping for a baby.

**she** *pron* (*obj* her, *poss* her, hers) the female person or thing named before or in question. • *n* a female person or animal.

**sheaf** *n* (*pl* sheaves) a bundle of reaped corn bound together; a collection of papers, etc, tied in a bundle.

**shear** *vti* (*pp* sheared *or* shorn) to clip or cut (through); to remove (a sheep's fleece) by clipping; to divest; (*metal*) to break off because of a heavy force or twist. • *n* a stress acting sideways on a rivet and causing a break, etc; a machine for cutting metal; (*pl*) large scissors; (*pl*) a tool for cutting hedges, etc.

**sheath** *n* a close-fitting cover, esp for a blade; a condom; a closefitting dress usu worn without a belt.

**shed**[1] *n* a hut for storing garden tools; a large roofed shelter often with one or more sides open; a warehouse.

**shed**[2] *vt* (*pr p* shedding, *pt* shed) (*tears*) to let fall; (*skin, etc*) to lose or cast off; to allow or cause to flow; to diffuse, radiate. • *n* a parting in the hair.

**sheep** *n* (*pl* sheep) a cud-chewing four-footed animal with a fleece and edible flesh called mutton; a bashful, submissive person.

**sheepdog** *n* a dog trained to tend, drive, or guard sheep.

**sheepish** *adj* bashful, embarrassed.—**sheepishly** *adv.*—**sheepishness** *n*.

**sheepskin** *n* the skin of a sheep, esp with the fleece; a rug, parchment, or leather made from it; a garment made of or lined with sheepskin.

**sheer**[1] *adj* pure, unmixed; downright, utter; perpendicular, extremely steep; (*fabric*) delicately fine, transparent. • *adv* outright; perpendicularly, steeply.

**sheer**[2] *vti* to deviate or cause to deviate from a course; to swerve. • *n* the act of sheering; the upward curve of a deck towards bow or stern; a change in a ship's course.

**sheet** *n* a broad thin piece of any material, as glass, plywood, metal, etc; a large rectangular piece of cloth used as inner bed clothes; a single piece of paper; (*inf*) a newspaper; a broad, flat expanse; a suspended or moving expanse (as of fire or rain).

**sheet lightning** *n* lightning that has the appearance of a broad sheet due to reflection and diffusion by the clouds and sky.

**sheikh** *n* an Arab chief.

**shelf** *n* (*pl* **shelves**) a board fixed horizontally on a wall or in a cupboard for holding articles; a ledge on a cliff face; a reef, a shoal.

**shell** *n* a hard outside covering of a nut, egg, shellfish, etc; an explosive projectile; an external framework; a light racing boat; outward show; a cartridge. • *vt* to remove the shell from; to bombard (with shells); (*with* out) (*inf*) to pay out (money).

**shellfish** *n* an aquatic animal with a shell, esp an edible one.

**shelter** *n* a structure that protects, esp against weather; a place giving protection, a refuge; protection. • *vti* to give shelter to, to shield, to cover; to take shelter.

**shelve** *vti* to place on a shelf; to defer consideration, to put aside; to slope gently, to incline.

**shelving** *n* material for making shelves; shelves collectively.

**shepherd** *n* a person who looks after sheep; a pastor. • *vt* to look after, as a shepherd; to manouevre or marshal in a particular direction.—**shepherdess** *nf*.

**shepherd's pie** *n* a dish of minced meat covered with a mashed potato crust.

**sheriff** *n* in US, the chief law enforcement officer of a county; in Scotland,

a judge in an intermediate law court; in England and Wales, the chief officer of the Crown, a ceremonial post.

**sherry** *n* a fortified wine originally made in Spain.

**Shetland pony** *n* a breed of small sturdy pony with a shaggy mane.

**shield** *n* a broad piece of armour carried for defence, usu on the left arm; a protective covering or guard; a thing or person that protects; a trophy in the shape of a shield. • *vti* to defend; to protect; to screen.

**shift** *vti* (**shiftier, shiftiest**) to change position (of); to contrive, to manage; to remove, to transfer; to replace by another or others; (*gears*) to change the arrangement of. • *n* a change in position; an expedient; a group of people working in relay with others; the time worked by them; a change or transfer; a straight dress.

**shifty** *adj* artful, tricky; evasive.—**shiftiness** *n*.

**shilling** *n* a former unit of currency of the UK and other countries, worth one twentieth of a pound.

**shillyshally** *vi* to vacillate, to hesitate. • *n* the inability to make up one's mind.

**shimmer** *vi* to glisten softly, to glimmer.—*also n*.

**shin** *n* the front part of the leg from the knee to the ankle; the shank. • *vi* (*with* up) to climb (a pole, etc) by gripping with legs and hands.

**shine** *vti* (*pt* **shone**) to emit light; to be bright, to glow; to be brilliant or conspicuous; to direct the light of; to cause to gleam by polishing. • *n* a lustre, a gloss; (*sl*) a liking.

**shingle**[1] *n* a thin wedge-shaped roof tile; a small signboard.

**shingle**[2] *n* waterworn pebbles as on a beach; an area covered with these.—**shingly** *adj*.

**shingles** *npl* a virus disease marked by a painful rash of red spots.

**shiny** *adj* (**shinier, shiniest**) glossy, polished; worn smooth.

**ship** *n* a large vessel navigating deep water; its officers and crew; a spacecraft. • *vti* (*pt* **shipped**) to transport by any carrier; to take in (water) over the side; to lay (oars) inside a boat; to go on board; to go or travel by ship.

**shipbuilder** *n* a person or company that designs or constructs ships. **shipbuilding** *n*.

**shipment** *n* goods shipped; a consignment.

**shipping** *n* the business of transporting goods; ships collectively.

**shipshape** *adj* in good order, tidy.

**shipwreck** *n* the loss of a vessel at sea; the remains of a wrecked ship; ruin, destruction. • *vti* to destroy by or suffer shipwreck; to ruin.

**shipyard** *n* a yard or shed where ships are built or repaired.

**shire** *n* in the UK, a county; a strong draft horse.

**shirk** *vti* to neglect or avoid work; to refuse to face (duty, danger, etc).—**shirker** *n*.

**shirt** *n* a sleeved garment of cotton, etc, for the upper body, typically having a fitted collar and cuffs and front buttons; (*inf*) one's money or resources.

**shiver**[1] *n* a small fragment, a splinter.

**shiver**[2] *vi* to shake or tremble, as with cold or fear, to shudder.—*also n.*—**shivery** *adj*.

**shoal**[1] *n* a large number of fish swimming together; a large crowd. • *vi* to form shoals.

**shoal**[2] *n* a submerged sandbank, esp one that shows at low tide; a shallow place; a hidden danger. • *vti* to come to a less deep part; to become shallower.

**shock**[1] *n* a shaggy mass of hair.

**shock**[2] *n* a violent jolt or impact; a sudden disturbance to the emotions; the event or experience causing this; the nerve sensation caused by an electrical charge through the body; a disorder of the blood circulation, produced by displacement of body fluids (due to injury); (*sl*) a paralytic stroke. • *vt* to outrage, horrify. • *vi* to experience extreme horror, outrage, etc.

**shock absorber** *n* a device, as on the springs of a car, that absorbs the force of bumps and jars.

**shocking** *adj* revolting; scandalous, improper; very bad.—**shockingly** *adv*.

**shod** *see* **shoe**.

**shoddy** *adj* (**shodier, shoddiest**) made of inferior material; cheap and nasty, trashy.—**shoddily** *adv*.—**shoddiness** *n*.

**shoe** *n* an outer covering for the foot not enclosing the ankle; a thing like a shoe, a partial casing; a horseshoe; a drag for a wheel; a device to guide movement, provide contact, or protect against wear or slipping; a dealing box that holds several decks of cards. • *vt* (*pr p* **shoeing**, *pt* **shod**) to provide with shoes; to cover for strength or protection.

**shoehorn** *n* a curved piece of plastic, metal, or horn used for easing the heel into a shoe.

**shoelace** *n* a cord that passes through eyelets in a shoe and is tied to keep the shoe on the foot.

**shoetree** *n* a block of wood, plastic or metal for preserving the shape of a shoe.

**shone** *see* **shine**.

**shook** *see* **shake**.

**shoot** *vb* (*pt* **shot**) *vt* to discharge or fire (a gun etc); to hit or kill with a bullet, etc; (*rapids*) to be carried swiftly over; to propel quickly; to thrust out; (*bolt*) to slide home; to variegate (with another colour, etc); (*a film scene*) to photograph; (*sport*) to kick or drive (a ball, etc) at goal; (*with* **down**) to disprove (an argument); (*with* **up**) to grow rapidly, to rise abruptly. • *vi* to move swiftly, to dart; to emit; to put forth buds, to sprout; to attack or kill indiscriminately; (*sl*) to inject a narcotic into a vein. • *n* a contest, a shooting trip, etc; a new growth or sprout.

**shooting** *n* the act of firing a gun or letting off an arrow.

**shooting star** *n* a meteor.

**shop** *n* a building were retail goods are sold or services provided; a factory; a workshop; the details and technicalities of one's own work, and talk about these. • *vti* (*pt* **shopped**) to visit shops to examine or buy; (*sl*) to inform on (a person) to the police; (*with* **around**) to hunt for the best buy.

**shop floor** *n* the part of a factory where goods are manufactured; the work force employed there, usu unionized.

**shopkeeper** *n* a person who owns or runs a shop.—**shopkeeping** *n*.

**shoplifting** *n* stealing from a shop during shopping hours.—**shoplifter** *n*.

**shopper** *n* a person who shops; a bag for carrying shopping.

**shopping** *n* the act of shopping; the goods bought.—*also adj*.

**shopping centre** *n* a complex of shops, restaurants, and service establishments with a common parking area.

**shopsoiled** *adj* faded, etc, from being on display in a shop.

**shop steward** *n* a union member elected to negotiate with management on behalf of his colleagues.

**shore**[1] *n* land beside the sea or a large body of water; beach.

**shore**[2] *n* a prop or beam used for support. • *vt* to prop (up), to support with a shore.

**shorn** *see* **shear**.

**short** *adj* not measuring much; not long or tall; not great in range or scope; brief; concise; not retentive; curt; abrupt; less than the correct amount; below standard; deficient; lacking; (*pastry*) crisp or flaky; (*vowel*) not prolonged, unstressed; (*drink*) undiluted, neat. • *n* something short; (*pl*) trousers not covering the knee; (*pl*) an undergarment like these; a short circuit. • *adv* abruptly; concisely; without reaching the end. • *vti* to give less than what is needed; to short-change; to short-circuit.—**shortness** *n*.

**shortage** *n* a deficiency.

**shortbread** *n* a rich, crumbly cake or biscuit made with much shortening.

**short-circuit** *n* the deviation of an electric current by a path of small resistance; an interrupted electric current. • *vti* to establish a short-circuit in; to cut off electric current; to provide with a short cut.

**shortcoming** *n* a defect or inadequacy.

**short cut** *n* a shorter route; any way of saving time, effort, etc.

**shorten** *vt* to make or become short or shorter; to reduce the amount of (sail) spread; to make (pastry, etc) crisp and flaky by adding fat.

**shorthand** *n* a method of rapid writing using signs or contractions.—*also adj*.

**short-lived** *adj* not lasting or living for long.

**shortly** *adv* soon, in a short time; briefly; rudely.

**short-sighted** *adj* not able to see well at a distance; lacking foresight.—**short-sightedness** *n*.

**shortwave** *n* a radio wave 60 metres or less in length.

**shot**[1] *see* **shoot**.

**shot**[2] *n* the act of shooting; range, scope; an attempt; a solid projectile for a gun; projectiles collectively; small lead pellets for a shotgun; a marksman; a photograph or a continuous film sequence; a hypodermic injection, as of vaccine; a drink of alcohol.

**shotgun** *n* a smooth-bore gun for firing small shot at close range.

**should** *vb aux* used to express obligation, duty, expectation or probability, or a future condition.—*also-pt of* **shall**.

**shoulder** *n* the joint connecting the arm with the trunk; a part like a shoulder; (*pl*) the upper part of the back; (*pl*) the capacity to bear a task or blame; a projecting part; the strip of land bordering a road. • *vti* to place on the shoulder to carry; to assume responsibility; to push with the shoulder, to jostle.

**shoulder blade** *n* the large flat triangular bone on either side of the back part of the human shoulder.

**shout** *n* a loud call; a yell. • *vti* to call loudly, to yell.

**shove** *vti* to drive forward; to push; to jostle. • *n* a forceful push.

**shovel** *n* an broad tool like a scoop with a long handle for moving loose material. • *vt* (*pt* **shovelled**) to move or lift with a shovel.

**show** *vti* (*pt* **showed**, *pp* **shown**) to present to view, to exhibit; to demonstrate, to make clear; to prove; to manifest, to disclose; to direct, to guide; to appear, to be visible; to finish third in a horse race; (*inf*) to arrive; (*with* **off**) to display to advantage; to try to attract admiration; to behave pretentiously; (*with* **up**) to put in an appearance, to arrive; to expose to ridicule. • *n* a display, an exhibition; an entertainment; a theatrical performance; a radio or television programme; third place at the finish (as a horse race).

**show business** *n* the entertainment industry.—*also* **show biz**.

**showdown** *n* (*inf*) a final conflict; a disclosure of cards at poker.

**shower** *n* a brief period of rain, hail, or snow; a similar fall, as of tears, meteors, arrows, etc; a great number; a method of cleansing in which the body is sprayed with water from above; a wash in this; a party for the presentation of gifts, esp to a bride. • *vt* to pour copiously; to sprinkle; to bestow (with gifts). • *vi* to cleanse in a shower.

**showjumping** *n* the competitive riding of horses to demonstrate their skill in jumping.

**showroom** *n* a room where goods for sale are displayed.

**shrank** *see* **shrink**.

**shrapnel** *n* an artillery shell filled with small pieces of metal that scatter on impact.

**shred** *n* a strip cut or torn off; a fragment, a scrap. • *vt* (*pt* **shredded**) to cut or tear into small pieces.

**shrewd** *adj* astute, having common sense; keen, penetrating.—**shrewdly** *adv*.—**shrewdness** *n*.

**shriek** *n* a loud, shrill cry, a scream. • *vti* to screech, to scream.

**shrill** *adj* high-pitched and piercing in sound; strident.

**shrimp** *n* a small edible shellfish with a long tail.

**shrine** *n* a container for sacred relics; a saint's tomb; a place of worship; a hallowed place.

**shrink** *vti* (*pt* **shrank**, *pp* **shrunk**) to become smaller, to contract as from cold, wetting, etc; to recoil (from), to flinch; to cause (cloth, etc) to contract by soaking. • *n* (*sl*) a psychiatrist.

**shrinkage** *n* contraction; diminution.

**shrivel** *vti* (*pt* **shrivelled**) to dry up or wither and become wrinkled; to curl up with heat, etc.

**shroud** *n* a burial cloth; anything that envelops or conceals; (*naut*) a supporting rope for a mast. • *vt* to wrap in a shroud; to envelop or conceal.

**Shrove Tuesday** *n* the last day before Lent.

**shrub** *n* a woody plant smaller than a tree with several stems rising from the same root; a bush.—**shrubby** *adj*.

**shrubbery** *n* an area of land planted with shrubs.

**shrug** *vti* (*pt* **shrugged**) to draw up and contract (the shoulders) as a sign of doubt, indifference, etc; (*with* **off**) to brush aside; to shake off; (*a garment*) to remove by wriggling out. • *n* the act of shrugging.

**shrunk** *see* **shrink**.

**shrunken** *adj* shrivelled, pinched; reduced.

**shudder** *vi* to tremble violently, to shiver; to feel strong repugnance. • *n* a convulsive shiver of the body; a vibration.

**shuffle** *vt* to scrape (the feet) along the ground; to walk with dragging steps; (*playing cards*) to change the order of, to mix; to intermingle, to mix up; (*with* **off**) to get rid of.—*also n*.

**shun** *vt* (*pt* **shunned**) to avoid scrupulously; to keep away from.

**shunt** *vti* to move to a different place; to put aside, to shelve; (*trains*) to switch from one track to another; (*sl*) to collide.—*also n*.

**shut** *vti* (*pr p* **shutting**, *pt* **shut**) to close; to lock, to fasten; to close up parts of, to fold together; to bar; (*with* **down**) to (cause to) stop working or operating; (*with* **in**) to confine; to enclose; to block the view from; (*with* **off**) to check the flow of; to debar; (*with* **out**) to exclude; (*with* **up**) to confine; (*inf*) to stop talking; (*inf*) to silence.

**shutdown** *n* a stoppage of work or activity, as in a factory.

**shutter** *n* a movable cover for a window; a flap device for regulating the exposure of light to a camera lens.

**shuttle** *n* a device in a loom for holding the weft thread and carrying it between the warp threads; a bus, aircraft, etc, making back-and-forth trips over a short route. • *vti* to move back and forth rapidly.

**shuttlecock** *n* a cork stuck with feathers, or a plastic imitation, hit with a racket in badminton.

**shy** *adj* (**shyer, shyest** *or* **shier, shiest**) very self-conscious, timid; bashful; wary, suspicious (of); (*sl*) lacking. • *vi* to move suddenly, as when startled; to be or become cautious, etc. • *n* a sudden movement.—**shyly** *adv*.—**shyness** *n*.

**Siamese cat** *n* a breed of domestic shorthaired cat with a fawn or grey coat, darker ears, paws, tail and face, and blue eyes.

**sick** *adj* unhealthy, ill; having nausea, vomiting; thoroughly tired (of); disgusted by or suffering from an excess; (*inf*) of humour, sadistic, gruesome.—**sickness** *n*.

**sick bay** *n* an area in a ship used as a hospital or dispen- sary; a room used for the treatment of the sick.

**sicken** *vti* to make or become sick or nauseated; to show signs of illness; to nauseate.

**sickening** *adj* disgusting.

**sickle** *n* a tool with a crescent-shaped blade for cutting tall grasses; anything shaped like this.

**sick leave** *n* absence from work due to illness.

**sickly** *adj* (**sicklier, sickliest**) inclined to be ill; unhealthy; causing nausea; mawkish; pale, feeble.—**sickliness** *n*.

**side** *n* a line or surface bounding anything; the left or right part of the body; the top or underneath surface; the slope of a hill; an aspect, a direction; a party or faction; a cause; a team; a line of descent; (*sl*) conceit. • *adj* towards or at the side, lateral; incidental. • *vi* to associate with a particular faction.

**sideboard** *n* a long table or cabinet for holding cutlery, crockery, etc; (*pl*) two strips of hair growing down a man's cheeks (—also **sideburns**).

**side effect** *n* a secondary and usu adverse effect, as of a drug or medical treatment.

**sidelight** *n* light coming from the side; a light on the side of a car, etc; incidental information.

**sideline** *n* a line marking the side limit of a playing area; a minor branch of business; a subsidiary interest.

**sidelong** *adj* oblique, not direct. • *adv* obliquely.

**side-saddle** *n* a saddle that enables a rider to sit with both feet on the same side of a horse. • *adv* as if sitting on a side-saddle.

**sideshow** *n* a minor attraction at a fair, etc; a subsidiary event.

**sidetrack** *vt* to prevent action by diversionary tactics; to shunt aside, to shelve. • *n* a railway siding.

**sidewalk** *n* a path, usu paved, at the side of a street, pavement.

**sideways** *adj*, *adv* towards or from one side; facing to the side.

**siding** *n* a short line beside a main railway track for use in shunting; a covering as of boards for the outside of a frame building.

**sidle** *vi* to move sideways, esp to edge along.

**siege** *n* the surrounding of a fortified place to cut off supplies and compel its surrender; the act of besieging; a continued attempt to gain something.

**sieve** *n* a utensil with a meshed wire bottom for sifting and straining; a person who cannot keep secrets. • *vt* to put through a sieve, to sift.

**sift** *vti* to separate coarser parts from finer with a sieve; to sort out; to examine critically; to pass as through a sieve.

**sigh** *vti* to draw deep audible breath as a sign of weariness, relief, etc; to make a sound like this; to pine or lament (for); to utter with a sigh.— *also n*.

**sight** *n* the act or faculty of seeing; what is seen or is worth seeing, a spectacle; a view or glimpse; range of vision; a device on a gun etc to guide the eye in aiming it; aim taken with this; (*inf*) anything that looks unpleasant, odd, etc. • *vti* to catch sight of; to aim through a sight.

**sightless** *adj* without sight, blind.— **sightlessly** *adv*.

**sightseeing** *n* the viewing or visitng of places of interest.—**sightseer** *n*.

**sign** *n* a mark or symbol; a gesture; an indication, token, trace, or symptom (of); an omen; (*math*) a conventional mark used to indicate an operation to be performed; a board or placard with publicly displayed information. • *vi* to append one's signature; to ratify thus • *vt* to engage by written contract; to write one's name on; to make or indicate by a sign; to signal; to communicate by sign language; (*with* **away**) to relinquish by signing a deed, etc; (*with* **on**) to accept employment; to register; (*with* **off**) to complete a broadcast.

**signal** *n* a sign, device or gesture to intimate a warning or to give information, esp at a distance; a message so conveyed; a semaphore system used by railways; in radio, etc, the electrical impulses transmitted or received; a sign or event that initiates action. • *vti* (*pt* **signalled**) to make a signal or signals (to); to communicate by signals. • *adj* striking, notable.

**signature** *n* a person's name written by himself or herself; the act of signing one's own name; a characteristic mark; (*mus*) the flats and sharps after the clef showing the key; (*print*) a mark on the first pages of each sheet of a book as a guide to the binder; such a sheet when folded.

**signature tune** *n* a tune associated with a performer or a TV, radio programme, etc.

**signet ring** *n* a ring with a seal set in it.

**significant** *adj* full of meaning, esp a special or hidden one; momentous, important; highly expressive; indicative (of).—**significance** *n.*—**significantly** *adv.*

**silence** *n* absence of sound; the time this lasts; refusal to speak or make a sound; secrecy. • *vt* to cause to be silent. • *interj* be silent!

**silencer** *n* a device for reducing the noise of a vehicle exhaust or gun.

**silent** *adj* not speaking; taciturn; noiseless; still.—**silently** *adv.*

**silhouette** *n* the outline of a shape against light or a lighter background; a solid outline drawing, usu in solid black on white, esp of a profile. • *vt* to show up in outline; to depict in silhouette.

**silk** *n* a fibre produced by silkworms; lustrous textile cloth, thread or a garment made of silk; (*pl*) silk garments; (*pl*) the colours of a racing stable, worn by a jockey, etc. • *adj* of, relating to or made of silk.

**silky** *adj* (**silkier, silkiest**) soft and smooth like silk; glossy; suave.—**silkiness** *n.*

**silly** *adj* (**sillier, silliest**) foolish, stupid; frivolous; lacking in sense or judgment; being stunned or dazed. • *n* a silly person.

**silt** *n* a fine-grained sandy sediment carried or deposited by water. • *vti* to fill or choke up with silt.

**silver** *n* a ductile, malleable, greyish-white metallic element used in jewellery, cutlery, tableware, coins, etc; a lustrous, greyish white. • *adj* made of or plated with silver; silvery; (*hair*) grey; marking the 25th in a series • *vt* to coat with silver or a substance resembling silver; to make or become silvery or grey.

**silver paper** *n* a metallic paper coated or laminated to resemble silver, tinfoil.

**silver plate** *n* a plating of silver; domestic utensils made of silver or of silver-plated metal.

**silversmith** *n* a worker in silver.

**similar** *adj* having a resemblance to, like; nearly corresponding; (*geom*) corresponding exactly in shape if not size.—**similarity** *n.*—**similarly** *adv.*

**simile** *n* a figure of speech likening one thing to another by the use of like, as, etc.

**simmer** *vti* to boil gently; to be or keep on the point of boiling; to be in a state of suppressed rage or laughter; (*with* down) to abate. • *n* the state of simmering.

**simple** *adj* single, uncompounded; plain, not elaborate; clear, not complicated; easy to do, understand, or solve; artless, not sophisticated; weak in intellect; unsuspecting, credulous; sheer, mere.—**simpleness** *n.*

**simplicity** *n* the quality or state of being simple; absence of complications; easiness; lack of ornament, plainness, restraint; artlessness; directness; guilelessness, openness, naivety.

**simplify** *vt* to make simple or easy to understand.

**simply** *adv* in a simple way; plainly; merely; absolutely.

**simulate** *vt* to pretend to have or feel, to feign; (*conditions*) to reproduce in order to conduct an experiment; to imitate.—**simulation** *n*.

**simulator** *n* a device that simulates specific conditions in order to test actions or reactions.

**simultaneous** *adj* done or occurring at the same time.—**simultaneously** *adv*.

**sin** *n* an offence against a religious or moral principle; transgression of the law of God; a wicked act, an offence; a misdeed, a fault. • *vi* (*pt* **sinned**) to commit a sin; to offend (against).

**since** *adv* from then until now; subsequently; ago. • *prep* during, or continuously from (then) until now; after. • *conj* from the time that; because, seeing that.

**sincere** *adj* genuine, real, not pretended; honest, straightforward.— **sincerely** *adv*.

**sincerity** *n* the quality or state of being sincere; genuineness, honesty, seriousness.

**sinew** *n* a cord of fibrous tissue, a tendon; (*usu pl*) the chief supporting force, a mainstay; (*pl*) muscles, brawn.

**sinful** *adj* guilty of sin, wicked.

**sing** *vti* (*pt* **sang**, *pp* **sung**) to utter (words) with musical modulations; (*a song*) to perform; to hum, to ring; to write poetry (about), to praise.— **singer** *n*.—**singing** *n*.

**singe** *vt* (*pr p* **singeing**, *pt* **singed**) to burn slightly; to scorch, esp to remove feathers, etc.—*also n*.

**singing** *n* the art or an act of singing.

**single** *adj* one only, not double; individual; composed of one part; alone, sole; separate; unmarried; for one; with one contestant on each side; simple; whole, unbroken; (*tennis*) played between two only; (*ticket*) for the outward journey only. • *n* a single ticket; a game between two players; a hit scoring one; a record with one tune on each side. • *vt* (*with* out) to pick out, to select.

**single file** *n* a single column of persons or things, one behind the other.

**single-handed** *adj*, *adv* without assistance, unaided.

**single-minded** *adj* having only one aim in mind.

**singlet** *n* an undervest.

**singly** *adv* alone; one by one.

**singular** *adj* remarkable; exceptional; unusual; eccentric, odd; (*gram*) referring to only one person or thing. • *n* (*gram*) the singular number or form of a word.

**sinister** *adj* inauspicious; ominous; ill-omened; evil-looking; malignant; wicked; left; (*her*) on the left side of the shield.

**sink** *vti* (*pt* **sank**, *pp* **sunk** *or* **sunken**) to go under the surface or to the bottom (of a liquid); to submerge in water; to go down slowly; (*wind*) to subside; to pass to a lower state; to droop, to decline; to grow weaker; to become hollow; to lower, to degrade; to cause to sink; to make by digging out; to invest; (*with* in) to penetrate; to thrust into; (*inf*) to be understood in full. • *n* a basin with an outflow pipe, usu in a kitchen; a cesspool; an area of sunken land.—**sinking** *n*.

**sinner** *n* a person who sins.

**sinuous** *adj* curving; winding; tortuous.—**sinuously** *adv*.

**sinus** *n* (*pl* **sinuses**) an air cavity in the skull that opens in the nasal cavities.

**sip** *vti* (*pt* **sipped**) to drink in small mouthfuls. • *n* the act of sipping; the quantity sipped.

**siphon** *n* a bent tube for drawing off liquids from a higher to a lower level by atmospheric pressure; a bottle with an internal tube and tap at the top for aerated water. • *vti* to draw off, or be drawn off, with a siphon.— *also* **syphon**.

**sir** *n* a title of respect used to address a man in speech or correspondence; (*with cap*) a title preceding the first name of a knight or baronet. • *vt* to address as "sir".

**siren** *n* a device producing a loud wailing sound as a warning signal; a fabled sea nymph who lured sailors to destruction with a sweet song; a seductive or alluring woman.

**sirloin** *n* the upper part of a loin of beef.

**sirocco** *n* a hot, oppressive wind that blows across southern Europe from North Africa.

**sister** *n* a female sibling, a daughter of the same parents; a female member or associate of the same race, creed, trade union, etc; a member of a religious sisterhood; one of the same kind, model, etc; a senior nurse. • *adj* (*ship, etc*) belonging to the same type.

**sister-in-law** *n* the sister of a husband or wife; the wife of a brother.

**sisterly** *adj* like a sister, kind, affectionate.

**sit** *vti* (*pr p* **sitting**, *pt* **sat**) to rest oneself on the buttocks, as on a chair; (*bird*) to perch; (*hen*) to cover eggs for hatching; (*legislator, etc*) to occupy a seat; (*court*) to be in session; to pose, as for a portrait; to ride (a horse); to press or weigh (upon); to be located; to rest or lie; to take an examination; to take care of a child, pet, etc, while the parents or owners are away; to cause to sit; to provide seats or seating room for; (*with* **down**) to take a seat; (*with* **for**) to represent in parliament; (*with* **in**) to attend a discussion or a musical session; to participate in a sit-in; (*with* **on**) to hold a meeting to discuss; to delay action on something; (*inf*) to suppress; to rebuke; (*with* **out**) to sit through the whole; to abstain from dancing; (*with* **up**) to straighten the back while sitting; not to go to bed; (*inf*) to be astonished.

**site** *n* a space occupied or to be occupied by a building; a situation; the place or scene of something. • *vt* to locate, to place.

**sit-in** *n* a strike in which the strikers refuse to leave the premises; civil disobedience in which demonstrators occupy a public place and refuse to leave voluntarily.

**sitting** *n* the state of being seated; a period of being seated, as for a meal, a portrait; a session, as of a court; a clutch of eggs. • *adj* that is sitting; being in a judicial or legislative seat; used in or for sitting; performed while sitting.

**sitting room** *n* a room other than a bedroom or kitchen; a parlour.

**situated** *adj* having a site, located; placed; provided with money, etc.

**situation** *n* a place, a position; a state of affairs, circumstances; a job or post.

**sit-up** *n* an exercise of sitting up from a prone position without using hands or legs.

**six** *adj, n* one more than five. • *n* the symbol for this (6, VI, vi); the sixth in a series or set; something having six units as members.

**sixteen** *adj, n* one more than fifteen. • *n* the symbol for this (16, XVI, xvi).—**sixteenth** *adj, n.*

**sixth** *n* one of six equal parts of a thing; (*mus*) an interval of six diatonic degrees; the sixth tone of a diatonic scale.—*also* *adv.* • *adj* next after fifth.—**sixthly** *adv.*

**sixty** *n* six times ten. • *n* the symbol for this (60, LX, lx); (*in pl*) sixties (60s), the numbers for 60 to 69; the same numbers in a life or century.— **sixtieth** *adj, adv.*

**sizable, sizeable** *adj* of some size; large.—**sizably, sizeably** *adv*.—**sizableness, sizeableness** *n*.

**size**[1] *n* magnitude; the dimensions or proportions of something; a graduated measurement, as of clothing or shoes. • *vt* to sort according to size; to measure; (*with* **up**) (*inf*) to make an estimate or judgment of; to meet requirements.

**size**[2] *n* a thin pasty substance used to glaze paper, stiffen cloth, etc. • *vt* to treat with size.

**sizzle** *vti* to make a hissing spluttering noise, as of frying; to be extremely hot; to be very angry; to scorch, sear or fry with a sizzling sound. • *n* a hissing sound.

**skate**[1] *n* a steel blade attached to a boot for gliding on ice; a boot with such a runner; a roller skate. • *vi* to move on skates.—**skater** *n*.

**skate**[2] *n* an edible fish of the ray family with a broad, flat body and short, spineless tail.

**skateboard** *n* a short, oblong board with two wheels at each end for standing on and riding.—*also vi.*

**skeleton** *n* the bony framework of the body of a human, an animal or plant; the bones separated from flesh and preserved in their natural position; a supporting structure, a framework; an outline, an abstract; a very thin person; something shameful kept secret. • *adj* (*staff, crew, etc*) reduced to the lowest possible level.—**skeletal** *adj*.

**sketch** *n* a rough drawing, quickly made; a preliminary draft; a short literary piece or essay; a short humorous item for a revue, etc; a brief outline. • *vti* to make a sketch (of); to plan roughly.

**sketchy** *adj* (**sketchier, sketchiest**) incomplete; vague; inadequate.—**sketchily** *adv.*—**sketchiness** *n*.

**skewer** *n* a long wooden or metal pin on which pieces of meat and vegetables are cooked. • *vt* to pierce and fasten on a skewer; to transfix.

**ski** *n* (*pl* **skis**) a long narrow runner of wood, metal or plastic that is fastened to a boot for moving across snow; a water-ski. • *vi* (*pr p* **skiing**, *pt* **skied**) to travel on skis.—**skier** *n*.

**skid** *vti* (*pt* **skidded**) to slide without rotating; to slip sideways; (*vehicle*) to slide sideways out of control; to cause (a vehicle) to skid. • *n* the act of skidding; a drag to reduce speed; a ship's fender; a movable support for a heavy object; a runner on an aircraft's landing gear.

**skilful, skillful** (*U.S*) *adj* having skill; proficient, adroit.—**skilfully** *adv.*—**skilfulness** *n*.

**skill** *n* proficiency; expertness, dexterity; a developed aptitude or ability; a type of work or craft requiring specialist training.

**skilled** *adj* fully trained, expert.

**skim** *vti* (*pt* **skimmed**) to remove (cream, scum) from the surface of; to glide lightly over, to brush the surface of; to read superficially.

**skimp** *vti* to give scant measure (of), to stint; to be sparing or frugal (with).

**skimpy** *adj* (**skimpier, skimpiest**) small in size; inadequate, scant, meagre.—**skimpily** *adv.*—**skimpiness** *n*.

**skin** *n* the tissue forming the outer covering of the body; a hide; the rind of a fruit; an outer layer or casing; a film on the surface of a liquid; a vessel for water, etc, made of hide. • *vti* (*pt* **skinned**) to remove the skin from, to peel; to injure by scraping (the knee, etc); to cover or become covered with skin; (*inf*) to swindle.

**skin-deep** *adj* superficial.

**skin diving** *n* the sport of swimming underwater with scuba equipment.—**skin-diver** *n*.

**skinny** *adj* (**skinnier, skinniest**) very thin; emaciated.—**skinniness** *n*.

**skip**[1] *vti* (*pt* **skipped**) to leap or hop lightly over; to keep jumping over a rope as it is swung under one; to make omissions, to pass over, esp in reading; (*inf*) to leave (town) hurriedly, to make off; (*inf*) to miss deliberately. • *n* a skipping movement; a light jump.

**skip**[2] *n* a large metal container for holding building debris; a cage or bucket for hoisting workers or materials in a mine, quarry, etc.

**skipper** *n* the captain of a boat, aircraft, or team. • *vt* to act as skipper; to captain.

**skipping rope** *n* a light rope, usu with a handle at each end, that is swung over the head and under the feet while jumping.

**skirmish** *n* a minor fight in a war; a conflict or clash. • *vi* to take part in a skirmish.

**skirt** *n* a woman's garment that hangs from the waist; the lower part of a dress or coat; an outer edge, a border; (*sl*) a woman. • *vti* to border; to move along the edge (of); to evade.

**skirting board** *n* a narrow panel of wood at the foot of an interior wall.

**skit** *n* a short humorous sketch, as in the theatre.

**ski tow** *n* a motor-driven device that pulls skiers uphill.

**skittles** *n* a game in which a wooden or plastic bottle-shaped pin is knocked down by a ball.

**skulk** *vi* to move in a stealthy manner; to lurk.

**skull** *n* the bony casing enclosing the brain; the cranium.

**skunk** *n* a small black-and-white mammal that emits a foul-smelling liquid when frightened; its fur; (*sl*) an obnoxious or mean person.

**sky** *n* the apparent vault over the earth; heaven; the upper atmosphere; weather, climate.

**skylight** *n* a window in the roof or ceiling.

**skyscraper** *n* a very tall building.

**skyward** *adj, adv* towards the sky.— **skywards** *adv*.

**slab** *n* a flat, broad, thick piece (as of stone, wood, or bread, etc); something resembling this. • *vt* to cut or form into slabs; to cover or support with slabs; to put on thickly.

**slack** *adj* loose, relaxed, not tight; (*business*) slow, not brisk; sluggish; inattentive, careless. • *n* the part (of a rope, etc) that hangs loose; a dull period; a lull; (*pl*) trousers for casual wear. • *vti* to neglect (one's work, etc), to be lazy; (*with* **off**) to slacken (a rope, etc).—**slackness** *n*.

**slacken** *vti* to make or become less active, brisk, etc; to loosen or relax, as a rope; to diminish, to abate.— **slackening** *n, adj*.

**slag** *n* the waste product from the smelting of metals; volcanic lava.

**slam** *vti* (*pt* **slammed**) to shut with a loud noise, to bang; to throw (down) violently; (*inf*) to criticize severely. • *n* a sound or the act of slamming, a bang; (*inf*) severe criticism; (*bridge*) the taking of 12 or 13 tricks.

**slander** *n* a false and malicious statement about another; the uttering of this. • *vt* to utter a slander about, to defame.—**slanderous** *adj*.

**slang** *n* words or expressions used in familiar speech but not regarded as standard English; jargon of a particular social class, age group, etc. • *adj* relating to slang.

**slant** *vti* to incline, to slope; to tell in such way as to have a bias. • *n* a slope; an oblique position; a bias, a point of view. • *adj* sloping.—**slantly** *adv*.

**slanted** *adj* prejudiced, biased; sloping.

**slap** n a smack with the open hand; an insult; a rebuff. • vt (pt **slapped**) to strike with something flat; to put, hit, etc, with force. • adv directly, full.

**slapdash** adj impetuous; hurried; careless; haphazard. • adv carelessly.

**slapstick** n boisterous humour of a knockabout kind.

**slash** vti to cut gashes in, to slit; to strike fiercely (at) with a sword, etc; to reduce (prices) sharply. • n a cutting blow; a long slit, a gash.

**slate**[1] vt to criticize or punish severely.

**slate**[2] n a fine-grained rock easily split into thin layers; a flat plate of this or other material used in roofing; a tablet (as of slate) for writing on; a list of proposed candidates. • adj the colour of slate, a deep bluish-grey colour; made of slate. • vt to cover with slates; to suggest as a political candidate.

**slaughter** n the butchering of animals; a wholesale killing, a massacre.— also vt.—**slaughterer** n.

**slaughterhouse** n a place where animals are slaughtered, an abattoir.

**slave** n a person without freedom or personal rights, who is legally owned by another; a person under domination, esp of a habit or vice; a person who works like a slave, a drudge. • vti to toil hard, as a slave.

**slavery** n the condition of being a slave; bondage; drudgery; slave-owning as an institution.

**sled**, **sledge** n a framework on runners for travelling over snow or ice; a toboggan. • vti to go or convey by sledge.

**sledgehammer** n a large, heavy hammer for two hands.

**sleek** adj smooth, glossy; having a prosperous or well-groomed appearance; plausible.

**sleep** n a natural, regularly recurring rest for the body, with little or no consciousness; a period spent sleeping; a state of numbness followed by tingling. • vti (pt **slept**) to rest in a state of sleep; to be inactive; to provide beds for; (with **in**) to sleep on the premises; to sleep too long in the morning; (with **on**) to have a night's rest before making a decision; (with **off**) to get rid of by sleeping; (with **over**) to pass the night in someone else's house; (with **with**) to have sexual relations with.

**sleeper** n a person or thing that sleeps; a horizontal beam that carries and spreads a weight; a sleeping car; something that suddenly attains prominence or value.

**sleeping bag** n a padded bag for sleeping in, esp outdoors.

**sleeping car** n a railway carriage with berths.

**sleeping pill** n a pill that induces sleep.

**sleepwalker** n a person who walks while asleep, a somnambulist.— **sleepwalking** n.

**sleepy** adj (**sleepier**, **sleepiest**) drowsy; tired; lazy, not alert.—**sleepily** adv.— **sleepiness** n.

**sleet** n snow or hail mixed with rain. • vi to rain in the form of sleet.

**sleeve** n the part of a garment enclosing the arm; (mech) a tube that fits over a part; an open-ended cover, esp a paperboard envelope for a record.

**sleeveless** adj (garment) without sleeves.

**sleigh** n a light vehicle on runners for travelling over snow; a sledge.

**sleight of hand** n manual dexterity, such as in conjuring or juggling; a deception.

**slender** adj thin; slim; slight; scanty.— **slenderly** adv.—**slenderness** n.

**slept** see **sleep**.

**slice** n a thin flat piece cut from something (as bread, etc); a wedge-shaped piece (of cake, pie, etc); a portion, a share; a broad knife for serving fish, cheese, etc; (*golf*) a stroke that makes the ball curl to the right. • *vti* to divide into parts; to cut into slices; to strike (a ball) so that it curves.—**slicer** *n* —**slicing** *adj, n*.

**slick** *adj* clever, deft; smart but unsound; insincere; wily; (*inf*) smooth but superficial, tricky, etc. • *n* a patch or area of oil floating on water. • *vt* to make glossy; (*with* **up**) (*inf*) to make smart, neat, etc.

**slide** *vti* (*pt* **slid**) to move along in constant contact with a smooth surface, as on ice, to glide; to coast over snow and ice; to pass gradually (into); to move (an object) unobtrusively. • *n* the act of sliding, a glide; a strip of smooth ice for sliding on; a chute; the glass plate of a microscope; a photographic transparency; a landslide.

**slide rule** *n* a ruler with a graduated sliding part for making calculations.

**sliding scale** *n* a schedule for automatically varying one thing (eg wages) according to the fluctuations of another thing (eg cost of living); a flexible scale.

**slight** *adj* small, inconsiderable; trifling; slim; frail, flimsy. • *vt* to disregard as insignificant; to treat with disrespect, to snub. • *n* intentional indifference or neglect, discourtesy.

**slightly** *adv* to a small degree; slenderly.

**slim** *adj* slender, not stout; small in amount, degree, etc; slight. • *vti* (slimming, slimmed) to make or become slim; to reduce one's weight by diet, etc.—**slimness** *n*.

**slime** *n* a sticky slippery, half-liquid substance; a glutinous mud; mucus secreted by various animals (eg slugs).

**sling** *n* a loop of leather with a string attached for hurling stones; a rope

for lifting or hoisting weights; a bandage suspended from the neck for supporting an injured arm. • *vt* (*pt* **slung**) to throw, lift, or suspend (as) with a sling; to hurl.

**slingshot** *n* a catapult.

**slip**[1] *vti* (*pt* **slipped**) to slide, to glide; to lose one's foothold and slide; to go or put quietly or quickly; to let go, to release; to escape from; (*with* **up**) to make a slight mistake. • *n* the act of slipping; a mistake, a lapse; a woman's undergarment; a pillowcase; a slipway.

**slip**[2] *n* a small piece of paper; a young, slim person; a long seat or narrow pew; a shoot for grafting, a cutting; a descendant, an offspring.

**slipped disc** *n* a ruptured cartilaginous disc between vertebrae.

**slipper** *n* a light, soft, shoe worn in the house.

**slippery** *adj* so smooth as to cause slipping; difficult to hold or catch; evasive, unreliable, shifty.

**slip road** *n* a road that gives access to a main road or motorway.

**slipshod** *adj* having the shoes down at heel; slovenly, careless.

**slip-up** *n* (*inf*) an error, a lapse.

**slipway** *n* an inclined surface for launching or repairing ships; a sloped landing stage.

**slit** *vt* (*pr p* **slitting**, *pt* **slit**) to cut open or tear lengthways; to slash or tear into strips. • *n* a long cut, a slash; a narrow opening.

**slither** *vi* to slide, as on a loose or wet surface; to slip or slide like a snake.

**slog** *vti* (*pt* **slogged**) to hit hard and wildly; to work laboriously; to trudge doggedly. • *n* a hard, boring spell of work; a strenuous walk or hike; a hard, random hit.

**slogan** *n* a catchy phrase used in advertising or as a motto by a political party, etc.

**slop** *n* a puddle of spilled liquid; un-appetizing semi-liquid food; (*pl*) liquid kitchen refuse. • *vti* (*pt* **slopped**) to spill or be spilled.

**slope** *n* rising or falling ground; an inclined line or surface; the amount or degree of this. • *vti* to incline, to slant; (*inf*) to make off, to go.

**sloppy** *adj* (**sloppier, sloppiest**) slushy; (*inf*) maudlin, sentimental; (*inf*) careless, untidy.—**sloppily** *adv*.—**sloppiness** *n*.

**slot** *n* a long narrow opening in a mechanism for inserting a coin, a slit. • *vt* (*pt* **slotted**) to fit into a slot; to provide with a slot; (*inf*) to place in a series.

**slot machine** *n* a machine operated by the insertion of a coin, used for gambling or dispensing drinks, etc.

**slouch** *vti* to sit, stand or move in a drooping, slovenly way. • *n* a drooping slovenly posture or gait; the downward droop of a hat brim; (*inf*) a poor performer, a lazy or incompetent person.

**slovenly** *adj* untidy, dirty; careless.—**slovenliness** *n*.

**slow** *adj* moving at low speed, not fast; gradual; not quick in understanding; reluctant, backward; dull, sluggish; not progressive; (*clock*) behind in time; tedious, boring; (*surface*) causing slowness. • *vti* (*also with* **up, down**) to reduce the speed (of).—**slowly** *adv*.—**slowness** *n*.

**slow-motion** *adj* moving slowly; denoting a filmed or taped scene with the original action slowed down.

**sludge** *n* soft mud or snow; sediment; sewage.

**slug**[1] *n* a mollusc resembling a snail but with no outer shell.

**slug**[2] *n* a small bullet; a disc for inserting into a slot machine; a line of type; (*inf*) a hard blow; a drink of spirits. • *vt* (*pt* **slugged**) (*inf*) to hit hard with a fist or a bat.

**sluice** *n* a gate regulating a flow of water; the water passing through this; an artificial water channel. • *vti* to draw off through a sluice; to wash with a stream of water; to stream out as from a sluice.

**slum** *n* a squalid, rundown house; (usu *pl*) an overcrowded area characterized by poverty, etc. • *vi* (*pt* **slummed**) to make do with less comfort.

**slumber** *vi* to sleep. • *n* a light sleep.

**slump** *n* a sudden fall in value or slackening in demand; (*sport*) a period of poor play. • *vi* to fall or decline suddenly; to sink down heavily; to collapse; to slouch.

**slung** *see* **sling**.

**slur** *vti* (*pt* **slurred**) to pronounce or speak indistinctly; (*letters, words*) to run together; (*mus*) to produce by gliding without a break; to make disparaging remarks. • *n* the act of slurring; a stigma, an imputation of disgrace; (*mus*) a curved line over notes to be slurred.

**slush** *n* liquid mud; melting snow; (*inf*) sentimental language.—**slushy** *adj*.

**slut** *n* a slovenly or immoral woman.—**sluttish** *adj*.

**sly** *adj* (**slyer, slyest** *or* **slier, sliest**) secretively cunning, wily; underhand; knowing.—**slyly** *adv*.—**slyness** *n*.

**smack**[1] *n* a taste; a distinctive smell or flavour; small quantity, a trace. • *vi* to have a smell or taste (of); to have a slight trace of something.

**smack**[2] *vt* to strike or slap with the open hand; to kiss noisily; to make a sharp noise with the lips.—*also n*.

**small** *adj* little in size, number, importance, etc; modest, humble; operating on a minor scale; young; petty. • *adv* in small pieces. • *n* the narrow, curving part of the back.

**smallpox** *n* an acute contagious viral

disease, now rare, causing the eruption of pustules which leave the skin scarred and pitted.

**small talk** *n* light, social conversation.

**smart** *n* a sudden, stinging pain. • *vi* to have or cause a sharp, stinging pain (as by a slap); to feel distress. • *adj* stinging; astute; clever, witty; fashionable; neatly dressed; (*equipment, etc*) capable of seemingly intelligent action through computer control; (*bombs, missiles*) guided to the target by lasers ensuring pinpoint accuracy.—**smartly** *adv.*—**smartness** *n.*

**smarten** *vti* to make or become smart.

**smash** *vti* to break into pieces with noise or violence; to hit, collide, or move with force; to destroy or be destroyed. • *n* a hard, heavy hit; a violent, noisy breaking; a violent collision; total failure, esp in business; (*inf*) a popular success.

**smashing** *n* (*inf*) excellent.

**smattering** *n* a slight superficial knowledge; a small number.

**smear** *vt* to cover with anything greasy or sticky; to make a smudge; to slander. • *n* a smudge; a slanderous attack; a deposit of blood, secretion, etc on a glass slide for examination under a microscope.

**smell** *n* the sense by which odours are perceived with the nose; a scent, odour, or stench; a trace. • *vti* (*pt* **smelt** *or* **smelled**) to have or perceive an odour.—**smelly** *adj.*

**smile** *vti* to express amusement, friendship, pleasure, etc, by a slight turning up of the corners of the mouth.—*also n.*

**smirk** *vi* to smile in an expression of smugness or scorn.—*also n.*

**smith** *n* a person who works in metal; a blacksmith.

**smithy** *n* a blacksmith's workshop.

**smock** *n* a loose shirtlike outer garment to protect the clothes.

**smog** *n* a mixture of fog and smoke.

**smoke** *n* a cloud or plume of gas and small particles emitted from a burning substance; any similar vapour; an act of smoking tobacco, etc; (*inf*) a cigar or cigarette. • *vi* to give off smoke; to (habitually) draw in and exhale the smoke of tobacco, etc. • *vt* to fumigate; to cure food by treating with smoke; to darken (eg glass) using smoke.

**smoker** *n* a person who habitually smokes tobacco; a train compartment where smoking is permitted.

**smoky** *adj* (**smokier, smokiest**) emitting smoke, esp excessively; filled with smoke; resembling smoke in appearance, flavour, smell, colour, etc.

**smooth** *adj* having an even or flat surface; silky; not rough or lumpy; hairless; of even consistency; calm, unruffled; gently flowing in rhythm or sound. • *vti* to make smooth; to calm; to make easier.—**smoothly** *adv.*—**smoothness** *n.*

**smother** *vt* to stifle, to suffocate; to put out a fire by covering it to remove the air supply; to cover over thickly; to hold back, suppress. • *vi* to undergo suffocation.—*also n.*

**smoulder, smolder** (*US*) *vi* to burn slowly or without flame; (*feelings*) to linger on in a suppressed state; to have concealed feelings of anger, jealousy, etc.

**smudge** *n* a dirty or blurred spot or area; in US, a fire made to produce dense smoke. • *vt* to make a smudge; to smear; to blur; in US, to produce smoke to protect against insects, etc. • *vi* to become smudged.

**smug** *adj* (**smugger, smuggest**) complacent, self-satisfied.—**smugly** *adv.*—**smugness** *n.*

**smuggle** *vt* to import or export (goods)

secretly without paying customs duties; to convey or introduce secretly.—**smuggler** n.

**smut** n a speck or smudge of dirt, soot, etc; indecent talk, writing, or pictures; a fungous disease of crop plants that covers the leaves in sooty spores. • vti (pt **smutted**) to stain or become stained with smut; (crops, etc) to infect or become infected with smut.—**smutty** adj.

**snack** n a light meal between regular meals.

**snag** n a sharp point or projection; a tear, as in cloth, made by a snag, etc; an unexpected or hidden difficulty.—also vti.

**snail** n a mollusc having a wormlike body and a spiral protective shell; a slow-moving person or thing.

**snake** n a limbless, scaly reptile with a long, tapering body, often with salivary glands modified to produce venom; a sly, treacherous person. • vt to twist along like a snake. • vi to crawl silently and stealthily.—**snaky** adj.

**snap** vti (pt **snapped**) (with at) to bite or grasp suddenly; (with at) to speak or utter sharply; to break suddenly; to make or cause to make a sudden, cracking sound; to close, fasten, etc with this sound. • adj sudden. • n a sharp, cracking sound; a fastener that closes with a snapping sound; a crisp biscuit; a snapshot; a sudden spell of cold weather; (inf) vigour, energy.

**snappy** adj (**snappier**, **snappiest**) speaking sharply; brisk; lively; smart, fashionable.—**snappily** adv.

**snapshot** n a photograph taken casually with a simple camera.

**snare** n a loop of string or wire for trapping birds or animals; something that catches one unawares, a trap; a loop of gut wound with wire stretched around a snare drum that produces a rattling sound. • vt to trap using a snare.

**snarl**[1] vi to growl with bared teeth; to speak in a rough, angry manner. • vt to express in a snarling manner.—also n.

**snarl**[2] vti to make or become entangled or complicated. • n a tangle; disorder.

**snatch** vt to seize or grasp suddenly; to take as opportunity occurs. • n the act of snatching; a brief period; a fragment; (inf) a robbery.

**sneak** vti to move, act, give, put, take, etc, secretly or stealthily. • n a person who acts secretly or stealthily; (inf) a person who tells or informs on others. • adj without warning.—**sneaky** adj.

**sneer** vi to show scorn or contempt by curling up the upper lip.—also n.

**sneeze** vi to expel air through the nose violently and audibly.—also n.

**snide** adj malicious; superior in attitude; sneering.

**sniff** vti to inhale through the nose audibly; to smell by sniffing; to scoff.—also n.

**snigger** vti to laugh disrespectfully.—also n.

**snip** vti (pt **snipped**) to cut or clip with a single stroke of the scissors, etc. • n a small piece cut off; the act or sound of snipping; (inf) a bargain; (inf) a certainty, cinch.

**snipe** n (pl **snipe**) any of various birds with long straight flexible bills. • vi to shoot at individuals from a hidden position; to make sly criticisms of.—**sniper** n.

**snippet** n a scrap of information.

**snob** n a person who wishes to be associated with those of a higher social status, whilst acting condescendingly to those whom he or she regards as inferior.—**snob-bery** n.—**snobbish** adj.

**snooker** n a game played on a billiard table with 15 red balls, 6 variously coloured balls, and a white cue ball; a position in the game where a ball lies directly between the cue ball and target ball. • vt to place in a snooker; (inf) to obstruct, thwart.

**snoop** vi (inf) to pry about in a sneaking way. • n an act of snooping; a person who pries into other people's business.—**snooper** n.

**snooze** vi (inf) to sleep lightly. • n (inf) a nap.

**snore** vi to breathe roughly and noisily while asleep.—also n.

**snorkel** n a breathing tube extending above the water, used in swimming just below the surface. • vi to swim using a snorkel.

**snort** vi to exhale noisily through the nostrils, esp as an expression of contempt or scorn. • vt to inhale (a drug) through the nose.

**snout** n the nose or muzzle of an animal.

**snow** n frozen water vapour in the form of white flakes; a snowfall; a mass of snow; (sl) cocaine or heroin. • vi to fall as snow.

**snowball** n snow pressed together in a ball for throwing; a drink made with advocaat and lemonade. • vi to throw snowballs; to increase rapidly in size.

**snowdrift** n a bank of drifted snow.

**snowfall** n a fall of snow; the amount of snow that falls in a given time or area.

**snowman** n snow piled into the shape of a human figure.

**snowplough, snowplow** (US) n a vehicle designed for clearing away snow.

**snub**[1] vt (pt **snubbed**) to insult by ignoring or making a cutting remark.—also n.

**snub**[2] adj short and turned up, as a nose.

**snuff**[1] n a powdered preparation of tobacco inhaled through the nostrils.

**snuff**[2] n the charred portion of a wick. • vt to extinguish (a candle flame).

**snug** adj (**snugger, snuggest**) cosy; warm; close-fitting.

**so** adv in this way; as shown; as stated; to such an extent; very; (inf) very much; therefore; more or less; also, likewise; then.

**soak** vt to submerge in a liquid; to take in, absorb; (sl) to extract large amounts of money from. • vi to become saturated; to penetrate. • n the act or process of soaking.

**soap** n a substance used with water to produce suds for washing; (inf) a soap opera. • vt to rub with soap.—**soapy** adj.

**soar** vi to rise high in the air; to glide along high in the air; to increase; to rise in status.

**sob** vi to weep with convulsive gasps. • vt to speak while sobbing.

**sober** adj not drunk; serious and thoughtful; realistic, rational; subdued in colour. • vt to make or become sober (often with **up** or **down**).—**soberly** adv.

**so-called** adj commonly named or known as.

**soccer** n a football game played on a field by two teams of 11 players with a round inflated ball.

**sociable** adj friendly; companionable.—**sociability** n.—**sociably** adv.

**social** adj living or organized in a community, not solitary; relating to human beings living in society; of or intended for communal activities; sociable. • n an informal gathering of people, such as a party.—**socially** adv.

**socialism** n (a system based on) a political and economic theory advocating state ownership of the means of production and distribution.—**socialist** n.—**socialistic** adj.

**social science** n the study of human social organization and relationships using scientific methods.

**social security** n financial assistance for the unemployed, the disabled, etc to alleviate economic distress.

**social work** n any of various professional welfare services to aid the underprivileged in society.—**social worker** n.

**society** n the social relationships between human beings or animals organized collectively; the system of human institutional organization; a community with the same language and customs; an interest group or organization; the fashionable or privileged members of a community; companionship.

**sociology** n the study of the development and structure of society and social relationships.—**sociologist** n.—**sociological** adj.

**sock**[1] n a kind of short stocking covering the foot and lower leg.

**sock**[2] vt (sl) to punch hard.—also n.

**socket** n a hollow part into which something is inserted, such as an eye, a bone, a tooth, an electric plug, etc.

**sod**[1] n a lump of earth covered with grass; turf.

**sod**[2] n (sl) an obnoxious person; (loosely) a person, man.

**soda** n sodium bicarbonate; sodium carbonate; soda water.

**soda water** n a fizzy drink made by charging water with carbon dioxide under pressure.

**sodden** adj completely soaked through.

**sodium** n a metallic element.

**sofa** n an upholstered couch or settee with fixed back and arms.

**soft** adj malleable; easily cut, shaped, etc; not as hard as normal, desirable, etc; smooth to the touch; (drinks) nonalcoholic; mild, as a breeze; lenient; (sl) easy, comfortable; (colour, light) not bright; (sound) gentle, low; (drugs) non-addictive.—**softly** adv.—**softness** n.

**soften** vti to make or become soft or softer.—**softener** n.

**software** n the programs used in computers.

**soggy** adj (soggier, soggiest) soaked with water; moist and heavy.

**soil**[1] n the ground or earth in which plants grow; territory.

**soil**[2] vt to make or become dirty or stained.

**solar** adj of or from the sun; powered by light or heat from the sun; reckoned by the sun.

**sold** see **sell**.

**solder** n a metal alloy used when melted to join or patch metal parts, etc.—also vti.

**soldier** n a person who serves in an army, esp a non-commissioned officer. • vi to serve as a soldier.—**soldierly** adj.

**sole**[1] n the underside of the foot or shoe. • vt to put a new sole on (a shoe).

**sole**[2] n (pl sole) a type of flatfish used as food.

**sole**[3] adj only, being the only one; exclusive.—**solely** adv.

**solemn** adj serious; formal; sacred; performed with religious ceremony.—**solemnly** adv.—**solemnness** n.

**solicitor** n a lawyer.

**solid** adj firm; compact; not hollow; strongly constructed; having three dimensions; neither liquid nor gaseous; unanimous. • n a solid substance (not liquid or gas); a three dimensional figure.—**solidly** adv.—**solidity** n.

**solidarity** n unity of interest and action.

**solidify** vti to make or become solid, compact, hard, etc.

**solitaire** n a single gemstone, esp a diamond; a card game for one (—also **patience**).

**solitary** adj alone; only; single; living alone; lonely.

**solitude** n the state of being alone; lack of company.

**solo** n (pl **solos**) a musical composition for performance by one voice or instrument; a flight by a single person in an aircraft, esp a first flight. • vi to perform by oneself. • adv alone. • adj unaccompanied.—**soloist** n.

**solstice** n either of the two times in the year at which the sun is farthest from the equator (21 June and 21 December).

**soluble** adj capable of being dissolved (usu in water); capable of being solved or answered.—**solubility** n.

**solution** n the act or process of answering a problem; the answer found; the dispersion of one substance in another, usu a liquid; so as to form a homogeneous mixture.

**solve** vt to work out the answer to; to clear up, resolve.

**solvent** adj capable of dissolving a substance; able to pay all debts. • n a liquid that dissolves substances.—**solvency** n.

**sombre, somber** (US) adj dark, gloomy or dull; dismal; sad.

**some** adj certain but not specified or known; of a certain unspecified quantity, degree, etc; a little; (inf) remarkable, striking, etc. • pron a certain unspecified quantity, number, etc.

**somebody** n an unspecified person; an important person.—also pron.

**someday** adv at some future day or time.

**somehow** adv in a way or by a method not known or stated.

**someone** n somebody.—also pron.

**someplace** adv somewhere.

**somersault** n a forward or backward roll head over heels along the ground or in mid-air.—also vi.

**something** n, pron a thing not definitely known, understood, etc; an important or notable thing. • adv to some degree. • adj having been formerly; being so occasionally or in only some respects.

**sometime** adj former. • adv at some unspecified future date.

**sometimes** adv at times, now and then.

**somewhat** adv to some extent, degree, etc; a little.

**somewhere** adv in, to or at some place not known or specified.

**son** n a male offspring or descendant.

**song** n a piece of music composed for the voice; the act or process of singing; the call of certain birds.

**sonic** adj of, producing, or involving sound waves.

**son-in-law** n a daughter's husband.

**sonnet** n a rhyming poem in a single stanza of fourteen lines.

**sonny** n a patronizing form of address to a boy.

**soon** adv in a short time; before long.

**sooner or later** adv at some future unspecified time, eventually.

**soot** n a black powder produced from flames.—**sooty** adj.

**soothe** vt to calm or comfort; to alleviate; to relieve (pain, etc).—**soothing** adj.

**sophisticated** adj refined; worldly-wise; intelligent; complex.—**sophistication** n.

**soppy** adj (**soppier, soppiest**) wet; (inf) sickly sentimental.—**soppily** adv.—**soppiness** n.

**sorcerer** *n* person who uses magic powers; a magician or wizard.—**sorceress** *nf*.

**sordid** *adj* filthy, squalid; vile; base; selfish.

**sore** *n* a painful or tender injury or wound; an ulcer or boil; grief; a cause of distress. • *adj* painful; tender; distressed.—**soreness** *n*.

**sorely** *adv* seriously, urgently.

**sorrow** *n* sadness; regret; an expression of grief. • *vi* to mourn, to grieve.— **sorrowful** *adj*.—**sorrowfully** *adv*.

**sorry** *adj* (**sorrier, sorriest**) feeling pity, sympathy, remorse or regret; pitiful; poor.

**sort** *n* a class, kind, or variety; quality or type. • *vt* to arrange according to kind; to classify.—**sorter** *n*.

**SOS** *n* an international signal code of distress; an urgent call for help or rescue.

**souffle** *n* a baked dish made light and puffy by adding beaten egg whites before baking.

**sought** *see* **seek**.

**soul** *n* a person's spirit; the seat of the emotions, desires; essence; character; a human being.

**soul-destroying** *adj* extremely boring, depressing.

**soulful** *adj* expressing profound sentiment.—**soulfully** *adv*.

**sound**[1] *adj* healthy; free from injury or damage; substantial; stable; deep (as sleep) solid; thorough.—**soundly** *adv*.—**soundness** *n*.

**sound**[2] *n* a narrow channel of water connecting two seas or between a mainland and an island.

**sound**[3] *n* vibrations transmitted through the air and detected by the ear; the sensation of hearing; any audible noise; the impression given by something. • *vi* to make a sound; to give a summons by sound. • *vt* to cause to make a sound; to voice; to make a signal or order by sound.

**sound**[4] *vt* to measure the depth of; to seek to discover the views and intentions of.

**sound barrier** *n* the increase in air resistance experienced by objects travelling close to the speed of sound.

**sounding**[1] *n* measurement of the depth of water; a test, sampling, eg of public opinion.

**sounding**[2] *adj* resounding.

**soundproof** *adj* unable to be penetrated by sound. • *vt* to make soundproof by insulation, etc.

**soundtrack** *n* the sound accompanying a film; the area on cinema film that carries the sound recording.

**soup** *n* a liquid food made from boiling meat, fish, vegetables, etc, in water; (*inf*) a difficult or embarrassing situation.—**soupy** *adj*.

**sour** *adj* having a sharp, biting taste; spoiled by fermentation; cross; badtempered; distasteful or unpleasant; (*soil*) acid in reaction. • *vti* to make or become sour.—**sourly** *adv*.—**sourness** *n*.

**source** *n* a spring forming the head of a stream; an origin or cause; a person, book, etc, that provides information.

**south** *n* the direction to one's right when facing the the direction of the rising sun; the region, country, continent, etc, lying relatively in that direction. • *adj*, *adv* facing towards or situated in the south.

**southeast** *n* the point on a compass midway between south and east. • *adj*, *adv* at, towards, or from the southeast.—*also* **southeastern**.

**southerly** *adj* in, towards, or from the south. • *n* a wind from the south.

**southern** *adj* in, towards, or from the south; inhabiting or characteristic of the south.—**southernmost** *adj*.

**southward** *adj* towards the south.—
**southwards** *adv*.

**southwest** *n* the point on a compass midway between south and west. • *adj, adv* at, towards, or from the southwest.—*also* **southwestern**.

**souvenir** *n* a keepsake, a memento.

**sovereign** *adj* supreme in authority or rank; (*country, state, etc*) independent. • *n* a supreme ruler; a monarch.—**sovereignty** *n*.

**sow**[1] *n* an adult female pig.

**sow**[2] *vt* (*pt* **sowed**, *pp* **sown** *or* **sowed**) to plant or scatter seed on or in the ground; to disseminate; to implant.—**sower** *n*.

**soya bean, soybean** (*US*) *n* a type of bean (orig from Asia) used as a source of food and oil.

**spa** *n* a mineral spring; a resort where there is a mineral spring.

**space** *n* the limitless three-dimensional expanse within which all objects exist; outer space; a specific area; an interval, empty area; room; an unoccupied area or seat. • *vt* to arrange at intervals.

**spacecraft** *n* a vehicle for travel in outer space.

**spacious** *adj* large in extent; roomy.—**spaciousness** *n*.

**spade**[1] *n* a tool with a broad blade and a handle used for digging.

**spade**[2] *n* a black symbol resembling a stylized spearhead marking one of the four suits of playing cards; a card of this suit.

**span** *n* a unit of length equal to a hand's breadth (about 9 inches/23 cm); the full extent between any two limits, such as the ends of a bridge or arch. • *vt* (*pt* **spanned**) to extend across.

**spaniel** *n* any of various breeds of dog with large drooping ears and a long silky coat.

**Spanish** *adj* of or pertaining to Spain.

• *n* the language of Spain and Spanish Americans.

**spank** *vt* to slap with the flat of the hand, esp on the buttocks.—*also n*.

**spanner** *n* a tool with a hole or (often adjustable) jaws to grip and turn nuts or bolts, a wrench.

**spare** *vt* to refrain from harming or killing; to afford; to make (something) available (eg time). • *adj* kept as an extra, additional; scanty. • *n* a spare part; a spare tyre —
**sparely** *adv*.—**spareness** *n*.

**sparing** *adj* frugal, economical.—**sparingly** *adv*.

**spark** *n* a fiery or glowing particle thrown off by burning material or by friction; a flash of light from an electrical discharge; a trace. • *vt* to stir up;. to activate. • *vi* to give off sparks.

**sparrow** *n* any of various small brownish songbirds related to the finch.

**sparse** *adj* spread out thinly; scanty.—**sparsely** *adv*.—**sparseness, sparsity** *n*.

**spasm** *n* a sudden, involuntary muscular contraction; any sudden burst (of emotion or activity).

**spasmodic** *adj* intermittent; of or like a spasm.—**spasmodically** *adv*.

**spastic** *n* a person who suffers from cerebral palsy. • *adj* affected by muscle spasm.—**spasticity** *n*.

**spat** *see* **spit**[2].

**spate** *n* a large amount; a sudden outburst (as of words); a sudden flood.

**spatter** *vti* to scatter or spurt out in drops; to splash.—*also n*.

**spatula** *n* a tool with a broad, flexible blade for spreading or mixing foods, paints, etc.

**spawn** *n* a mass of eggs deposited by fish, frogs, or amphibians; offspring. • *vti* to lay eggs; to produce, esp in great quantity.

**spay** *vt* to render (a female animal) sterile by removing the ovaries.

**speak** vi (pt **spoke**, pp **spoken**) to utter words; to talk; to to converse with; to deliver a speech; to be suggestive of something; to produce a characteristic sound.

**speaker** n a person who speaks, esp before an audience; the presiding official in a legislative assembly; a loudspeaker.

**spear** n a weapon with a long shaft and a sharp point; a blade or shoot (of grass, broccoli, etc). • vt to pierce with a spear.

**spec** vt to write specifications for.

**special** adj distinguished; uncommon; designed for a particular purpose; peculiar to one person or thing.— **specially** adv.

**specialist** n a person who concentrates on a particular area of study or activity, esp in medicine.

**speciality**, **specialty** (US) n a special skill or interest; a special product.

**specialize** vi to concentrate on a particular area of study or activity. • vt to adapt to a particular use or purpose.—**specialization** n.

**species** n (pl **species**) a class of plants or animals with the same main characteristics, enabling interbreeding; a distinct kind or sort.

**specific** adj explicit; definite; of a particular kind. • n a characteristic quality or influence; a drug effective in treating a particular disease.— **specifically** adv.

**specification** n a requirement; (pl) detailed description of dimensions, materials, etc of something.

**specify** vt to state specifically; to set down as a condition.

**specimen** n (plant, animal, etc) an example of a particular species; a sample; (inf) a person.

**speck** n a small spot; a fleck.

**speckle** n a small mark of a different colour. • vt to mark with speckles.

**spectacle** n an unusual or interesting scene; a large public show; an object of derision or ridicule; (pl) a pair of glasses.—**spectacled** adj.

**spectacular** adj impressive; astonishing.

**spectator** n an onlooker.

**spectre**, **specter** (US) n an apparition or ghost; a haunting mental image.

**spectrum** n (pl **spectra**) the range of colour which is produced when a white light is passed through a prism; any similar distribution of wave frequencies; a broad range.

**speculate** vi to theorize, to conjecture; to make investments in the hope of making a profit.—**speculation** n.— **speculator** n.

**speculative** adj of or based on speculation; engaging in speculation in finance, etc.—**speculatively** adv.

**speech** n the action or power of speaking; a public address or talk; language, dialect.

**speechless** adj unable to speak; silent, as from shock; impossible to express in words.—**speechlessly** adv.

**speed** n quickness; rapidity or rate of motion; (photog) the sensitivity of film to light; (sl) an amphetamine drug. • vi (pt **sped**) to go quickly, to hurry; (pt **speeded**) to drive (a vehicle) at an illegally high speed.

**speedometer** n an instrument in a motor vehicle for measuring its speed.

**speedway** n the sport of racing light motorcycles around dirt or cinder tracks; a stadium for motorcycle racing; in US, a road reserved for fast traffic.

**speedy** adj (**speedier**, **speediest**) quick; prompt.—**speedily** adv.

**spell**[1] n a sequence of words used to perform magic; fascination.

**spell**[2] vb (pt **spelt** or **spelled**) vt to name or write down in correct order the letters to form a word; (*letters*) to form a word when placed in the correct order; to indicate. • *vi* to spell words.

**spell**³ *n* a usu indefinite period of time; a period of duty in a certain occupation or activity. • *vt* to relieve, stand in for.

**spellbound** *adj* entranced, enthralled.

**spend** *vb* (*pt* **spent**) *vt* to pay out (money); to concentrate (one's time or energy) on an activity; to pass, as time; to use up. • *vi* to pay out money.—**spender** *n*.

**spendthrift** *n* a person who spends money wastefully or extravagantly.

**spent** *adj* consumed, used up; physically drained, exhausted.

**sperm** *n* semen; the male reproductive cell.

**spew** *vti* to vomit; to flow or gush forth. • *n* something spewed.

**sphere** *n* a ball, globe or other perfectly round object; a field of activity or interest; a social class.—**spherical, spheric** *adj*.—**spherically** *adv*.

**spice** *n* an aromatic vegetable substance used for flavouring and seasoning food; these substances collectively; something that adds zest or interest. • *vt* to flavour with spice; to add zest to.

**spicy** *adj* (**spicier, spiciest**) flavoured with spice; pungent; (*inf*) somewhat scandalous or indecent.—**spicily** *adv*.—**spiciness** *n*.

**spider** *n* a small wingless creature (arachnid) with eight legs, and abdominal spinnerets for spinning silk threads to make webs.

**spike** *n* long heavy nail; a sharp-pointed projection, as on a shoe to prevent slipping; an ear of corn, etc; a cluster of stalkless flowers arranged on a long stem. • *vt* to pierce with a spike.—**spiky** *adj*.

**spill**¹ *vti* (*pt* **spilt** *or* **spilled**) to cause, esp unintentionally, to flow out of a container; to shed (blood). • *n* something spilled.—**spillage** *n*.

**spill**² *n* a splinter or thin strip of wood or twisted paper for lighting a fire, etc.

**spin** *vb* (*pr p* **spinning**, *pt* **spun**) *vt* to rotate rapidly; to draw out and twist fibres into thread or yarn; (*spiders, silkworm, etc*) to make a web or cocoon; to draw out (a story) to a great length; (*with* **out**) to prolong, extend; to cause to last longer, eg money. • *vi* to seem to be spinning from dizziness; (*wheels*) to turn rapidly without imparting forward motion. • *n* a swift rotation; (*inf*) a brief, fast ride in a vehicle.

**spinach** *n* a plant with large, green edible leaves.

**spinal** *adj* of or relating to the spine or spinal cord.

**spinal cord** *n* the cord of nerves enclosed by the spinal column.

**spindly** *adj* (**spindlier, spindliest**) tall and slender; frail.

**spine** *n* a sharp, stiff projection, as a thorn of the cactus or quill of a porcupine; a spinal column; the backbone of a book.

**spineless** *adj* lacking a spine; weak-willed; irresolute.—**spinelessness** *n*.

**spinning wheel** *n* a small household machine with a wheel-driven spindle for spinning yarn from fibre.

**spinster** *n* an unmarried woman.

**spiral** *adj* winding round in a continuous curve up or down a centre or pole. • *n* a helix; a spiral line or shape; a continuous expansion or decrease, eg in inflation. • *vi* (*pt* **spiralled**) to move up or down in a spiral curve; to increase or decrease steadily.

**spire** *n* the tapering point of a steeple.

**spirit** *n* soul; a supernatural being, as a ghost, angel, etc; (*pl*) disposition;

mood; vivacity, courage, etc; real meaning; essential quality; (*usu pl*) distilled alcoholic liquor. • *vt* to carry (away, off, etc) secretly and swiftly.

**spirited** *adj* full of life; animated.— **spiritedly** *adv*.

**spirit level** *n* a glass tube filled with liquid containing an air bubble and mounted in a frame, used for testing whether a surface is level.

**spiritual** *adj* of the soul; religious; sacred. • *n* an emotional religious song, originating among the Black slaves in the American South.—**spirituality** *n*.—**spiritually** *adv*.

**spiritualism** *n* the belief that the spirits of the dead can communicate with the living, as through mediums.—**spiritualist** *n*.

**spirt** *see* **spurt**.

**spit**[1] *n* a pointed iron rod on which meat is roasted; a long narrow strip of land projecting into the water. • *vt* (*pr p* **spitting**, *pt* **spitted**) to fix as on a spit, impale.

**spit**[2] *vb* (*pr p* **spitting**, *pt* **spat** *or* **spit**) *vt* to eject from the mouth; to utter with scorn. • *vi* to expel saliva from the mouth; (*hot fat*) to splutter; to rain lightly. • *n* saliva.

**spite** *n* ill will; malice. • *vt* to annoy spitefully, to vex.—**spiteful** *adj*.

**spittle** *n* saliva ejected form the mouth.

**splash** *vt* to spatter with liquid; to move with a splash; to display prominently. • *n* something splashed; a patch of colour; a small amount, esp of a mixer added to an alcoholic drink.—**splashy** *adj*.

**spleen** *n* a large lymphatic organ in the upper left part of the abdomen which modifies the blood structure; spitefulness; ill humour.

**splendid** *adj* brilliant; magnificent; (*inf*) very good.—**splendidly** *adv*.

**splendour, splendor** (*US*) *n* brilliance; magnificence; grandeur.

**splice** *vt* to unite (two ends of a rope) by intertwining the strands; to connect (two pieces of timber) by overlapping.—*also n*.

**splint** *n* a rigid structure used to immobilize and support a fractured limb; a splinter of wood for lighting fires. • *vt* to put in splints.

**splinter** *n* a thin, sharp piece of wood, glass, or metal broken off. • *vti* to break off into splinters.—**splintery** *adj*.

**split** *vti* (*pr p* **splitting**, *pt* **split**) to break apart (usu into two pieces); to separate into factions; to divide into shares; to burst or tear. • *n* the act or process of splitting; a narrow gap made (as if) by splitting; a dessert consisting of sliced fruit, esp banana, with ice cream, nuts, etc; (*often pl*) the act of extending the legs in opposite directions and lowering the the body to the floor. • *adj* divided; torn; fractured.

**splutter** *vi* to spit out food or drops of liquid noisily; to utter words confusedly and hurriedly.—*also n*.

**spoil** *vb* (*pt* **spoilt** *or* **spoiled**) *vt* to damage as to make useless, etc; to impair the enjoyment, etc, of; to overindulge (a child). • *vi* to become spoiled; to decay, etc, as food. • *npl* booty, valuables seized in war; the opportunities for financial gain from holding public office.

**spoil-sport** *n* (*inf*) a person who spoils the fun of others.

**spoke**[1], **spoken** *see* **speak**.

**spoke**[2] *n* any of the braces extending from the hub to the rim of a wheel.

**spokesman** *n* a person authorized to speak on behalf of others.—**spokeswomen** *nf*.

**sponge** *n* a plantlike marine animal with an internal skeleton of elastic interlacing horny fibres; a piece of natural or manmade sponge for washing or cleaning. • *vt* to wipe with a sponge. •*vi* (*inf*) to scrounge. —**sponginess** *n.*—**spongy** *adj.*

**sponge cake** *n* a sweet cake with a light porous texture.

**sponsor** *n* a person or organization that pays the expenses connected with an artistic production or sports event in return for advertising; in US, a business firm, etc that pays for a radio or TV programme advertising its product. • *vt* to act as sponsor for.—**sponsorship** *n.*

**spontaneous** *adj* arising naturally; unpremeditated.—**spontaneously** *adv.*—**spontaneity** *n.*

**spook** *n* (*inf*) a ghost; (*inf*) a spy. • *vt* to frighten.—**spooky** *adj.*

**spool** *n* a cylinder, bobbin, or reel, upon which thread, photographic film, etc, are wound. • *vt* to wind on a spool.

**spoon** *n* utensil with a shallow bowl and a handle, for eating, stirring, etc.—**spoonful** *n.*

**sporadic** *adj* occurring here and there; intermittent.—**sporadically** *adv.*

**sport** *n* an athletic game or pastime, often competitive and involving physical capability; good-humoured joking; (*inf*) a person regarded as fair and abiding by the rules. • *vi* to play, frolic. • *vt* (*inf*) to display, flaunt.

**sporting** *adj* interested in, concerned with, or suitable for sport; exhibiting sportsmanship; willing to take a risk.

**sportsman** *n* a person engaged in sport; a person who plays by the rules, is fair, is a good loser, etc.— **sportswoman** *nf.*—**sportsmanlike**, **sportsmanly** *adj.*—**sportsmanship** *n.*

**sporty** *adj* (**sportier, sportiest**) (*inf*) fond of sport; flashy, ostentatious. — **sportily** *adv.*—**sportiness** *n.*

**spot** *n* a small area differing in colour, etc, from the surrounding area; a

stain, speck, etc; a taint on character or reputation; a small quantity or amount; a locality; (*inf*) a difficult or embarrassing situation; a place on an entertainment programme; a spotlight. • *vt* (*pt* **spotted**) to mark with spots; (*inf*) to identify or recognise; to glimpse.

**spot check** *n* a sudden random examination.

**spotless** *adj* immaculate.—**spotlessly** *adv.*

**spotty** *adj* (**spottier, spottiest**) marked with spots, esp on the skin; intermittent, uneven.—**spottiness** *n.*

**spouse** *n* (one's) husband or wife.

**spout** *vti* to eject in a strong jet or spurts; (*inf*) to drone on boringly. • *n* a projecting lip or tube for pouring out liquids.

**sprain** *n* a wrenching of a joint by sudden twisting or tearing of ligaments.—*also vt.*

**sprang** *see* **spring**.

**sprawl** *vi* to lie down with the limbs stretched out in an untidy manner; to spread out in a straggling way.— *also n.*

**spray**[1] *n* fine particles of a liquid; mist; an aerosol or atomizer. • *vti* to direct a spray (on); to apply as a spray.

**spray**[2] *n* a number of flowers on one branch; a decorative flower arrangement; an ornament resembling this.

**spread** *vt* (*pt* **spread**) to extend; to unfold or open; to disseminate; to distribute; to apply a coating (eg butter). • *vi* to expand in all directions. • *n* an expanse; (*inf*) a feast; food which can be spread on bread; a bed cover.

**spree** *n* (*inf*) excessive indulgence, eg in spending money, alcohol consumption, etc.

**sprig** *n* a twig with leaves on it.

**sprightly** *adj* (**sprightlier, sprightliest**) full of life or energy.—**sprightliness** *n.*

**spring** vb (pt **sprang** or **sprung**, pp **sprung**) vi to move suddenly, as by elastic force; to arise suddenly; to originate. • vt to cause to spring up, to cause to operate suddenly. • n a leap; the season between winter and summer; a coiled piece of wire that springs back to its original shape when stretched; the source of a stream.—**springiness** n.—**springy** adj.

**springboard** n a flexible board used by divers and in gymnastics to provided added height or impetus.

**spring-clean** vi to clean (a house, etc) thoroughly.—also n.

**sprinkle** vt to scatter in droplets or particles (on something).—also n.

**sprint** n a short run or race at full speed. • vi to go at top speed.—**sprinter** n.

**sprite** n an elf or imp; a dainty person.

**sprout** n a new shoot on a plant; a small cabbage-like vegetable. • vt to put forth (shoots). • vi to begin to grow.

**spruce**[1] adj smart, neat, trim. • vt to smarten.

**spruce**[2] n an evergreen tree of the pine family with a conical head and soft light wood.

**sprung** see **spring**.

**spry** adj (**spryer**, **spryest** or **sprier**, **spriest**) vigorous, agile.

**spun** see **spin**.

**spur** n a small metal wheel on a rider's heel, with sharp points for urging on the horse; encouragement, stimulus; a hard sharp projection. • vt (pt **spurred**) to urge on.

**spurious** adj not legitimate or genuine; false.—**spuriously** adv.—**spuriousness** n.

**spurn** vt to reject with disdain. • n disdainful rejection.

**spurt** vt to gush forth in a sudden stream or jet. • n a sudden stream or jet; a burst of activity.—also **spirt**.

**spy** n a secret agent employed to collect information on rivals. • vi to keep under secret surveillance, act as a spy (usu with **on**). • vt to catch sight of.

**sq.** abbr = square.

**squabble** vi to quarrel noisily. • n a noisy, petty quarrel.—also n.

**squad** n a small group of soldiers which form a working unit; a section of a police force; (sport) a group of players from which a team is selected.

**squadron** n a unit of warships, cavalry, military aircraft, etc.

**squalid** adj filthy; neglected, sordid; degrading.—**squalidly** adv.—**squalor** n.

**squander** vt to spend extravagantly or wastefully.

**square** n a shape with four sides of equal length and four right angles; an open space in a town, surrounded by buildings; (inf) an old-fashioned person; an instrument for drawing right angles; the product of a number multiplied by itself. • adj square-shaped; (financial account) settled; fair, honest; equal in score; (inf) old-fashioned. • vt to make square; to multiply by itself. • vi to agree.—**squarely** adv. **squareness** n.

**squash**[1] vt to squeeze, press, or crush; to suppress. • vi to squelch; to crowd. • n a crushed mass; a crowd of people pressed together; a fruit-flavoured drink; a game played in a walled court with rackets and rubber ball.—**squashy** adj.

**squash**[2] n (pl **squashes**, **squash**) a marrow or gourd eaten as a vegetable.

**squat** vi (pt **squatted**) to crouch down upon the heels; to occupy land or property, without permission or title. • adj short and dumpy. • n the act of squatting; a house that is occupied by squatters.

**squatter** *n* a person who squats.

**squawk** *n* a loud, raucous call or cry, as of a bird; (*inf*) a loud protest.— *also vi*.

**squeak** *vi* to make a high-pitched cry. • *n* a squeaky noise.—**squeaker** *n*.—**squeaky** *adj*.

**squeal** *vi* to make a shrill and prolonged cry or sound; (*sl*) to be an informer; to protest.

**squeamish** *adj* easily nauseated; easily shocked or disgusted.—**squeamishly** *adv*.—**squeamishness** *n*.

**squeeze** *vt* to press firmly, compress; to grasp tightly; to hug; to force (through, into) by pressing; to extract liquid, juice, from by pressure; to obtain (money, etc) by force, to harass. • *n* squeezing or being squeezed; a hug; a small amount squeezed from something; a crowding together; financial pressure or hardship.

**squelch** *vi* to walk through soft, wet ground, making a sucking noise. • *vt* to crush or squash completely. • *n* a squelching sound.

**squid** *n* (*pl* **squid, squids**) an edible mollusc, related to the cuttlefish, with a long body and ten arms.

**squint** *vi* to half close or cross the eyes; to glance sideways. • *n* crossed eyes, as caused by a visual disorder; a glance sideways; (*inf*) a look. • *adj* squinting; (*inf*) crooked.

**squire** *n* a country gentleman, esp the leading landowner in a district.

**squirm** *vi* to writhe; to wriggle; to feel embarrassed or ashamed.

**squirrel** *n* a bushy tailed rodent with grey or reddish fur which lives in trees and feeds on nuts.

**squirt** *vt* to eject liquid in a jet. • *vi* to spurt. • *n* a jet of liquid; (*inf*) an insignificant person.

**St** *abbr* = Saint.

**St.** *abbr* = Street.

**stab** *vt* (*pt* **stabbed**) to injure with a knife or pointed weapon; to pain suddenly and sharply. • *vi* to thrust at (as if) with a pointed weapon. • *n* an act or instance of stabbing; a wound made by stabbing; a sudden sensation, as of emotion, pain, etc; (*inf*) an attempt.

**stabilize** *vti* to make or become stable or steady.

**stable**[1] *adj* steady or firm; firmly established; permanent; not decomposing readily.—**stability** *n*.

**stable**[2] *n* a building where horses or cattle are kept; a group of racehorses belonging to one owner; a group of people working for or trained by a specific establishment, as writers, performers, etc. • *vti* to put, keep, or live in a stable.

**stack** *n* a large neatly arranged pile (of hay, papers, records, etc); a chimney stack; (*inf*) a large amount of; a number of aircraft circling an airport waiting for permission to land. • *vt* to pile, arrange in a stack.

**stadium** *n* a sports ground surrounded by tiers of seats.

**staff** *n* (*pl* **staves**) a strong stick or pole; (*mus*) one of the five horizontal lines upon which music is written (—*also* **stave**); (*pl* **staffs**) a body of officers who help a commanding officer, or perform special duties; the workers employed in an establishment; the teachers or lecturers of an educational institution. • *vt* to provide with staff.

**stag** *n* a full-grown male deer. • *adj* (*party*) for men only.

**stage** *n* a degree or step in a process; a raised platform, esp for acting on; (*with* **the**) the theatre, the theatrical calling; any field of action or setting; a portion of a journey; a propulsion unit of a space rocket discarded when its fuel is spent. • *vt* to perform a play on the stage; to plan, organize (an event).

**stage fright** *n* nervousness at appearing before an audience.

**stage manager** *n* a person responsible for the stage arrangements prior to and during the performance of a play.

**stagger** *vi* to walk unsteadily, to totter. • *vt* to astound; to give a shock to; to arrange so as not to overlap; to alternate.

**staggering** *adj* astounding.—**staggeringly** *adv*.

**stagnant** *adj* (*water*) not flowing, standing still with a revolting smell; unchanging, dull.—**stagnancy** *n*.

**stagnate** *vi* to be, or become, stagnant.—**stagnation** *n*.

**stagy, stagey** *adj* (**stagier, stagiest**) theatrical, dramatic.

**staid** *adj* sober; sedate; old-fashioned.

**stain** *vt* to dye; to discolour with spots of something which cannot be removed. • *vi* to become stained; to produce stains. • *n* a discoloured mark; a moral blemish; a dye or liquid for staining materials, eg wood.

**stained glass** *n* coloured glass used in windows.

**stainless** *adj* free from stain; (materials) resistant to staining.

**stair** *n* a flight of stairs; a single step; (*pl*) a stairway.

**staircase** *n* a flight of stairs with banisters.

**stairway** *n* a staircase.

**stake**[1] *n* a sharpened metal or wooden post driven into the ground, as a marker or fence post; a post to which persons were tied for execution by burning; this form of execution. • *vt* to support with, tie or tether to a stake; to mark out (land) with stakes; (*with* **out**) to put under surveillance.

**stake**[2] *vt* to bet; (*inf*) to provide with

money or resources. • *n* a bet; a financial interest; (*pl*) money risked on a race; (*pl*) the prize in a race

**stalactite** *n* an icicle-like calcium deposit hanging from the roof of a cave.

**stalagmite** *n* a cylindrical deposit projecting upwards from the floor of a cave, caused by the dripping of water and lime from the roof.

**stale** *adj* deteriorated from age; tainted; musty; stagnant; jaded.—**staleness** *n*.

**stalemate** *n* (*chess*) a situation in which a king can only be moved in and out of check, thus causing a draw; a deadlock.—*also vt*.

**stalk**[1] *n* the stem of a plant.

**stalk**[2] *vi* to stride in a stiff or angry way; to hunt (game, prey) stealthily.—**stalker** *n*.

**stall**[1] *n* a compartment for one animal in a stable; a table or stand for the display or sale of goods; a stalling of an engine; (*aircraft*) a loss of lift and downward plunge due to an excessive decrease in airspeed; (*pl*) the seats on the ground floor of a theatre. • *vti* (*car engine*) to stop or cause to stop suddenly, eg by misuse of the clutch; (*aircraft*) to lose or cause to lose lift because of an excessive reduction in airspeed.

**stall**[2] *vti* to play for time; to postpone or delay. • *n* (*inf*) any action used in stalling.

**stalwart** *adj* strong, sturdy; resolute; dependable. • *n* a loyal, hardworking supporter.

**stamina** *n* strength; staying power.

**stammer** *vti* to pause or falter in speaking; to stutter.—*also n*.—**stammerer** *n*.

**stamp** *vt* to put a mark on; to imprint with an official seal; to affix a postage stamp; (*with* **out**) to extinguish by stamping; to suppress, eradicate, by force. • *vi* to bring the foot down heavily (on). • *n* a postage stamp; the mark cancelling a postage stamp; a block for imprinting.

**stampede** *n* an impulsive rush of a panic-stricken herd; a rush of a crowd.—*also vti*.

**stance** *n* posture; the attitude taken in a given situation.

**stand** *vb* (*pt* **stood**) *vi* to be in an upright position; to be on, or rise to one's feet; to make resistance; to remain unchanged; to endure, tolerate; (*with* by) to look on without interfering; to be available for use if required; (*with* down) to withdraw, resign; to leave a witness box after testifying in court; (*soldier*) to go off duty; (*with* off) to remain at a distance; to reach a deadlock; (*with* up) to rise to one's feet. • *vt* to put upright; to endure, tolerate; (*with* by) to remain loyal to, to defend; (*with* off) to (cause to) keep at a distance; to lay off (employees) temporarily; (*with* up) to resist; to withstand criticism, close examination, etc; (*inf*) to fail to keep an appointment with. • *n* a strong opinion; a standing position; a standstill; a place for taxis awaiting hire; (*pl*) a structure for spectators; the place taken by a witness for testifying in court; a piece of furniture for hanging things from; a stall or booth for a small retail business.

**standard** *n* a flag, banner, or emblem; an upright pole, pillar; an authorized weight or measure; a criterion; an established or accepted level of achievement; (*pl*) moral principles. • *adj* serving as a standard; typical.—**standardize** *vt*.

**stand-by** *n* a person or thing held in readiness for use in an emergency, etc.—*also adj*.

**stand-in** *n* a substitute; a person who takes the place of an actor during the preparation of a scene or in stunts.—*also vi*.

**standing** *n* status or reputation; length of service, duration. • *adj* upright; permanent; (*jump*) performed from a stationary position.

**standoffish** *adj* aloof, reserved.

**standpoint** *n* a point of view, opinion.

**standstill** *n* a complete halt.

**stand-up** *adj* (*collar*) upright; (*fight*) furious; (*comedian*) telling jokes standing alone in front of an audience.

**stank** *see* **stink**.

**staple**[1] *n* a principal commodity of trade or industry of a region, etc; a main constituent. • *adj* chief.

**staple**[2] *n* a U-shaped thin piece of wire for fastening. • *vt* to fasten with a staple.

**star** *n* any one of the celestial bodies, esp those visible by night which appear as small points of light, including planets, comets, meteors, and less commonly the sun and moon; a figure with five points; an exceptionally successful or skilful person; a famous actor, actress, musician, dancer, etc. • *vti* (*pt* **starred**) to feature or be featured as a star.

**starboard** *n* the right side of a ship or aircraft when facing the bow.

**starch** *n* a white, tasteless, food substance found in potatoes, cereal, etc; a fabric stiffener based on this. • *vt* to stiffen with starch.—**starchy** *adj*.

**stare** *vi* to gaze fixedly, as in horror, astonishment, etc; to glare. • *n* a fixed gaze.

**stark** *adj* bare; plain; blunt; utter. • *adv* completely.—**starkly** *adv*.—**starkness** *n*.

**start** *vi* to commence, begin; to jump involuntarily, from fright. • *vt* to begin. • *n* a beginning; a slight involuntary body movement; a career opening.

**starter** n a person who starts something, esp an official who signals the beginning of a race; a competitor in a race; the first course of a meal; a small electric motor used to start an internal combustion engine.

**startle** vti to be, or cause to be, frightened or surprised.—**startling** adj.

**starve** vi to die or suffer from a lack of food. • vt deprive (a person) of food; to deprive (of) anything necessary.—**starvation** n.

**state** n condition; frame of mind; position in society; ceremonious style; (with cap) an area or community with its own government, or forming a federation under a sovereign government. • adj of the state or State; public; ceremonial. • vt to express in words; to specify, declare officially.

**stately** adj (**statelier, stateliest**) dignified; majestic.—**stateliness** n.

**statement** n a formal announcement; a declaration; a document showing one's bank balance.

**statesman** n a well-known and experienced politician.—**statesmanship** n.

**static** adj fixed; stationary; at rest. • n electrical interference causing noise on radio or TV.

**station** n a railway or bus terminal or stop; headquarters (of the emergency services); military headquarters; (inf) a TV channel; position in society, standing. • vt to assign to a post, place, office.

**stationary** adj not moving.

**stationer** n a dealer in stationery, office supplies, etc.

**stationery** n writing materials, esp paper and envelopes.

**station wagon** n an estate car.

**statistic** n a fact obtained from analysing information expressed in numbers.

**statistics** n (used as sing) the branch of mathematics dealing with the collection, analysis and presentation of numerical data.—**statistical** adj.—**statistician** n.

**statue** n a representation of a human or animal form that is carved or moulded.

**stature** n the standing height of a person; level of attainment.

**status** n (pl **statuses**) social or professional position or standing; prestige; condition or standing from the point of view of the law, position of affairs.

**status quo** n the existing state of affairs.

**statute** n a law enacted by a legislature; a regulation.

**statutory** adj established, regulated, or required by statute.

**staunch** adj loyal; dependable.—**staunchly** adv.

**stave** n a piece of wood of a cask or barrel; (mus) a staff. • vt (pt **staved** or **stove**) (usu with **in**) to smash or dent inwards.

**stay**[1] n a rope supporting a mast

**stay**[2] vi to remain in a place; to wait; to reside temporarily. • vt to support; to endure; to stop, restrain. • n a suspension of legal proceedings; a short time spent as a visitor or guest.

**STD** abbr = sexually transmitted disease; subscriber trunk dialling.

**steadfast** adj firm, fixed; resolute.—**steadfastly** adv.

**steady** adj (**steadier, steadiest**) firm, stable; regular, constant; calm, unexcitable. • n (inf) a regular boyfriend or girlfriend. • vti to make or become steady.—**steadily** adv.—**steadiness** n.

**steak** n a slice of meat, esp beef or fish, for grilling or frying.

**steal** vt (pt **stole**, pp **stolen**) to take (from someone) dishonestly; to obtain secretly. • n (inf) an unbelievable bargain.

**stealth** n a manner of moving quietly and secretly.

**stealthy** adj (**stealthier, stealthiest**) acting or performed in a quiet, secret manner; unobtrusive, furtive.—**stealthily** adv.—**stealthiness** n.

**steam** n the hot mist or vapour created by boiling water. • vi to give off steam; to move by steam power; to cook with steam; (with up) (glasses, windows, etc) to become covered in condensation. • adj driven by steam.

**steel** n an alloy of iron and carbon; strength or courage. • adj of, or like, steel. • vt to cover with steel; to harden; to nerve (oneself).—**steely** adj.

**steep**[1] adj sloping sharply; (inf) excessive, exorbitant.—**steeply** adv.—**steepness** n.

**steep**[2] vti to soak or be soaked in a liquid; to saturate; to imbue.—also n.

**steeple** n a tower of a church, with or without a spire; the spire alone.

**steeplechase** n a horse race across country or on a course over jumps; a track race over hurdles and water jumps.—**steeplechaser** n.

**steer**[1] n a castrated male of the cattle family.

**steer**[2] vti to direct (a vehicle, ship, bicycle, etc) in the correct direction of travel.

**stem**[1] n a plant stalk; the upright slender part of anything, such as a wineglass; the root of a word. • vi (pt **stemmed**) to originate (from).

**stem**[2] vt (pt **stemmed**) to stop, check (the flow or tide).

**stench** n a foul odour.

**stencil** n a pierced sheet of card or metal for reproducing letters by applying paint; a design so made. • vti (pt **stencilled**) to produce (letters, etc) or designs using a stencil.

**step** n one movement of the foot ahead in walking, running, or dancing; a pace; a grade or degree; a stage towards a goal; one tread of a stair, rung of a ladder. • vti (pt **stepped**) to take a step or a number of paces.

**step-** prefix related by remarriage of a spouse or parent.

**stepladder** n a short portable ladder with flat steps fixed within a frame.

**stereo** n (pl **stereos**) a hi-fi or record player with two loudspeakers; stereophonic sound. • adj stereophonic.

**stereophonic** adj (sound reproduction system) using two separate channels for recording and transmission to create a spatial effect.—**stereophonically** adv.—**stereophony** n.

**stereotype** n a fixed, general image of a person or thing shared by many people.—also vt.

**sterile** adj unable to produce offspring, fruit, seeds, or spores; fruitless; free from germs.

**sterilize** vt to render incapable of reproduction; to free from germs.—**sterilization** n.

**sterling** n the British system of money. • adj of excellent character.

**stern**[1] adj severe; austere, harsh.—**sternly** adv.—**sternness** n.

**stern**[2] n the rear part of a boat or ship.

**stethoscope** n an instrument used to detect body sounds.—**stethoscopic** adj.

**stew** n a meal of cooked meat with vegetables. • vt to cook slowly.

**steward** n a manager (of property); a race organizer; a person who serves food on an aircraft or ship and looks after passengers.

**stewardess** n a woman steward on an aircraft or ship.

**stick**[1] vb (pt **stuck**) vt to pierce or stab; to attach with glue, adhesive tape, etc. • vi to cling to, to adhere; to stay close to; to be held up.

**stick**[2] n a broken off shoot or branch

of a tree; a walking stick; a hockey stick; a rod.

**sticker** *n* an adhesive label or poster.

**stickler** *n* a person who is scrupulous or obstinate about something.

**sticky** *adj* (**stickier, stickiest**) covered with adhesive or something sweet; (*weather*) warm and humid; (*inf*) difficult.—**stickiness** *n*.

**stiff** *adj* not flexible or supple; rigid; firm; moving with difficulty; having aching joints and muscles; formal, unfriendly; (*drink*) potent; (*breeze*) strong; (*penalty*) severe. • *n* (*sl*) a corpse. • *adv* utterly.—**stiffly** *adv*.—**stiffness** *n*.

**stiffen** *vti* to make or become stiff.—**stiffener** *n*.

**stifle** *vt* to suffocate; to smother; to suppress, hold back.

**stifling** *adj* excessively hot and stuffy.—**stiflingly** *adv*.

**stigma** *n* (*pl* **stigmas**) a social disgrace; the part of a flower that receives pollen; (*pl* **stigmata**) (*Christianity*) marks resembling the wounds of Christ thought to appear on the bodies of saintly people.

**stile** *n* a step, or set of steps, for climbing over a wall or fence.

**still**[1] *adj* motionless; calm; silent; (*drink*) not carbonated. • *n* a single photograph taken from a cinema film. •*vti* to make or become still. • *adv* continuously; nevertheless.—**stillness** *n*.

**still**[2] *n* an apparatus for distilling liquids, esp spirits.

**stillborn** *adj* born dead; (*idea, project, etc*) a failure from the start, abortive.

**still life** *n* (*pl* **still lifes**) a painting of inanimate objects, such as flowers, fruit, etc.

**stilt** *n* either of a pair of poles with footrests on which one can walk, as in a circus; a supporting column.

**stilted** *adj* (*speech, writing*) pompous, unnaturally formal; (*conversation*) forced, intermittent.

**stimulate** *vt* to excite, arouse.—**stimulation** *n*.

**stimulus** *n* (*pl* **stimuli**) something that acts as an incentive; an agent that arouses or provokes a response in a living organism.

**sting** *n* a sharp pointed organ of a bee, wasp, etc, or hair on a plant, used for injecting poison; a skin wound caused by injected poison from an insect or plant; (*sl*) a swindle. • *vt* to wound with a sting; to cause to suffer mentally; to goad, incite; (*sl*) to cheat by overcharging. • *vi* to feel a sharp pain.

**stingy** *adj* (**stingier, stingiest**) miserly, mean.—**stingily** *adv*.—**stinginess** *n*.

**stink** *vi* (*pt* **stank** *or* **stunk**) to give out an offensive smell; (*sl*) to possess something in an excessive amount; (*sl*) to be extremely bad in quality. • *n* a foul smell.

**stipulate** *vt* to specify as a condition of an agreement.—**stipulation** *n*.

**stir**[1] *vb* (*pt* **stirred**) *vt* to mix, as with a spoon; to rouse; to stimulate or excite. • *vi* to be disturbed; to move oneself; to be active. • *n* a stirring movement; tumult.

**stir**[2] *n* (*sl*) prison.

**stirring** *adj* rousing, exciting.

**stirrup** *n* a strap and flat-bottomed ring hanging from a saddle, for a rider's foot.

**stitch** *n* a single in-and-out movement of a threaded needle in sewing; a single loop of a yarn in knitting or crocheting; a sudden, sharp pain, esp in the side. • *vti* to sew.

**stock** *n* raw material; goods on hand; shares of corporate capital, or the certificates showing such ownership; lineage, family, race; a store; the cattle, horses, etc, kept on a farm; the broth obtained by boiling meat, bones, and vegetables as a foundation for soup, etc. • *vt* to supply; to keep in store. • *adj* standard; hackneyed.

**stockade** *n* a defensive enclosure or barrier of stakes fixed in the ground.

**stockbroker** *n* a person who deals in stocks.

**stocking** *n* a sock; a nylon covering for a woman's leg, supported by suspenders.

**stock market, stock exchange** *n* the market for dealing in stocks and shares.

**stockpile** *n* a reserve supply of essentials.—*also vt.*

**stocky** *adj* (**stockier, stockiest**) short and sturdy.—**stockily** *adv.*—**stockiness** *n.*

**stodgy** *adj* (**stodgier, stodgiest**) (*food*) thick, heavy and indigestible; uninteresting.

**stoke** *vt* to stir and feed (a fire) with fuel.

**stole**[1], **stolen** *see* **steal**.

**stole**[2] *n* a long scarf or piece of fur worn on the shoulders.

**stolid** *adj* impassive; unemotional.—**stolidity** *n.*—**stolidly** *adv.*

**stomach** *n* the organ where food is digested; the belly. • *vt* to put up with.

**stone** *n* a small lump of rock; a precious stone or gem; the hard seed of a fruit; (*pl* **stone**) a unit of weight (14 lb./6.35 kg). • *vt* to throw stones at; to remove stones from (fruit).

**stony, stoney** *adj* (**stonier, stoniest**) of, like, or full of stones; unfeeling, heartless.

**stood** *see* **stand**.

**stool** *n* a seat or a support for the back when sitting, with no back or arms; matter evacuated from the bowels.

**stoop** *vti* to bend the body forward and downward; to degrade oneself; to deign.—*also n.*

**stop** *vb* (*pt* **stopped**) *vt* to halt; to prevent; to intercept; to plug or block.

• *vi* to cease; to come to an end; to stay. • *n* an act or instance of stopping; an impediment; (a knob controlling) a set of organ pipes; any of the standard settings of the aperture in a camera lens (—*also* **f-stop**); a regular stopping place for a bus or train; a punctuation mark, esp full stop.

**stopover** *n* a short break in a journey.

**stoppage** *n* stopping or being stopped; an obstruction; a deduction from pay; a concerted cessation of work by employees, as during a strike.

**stopper** *n* a cork or bung.

**storage** *n* storing or being stored; an area reserved for storing; (*comput*) the storing of data in a computer memory or on disk, tape, etc.

**store** *n* a large supply of goods for future use; a warehouse; a shop. • *vt* to set aside; to put in a warehouse, etc; (*comput*) to put (data) into a computer memory or onto a storage device.

**storey, story** (*US*) *n* a horizontal division of a building; a set of rooms occupying this space.

**stork** *n* a long-necked and long-legged wading bird.

**storm** *n* a heavy fall of rain, snow, etc with strong winds; a violent commotion; a furore; (*mil*) an attack on a fortified place. • *vt* to rush, invade. • *vi* to be angry; to rain, snow hard.—**stormy** *adj.*

**story** *n* a narrative of real or imaginary events; a plot of a literary work; an anecdote; an account; (*inf*) a lie; a news article.

**stout** *adj* strong; short and plump; sturdy. • *n* strong dark beer.—**stoutly** *adv.*—**stoutness** *n.*

**stove**[1] *n* a cooker; heating apparatus.

**stove**[2] *see* **stave**.

**stow** *vt* to store, pack, in an orderly way

**stowaway** *n* a person who hides on a

ship, car, aircraft, etc to avoid paying the fare.

**straddle** vt to have one leg or support on either side of something.

**strafe** vt to machine-gun (troops, vehicles, etc) from the air.—also n.

**straggle** vi to stray; to wander.—**straggler** n.—**straggly** adj.

**straight** adj (line) continuing in one direction, not curved or bent; direct; honest; (sl) heterosexual; (alcoholic drinks) neat, not diluted. • adv directly; without delay. • n being straight; a straight line, form, or position; a straight part of a racetrack; (poker) a hand containing five cards in sequence.—**straightness** n.

**straighten** vti to make or become straight.

**straightforward** adj honest, open; simple; easy.—**straightforwardly** adv.— **straightforwardness** n.

**strain**[1] vt to tax; to stretch; to overexert; to stress; to injure (a muscle) by overstretching; (food) to drain or sieve. • n overexertion; tension; an injury from straining.

**strain**[2] n a plant or animal within a species having a common characteristic; a trait; a trace.

**strained** adj (action, behaviour) produced by excessive effort; (mood, atmosphere) tense, worried.

**strainer** n a sieve or colander used for straining liquids, pasta, tea, etc.

**strait** n a channel of sea linking two larger seas; (usu pl) difficulty, distress.

**straitjacket, straightjacket** n a coatlike device for restraining violent people; something that restricts or limits.— also vt.

**strait-laced, straight-laced** adj prim, morally strict.

**strand**[1] vt to run aground; to leave helpless, without transport or money.

**strand**[2] n a single piece of thread or

wire twisted together to make a rope or cable; a tress of hair.—also vt.

**strange** adj peculiar; odd; unknown; unfamiliar.—**strangely** adv.— **strangeness** n.

**stranger** n a person who is unknown; a new arrival to a place, town, social gathering, etc; a person who is unfamiliar with or ignorant of something.

**strangle** vt to kill by compressing the windpipe, to choke; to stifle, suppress.—**strangler** n.

**strap** n a narrow strip of leather or cloth for carrying or holding (a bag, etc); a fastening, as on a shoe, wristwatch. • vti (pt **strapped**) to fasten with a strap; to beat with a strap.

**strapping** adj tall, well-built.

**strata** see stratum.

**strategic, strategical** adj of, relating to, or important in strategy; (weapons) designed to strike at the enemy's homeland, not for use on the battlefield.—**strategically** adv.

**strategy** n the planning and conduct of war; a political, economic, or business policy.—**strategist** n.

**stratum** n (pl **strata, stratums**) a layer of sedimentary rock; a level (of society).

**straw** n the stalks of threshed grain; a tube for sucking up a drink.

**strawberry** n a soft red fruit used in desserts and jam.

**stray** vi to wander; to deviate; to digress. • n a domestic animal that has become lost. • adj random.

**streak** n a line or long mark of contrasting colour; a flash of lightning; a characteristic, a trace. • vti to mark with or form streaks; to run naked in public as a prank.— **streaker** n.

**streaky** adj (**streakier, streakiest**) marked with streaks; (bacon) having alternate layers of fat and lean.

**stream** n a small river, brook, etc; a flow of liquid; anything flowing and continuous. • vi to flow, gush.

**streamer** n a banner; a long decorative ribbon.

**streamline** vt to shape (a car, boat, etc) in a way that lessens resistance through air or water; to make more efficient, to simplify.—**streamlined** adj.

**street** n a public road in a town or city lined with houses; such a road with its buildings and pavements; the people living, working, etc, along a given street.

**streetcar** n a tram.

**strength** n the state or quality of being physically or mentally strong; power of exerting or withstanding pressure, stress, force; potency; effectiveness.

**strengthen** vti to make or become stronger.

**strenuous** adj vigorous; requiring exertion.—**strenuously** adv.—**strenuousness** n.

**stress** n pressure; mental or physical tension or strain; emphasis; (physics) a system of forces producing or sustaining strain. • vt to exert pressure on; to emphasize.

**stretch** vt to extend, to draw out. • vi to extend, spread; to extend (the limbs, body); to be capable of expanding, as in elastic material. • n the act of stretching or instance of being stretched; the capacity for being stretched; an expanse of time or space; (sl) a period of imprisonment.—**stretchy** adj.

**stretcher** n a portable frame for carrying the sick or injured.

**strew** vt (pt **strewed**, pp **strewn** or **strewed**) to scatter; to spread.

**stricken** adj suffering (from an illness); afflicted, as by something painful.

**strict** adj harsh, firm; enforcing rules

rigorously; rigid.—**strictly** adv.—**strictness** n.

**stride** vi (pt **strode**, pp **stridden**) to walk with long steps. • vt to straddle.—also n.

**strident** adj loud and harsh.—**stridency** n.—**stridently** adv.

**strife** n a fight, quarrel; struggle.

**strike** vb (pt **struck**) vt to hit; to crash into; (mil) to attack; to ignite (a match) by friction; (disease, etc) to afflict suddenly; to come upon, esp unexpectedly; to delete; (clock) to indicate by sounding; to assume (eg an attitude); to occur to; (medal, coin) to produce by stamping; (flag, tent) to lower, take down; to come upon (oil, ore, etc) by drilling or excavation. • vi to cease work to enforce a demand (for higher wages or better working conditions). • n a stoppage of work; a military attack.

**striker** n a worker who is on strike; a mechanism that strikes, as in a clock; (soccer) a forward player whose primary role is to score goals.

**striking** adj impressive.—**strikingly** adv.

**string** n a thin length of cord or twine used for tying, fastening, etc; a stretched length of catgut, wire, or other material in a musical instrument; (pl) the stringed instruments in an orchestra; their players; a line or series of things. • vt (pt **strung**) to thread on a string.

**stringent** adj strict.—**stringently** adv.—**stringency** n.

**strip** vb (pt **stripped**) vt to peel off; to divest; to take away removable parts. • vi to undress. • n a long, narrow piece (of cloth, land, etc); an airstrip or runway.

**stripe** n a narrow band of a different colour form the background; a chevron worn on a military uniform to indicate rank. • *vt* to mark with a stripe.—**striped** *adj*.—**stripy** *adj*.

**stripper** *n* a striptease artist; a device or solvent that removes paint.

**striptease** *n* an erotic show where a person removes their clothes slowly and seductively to music.

**strive** *vi* (*pt* **strove**, *pp* **striven**) to endeavour earnestly, labour hard, to struggle, contend.

**strode** *see* **stride**.

**stroke**[1] *n* a blow or hit; (*med*) a seizure; the sound of a clock; (*sport*) an act of hitting a ball; a manner of swimming; the sweep of an oar in rowing; a movement of a pen, pencil, or paintbrush.

**stroke**[2] *vt* to caress; to do so as a sign of affection.

**stroll** *vi* to walk leisurely, to saunter.—*also n*.

**strong** *adj* physically or mentally powerful; potent; intense; healthy; convincing; powerfully affecting the sense of smell or taste, pungent. • *adv* effectively, vigorously.—**strongly** *adv*.

**stronghold** *n* a fortress; a centre of strength or support.

**strove** *see* **strive**.

**struck** *see* **strike**.

**structure** *n* organization; construction; arrangement of parts in an organism, or of atoms in a molecule of a substance; system, framework; order. • *vt* to organize, to arrange; to build up.—**structural** *adj*.—**structurally** *adv*.

**struggle** *vi* to move strenuously so as to escape; to strive; to fight; to exert strength; to make one's way (along, through, up, etc) with difficulty. • *n* a violent effort; a fight.

**strum** *vt* (*pt* **strummed**) to play on (a guitar, etc), by moving the thumb across the strings.

**strung** *see* **string**.

**strut**[1] *vi* (*pt* **strutted**) to walk in a proud or pompous manner.

**strut**[2] *n* a brace or structural support. • *vt* to brace.

**stub** *n* a short piece left after the larger part has been removed or used; the counterfoil of a cheque, receipt, etc. • *vt* (*pt* **stubbed**) to knock (one's toe or foot) painfully; to extinguish (a cigarette).

**stubble** *n* the stubs or stumps left in the ground when a crop has been harvested; any short, bristly growth, as of beard.—**stubbly** *adj*.

**stubborn** *adj* obstinate; persevering; determined, inflexible.—**stubbornly** *adv*.—**stubbornness** *n*.

**stuck** *see* **stick**.

**stuck-up** *adj* (*inf*) conceited; proud; snobbish.

**stud**[1] *n* a male animal, esp a horse, kept for breeding; a collection of horses and mares for breeding; a farm or stable for stud animals.

**stud**[2] *n* a large-headed nail; an ornamental fastener. • *vt* (*pt* **studded**) to cover with studs.

**student** *n* a person who studies or investigates a particular subject; a person who is enrolled for study at a school, college, university, etc.

**studied** *adj* carefully planned.

**studio** *n* (*pl* **studios**) the workshop of an artist, photographer, etc; (*pl*) a building where motion pictures are made; a room where TV or radio programmes are recorded.

**studious** *adj* given to study; careful.

**study** *vt* to observe an investigate (eg phenomena) closely; to learn (eg a language); to scrutinize; to follow a course (at college, etc). • *n* the process of studying; a detailed investigation and analysis of a subject; the written report of a study of something; a room for studying.

**stuff**[1] *n* material; matter; textile fabrics;

cloth, esp when woollen; personal possessions generally. • *vt* to cram or fill.

**stuffing** *n* material used to stuff or fill anything; a seasoned mixture put inside poultry, meat, vegetables etc before cooking.

**stuffy** *adj* (**stuffier, stuffiest**) badly ventilated; lacking in fresh air; dull, uninspired.—**stuffiness** *n*.

**stumble** *vi* to trip up or lose balance when walking; to falter; (*with* **across** *or* **on**) to discover by chance. • *n* a trip; a blunder.

**stump** *n* the part of a tree remaining in the ground after the trunk has been felled; the part of a limb, tooth, that remains after the larger part is cut off or destroyed. • *vt* (*inf*) to confuse, baffle; to campaign for an election.

**stun** *vt* (*pt* **stunned**) to render unconscious due to a fall or blow; to surprise completely; to shock.

**stung** *see* **sting**.

**stunk** *see* **stink**.

**stunning** *adj* (*inf*) strikingly attractive.

**stunt**[1] *vt* to prevent the growth of, to dwarf.

**stunt**[2] *n* a daring or spectacular feat; a project designed to attract attention. • *vi* to carry out stunts.

**stupefy** *vt* to dull the senses of.—**stupefaction** *n*.

**stupendous** *adj* wonderful, astonishing.

**stupid** *adj* lacking in understanding or common sense; silly; foolish; stunned.—**stupidity** *n*.—**stupidly** *adv*.

**stupor** *n* extreme lethargy; mental dullness.

**sturdy** *adj* (**sturdier, sturdiest**) firm; strong, robust.—**sturdily** *adv*.—**sturdiness** *n*.

**stutter** *vi* to stammer.—*also n*.

**sty**[1], **stye** *n* (*pl* **sties, styes**) an inflamed swelling on the eyelid.

**sty**[2] *n* (*pl* **sties**) a pen for pigs; any filthy place.

**style** *n* the manner of writing, painting, composing music peculiar to an individual or group; fashion, elegance. • *vt* to design or shape (eg hair).

**stylish** *adj* having style; fashionable.—**stylishly** *adv*.—**stylishness** *n*.

**stylize** *vt* to give a conventional style to.—**stylization** *n*.

**stylus** *n* (*pl* **styli, styluses**) the device attached to the cartridge on the arm of a record-player that rests in the groove of a record and transmits the vibrations that are converted to sound.

**suave** *adj* charming, polite.—**suavely** *adv*.—**suaveness, suavity** *n*.

**sub** *n* (*inf*) a submarine; a substitute; a subscription; a subeditor.

**sub-** *prefix* under, below; subordinate, next in rank to.

**subconscious** *adj* happening without one's awareness. • *n* the part of the mind that is active without one's conscious awareness.—**subconsciously** *adv*.

**subdue** *vt* to dominate; to render submissive; to repress (eg a desire); to soften, tone down (eg colour, etc).

**subject** *adj* under the power of; liable. • *n* a person under the power of another; a citizen; a topic; a theme; the scheme or idea of a work of art. • *vt* to bring under control; to make liable; to cause to undergo something.—**subjection** *n*.

**subjective** *adj* determined by one's own mind or consciousness; relating to reality as perceived and not independent of the mind; arising from one's own thoughts and emotions, personal.—**subjectively** *adv*.

**subjunctive** *adv* denoting that mood of a verb which expresses doubt, condition, wish, or hope. • *n* the subjunctive mood.

**sublime** *adj* noble; exalted.—**sublimely** *adv*.—**sublimity** *n*.

**submarine** *adj* underwater, esp under the sea. • *n* a naval vessel capable of being propelled under water, esp for firing torpedoes or missiles.

**submerge, submerse** *vt* to plunge or sink under water; to cover, hide.—**submergence, submersion** *n*.

**submission** *n* an act of submitting; something submitted, as an idea or proposal; the state of being submissive, compliant; the act of referring something for another's consideration, criticism, etc.—**submissively** *adv*.—**submissiveness** *n*.

**submit** *vb* (*pt* **submitted**) *vt* to surrender (oneself) to another person or force; to refer to another for consideration or judgment; to offer as an opinion. • *vi* to yield, to surrender.

**subordinate** *adj* secondary; lower in order, rank. • *n* a subordinate person. • *vt* to put in a lower position or rank.—**subordination** *n*.

**subscribe** *vt* to pay to receive regular copies (of a magazine, etc); to donate money (to a charity, campaign); to support or agree with (an opinion, faith).—**subscriber** *n*.—**subscription** *n*.

**subsequent** *adj* occurring or following after.—**subsequently** *adv*.

**subside** *vi* to sink or fall to the bottom; to settle; to diminish; to abate.—**subsidence** *n*.

**subsidiary** *adj* secondary; supplementary; (*company*) owned or controlled by another.—*also n*.

**subsidy** *n* government financial aid to a private person or company to assist an enterprise.—**subsidize** *vt*.

**subsistence** *n* existence; livelihood.

**substance** *n* matter (such as powder, liquid); the essential nature or part; significance.

**substantial** *adj* of considerable value or size; important; strongly built.—**substantially** *adv*.

**substantiate** *vt* to prove, to verify.—**substantiation** *n*.

**substitute** *vt* to put or act in place of another person or thing (*with* **for**); to replace (by). • *n* a person or thing that serves in place of another.—*also adj*.—**substitution** *n*.

**subtitle** *n* an explanatory, usu secondary, title to a book; a printed translation superimposed on a foreign language film.—*also vt*.

**subtle** *adj* delicate; slight; not noticeable; difficult to define, put into words; ingenious.—**subtlety** *n*.—**subtly** *adv*.

**subtract** *vti* to take away or deduct, as one quantity from another.—**subtraction** *n*.

**suburb** *n* a residential district on the outskirts of a large town or city.—**suburban** *adj*.—**suburbia** *n*.

**subversive** *adj* liable to subvert established authority. • *n* a person who engages in subversive activities.

**subway** *n* a passage under a street; an underground metropolitan electric railway.

**succeed** *vt* to come after, to follow; to take the place of. • *vi* to accomplish what is attempted; to prosper.

**success** *n* the gaining of wealth, fame, etc; the favourable outcome (of anything attempted); a successful person or action.

**successful** *adj* having success.—**successfully** *adv*.

**succession** *n* following in sequence; a number of persons or things following in order; the act or process of succeeding to a title, throne, etc; the line of descent to succeed to something.

**successive** *adj* following in sequence.—**successively** *adv*.

**successor** *n* a person who succeeds anothe.

**succinct** *adj* clear, concise.—**succinctly** *adv*.—**succinctness** *n*.

**succulent** *adj* juicy; moist and tasty; (*plant*) having fleshy tissue. • *n* a succulent plant (eg cactus).—**succulence** *n*.

**succumb** *vi* to yield to superior strength or overpowering desire; to die.

**such** *adj* of a specified kind (eg such people, such a film); so great. • *adv* so; very.

**suck** *vt* to draw (a liquid, air) into the mouth; to dissolve or roll about in the mouth (as a sweet); to draw in as if by sucking (*with* **in, up** etc).—*also n*.

**sucker** *n* (*sl*) a person who is easily taken in or deceived; a cup-shaped piece of rubber that adheres to surfaces.

**suckle** *vt* to feed at the breast or udder.

**sucrose** *n* sugar.

**suction** *n* the act or process of sucking; the exertion of a force to form a vacuum.

**sudden** *adj* happening quickly and unexpectedly, abrupt.—**suddenly** *adv*.—**suddenness** *n*.

**sue** *vt* (*pr p* **suing**, *pt* **sued**) to bring a legal action against.

**suede** *n* leather finished with a soft nap.

**suet** *n* white, solid fat in animal tissue, used in cooking.

**suffer** *vt* to undergo; to endure; to experience. • *vi* to feel pain or distress.—**sufferer** *n*.—**suffering** *n*.

**sufferable** *adj* endurable.

**suffice** *vi* to be sufficient, adequate (for some purpose).

**sufficient** *adj* enough; adequate—**sufficiency** *n*.—**sufficiently** *adv*.

**suffix** *n* (*pl* **suffixes**) a letter, syllable, or syllables added to the end of a word to modify its meaning or to form a new derivative.

**suffocate** *vti* to kill or be killed by depriving of oxygen, or by inhaling a poisonous gas; to feel hot and uncomfortable due to lack of air; to prevent from developing.—**suffocation** *n*.

**sugar** *n* a sweet white, crystalline substance obtained from sugarcane and sugar beet • *vi* to sweeten.

**sugary** *adj* resembling or containing sugar; cloyingly sweet in manner, content, etc.—**sugariness** *n*.

**suggest** *vt* to put forward for consideration; to bring to one's mind; to evoke.—**suggestion** *n*.

**suggestible** *adj* easily influenced by others.—**suggestibility** *n*.

**suggestive** *adj* evocative; rather indecent, risqué.—**suggestively** *adv*.—**suggestiveness** *n*.

**suicide** *n* a person who kills himself intentionally; the act or instance of killing oneself intentionally; ruin of one's own interests.

**suit** *n* a set of matching garments, such as a jacket and trousers or skirt; one of the four sets of thirteen playing cards; a lawsuit. • *vt* to be appropriate; to be convenient or acceptable to.

**suitable** *adj* fitting; convenient (to, for).—**suitably** *adv*.—**suitability** *n*.

**suitcase** *n* a portable, oblong travelling case.

**suite** *n* a number of followers or attendants; a set, esp of rooms, furniture, pieces of music.

**sulk** *vi* to be sullen.

**sulky** *adj* (**sulkier, sulkiest**) bad-tempered, quiet and sullen, because of resentment.

**sullen** *adj* moody and silent; gloomy, dull.—**sullenly** *adv*.—**sullenness** *n*.

**sulphur, sulfur** (*US*) *n* a yellow non-metallic element that is inflammable and has a strong odour.—**sulphuric** *adj*.

**sulphuric acid** *n* a powerfully corrosive acid.

**sultana** *n* a dried, white grape used in cooking; the wife or female relative of a sultan.

**sultry** *adj* (**sultrier, sultriest**) (*weather*) very hot, humid and close; (*person*) sensual; passionate.—**sultriness** *n*.

**sum** *n* the result of two or more things added together; the total, aggregate; a quantity of money; essence, gist. • *vt* (*pt* **summed**) to add (*usu with* up); to encapsulate; to summarize.

**summarize** *vt* to make or be a summary of.

**summary** *adj* concise; performed quickly, without formality. • *n* a brief account of the main points of something.—**summarily** *adv*.

**summer** *n* the warmest season of the year, between spring and autumn.—**summery** *adj*.

**summit** *n* the highest point, the peak; a meeting of world leaders.

**summon** *vt* to order to appear, esp in court; to convene; to gather (strength, enthusiasm, etc).

**summons** *n* a call to appear (in court). • *vt* to serve with a summons.

**sump** *n* a section of an engine for the oil to drain into.

**sumptuous** *adj* lavish; luxurious.—**sumptuously** *adv*.—**sumptuousness** *n*.

**sun** *n* the star around which the earth and other planets revolve which gives light and heat to the solar system; the sunshine. • *vt* (*pt* **sunned**) to expose oneself to the sun's rays.

**sunbathe** *vi* to lie in the rays of the sun or a sun lamp to get a suntan.—*also n*.

**sunburn** *n* inflammation of the skin from exposure to sunlight.—*also vti*.

**Sunday** *n* the day of the week after Saturday, regarded as a day of worship by Christians; a newspaper published on a Sunday.

**sundial** *n* a device that shows the time by casting a shadow on a graduated dial.

**sundry** *adj* miscellaneous, various. • *n* (*pl*) miscellaneous small things.

**sunflower** *n* a tall plant with large yellow flowers whose seeds yield oil.

**sung** *see* **sing**.

**sunglasses** *npl* tinted glasses to protect the eyes from sunlight.

**sunk** *see* **sink**.

**sunny** *adj* (**sunnier, sunniest**) (*weather*) bright with sunshine; (*person, mood*) cheerful.

**sunrise** *n* dawn.

**sunset** *n* dusk.

**sunshine** *n* the light and heat from the sun.

**sunstroke** *n* illness caused by exposure to the sun.

**suntan** *n* browning of the skin by the sun.

**super** *adj* (*inf*) fantastic, excellent; (*inf*) a superintendent, as in the police. • *n* a variety of high-octane petrol.

**superannuation** *n* regular contributions from employees' wages towards a pension scheme.

**superb** *adj* grand; excellent; of the highest quality.—**superbly** *adv*.

**supercilious** *adj* arrogant; haughty; disdainful.—**superciliously** *adv*. —**superciliousness** *n*.

**superficial** *adj* near the surface; slight, not profound; (*person*) shallow in nature.—**superficiality** *n*.—**superficially** *adv*.

**superfluous** *adj* exceeding what is required; unnecessary.—**superfluity** *n*.

**superimpose** *vt* to put or lay upon something else.

**superintendent** *n* a person who manages or supervises; a British police officer next above the rank of inspector.

**superior** *adj* higher in place, quality, rank, excellence; greater in number, power. • *n* a person of higher rank.—**superiority** *n*.

**superlative** *adj* of outstanding quality; (*gram*) denoting the extreme degree of comparison of adjectives and adverbs.—**superlatively** *adv*.

**supermarket** *n* a large self-service, shop selling food and household goods.

**supernatural** *adj* relating to things that cannot be explained by nature; involving ghosts, spirits, etc.— **supernaturally** *adv*.

**superpower** *n* a nation with great economic and military strength.

**supersede** *vt* to take the place of, replace.

**supersonic** *adj* faster than the speed of sound.—**supersonically** *adv*.

**superstition** *n* irrational belief based on ignorance or fear.—**superstitious** *adj*.

**supervise** *vti* to have charge of, direct, to superintend.—**supervision** *n*.—**supervisor** *n*.—**supervisory** *adj*.

**supper** *n* a meal taken in the evening, esp when dinner is eaten at midday; an evening social event; the food served at a supper; a light meal served late in the evening.

**supple** *adj* flexible, easily bent; lithe; (*mind*) adaptable.—**suppleness** *n*.

**supplement** *n* an addition or extra amount (usu of money); an additional section of a book, periodical or newspaper. • *vt* to add to.—**supplemental** *adj*.

**supply** *vt* to provide, meet (a deficiency, a need); to fill (a vacant place). • *n* a stock; (*pl*) provisions.—**supplier** *n*.

**support** *vt* to hold up, bear; to tolerate, withstand; to assist; to advocate (a cause, policy); to provide for (financially). • *n* a means of support; maintenance.

**supporter** *n* a person who backs a political party, sports team, etc.

**suppose** *vt* to assume; to presume as true without definite knowledge; to think probable; to expect. • *vi* to conjecture.

**supposed** *adj* believed to be on available evidence.

**supposedly** *adv* allegedly.

**supposition** *n* an assumption, hypothesis.

**suppress** *vt* to crush, put an end to (eg a rebellion); to restrain (a person); to subdue.—**suppression** *n*.—**suppressor** *n*.

**supreme** *adj* of highest power; greatest; final; ultimate.—**supremacy** *n*.

**surcharge** *vt* to overcharge (a person); to charge an additional sum; to overload. • *n* an additional tax or charge; an additional or excessive load.

**sure** *adj* certain; without doubt; reliable, inevitable; secure; safe; dependable. • *adv* certainly.

**surely** *adv* certainly; securely; it is to be hoped or expected that.

**surety** *n* a person who undertakes responsibility for the fulfilment of another's debt; security given as a guarantee of payment of a debt.

**surf** *n* the waves of the sea breaking on the shore or a reef.

**surface** *n* the exterior face of an object; any of the faces of a solid; the uppermost level of sea or land; a flat area, such as the top of a table; superficial features. • *adj* superficial; external. • *vt* to cover with a surface, as in paving. • *vi* to rise to the surface of water.

**surfboard** *n* a long, narrow board used in the sport of surfing.

**surfeit** *n* an excessive amount.

**surfing** *n* the sport of riding in toward shore on the crest of a wave, esp on a surfboard.

**surge** *n* the rolling of the sea, as after

a large wave; a sudden, strong increase, as of power.—*also vi.*

**surgeon** *n* a medical specialist who practices surgery.

**surgery** *n* the treatment of diseases or injuries by manual or instrumental operations; the consulting room of a doctor or dentist; the daily period when a doctor is available for consultation; the regular period when an MP, lawyer, etc is available for consultation.—**surgical** *adj.*—**surgically** *adv.*

**surmise** *n* guess, conjecture. • *vt* to infer the existence of from partial evidence.

**surmount** *vt* to overcome; to rise above.

**surname** *n* the family name. • *vt* to give a surname to.

**surpass** *vt* to outdo, to outshine; to excel; to exceed.

**surplus** *n* an amount in excess of what is required; an excess of revenues over expenditure in a financial year.

**surprise** *n* the act of catching unawares; an unexpected gift, event; astonishment. • *vt* to cause to feel astonished; to attack unexpectedly; to take unawares.—**surprising** *adj.*—**surprisingly** *adv.*

**surreal** *adj* bizarre.

**surrender** *vt* to relinquish or give up possession or power. • *vi* to give oneself up (to an enemy).—*also n.*

**surreptitious** *adj* done by stealth; clandestine, secret.—**surreptitiously** *adv.*

**surround** *vt* to encircle on all or nearly all sides; (*mil*) to encircle. • *n* a border around the edge of something.

**surroundings** *npl* the conditions, objects, etc around a person or thing; the environment.

**surveillance** *n* a secret watch kept over a person, esp a suspect.

**survey** *vt* to take a general view of; to appraise; to examine carefully; to measure and make a map of an area.

• *n* a detailed study, as by gathering information and analysing it, a general view; the process of surveying an area or a house.

**surveyor** *n* a person who surveys land or buildings.

**survival** *n* surviving; a person or thing that survives; a relic.

**survive** *vt* to live after the death of another person; to continue, endure; to come through alive. • *vi* to remain alive (after experiencing a dangerous situation).—**survivor** *n.*

**susceptible** *adj* ready or liable to be affected by; impressionable.—**susceptibility** *n.*—**susceptibly** *adv.*

**suspect** *vt* to mistrust; to believe to be guilty; to think probable. • *n* a person under suspicion. • *adj* open to suspicion.

**suspend** *vt* to hang; to discontinue, or cease temporarily; to postpone; to debar temporarily from a privilege, etc.

**suspender** *n* a fastener for holding up stockings; (*pl*) braces.

**suspense** *n* mental anxiety or uncertainty; excitement.

**suspension** *n* suspending or being suspended; a temporary interruption or postponement; a temporary removal from office, privileges, etc; the system of springs, shock absorbers, etc that support a vehicle on its axles; (*chem*) a dispersion of fine particles in a liquid.

**suspension bridge** *n* a bridge carrying a roadway suspended by cables anchored to towers at either end.

**suspicion** *n* act of suspecting; a belief formed or held without sure proof; mistrust; a trace.—**suspicious** *adj.*—**suspiciously** *adv.*

**sustain** *vt* hold up, support; to maintain; to suffer (eg an injury); to nourish.

**sustenance** *n* nourishment.

**swab** n a wad of absorbent material, usu cotton, used to clean wounds, take specimens, etc; a mop.—*also vt*.

**swagger** vi to strut; to brag loudly. • n boastfulness; swinging gait.

**swallow**[1] n a small migratory bird with long wings and a forked tail.

**swallow**[2] vt to cause food and drink to move from the mouth to the stomach; to endure; to engulf; (*inf*) to accept gullibly; (*emotion, etc*) to repress.—*also n*.

**swam** *see* **swim**.

**swamp** n wet, spongy land; bog. • vt to overwhelm; to flood as with water. **swampy** adj.

**swan** n a large, usu white, bird with a very long neck that lives on rivers and lakes. • vi (*pt* **swanned**) (*inf*) to wander aimlessly.

**swap** vti (*pt* **swapped**) (*inf*) to trade, barter. • n (*inf*) the act of exchanging one thing for another.—*also* **swop**.

**swarm** n a colony of migrating bees; a moving mass, crowd or throng. • vi to move in great numbers; to teem.

**swarthy** adj (**swarthier, swarthiest**) dark-complexioned.—**swarthiness** n.

**swat** vt (*pt* **swatted**) (*inf*) to hit with a sharp blow; to swipe.—*also n*.— **swatter** n.

**sway** vi to swing or move from one side to the other or to and fro; to lean to one side; to vacillate in judgment or opinion. • n influence; control.

**swear** vi (*pt* **swore**, *pp* **sworn**) to make a solemn affirmation, promise, etc, calling God as a witness; to give evidence on oath; to curse, blaspheme or use obscene language; to vow.

**sweat** n perspiration; (*inf*) hard work; (*inf*) a state of eagerness, anxiety.— *also vti*.—**sweaty** adj.

**sweater** n a knitted pullover.

**Swede** n a native of Sweden.

**swede** n a round root vegetable with yellow flesh.

**Swedish** adj pertaining to Sweden, its people or language. • n the language of Sweden.

**sweep** vb (*pt* **swept**) vt to clean with a broom; to remove (rubbish, dirt) with a brush. • vi to pass by swiftly. • n a movement, esp in an arc; a stroke; scope, range; a sweepstake.

**sweeping** adj wide-ranging; indiscriminate.—**sweepingly** adv.

**sweet** adj having a taste like sugar; pleasing to other senses; gentle; kind. • n a small piece of confectionery; a dessert.—**sweetly** adv.— **sweetness** n.

**sweetbread** n the pancreas or thymus of an animal used for food.

**sweetcorn** n maize, corn on the cob.

**sweeten** vti to make or become sweet or sweeter; to mollify.

**sweetheart** n a lover.

**swell** vi (*pt* **swelled**, *pp* **swollen** or **swelled**) to increase in size or volume; to rise into waves; to bulge out. • n the movement of the sea; a bulge; a gradual increase in the loudness of a musical note; (*inf*) a socially prominent person. • adj excellent.

**swelling** n inflammation.

**swelter** vi to suffer from heat. • n humid, oppressive heat.

**swept** *see* **sweep**.

**swerve** vi to turn aside suddenly from a line or course; to veer.—*also n*.

**swift** adj moving with great speed; rapid. • n a swallow-like bird.— **swiftly** adv.—**swiftness** n.

**swig** vt (*pt* **swigged**) (*inf*) to take a long drink, esp from a bottle.—*also n*.

**swill** vti to drink greedily; to guzzle; to rinse with a large amount of water. • n liquid refuse fed to pigs.

**swim** vi (*pt* **swam**, *pp* **swum**) to move through water by using limbs or fins;

to be dizzy; to be flooded with. • *n* the act of swimming.—**swimmer** *n*.

**swimming costume, swimsuit** *n* a one-piece garment for swimming in.

**swindle** *vti* to cheat (someone) of money or property.—*also n*.—**swindler** *n*.

**swine** *n* (*pl* **swine**) a pig; (*inf*) an contemptible person; (*inf*) an unpleasant thing.

**swing** *vb* (*pt* **swung**) *vi* to sway or move to and fro, as an object hanging in air; to pivot; to shift from one mood or opinion to another; (*music*) to have a lively rhythm; (*sl*) to be hanged. • *vt* to whirl; to play swing music; to influence; to achieve, bring about. • *n* a swinging, curving or rhythmic movement; a suspended seat for swinging in; a shift from one condition to another; a type of popular jazz played by a large band and characterized by a lively, steady rhythm.

**swinging** *adj* (*inf*) up-to-date; lively.

**swipe** *n* (*inf*) a hard, sweeping blow. • *vt* (*inf*) to hit with a swipe; (*sl*) to steal.

**swirl** *vti* to turn with a whirling motion.—*also n*.

**swish** *vi* to move with a soft, whistling, hissing sound. • *n* a swishing sound. • *adj* (*inf*) smart, fashionable.

**Swiss** *adj* of or belonging to Switzerland. • *n* (*pl* **Swiss**) a native of Switzerland.

**switch** *n* a control for turning on and off an electrical device; a sudden change; a swap. • *vt* to shift, change, swap; to turn on or off (as of an electrical device).

**switchback** *n* a zigzag road in a mountain region; a roller coaster.

**switchboard** *n* an installation in a building where telephone calls are connected.

**swivel** *n* a coupling that permits parts to rotate. • *vi* (*pt* **swivelled**) to turn (as if) on a pin or pivot.

**swoon** *vt* to faint.—*also n*.

**swoop** *vt* to carry off abruptly. • *vi* to make a sudden attack (*usu with* **down**) as a bird in hunting.—*also n*.

**swop** *see* **swap**.

**sword** *n* a weapon with a long blade and a handle a one end.

**swordfish** *n* a large marine fish with a sword-like upper jaw.

**swore, sworn** *see* **swear**.

**swot** *vi* (*pt* **swotted**) (*inf*) to study hard for an examination. • *n* (*inf*) a person who studies hard.

**syllable** *n* word or part of a word uttered by in a single sound; one or more letters written to represent a spoken syllable.

**syllabus** *n* (*pl* **syllabuses**) a summary or outline of a course of study or of examination requirements; the subjects studied for a particular course.

**symbol** *n* a representation; an object used to represent something abstract; an arbitrary or conventional sign standing for a quality, process, relation, etc as in music, chemistry, mathematics, etc.

**symbolic, symbolical** *adj* of, using, or constituting a symbol.—**symbolically** *adv*.

**symbolism** *n* the use of symbols; a system of symbolic representation.—**symbolist** *n*.

**symbolize** *vt* to be a symbol; to represent by a symbol.—**symbolization** *n*.

**symmetrical, symmetric** *adj* having symmetry.

**symmetry** *n* the corresponding arrangement of one part to another in size, shape and position; balance or harmony of form resulting form this.

**sympathetic** *adj* having sympathy; compassionate.—**sympathetically** *adv*.

**sympathize** *vi* feel sympathy for; to commiserate; to be in sympathy (with).

**sympathy** *n* agreement of ideas and opinions; compassion; (*pl*) support for an action or cause.

**symphony** *n* an orchestral composition in several movements; a large orchestra for playing symphonic works.—**symphonic** *adj.*—**symphonically** *adv.*

**symposium** *n* (*pl* **symposiums, symposia**) a conference at which several specialists deliver short addresses on a topic; an anthology of scholarly essays.

**symptom** *n* a bodily sensation experienced by a patient indicative of a particular disease; an indication.

**synagogue** *n* the building where Jews assemble for worship and religious study.

**synchronize** *vti* to occur at the same time and speed; (*watches*) to adjust to show the same time.—**synchronization** *n*.

**syndicate** *n* an association of individuals or corporations formed for a project requiring much capital; any group, as of criminals, organized for some undertaking; an organization selling articles or features to many newspapers, etc. • *vt* to manage as or form into a syndicate; to sell (an article, etc) through a syndicate. • *vi* to form a syndicate.—**syndication** *n*.

**syndrome** *n* a characteristic pattern of signs and symptoms of a disease.

**synonym** *n* a word that has the same, or similar, meaning as another or others in the same language.

**synonymous** *adj* having the same meaning; equivalent.

**synopsis** *n* (*pl* **synopses**) a summary or brief review of a subject.

**syntax** *n* (*gram*) the arrangement of words in the sentences and phrases of language; the rules governing this.—**syntactic** *adj.*—**syntactically** *adv.*

**synthesis** *n* (*pl* **syntheses**) the process of combining separate elements of thought into a whole; the production of a compound by a chemical reaction.

**synthetic** *adj* produced by chemical synthesis; artificial.—**synthetically** *adv.*

**syphilis** *n* a contagious, infectious venereal disease.—**syphilitic** *adj*.

**syphon** *see* **siphon**.

**syringe** *n* a hollow tube with plunger at one end and a sharp needle at the other by which liquids are injected or withdrawn, esp in medicine. • *vt* to inject or cleanse with a syringe.

**syrup** *n* a thick sweet substance made by boiling sugar with water; the concentrated juice of a fruit or plant.—**syrupy** *adj*.

**system** *n* a method of working or organizing by following a set of rules; routine; organization; structure; a political regime; an arrangement of parts fitting together.

**systematic** *adj* constituting or based on a system; according to a system.—**systematically** *adv*.

**systems analysis** *n* analysis of a particular task or operation to determine how computer hardware and software may best perform it. —**systems analyst** *n*.

# T

**tab** *n* a small tag, label or flap; (*inf*) a bill, as for expenses. • *vt* to fix a tab on.

**tabby** *n* a domestic cat with a striped coat, esp a female.

**table** 459 **take**

**table** n a piece of furniture consisting of a slab or board on legs; the people seated round a table; supply of food; a list arranged for reference or comparison. • vt to submit, put forward; to postpone indefinitely. • adj of, on or at a table.

**tablecloth** n a cloth for covering a table.

**table d'hôte** n (pl **tables d'hôte**) a meal at a fixed price for a set number of courses.—also adj.

**tablespoon** n a large serving spoon; a unit of measure in cooking.—**table-spoonful** n.

**tablet** n a pad of paper; a medicinal pill; a cake of solid substance, such as soap; a slab of stone.

**table tennis** n a game like tennis played on a table with small bats and balls.

**taboo, tabu** n a religious or social prohibition.—also adj.

**tabulate** vt to arrange (written material) in the form of a table.—**tabulation** n

**tacit** adj implied without being spoken; understood.—**tacitly** adj.

**taciturn** adj habitually silent and reserved.—**taciturnity** n.

**tack**[1] n a short, flat-headed nail; the course of a sailing ship; a course of action, approach; adhesiveness. • vt to fasten with tacks. • vi to change direction.

**tack**[2] n (inf) food.

**tackle** n a system of ropes and pulleys for lifting; equipment; rigging; (sport) an act of grabbing and stopping an opponent. • vt (task, etc) to attend to, undertake; (a person) to confront; (sport) to challenge with a tackle.

**tacky** adj (**tackier, tackiest**) (paint, etc) sticky.

**tact** n discretion in managing the feelings of others.—**tactful** adj.—**tactless** adj.

**tactics** n sing stratagem; ploy; the science or art of manoeuvring troops in the presence of the enemy.—**tactical** adj.—**tactician** n.

**tadpole** n the larva of a frog or toad, esp at the stage when the head and tail have developed.

**tag**[1] n a strip or label for identification. • vt to attach a tag; to mark with a tag. • vi (with **onto, after**) to trail along (behind).

**tag**[2] n a children's chasing game.

**tail** n the appendage of an animal growing from the rear; the rear part of anything; (pl) the side of a coin without a head on it; (inf) a person who keeps another under surveillance, esp a detective. • vt to follow closely, shadow.

**tail coat** n a man's black or grey coat cut horizontally just below the waist at the front with two long tails at the back.

**tail-end** adj tardy; being the last in line. • n the last.

**tailor** n a person who makes and repairs outer garments, esp. men's suits. • vi to work as a tailor. • vt to adapt to fit a particular requirement.

**tailor-made** adj specially designed for a particular purpose or person.

**taint** vt to contaminate; to infect. • vi to be corrupted or disgraced. • n a stain; corruption.

**take** vb (pt **took**, pp **taken**) vt to lay hold of; to grasp or seize; to gain, win; to choose, select; (attitude, pose) to adopt; to understand; to consume; to accept or agree to; to lead or carry with one; to use as a means of travel; (math) to subtract (from); to use; to steal; (gram) to be used with; to endure calmly. • vi (plant, etc) to start growing successfully; to become effective; to catch on; to have recourse to; to go to. • n (film, TV) the amount of film used without stopping the camera.

**takeoff** *n* the process of an aircraft becoming airborne.

**takeover** *n* the taking over of control, as in business.

**taking** *adj* attractive, charming; (*inf*) catching, contagious. • *n* the act of one that takes; (*pl*) earnings; profits.

**talc** *n* a type of smooth mineral used in ceramics and talcum powder; talcum powder.

**talcum powder** *n* perfumed powdered talc for the skin.

**tale** *n* a narrative or story; a fictitious account, a lie; idle or malicious gossip.

**talent** *n* any innate or special aptitude.—**talented** *adj*.

**talk** *vti* to speak; to converse; to discuss; to gossip; to divulge information. • *n* a discussion; a lecture; gossip; (*pl*) negotiations.

**talkative** *adj* given to talking a great deal.

**tall** *adj* above average in height; (*inf: story*) exaggerated.—**tallness** *n*.

**tallboy** *n* a high chest of drawers.

**tally** *n* reckoning, account; one score in a game. • *vi* to correspond; to keep score.

**tambourine** *n* a percussion hand instrument made of skin stretched over a circular frame with small jingling metal discs around the edge.

**tame** *adj* (*animal*) not wild, domesticated; compliant; dull, uninteresting. • *vt* (*animal*) to domesticate; to subdue; to soften.

**tamper** *vi* to meddle (with); to interfere (with).

**tampon** *n* a firm plug of cotton wool inserted in the vagina during menstruation.

**tan** *n* a yellowish-brown colour; suntan. • *vti* (*pt* **tanned**) to acquire a

suntan through sunbathing; (*skin, hide*) to convert into leather by processing.

**tandem** *n* a bicycle for two riders, one behind the other.

**tang** *n* sharp smell or a strong taste.—**tangy** *adj*.

**tangent** *n* a line that touches a curve or circle at one point, without crossing it. • *adj* touching at one point.

**tangerine** *n* a small, sweet orange with a loose skin; the colour of this.—*also adj*.

**tangible** *adj* capable of being felt, seen or noticed; substantial; real.—**tangibility** *n*.

**tangle** *n* a mass of hair, string or wire knotted together confusedly; a complication. • *vi* to become tangled or complicated; (*with* **with**) to become involved in argument with.

**tango** *n* (*pl* **tangos**) a Latin American dance.—*also vi*.

**tank** *n* a large container for storing liquids or gases; an armoured combat vehicle, mounted with guns and having caterpillar tracks.

**tankard** *n* a tall, one-handled beer mug, often with a hinged lid.

**tanker** *n* a large ship or truck for transporting oil and other liquids.

**tantalize** *vt* to tease or torment by presenting something greatly desired, but keeping it inaccessible.

**tantamount** *adj* equivalent (to) in effect; as good as.

**tantrum** *n* a childish fit of bad temper.

**tap**[1] *n* a quick, light blow or touch; a piece of metal attached to the heel or toe of a shoe for reinforcement or to tap-dance. • *vti* (*pt* **tapped**) to strike lightly; to make a tapping sound.

**tap**[2] *n* a device controlling the flow of liquid through a pipe or from a container. • *vt* to pierce in order to draw fluid from; to connect a secret listening device to a telephone; (*inf*) to ask for money from; (*resources, etc*) to draw on.

**tap-dance** *vi* to perform a step dance in shoes with taps.—**tap-dancer** *n*.—**tap-dancing** *n*.

**tape** *n* a strong, narrow strip of cloth, paper, etc, used for tying, binding, etc; a tape measure; magnetic tape, as in a cassette or videotape. • *vt* to wrap with tape; to record on magnetic tape.

**tape measure** *n* a tape marked in inches or centimetres for measuring.

**taper** *n* a long thin candle. • *vti* to make or to become gradually narrower towards one end.—**tapering** *adj*.

**tape recorder** *n* a machine for recording and reproducing sounds or music on magnetic tape.—*also* **tape deck**.

**tapestry** *n* a heavy fabric woven with patterns or figures, used for wall hangings and furnishings.

**tapioca** *n* a starch extracted from the root of a tropical plant and used in puddings, etc.

**tar** *n* a thick, dark gluey substance obtained from wood, coal, peat, etc., used for surfacing roads. • *vt* to coat with tar.—**tarry** *adj*.

**tarantula** *n* a large, hairy spider with a poisonous bite.

**tardy** *adj* (**tardier, tardiest**) slow; later than expected.—**tardily** *adv*.—**tardiness** *n*.

**target** *n* a mark to aim at, esp in shooting; an objective or ambition.

**tariff** *n* a tax on imports; (*in a hotel*) a list of prices; the rate of charge for public services, such as gas or electricity.

**Tarmac, Tarmacadam** *n* (*trademark*) a material for surfacing roads made from crushed stones and tar; an airport runway. • *vti* (*pt* **tarmacked**) to lay down a tarmac surface.

**tarnish** *vi* (*metal*) to lose its lustre or discolour due to exposure to the air. • *vt* (*reputation*) to taint.—*also n*.

**tarpaulin** *n* canvas cloth coated with a waterproof substance.

**tart**[1] *adj* having a sour, sharp taste; (*speech*) sharp, severe. —**tartly** *adv*.—**tartness** *n*.

**tart**[2] *n* an open pastry case containing fruit, jam or custard; (*inf*) a prostitute.

**tartan** *n* a woollen cloth with a chequered pattern, having a distinctive design for each Scottish clan.

**tartar** *n* a hard, yellow, crusty deposit that forms on the teeth; a salty deposit on the sides of wine casks.

**tartar sauce** *n* a mayonnaise sauce with herbs, etc, eaten esp with fish.

**task** *n* a specific amount of work to be done; a chore.

**task force** *n* a small unit with a specific mission, usu military.

**tassel** *n* an ornamental tuft of silken threads decorating soft furnishings, clothes, etc.—**tasselled** *adj*.

**taste** *vt* to perceive (a flavour) by taking into the mouth; to try by eating and drinking a little; to sample; to experience. • *vi* to try by the mouth; to have a specific flavour. • *n* the sense by which flavours are perceived; a small portion; the ability to recognize what is beautiful, attractive, etc; liking; a brief experience.

**tasteful** *adj* showing good taste.—**tastefully** *adv*.—**tastefulness** *n*.

**tasteless** *adj* without taste, bland; in bad taste.—**tastelessly** *adv*.

**tasty** *adj* (**tastier, tastiest**) savoury; having a pleasant flavour.

**tatter** *n* a torn or ragged piece of cloth.—**tattered** *adj*.

**tattoo**[1] *n* (*pl* **tattoos**) a continuous beating of a drum; a military display of exercises and music.

**tattoo**[2] *vt* to make permanent patterns or pictures on the skin by pricking and marking with dyes. • *n* (*pl* **tattoos**) marks made on the skin in this way.

**tatty** *adj* (**tattier, tattiest**) shabby, ragged.

**taught** *see* **teach**.

**taunt** *vt* to provoke with mockery or contempt; to tease. • *n* an insult.

**Taurus** *n* the Bull, the second sign of the zodiac; a star sign which applies to those with birthdays between April 21 and May 20.

**taut** *adj* stretched tight; tense; stressed.

**tavern** *n* a pub, an inn.

**tawdry** *adj* (**tawdrier, tawdriest**) showy, cheap, and of poor quality.

**tawny** *adj* yellowish brown.

**tax** *n* a rate imposed by the government on property or persons to raise revenues; a strain. • *vt* to impose a tax (upon); to strain.

**taxation** *n* the act of levying taxes; the amount so raised.

**taxi, taxicab** *n* a car, usu fitted with a taximeter, that may be hired to transport passengers. • *vi* (*pr p* **taxiing,** *pt* **taxied**) (*aircraft*) to move along the runway before takeoff or after landing.

**taxpayer** *n* a person who or an organization that pays taxes.

**TB** *abbr* = tuberculosis.

**tea** *n* a shrub growing in China, India, Sri Lanka, etc; its dried, shredded leaves, which are infused in boiling water for a beverage; a light meal taken in mid-afternoon; a main meal taken in the early evening.

**tea bag** *n* a small porous bag containing tea leaves for infusing.

**teach** *vb* (*pt* **taught**) *vt* to impart knowledge to; to give lessons (to); to train; to help to learn. • *vi* to give instruction, esp as a profession.— **teachable** *adj*.

**teacher** *n* a person who instructs others, esp as an occupation.

**teaching** *n* the profession or practice of being a teacher; the act of giving instruction.

**teacup** *n* a small cup for drinking tea.

**teak** *n* a type of hard wood from an East Indian tree.

**team** *n* a group of people participating in a sport together; a group of people working together; two or more animals pulling a vehicle. • *vi* (*with* **up**) to join in cooperative activity.

**teamwork** *n* cooperation of individuals for the benefit of the team; the ability of a team to work together.

**teapot** *n* a vessel in which tea is made.

**tear**[1] *n* a drop of salty liquid appearing in the eyes when crying; anything tear-shaped.

**tear**[2] *vb* (*pt* **tore,** *pp* **torn**) *vt* to pull apart by force; to split. • *vi* to move with speed. • *n* a hole or split.

**tearful** *adj* weeping; sad.—**tearfully** *adv*.

**tear gas** *n* gas that irritates the eyes and nasal passages, used in riot control.

**tease** *vt* to separate the fibres of; to torment or irritate; to taunt playfully. • *n* a person who teases or torments; (*inf*) a flirt.—**teaser** *n*.

**tea service, tea set** *n* the set of cups and saucers, etc for serving tea.

**teaspoon** *n* a small spoon for use with tea or as a measure; the amount measured by this.—**teaspoonful** *n*.

**teat** *n* the nipple on a breast or udder; the mouthpiece of a baby's feeding bottle.

**tea towel, tea cloth** *n* a towel for drying dishes.

**technical** *adj* relating to, or specializing in practical, industrial, mechanical or applied sciences; (*expression, etc*) belonging to or peculiar to a particular field of activity.—**technically** *adv*.

**technicality** *n* a petty formality or technical point.

**technician** *n* a person skilled in the practice of any art, esp in practical work with scientific equipment.

**technique** *n* method of performing a particular task; knack.

**technology** *n* the application of mechanical and applied sciences to industrial use.—**technological** *adj.*—**technologist** *n.*

**teddy bear** *n* a stuffed toy bear.

**tedious** *adj* monotonous; boring.—**tedium** *n.*

**tee** *n* (*golf*) the place from where the first stroke is played at each hole; a small peg from which the ball is driven. • *vti* to position (the ball) on the tee.

**teem**[1] *vi* (*with* **with**) to be prolific or abundant in.

**teem**[2] *vi* to pour (with rain).

**teenager** *n* (*inf*) a person who is in his or her teens.

**teens** *npl* the years of one's life from thir*teen* to nine*teen*.—**teenage** *adj.*—**teenaged** *adj.*

**tee-shirt** *see* **T-shirt**.

**teeter** *vi* to move or stand unsteadily.

**teeth** *see* **tooth**.

**teethe** *vi* to cut one's first teeth.

**teething** *n* the condition in babies of the first growth of teeth.

**teething troubles** *npl* problems encountered in the early stages of a project, etc; pain caused by growing teeth.

**teetotaller, teetotaler** (*US*) *n* a person who abstains from alcoholic drinks.—**teetotal** *adj.*

**telecommunication** *n* communication of information over long distances by telephone and radio; (*pl*) the technology of telephone and radio communication.

**telegram** *n* a message sent by telegraph.

**telegraph** *n* a system for transmitting messages over long distances using electricity, wires and a code. • *vt* to transmit by telegraph.—**telegraphic** *adj.*—**telegraphy** *n.*

**telepathy** *n* the communication between people's minds of thoughts and feelings, without the need for speech or proximity.—**telepathic** *adj.*

**telephone** *n* an instrument for transmitting speech at a distance, esp by means of electricity. • *vt* (*someone*) to call by telephone.

**telephonist** *n* a person who operates a telephone switchboard.—*also* **telephone operator**.

**telephoto lens** *n* a camera lens that magnifies distant objects.

**teleprinter** *n* a telegraph apparatus with a keyboard that transmits and a printer that receives messages over a distance.

**telescope** *n* a tubular optical instrument for viewing objects at a distance.

**televise** *vt* (*a programme*) to transmit by television.

**television** *n* the transmission of visual images and accompanying sound through electrical and sound waves; a television receiving set; television broadcasting.

**tell** *vb* (*pt* **told**) *vt* to narrate; to disclose; to inform; to notify; to instruct to distinguish. • *vi* to tell tales, to inform on; to produce a marked effect.

**teller** *n* a bank clerk; a person appointed to count votes in an election.

**telling** *adj* having great impact.

**telltale** *n* a person who tells tales about others. • *adj* revealing what is meant to be hidden.

**telly** *n* (*inf*) television.

**temerity** *n* rashness.

**temp** *n* (*inf*) a temporary employee.

**temp.** *abbr* = temperature.

**temper** n a frame of mind; a fit of anger. • vt to tone down, moderate; (steel) to heat and cool repeatedly to bring to the correct hardness.

**temperament** n one's disposition.

**temperamental** adj easily irritated; erratic.—**temperamentally** adv.

**temperance** n moderation; abstinence from alcohol.

**temperate** adj mild or moderate in temperature; (behaviour) moderate, self-controlled.

**temperature** n degree of heat or cold; body heat above the normal.

**tempest** n a violent storm.

**template** n a pattern, gauge or mould used as a guide esp in cutting metal, stone or plastic.

**temple**[1] n a place of worship.

**temple**[2] n the region on either side of the head above the cheekbone.

**tempo** n (pl **tempos, tempi**) (mus) the speed at which music is meant to be played; rate of any activity.

**temporal**[1] adj relating to time; secular, civil.

**temporal**[2] adj of or relating to the temples of the head.

**temporary** adj lasting or used for a limited time only; not permanent.— **temporarily** adv.

**tempt** vt to entice to do wrong; to invite, attract, induce.—**tempter** n.— **temptress** nf.

**temptation** n the act of tempting or the state of being tempted; something or someone that tempts.

**tempting** adj attractive, inviting.

**ten** adj, n the cardinal number next above nine. • n the symbol for this (10, X, x).

**tenacious** adj grasping firmly; persistent; retentive; adhesive.

**tenacity** n the state or quality of being tenacious; doggedness, obstinacy; adhesiveness, stickiness.

**tenancy** n the temporary possession by a tenant of another's property; the period of this.

**tenant** n a person who pays rent to occupy a house or flat or for the use of land or buildings; an occupant.

**tend**[1] vt to take care of; to attend (to).

**tend**[2] vi to be inclined; to move in a specific direction.

**tendency** n an inclination or leaning.

**tender**[1] n a wagon attached to locomotives to carry fuel and water; a small ship that brings stores to a larger one.

**tender**[2] vt to present for acceptance; to offer as payment. • vi to make an offer. • n an offer to provide goods or services at a fixed price.

**tender**[3] adj soft, delicate; fragile; painful, sore; sensitive; sympathetic.— **tenderly** adv.—**tenderness** n.

**tenderize** vt (meat) to make more tender, esp by pounding.

**tendon** n fibrous tissue attaching a muscle to a bone.

**tenement** n a building divided into flats, each occupied by a separate owner or tenant.

**tenet** n any belief or doctrine.

**tennis** n a game for two or four people, played by hitting a ball over a net with a racket.

**tennis court** n a court surfaced with clay, asphalt or grass on which tennis is played.

**tenor** n a general purpose or intent; the highest regular adult male voice, higher than a baritone and lower than an alto; a man who sings tenor.

**tense**[1] n (gram) the verb form that indicates the time of an action or the existence of a state.

**tense**[2] adj stretched, taut; apprehensive; nervous and highly strung. • vti to make or become tense.— **tensely** adv.—**tenseness** n.

**tension** n the act of stretching; the state of being stretched; (between *forces, etc*) opposition; stress; mental strain.

**tent** *n* a portable shelter of canvas, plastic or other waterproof fabric, which is erected on poles and fixed to the ground by ropes and pegs.

**tentacle** *n* a long, slender, flexible growth near the mouth of invertebrates, used for feeling, grasping or handling.

**tentative** *adj* provisional; not definite.—**tentatively** *adv*.—**tentativeness** *n*.

**tenterhook** *n* one of a series of hooks on which cloth is stretched to dry; (*pl: with* on) in a tense or anxious state.

**tenth** *adj* the last of ten; being one of ten equal parts. • *n* one of ten equal parts.

**tenuous** *adj* slight, flimsy, insubstantial.—**tenuousness** *n*.

**tenure** *n* the holding of property or a position; the period of time which a position lasts; a permanent job at a university.

**tepid** *adj* slightly warm, lukewarm.

**term** *n* a limit; any prescribed period of time; a division of an academic year; a word or expression, esp in a specialized field of knowledge; (*pl*) mutual relationship between people; (*pl*) conditions of a contract, etc. • *vt* to call, designate.

**terminal** *adj* being or situated at the end or extremity; (*disease*) fatal, incurable. • *n* a bus, coach or railway station at the end of the line; the point at which an electrical current enters or leaves a device; a device with a keyboard and monitor for inputting data into, or viewing it from, a computer.—**terminally** *adv*.

**terminate** *vti* to bring or come to an end.—**termination** *n*.

**terminology** *n* the terms used in any specialized subject.

**terminus** *n* (*pl* **termini, terminuses**) the final part; a limit; end of a transportation line.

**termite** *n* a wood-eating, white, ant-like insect.

**terrace** *n* a raised level area of earth, often part of a slope; an unroofed paved area between a house and a lawn; a row of houses; a patio or balcony; (*pl*) unroofed tiers in a football ground. • *vt* to make into a terrace.

**terrain** *n* the surface features of a tract of land; (*fig*) field of activity.

**terrible** *adj* causing great fear; dreadful; (*inf*) very unpleasant.

**terribly** *adv* frighteningly; (*inf*) very.

**terrier** *n* a type of small, active dog.

**terrific** *adj* of great size; (*inf*) excellent.

**terrify** *vt* to fill with terror, to frighten greatly.

**territory** *n* an area under the jurisdiction of a city or state; a wide tract of land; an area assigned to a sales person; an area of knowledge.

**terror** *n* great fear; an object or person inspiring fear or dread.

**terrorism** *n* the use of terror and violence to intimidate.— **terrorist** *n*.

**terrorize** *vt* to terrify; to control by terror.—**terrorization** *n*.

**terse** *adj* abrupt, to the point, concise.—**tersely** *adv*.

**test** *n* an examination; trial; a chemical reaction to test a substance or to test for an illness; a series of questions or exercises. • *vt* to examine critically.

**testament** *n* a will; proof; tribute; a covenant made by God with men; (*with cap*) one of the two main parts of the Bible.

**test case** *n* a legal action that establishes a precedent.

**testicle** *n* either of the two male reproductive glands that produce sperm.

**testify** *vti* to give evidence under oath;

to serve as witness (to); (*with* **to**) to be evidence of.

**testimonial** *adj* relating to a testimony. • *n* a recommendation of one's character or abilities.

**testimony** *n* evidence; declaration of truth or fact.

**testis** *n* (*pl* **testes**) testicle.

**test match** *n* one of a series of international cricket or Rugby football matches.

**test pilot** *n* someone who flies new types of aircraft to test their performance and characteristics.

**test tube** *n* a cylinder of thin glass closed at one end, used in scientific experiments.

**testy** *adj* (**testier, testiest**) touchy, irritable.

**tetanus** *n* an intense and painful spasm of muscles, caused by the infection of a wound by bacteria; lockjaw.

**tether** *n* a rope or chain for tying an animal; the limit of one's endurance. • *vt* to fasten with a tether; to limit.

**text** *n* the main part of a printed work; the original or exact wording; a passage from the Bible forming the basis of a sermon; a subject or topic; a textbook.—**textual** *adj*.

**textbook** *n* a book used as a basis for instruction.

**textile** *n* a woven fabric or cloth. • *adj* relating to the making of fabrics.

**texture** *n* the characteristic appearance, arrangement or feel of a thing; the way in which threads in fabric are woven together.—**textural** *adj*.

**than** *conj* introducing the second element of a comparison.

**thank** *vt* to express gratitude to or appreciation for. • *npl* an expression of gratitude.—**thankful** *adj*.—**thankfully** *adv*.

**thankless** *adj* without thanks; unappreciated; fruitless, unrewarding.—**thanklessness** *n*.

**Thanksgiving Day** *n* a US legal holiday observed on the fourth Thursday of November.

**that** *demons adj, pron* (*pl* **those**) the (one) there or then, esp the latter or more distant thing. • *rel pron* who or which. • *conj* introducing noun clause or adverbial clause of purpose or consequence; because; in order that; (*preceded by* **so, such**) as a result.

**thatch** *n* roofing straw. • *vt* to cover a roof with thatch.

**thaw** *vi* to melt or grow liquid; to become friendly. • *vt* to cause to melt. • *n* the melting of ice or snow by warm weather.

**the** *demons adj* denoting a particular person or thing. • *adv* used before comparative adjectives or adverbs for emphasis.

**theatre, theater** (*US*) *n* a building where plays and operas are performed; the theatrical world as a whole; a setting for important events; field of operations.

**theatrical** *adj* relating to the theatre; melodramatic, affected.—**theatrically** *adv*.

**theft** *n* act or crime of stealing.

**their** *poss adj* of or belonging to them; his, hers, its.

**theirs** *poss pron* of or belonging to them; his, hers, its.

**them** *pron* the objective case of **they**.

**theme** *n* the main subject of a discussion; an idea or motif in a work; a short essay; a leading melody.—**thematic** *adj*.

**themselves** *pron* the reflexive form of **they** or **them**.

**then** *adv* at that time; afterwards; immediately; next in time. • *conj* for that reason; in that case.

**theologian** *n* a person who studies and interprets religious texts, etc; a teacher of theology.

**theology** n the study of God and of religious doctrine and matters of divinity.

**theorem** n a proposition that can be proved from accepted principles; law or principle.

**theoretical** adj of or based on theory, not practical application; hypothetical; conjectural.

**theorize** vi to form theories; to speculate.—**theorist** n.

**theory** n an explanation or system of anything; ideas and abstract principles of a science or art; speculation; a hypothesis.

**therapeutic** adj relating to the treatment of disease; beneficial.

**therapy** n the treatment of physical or mental illness.—**therapist** n.

**thero** adv in, at or to, that place or point; in that respect; in that matter.

**thereabouts** adv at or near that place or number.

**thereafter** adv after that; according to that.

**therefore** adv for that or this reason; consequently.

**therein** adv in that place or respect.

**thereon** adv on that or it; immediately following that.

**therm** n a measurement of heat.

**thermal** adj generating heat; hot, warm; (underwear) of a knitted material with air spaces for insulation. • n a rising current of warm air.

**thermometer** n an instrument for measuring temperature.

**thermonuclear** adj of or relating to nuclear fusion or nuclear weapons that utilize fusion reactions.

**Thermos** n (trademark) a brand of vacuum flask.

**thermostat** n an automatic device for regulating temperature.

**thesaurus** n (pl **thesauri, thesauruses**) a reference book of synonyms.

**these** see **this**.

**thesis** n (pl **theses**) a detailed essay written as part of a university degree; a theory expressed as a statement for discussion.

**they** pers pron, pl of **he, she** or **it**.

**thick** adj dense; fat, broad; abundant, closely set; in quick succession; crowded; (inf) stupid. • adv closely; frequently.

**thicken** vti to make or become thick.

**thickset** adj having a short, stocky body.

**thick-skinned** adj not sensitive.

**thief** n (pl **thieves**) a person who steals.

**thigh** n the thick part of the leg from the hip to the knee.

**thimble** n a cap or cover worn to protect the finger when sewing.

**thin** adj (**thinner, thinnest**) narrow; slim; lean; sparse, weak, watery; (material) fine; not dense. • vt to make thin; to make less crowded; to water down.—**thinly** adv.—**thinness** n.

**thing** n an inanimate object; an event; an action; (pl) possessions; (inf) an obsession.

**think** vb (pt **thought**) vi to exercise the mind in order to make a decision; to revolve ideas in the mind, to ponder; to remember; to consider. • vt to judge, to believe or consider; (with up) to concoct, devise.—**thinker** n.

**third** adj the last of three; being one of three equal parts. • n one of three equal parts.

**thirdly** adv in the third place; as a third point.

**third party** n (insurance) involving a third person.

**third rate** adj inferior.

**Third World** n the underdeveloped countries of the world (usu refers to Africa, Asia and South America).

**thirst** n a craving for drink; a longing. • vi to feel thirst; to have a longing.

**thirsty** *adj* (**thirstier, thirstiest**) having a desire to drink; dry, arid; longing or craving for.—**thirstily** *adv*.—**thirstiness** *n*.

**thirteen** *adj*, *n* three and ten.—**thirteenth** *adj*, *n*.

**thirty** *adj*, *n* three times ten.—**thirtieth** *adj*, *n*.

**this** *demons pron or adj* (*pl* **these**) denoting a person or thing near, just mentioned, or about to be mentioned.

**thistle** *n* a wild plant with prickly leaves and a purple flower.

**thong** *n* a piece or strap of leather to lash things together; the lash of a whip.

**thorn** *n* a shrub or small tree having thorns, esp hawthorn; a sharp point or prickle on the stem of a plant or the branch of a tree.

**thorny** *adj* (**thornier, thorniest**) prickly; (*problem*) knotty.

**thorough** *adj* complete, very detailed and painstaking, exhaustive.—**thoroughness** *n*.

**thoroughbred** *adj* bred from pure stock. • *n* a pedigree animal, esp a horse.

**thoroughfare** *n* a way through; a street; right of passing through.

**thoroughly** *adv* completely, fully; entirely, absolutely.

**those** *adj*, *pron*, *pl* of **that**.

**though** *conj* yet, even if. • *adv* however; nevertheless.

**thought** *pt*, *pp of* **think**. • *n* the act of thinking; reasoning; serious consideration; an idea; opinions collectively; design, intention.

**thoughtful** *adj* pensive; considerate.

**thoughtless** *adj* without thought; inconsiderate.

**thousand** *adj* ten times one hundred; (*pl*) denoting any large but unspecified number. • *n* the number 1000.—**thousandth** *adj*, *n*.

**thrash** *vt* to beat soundly; to defeat; (*with* **out**) to discuss thoroughly, until agreement is reached. • *vi* to thresh grain; to writhe.

**thread** *n* a fine strand or filament; a long thin piece of cotton, silk or nylon for sewing; the spiral part of a screw; (*of reasoning*) a line. • *vt* to pass a thread through the eye of a needle; to make one's way (through).

**threadbare** *adj* worn, shabby.

**threat** *n* a declaration of an intention to inflict harm or punishment upon another.

**threaten** *vti* to utter threats to; to be a threat.

**three** *adj*, *n* the cardinal number next above two. • *n* the symbol (3, III, iii) expressing this.

**three-dimensional** *adj* having three dimensions.

**thresh** *vti* to beat out (grain) from (husks).

**threshold** *n* the sill at the door of a building; doorway, entrance; the starting point, beginning.

**threw** *see* **throw**.

**thrift** *n* careful management of money.—**thrifty** *adj*.

**thrill** *vti* to tingle with pleasure or excitement. • *n* a sensation of pleasure and excitement; a trembling or quiver.

**thriller** *n* a novel, film or play depicting an exciting story of mystery and suspense.

**thrive** *vi* (*pt* **thrived** *or* **throve**, *pp* **thrived** *or* **thriven**) to prosper, to be successful; to grow vigorously.—**thriving** *adj*.

**throat** *n* the front part of the neck; the passage from back of the mouth to the top part of the tubes into the lungs and stomach; an entrance.

**throb** *vi* (*pt* **throbbed**) to beat or pulsate rhythmically, with more than usual force; to vibrate.—*also n*.

**throes** *npl* violent pangs or pain.

**thrombosis** *n* (*pl* **thromboses**) the forming of a blood clot in the heart or in a blood vessel.

**throne** *n* a chair of state occupied by a monarch; sovereign power. • *vt* to place on a throne.

**throttle** *n* a valve controlling the flow of fuel or steam to an engine. • *vt* to choke or strangle.

**through** *prep* from one side or end to the other; into and then out of; covering all parts; from beginning to end of; by means of; in consequence of; up to and including. • *adv* from one end or side to the other; completely. • *adj* going without interruption; unobstructed.

**throughout** *prep* in every part of; from beginning to end. • *adv* everywhere; at every moment.

**throw** *vb* (*pt* **threw**, *pp* **thrown**) *vt* to hurl, to fling; to cast off; (*party*) to hold; (*inf*) to confuse or disconcert. • *vi* to cast or hurl through the air (with the arm and wrist); to cast dice. • *n* the act of throwing; the distance to which anything can be thrown; a cast of dice.

**throwaway** *adj* disposable.

**throw-in** *n* (*soccer*) a throw from touch to resume play.

**thrush**[1] *n* a bird with a brown back and spotted breast.

**thrush**[2] *n* a fungal disease occurring in the mouths of babies or in women's vaginas.

**thrust** *vti* (*pt* **thrust**) to push with force; to stab, pierce; to force into a situation. • *n* a forceful push or stab; pressure; the driving force of a propeller; forward movement; the point or basic meaning.

**thud** *n* a dull, heavy sound, caused by a blow or a heavy object falling. • *vi* (*pt* **thudded**) to make such a sound.

**thug** *n* a violent and rough person, esp a criminal.

**thumb** *n* the first, short, thick finger of the human hand. • *vt* (*book*) to turn (the pages) idly.

**thumb index** *n* a series of semicircular notches cut in the edge of a book for easier reference to particular parts.

**thumbtack** *n* a drawing pin.

**thump** *n* a heavy blow; a thud. • *vt* to strike with something heavy. • *vi* to throb or beat violently.

**thunder** *n* the deep rumbling or loud cracking sound after a flash of lightning; any similar sound. • *vi* to sound as thunder. • *vt* (*words*) to utter loudly.

**thunderclap** *n* a loud bang of thunder.

**thunderous** *adj* very loud; producing thunder.

**thunderstorm** *n* a storm with thunder and lightning.

**thundery** *adj* indicating thunder.

**Thursday** *n* the fifth day of the week.

**thus** *adv* in this or that way; to this degree or extent; so; therefore.

**thwart** *vt* to prevent, to frustrate.

**thyme** *n* a herb with small leaves used for flavouring savoury food.

**thyroid** *n* the gland in the neck affecting growth and metabolism.

**tiara** *n* a semicircular crown decorated with jewels.

**tic** *n* any involuntary, regularly repeated, spasmodic contraction of a muscle.

**tick**[1] *n* a small bloodsucking insect that lives on people and animals.

**tick**[2] *vi* to make a regular series of short sounds; to beat, as a clock; (*inf*) to work, function. • *n* the sound of a clock; a moment.

**tick**[3] *n* (*inf*) account, credit.

**tick**[4] *vt* (*often with* **off**) to check off, as items in a list. • *n* a check mark ($\sqrt{}$) to check off items on a list or to indicate correctness.

**ticket** *n* a printed card, etc, giving right of travel or entry; a label on merchandise giving size, price, etc.

**tickle** *vt* to touch lightly to provoke pleasure or laughter; to please or delight.

**ticklish, tickly** *adj* sensitive to being tickled; easily offended; difficult or delicate.

**tidal** *adj* relating to, or having, tides.

**tiddlywinks** *npl* a game whose object is to flick small plastic discs into a container by snapping them with a larger disc.

**tide** *n* the regular rise and fall of the seas, oceans, etc usu twice a day; a current of water; a tendency; a flood. • *vt* (*with* **over**) to help along temporarily.

**tidy** *adj* (**tidier, tidiest**) neat; orderly. • *vt* to make neat; to put things in order.—**tidily** *adv*.—**tidiness** *n*.

**tie** *vb* (*pr p* **tying**, *pt* **tied**) *vt* to bind; to fasten with a string or thread; to make a bow or knot in; to restrict. • *vi* to score the same number of points (as an opponent). • *n* a knot, bow, etc; a bond; a long narrow piece of cloth worn with a shirt; an equality in score.

**tier** *n* a row or rank in a series when several rows are placed one above another.

**tiff** *n* a petty quarrel or disagreement.

**tiger** *n* a large, fierce carnivorous animal of the cat family, having orange and black stripes.—**tigress** *nf*.

**tight** *adj* taut; fitting closely; not leaky; constricted; miserly; difficult; providing little space or time for variance; (*contest*) close; (*inf*) drunk.

**tighten** *vti* to make or grow tight or tighter

**tightrope** *n* a taut rope on which acrobats walk.

**tights** *npl* a one-piece garment covering the legs and lower body.

**tile** *n* a thin slab of baked clay used for covering roofs, floors, etc. • *vt* to cover with tiles.

**till**[1] *n* a drawer inside a cash register for keeping money.

**till**[2] *prep* until. • *conj* until.

**till**[3] *vt* (*land*) to cultivate for raising crops, as by ploughing.

**tiller** *n* the handle or lever for turning a rudder in order to steer a boat.

**tilt** *vi* to slope, incline, slant. • *vt* to raise one end of. • *n* a slope or angle.

**timber** *n* wood when used as construction material; a beam; trees collectively. • *vt* to provide with timber or beams.

**time** *n* the past, present and future; a particular moment; hour of the day; an opportunity; the right moment; duration; occasion; musical beat. • *vt* to regulate as to time; to measure or record the duration of.

**time bomb** *n* a bomb designed to explode at a predetermined time; something with a potentially delayed reaction.

**timekeeper** *n* a person or instrument that records or keeps time; an employee who records the hours worked by others.—**timekeeping** *n*.

**time lag** *n* the interval between two connected events.

**timeless** *adj* eternal; ageless.

**timely** *adj* at the right time, opportune.—**timeliness** *n*.

**timer** *n* a device for measuring, recording or controlling time; a device for controlling lights, heating, etc by setting an electrical clock to regulate their operations.

**timetable** *n* a list of times of arrivals and departures or trains, aeroplanes, etc; a schedule showing a planned order or sequence.

**time zone** *n* a geographical region throughout which the same standard time is used.

**timing** *n* the control and expression of speech or actions to create the best effect, esp in the theatre, etc.

**timpani** *npl* a set of kettledrums.

**tin** *n* a malleable metallic element; a container of tin, a can. • *adj* made of tin or tin plate. • *vt* (*pt* **tinned**)to put food into a tin.

**tinfoil** *n* baking foil for wrapping food; silver paper.

**tinge** *vt* to tint or colour. • *n* a slight tint, colour or flavour.

**tingle** *vi* to feel a prickling, itching or stinging sensation.—*also n.*

**tinker** *n* (*formerly*) a travelling mender of pots and pans. • *vi* to fiddle with; to attempt to repair.

**tinkle** *vi* to make a sound like a small bell ringing; to clink, to jingle; to clink repeatedly. • *n* a tinkling sound; (*inf*) a telephone call.

**tin plate** *n* thin sheets of iron or steel plated with tin.

**tinsel** *n* a shiny Christmas decoration made of long pieces of thread wound round with thin strips of metal or plastic foil; something showy but of low value.

**tint** *n* a shade of any colour, esp a pale one; a tinge; a hair dye. • *vt* to colour or tinge.

**tiny** *adj* (**tinier, tiniest**) very small.

**tip**[1] *n* the pointed end of anything; the end, as of a billiard cue, etc. • *vt* (*pt* **tipped**) to put a tip on.

**tip**[2] *vti* (*pt* **tipped**) to tilt or cause to tilt; to overturn; to empty (out, into, etc.); to give a gratuity to, as a waiter, etc; (*rubbish*) to dump; to give a helpful hint or inside information to. • *n* a light tap; a gratuity; a rubbish dump; an inside piece of information; a helpful hint.

**tip-off** *n* a warning based on inside information.

**tipple** *vi* to drink alcohol regularly in small quantities. • *n* an alcoholic drink.

**tipsy** *adj* (**tipsier, tipsiest**) slightly drunk.

**tiptoe** *vi* (*pt* **tiptoed**) to walk very quietly or carefully.

**tire** *vt* to exhaust the strength of, to weary. • *vi* to become weary; to lose patience; to become bored.

**tired** *adj* weary, sleepy; hackneyed, conventional, flat; (*with* **of**) exasperated by, bored with.

**tiresome** *adj* tedious.

**tissue** *n* thin, absorbent paper used as a disposable handkerchief, etc; a very finely woven fabric; a mass of organic cells of a similar structure and function.

**tit**[1] *n* a songbird such as a blue tit or great tit.

**tit**[2] *n* (*vulg*) a woman's breast.

**titanic** *adj* monumental; huge.

**titbit** *n* a tasty morsel of food; a choice item of information.

**titillate** *vt* to tickle; to arouse or excite pleasurably.

**title** *n* the name of a book, play, piece of music, work of art, etc; the heading of a section of a book; a name denoting nobility or rank or office held, or attached to a personal name; (*law*) that which gives a legal right (to possession).

**title deed** *n* a deed or document proving a title or right to possession.

**title role** *n* the character in a play, film, etc after whom it is named.

**titter** *vi* to giggle, snigger. • *n* a suppressed laugh.

**tittle-tattle** *n* idle chat, empty gossip.

**to** *prep* in the direction of; towards; as far as; expressing the purpose of an action; indicating the infinitive; introducing the indirect object; in comparison with. • *adv* towards.

**toad** *n* an amphibious reptile, like a frog, but having a drier skin and spending less time in water.

**toadstool** *n* a mushroom, esp a poisonous or inedible one.

**toady** *n* a person who flatters

insincerely. • *vi* (*with* **to**) to act in a servile manner.

**toast** *vt* to brown over a fire or under a grill; to warm; to drink to the health of. • *n* toasted bread; the sentiment or person to which one drinks.

**toaster** *n* a person who toasts; a thing that toasts, esp an electrical appliance.

**toastmaster** *n* the proposer of toasts at public dinners.—**toastmistress** *nf*.

**tobacco** *n* a plant whose dried leaves are used for smoking, chewing or snuff.

**tobacconist** *n* a person or shop that sells cigarettes, etc.

**toboggan** *n* a sledge, sled.

**today** *n* this day; the present age. • *adv* on this day; nowadays.

**toddler** *n* a young child.

**toddy** *n* a drink of whisky, sugar, and hot water.

**toe** *n* one of the five digits on the foot; the part of the shoe or sock that covers the toes.

**toenail** *n* the thin, hard, covering on the end of the toes.

**toffee, toffy** *n* a sweet of brittle but tender texture made by boiling sugar and butter together.

**toga** *n* a piece of cloth draped around the body, as worn by citizens in ancient Rome.

**together** *adv* in one place or group; in cooperation with; in unison; jointly.

**toil** *vi* to work strenuously; to move with great effort. • *n* hard work.

**toilet** *n* a lavatory; the room containing a lavatory; the act of washing and dressing oneself.

**toilet paper, toilet tissue** *n* an absorbent paper for cleansing after urination, etc.

**toilet roll** *n* a cardboard cylinder around which toilet paper is wound.

**toiletry** *n* a lotion, perfume, etc used in washing and dressing oneself.

**toilet water** *n* a diluted perfume.

**token** *n* a symbol, sign; an indication; a metal disc for a slot machine; a souvenir; a gift voucher. • *adj* nominal; symbolic.

**told** *see* **tell**.

**tolerable** *adj* bearable; fairly good.— **tolerably** *adv*.

**tolerance** *n* open-mindedness; forbearance; (*med*) ability to resist the action of a drug, etc; ability of a substance to endure heat, stress, etc without damage.

**tolerant** *adj* able to put up with the beliefs, actions, etc of others; broadminded; showing tolerance to a drug, etc; capable of enduring stress, etc.

**tolerate** *vt* to endure, put up with, suffer.

**toll**[1] *n* money levied for passing over a bridge or road; the number of people killed in an accident or disaster.

**toll**[2] *vt* (*bell*) to ring slowly and repeatedly, as a funeral bell. • *vi* to sound, as a bell. • *n* the sound of a bell when tolling.

**tomato** *n* (*pl* **tomatoes**) a plant with red pulpy fruit used as a vegetable.

**tomb** *n* a vault in the earth for the burial of the dead.

**tomboy** *n* a girl who likes rough outdoor activities.

**tombstone** *n* a memorial stone over a grave.

**tomcat** *n* a male cat.

**tomorrow** *n* the day after today; the future.—*also adv*.

**ton** *n* a unit of weight equivalent to 2,000 pounds in US or 2,240 pounds in UK; (*inf*) 100 mph; (*inf: pl*) a great quantity.

**tone** *n* the quality of a sound; pitch or inflection of the voice; colour, shade; body condition. • *vt* to give tone to. • *vi* to harmonize (with).

**tongs** *npl* an instrument consisting of

two arms that are hinged, used for grasping and lifting.

**tongue** *n* the soft, moveable organ in the mouth, used in tasting, swallowing, and speech; the ability to speak; a language; (*shoe*) a piece of leather under the laces; a jet of flame; the tongue of an animal served as food; the catch of a buckle.

**tongue-tied** *adj* speechless.

**tongue-twister** *n* a sequence of words that it is difficult to pronounce quickly and clearly.

**tonic** *n* a medicine that improves physical well-being; something that imparts vigour; a fizzy mineral water with a bitter taste. • *adj* relating to tones or sounds.

**tonight** *n* this night; the night or evening of the present day.—*also adv.*

**tonnage** *n* a merchant ship's capacity measured in tons; the weight of its cargo; the amount of shipping of a country or port; merchant ships collectively; a duty levied on ships based on tonnage or capacity.

**tonne** *n* metric ton, 1,000 kg.

**tonsil** *n* one of the two oval organs of soft tissue situated one on each side of the throat.

**tonsillitis** *n* inflammation of the tonsils.

**too** *adv* in addition; also, likewise; extremely; very.

**took** *see* **take**.

**tool** *n* an implement that is used by hand; a means for achieving any purpose.

**toot** *vi* to hoot a car horn, whistle, etc in short blasts. • *n* a hoot.—*also vt.*

**tooth** *n* (*pl* **teeth**) one of the white, bone-like structures arranged in rows in the mouth, used in biting and chewing; the palate; a tooth-like projection on a comb, saw, or wheel.

**toothache** *n* a pain in a tooth.

**toothbrush** *n* a small brush for cleaning teeth.

**toothpaste** *n* a paste for cleaning teeth, used with a toothbrush.

**toothpick** *n* a sliver of wood or plastic for removing food particles from between the teeth.

**top**[1] *n* the highest, or uppermost, part or surface of anything; the highest in rank; the crown of the head; the lid. • *adj* highest; greatest. • *vt* to cover on the top; to remove the top of or from; to rise above; to surpass.

**top**[2] *n* a child's toy, which is spun on its pointed base.

**top hat** *n* a man's tall, silk hat.

**top-heavy** *adj* having an upper part too heavy for the lower, causing instability.

**topic** *n* a subject for discussion; the theme of a speech or writing.

**topical** *adj* of current interest.

**topless** *adj* lacking a top; (*garment*) revealing the breasts; wearing such a garment.

**topmost** *adj* nearest the top, highest.

**topple** *vi* to fall over. • *vt* to cause to overbalance and fall; (*government*) to overthrow.

**topsy-turvy** *adj, adv* turned upside down; in confusion.

**torch** *n* a portable light powered by batteries; a device for giving off a hot flame.

**torment** *n* torture, anguish; a source of pain. • *vt* to afflict with extreme pain, physical or mental.—**tormentor, tormenter** *n*.

**torn** *see* **tear**[2].

**tornado** *n* (*pl* **tornadoes**) a violently whirling column of air seen as a funnel-shaped cloud that usu destroys everything in its narrow path.

**torpedo** *n* (*pl* **torpedoes**) a self-propelled submarine offensive weapon, carrying an explosive charge. • *vt* to attack, hit, or destroy with torpedo(es).

**torpor** n a state of lethargy.

**torque** n (*physics*) a force that causes rotation around a central point, such as an axle.

**torrent** n a rushing stream; a flood of words.—**torrential** adj.

**torso** n (*pl* **torsos**) the trunk of the human body.

**tortoise** n a slow-moving reptile with a dome-shaped shell into which it can withdraw.

**tortoiseshell** n a brown and yellow colour.

**tortuous** adj full of twists, involved.—**tortuously** adv.

**torture** n subjection to severe physical or mental pain to extort a confession, or as a punishment. —*also vt*. —**torturer** n.

**Tory** n a member of the Conservative Party in UK politics.—*also adj*.

**toss** vt to throw up; to pitch; to fling; (*head*) to throw back. • vi to be tossed about; to move restlessly.—*also n*.

**toss**-up n the throwing of a coin to decide a question.

**tot**[1] n anything little, esp a child; a small measure of spirits.

**tot**[2] vt (*pt* **totted**) (*with* up) to add up or total.

**total** adj whole, complete; absolute. • n the whole sum; the entire amount. • vt (*pt* **totalled**) to add up.—**totally** adv.

**totalitarian** adj relating to a system of government in which one political group maintains complete control, esp under a dictator. —**totalitarianism** n.

**totter** vi to walk unsteadily; to shake or sway as if about to fall.—**tottery** adj.

**touch** vt to come in contact with, esp with the hand or fingers; to reach; to affect with emotion; to tinge or tint; to border on; (*sl*) to ask for money (from). • vi to be in contact; to be adjacent; to allude to. • n the act of touching; the sense by which something is perceived through contact; a trace; understanding; a special quality or skill.

**touch-and-go** adj precarious, risky.

**touchdown** n the moment when an aircraft or spaceship lands; (*Rugby football, American football*) a placing of the ball on the ground to score.

**touched** adj emotionally affected; mentally disturbed.

**touching** adj affecting, moving.

**touchline** n (*football, etc*) the side boundary of a pitch.

**touchy** adj (**touchier, touchiest**) irritable; very risky.

**tough** adj strong; durable; hardy; rough and violent; difficult; (*inf*) unlucky.—**toughen** vti.—**toughness** n.

**toupee** n a wig or section of hair to cover a bald spot, esp worn by men.

**tour** n a turn, period, etc as of military duty; a long trip, as for sightseeing. • vti to go on a tour (through).

**tourism** n travelling for pleasure; the business of catering for people who do this; the encouragement of touring.

**tourist** n one who makes a tour, a sightseer, travelling for pleasure.—*also adj*.

**tournament** n a sporting event involving a number of competitors and a series of games.

**tousle** vt to make untidy, ruffle, make tangled (esp hair).

**tout** vti (*inf*) to praise highly; (*inf*) to sell betting tips on (race horses); (*inf*) to solicit business in a brazen way. • n (*inf*) a person who does so.

**tow** vt to pull or drag with a rope. • n the act of towing; a towrope.

**towards, toward** (*US*) prep in the direction of; concerning; just before; as a contribution to.

**towel** n an absorbent cloth for drying the skin after it is washed, and for other purposes.

**towelling, toweling** (US) n cloth for towels; a rubbing with a towel.

**tower** n a tall, narrow building, standing alone or forming part of another; a fortress. • vi (with over) to rise above; to loom.

**tower block** n a skyscraper.

**town** n a densely populated urban centre, smaller than a city and larger than a village; the people of a town.

**townhall** n a large building housing the offices of the town council, often with a hall for public meetings.

**towpath** n the footpath beside a river or canal.

**towrope, towline** n a strong rope or cable for towing a wheeled vehicle, ship, etc.

**toxic** adj poisonous; harmful; deadly.

**toy** n an object for children to play with; a replica; a miniature. • vi to trifle; to flirt.

**trace** n a mark etc left by a person, animal or thing; a barely perceptible footprint; a small quantity. • vt to follow by tracks; to discover the whereabouts of; (map, etc) to copy by following the lines on transparent paper.

**track** vt to follow the tracks of; (satellite, etc) to follow by radar and record position. • n a mark left; a footprint; parallel steel rails on which trains run; a course for running or racing; sports performed on a track, as running, hurdling; the band on which the wheels of a tractor or tank run; one piece of music on a record; a soundtrack.

**tracksuit** n a loose suit worn by athletes to keep warm.

**tract**[1] n an expanse of land or water; a part of a bodily system or organ.

**tract**[2] n a treatise.

**tractor** n a motor vehicle for pulling heavy loads and for working ploughs.

**trade** n buying and selling (of commodities); commerce; occupation; customers; business. • vi to buy and sell; to exchange.—**trader** n.

**trade-in** n a used item given in part payment when buying a replacement.

**trademark** n a name used on a product by a manufacturer to distinguish it from its competitors, esp when legally protected.—also vt.

**tradesman** n (pl **tradesmen**) a shopkeeper; a skilled worker.

**trade(s) union** n an organized association of employees of any trade or industry for the protection of their income and working conditions.

**tradition** n the handing down from generation to generation of opinions and practices; the belief or practice thus passed on; custom.—**traditional** adj.—**traditionally** adv.

**traffic** n trade; the movement or number of vehicles, pedestrians, etc, along a street, etc. • vi (pt **trafficked**) to do business (esp. in illegal drugs).

**traffic circle** n a roundabout.

**traffic light** n one of a set of coloured lights used to control traffic at street crossings, etc.

**traffic warden** n a person who is authorized to control traffic and to report parking violations, etc.

**tragedy** n a play or drama that is serious and sad, and the climax a catastrophe; an accident or situation involving death or suffering.—**tragic** adj.—**tragically** adv.

**trail** vt to drag along the ground; to have in its wake; to follow behind. • vi to hang or drag loosely behind; (plant) to climb; (with off or away) to grow weaker or dimmer. • n a path or track; the scent of an animal; something left in the wake.

**trailer** *n* a wagon, van, etc designed to be towed by a motor vehicle; a caravan; an advertisement for a film or television programme.

**train** *vt* to teach, to guide; to tame for use, as animals; to prepare for racing, etc; (*gun, etc*) to aim. • *vi* to do exercise or preparation. • *n* a series of railway carriages pulled by a locomotive; a sequence; the back part of a dress that trails along the floor; a retinue.

**trained** *adj* skilled.

**trainee** *n* a person who is being trained.

**trainer** *n* a coach or instructor in sports; a person who prepares horses for racing.

**training** *n* practical instruction; a course of physical exercises.

**trait** *n* a characteristic feature.

**traitor** *n* a person who commits treason or betrays his country, friends, etc.—**traitorous** *adj*.

**tram** *n* an electrically powered vehicle for public transport that travels along rails set into the ground.

**tramlines** *npl* rails for trams; the sidelines on a tennis court.

**tramp** *vti* to walk heavily; to tread or trample; to wander about as a tramp. • *n* a vagrant.

**trample** *vti* to tread under foot.

**trampoline** *n* a sheet of strong canvas stretched tightly on a frame, used in acrobatic tumbling.

**trance** *n* a state of unconsciousness, induced by hypnosis, in which some of the powers of the waking body, such as response to commands, may be retained.

**tranquil** *adj* quiet, calm, peaceful.—**tranquillity, tranquility** *n*.

**tranquillizer** *n* a drug that calms.

**transact** *vt* (*business*) to conduct or carry out.

**transaction** *n* the act of transacting; something transacted, esp a business deal; (*pl*) a record of the proceedings of a society.

**transatlantic** *adj* crossing the Atlantic Ocean; across, beyond the Atlantic.

**transcend** *vt* to rise above or beyond; to surpass.—**transcendent** *adj*.

**transcript** *n* a written or printed copy made by transcribing; an official copy of proceedings, etc.

**transcription** *n* the act of transcribing; something transcribed, esp a piece of music; a transcript; a recording made for broadcasting.

**transept** *n* one of the two wings of a church, at right angles to the nave.

**transfer** *vb* (*pt* **transferred**) *vt* to carry, convey, from one place to another; (*law*) to make over (property) to another; (*money*) to move from the control of one institution to another. • *vi* to change to another bus, etc. • *n* the act of transferring; the state of being transferred; someone or something that is transferred; a design that can be moved from one surface to another.—**transferable** *adj*.

**transform** *vti* to change the shape, appearance, or condition of; to convert.—**transformation** *n*.

**transformer** *n* a device for changing alternating current with an increase or decrease of voltage.

**transfusion** *n* the injection of blood into the veins of a sick or injured person.—**transfuse** *vt*.

**transient** *adj* temporary; of short duration, momentary.—**transience** *n*.

**transistor** *n* a device for amplifying sound, as in a radio or television; a small portable radio.

**transit** *n* a passing over or through; the carrying of people or goods.

**transition** *n* passage from one place or state to another; change.—**transitional** *adj*.

**transitive** *adj* (*gram*) denoting a verb

that requires a direct object; of or relating to transition.

**transitory** *adj* lasting only a short time.

**translate** *vti* to express in another language; to explain, interpret.—**translator** *n*.

**translation** *n* the act of translating; something translated into another language or state; an interpretation.

**transmission** *n* the act of transmitting; something transmitted; a system using gears, etc, to transfer power from an engine to a moving part, esp wheels of a car; a radio or television broadcast.

**transmit** *vt* (*pt* **transmitted**) to send from one place or person to another; to communicate; to convey; (*radio or TV signals*) to send out.

**transmitter** *n* an apparatus for broadcasting television or radio programmes.

**transparency** *n* the state of being transparent; (*photog*) a slide.

**transparent** *adj* that may be easily seen through; clear, easily understood.

**transplant** *vt* (*plant*) to remove and plant in another place; (*med*) to remove an organ from one person and transfer it to another.—*also n*.

**transport** *vt* to convey from one place to another; to delight. • *n* the system of transporting goods or passengers; the carrying of troops and their equipment by sea or land; a vehicle for this purpose.—**transportable** *adj*.—**transportation** *n*.

**transvestite** *n* a person who gains sexual pleasure from wearing the clothes of the opposite sex.—**transvestism** *n*.

**trap** *n* a mechanical device or pit for snaring animals; an ambush; a trick to catch someone out; a two-wheeled horsedrawn carriage. • *vt* (*pt* **trapped**) to catch in a trap; to trick.

**trapdoor** *n* a hinged or sliding door in a roof, ceiling or floor.

**trapeze** *n* a gymnastic apparatus consisting of a horizontal bar suspended by two parallel ropes.

**trapper** *n* a person who traps animals, esp for their skins.

**trappings** *npl* trimmings; additions; ornaments.

**trash** *n* nonsense; refuse; rubbish.

**trash can** *n* a dustbin.

**trauma** *n* an emotional shock that may cause long-term psychological damage; an upsetting experience.—**traumatic** *adj*.

**travel** *vb* (*pt* **travelled**) *vi* to journey or move from one place to another. • *vt* to journey across, through. • *n* journey.

**traveller, traveler** (*US*) *n* a person who travels; a salesman who travels for a company.

**traveller's cheque** *n* a draft purchased from a bank, etc signed at the time of purchase and signed again at the time of cashing.

**travesty** *n* a misrepresentation; a poor imitation; a parody.

**trawler** *n* a boat used for trawling.

**tray** *n* a flat board, or sheet of metal or plastic, surrounded by a rim, used for carrying food or drink.

**treacherous** *adj* untrustworthy, disloyal; unstable, dangerous.

**treachery** *n* disloyalty, betrayal of trust.

**treacle** *n* a thick sticky substance obtained during the refining of sugar.—**treacly** *adj*.

**tread** *vti* (*pt* **trod**, *pp* **trodden**) to step or walk on, along, in, over or across; to crush or squash (with the feet); to trample (on). • *n* a step, way of walking; the part of a shoe, wheel, or tyre that touches the ground.

**treason** *n* the crime of betraying one's government or attempting to overthrow it; treachery.—**treasonable** *adj*.

**treasure** *n* wealth and riches hoarded

up; a person or thing much valued. • *vt* to hoard up; to prize greatly.

**treasurer** *n* a person appointed to take charge of the finances of a society, government or city.

**treasury** *n* a place where valuable objects are deposited; the funds or revenues of a government.

**treat** *vt* to deal with or regard; to subject to the action of a chemical; to apply medical treatment to; to pay for another person's entertainment; to deal with in speech or writing. • *n* an entertainment paid for by another person; a pleasure seldom indulged; a unusual cause of enjoyment.

**treatise** *n* a formal essay in which a subject is treated systematically.

**treatment** *n* the application of drugs, etc, to a patient; the manner of dealing with a person or thing, esp in a novel or painting; behaviour towards someone.

**treaty** *n* a formal agreement between states.

**treble** *adj* triple, threefold; (*mus*) denoting the treble. • *n* the highest range of musical notes in singing. • *vti* to make or become three times as much.

**tree** *n* a tall, woody, perennial plant having a single trunk, branches and leaves.

**trek** *vi* (*pt* **trekked**) to travel slowly or laboriously; (*inf*) to go on foot (to). • *n* a long and difficult journey; a migration.

**trellis** *n* a structure of lattice work, for supporting climbing plants, etc.— **trelliswork** *n*.

**tremble** *vi* to shake, shiver from cold or fear; to quiver.—*also n*.

**tremendous** *adj* awe-inspiring; very large or great; (*inf*) wonderful; marvellous.

**tremor** *n* a vibration; an involuntary shaking.

**trench** *n* a long narrow channel in the earth, used for drainage; such an excavation made for military purposes.

**trend** *n* tendency; a current style or fashion.

**trendy** *adj* (**trendier, trendiest**) (*inf*) fashionable. • *n* (*inf*) a person who tries to be fashionable.— **trendily** *adv*.— **trendiness** *n*.

**trepidation** *n* a state of fear or anxiety.

**trespass** *vi* to intrude upon another person's property without their permission; to encroach upon, or infringe, another's rights. • *n* act of trespassing.— **trespasser** *n*.

**trestle** *n* a wooden framework for supporting a table top.

**trial** *n* a test or experiment; judicial examination; an attempt; a preliminary race, game in a competition; suffering; hardship; a person causing annoyance.

**triangle** *n* (*math*) a plane figure with three angles and three sides; a percussion instrument consisting of a triangular metal bar beaten with a metal stick.— **triangular** *adj*.

**tribe** *n* a group of people of the same race, sharing the same customs, religion, language or land.— **tribal** *adj*.— **tribesman** *n*.

**tribulation** *n* distress, difficulty, hardship.

**tribunal** *n* a court of justice; a committee that investigates and decides on a particular problem.

**tribune**[1] *n* in ancient Rome, a magistrate appointed to protect the rights of common people; a champion of the people.

**tribune**[2] *n* a raised platform or dais from which speeches are delivered.

**tributary** *n* a stream or river flowing into a larger one.

**tribute** *n* a speech, gift or action to show one's respect or thanks to someone; a payment made at certain intervals by one nation to another in return for peace.

**trick** *n* fraud; deception; a mischievous plan or joke; a magical illusion; a clever feat; skill, knack; the playing cards won in a round. • *adj* using fraud or clever contrivance to deceive. • *vt* to deceive, cheat.—**trickster** *n*.

**trickery** *n* the practice or an act of using underhand methods to achieve an aim; deception.

**trickle** *vti* to flow or cause to flow in drops or in a small stream.—*also n*.

**tricky** *adj* (**trickier, trickiest**) complicated, difficult to handle; risky; cunning, deceitful.—**trickily** *adv*.—**trickiness** *n*.

**tricycle** *n* a three-wheeled pedal cycle, esp for children.

**trifle** *vi* to treat lightly; to dally. • *n* anything of little value; a dessert of whipped cream, custard, sponge cake, sherry, etc.

**trifling** *adj* insignificant.

**trigger** *n* a catch that when pulled activates the firing mechanism of a gun. • *vt* (*with* **off**) to initiate; to set (off).

**trigonometry** *n* the branch of mathematics concerned with calculating the angles of triangles or the lengths of their sides.

**trim** *adj* (**trimmer, trimmest**) in good condition; tidy, neat; slim. • *vt* (*pt* **trimmed**) to neaten; to cut or prune; to decorate; (*aircraft*) to balance the cargo weight in. • *n* a decorative edging; a haircut that tidies.

**trimming** *n* decorative part of clothing; (*pl*) accompaniments.

**trinity** *n* a group of three; (*with cap*) in Christianity, the union of Father, Son and Holy Spirit in one God.

**trinket** *n* a small or worthless ornament.

**trio** *n* (*pl* **trios**) a set of three; (*mus*) a group of three singers or instrumentalists.

**trip** *vb* (*pt* **tripped**) *vi* to move or tread lightly; to stumble and fall; to make a blunder. • *vt* (*a person: often with* **up**) to cause to stumble; to activate a trip. • *n* a stumble; a journey, tour, or voyage; a slip; a mistake; a light step; a mechanical switch; (*sl*) a hallucinatory experience under the influence of a drug.

**tripe** *n* the stomach lining of an ox, prepared for cooking; (*inf*) rubbish, nonsense.

**triple** *adj* threefold; three times as many. • *vti* to treble.

**triplet** *n* one of three children born at one birth.

**triplicate** *adj* threefold.

**tripod** *n* a three-legged stand, as for supporting a camera.

**trite** *adj* dull; hackneyed.

**triumph** *n* a victory; success; a great achievement. • *vi* to win a victory or success; to rejoice over a victory.—**triumphal** *adj*.

**triumphant** *adj* feeling or showing triumph; celebratory; victorious.—**triumphantly** *adv*.

**trivia** *npl* unimportant details.

**trivial** *adj* unimportant; commonplace.

**trod, trodden** *see* **tread**.

**trolley** *n* (*pl* **trolleys**) a table on wheels for carrying or serving food; a cart for transporting luggage or shopping in a supermarket; a device that transmits electric current from an overhead wire.

**trolleybus, trolley car** *n* an electric bus powered from an overhead wire by means of a trolley.

**trombone** *n* a brass musical wind instrument whose length is varied with a U-shaped sliding section.

**troop** *n* a crowd of people; a group of soldiers within a cavalry regiment;

(*pl*) armed forces; soldiers. • *vi* to go in a crowd.

**trooper** *n* a cavalryman; in US, a mounted policeman or a state policeman.

**trophy** *n* a cup or shield won as a prize in a competition or contest; a memento , as taken in battle or hunting.

**tropic** *n* one of the two parallel lines of latitude north and south of the equator; (*pl*) the regions lying between these lines.

**tropical** *adj* relating to the tropics; (*weather*) hot and humid.

**trot** *vi* (*pt* **trotted**) (*horse*) to go, lifting the feet higher than in walking and moving at a faster rate. • *n* the gait of a horse; a brisk pace.

**trouble** *vti* to cause trouble to; to worry; to pain; to upset; to cause inconvenience; to take pains (to). • *n* an anxiety; a medical condition causing pain; a problem; unrest or disturbance.—**troublesome** *adj*.

**troubleshooter** *n* a person whose work is to locate and eliminate a source of trouble or conflict.—**troubleshooting** *n*.

**trough** *n* a long, narrow container for water or animal feed; a channel in the ground; an elongated area of low barometric pressure.

**trounce** *vt* to defeat completely.

**troupe** *n* a travelling company, esp of actors, dancers or acrobats.—**trouper** *n*.

**trousers** *npl* an item of clothing covering the body from waist to ankle, with two tubes of material for the legs; pants.

**trousseau** *n* (*pl* **trousseaux**) the clothes and linen a bride collects for her marriage.

**trout** *n* (*pl* **trout**) a game fish of the salmon family living in fresh water.

**trowel** *n* a hand tool for gardening; a

flat-bladed tool for spreading cement, etc.

**truant** *n* a pupil who is absent from school without permission. • *vi* to play truant.—*also adj*.—**truancy** *n*.

**truce** *n* an agreement between two armies or states to suspend hostilities.

**truck** *n* a heavy motor vehicle for transporting goods; a lorry; a vehicle open at the back for moving goods or animals. • *vt* (*goods*) to convey by truck. • *vi* to drive a truck.

**trudge** *vti* to travel on foot, heavily or wearily. • *n* a tiring walk.

**true** *adj* (**truer, truest**) conforming with fact; correct; accurate; genuine; loyal; perfectly in tune. • *adv* truthfully; rightly.

**truffle** *n* a round, edible underground fungus; a sweet made with chocolate, butter and sugar.

**truly** *adv* completely; genuinely; to a great degree.

**trump** *n* (*cards*) the suit that is chosen to have the highest value in one game. • *vt* to play a trump card on.

**trumpet** *n* a brass wind instrument consisting of a long tube with a flared end and three buttons. • *vti* to proclaim loudly.—**trumpeter** *n*.

**truncate** *vt* to cut the top end off; to shorten.—**truncation** *n*.

**truncheon** *n* a short, thick club carried by a policeman.

**trundle** *vt* (*an object*) to push or pull on wheels. • *vi* to move along slowly.

**trunk** *n* the main stem of a tree; the torso; the main body of anything; the long nose of an elephant; a strong box or chest for clothes, etc, esp on a journey; the boot of a car.

**trunks** *npl* a man's short, light pants for swimming.

**truss** *n* a supporting framework for a roof or bridge; a hernia brace. • *vt* to bind (up).

**trust** *n* firm belief in the truth of

anything, faith in a person; confidence in; custody; a financial arrangement of investing money for another person; a business syndicate. • *adj* held in trust. • *vti* to have confidence in; to believe.—**trustful** *adj*.

**trustee** *n* a person who has legal control of money or property that they are keeping or investing for another.—**trusteeship** *n*.

**trustworthy** *adj* reliable, dependable.

**trusty** *adj* (**trustier, trustiest**) trustworthy, faithful. • *n* a prisoner granted special privileges as a trustworthy person.—**trustily** *adv*.—**trustiness** *n*.

**truth** *n* that which is true, factual or genuine; agreement with reality.

**truthful** *adj* telling the truth; accurate, realistic; honest, frank.—**truthfulness** *n*.

**try** *vt* to test the result or effect by experiment; to determine judicially; to put strain on. • *vi* to attempt; to make an effort. • *n* an attempt, an effort; (*Rugby football*) a score made with a touchdown.

**trying** *adj* exasperating.

**tsar** *n* the title of the former ruler of Russia.—*also* **czar**.

**T-shirt** *n* an informal knitted cotton sweater.—*also* **tee-shirt**.

**T-square** *n* a T-shaped instrument for drawing and determining right angles.

**tub** *n* a circular container, esp for holding water.

**tuba** *n* a large brass instrument of bass pitch.

**tubby** *adj* (**tubbier, tubbiest**) plump.

**tube** *n* a long, thin, hollow pipe; a soft metal or plastic cylinder in which thick liquids or pastes are stored; (*inf*) in UK, the underground railway system.—**tubular** *adj*.

**tuberculosis** *n* an infectious disease of the lungs.—**tubercular** *adj*.

**tubing** *n* tubes collectively; a length of tube; the material from which tubes are made; a circular fabric.

**TUC** *abbr* = Trades Union Congress.

**tuck** *vt* to draw or gather together in a fold; (*with* up) to wrap snugly. • *vi* (*inf*) (*with* into) to eat greedily. • *n* a fold in a garment.

**Tuesday** *n* the third day of the week.

**tuft** *n* a bunch of grass, hair or feathers held together at the base; a clump.

**tug** *vti* (*pt* **tugged**) to pull with effort or to drag along. • *n* a strong pull; a tugboat.

**tugboat** *n* a small powerful boat for towing ships.

**tug of war** *n* a contest in which two teams tug on opposite ends of a rope to pull the opposing team over a central line; a struggle for supremacy between two opponents.

**tuition** *n* teaching, instruction.

**tulip** *n* a highly-coloured cup-shaped flower grown from bulbs.

**tumble** *vi* to fall over; to roll or to twist the body, as an acrobat. • *vt* to push or cause to fall. • *n* a fall; a somersault.

**tumble-drier, tumble dryer** *n* a machine for drying clothes with warm air.

**tumbler** *n* a large drinking glass without a handle or stem; an acrobat.

**tummy** *n* (*inf*) stomach.

**tumour, tumor** (*US*) *n* an abnormal growth of tissue in any part of the body.

**tumult** *n* a commotion; an uproar.

**tumultuous** *adj* disorderly; rowdy, noisy; restless.—**tumultuously** *adv*.—**tumultuousness** *n*.

**tuna** *n* (*pl* **tuna, tunas**) a large ocean fish of the mackerel group.

**tune** *n* a melody; correct musical pitch; harmony. • *vt* (*musical instrument*) to adjust the notes of; (*radio, TV etc*) to adjust the resonant frequency, etc,

to a particular value.—**tuneful** *adj.*—
**tunefully** *adv*.

**tungsten** *n* a hard malleable greyish
white metallic element used in
lamps, etc, and in alloys with steel.

**tunic** *n* a hip or knee-length loose, usu
belted blouse-like garment; a close-
fitting jacket worn by soldiers and
policemen.

**tunnel** *n* an underground passage, esp
one for cars or trains. • *vb* (*pt* **tun-
nelled**) *vt* to make a way through.
• *vi* to make a tunnel.

**tunny** *n* (*pl* **tunnies, tunny**) tuna.

**turban** *n* a headdress consisting of
cloth wound in folds around the head
worn by men; a woman's hat of this
shape.

**turbine** *n* a machine in which power is
produced when the forced passage
of steam, water, etc causes the blades
to rotate.

**turbot** *n* a large, flat, round edible fish.

**turbulent** *adj* disturbed, in violent
commotion.

**tureen** *n* a large dish for serving soup,
etc.

**turf** *n* (*pl* **turf, turves**) the surface layer
of grass and its roots; (*with* **the**)
horse racing; a racetrack. • *vt* to
cover with turf.

**turgid** *adj* swollen; pompous, bombastic.—**turgidity** *n*.—**turgidness** *n*.

**turkey** *n* (*pl* **turkeys, turkey**) a large
bird farmed for its meat.

**Turkish bath** *n* a bath with steam
rooms, showers, massage, etc.

**turmoil** *n* agitation; disturbance, confusion.

**turn** *vi* to revolve; to go in the opposite
direction; to depend on; to appeal
(to) for help; to direct (thought or
attention) away from; to change in
character; to be shaped on the lathe.
• *vt* to change the position or direction of by revolving; to reverse; to
transform; (*age, etc*) to have just

passed; to change or convert; to invert. • *n* a rotation; new direction or
tendency; a place in sequence; a turning point, crisis; performer's act; an
act of kindness or malice; a bend.

**turning point** *n* the point at which a significant change occurs.

**turnip** *n* a plant with a large white or
yellow root, cultivated as a vegetable.

**turnout** *n* a gathering of people.

**turnover** *n* the volume of business
transacted in a given period; a fruit
or meat pasty; the rate of replacement of workers.

**turnpike** *n* a toll road, esp one that is
an expressway.

**turnstile** *n* a mechanical gate across a
footpath or entrance, which admits
only one person at a time.

**turntable** *n* a circular, horizontal revolving platform, as in a record player.

**turn-up** *n* the cuff of a trouser; (*inf*) a
surprise.

**turpentine** *n* an oily resin secreted by
coniferous trees, used as a solvent
and thinner for paints.—*also* **turps**.

**turquoise** *n* an opaque greenish-blue
mineral, valued as a gem; the colour
of turquoise.—*also adj*.

**turret** *n* a small tower on a building rising above it; a dome or revolving
structure for guns, as on a warship,
tank or aeroplane.—**turreted** *adj*.

**turtle** *n* any of an order of land , freshwater or marine reptiles having a soft
body encased in a hard shell.

**turtleneck** *n* a high close-fitting neck-
line on a sweater.

**tusk** *n* a long, projecting tooth on either side of the mouth, as of the elephant.—**tusked** *adj*.

**tussle** *n* a scuffle.

**tutor** *n* a private teacher who instructs
pupils individually; a member of staff
responsible for the supervision and
teaching of students in a university.
• *vt* to instruct; to act as a tutor.

**tutorial** *n* a period of tuition by a tutor to an individual or a small group. • *adj* of or pertaining to a tutor.

**tuxedo** *n* a man's semi-formal suit with a tailless jacket; a dinner jacket.

**TV** *abbr* = television.

**twang** *n* a sharp, vibrant sound, as of a taut string when plucked; a nasal tone of voice. • *vt* to make a twanging sound.

**tweed** *n* a twilled woollen fabric used in making clothes.

**tweezers** *n sing* small pincers.

**twelfth** *adj* the last of twelve; being one of twelve equal parts.

**twelve** *adj* the cardinal number next after eleven. • *n* the symbol for this (12, XII, xii).

**twenty** *adj*, *n* two times ten. • *n* the symbol for this (20, XX, xx). —**twentieth** *adj*.

**twice** *adv* two times; two times as much; doubly.

**twig**[1] *n* a small branch or shoot of a tree.—**twiggy** *adj*.

**twig**[2] *vti* (*pt* **twigged**) (*inf*) to grasp the meaning of.

**twilight** *n* the dim light just after sunset and before sunrise; the final stages of something.

**twill** *n* a cloth woven in such a way as to produce diagonal lines across it.— **twilled** *adj*.

**twin** *n* either of two persons or animals born at the same birth; one thing resembling another. • *adj* double; very like another; consisting of two parts nearly alike. • *vt* (*pt* **twinned**) to pair together.

**twine** *n* a string of twisted fibres or hemp. • *vti* to twist together; to wind around.

**twinge** *n* a sudden, stabbing pain; an emotional pang.

**twinkle** *vi* to sparkle; to flicker.

**twirl** *vt* to whirl; to rotate; to wind or twist. • *vi* to turn around rapidly.

**twist** *vt* to unite by winding together; to coil; to confuse or distort (the meaning of); to bend. • *vi* to revolve; to write. • *n* the act or result of twisting; a twist of thread; a curve or bend; an unexpected event; a wrench.

**twitch** *vt* to pull with a sudden jerk. • *vi* to be suddenly jerked. • *n* a sudden muscular spasm.

**two** *adj*, *n* the cardinal number next above one. • *n* the symbol for this (2, II, ii).

**two-faced** *adj* deceitful, hypocritical.

**two-piece** *n* a garment consisting of two separate matching bits.—*also adj*.

**twosome** *n* a group of two; a game for two people.

**tycoon** *n* a powerful industrialist, etc.

**type** *n* a kind, class or group; sort; model; a block of metal for printing letters; style of print. • *vt* to write by means of a typewriter; to classify.

**typecast** *vt* (*pt* **typecast**) (*actor*) to cast in the same role repeatedly because of physical appearance, etc.

**typescript** *n* a typed copy of a book, document, etc.

**typewriter** *n* a keyboard machine for printing characters.

**typhoid** *n* an acute infectious disease acquired from contaminated food or water.

**typhoon** *n* a violent tropical cyclone originating in the western Pacific.

**typhus** *n* a highly contagious acute disease spread by body lice and characterized by fever, a rash and headache.—**typhous** *adj*.

**typical** *adj* representative of a particular type; characteristic.—**typically** *adv*.

**typify** *vt* to characterize.

**typist** *n* a person who uses a typewriter, esp as a job.

**tyranny** *n* the government or authority of a tyrant; harshness; oppression.

**tyrant** *n* a person who uses his or her power arbitrarily and oppressively.—**tyrannical** *adj*.

**tyre, tire** (*US*) *n* a protective, usu rubber, covering around the rim of a wheel.

# U

**ubiquitous** *adj* existing, or seeming to exist everywhere at once.—**ubiquity** *n*.

**udder** *n* a milk-secreting organ containing two or more teats, as in cows.

**UFO** *abbr* = unidentified flying object.

**ugly** *adj* (**uglier, ugliest**) unsightly; unattractive; repulsive; ill tempered.—**ugliness** *n*.

**UHF** *abbr* = ultrahigh frequency.

**UK** *abbr* = United Kingdom.

**ulcer** *n* an open sore on the surface of the skin or a mucous membrane.—**ulcerous** *adj*

**ulterior** *adj* (*motives*) hidden, not evident; subsequent.

**ultimate** *adj* last; final; most significant; essential. • *n* the most significant thing.—**ultimately** *adv*.

**ultimatum** *n* (*pl* **ultimatums**) the final proposal, condition or terms in negotiations.

**ultraviolet** *adj* of light waves shorter than the wavelengths of visible light and longer than X-rays.

**umbilical cord** *n* the vascular tube connecting a foetus with the placenta through which oxygen and nutrients are passed.

**umbrage** *n* resentment; offence.

**umbrella** *n* a cloth-covered collapsible frame carried in the hand for protection from rain or sun; a general protection.

**umpire** *n* an official who enforces the rules in sport; an arbiter.—*also vti*.

**umpteen** *adj* (*inf*) an undetermined large number.—**umpteenth** *adj*.

**UN** *abbr* = United Nations.

**un-** *prefix* not; opposite of; contrary to; reversal of an action or state.

**unable** *adj* not able; lacking the strength, skill, power or opportunity (to do something).

**unanimous** *adj* showing complete agreement.—**unanimity** *n*.—**unanimously** *adv*.

**unassuming** *adj* unpretentious; modest.

**unattached** *adj* unmarried, not engaged to be married; not belonging to a particular group, organization, etc.

**unattended** *adj* not supervised; not accompanied.

**unauthorized** *adj* not endorsed by authority.

**unavoidable** *adj* bound to happen, inevitable; necessary, compulsory.—**unavoidably** *adv*.

**unaware** *adj* not conscious or aware (of); ignorant (of).

**unawares** *adv* by surprise; unexpectedly, without warning.

**unbalanced** *adj* mentally unstable; having bias or over-representing a particular view, group, interest, etc; (*bookkeeping*) not having equal debit and credit totals.

**unbeliever** *n* a person who does not believe, esp in a religion.

**unbending** *adj* severe, stern; inflexible, unchanging; rigid in behaviour or attitude.

**unbridled** *adj* unrestrained; (*horse*) having no bridle.

**unburden** *vt* to reveal or confess one's troubles, secrets, etc to another in order to relieve the mind; to take off a burden.

**uncalled-for** *adj* unnecessary, unwanted, unwarranted.

**uncanny** *adj* (**uncannier, uncanniest**) odd; unexpected; suggestive of supernatural powers; unearthly.

**uncertain** *adj* not knowing accurately, doubtful; (*with* **of**) not confident or sure; not fixed, variable, changeable.—**uncertainty** *n*.

**uncle** *n* the brother of one's father or mother; the husband of one's aunt.

**uncommon** *adj* rare, unusual; extraordinary.

**uncompromising** *adj* not prepared to compromise; inflexible, obstinate.

**unconditional** *adj* without restrictions or conditions, absolute.

**unconscious** *adj* not aware (of); lacking normal perception by the senses, insensible; unintentional. • *n* the deepest level of mind containing feelings and emotions of which one is unaware and unable to control.—

**unconsciously** *adv*.

**uncouth** *adj* lacking in manners; rough; rude.—**uncouthness** *n*.

**unctuous** *adj* oily; smarmy,; too suave; insincerely charming.—**unctuously** *adv*.—**unctuousness** *n*.

**undaunted** *adj* fearless; not discouraged.—**undauntedly** *adv*.

**undecided** *adj* doubtful, hesitant; (*solution, etc*) not determined.—**undecidedly** *adv*.

**under** *prep* lower than; beneath the surface of; below; covered by; subject to; less than, falling short of. • *adv* beneath, below, lower down. • *adj* lower in position, degree or rank; subordinate.

**under-** *prefix* beneath, below.

**undercarriage** *n* the landing gear of an aeroplane; a car's supporting framework.

**underclothes** *npl* underwear.—*also* **underclothing**.

**undercoat** *n* a coat of paint, etc, applied as a base below another; a growth of hair or fur under another; a coat worn under an overcoat.

**undercover** *adj* done or operating secretly.

**undercurrent** *n* a hidden current under water; an emotion, opinion, etc, not apparent.

**undercut** *vt* (*pt* **undercut**) to charge less than a competitor; to undermine.

**underdog** *n* the loser in an encounter, contest, etc; a person in an inferior position.

**underdone** *adj* not sufficiently or completely cooked.

**underestimate** *vti* to set too low an estimate on or for. • *n* too low an estimate.

**underexpose** *vt* (*photog*) to fail to expose (film) to light sufficiently long to produce a good image.—**underexposed** *adj*.—**underexposure** *n*.

**underfoot** *adv* underneath the foot or feet; on the ground.

**undergo** *vt* (*pt* **underwent**, *pp* **undergone**) to experience, suffer, endure.

**undergraduate** *n* a student at a college or university studying for a first degree.

**underground** *adj* situated under the surface of the ground; secret; of noncommercial newspapers, movies, etc that are unconventional, radical, etc. • *n* a secret group working for the overthrow of the government or the expulsion of occupying forces; an underground railway system; a subway.

**undergrowth** *n* shrubs, plants, etc growing beneath trees.

**underhand** *adv* (*sport*) with an underarm motion; underhandedly.

**underhanded** *adj* sly, secret, deceptive.—**underhandedly** *adv*.

**underlie** *vt* (*pr p* **underlying**, *pt* **underlay**, *pp* **underlain**) to be situated under; to form the basis of.

**underline** vt to put a line underneath; to emphasize.

**underling** n a person of inferior rank or status to someone else; a subordinate.

**undermine** vt to wear away, or weaken; to injure or weaken, esp by subtle or insidious means.

**underneath** adv under. • adj lower. • n the underside.—also prep.

**underpants** npl pants worn as an undergarment by men and boys.

**underpass** n a section of road running beneath another road, a railway, etc.

**underprivileged** adj lacking the basic rights of other members of society; poor.

**underrate** vt to undervalue, to underestimate.

**underside** n the lower surface.

**underskirt** n a woman's undergarment worn beneath the skirt, a petticoat.

**understand** vb .(pt **understood**) vt to comprehend; to realize; to believe; to assume; to know thoroughly (eg a language); to accept; to be sympathetic with. • vi to comprehend; to believe.—**understandable** adj.

**understanding** n comprehension; compassion, sympathy; personal opinion, viewpoint; mutual agreement. • adj sympathetic.

**understate** vt to state something in restrained terms; to represent as less than is the case.—**understatement** n.

**understudy** vti to learn a role or part so as to be able to replace (the actor playing it); to act as an understudy (to).—also n

**undertake** vt (pt **undertook**, pp **undertaken**) to attempt to; to agree to; to commit oneself; to promise; to guarantee.

**undertaker** n a funeral director.

**undertaking** n enterprise; task; promise; obligation.

**underwater** adj being, carried on under the surface of the water, esp the sea; submerged; below the water line of a vessel.—also adv.

**underwear** n garments worn underneath one's outer clothes, next to the skin.

**underworld** n criminals as an organized group; (myth) Hades.

**undesirable** adj not desirable; not pleasant; objectionable.—**undesirability** n.—**undesirably** adv.

**undies** npl (inf) women's underwear.

**undo** vt (pt **undid**, pp **undone**) to untie or unwrap; to reverse (what has been done); to bring ruin on.

**undoubted** adj without doubt; definite, certain.—**undoubtedly** adv.

**undress** vt to remove the clothes from. • vi to take off one's clothes.

**undue** adj improper; excessive.

**unduly** adv too; excessively; improperly.

**unearth** vt to dig up from the earth; to discover; to reveal.

**unearthly** adj mysterious; eerie; supernatural; absurd, unreasonable.

**uneasy** adj uncomfortable; restless; anxious; disquieting.—**uneasily** adv.—**uneasiness** n.

**uneconomic** adj wasteful; unprofitable.

**unemployed** adj not having a job, out of work.—**unemployment** n.

**unerring** adj sure, unfailing.

**uneven** adj not level or smooth; variable; not divisible by two without leaving a remainder.—**unevenness** n.

**unexpected** adj not looked for, unforeseen.—**unexpectedly** adv.

**unfailing** adj not failing or giving up; persistent; constant, dependable.—**unfailingly** adv.

**unfair** adj unjust; unequal; against the rules.—**unfairly** adv.—**unfairness** n.

**unfaithful** adj disloyal; not abiding by

a promise; adulterous.—**unfaithfully** *adv.*—**unfaithfulness** *n.*

**unfasten** *vt* to open or become opened; to undo or become undone; to loose.

**unfeeling** *adj* callous, hardhearted.—**unfeelingly** *adv.*

**unfinished** *adj* not finished, incomplete; in the making; crude, sketchy.

**unfit** *adj* unsuitable; in bad physical condition.

**unflappable** *adj* (*inf*) calm, not easily agitated.

**unfold** *vti* to open or spread out; to become revealed; to develop.

**unforeseen** *adj* unsuspected.

**unfortunate** *adj* unlucky; disastrous; regrettable. • *n* an unlucky person.

**unfortunately** *adv* regrettably, unluckily, unhappily.

**unfounded** *adj* groundless; baseless.

**ungainly** *adj* (**ungainlier, ungainliest**) awkward; clumsy.— **ungainliness** *n.*

**ungodly** *adj* (**ungodlier, ungodliest**) not religious; sinful; wicked; (*inf*) outrageous.

**unguarded** *adj* without protection, vulnerable; open to attack; careless; candid, frank.—**unguardedly** *adv.*

**unguent** *n* a lubricant or ointment.

**unhappy** *adj* (**unhappier, unhappiest**) not happy or fortunate; sad; wretched; not suitable.—**unhappily** *adv.*—**unhappiness** *n.*

**unhealthy** *adj* (**unhealthier, unhealthiest**) not healthy or fit, sick; encouraging or resulting from poor health; harmful, degrading; dangerous.—**unhealthily** *adv.*—**unhealthiness** *n.*

**unicorn** *n* an imaginary creature with a body like a horse and a single horn on the forehead.

**uniform** *adj* unchanging in form; consistent; identical. • *n* the distinctive clothes worn by members of the same organization, such as soldiers, schoolchildren.—**uniformly** *adv.*

**uniformity** *n* the state of being consistent or the same; dullness, monotony.

**unify** *vt* to make into one; to unite.—**unification** *n.*

**unilateral** *adj* involving one only of several parties; not reciprocal.—**unilateralism** *n.*—**unilaterally** *adv.*

**uninhibited** *adj* not repressed or restrained; relaxed, spontaneous.—**uninhibitedly** *adv.*

**union** *n* the act of uniting; a combination of several things; a confederation of individuals or groups; marriage; a trades union.

**unique** *adj* without equal; the only one of its kind.—**uniquely** *adv.*

**unison** *n* accordance of sound, concord, harmony; **in unison** simultaneously; in agreement; in harmony.

**unit** *n* the smallest whole number, one; a single or whole entity; (*measurement*) a standard amount; an establishment or group of people who carry out a specific function; a piece of furniture fitting together with other pieces.—**unitary** *adj.*

**unite** *vti* to join into one, to combine; to be unified in purpose.

**United Nations** *n sing or pl* an international organization of nations for world peace and security formed in 1945.

**United States** *n* a federation of states, esp the United States of America.

**unit trust** *n* a company that manages a range of investments on behalf of members of the public whose interests are looked after by an independent trust.

**unity** *n* oneness; harmony; concord.

**universal** *adj* widespread; general; relating to all the world or the universe; relating to or applicable to all mankind.—**universally** *adv.*—**universality** *n.*

**universe** *n* all existing things; (*astron*) the totality of space, stars, planets and other forms of matter and energy; the world.

**university** *n* an institution of higher education which confers bachelors' and higher degrees; the campus or staff of a university.

**unkempt** *adj* uncombed; slovenly, dishevelled

**unkind** *adj* lacking in kindness or sympathy; harsh; cruel.—**unkindly** *adv.*—**unkindness** *n*.

**unknown** *adj* not known; not famous; not understood; with an unknown value. • *n* an unknown person or thing.

**unleash** *vt* to release from a leash; to free from restraint.

**unless** *conj* if not; except that.

**unlikely** *adj* improbable; unpromising.

**unlimited** *adj* without limits; boundless; not restricted.—**unlimitedly** *adv.*

**unload** *vti* to remove a load, discharge freight from a truck, ship, etc; to relieve of or express troubles, etc; to dispose of, dump; to empty, esp a gun.

**unlock** *vt* (*door, lock, etc*) to unfasten; to let loose; to reveal; to release.

**unlucky** *adj* (**unluckier, unluckiest**) not lucky, not fortunate; likely to bring misfortune; regrettable.—**unluckily** *adv.*

**unmask** *vti* to remove the mask from; to expose, show up.

**unmitigated** *adj* unqualified, absolute.

**unnatural** *adj* abnormal; contrary to nature; artificial; affected; strange; wicked.—**unnaturally** *adv.*

**unpack** *vti* (*suitcase, etc*) to remove the contents of; (*container, etc*) to take things out of; to unload.

**unpleasant** *adj* not pleasing or agreeable; nasty; objectionable.—**unpleasantly** *adv.*—**unpleasantness** *n*.

**unpopular** *adj* disliked; lacking general approval.—**unpopularity** *n*.

**unprecedented** *adj* having no precedent; unparalleled.

**unpretentious** *adj* modest, not boasting.

**unqualified** *adj* lacking recognized qualifications; not equal to; not restricted, complete.

**unravel** *vt* (*pt* **unravelled**) to disentangle; to solve.

**unreasonable** *adj* contrary to reason; lacking reason; immoderate; excessive.—**unreasonably** *adv.*

**unrelenting** *adj* relentless; continuous.—**unrelentingly** *adv.*

**unremitting** *adj* incessant.

**unrest** *n* uneasiness; anxiety; angry discontent verging on revolt.

**unroll** *vti* to open out or down from a roll; to unfold; to straighten out; to reveal or become revealed.

**unruly** *adj* (**unrulier, unruliest**) hard to control, restrain, or keep in order; disobedient.

**unsavoury, unsavory** (*US*) *adj* distasteful; disagreeable; offensive.

**unscathed** *adj* unharmed.

**unscrew** *vti* to remove a screw from; (*lid, etc*) to loosen by turning.

**unscrupulous** *adj* without principles.

**unseemly** *adj* unbecoming; inappropriate.

**unsettled** *adj* changeable; lacking stability; unpredictable; not concluded.

**unsightly** *adj* unattractive; ugly.

**unskilled** *adj* without special skill or training.

**unspeakable** *adj* bad beyond words, indescribable.

**unsteady** *adj* (**unsteadier, unsteadiest**) shaky, reeling; facillating.—**unsteadily** *adv.*

**unthinkable** *adj* inconceivable; out of the question; improbable.—**unthinkably** *adv.*

**untidy** *adj* (**untidier, untidiest**) not neat, disordered. • *vt* to make untidy.—**untidily** *adv.*

**untie** vt to undo a knot in, unfasten.

**until** prep up to the time of; before.
• conj up to the time when or that; to the point, degree, etc that; before.

**untimely** adj premature; inopportune.

**untold** adj not told; too great to be counted; immeasurable.

**untoward** adj unseemly; unfavourable; adverse.

**unusual** adj uncommon; rare.

**unveil** vt to reveal; to disclose.

**unwell** adj ill, not well; (inf) suffering from a hangover.

**unwieldy** adj not easily moved or handled, as because of large size; awkward.—**unwieldily** adv.—**unwieldiness** n.

**unwilling** adj not willing, reluctant; said or done with reluctance.—**unwillingly** adv.—**unwillingness** n.

**unwind** vt to untangle; to undo. • vi to relax.

**unwitting** adj not knowing; unintentional.—**unwittingly** adv.

**unworldly** adj spiritual, not concerned with the material world.

**unwritten** adj not written or printed; traditional; oral.

**up** adv to, towards, in or on a higher place; to a later period; so as to be even with in time, degree, etc. • prep from a lower to a higher point on or along. • adj moving or directed upward; at an end; (inf) well informed. • vt (pt **upped**) to raise; to increase; to take up. • n ascent; high point.

**up-and-coming** adj promising for the future; likely to succeed.

**upbringing** n the process of educating and nurturing (a child).

**update** vt to bring up to date.

**upgrade** vt to improve, raise to a higher grade.

**upheaval** n radical or violent change.

**uphill** adj ascending, rising; difficult, arduous. • adv up a slope or hill; against difficulties.

**uphold** vt (pt **upheld**) to support, sustain; to defend.

**upholstery** n materials used to make a soft covering esp for a seat.

**upkeep** n maintenance; the cost of it.

**upon** prep on, on top of.

**upper** adj farther up; higher in position, rank, status. • n the part of a boot or shoe above the sole; (sl) a drug used as a stimulant.—also **upmost**.

**upper case** n capital letters.—**uppercase** adj.

**upper class** n people occupying the highest social rank.—also adj.

**upright** adj vertical, in an erect position; righteous, honest, just. • n a vertical post or support. • adv vertically.

**uprising** n a revolt; a rebellion.

**uproar** n a noisy disturbance; a commotion; an outcry.

**uproot** vt to tear out by the roots; to remove from established surroundings.

**upset**[1] vt (pr p **upsetting**, pt **upset**) to overturn; to spill; to disturb; to put out of order; to distress; to overthrow; to make physically sick.

**upset**[2] n an unexpected defeat; distress or its cause. • adj distressed; confused; defeated.

**upshot** n the conclusion; the result.

**upside down** adj inverted; the wrong way up; (inf) topsy turvy.

**upstairs** adv up the stairs; to an upper level or storey. • n an upper floor.

**upstart** n a person who has suddenly risen to a position of wealth and power; an arrogant person.

**up-to-date** adj modern; fashionable.

**upturn** n an upward trend; an (economic) improvement. • vt to turn upside down.

**upward, upwards** adj from a lower to a higher place.—also adv.

**uranium** n a metallic element used as a source of nuclear energy.

**urban** *adj* of or relating to a city.—**urbanization** *n*.

**urbane** *adj* sophisticated; refined.—**urbanity** *n*.

**urchin** *n* a raggedly dressed mischievous child; a sea urchin.

**urge** *vt* to drive forward; to press, plead with. • *n* an impulse, yearning.

**urgency** *n* the quality or condition of being urgent; compelling need; importance.

**urgent** *adj* impelling; persistent; calling for immediate attention.—**urgently** *adv*.

**urinate** *vi* to pass urine.

**urn** *n* a vase or large vessel; a receptacle for preserving the ashes of the dead; a large metal container for boiling water for tea or coffee.

**US** *abbr* = United States.

**us** *pron* the objective case of **we**.

**USA** *abbr* = United States of America.

**usage** *n* customary use; practice, custom; use of language.

**use**[1] *vt* to put to some purpose; to utilize; to exploit (a person); to partake of (drink, drugs, tobacco, etc).

**use**[2] *n* act of using or putting to a purpose; usage; usefulness; need (for); advantage; practice, custom.—**usable, useable** *adj*.

**used** *adj* not new; second-hand.

**useful** *adj* able to be used to good effect; (*inf*) capable, commendable.—**usefully** *adv*.

**useless** *adj* of no use.—**uselessly** *adv*.—**uselessness** *n*.

**usher** *n* one who shows people to their seats in a theatre, church, etc; a doorkeeper in a law court. • *vt* to escort to seats, etc.

**USSR** *abbr* = (*formerly*) Union of Soviet Socialist Republics.

**usual** *adj* customary; ordinary; normal.—**usually** *adv*.

**usurer** *n* a person who lends money at an excessively high rate of interest.

**usurp** *vt* to seize or appropriate unlawfully.—**usurper** *n*.

**utensil** *n* an implement or container, esp one for use in the kitchen.

**uterus** *n* (*pl* **uteri**) the womb.—**uterine** *adj*.

**utilitarian** *adj* designed to be of practical use.

**utility** *n* usefulness; a public service, such as telephone, electricity, etc; a company providing such a service.

**utilize** *vt* to make practical use of.—**utilization** *n*.

**utmost** *adj* of the greatest degree or amount; furthest. • *n* the most possible.

**utter**[1] *adj* absolute; complete.

**utter**[2] *vt* to say; to speak.—**utterance** *n*.

# V

**V** *abbr* = volt(s).

**v** *abbr* = velocity; *versus* against; *vide* see; verb.

**vacancy** *n* emptiness; an unoccupied job or position.

**vacant** *adj* empty; unoccupied; (*expression*) blank.—**vacantly** *adv*.

**vacate** *vt* to leave empty; to give up possession of.

**vacation** *n* a holiday; a period of the year when universities, colleges and law courts are closed. • *vi* to go on holiday.—**vacationer** *n*

**vaccinate** *vt* to inoculate with vaccine as a protection against a disease.—**vaccination** *n*

**vaccine** *n* a preparation used for inoculation to give immunity from certain diseases.

**vacuum** *n* (*pl* **vacuums**) a region devoid of all matter; a region in which gas is present at low pressure; a vacuum cleaner. • *vt* to clean with a vacuum cleaner.

**vacuum cleaner** *n* an electrical appliance for removing dust from carpets, etc, by suction.

**vacuum flask** *n* a container for keeping liquids hot or cold.

**vagina** *n* in female mammals and humans, the canal connecting the uterus and the external sex organs.—**vaginal** *adj*.

**vagrant** *n* a person who has no settled home, a tramp.—**vagrancy**.

**vague** *adj* unclear; indistinct, imprecise; (*person*) absent minded.—**vaguely** *adv*.—**vagueness** *n*.

**vain** *adj* conceited; excessively concerned with one's appearance; senseless; worthless.—**vainly** *adv*.

**valentine** *n* a lover or sweetheart chosen on St Valentine's Day, 14th February; a card or gift sent on that day.

**valiant** *adj* courageous; brave.—**valiantly** *adv*.

**valid** *adj* based on facts; (*objection, etc*) sound; legally acceptable; binding.—**validity** *n*.—**validly** *adv*.

**valley** *n* (*pl* **valleys**) low land between hills or mountains.

**valuable** *adj* having considerable importance or monetary worth. • *n* a personal possession of value, esp jewellery; (*pl*) valuable possessions.

**valuation** *n* the act of valuing; an estimated price or worth; an estimation.—**valuator** *n*.

**value** *n* worth, merit, importance; market value; purchasing power; relative worth; (*pl*) moral principles. • *vt* to estimate the worth of; to regard highly; to prize.—**valued** *adj*.—**valuer** *n*.

**value added tax** *n* a tax levied on the difference between the production cost of an item and its selling price.

**valve** *n* a device for controlling the flow of a gas or liquid through a pipe; (*anat*) a tube allowing blood to flow in one direction only.

**van** *n* a covered motor vehicle for transporting goods, etc.

**vandal** *n* a person who wilfully damages property.—**vandalism** *n*.—**vandalize** *vt*.

**vanguard** *n* the front part of an army; the leading position of any movement.

**vanilla** *n* extract from the orchid pod used as a flavouring.

**vanish** *vi* to disappear; to fade away.

**vanity** *n* conceit; worthlessness; something worthless.

**vanity case, vanity box** *n* a small case used for carrying cosmetics, etc.

**vantage** *n* a favourable position; a position allowing a clear view or understanding.

**vapour, vapor** (*US*) *n* the gaseous state of a substance normally liquid or solid; particles of water or smoke in the air.

**variable** *adj* liable to change; not constant. • *n* (*math*) a quantity that varies.—**variability** *n*.

**variance** *n* discrepancy.

**variant** *n* a different form.—*also adj*.

**variation** *n* diversity; deviation; modification.

**varicose** *adj* (*veins*) abnormally swollen and dilated.

**variety** *n* diversity; an assortment.

**variety show** *n* an entertainment made up of various acts, such as songs, comedy turns, etc.

**various** *adj* varied, different; several.—**variously** *adv*.

**varnish** *n* a sticky liquid which dries and forms a hard, glossy coating. • *vt* to coat with varnish.

**vary** *vti* to change, to diversify, modify; to become altered.

**vase** *n* a vessel for displaying flowers.

**vast** *adj* immense.—**vastly** *adv*.—*n* **vastness**.

**VAT** *abbr* = value added tax.

**vat** *n* a large barrel or tank.

**Vatican** *n* the residence of the pope in Rome; papal authority.

**vault**[1] *n* an arched ceiling or roof; a burial chamber; a strongroom for valuables; a cellar.—**vaulted** *adj*.

**vault**[2] *vti* to leap or jump over an obstacle.—*also n*.

**VD** *abbr* = venereal disease.

**veal** *n* the edible flesh of a calf.

**veer** *vi* (*wind*) to change direction; to swing around; to change from one mood or opinion to another.

**vegetable** *n* a herbaceous plant grown for food; (*inf*) a person who has suffered brain damage.—*also adj*.

**vegetarian** *n* a person who consumes a diet that excludes meat and fish. —*also adj*.—**vegetarianism** *n*.

**vegetate** *vi* to grow like a plant; to sprout; to lead a mentally inactive, aimless life.

**vegetation** *n* vegetable growth; plants in general.

**vehement** *adj* passionate; forceful; furious.—**vehemence** *n*.

**vehicle** *n* a conveyance, such as a car, bus or truck, for carrying people or goods; a medium.—**vehicular** *adj*.

**veil** *n* a thin fabric worn over the head or face of a woman; a nun's headdress; anything that conceals. • *vt* to put on a veil; to cover; to conceal.

**vein** *n* one of the vessels that convey the blood back to the heart; a seam of mineral within a rock; a branching rib in a leaf; a streak of different colour; a style or mood. • *vt* to streak.

**velocity** *n* speed.

**velvet** *n* a fabric made from silk, rayon, etc with a soft, thick pile; anything like velvet in texture.

**vending machine** *n* a coin-operated machine which dispenses goods.

**vendor, vender** *n* a person selling something.

**veneer** *n* an overlay of fine wood or plastic; a superficial appearance. • *vt* to cover with veneer.

**venerable** *adj* worthy of reverence or respect.

**venereal** *adj* (*disease*) resulting from sexual intercourse.

**Venetian blind** *n* a window blind formed of long thin horizontal slips of wood that can be pivoted.

**vengeance** *n* the act of taking revenge; retribution.—**vengeful** *adj*.

**venison** *n* the edible flesh of the deer.

**venom** *n* poison; spite, malice.—**venomous** *adj*.

**vent** *n* a small opening or slit; an outlet or flue for the escape of fumes. • *vt* to release; (*temper*) to give expression to.

**ventilate** *vt* to supply with fresh air; to express, to discuss.

**ventilation** *n* the act of ventilating; the state of being ventilated; free discussion.

**ventilator** *n* an appliance for ventilating a room, etc.

**ventriloquism** *n* the act or art of speaking so that the sounds appear to come from a source other than the actual speaker.

**venture** *n* a dangerous expedition; a risky undertaking. • *vti* to risk; to dare.—**venturesome** *adj*.

**venue** *n* the place of an action or event.

**veranda, verandah** *n* a roofed porch, supported by light pillars.

**verb** *n* (*gram*) the part of speech that expresses an action, a process, state or condition or mode of being.

**verbal** *adj* spoken; literal; pertaining to or characteristic of a verb.—**verbally** *adv*.

**verbiage** *n* use of too many words.

**verbose** *adj* wordy.

**verdict** *n* the decision of a jury at the end of a trial; decision, judgment.

**verge** *n* the brink; the extreme edge

or margin; a grass border beside a road. • *vi* to border (on).

**verger** *n* a church official.

**verify** *vt* to confirm the truth of; to substantiate.—**verifiable** *adj.*—**verification** *n*.

**vermin** *n* (*used as pl*) pests, such as insects and rodents; persons dangerous to society.—**verminous** *adj*.

**vermouth** *n* a white wine flavoured with herbs, used in cocktails and as an aperitif.

**vernacular** *n* the commonly spoken language or dialect of a country or region. • *adj* native.

**versatile** *adj* changeable, adaptable; able to move or turn freely.—**versatility** *n*.

**verse** *n* a line of poetry; a stanza of a poem; a short section of a chapter in the Bible.

**versed** *adj* skilled or learned in a subject.

**version** *n* a translation from one language into another; a particular account or description.

**versus** *prep* against; in contrast to.

**vertebra** *n* (*pl* **vertebrae, vertebras**) one of the interconnecting bones of the spinal column.

**vertebrate** *n* an animal with a backbone.

**vertical** *adj* perpendicular to the horizon; upright. • *n* a vertical line or plane.

**vertigo** *n* a sensation of dizziness and sickness caused by a disorder of the sense of balance.—**vertiginous** *adj*.

**verve** *n* enthusiasm; liveliness; energy.

**very** *adj* complete; absolute; same. • *adv* extremely; truly; really.

**vespers** *npl* (*used as sing*) an Anglican service held daily in the evening.

**vessel** *n* a container; a ship or boat; a tube in the body along which fluids pass.

**vest** *n* a sleeveless undergarment; a

waistcoat. • *vt* to place or settle (power, authority, etc.); to confer.

**vested interest** *n* a strong reason for acting in a certain way, usu for personal gain.

**vestibule** *n* an entrance hall or lobby.

**vestige** *n* a hint; a trace.

**vestry** *n* a room in a church where vestments, etc, are kept and parochial meetings held; a meeting for parish business.

**vet** *n* a veterinary surgeon. • *vt* (*pt* **vetted**) to examine, check for errors, etc.

**veteran** *adj* old, experienced; having served in the armed forces. • *n* a person who has served in the armed forces; a person who has given long service in a particular activity.

**veterinary surgeon** *n* a person trained in treating sick or injured animals.—*also* **veterinarian**.

**veto** *n* (*pl* **vetoes**) the right of a person or group to prohibit an action or legislation; a prohibition. • *vt* to refuse to agree to; to prohibit.

**vex** *vt* to annoy; to puzzle, confuse.—**vexation** *n*.

**VHF** *abbr* = very high frequency.

**via** *prep* by way of.

**viable** *adj* capable of growing or developing; workable; practicable.—**viability** *n*.

**viaduct** *n* a road or railway carried by a bridge with arches over a valley, river, etc.

**vibrate** *vti* to shake; to move quickly backwards and forwards; to quiver; to oscillate.—**vibration** *n*.—**vibratory** *adj*.

**vicar** *n* a parish priest; a clergyman in charge of a chapel.

**vice**[1] *n* an evil action or habit.

**vice**[2], **vise** (*US*) *n* a clamping device with jaws, used for holding objects firmly.

**vice-** *prefix* who acts in place of, or as a deputy to, another.

**vice versa** *adv* conversely; the other way round.

**vicinity** *n* a nearby area; proximity.

**vicious** *adj* cruel; violent; malicious; ferocious.—**viciously** *adv*.

**vicissitudes** *npl* ups and downs; successive changes of fortune.

**victim** *n* a person who has been killed or injured by an action beyond his or her control; a dupe.

**victimize** *vt* to make a victim.—**victimization** *n*.

**victor** *n* a winner; a conqueror.

**Victorian** *adj* of or living in the reign of Queen Victoria; old-fashioned, prudish.

**victorious** *adj* having won in battle or contest; emblematic of victory; triumphant.—**victoriously** *adv*.

**victory** *n* triumph in battle; success; achievement.

**video** *n* (*pl* **videos**) the transmission or recording of television programmes or films, using a television set and a video recorder and tape. • *vt* to record on video tape.

**video recorder** *n* the machine that plays or records on video tape.

**video tape** *n* a magnetic tape on which images and sounds can be recorded for reproduction on television.—**video-tape** *vt*.

**vie** *vi* (*pr p* **vying**, *pt* **vied**) to contend or strive for superiority.

**view** *n* sight; range of vision; inspection, examination; intention; scene; opinion. • *vt* to see; to consider; to examine intellectually.

**viewer** *n* a person who views, esp television; an optical device used in viewing.

**viewfinder** *n* a device in a camera showing the view to be photographed.

**viewpoint** *n* opinion; a place from which something can be viewed, esp a scenic panorama.

**vigil** *n* keeping watch at night.

**vigilance** *n* watchfulness; alertness.—**vigilant** *adj*.

**vigour, vigor** (*US*) *n* physical or mental strength; vitality.—**vigorous** *adj*.—**vigorously** *adv*.

**vile** *adj* wicked; evil; offensive; very bad.

**villa** *n* a large country or suburban house.

**village** *n* a collection of houses smaller than a town.

**villager** *n* an inhabitant of a village.

**villain** *n* a scoundrel; the main evil character in a play, film or novel.—**villainous** *adj*.

**vindicate** *vt* to justify; to absolve from blame.—**vindication** *n*.—**vindicator** *n*.

**vindictive** *adj* vengeful; spiteful.—**vindictiveness** *n*.

**vine** *n* any climbing plant, or its stem; a grapevine.

**vinegar** *n* a sour-tasting liquid containing acetic acid, used as a condiment and preservative.

**vineyard** *n* a plantation of grapevines.

**vintage** *n* the grape harvest of one season; wine, esp of good quality made in a particular year; wine of a particular region; the product of a particular period. • *adj* (*cars*) classic; (*wine*) of a specified year and of good quality; (*play*) characteristic of the best.

**vinyl** *n* a strong plastic used in floor coverings, furniture, records, etc.

**viola** *n* a stringed instrument of the violin family, and tuned a fifth below it.

**violate** *vt* to break or infringe (an agreement); to rape; to disturb (one's privacy).

**violence** *n* physical force intended to cause injury or destruction; natural force; passion, intensity.

**violent** *adj* urged or driven by force; vehement; impetuous; forcible; furious; severe.—**violently** *adv*.

**violet** *n* a small plant with bluish-purple flowers; a bluish-purple colour.

**violin** *n* a four-stringed musical instrument, played with a bow.

**violinist** *n* a person who plays the violin.

**VIP** *abbr* = Very Important Person.

**viper** *n* a common European venomous snake.

**virgin** *n* a person (esp a woman) who has never had sexual intercourse. • *adj* chaste; pure; untouched.— **virginal** *adj*.

**virginity** *n* the state of being a virgin; the state of being chaste, untouched, etc.

**Virgo** *n* the Virgin, the 6th sign of the zodiac.

**virile** *adj* manly; sexually potent.— **virility** *n*.

**virtual** *adj* in effect or essence, though not in fact or strict definition.— **virtually** *adv*.

**virtue** *n* moral excellence; any admirable quality; chastity; merit.

**virtuoso** *n* (*pl* **virtuosi**, **virtuosos**) a person highly skilled in an activity, esp in playing a musical instrument.— *also adj*.— **virtuosity** *n*.

**virtuous** *adj* righteous; upright; pure.— **virtuously** *adv*.

**virus** *n* (*pl* **viruses**) a very simple microorganism capable of replicating within living cells, producing disease; the disease caused by a virus; a harmful influence.

**visa** *n* an endorsement on a passport allowing the bearer to travel in the country of the government issuing it.

**vis-à-vis** *prep* opposite to; in face of. • *adv* facing.

**viscount** *n* in UK, a title of nobility next below an earl.— **viscountess** *nf*.

**visibility** *n* clearness of seeing or being seen.

**visible** *adj* that may be seen; evident.

**vision** *n* the power of seeing; sight; a supernatural appearance; foresight; imagination.

**visionary** *adj* imaginative; having foresight; existing in imagination only, not real. • *n* an imaginative person.

**visit** *vt* to go to see; to pay a call upon a person or place; to punish or reward with. • *vi* to see or meet someone regularly. • *n* act of going to see.

**visiting card** *n* a small card with the name left when paying visits.

**visitor** *n* a person who visits; a caller.

**visor** *n* a movable part of a helmet protecting the face; the peak of a cap.

**vista** *n* a view, as from a high place; a mental picture.

**visual** *adj* relating to vision or sight; visible.

**visual aid** *n* a film, slide or overhead projector, etc used to aid teaching.

**visualize** *vt* to form a mental picture of.— **visualization** *n*.

**vital** *adj* necessary to life; essential; lively.— **vitally** *adv*.

**vitality** *n* vigour; spirits; animation.

**vitamin** *n* organic substance, occurring naturally in foods, which is essential for good health.

**vivacious** *adj* lively; animated; spirited.— **vivacity** *n*.

**vivid** *adj* brightly coloured, graphic; lively; intense.— **vividly** *adv*.

**vivisection** *n* the practice of performing surgical operations on living animals for scientific research.

**vocabulary** *n* an alphabetical list of words with their meanings; the words of a language; an individual's use of particular words.

**vocal** *adj* relating to the voice; outspoken; noisy; (*phonetics*) having a vowel function.— **vocally** *adv*.

**vocalist** *n* a singer.

**vocation** *n* calling to a particular career or occupation.— **vocational** *adj*.

**vociferous** *adj* clamorous, noisy.— **vociferously** *adv*.

**vodka** *n* a spirit distilled from rye.

**vogue** *n* the fashion at a specified time; popularity.

**voice** *n* sound from the mouth; sound produced by speaking or singing; expressed opinion; the relation between a verb and its subject. • *vt* to express; to speak.

**void** *adj* unoccupied, empty; not legally binding. • *n* an empty space, a vacuum. • *vt* to empty; to make invalid.

**volatile** *adj* evaporating very quickly.

**volcano** *n* (*pl* **volcanoes, volcanos**) a hill or mountain formed by ejection of lava, ashes, etc through an opening in the earth's crust.—**volcanic** *adj*.

**volition** *n* the exercise of the will; choice.

**volley** *n* (*pl* **volleys**) the multiple discharge of many missiles or small arms; a barrage; (*tennis, volleyball*) the return of the ball before it reaches the ground. • *vt* to return (a ball) before it hits the ground.

**volleyball** *n* a team game played by hitting a large inflated ball over a net with the hands; the ball used.

**volt** *n* the unit of measure of the force of an electrical current.

**voltage** *n* electrical force measured in volts.

**volume** *n* the amount of space occupied by an object; quantity, amount; intensity of sound; a book; one book of a series.

**voluntary** *adj* acting by choice; willing; brought about by free will; without remuneration.—**voluntarily** *adv*.

**volunteer** *n* a person who carries out work voluntarily; a person who freely undertakes military service.—*also vti*.

**voluptuous** *adj* excessively fond of pleasure; having an attractive figure.

**vomit** *vi* (*pt* **vomited**) to eject the contents of the stomach through the mouth, to spew. • *n* matter ejected from the stomach when vomiting.

**vote** *n* an indication of a choice or opinion as to a matter on which one has a right to be consulted; a ballot; decision by a majority; the right to vote; franchise. • *vi* to cast one's vote. • *vt* to elect.—**voter** *n*.

**vouch** *vt* to provide evidence or proof of. • *vi* to give assurance; to guarantee.

**voucher** *n* a written record of a transaction; a receipt; a token that can be exchanged for something else.

**vow** *n* a solemn or binding promise. • *vt* to promise; to resolve.

**vowel** *n* an open speech sound produced by continuous passage of the breath; a letter representing such a sound, as *a, e, i, o, u*.

**voyage** *n* a long journey, esp by ship or spacecraft. • *vi* to journey.—**voyager** *n*.

**vulgar** *adj* common; coarse; offensive; vernacular.—**vulgarly** *adv*.

**vulnerable** *adj* capable of being wounded physically or mentally; open to persuasion; easily influenced.—**vulnerability** *n*.

**vulture** *n* a large bird of prey having no feathers on the neck or head.

# W

**wad** *n* a small, soft mass, as of cotton or paper; a bundle of paper money.

**wade** *vti* to walk through water; to pass (through) with difficulty.

**wader** *n* a bird that wades, eg the heron.

**waffle**[1] *n* a thick, crisp pancake baked in a waffle iron.

**waffle**[2] *vi* (*inf*) to speak or write at length without saying anything substantial.

**waft** *vt* to drift or float through the air.
• *n* a breath, scent or sound carried through the air.

**wag**[1] *vti* (*pt* **wagged**) to move rapidly from side to side or up and down (as of a finger, tail).—*also n.*

**wag**[2] *n* a joker, a wit.

**wage** *vt* to carry on, esp war. • *n* (*often pl*) payment for work or services.

**wager** *n* a bet. • *vti* to bet.

**waggle** *vti* to wag.—*also n.*

**wagon, waggon** *n* a four-wheeled vehicle pulled by a horse or tractor, for carrying heavy goods.

**wail** *vi* to make a long, loud cry of sorrow or grief; to howl, to moan.—*also n.*

**waist** *n* the narrowest part of the human trunk, between the ribs and the hips; the narrow part of anything that is wider at the ends; the part of a garment covering the waist.

**waistcoat** *n* a waist-length, sleeveless garment worn immediately under a suit jacket; a vest.

**waistline** *n* the narrowest part of the waist; its measurement; the seam that joins the bodice and skirt of a dress, etc; the level of this.

**wait** *vti* to stay, or to be, in expectation or readiness; to defer or to be postponed; to remain; (*with* **at** *or* **on**) to serve food at a meal. • *n* act or period of waiting.

**waiter** *n* a man or woman who serves at table, as in a restaurant.—**waitress** *nf.*

**waiting list** *n* a list of people applying for or waiting to obtain something.

**waiting room** *n* a room for people to wait in at a station, hospital, etc.

**waive** *vt* to refrain from enforcing; to relinquish voluntarily.

**wake**[1] *vb* (*pt* **woke** *or* **waked**, *pp* **woken** *or* **waked**) *vi* to emerge from sleep; to become awake. • *vt* to rouse from sleep. • *n* a watch or vigil beside a corpse, on the eve of the burial.—**wakeful** *adj.*—**waken** *vti.*

**wake**[2] *n* the waves or foamy water left in the track of a ship; a trail.

**walk** *vi* to travel on foot with alternate steps. • *vt* to pass through or over; (*a dog*) to exercise; to escort on foot. • *n* the act of walking; distance walked over; gait; a ramble or stroll; a profession.—**walker** *n.*

**walkie-talkie** *n* a portable two-way radio transmitter and receiver.

**walking stick** *n* a stick used in walking, a cane.

**walkover** *n* an unopposed or easy victory; a horse race with only one starter.

**wall** *n* a vertical structure of brick, stone, etc for enclosing, dividing or protecting. • *vt* to enclose with a wall; to close up with a wall.

**wallet** *n* a flat pocketbook for paper money, cards etc.

**wallflower** *n* a fragrant plant with red or yellow flowers; a person who does not dance for lack of a partner.

**wallop** *vt* (*pt* **walloped**) (*inf*) to beat or defeat soundly; (*inf*) to strike hard. • *n* (*inf*) a hard blow.

**wallow** *vi* (*animal*) to roll about in mud; to indulge oneself in emotion.—*also n.*

**wallpaper** *n* decorated paper for covering the walls of a room.

**walnut** *n* a tree producing an edible nut with a round shell and wrinkled seed; its nut; its wood used for furniture.

**walrus** *n* (*pl* **walruses, walrus**) a large, thick-skinned aquatic animal, related to the seals, having long canine teeth and coarse whiskers.

**waltz** *n* a piece of music with three beats to the bar; a whirling or slowly circling dance. • *vti* to dance a waltz; to lead (someone) in waltz time.

**wan** *adj* (**wanner, wannest**) pale and sickly; feeble or weak.—**wanly** *adv*.—**wanness** *n*.

**wand** *n* a magician's rod.

**wander** *vi* to ramble with no definite destination; to go astray; to lose concentration.—*also n*.

**wane** *vi* to decrease, esp of the moon; to decline. • *n* decrease, decline.

**want** *n* lack; poverty. • *vt* to need; to require; to lack; to wish (for).

**wanted** *adj* sought after.

**wanting** *adj* lacking.

**wanton** *adj* malicious; wilful; sexually provocative.

**war** *n* military conflict between nations or parties; a conflict; a contest. • *vi* (*pt* **warred**) to make war.

**ward** *n* a section of a hospital; an electoral district; a division of a prison; a child placed under the supervision of a court.—**wardship** *n*.

**warden** *n* an official; a person in charge of a building or home; a prison governor;

**warder** *n* a prison officer.

**wardrobe** *n* a cupboard for clothes; one's clothes.

**ware** *n* (*pl*) merchandise, goods for sale; pottery.

**warehouse** *n* a building for storing goods.

**warfare** *n* armed hostilities; conflict.

**warhead** *n* the section of a missile containing the explosive.

**warlike** *adj* hostile.

**warm** *adj* moderately hot; friendly, kind; (*colours*) rich; enthusiastic. • *vt* to make warm. • *vi* to become enthusiastic (about). —**warmly** *adv*.—**warmth** *n*.

**warm-hearted** *adj* kind, sympathetic; affectionate.

**warn** *vt* to notify of danger; to caution or advise (against).—**warning** *n*.

**warp** *vti* to twist out of shape; to distort; to corrupt. • *n* the threads arranged lengthwise on a loom across which other threads are passed.

**warrant** *vt* to guarantee; to justify. • *n* a document giving authorization; a writ for arrest.

**warranty** *n* a pledge to replace something if it is not as represented, a guarantee.

**warrior** *n* a soldier, fighter.

**warship** *n* a ship equipped for war.

**wart** *n* a small, hard projection on the skin.—**warty** *adj*.

**wartime** *adj, n* (of) a period or time of war.

**wary** *adj* (**warier, wariest**) watchful; cautious.—**warily** *adv*.—**wariness** *n*.

**was** *see* **be**.

**wash** *vti* to cleanse with water and soap; to flow against or over; to sweep along by the action of water; to separate gold, etc, from earth by washing; to cover with a thin coat of metal or paint. • *n* a washing; the break of waves on the shore; the waves left behind by a boat; a liquid used for washing.

**washbasin, washbowl** *n* a basin or bowl, esp a bathroom fixture, for use in washing one's hands, etc.—*also* **wash-hand basin**.

**washed-out** *adj* faded; limp; exhausted.

**washer** *n* a flat ring of metal, rubber, etc, to give tightness to joints; a washing machine.

**washing** *n* the act of cleansing with water; a number of items washed together.

**washing machine** *n* a device for washing clothes.

**washroom** *n* cloakroom, lavatory.

**wasp** *n* a winged insect with a black and yellow striped body, which can sting.

**wastage** *n* anything lost by use or natural decay; wasteful or avoidable loss of something valuable.

**waste** *adj* useless; left over; uncultivated or uninhabited. • *vt* to ravage; to squander; to use foolishly; to fail to use. • *vi* to lose strength, etc as by disease. • *n* uncultivated or uninhabited land; discarded material, garbage, excrement.—**wasteful** *adj.*—**wastefully** *adv.*—**wastefulness** *n.*

**watch** *n* surveillance; close observation; vigil; guard; a small timepiece worn on the wrist, etc; (*naut*) a period of duty. • *vi* to look with attention; to wait for; to keep vigil. • *vt* to keep one's eyes fixed on; to guard; to tend; to observe closely; (*chance, etc*) to wait for.—**watcher** *n.*—**watchful** *adj.*—**watchfully** *adv.*—**watchfulness** *n.*

**watchdog** *n* a dog that guards property; a person or group that monitors safety, standards, etc.

**watchmaker** *n* a person who makes and repairs watches.

**water** *n* the substance H2O, a clear, thin liquid, lacking taste or smell, and essential for life; any body of it, as the ocean, a lake, river, etc; bodily secretions such as tears, urine. • *vt* to moisten with water; to irrigate; to dilute with water. • *vi* (*eyes*) to smart; to salivate; to take in water.

**water-closet** *n* a lavatory.

**watercolour, watercolor** (*US*) *n* a water-soluble paint; a picture painted with watercolours.

**watercress** *n* a plant growing in ponds and streams, used in a salad.

**waterfall** *n* a fall of water over a precipice or down a hill.

**watering can** *n* a container with a spout for watering plants.

**water line** *n* a line up to which a ship's hull is submerged.

**waterlogged** *adj* soaked or saturated with water.

**water main** *n* a main pipe or conduit for carrying water.

**watermark** *n* a line marking the height to which water has risen; a mark impressed on paper which can only be seen when held up to the light.

**watermelon** *n* a large fruit with a hard green rind and edible red watery flesh.

**waterproof** *adj* impervious to water; watertight.—*also vt.*

**watershed** *n* a turning point.

**water-skiing** *n* the sport of planing on water by being towed by a motorboat—**water-skier** *n.*

**watertight** *adj* not allowing water to pass through; foolproof.

**waterworks** *n* (*as sing*) an establishment that supplies water to a district; (*pl: inf*) the urinary system; (*inf*) tears.

**watt** *n* a unit of electrical power.

**wave** *n* an undulation travelling on the surface of water; the form in which light and sound are thought to travel; an increase or upsurge (eg of crime); a hair curl; a movement of the hand in greeting or farewell. • *vti* to move freely backward and forward; to flutter; to undulate; to move the hand to and fro in greeting, farewell, etc.—**wavy** *adj.*

**wavelength** *n* the distance between the crests of successive waves of light or sound; radio frequency.

**waver** *vi* to hesitate; to falter.—**waverer** *n.*

**wax**[1] *n* beeswax; an oily substance used to make candles, polish, etc. • *vt* to rub, polish, cover or treat with wax.

**wax**[2] *vi* to increase in strength, size, etc.

**waxwork** *n* a figure or model formed of wax; (*pl*) an exhibition of such figures.

**way** *n* path, route; road; distance; room to advance; direction; state; means; possibility; manner of living; (*pl*) habits.

**waylay** *vt* (*pt* **waylaid**) to lie in wait for; to accost.

**wayward** *adj* wilful, stubborn; unpredictable.—**waywardness** *n*.

**WC** *abbr* = water-closet.

**we** *pron pl* of **I**; I and others.

**weak** *adj* lacking power or strength; feeble; ineffectual.—**weakness** *n*.

**weaken** *vti* to make or grow weaker.

**weakling** *n* a person who lacks strength of character.

**wealth** *n* a large amount of possessions or money; affluence; an abundance (of).—**wealthy** *adj*.

**wean** *vt* (*baby, animal*) to replace the mother's milk with other nourishment; to dissuade (from indulging a habit).

**weapon** *n* any instrument used in fighting.

**wear** *vb* (*pt* **wore**, *pp* **worn**) *vt* to have on the body as clothing; (*hair, etc*) to arrange in a particular way; to display; to rub away; to impair by use; to exhaust, tire. • *vi* to be impaired by use or time; to be spent tediously. • *n* deterioration from frequent use; articles worn.—**wearer** *n*.

**weary** *adj* (**wearier, weariest**) tired; bored. • *vti* to make or become tired.—**weariness** *n*.—**wearisome** *adj*.

**weasel** *n* a small carnivorous animal with a long slender body and reddish fur.

**weather** *n* atmospheric conditions, such as temperature, rainfall, cloudiness, etc. • *vt* to expose to the action of the weather; to survive. • *vi* to withstand the weather.

**weathercock** *n* a weather vane in the form of a cock to show the wind direction.

**weave** *vb* (*pt* **wove**, *pp* **woven**) *vt* to interlace threads in a loom to form fabric; to construct. • *vi* to make a way through (eg a crowd), to zigzag.—**weaver** *n*.

**web** *n* a woven fabric; the network of fine threads spun by a spider; the membrane joining the digits of birds and animals.

**webbed** *adj* (*ducks, etc*) having the digits connected by a fold of skin.

**wed** *vti* (*pt* **wedded** *or* **wed**) to marry; to join closely.

**wedding** *n* marriage; the ceremony of marriage.

**wedge** *n* a v-shaped block of wood or metal for splitting or fastening; a wedge-shaped object. • *vti* to split or secure with a wedge; to thrust (in) tightly; to become fixed tightly.

**wedlock** *n* marriage.

**Wednesday** *n* fourth day of the week, between Tuesday and Thursday.

**wee** *adj* small, tiny.

**weed** *n* any undesired plant, esp one that crowds out desired plants; (*sl*) marijuana. • *vt* to remove weeds or anything troublesome.

**weedkiller** *n* a chemical or hormonal substance used to kill weeds.

**week** *n* the period of seven consecutive days, esp from Sunday to Sunday.

**weekday** *n* a day of the week other than Saturday or Sunday.

**weekend** *n* the period from Friday night to Sunday night—*also adv*.

**weekly** *adj* happening once a week or every week.

**weep** *vti* (*pt* **wept**) to shed tears, to cry; (*wound*) to ooze.—**weepy** *adj*.

**weigh** *vt* to measure the weight of; to consider carefully. • *vi* to have weight; to be burdensome.

**weight** *n* the amount which anything weighs; influence; any unit of heaviness. • *vt* to attach a weight to.

**weightlessness** *n* the state of having no or little reaction to gravity, esp in space travel.

**weightlifting** *n* the sport of lifting weights of a specific amount in a particular way.—**weightlifter** *n*.

**weighty** *adj* (**weightier, weightiest**) heavy; serious.—**weightily** *adv*.

**weir** *n* a low dam across a river which controls the flow of water.

**weird** *adj* unearthly, mysterious; eerie; bizarre.—**weirdly** *adv*.

**welcome** *adj* gladly received; pleasing. • *n* reception of a person or thing. • *vt* to greet kindly.

**welch** *see* **welsh**.

**weld** *vt* to unite, as metal by heating until fused or soft enough to hammer together; to join closely. • *n* a welded joint.

**welfare** *n* wellbeing; health; assistance or financial aid granted to the poor, the unemployed, etc.

**well**[1] *n* a spring; a hole bored in the ground to provide a source of water, oil, gas, etc; the open space in the middle of a staircase. • *vi* to pour forth.

**well**[2] *adj* (**better, best**) agreeable; comfortable; in good health. • *adv* in a proper, satisfactory, or excellent manner; thoroughly; prosperously; with good reason; to a considerable degree; fully. • *interj* an expression of surprise, etc.

**well-heeled** *adj* (*inf*) wealthy.

**wellies** *npl* (*sl*) wellingtons.

**wellington (boot)** *n* a rubber, waterproof boot.

**well-off** *adj* in comfortable circumstances; prosperous.

**well-to-do** *adj* prosperous.

**Welsh** *adj* relating to the people of Wales or their language.—*also n*.

**welsh** *vti* to avoid paying a gambling debt; to run off without paying.—*also* **welch**.—**welsher, welcher** *n*.

**went** *see* **go**.

**wept** *see* **weep**.

**were** *see* **be**.

**we're** = we are.

**weren't** = were not.

**west** *n* the direction of the sun at sunset; one of the four points of the compass; the region in the west of any country; (*with cap*) Europe and the Western Hemisphere. • *adj* situated in, or toward the west. • *adv* in or to the west.

**westerly** *adj* towards the west; blowing from the west. • *n* a wind blowing from the west.—*also adv*.

**western** *adj* of or in the west. • *n* a film, novel, etc about the usu pre-20th century American West.

**westward** *adj* towards the west.—*also adv*.

**wet** *adj* (**wetter, wettest**) covered or saturated with water or other liquid; rainy; misty; not yet dry. • *n* water or other liquid; rain or rainy weather. • *vti* (*pt* **wet** *or* **wetted**) to soak; to moisten.—**wetness** *n*.

**wet suit** *n* a close-fitting suit worn by divers, etc, to retain body heat.

**whack** *vti* (*inf*) to strike sharply, esp making a sound. • *n* (*inf*) a sharp blow.

**whale** *n* a very large sea mammal that breathes through a blowhole, and resembles a fish in shape. • *vi* to hunt whales.

**wharf** *n* (*pl* **wharfs, wharves**) a platform for loading and unloading ships in harbour.

**what** *adj* of what sort, how much, how great. • *relative pron* that which; as much or many as. • *interj* used as an expression of surprise or astonishment.

**whatever** *pron* anything that; no matter what.

**whatsoever** *adj* whatever.

**wheat** *n* a cereal grain usu ground into flour for bread.

**wheel** *n* a solid disc or circular rim turning on an axle; a steering wheel; (*pl*) the moving forces. • *vt* to transport on wheels. • *vi* to turn round or on an axis; to move in a circular direction, as a bird.

**wheelbarrow** *n* a cart with one wheel in front and two handles and legs at the rear.

**wheelchair** *n* a chair with large wheels for invalids.

**wheeze** *vi* to breathe with a rasping sound; to breathe with difficulty.—*also n.*

**when** *adv* at what or which time • *conj* at the time at which; although; *relative pron* at which.

**where** *adv* at which or what place; to which place; from what source; *relative pron* in or to which.

**whereabouts** *adv* near or at what place; about where. • *n* approximate location.

**whereas** *conj* since; on the contrary.

**wherever** *adv* at or to whatever place.

**whet** *vt* (*pt* **whetted**) to sharpen by rubbing, to stimulate.

**whether** *conj* introducing an alternative possibility or condition.

**which** *adj* what one (of). • *pron* which person or thing; that. • *relative pron* person or thing referred to.

**whichever** *pron* whatever one that; whether one or the other; no matter which.—*also adj.*

**whiff** *n* a sudden puff of air, smoke or odour.

**while** *n* a period of time. • *conj* during the time that; whereas; although. • *vt* to pass (the time) pleasantly.

**whim** *n* a fancy; an irrational thought.

**whimper** *vi* to make a low, unhappy cry.—*also n.*

**whimsical** *adj* unusual, odd, fantastic.—**whimsicality** *n.*

**whine** *vi* (*dog*) to make a long, high-pitched cry; (*person*) to complain childishly. • *n* a plaintive cry.

**whip** *n* a piece of leather attached to a handle used for punishing people or driving on animals; an officer in parliament who maintains party discipline. • *vb* (*pt* **whipped**) *vt* to move,

pull, throw, etc suddenly; to strike, as with a lash; (*eggs, etc*) to beat into a froth. • *vi* to move rapidly.

**whip-round** *n* (*inf*) an appeal among friends for contributions.

**whir, whirr** *n* a humming or buzzing sound. • *vti* to revolve with a buzzing noise.

**whirl** *n* a swift turning; confusion, commotion; (*inf*) an attempt or try. • *vti* to turn around rapidly; to spin.

**whirlpool** *n* a circular current or vortex of water.

**whirlwind** *n* a whirling column of air; rapid activity.

**whisk** *vt* to make a quick sweeping movement; (*eggs, cream*) to beat, whip. • *vi* to move nimbly and efficiently. • *n* a kitchen utensil for whisking; (*inf*) a small amount.

**whisker** *n* any of the sensory bristles on the face of a cat, etc; (*pl*) the hair growing on a man's face, esp the cheeks.—**whiskered** *adj.*

**whiskey** *n* whisky distilled in the US or Ireland.

**whisky** *n* a spirit distilled from barley or rye.

**whisper** *vti* to speak softly; to spread a rumour. • *n* a hushed tone; a hint, trace.

**whist** *n* a card game for four players in two sides, each side attempting to win the greater number of the 13 tricks.

**whistle** *vti* to make a shrill sound by forcing the breath through the lips; to make a similar sound with a whistle; (*wind*) to move with a shrill sound. • *n* a whistling sound; a musical instrument; a metal tube that is blown to make a shrill warning sound.

**white** *adj* of the colour of snow; pure; bright; (*skin*) light-coloured. • *n* the colour white; the white part of an egg or the eye.—**whiten** *vti.*

**white-collar** *adj* of office and professional workers.

**whitewash** *n* a mixture of lime and water, used for whitening walls; concealment of the truth.—*also vt.*

**Whitsun** *n* the seventh Sunday after Easter; the following week.—*also* **Whit Sunday, Whitsuntide.**

**whittle** *vt* to pare or cut thin shavings from (wood) with a knife; (*with* **away** *or* **down**) to reduce.

**whiz, whizz** *vi* (*pt* **whizzed**) to make a humming sound. • *n* (*pl* **whizzes**) a humming sound; (*inf*) an expert.

**WHO** *abbr* = World Health Organization.

**who** *pron* what or which person; that.

**whodunit, whodunnit** *n* (*inf*) a detective novel, play, etc.

**whoever** *pron* anyone who; whatever person.

**whole** *adj* not broken, intact; containing the total amount, number, etc.; complete. • *n* the entire amount; a thing complete in itself.

**wholehearted** *adj* sincere, single-minded, enthusiastic.—**wholeheartedly** *adv.*

**whole note** *n* a semibreve.

**wholesale** *n* selling of goods, usu at lower prices and in quantity, to a retailer.

**wholesome** *adj* healthy; mentally beneficial.—**wholesomeness** *n.*

**whom** *pron* objective case of **who.**

**whoop** *n* a loud cry of excitement.

**whooping cough** *n* an infectious disease, esp of children, causing coughing spasms.

**whore** *n* a prostitute.

**whose** *pron* the possessive case of **who** or **which.**

**why** *adv* for what cause or reason? • *interj* exclamation of surprise. • *n* (*pl* **whys**) a cause.

**wick** *n* a cord, as in a candle or lamp, that supplies fuel to the flame.

**wicked** *adj* evil, immoral, sinful.—**wickedly** *adv.*—**wickedness** *n.*

**wicker** *n* a long, thin, flexible twig; such twigs woven together, as in making baskets.—**wickerwork** *n.*

**wicket** *n* a small door or gate; (*croquet*) any of the small wire arches through which the balls must be hit; (*cricket*) the stumps at which the bowler aims the ball; the area between the bowler and the batsman; a batsman's innings.

**wide** *adj* broad; extensive; of a definite distance from side to side; (*with* **of**) far from the aim; open fully. • *n* (*cricket*) a ball bowled beyond the reach of the batsman.—**widely** *adv.*

**wide-angle** *adj* (*photog*) with an angle of view of 60 degrees or more.

**wide-awake** *adj* fully awake; ready, alert.

**widen** *vti* to make or grow wide or wider.

**widespread** *adj* widely extended; general.

**widow** *n* a woman whose husband has died. • *vt* to cause to become a widow.—**widowhood** *n.*

**widower** *n* a man whose wife has died.

**width** *n* breadth.

**wield** *vt* (*a weapon, etc*) to brandish; to exercise power.

**wife** *n* (*pl* **wives**) a married woman.

**wig** *n* an artificial covering of real or synthetic hair for the head.

**wiggle** *vti* to move from side to side with jerky movements.

**wild** *adj* in its natural state; not tamed or cultivated; uncivilized; lacking control; disorderly; furious. —**wildly** *adv.*—**wildness** *n.*

**wilderness** *n* an uncultivated and desolate place.

**wild-goose chase** *n* a futile pursuit of something.

**wildlife** *n* animals in the wild.

**wilful, willful** (*US*) *adj* stubborn; done

intentionally.—**wilfully** adv. —**wilful-ness** n.

**will**[1] n power of choosing or determin-ing; desire; determination; desire; attitude, disposition; a legal docu-ment directing the disposal of one's property after death. • vt to be-queath; to command.

**will**[2] aux vb used in constructions with 2nd and 3rd persons; used to show futurity, determination, obligation.

**willow** n a tree or shrub with slender, flexible branches; the wood of the willow.

**willpower** n the ability to control one's emotions and actions.

**wilt** vi to become limp, as from heat; (plant) to droop; to become weak or faint.

**wily** adj (**wilier, wiliest**) crafty; sly.— **wiliness** n.

**win** vti (pr p **winning**, pt **won**) to gain with effort; to succeed in a contest; to gain eg by luck; to achieve influ-ence over. • n a success.—**winner** n.

**wince** vi to shrink back; to flinch (as in pain).—also n.

**winch** n a hoisting machine. • vt to hoist or lower with a winch.

**wind**[1] n a current of air; breath; scent of game; (inf) flatulence; tendency; (mus) wind instrument(s). • vt (pt **winded**) to cause to be short of breath; to perceive by scent.

**wind**[2] vb (pt **wound**) vt to turn by crank-ing; to tighten the spring of a clock; to coil around something else; to en-circle or cover, as with a bandage. • vi to turn, to twist, to meander.

**windbreak** n a shelter that breaks the force of the wind, as a line trees.

**windfall** n fruit blown off a tree; any unexpected gain, esp financial.

**winding** adj meandering.

**wind instrument** n a musical instru-ment played by blowing into it or by passing a current of air through it.

**windmill** n a machine operated by the force of the wind turning a set of sails.

**window** n a framework containing glass in the opening in a wall of a building, or in a vehicle, etc, for air and light.

**window box** n a narrow box on a win-dowsill for growing flowers, etc.

**windowsill** n a sill beneath a window.

**windpipe** n the air passage from the mouth to the lungs.

**windscreen, windshield** n a protective shield of glass in the front of a vehi-cle.

**windscreen wiper, windshield wiper** n a metal blade with a rubber edge that removes rain, etc, from a wind-screen.

**windy** adj (**windier, windiest**) exposed to the winds; stormy; verbose.

**wine** n fermented grape juice used as an alcoholic beverage; the fermented juice of other fruits or plants.

**wineglass** n a glass, usu with a stem, for drinking wine.

**wing** n the forelimb of a bird, bat or insect, by which it flies; the main lat-eral surface of an aeroplane; a pro-jecting part of a building; the side of a stage; a section of a political party. • vti to make one's way swiftly; to wound without killing.

**wink** vi to quickly open and close one's eye; to give a hint by winking. • n the act of winking; an instant.

**winning** n a victory; (pl) money won in gambling. • adj charming.

**winter** n the coldest season of the year: in the northern hemisphere from November or December to January or February. • vi to spend the win-ter.

**wintry, wintery** adj (**wintrier, wintriest**) typical of winter, cold, stormy, snowy; unfriendly, frigid.

**wipe** vt to rub a surface with a cloth in

order to clean or dry it; (*with* **out**) to remove; to erase; to kill off; to destroy. • *n* a wiping.

**wire** *n* a flexible thread of metal; a length of this; (*US horse racing*) the finish line of a race; a telegram. • *adj* formed of wire. • *vt* to fasten, furnish, connect, etc with wire; in US, to send a telegram.

**wireless** *n* (*formerly*) a radio.

**wiry** *adj* (**wirier, wiriest**) lean, supple and sinewy.—**wiriness** *n*.

**wisdom** *n* the ability to use knowledge; sound judgment.

**wisdom tooth** *n* one of four teeth set at the end of each side of the upper and lower jaw in humans and grown last.

**wise** *adj* having knowledge or common sense; learned; prudent.— **wisely** *adv*.

**wish** *vti* to long for; to express a desire. • *n* desire; thing desired.

**wishful** *adj* having a wish; hopeful.

**wisp** *n* a thin strand; a small bunch, as of hay; anything slender.—**wispy** *adj*.

**wistful** *adj* pensive; sad; yearning.— **wistfully** *adv*.—**wistfulness** *n*.

**wit** *n* (*speech, writing*) the facility of combining ideas with humorous effect; a person with this ability; (*pl*) ability to think quickly.

**witch** *n* a woman who practises magic and is considered to a have dealings with the devil.

**witchcraft** *n* the practice of magic.

**with** *prep* denoting nearness or agreement; in the company of, in the same direction as; among; by means of; possessing.

**withdraw** *vb* (*pt* **withdrew**, *pp* **withdrawn**) *vt* to draw back or away; to remove; to retract. • *vi* to retire; to retreat.—**withdrawal** *n*.

**wither** *vi* to fade or become limp or dry, as of a plant. • *vt* to cause to dry up or fade.

**withhold** *vt* (*pt* **withheld**) to hold back; to deduct; to restrain; to refuse to grant.

**within** *prep* inside; not exceeding; not beyond.

**without** *prep* outside or out of, beyond; not having, lacking. • *adv* outside.

**withstand** *vt* (*pt* **withstood**) to oppose or resist, esp successfully; to endure.

**witness** *n* a person who gives evidence or attests a signing; testimony (of a fact). • *vt* to have first hand knowledge of; to see; to be the scene of; to serve as evidence of; to attest a signing. • *vi* to testify.

**witness box, witness stand** *n* an enclosure for witnesses in a court of law.

**witticism** *n* a witty remark.

**witty** *adj* (**wittier, wittiest**) full of wit.— **wittily** *adv*.—**wittiness** *n*.

**wives** *see* **wife**.

**wizard** *n* a magician; a man who practises witchcraft or magic; an expert.—**wizardry** *n*.

**wk** *abbr* = week.

**wobble** *vi* to sway unsteadily from side to side; to waver, to hesitate.—**wobbly** *adj*.

**woe** *n* grief, misery; (*pl*) misfortune.— **woeful** *adj*.—**woefully** *adv*.

**wok** *n* a large, metal, hemispherical pan used for Chinese-style cooking.

**woke, woken** *see* **wake**[1].

**wolf** *n* (*pl* **wolves**) a wild animal of the dog family that hunts in packs; a flirtatious man.

**woman** *n* (*pl* **women**) an adult human female; the female sex.

**womanly** *adj* having the qualities of a woman.

**womb** *n* the female organ in which offspring are developed until birth, the uterus; any womb-like cavity; a place where something is produced.

**women** *see* **woman**.

**won** *see* **win**.

**wonder** *n* a feeling of surprise or

astonishment; something that excites such a feeling; a prodigy. • *vi* to feel wonder; to be curious; to speculate; to marvel.

**wonderful** *adj* marvellous.—**wonderfully** *adv*.

**won't** = will not.

**woo** *vt* to seek to attract with a view to marriage; to court; to solicit eagerly.—**wooer** *n*.

**wood** *n* the hard fibrous substance under the bark of trees; trees cut or sawn, timber; a thick growth of trees.

**wooded** *adj* covered with trees.

**woodpecker** *n* a bird that pecks holes in trees to extract insects.

**woodwind** *n* section of an orchestra in which wind instruments, originally made of wood, are played.

**woodwork** *n* carpentry.

**woodworm** *n* an insect larva that bores into wood; the damage in furniture so caused.

**wool** *n* the fleece of sheep and other animals; thread or yarn spun from the coats of sheep; cloth made from this yarn.

**woollen, woolen** (*US*) *adj* made of wool.

**woolly** *adj* (**woollier, woolliest**) of, like or covered with wool; indistinct, blurred; muddled. • *n* (*inf*) a woollen garment.—**woolliness** *n*.

**word** *n* a single unit of language in speech or writing; talk, discussion; a message; a promise; a command; information; a password; (*pl*) lyrics; (*pl*) a quarrel. • *vt* to put into words, to phrase; to flatter.

**wording** *n* the way in which words are used, esp in written form; a choice of words.

**wordy** *adj* (**wordier, wordiest**) verbose.

**wore** *see* **wear**.

**work** *n* employment, occupation; a task; the product of work; manner of working; place of work; a literary composition; (*pl*) a factory, plant. • *vi* to be employed, to have a job; to operate (a machine, etc); to produce effects. • *vt* to effect, to achieve.—**workable** *adj*.—**worker** *n*.

**working** *adj* spent in or used for work; functioning. • *n* operation; mode of operation; (*pl*) the manner of functioning or operating; (*pl*) the parts of a mine that are worked.

**working class** *n* people who work for wages, esp manual workers.

**workmanship** *n* technical skill; the way a thing is made, style.

**work-out** *n* a session of strenuous physical exercises.

**workshop** *n* a room or building where work is done; a seminar for specified intensive study, work, etc.

**world** *n* the planet earth and its inhabitants; mankind; the universe; a sphere of existence; the public.

**worldly** *adj* (**worldlier, worldliest**) earthly, rather than spiritual; material; experienced.

**worldwide** *adj* universal.

**worm** *n* an earthworm; an insect larva; the thread of a screw. • *vt* to work (oneself into a position) slowly or secretly; to extract information by slow and persistent means.

**worn** *see* **wear**.

**worn-out** *adj* (*machine, etc*) past its useful life; (*person*) depressed, tired.

**worry** *vb* to bother, pester, harass. • *vi* to be uneasy or anxious; to fret. • *n* a cause or feeling of anxiety.—**worrier** *n*.

**worse** *adj* (*used as compar of* **bad** *and* **ill** ) less favourable; not so well as before. • *adv* with great severity. — **worsen** *vti*.

**worship** *n* religious adoration; a religious ritual, eg prayers; devotion. • *vb* (*pt* **worshipped**) *vt* to adore or idolize. • *vi* to participate in a religious service.—**worshipper** *n*.

**worst** *adj* (*used as superl of* **bad** *or* **ill**; *see also* **worse**) bad or ill in the highest degree; of the lowest quality. • *adv* to the worst degree. • *n* the least good part.

**worsted** *n* twisted thread or yarn made from long, combed wool.

**worth** *n* value; price; excellence; importance. • *adj* equal in value to; meriting.

**worthless** *adj* valueless; useless; of bad character.—**worthlessness** *n*.

**worthwhile** *adj* important or rewarding enough to justify effort.

**worthy** *adj* (**worthier, worthiest**) virtuous; deserving. • *n* a worthy person, a local celebrity.—**worthily** *adv*.

**would** *see* **will**[2].

**would-be** *adj* aspiring or professing to be.

**wound**[1] *n* any cut, bruise, hurt, or injury caused to the skin; hurt feelings. • *vt* to injure.

**wound**[2] *see* **wind**[2].

**wove, woven** *see* **weave**.

**wrangle** *vi* to argue; to dispute noisily. • *n* a noisy argument.

**wrap** *vt* (*pt* **wrapped**) to fold (paper) around (a present, purchase etc); to wind (around); to enfold. • *n* a shawl.

**wrapper** *n* one who or that which wraps; a book jacket; a light dressing gown.

**wrath** *n* intense anger; rage.—**wrathful** *adj*.

**wreak** *vt* inflict or exact (eg vengeance, havoc).

**wreath** *n* (*pl* **wreaths**) a twisted ring of leaves, flowers, etc; something like this in shape.

**wreck** *n* accidental destruction of a ship; a badly damaged ship; a rundown person or thing. • *vt* to destroy; to ruin.

**wreckage** *n* the process of wrecking; remnants from a wreck.

**wren** *n* small brownish songbird, with a short erect tail.

**wrench** *vt* to give something a violent pull or twist; to injure with a twist, to sprain; to distort. • *n* a forceful twist; a sprain; a spanner; emotional upset caused by parting.

**wrestle** *vti* to fight by holding and trying to throw one's opponent down; to struggle.—**wrestler** *n*.

**wretch** *n* a miserable or despised person.

**wretched** *adj* very miserable; in poor circumstances; despicable.—**wretchedly** *adv*.—**wretchedness** *n*.

**wriggle** *vi* to move with a twisting motion; to squirm, to writhe; to use evasive tricks.—*also n*.—**wriggler** *n*.

**wring** *vt* (*pt* **wrung**) to twist; to compress by twisting to squeeze water from; to pain; to obtain forcibly.

**wrinkle** *n* a small crease or fold on a surface. • *vti* to make or become wrinkled.

**wrist** *n* the joint connecting the hand with the forearm.

**writ** *n* (*law*) a written court order.

**write** *vb* (*pr p* **writing,** *pt* **wrote,** *pp* **written**) *vt* to form letters on paper with a pen or pencil; to express in writing; to compose (music, literary work,etc); to communicate by letter; (*with* **off**) to cancel a bad debt as a loss; (*inf*) to damage (a vehicle) beyond repair. • *vi* to be a writer.

**write-off** *n* a debt cancelled as a loss; (*inf*) a badly damaged car.

**writer** *n* an author; a scribe or clerk.

**writhe** *vi* to twist the body violently, as in pain; to squirm (under, at).

**writing** *n* the act of forming letters on paper, etc; a written document; authorship; (*pl*) literary works.

**writing paper** *n* paper treated to accept ink and used esp for letters.

**written** *see* **write**.

**wrong** *adj* not right, incorrect; mistaken, misinformed; immoral. • *n* harm; injury done to another. • *adv* incorrectly. • *vt* to do wrong to.— **wrongly** *adv*.

**wrongful** *adj* unwarranted, unjust.— **wrongfully** *adv*.

**wrote** *see* **write**.

**wrought** *adj* formed; made; (*metals*) shaped by hammering, etc.

**wrung** *see* **wring**.

**wry** *adj* (**wryer, wryest** *or* **wrier, wriest**) twisted, contorted; ironic.—**wryly** *adv*.—**wryness** *n*.

**wt** *abbr* = weight.

# XYZ

**Xmas** *abbr* = Christmas.

**X-ray, x-ray** *n* radiation of very short wavelengths, capable of penetrating solid bodies, and printing on a photographic plate a shadow picture of objects not permeable by light rays. • *vt* to photograph by x-rays.

**xylophone** *n* a percussion instrument consisting of a series of wooden bars which are struck with small hammers.

**yacht** *n* a sailing or mechanically driven vessel, used for pleasure cruises or racing. • *vi* to race or cruise in a yacht.—**yachting** *n*.—**yachtsman** *n*.—**yachtswoman** *nf*.

**Yank, Yankee** *n* (*inf*) a citizen of the US, an American.

**yank** *vti* to pull suddenly, to jerk.—*also n*.

**yap** *vi* (*pt* **yapped**) to yelp, bark; (*sl*) to talk constantly, esp in a noisy or irritating manner.

**yard**[1] *n* a unit of measure of 3 feet and equivalent to 0.9144 metres.

**yard**[2] *n* an enclosed concrete area, esp near a building; an enclosure for a commercial activity (eg a shipyard); a garden.

**yardstick** *n* a standard used in judging.

**yarn** *n* fibres of wool, cotton etc spun into strands for weaving, knitting, etc; (*inf*) a tale or story. • *vi* to tell a yarn; to talk at length.

**yawn** *vi* to open the jaws involuntarily and inhale, as from drowsiness; to gape.—*also n*.

**yawning** *adj* gaping; wide-open; drowsy.—**yawningly** *adv*.

**yd., yds** *abbr* = yard(s).

**year** *n* a period of twelve months, or 365 or 366 days, beginning with 1 January and ending with 31 December.

**yearly** *adj* occurring every year; lasting a year. • *adv* once a year; from year to year.

**yearn** *vi* to feel desire (for); to long for.—**yearning** *n*.

**yeast** *n* a fungus that causes alcoholic fermentation, used in brewing and baking.

**yell** *vti* to shout loudly; to scream. • *n* a loud shout.

**yellow** *adj* of the colour of lemons, egg yolk, etc; having a yellowish skin; (*inf*) cowardly. • *n* the colour yellow. • *i* to become or turn yellow.

**yelp** *vti* to utter a sharp, shrill cry or bark.—*also n*.

**yen**[1] *n* (*pl* **yen**) the monetary unit of Japan.

**yen**[2] *n* (*inf*) a yearning, an ambition.

**yes** *adv* a word of affirmation or consent.

**yesterday** *n* the day before today; the recent past. • *adv* on the day before today; recently.

**yet** *adv* still; so far; even. • *conj* nevertheless; however; still.

**yew** *n* an evergreen tree or shrub with thin, sharp leaves and red berries.

**Yiddish** *n* a mixed German and Hebrew dialect spoken by Jews.

**yield** *vt* to resign; to give forth, to produce, as a crop, result, profit, etc.

• *vi* to submit; to give way to physical force, to surrender. • *n* the amount yielded; the profit or return on a financial investment.

**yodel** *vti* (*pt* **yodelled**) to sing, alternating from the ordinary voice to falsetto.

**yoga** *n* a system of exercises for attaining bodily and mental control and well-being.

**yoghurt, yogurt** *n* a semi-liquid food made from milk curdled by bacteria.

**yoke** *n* a bond or tie; slavery; the wooden frame joining oxen to make them pull together; part of a garment that is fitted below the neck. • *vt* to put a yoke on; to join together.

**yolk** *n* the yellow part of an egg.

**yonder** *adv* over there.

**you** *pron* (*gram*) 2nd person singular or plural; the person or persons spoken to.

**you'd** = you would; you had.

**you'll** = you will; you shall.

**young** *adj* in the early period of life; in the first part of growth; new; inexperienced. • *n* young people; offspring.

**youngster** *n* a young person; a youth.

**your** *poss adj* of or belonging to or done by you.

**you're** = you are.

**yours** *poss pron* of or belonging to you.

**yourself** *pron* (*pl* **yourselves**) the emphatic and reflexive form of **you**.

**youth** *n* the period between childhood and adulthood; young people collectively; the early stages of something; a young man or boy.—**youthful** *adj*.—**youthfully** *adv*.

**youth hostel** *n* a supervised lodging for usu young travellers.

**you've** = you have.

**zany** *adj* (**zanier, zaniest**) comical; eccentric.—**zaniness** *n*.

**zeal** *n* fervent devotion; fanaticism.

**zealous** *adj* full of zeal; ardent.—**zealously** *adv*.

**zebra** *n* (*pl* **zebras, zebra**) a black and white striped wild animal related to the horse.

**zebra crossing** *n* a street crossing for pedestrians marked by black and white strips on the road.

**zero** *n* (*pl* **zeros**) the symbol 0; nothing; the lowest point; freezing point, 0 degrees Celsius.

**zest** *n* the outer part of the skin of an orange or lemon used to give flavour; enthusiasm; excitement.—**zestful** *adj*.

**zigzag** *n* a series of short, sharp angles in alternate directions. • *adj* having sharp turns. • *vti* (*pt* **zigzagged**) to move or form in a zigzag.

**zinc** *n* a bluish-white metallic element used in alloys and batteries.

**zip** *n* a slide fastener on clothing, bags, etc with interlocking teeth. • *vt* (*pt* **zipped**) to fasten with a zip.

**zipper** *n* a zip.

**zither** *n* a stringed instrument played by plucking.

**zodiac** *n* an imaginary belt in the heavens, along which the sun, moon, and planets appear to move, divided into twelve equal areas; a diagram representing this.

**zombie** *n* a person who is lifeless and apathetic; an automaton.

**zone** *n* a region, area; a subdivision; any area with a specified use or restriction.—**zonal** *adj*.

**zoo** *n* (*pl* **zoos**) a place where wild animals are kept for public show.

**zoology** *n* the study of animals with regard to their classification, structure and habits.—**zoological** *adj*.—**zoologist** *n*.

**zoom** *vi* to go quickly, to speed; to climb upwards sharply in an aeroplane; to rise rapidly; (*photog*) to focus in on, using a zoom lens.

**zoom lens** *n* (*photog*) a camera lens

that makes distant objects appear closer without moving the camera.

**zoomorphism** *n* the representation (esp of a deity) in the form of or with the attributes of an animal.—zoomorphic *adj*.

**zoophyte** *n* any animal (eg coral, a sponge) that resembles a plant.—zoophytic *adj*.

**zootomy** *n* animal anatomy; the dissection of animals.—**zootomical** *adj*.—**zootomist** *n*.

**zorille, zoril** *n* a small African mammal that resembles and smells like a skunk.

**Zoroastrianism** *n* a religious system founded by the Persian prophet Zoroaster (*c*.628-551BC), based on the recognition of the dual principle of good and evil.—**Zoroastrian** *n*, *adj*.

**zounds** *interj* (*arch*) expressing anger and astonishment.

**zucchetto** *n* (*pl* **zucchettos**) a skullcap worn by Roman Catholic ecclesiastics, which varies in colour according to rank (black for a priest, purple for a bishop, red for a cardinal, white for the Pope).

**zucchini** *npl n* a type of small vegetable marrow.—also **courgette**.

**Zulu** *n* (*pl* **Zulus**, Zulu) a member of a Negroid people of South Africa, or their language.—also *adj*.

**zwieback** *n* a thin rusk.

**zyg-, zygo-** *prefix* yoked, paired.

**zygodactyl** *adj* (bird) with the toes in pairs, two pointing forward and two backward. • *n* a zygodactyl bird, eg the parrot.—**zygodactylous** *adj*.

**zygomorphic, zygomorphous** *adj* (flowers) bilaterally symmetrical.—**zygomorphism, zygomorphy** *n*.

**zygospore** *n* a spore formed from the fusion of gametes.—**zygosporic** *adj*.

**zygote** *n* the cell formed by the union of an ovum and a sperm; the developing organism from such a cell.

**zymosis** *n* (*pl* **zymoses**) an infectious disease caused by a virus or organism that acts like a ferment; fermentation.

**zymotic** *adj* caused by or relating to an infection or an infectious disease; producing fermentation.

**zymurgy** *n* the chemistry of fermentation in brewing, etc.